How to Make War

THIRD EDITION

THIRD EDITION

How to Make War

A Comprehensive Guide to Modern Warfare for the Post–Cold War Era

JAMES F. DUNNIGAN

WILLIAM MORROW AND COMPANY, INC.
New York

It is the policy of William Morrow and Company, Inc., and its imprints and affiliates, recognizing the importance of preserving what has been written, to print the books we publish on acid-free paper, and we exert our best efforts to that end.

Library of Congress Cataloging-in-Publication Data

Dunnigan, James F.
    How to make war : a comprehensive guide to modern warfare for the
  post–Cold War era / James F. Dunnigan. — 3rd ed.
      p.   cm.
    Includes bibliographical references and index.
    ISBN 0-688-12157-8
    1. Military art and science.   2. Military weapons.   3. War.
  I. Title.
  U102.D836   1993
  355—dc20   93-6568
                                                               CIP

Printed in the United States of America

1 2 3 4 5 6 7 8 9 10

To my parents, whose love of learning and hatred of weapons gave me the proper perspective. To all the professional military men I have known, for sharing their secrets with me and demonstrating how they can be pacifists, warriors and patriots without contradiction.

Contents

PART FIVE: SPECIAL WEAPONS

PART SIX: WARFARE BY THE NUMBERS

PART SEVEN: MOVING THE GOODS

PART EIGHT: TOOLS OF THE TRADE

Charts and Tables

How to
Make War

THIRD EDITION

Introduction to the New Edition

THE SECOND EDITION OF *How to Make War* was a huge success. One result of that success is that you now have a third edition, and the prospect of new editions every five or six years from now on. This third edition recognizes the major changes in military affairs brought about by the end of the Cold War. There is no longer an "East Bloc" and "West Bloc." What remains is the United States and its industrialized allies, plus more than 100 other nations scrambling to create and maintain whatever military force they can manage. To add to the confusion, we also have the 1991 Gulf War, which demonstrated that the more recent generations of weapons had decisively changed the World War II combat mentality that prevailed throughout the Cold War.

These changes are reflected throughout this edition. You will still see a lot of material on Soviet weapons, mainly because there are still so many of them out there. You will not see as much material on the armed forces of the former Soviet Union. The huge army, navy, and air force built up by the Soviet Union over the last 40 years has largely evaporated as a world-class combat force. Many of the troops and their equipment still exist, but with much diminished capability. Manpower in the former Soviet armed forces is rapidly shrinking, and units that still exist are often demoralized and no longer as capable as they once were. New and upgraded equipment is not forthcoming; existing equipment is being destroyed or left to decay from lack of maintenance. The text in this edition reflects these changes and approaches warfare from the viewpoint of a wider array of potential opponents. While we may have escaped from the shadow of World War III (for the moment, anyway), there are a larger number of nasty little wars.

A lot of work has gone into revising the second edition's charts, but a lot more went into the text. A combination of new information, new ways of looking at the subject, and a desire to improve things in general led to a pretty thorough rewrite. Hardly a page escaped significant change. Nearly all sections have been substantially done over.

Although not everyone agreed with all the conclusions in the first and second editions, many of you brought up points and perceptions that I had not thought of or considered enough. As I always enjoy hearing from readers and carefully consider their comments, you will find several items changed. Modifications are not radical, but incremental. Things change—this book shows it and is better for these evolutions.

One last item. I received numerous letters, electronic mail, and phone calls from readers of the first and second editions. The best way to get a quick response is via electronic mail. I can be reached on CompuServe (70425,232), GEnie (JDUNNIGAN) and MCIMail (JDUNNIGAN). I never got into USENET because I don't have the time. Some USENET users got to me via the CompuServe link, but I've had mixed success replying to those messages via CompuServe. Sometimes it works, sometimes it doesn't. Kind of reminds me about some of the things I write about in this book.

I appreciate the feedback, especially when it points out errors. There will likely be a fourth edition of this book, just in time for the millennium. So don't hesitate to let me know what you think, perferably via e-mail.

As with the first and second editions, I am indebted to a number of people for their advice and criticism of the manuscript. Among these are Austin Bay, Albert A. Nofi, Ray Macedonia, Alison Brown, Al Rehm, Doug MacCaskill, Stephen B. Patrick, Kathy Bay, Susan Leon, Sterling Hart, Ken Hoffman, Mark Herman, Jennifer Williams, E. Al Hattlestad, Jr., Kenneth B. Wheeler, Kurt B. Weinschenker, Phillip H. Feller, Richard M. Kirka, Steve Plegge, Tom Trinko, Trent J. Telenko, William S. Gross, Edward Ablon, James S. Elder, Mark Turnage, Pat F. Fogarty.

Illustrations are taken from U.S. Department of Defense publication *Soviet Military Power.*

1

How to Become an Effective Armchair General

WITH THE PROLIFERATION of smaller, and often more politically complex, conflicts, war is becoming more difficult to understand. Although the process of warfare is still clouded by obscurity and confused by myths, sense can be made of it nevertheless. The mass media may create and perpetuate many myths; appointed experts may be equally ill informed. But when a war breaks out, these myths gradually become apparent as distortions. Operating on these misunderstandings, leaders and citizens are much more likely to get involved in wars, or make ones they have forced on them even more expensive. One of the constants of history is that a nation rarely goes to war until it has convinced itself that victory is attainable and worth the cost. In reality, wars are never worth the cost for those who start them. Instigators of warfare invariably come to regret it. Those who resist aggression have a better case. Yet avoiding war typically leaves people feeling they have missed a golden opportunity to right some wrong. Real warfare is ugly, destructive, and remembered fondly only by those who survived it without getting too close. Time dims our memories and conjures up wishful myths. This book removes some of the obscurity and destroys a few of the myths.

The Principles of War

Understanding how the military mind operates requires familiarity with the central "truths" military commanders have learned over the centuries. These principles of war have been distilled from our long history of warfare. They reflect reality. Were they followed to the letter, there would probably be a lot less fighting. The principles of war preach, above all, that you must know what you are doing. Or at least know your business better than your opponent. These principles are codified, and applied, somewhat differently from nation to nation, but the following describes the more common and important ones as I define them.

1. **Mass.** This is best summed up by the old American saying "Get there first with the most." While superior troops can enable you to fight outnumbered and win, victory usually goes to the side that amasses the most combat power on the battlefield.
2. **Unity of Command.** Armed forces have always been large organizations—usually larger than one leader can command and control. Therefore, the leader must make arrangements to deal with different parts of the armed forces—all operating at cross-purposes with one another. While units should know and be ready to execute the same plan—or execute previously arranged actions if the plan doesn't work—this principle is one of the most difficult to practice.
3. **Maintenance of the Objective.** This means choosing a reason for being on the battlefield and sticking with it. In warfare, the commander regularly operates with very little information about what is going on. As the situation develops, there is a temptation to change objectives. This wastes time and energy. History has shown that the army that consistently pursues its original goal is likely to succeed. An example is found in the Arab-Israeli wars. The Israelis ruthlessly maintained their objectives, ignoring temptations to surround bypassed Arab formations. This straightforward attitude always resulted in the destruction of far larger Arab forces. By contrast, the Egyptians, in 1973, changed their plan after crossing the Suez Canal. Instead of digging in to receive the Israeli counterattack, they launched further attacks of their own. This resulted in heavy Egyptian losses, which set the stage for a successful Israeli crossing of the canal.
4. **Economy of Force.** Otherwise known as *not* putting all your eggs in one basket. No one ever has enough resources to accomplish everything. Economy of force dictates carefully parceling out forces for each phase of the operation. However, this means more than using small forces. For key operations, you will often need massive

ones, and they are obtained by maintaining a large reserve. Invariably, once all your committed forces get hopelessly tangled up, the reserve can snatch survival from the jaws of disaster. During World War II, for example, the German Army maintained a reserve no matter how desperate the situation. This habit alone may have prolonged the war by at least a year. Economy of force also allows *you* to amass sufficient combat power where it will do the most good.

5. **Flexibility.** This may seem to be a contradiction of the "Maintenance of the Objective" principle, but it isn't. Flexibility in planning, thought, and action is otherwise known as common sense. Maintenance of the objective does not imply ignoring the obvious. If your orders are to take a town, and you determine the easiest way to do this would be to surround it and then attack it from all sides instead of charging right in, that's being flexible. If, while moving around the town, you discover that a large relief force is coming to support the enemy troops in the town, you would go after this new relief force before it could unite with the enemy forces in the town. After the relief force is defeated, you can go back after the town. That's being flexible and maintaining the objective at the same time.

6. **Initiative.** Getting there first with the most and taking advantage of the situation is the principal quality of the combat leader, and not all of them have it. Being first off the mark most of the time leaves the other fellow with less opportunity to respond to your moves and plans. Defeat is the likely outcome for a commander who always waits for something to happen. Indeed, surprise is little more than an enormous disparity in initiative between two forces.

7. **Maneuver.** If you don't move your troops around, then you can, at best, achieve a stalemate. This may be sufficient, but victory is better, and often necessary. To win, you must outmaneuver your opponent, or cause your opponent to try some fancy maneuver that turns into a disaster. Maneuvering is always dangerous, as the other fellow may turn out to be better at it. For this reason, many otherwise-able commanders fail in battle because they do not have the proper mind-set for maneuver warfare. They are not willing to take risks. Successfully moving troops around in battle is the pinnacle of military art and the usual precursor of victory.

8. **Security.** It's not sheer bloody-mindedness that causes captured spies to be shot in wartime. Information can usually be calculated in lives saved or lost. If you know what the enemy is up to while concealing your own plans, your chances of success increase immensely. The crucial Battle of Midway in 1942 was won largely

because the United States had broken the Japanese codes. The Japanese, however, knew little of the U.S. forces' deployment, or that the Americans were reading their coded messages. Good security capability enables you to achieve the most crucial of combat advantages—surprise.

9. **Surprise.** One of the earliest lessons soldiers learn is that it's a lot safer, and potentially more successful, to hit the other guy when he's not expecting it. That's what surprise is, and that's why "Security" is also a principle of war.

10. **Simplicity.** Warfare is a chaotic and unpredictable undertaking. Elaborate plans quickly come apart under the stress of combat. Large, elaborate, and complex military organizations do require planning to keep them going, and it's not easy to keep the procedures simple. The quality of your leaders and their ability to do the right thing in unison is the key. Good leaders are another scarce resource. It's no easy thing waging war.

11. **Morale.** This is not generally considered one of the principles of war, but morale has always been one of those crucial items that overrule all others. Often taken for granted until it's too late, morale is the attitude of the officers and troops. It is generally much higher at the beginning of a battle than during and after. Once morale declines to a certain point, the troops lose their desire to fight. If this breaking point is reached during a battle, the side suffering from it loses.

12. **Entropy.** This is also not generally considered one of the principles of war, but entropy has been a constant throughout military history. In practice, entropy means that after an initial shock, the war or battle will settle down to a steady grind. Once a war gets started, casualty and movement rates become predictable. In combat, personnel losses average a few percent a day per division. Against enemy opposition, even mechanized forces rarely advance farther than some 20 km a day. There are exceptions, and the exceptions may win battles. Over the course of an entire war, however, entropy takes over. A technical way to put it is that "events tend to regress toward the mean." Don't let flashy press reports fool you—exceptions tend to get published far more than day-to-day averages. Commanders who are best able to cope with entropy develop a more realistic, and winning, attitude.

Rules of Thumb

As crass as it might seem, it is possible to boil this book down to a dozen rules of thumb on "how to make war." These are the historical outcomes that consistently repeat themselves.

1. An armed force's strength is calculated by multiplying numbers of men, weapons, munitions, and equipment by the quality factor. Quality is a seemingly nebulous thing, but it includes the effectiveness of leadership, training, morale, weapons, and equipment. Numbers alone are not the standard by which you can calculate a nation's combat strength. Units with equal numbers of men and equipment can vary substantially in terms of combat effectiveness. In other words, the soldier of one army can be worth several of another. It is also assumed that the armed forces in question have the proper ratios of infantry, tanks, aircraft, artillery, ships, trucks, etc. This is often a rash assumption, because the force with a higher quality rating possesses a more effective ration of forces.

2. Attack-strength ratios: The offensive needs three or more times as much combat *strength* (not just troops and weapons) in order to overcome a defender at the point of attack. This may vary with the size of the forces, because at the platoon level the required ratio can be as high as 10 to 1. At the theater level, where up to a million or more troops are involved, anything between 1 to 1 and 2 to 1 will often suffice because only a small part of the terrain in the theater will be fought over at any one time. You also have to take time into account. The larger the advantage, the less time it will take to win.

3. Climate and terrain have a severe effect on the tempo and effects of combat. Rough terrain, darkness, and winter all slow down operations and reduce the combat casualty rate, while losses from disease and sickness are increased. The cumulative effects can slow down operations by over 50 percent and reduce casualties by even more. Chemical weapons have the same general effect as bad weather, although with a slightly higher casualty rate. Flat, open terrain speeds up operations, particularly if the defender cannot put up substantial opposition. Such conditions can also reduce attackers' losses while enormously increasing those of the hapless defender.

4. Modern ground combat causes average losses per division (of 10,000–20,000 troops) to be from 1 to 5 percent per day during sustained combat. Losses vary enormously depending on the soldiers' jobs. The infantry units' casualty rate is two to three times the overall rate. Tank-unit losses are about the same as the overall rate. Artillery units suffer half the overall rate, and all other troops are lost at about one-sixth the rate of the division as a whole. Keep in mind that smaller combat units like battalions will have 50+ percent of their strength exposed to enemy fire, while a larger unit like a division will expose only 10 to 15 percent. You don't have to be a mathematician to figure out that a battalion will have a much higher rate of loss than a division.

5. Combat vehicles (tanks and personnel carriers) are lost in combat at a rate of 5 to 10 times the personnel-loss rate. If a division loses 2 percent of its troops a day in battle, it will lose over 10 percent of its armored vehicles. Highly mechanized forces tend to grind to a halt over time as their equipment breaks down. Low-tech forces can continue killing each other longer without being stopped by equipment failure. When low-tech troops (such as the Afghan resistance fighters) engaged high-tech troops (the Soviets), the low-tech force could keep going a lot longer with fewer resources. This is why guerrilla warfare is so difficult for a high-tech force and why most of the wars in the 1990s will be resistant to high-tech solutions.

6. The ratio of dead to wounded is about 1 to 4 in most armies. This varies according to the quantity of available medical resources. Armies with substantial resources get the ratio up to 1 dead for 5–10 wounded. Most of the wounded can then be returned to service in less than a month. Noncombat losses per month vary from 1 to 40 percent depending on living conditions, climate, and medical facilities available. Wars in the 1990s will generally be in unhealthy places. Noncombat losses are also liable to be higher than combat losses.

7. All things being equal, defending is easier than attacking. This is especially true if the defender is within fortifications that cannot be bypassed. By defending, a force doubles or triples its combat power. A stalemate can be achieved if both sides are too strong for the other to attack. World War I was a classic example, and many other campaigns in this century suffered from this problem. Guerrilla wars also often end up as stalemates. This unconventional warfare favors the guerrillas, as the other side usually runs out of capital in keeping these extended wars going.

8. Losses in aircraft average 1–5 per 1,000 sorties. The American experience in Vietnam and the Soviet record in Afghanistan demonstrated that noncombat losses amount to between 1 and 5 percent of all aircraft per month. If you manage to shut down the enemy air defenses right away, as happened in the 1991 Gulf War, you can get the losses down to less than 1 per 1,000 sorties (it was about .4 per 1,000 sorties in the Gulf).

9. Naval warfare today primarily involves nations that are dependent on maritime trade protecting their merchant shipping. It is largely a defensive exercise, more so than air or ground combat. The recent Gulf War was an example of this, with Allied naval forces shutting down Iraqi ports. The Allied naval forces then had to devote considerable resources to protecting themselves from possible Iraqi air or missile attack.

10. Surprise in battle can increase one side's combat power by a factor of 3 or more. The effect wears off after one to three days. This is

one of the key factors in battlefield success and is regularly underestimated or ignored.

11. Troops that have not been in combat, or have not undergone intensive and realistic training, underestimate the amount of time, effort, and casualties it will take to accomplish anything in battle. It is very difficult to break out of this habit. For most armies, only combat experience will provide a realistic attitude toward warfare. A welcome exception was the experience of U.S. forces in the Gulf War, who had spent millions of hours and billions of dollars on realistic training exercises. This preparation was close enough to real warfare to make the operations against Iraq highly successful. One aspect of this that went unnoticed by the American public was that U.S. ground troops, because of their intense and realistic training over the years, knew how to make use of the months of time spent in the Saudi Arabian desert. Here they perfected their techniques with training on the local terrain and detailed rehearsals for their advance north. As the U.S. experience in World War II demonstrated, spending a lot of time on inappropriate training is counterproductive when the shooting starts.

12. Warfare is expensive. Depending on how wealthy a nation is, and how many weapons and munitions it can buy, each enemy soldier killed can cost from several thousand to several million dollars. There's no such thing as a cheap war.

How to Find the Right Questions

Warfare, to put it bluntly, is just a job. There are techniques the successful practitioners must learn and tools they must master. As in any other profession, conditions change constantly. Practitioners must adapt to these changes by correctly answering the questions raised by changed conditions. But warfare, like testing flashbulbs, cannot be practiced. This makes it difficult to determine the important questions, much less the answers. Below are some of the ones that are raised in this book.

How many post–Cold War armed forces do you need? Not a whole lot. After we finish the analysis of the world's armed forces (at the end of the book), it will become clear that there are no nations powerful or angry enough to drag the United States into a major war during the rest of the decade. The world is a more peaceful place (in relative terms) than it has been in over a century. One of the benefits of the Cold War was the unity created among the industrialized nations (the "West," which also includes several Asian states). In previous centuries, the major powers were always at odds with each other, and often at war as well. The Cold War and its nuclear stalemate changed all that. Thus, it is not up to the United States alone to take care of military emergencies threatening many other nations as well as the United States. If America had not promptly responded to the Iraqi invasion of Kuwait in 1990, the other industrialized nations had more than sufficient military means to go there and sort things out. They would not have been able to do it as expeditiously as the United States, but the matter would have been cleared up. Before World War II, the United States spent about 2 percent of its GNP on defense. That is a third of what is being spent now. Could we go back to that level? Voters must study the matter and decide.

Why bother studying the Russians anymore? Well, it was nice, back in the Cold War days, to have two superpowers. Comparing the two made life simpler than measuring one superpower against dozens of potential, and much smaller, opponents. But the Russian (Soviet) armed forces have left a legacy that will color studies of warfare for the next decade. The Soviets supplied weapons and training to scores of nations, and many of the Soviet successor states continue to export military equipment and technology. Many of these smaller powers, like Iraq, may again face American and Western armed forces. Russia itself is still selling large quantities of weapons, as well as instructing and training buyers regarding their use. These sales will not diminish until the mid-1990s and will still be substantial at the end of the decade. So we have good reason to still keep an eye on military affairs inside Russia.

What were the lessons of the Gulf War? The principal lesson was that training pays large dividends. American troops underwent unprecedented (for peacetime American forces) training during the 1980s. Moreover, the troops were now all volunteers and carefully selected. This has been the traditional method of creating a highly effective armed force. The Iraqis were largely an army of ill-trained, ill-led, and ill-motivated conscripts. These training and troop-quality factors, not superior equipment, were the real reasons the United States did so well. The lesson yet to be learned is if the U.S. armed forces will choose to maintain their training levels or, as is more common, cut back training in favor of developing and producing new equipment. The choice will be hard, as U.S. defense budgets will likely suffer considerable shrinkage because of the end of the Cold War. There were several other lessons gleaned from the Gulf War. Some of the more prominent ones were:

- Spare parts and munitions were not at "big war" levels. The Gulf War was a medium-sized short war, and if it had gone on much longer, there would have been embarrassing shortages of spare parts and munitions on the U.S. side.
- Combat service support was not up to wartime standards. Although U.S. Army doctrine had preached maneuverability for over a decade, there were not enough trucks available to support it. Last-minute scrounging to improvise sufficient transportation was still not able to

prevent supply shortages once the three-day ground offensive got under way.

- The navy floats better than it fights. The U.S. Navy was revealed to have overlooked some key technologies during its 1980s expansion. The U.S. Air Force had a superior bombing technology, which the navy knew about but had declined to get involved with because of the expense, and the feeling was that the Navy Way was the Right Way. This can be seen as either good news or bad news for interservice rivalries. The good news is that while the navy took the wrong path, the air force went another way and proved extremely efficient. The bad news is that the United States had two air forces, one operating from the land and another from carriers. Only one of them fought smart.

- Massive amounts of money spent in peacetime can save lives. The low U.S. casualty rate in the Gulf was a direct result of the money spent on training and equipment during the 1980s. If this spending is cut back, as it will be, casualty rates will increase during the next war. This has historically been the case, especially since the money can usually be spent to save even more civilian lives during peacetime with health and training programs. Defense spending, no matter how essential, hurts the economy. Nondefense spending builds the economy and provides more jobs. A run-down economy together with unemployment causes lower living standards, increased disease, and shorter life spans. You may yet hear this one raised in the debates over 1990s defense spending. Americans want to win the "war" at home now.

- You can't see everything from the air in the desert. As spectacular as the air force performance was in the Gulf War, it typified the experiences of above-ground fighting in the desert. This suggests dire consequences for future wars. For example, the air force was stymied in finding and stopping the Scud missile attacks and demonstrates that an inability to find a few missiles could lead to large losses as missile technology continues to spread and potential enemies acquire chemical or nuclear missiles. Additionally, the chapters on combat and logistics will show that the conditions under which the Gulf War were fought were unique. Change those conditions a little, and you can change the results a lot.

What does war cost? Appalled by the size of the defense budget? With annual worldwide arms spending still in the neighborhood of a trillion dollars, you have plenty of company. The end of the Cold War has created pressure worldwide to cut defense spending. But there will still be wars, and wars are not getting any cheaper. The chapters on combat operations rate the relative worth of the various weapons bought. The chapter on logistics gives more details on the material needed to carry on a war. Using the chapters on the cost of war, logistics, and attrition, you can do your own calculations on the cost of a current or a future war. Although the cost of war is not frequently mentioned in the press, governments are well aware of it. This cost is a major element in the decision to wage war or to seek a less expensive means of achieving national goals. These chapters explain why modern wars are either short or will eventually bankrupt the participants. The Iran-Iraq War is a good example of a "war of bankruptcy." And even the 1991 Gulf War cost the winners $60 billion, and the losers much more.

The navy controls two thirds of the planet—75 percent of the world's surface area is water—because as the strongest naval power the United States holds sway over international waters. The USN is now more powerful than all the other navies of the world combined. No likely combination of foreign navies can challenge the USN—not now, or for the rest of the century. The chapters on naval power explain why and demonstrate how the growth of the USN since before World War II has resulted in the ultimate victory at sea.

The chapter on strategic nuclear weapons reveals a few surprises about what might happen: for example, it discusses the threat that ICBMs (Intercontinental Ballistic Missiles) with nerve-gas warheads could be used. What probably won't happen is the end of the world. The reasons? Primarily the world's fear of the massive use of atomic weapons and the unlikelihood that they will actually work. Although anything is possible, read and study the details. Then decide for yourself. The chapters on nuclear weapons point out a number of factors influencing the reliability and effects of weaponry that are not normally published in the open press. These weapons may even be used in the future, but not in the ways we currently anticipate. Read Chapters 20, 21, and 22 and draw your own conclusions on nuclear weapons and how they will be deployed.

Who's on first in Europe, the Middle East, Africa, Asia? Chapter 29, on the armed forces of the world, puts this topic into perspective. The information on each nation's armed forces indicates the potential resolution of such conflicts. Other chapters can be consulted to gain a more complete understanding of the possible outcomes. All countries have armed forces, but not all have an effective military organization. Except for the top 10 military nations in the world, effective offensive warfare is not a realistic possibility; the Iraqis thought otherwise, and look what happened to them. Actually, the most pressing danger today is that more militarily competent countries will be drawn into a local squabble. With the information contained in Chapter 29, you can quickly assess who might do what to whom.

In modern warfare, few people in the combat zone are exposed to enemy fire, and fewer still actually fight. They rarely even see an enemy soldier, except as a corpse or as a prisoner. The sections on ground, naval, and air combat demonstrate this in detail. These sections also add accurate detail to frequently misleading news accounts of combat. How are current wars being fought? Who gets hurt? The chapters on various aspects of military operations give details not ordinarily found in other sources. The chapters on the human factors are also crucial, as these items are repeatedly ignored or misinterpreted.

What is all this talk about electronic warfare? Chapter 19 lays it all out, step by step. The widespread introduction of electronics has profoundly changed the ways in which wars are fought. This electronic equipment has led to overconfidence and overspending, and sometimes increased military effectiveness. More than anything else, however, electronics have led to uncertainty, as there is no practical experience with these devices in a major war. Therefore, it is important to understand their potential, limitations, and current status.

Will Star Wars Work? The American SDI (Strategic Defense Initiative) proposes to put an antimissile defense system in orbit. Given the track record of high-tech military projects, this system's prospects are murky at best. What can be guaranteed is a cost that will endanger U.S. defense budgets and the very economy SDI is supposed to defend. One understated side effect is to endanger the existence of unfriendly satellites. See Chapters 20 and 22.

A Few Notes on Approach

A half-serious maxim among military historians contends that you can determine which army is more effective by looking at their uniforms. The best-dressed army is generally the least effective. A fresh coat of paint, however, makes any weapon appear awesome. How, then, do we determine which weapon is better than another? My solution is to collect enough data on enough nations over enough years to get an accurate picture of current and future military capabilities. This approach works well when combined with a study of trends in the quality of leadership and manpower. You may not agree with some of my evaluations, but at least you'll have a point from which to start your argument. This book is for those people who ask questions rather than simply accept the obvious answer. Because much of this book's subject matter is normally classified, secret, or worse, information had to be obtained from whatever sources were available. Because of my long experience with this type of information gathering, I am confident that this is as accurate a picture of modern warfare as you are going to get. Even access to classified information is shaded by doubts about its trustworthiness. But that's another story (see Chapter 15, "Intelligence"). Any errors in fact or interpretation are my own.

The metric system of measurements has been used in most instances. Units of distance are measured in kilometers. To convert to statute (British/American) miles, divide kilometers (or km) by 1.6. To convert to nautical miles (or knots), divide by 1.8. Weights are in metric tons (2,240 pounds).

Nonmetric measures are sometimes used to enable British or American readers to grasp scale better.

The following paragraph was included in both the first and second editions of this book. It's obsolete now, but I thought it of interest to reprint it. This is an example of the many things in political and military affairs that do not change over the centuries. Successful soldiers in the past would still be successful today, once they'd learned how to use modern weapons. Never lose sight of the many constants in history. They are among the few things you can depend on.

> Things Russian are called "Russian" throughout. Purists will insist that the proper term is "Soviet." The purists are correct. I thought it easier to call Russians Russians, for they have been around far longer than the Soviet Union. Russians consider themselves Russian, although the Ukrainians, Estonians, and hundred other ethnic groups in the Russian Empire may not. Russia's neighbors see no difference between czar and commissar. The Soviet Union may not last, but Russia will endure.

The world still has two major military systems, the "Western" and the "Russian." The United States and Western Europe produce the vast majority of the equipment used by the industrialized, and many Third World, nations. Those same nations tend also to use Western unit organizations, tactics, and doctrine. The same applies to countries that still obtain their equipment from Russia, or have received large quantities of equipment from the Soviet Union in the past. Therefore, frequent reference is made to Western and Russian nations. Since over half the planet's military might is found in the Western nations and Russia this is a reasonable, albeit somewhat simplistic, practice.

PART ONE

GROUND COMBAT

WARS ARE DECIDED on the ground. A war isn't over until your infantry, the ultimate arbiter of victory, walk into the other fellow's cities and take up residence. You can win a war with bombers or by blockading and bombarding ships. But that doesn't end the war. Only infantry can do that. Ground combat uses the majority of troops and produces most of the casualties.

2

The Poor Bloody Infantry

YOU ARE ON the outskirts of a largely abandoned town. The few remaining inhabitants take an occasional shot at you. More excitement comes from the seemingly random explosions caused by shells falling from the sky, or from objects equipped with time-delay fuses. Your only protection is to seek shelter in half-wrecked buildings or dig a hole in the rain-sodden ground. You have not had a hot meal or bath for five weeks and are living on cold food out of a can or pouch. Your small group of ragged companions waits for instructions over a radio. You will be told to either move toward an area experiencing more explosions or in the other direction, where the mayhem level is a bit less. Your only escape from this nightmare is to be injured or killed.

The above is not science fiction, just the life of the average infantryman. Those who have not been through it find the appalling stories of what infantrymen must endure hard to believe. The usual reaction is, "How do soldiers stand it?" The answer is, only for so long. Studies during World War II indicated that after as few as 100 to 200 days of combat—and the stress that goes with it—the average infantryman was a mental and physical wreck, incapable of further performance. Most infantrymen didn't survive that long. With an average daily casualty rate of 2 percent, the chances of keeping body and soul together for 100–200 days were slim. The infantry, by definition, take the brunt of the fighting. In ancient armies the infantry were often the poorest soldiers with the weakest weapons, typically spears and shields. They were put up front to absorb the enemies' arrows and spears, and to keep the other side's infantry occupied. Meanwhile, the wealthier, and usually noble, horsemen and more heavily armored infantry in the rear waited for the right moment to charge to victory or retreat from defeat. Win or lose, the infantry suffer the majority of the casualties.

Today, far more firepower is tossed about. Battles are now fought along continuous fronts hundreds or thousands of kilometers long instead of a few hundred meters of battle line on some dusty field. However, four thousand years have not changed the role of the infantry much.

Candidates for the Infantry

Studies during World War II revealed that the more effective infantryman was a fellow of average or better intelligence, with good mechanical skills, and in good physical shape. These were the same skills needed in the artillery, or to operate armored vehicles, but as complex infantry weapons have become more common, the demand for quality troops in the infantry has increased. The leaders of infantry units also must be of good quality; otherwise, the infantry is completely lost. These leaders, particularly the NCOs (sergeants), come from the ranks, and while infantry takes the recruits it can get, it is hoped that effective training of the NCOs and officers will compensate for the inexperience of the troops. The ancient truism "There are no bad troops, only bad officers" applies especially here.

Although the industrialized countries have greater demands for the best and the brightest infantry recruits, they also tend to have a higher level of education in their population. These nations also use relatively more firepower and fewer infantrymen. The solution of many industrialized nations is to have smaller, professional armies that can obtain carefully screened volunteers. This solution has worked, but cannot provide sufficient high-quality infantry for mass armies. But then, perhaps we don't need massive armies anymore.

The Infantry Unit

Every infantryman depends on his unit for physical, moral, mental, and medical support. The squad is made up of 8 to 15 men. It is customarily commanded by a sergeant and consists of two or more fire teams. Each team is organized around some sort of heavy weapon: machine gun, mortar, antitank or antiaircraft weapon. This form of organization developed from World War I experience, where it was noticed that most of the firepower of an infantry unit is in its crew-served heavy weapons, not the individual soldiers' rifles. A weapon requiring more than one person to operate, such as a machine gun that needs another man to feed the ammunition and look out for targets, is more likely to be fired—an isolated soldier will tend to not fire. The close proximity of another soldier, and the firepower of their larger weapon, reassures the troops and helps suppress anxiety. Loneliness and the presence of death are a devastating combination that plunges many isolated soldiers into a frozen panic. Under the stress and uncertainty of combat, individual infantrymen will tend to seek cover and not use their weapons, or at best fire blindly. It is not unusual for units new to combat to hit the ground en masse at the sound of a few rifle shots. Once on the ground, out of sight of its leaders, an entire battalion could take hours to get up and start moving again. Knowledgeable leadership, a spirit of co-operation, and mutual support can turn an infantry unit from a panic-stricken mob into a cohesive, effective combat unit.

The infantryman works with the other members of his squad and knows many other members of his platoon. When not in the field, the unmarried members of the platoon live in the same large room or building. When out in the field, the infantrymen live wherever they can, and feel even more isolated because the troops are spread out over a larger area. They might go days without seeing anyone but members of their squad or platoon.

Infantry Organization

One of the few things that have become standardized throughout the world is the organization of infantry units. What follows is a list of infantry units, from the smallest to the largest.

Fire Teams have two to six men and are sometimes called a section. They are based on the operation of a crew-served weapon such as a machine gun, mortar, antiaircraft or antitank missile. While only one man may be needed to operate the weapon, and another to assist with ammunition, the other members of the team provide security and replacements if the machine gunner is wounded. Heavy losses in combat will often shrink fire teams down to a minimal size of two men. Fire teams are commanded by the lowest grade of noncommissioned officer (NCO). When attacking, a fire team spreads out on a frontage under 50 meters. In defense, a fire team is responsible for an area that can be effectively covered by its primary weapon: If a machine gun or automatic rifle, this means a range of over 500 meters on an open plain to an area of a few meters in jungles. More important is the range at which the troops can detect, by eye or ear, the presence of enemy troops. Detection capability gets worse after a few hundred meters and is also reduced by rain, fog, night, and heavy winds. The foundation of any infantry force, whether or not they operate from armored personnel carriers (APCs), the fire teams must be efficient or the larger units will never be.

Squads have two or three fire teams (8 to 15 men) and are commanded by an NCO. In an attack, they advance on a front of 50 to 100 meters. In defense, they are responsible for an area generally 200 meters wide and

deep. The squad is the largest unit consisting of nothing but infantrymen—
it says so in the job classifications (in the U.S. Army, the code is 11B, or
"eleven bush.")

Platoons have three or four squads (30 to 50 men) and are commanded
by an NCO or the lowest grade of commissioned officer. Typically, if there
is a fourth squad, it contains special weapons, normally machine guns or
mortars. They attack on a front of 100 to 150 meters, normally with two
platoons side by side and a third behind acting as a reserve. A platoon
defends up to 500 meters' frontage, generally by concentrating several
squads for all-round defense. The platoon is the smallest unit with non-
infantry specialists, such as radio operators or medics. Still, it consists of
80 to 95 percent infantry.

Companies have three or four platoons (100 to 250 men). Always commanded by an officer and assisted by a senior NCO. The fourth platoon
typically contains mortars, heavy machine guns, and sometimes antitank
and/or antiaircraft missiles. Wealthier armies have electronic sensors and
other special equipment. A company attacks on a front of 500 to 1,000
meters. In defense, it holds twice that frontage. It is made up of from 60
to 90 percent infantry.

Battalions have three to five companies (400 to 1,500 men) and are
commanded by a major or lieutenant colonel along with a small staff.
Battalions sometimes have tanks and artillery and are the smallest
combined-arms unit capable of independent operations. In effect, a battalion is outfitted as a miniature army. In the attack, it advances on a
frontage of one to three kilometers (km), and defends twice that. Battalions
are from 40 to 80 percent infantry.

Regiments have three or four battalions (1,500–2,500 men). Commanded by a lieutenant colonel or colonel, they usually have small contingents of artillery, tanks, engineers, and other support units. Most
Western nations no longer have infantry regiments, but instead form brigades with smaller proportions of infantry in them. These brigades have
their own support units, which turn them into miniature divisions. They
are from 25 to 60 percent infantry.

Larger Units. Brigades, divisions, and armies contain smaller proportions of infantry and are frequently not referred to as infantry units. The
proportion of infantry declines rapidly as unit size increases. Most infantry
divisions are less than 10 percent infantry, the remainder being combat
and noncombat support troops.

Combat Engineers. Called "Pioneers" or "Sappers" by most armies,
combat engineers are specialists in exotic weapons and engineering equipment. They are also expected to be infantry-trained and in emergencies
are used just like infantry. Their weapons include mines, special explosives,
flamethrowers, and any new device that seems to fall within their area of
expertise. Their specialty is setting up elaborate defense quickly. Engineers
are also expert at demolishing enemy defenses quickly, which qualifies them

as combat troops. They are highly respected by the infantry. This is primarily because of their activities in front of the infantry when assisting in an assault on dense enemy defenses, specifically concrete-reinforced "fixed" defenses. Because of their specialists' training, combat engineers are used as regular infantry only in emergencies. They are highly trained and not as easily replaced as regular infantry.

Special Operations Forces (SOF), otherwise known as commandos, raiders, rangers, Spetsnaz, or special forces, are highly trained infantry who operate quietly in small groups. In theory, small groups of well-prepared infantry should be much more efficient. In practice, many nations try to have it both ways and use these troops in large groups. Under these conditions, they usually attract too much attention, and enemy firepower. These guys are good, but not bulletproof. SOF earn their keep when doing what they do best—raids, reconnaissance, and other special operations. These actions are expensive to support with the required aircraft, ships, and staging areas. Moreover, there are relatively few of these tasks to be done compared to the more massive operations of a major war. Larger-scale commando operations have long been proposed by the Soviets for their Spetsnaz troops. These troops are to operate in groups of 5 to 50 troops, going after airfields, missile launchers, headquarters, supply depots, radars, and the like in the early stages of a major war. Working with undercover agents in enemy nations, Spetsnaz expect to take high losses but to strike a paralyzing blow to the enemy's ability to resist. Such operations were mounted during World War II and the Soviet invasion of Afghanistan in 1979. The Tet Offensive during the Vietnam War was a Spetsnaz-type operation. These operations are a gamble, with a payoff far in excess of possible losses. The only problem is that they are a gamble, and failure may seriously compromise operations using friendly conventional forces.

The Infantryman's Job

Once a soldier is inducted, given some training, and sent to the combat zone, he can expect to encounter the following list of activities:

Reserve. Although available for combat, new reserve units arriving at the front wait until things quiet down to be given a "quiet" sector of the front. In this way, new units are eased into the horrors of combat. Reserve status is also an opportunity to rest units that have been in heavy fighting. The troops catch up on sleep, clean themselves up, send and receive mail, get hot food, receive replacements for lost men and equipment, and train. Normally, but not always, all this occurs in an area that is not under enemy fire. Often the accommodations aren't much better than those at the front.

Most of the units sent to Saudi Arabia in 1990 were, in effect, in reserve status until the fighting began.

Movement. Until the 1950s, the majority of the infantrymen walked. Some still do. Today, infantry ride in armored personnel carriers (APCs), trucks, or helicopters. Movement affords a good opportunity to sleep. Veterans learn this quickly and practice it diligently. It is not easy to sleep in APCs, especially cramped Russian ones, but it can be done. This is one reason why troops spend over 90 percent of their time outside their vehicles. But when the units are on the move, the troops practically live in their vehicles. The vehicle drivers are only human, and if great care is not taken, they also will doze off during long drives at night. A characteristic of mechanized units' continued movement are frequent accidents as driver fatigue increases. The risk of ambush from the air or ground also increases considerably, partially as a result of the greater fluidity of the battlefield and partially because air and ground sensors are more capable. Aircraft were always a problem, but now we have "smart" artillery munitions that can quickly pounce on the unsuspecting convoy and, at the very least, wake everyone up. These nasties operate at all times, even during weather conditions that ground aircraft. Some smart munitions even land and wait for a vehicle to pass by before detonating. Troop movements will never be as restful as they once were.

Meeting Engagement. In the early stages of a war, a lot of "meeting engagements" are anticipated between advancing units that encounter each other unexpectedly. They are expected to be spirited and hectic. Since the 1970s, many armies have come to believe that this will be the common form of combat in future wars. In any case, the infantryman will find himself either ambushed or, after a warning, sent off in some direction as if on patrol to ambush someone else. Only the most confident and experienced troops look forward to this form of combat. Too many things can go wrong in such chaotic engagements.

Construction. A soldier's best friend is not his weapons, but his shovel. Once a soldier gets a taste of infantry combat, he quickly develops protective attitudes. Even in an inactive situation, the infantry still have daily casualties from stray enemy and friendly fire. When this fire increases, so does the risk to life and limb. This provides a constant incentive to obtain better protection. This is where the shovel comes in. Even with the widespread use of armored personnel carriers, troops still dig. The armored carriers are not immune to all shells and bullets, and a disabled APC means the crew has to do without the amenities it provides. The APCs are dug in if time and resources, such as a bulldozer blade on some armored vehicles, permit. When a combat unit halts for more than a few hours, it works diligently to get "wired in" and "dug in." Preparing trenches and other protective positions comes first. The wiring consists of putting out sensors (trip flares, sound and motion detectors, ground radars, etc.), and laying—sometimes burying—telephone wires. If resources are available, mines are emplaced, barbed wire is laid down, and barricades are erected on vehicle routes. Weapons are positioned so that they can be fired quickly—and "blind" at night or in bad weather—to cover all likely avenues of enemy movement. Supporting artillery and air force units are contacted and arrangements made for their firepower to be delivered to key locations if needed. More important, these distant units are alerted where not to fire, so as to avoid hitting friendly units.

All of this is not enough. Enemy fire can cut the telephone wires, and jammers render the radios useless. Preparations must be made to use alternate forms of communication, such as colored flares or messengers. The emphasis is on making the defenders capable of executing defensive operations as quickly and tersely as possible. This is accomplished through considerable efforts by the troops. All troops in a position must be drilled on where everything is, including supplies. Routes protected from enemy fire are marked so that people can move safely, especially if a retreat is called for. Provision must be made for things going from bad to worse. The routes for withdrawal to another defensive position, and the new position itself, must be identified. The troops must be drilled on the sequence of a withdrawal; otherwise, it can easily turn into a rout and a great slaughter. These arrangements increase survivability during the chaos of an enemy attack. During the heat of battle, it is difficult to perform the simplest actions, such as moving 10 meters, pulling a trigger, or getting a fire request back to an artillery unit. All these preparations take skill, and considerable diligence. Twenty-four hours of effort will do wonders to prepare these safety measures. An ancient saying has it that "the more you sweat before the battle, the less you will bleed during it."

Patrol. Superior information gives you a lifesaving edge in combat. Patrolling is how to obtain it. Patrolling is also a tense and dangerous activity. Troops go into enemy territory to look around, and often try to capture one or more of the enemy troops for interrogation. Friendly and enemy forces are typically separated by a few hundred meters or up to a few kilometers of no-man's-land. This is the site of most patrol actions. Each side struggles to hide details of its own situation while discovering what its opponent is up to. Patrols attempt to prevent the enemy from gaining surprise. The patrol's biggest danger is an enemy ambush. Modern electronic sensors have helped somewhat—microphones or, more recently, devices that recognize the sound or heat signatures of men and equipment are currently being used. Battlefield radars are also used if the area is open enough. Troops on foot, however, remain difficult to detect. Also, it's dangerous to patrol wooded or built-up areas, where detection ranges are lowest.

Night is the preferred time for patrols, because in the dark it is possible to remain undetected longer, or more easily escape from an encounter. Ambushes are typically set up at night, as are booby traps and mines. At night, attempts are made to remove the enemy traps and mines. Patrols generally do not go looking for a fight—they just want information. But each side will fight to preserve its own secrets. Because patrolling comprises most of a soldier's time in combat, it becomes a terror-filled, deadly game of hide-and-seek. Just sitting in your hole can be dangerous enough; getting out and patrolling is very unhealthy.

The tactics of patrolling are simple enough. The size of a patrol averages from fire team to platoon strength. At the head of the patrol are one or two men who constitute the "point." Their job is to spot the enemy before the enemy spots them. Even if the point man is hit, the rest of the patrol, 30 to 100 meters behind, will have time, and space, to deploy and face the enemy on more even terms. Depending on the size of the patrol, the nature of the terrain, and the expected enemy opposition, additional "points" may be sent to the flanks or to the rear. Ideally, the rest of the troops try to maintain a distance of five meters from each other to minimize casualties should they be shelled, or run across booby traps or automatic-weapons fire. Patrols are done very systematically, or should be, and their routes are carefully plotted. The primary purpose is to find the enemy and determine what he is up to. Also, useful information about the local geography and population is gathered. And often there will be a secondary mission to seek out and destroy enemy patrols and outposts.

Sometimes the patrol is assigned an ambush position, or just a location from which to observe. Or patrols go out to set up booby traps, listening devices, or mines. Their missions may last from a few hours to a few days, and the patrol can go out and return by helicopter, by airplane, or on foot. Artillery and air-power support is sometimes arranged, although this requires that the patrol stick closely to the assigned route and continually know where the support is. Otherwise, the supporting fire will hit nothing, or perhaps even the patrol itself. Technology, in the form of GPS (Global Positioning System) hand-held locating devices (the device shows where you are via satellite signals, to within 50 meters or less) makes patrolling a lot safer for those who have them. The GPS devices were very welcome among the combat troops during their first battlefield use in the Gulf War.

Multiple patrols will support each other, or additional forces will be held ready to go after an endangered patrol. Patrolling is done day and night. Round-the-clock patrolling is an indicator that a force has good control over an area. Troops that know how to patrol effectively have mastered the most difficult aspect of soldiering and are usually superior in other ways to their opponents.

Defense. Soldiers sometimes attack, frequently patrol, but always defend. When the other fellow attacks, you might have received some warning from your patrols. Typically, the attack is announced by incoming artillery fire, which might include poison gas or nuclear weapons (gas shells have been used, but not nukes—still, the capability is still there). Survivors must quickly get out of the bottom of their holes or dugouts and set up antitank and other heavy weapons. These weapons are normally concealed to prevent damage during the initial enemy fire. The defenders must also emerge to observe the advancing enemy and direct the fire of their own artillery. Although now exposed to some enemy fire, the defenders are still in their positions, and have a chance of surviving. Their prospects are further increased by the "spread-out" nature of modern warfare.

As part of a platoon strong point, you would occupy one of 10 or so holes in the ground in a circular area 100 to 200 meters in diameter. The enemy might not even be coming your way. Instead, enemy artillery would be fired to prevent you from going to the aid of your comrades in the distance who are being overrun. If you have the misfortune of being in the way, you can only hope that your firepower, and that of your artillery, will stop them. You may survive being overrun, because the attack's initial goal is getting through your front-line positions and into the rear area to shoot up supply and artillery units. In the chaos of battle, it is easy enough to crawl off somewhere and hide or just keep your head down as the enemy's armored vehicles rumble past. Fighting to the death exists more as a fiction than as an infantryman's goal in battle.

Surrender is always a possibility, assuming the battered attacker is in a compassionate mood. However, given the fact that 70 percent of attacking troops in destroyed APCs are killed or injured, the enemy might try to kill off any survivors of the opposition. Although it is not often written about, prisoners are not usually taken during attacks, especially if individuals or small groups are trying to give up. The attacker doesn't want to spare any troops to guard prisoners, particularly since he needs all the help he can get to complete the attack successfully—his own troops that are wounded are in more need of attention than enemy prisoners. This is why defeated defenders attempt to hide or sneak away rather than test the questionable mercies of surrender. Veteran troops know this, otherwise they wouldn't be veterans. The 1991 Gulf War was not exceptional in this respect. The Iraqis, for the most part, did not resist. The coalition troops soon realized that they had achieved a rarely realized dream: a defender who didn't want to fight. The coalition troops celebrated by taking prisoner just about any Iraqi who wanted to surrender.

On the other hand, the defender has a number of advantages. First, he is under cover, customarily dug in. He is difficult to see. The attacker is nervously aware of this invisibility, and this frequently leads to panic. The attackers see their companions being hit by unseen defenders. The defender also sees this and is encouraged. Moreover, defender casualties are generally not seen by the attackers, or defenders, further widening the gap in morale. The defender knows that safety is as close as the bottom of his hole.

When attackers go for cover, the attack breaks down. You can't attack when you are flat on your face. Therefore, attacks succeed only if the troops are well trained and well led (a rare combination), and/or the defender has been all but obliterated by artillery and other firepower. If the defender cannot maintain a continuous front of firepower, the attacker will be stopped only in front of the surviving positions. These positions can then be hit from all sides and eliminated more easily. However, a continuous front does not require a large number of troops; in open terrain, one functioning machine gun can hold up infantry on a front of 200 meters or more. Defense rarely produces victory, only various degrees of defeat. If you stop the enemy attack once, there will likely be another one. If you do manage to really clobber the attacker, you are often rewarded with an order to counterattack. An astute commander attempts to have defending troops fall back before the next attack hits, especially if he calculates that this next attack will overwhelm his defenses. Even if he feels he can hold, a successful and well-timed fallback will force the enemy to waste a lot of firepower, fuel, and energy attacking an empty position, thus weakening the enemy for the next attack.

Attacking. Think of this as a large-scale patrol where you are almost certain to be ambushed. This is the most dreaded of infantry operations. No matter how well planned, an attack means that you must get up and expose yourself to enemy fire. Ideally, the artillery smashes the defender to the point where the infantry simply walks in, takes a few prisoners, and keeps on going. It rarely works out that way.

If patrolling and information gathering are first-rate, you will know the position of most, but never all, of the enemy positions. If the artillery fire is plentiful and accurate (it rarely is), you can destroy many of these positions. If the leaders planning and leading the attacks are skillful enough, they can destroy the key positions, allowing troops to bypass many of the remaining ones. This way, the assault can be carried out with minimal losses to the attacker. If the attacking troops are adept enough, they work as a deadly team, avoiding enemy fire and eliminating defending positions systematically. If, if, if . . .

The key ingredients are skill, preparation, and, above all, information. History demonstrates that a successful attack is won before it begins. The norm is not enough time, not enough resources, not enough skill, not enough information. Even against an unskilled defender, everything must go right to achieve minimal losses. Keep in mind that the defender can fire off a shot in relative safety and not even be detected. The attackers may get him, but not before they've had a few more casualties. Historically, the only way to truly "soften up" a defender is to destroy his morale. This is generally achieved more through psychological means than with firepower. It can be done, it is often done, but it depends a great deal on who the defender is. Defenders fighting for something they believe in are very difficult to demoralize.

In the attack, the quality of the troops is the critical factor. Poorly trained, poorly led troops do not press home an attack against even inept opposition, and when they do, they take heavy casualties. Some things never change, and this is one of them. Reckless bravery does not help, as it just gets more attackers killed. The security of armored personnel carriers has also proven to be false; most armies have reverted to infantry attacking on foot, with their tanks and APCs behind them providing fire support. The Arab-Israeli wars showed this, just as the Japanese banzai attacks in World War II showed the futility of blind courage. But attacks can be enormously successful. The most recent example was the Allied ground offensive in the Gulf War. The attacking troops, largely Americans, made all the right moves described above. They did it professionally, thoroughly, and relentlessly. Their reward was the quick defeat of the Iraqis, and an unprecedented low casualty rate among the attacking troops.

Pursuit. Once the enemy is on the run, you must chase down the defeated remnants before they can reform and defend again. Pursuit is deceptively dangerous. You never know when the enemy will stop and ambush you, and with what. The resistance might be just a few diehards unable, or unwilling, to retreat any further. It might also be fresh enemy units, strong enough to stop the pursuer cold. The watchword of pursuit is speed. Go so fast that you overtake the fleeing defender, along a parallel route if possible. The ideal situation is to set up your own ambush, then collect more prisoners or kill the enemy off in comparative safety. Again, the deciding factors are skill in patrolling and intelligence gathering, as well as the ability to deploy rapidly against any resistance despite fatigue.

Not all nations train their troops with equal intensity for all the above activities. Some emphasize the offense at the expense of the others. Many less powerful nations emphasize the defense. Some nations simply have strange priorities for any number of reasons. The U.S. Army, for example, does not train for "pursuit" operations. Why it doesn't is a long story, but the point is that "well-trained troops" can have quite different capabilities from one nation to the next.

The Standard of Living at the Front

It is very low, and the overriding goal is to not get hit by flying objects. This requires being inconspicuous, as what the enemy can't see is less likely to be shot at. Shellfire is less deliberate and more difficult to hide from. For this reason, infantry become like Hobbits—they live underground. Even so, it's an uneasy life. There's much work to be done. Defensive positions must be prepared and maintained. Equipment must be looked after, which is now a major chore since the infantry have been given armored vehicles. Enemy fire and Mother Nature conspire to keep everyone dirty, damaged, and generally on the verge of a breakdown.

Security is the major consideration. From 20 to 50 percent of the troops are on guard at all times, doing little more than manning their weapons and watching for the enemy to do something. Some of this guard time is spent in working on fortifications, an endless task. Depending on how aggressive, and capable, a unit is, 10 percent of the guard-duty time will be spent outside the unit positions setting up ambushes and listening posts (a few troops hunkered down near enemy positions to observe what the other guy is doing). This is also a form of patrol work. These activities are immediate, essential, and a matter of life and death. Competent armies have set routines for troops in the field, with the work divided up so that the troops have minimal time to eat and sleep, and little else. There are always emergencies and distractions to disrupt those not "at work"—from an enemy attack to random shellfire. Fatigue is usually the result.

The uneasy nature of life under enemy fire is not conducive to relaxation. About 10 percent of all casualties are attributed to combat fatigue, the cumulative effect of little sleep, poor food (typically cold and consumed in an unappetizing atmosphere), dreary living conditions, and the constant threat of random death or mutilation. If it rains, you normally get wet. If it's cold, you bundle up as best you can. If it stays damp, you are in constant danger of maladies like trench foot (your toes literally rot). If it's a tropical climate, you can rot all over, plus contract numerous diseases. These afflictions can be avoided only by energetic measures to keep dry and medicated, which requires discipline and the availability of medicines and dry clothing. Staying clean is nearly impossible, as you are living in the dirt. But a certain level of cleanliness (or "field sanitation") is critical. Otherwise, the troops get sick. Eventually, most of the troops get sick, and some begin to die. Normally, the only solution to the constant threat of wastage from these living conditions is rotating troops out of the front line periodically. Two weeks in, one week out is ideal. Rarely are there enough troops to go around; the ratio is often lower, and sometimes there is no relief for the infantry. Such a situation means that hardly any troops will survive prolonged combat alive or uninjured.

Even without the immediate presence of the enemy, life in the field in wartime is an ultimately degenerating experience. Modern infantry units have to maintain enormous quantities of equipment. A 700-man U.S. mechanized-infantry battalion has over 100 vehicles, mostly armored personnel carriers. These heavy, tracklaying (bulldozerlike) vehicles require at least four man-hours of maintenance a day to keep them going. And more than 100 machine guns, 50 antitank guided missiles, over 100 major electronic items (radios and sensors), plus generators, stoves, maintenance supplies, personal weapons, and other gear. When living in barracks, the troops can spend more than 20 hours a week per man just keeping their equipment in shape. The troops are capable of only so much. Eventually, they and their equipment begin to waste away. It's an eternal truth of warfare that when campaigning, even without deadly contact with the enemy, an army will eventually wear itself out.

Theory and Practice

Commanders must confront many ways of doing it wrong when preparing men for infantry combat. There is only one way to do it right. A handful of nations usually get it right. These include Germany, Britain, Israel, and a few others. America's record was spotty until the 1980s, primarily because of lapses in leadership and training. The reforms (largely unheralded) of the 1980s finally give the United States professional peacetime armed forces. The United States thus joins a very select club. Russia should not be forgotten simply because the Soviet Union has disappeared. Russia is still the largest, and most populous, nation in Europe. Russian infantry improves substantially after they have been battered around a bit, and Russia is already involved in more wars now than at any other time in the past 40 years.

Another problem with infantry is that there is a lot less of it. A Western mechanized-infantry division of 16,000 men has fewer than 1,000 infantrymen. Even many Third World infantry divisions have the same number of infantry. The chief cause of this is the introduction of the Infantry Fighting Vehicle (IFV) and a lot of other equipment that must be taken care of. The IFVs are actually light tanks, equipped with small cannon and ATGMs (Antitank Guided Missles). A crew is required to operate all this equipment, and the operators come from the infantry squad. Numerous other problems intrude. The vehicle and its additional equipment require a lot of attention, leaving less time for infantry training.

The armored IFV also prompts troops to stay near their vehicle, making them more vulnerable to enemy fire. IFVs are very vulnerable to a large number of modern weapons. Each IFV carries a cannon that is effective against other IFVs. All antitank weapons can destroy IFVs. Worst of all, IFVs have not seen a lot of action. It is not yet known, from actual experience, which tactics are most efficient for IFVs. The experience with Russian IFVs (BMPs) in Middle Eastern wars has not been encouraging. The experience of U.S. IFVs in the Gulf War was not conclusive because the IFVs did not get a sustained workout. Finding out what IFVs are best at is likely to be a painful and expensive process. The experience to date is not encouraging. After all, Israel went out of its way to produce a new tank, but saw no compelling reason to develop an IFV. Armies are not unmindful of the many problems created by the numerous armored vehicles their infantry now have.

In America, there has been an infatuation with the light-infantry concept, and several divisions of these troops have been formed. Lacking many armored vehicles, these units can be rapidly moved to distant battlefields on short notice. Supplying them in the typically lavish U.S. fashion is another matter, and this problem has been largely pushed aside. From this, one can concur that these lightly armed and not-very-mobile troops will take a beating should they encounter more traditionally equipped adversaries. Like a few Iraqi tank divisions, for example. This was a very real fear during the summer of 1990, when all that stood between the Iraqi armor and the Saudi Arabian oil fields were some U.S. light infantry. In light of that experience, the United States has arranged to get at least 5 or 10 M-1 tanks airlifted along with the next unit of light infantry sent to a hot spot. As the C-5 transport can only carry one M-1 at a time, this adds little armored support to the light infantry. But in light of the Persian Gulf situation of 1990, it now seems a reasonable move. For a long-range solution, the army is building 300 light tanks, half of which will equip a new light (or "air transportable") armored cavalry regiment. These vehicles provide more armored protection per C-5 load than the airborne M-1s. A more practical solution has also been instituted, and that is storing the equipment for an armored brigade in Kuwait, and, for a marine division, 2,500 miles to the south (in Diego Garcia).

Being a grunt has never been easy.

The Future

The future is bleak for the infantry, especially those that operate on a tight budget. A century ago, it was calculated that you had to fire a man's weight in bullets and shells to cause a casualty. This tonnage has increased several times in the last 50 years. But the tonnage has recently come down as much more efficient weapons became available. More cluster bombs and other ICM (Improved Conventional Munitions) will be blasting away at smaller numbers of infantry. Armored vehicles, many with improved lightweight armor, plus improved protective clothing for the troops, do not give sufficient protection against all of this. As long as the supplies of these high-tech weapons hold up, they will cause casualties more quickly and at higher rates than lower-tech weapons did in the past. This will be particularly true for infantry in the Third World, and in general with nations that cannot afford to lavish a lot of attention on their infantry.

Although the major powers seem increasingly reluctant to use chemical and nuclear weapons, Third World nations have found homemade chemical weapons an easily obtained means of inflicting massive casualties quickly and cheaply. Iraq did not hesitate to use chemicals against Iran and the Kurds in the 1980s. The Iraqis also used laser range finders as a weapon to deliberately blind Iranian troops. The increasing number of laser devices has given the battlefield a more sinister appearance as more troops wear protective glasses. Already, many European armies issue special "laser-proof" binoculars.

While protection is lagging, the infantry themselves are becoming more lethal. They are being equipped with more capable and appropriate weapons. After years of troops using antitank rockets as portable artillery against enemy fortifications, rocket launchers for that purpose—and much more effective at it—are coming into use. Better mines and sensors, as well as lighter, more powerful, and more reliable radios, and protective clothing are becoming standard in many armies. Another way of providing protection is to get the troops out of the way of all this new firepower. Electronic sensors are more common, thus reducing the need for patrols and manned listening posts. Robotic antitank weapons and lighter and more numerous mines also keep the grunts away from their nemesis, the tank. Despite all this, in the Gulf War, nearly all the casualties were infantry, including most of the friendly-fire losses. The infantry will still be needed to perform their principal function, occupying ground. If the troops feel more exposed and vulnerable in these situations, they are not imagining the increased danger. It is real, and growing.

While the Third World nations attempt to catch up with Western levels of infantry equipment, Western nations keep moving forward. The United States, in particular, is still keen on giving its infantry every possible edge. This involves moving U.S. infantry into the realm of what is currently considered science fiction. In addition to more effective protective clothing, the most significant new equipment will be electronic. In particular, miniaturized electronics and high-capacity batteries make it possible to put a short-range communications and navigation system in a soldier's helmet without unduly increasing weight. This would enable troops to keep in touch with each other and discuss their positions when visual contact is not possible. As battlefields and the troops become more spread out, this form of contact becomes more critical. Navigation aids, based on GPS technology, will be carried by platoon, or even squad, leaders. A few weapons (infrared or laser) have special electronic sighting equipment that allows for improved accuracy (image enhancement for seeing through dark and smoke).

A laser-spotting device can indicate where the weapon will hit out to 800 meters, which saves a lot of ammunition when you are trying to hit something. Also available for deployment is a six-pound thermal sight for rifles and machine guns. These sights have a range of 400–1,000 meters (depending on weather conditions) and would make high-tech infantry a devastating force at night. In the near future, a lightweight microcomputer (weighing less than a hand grenade and the size of a deck of cards) will be able to be carried like a grenade, with a wire going down the arm to the control panel on the arm. Such devices, in fact, exist now in commercial applications. This computer could handle communication, navigation, intel info, and logistics for the individual soldier. Lightweight sensors will also allow troops to better defend their positions, even if they stop only for a few hours. We saw a preview of these technical advantages in the 1991 Gulf War—the armored vehicles had them. Now, it is technically possible to equip individual infantry in the same way. With the cost of the U.S. infantryman's equipment currently at about $1,100, the high-tech grunt's gear could, with these additions, easily cost more than 10 times that amount. However, the new equipment would provide an edge in battlefield situations.

Naturally, all this electronic gear can be a liability if the opposition also has access to sophisticated electronics. For example, off-the-shelf electronics could be easily fashioned to provide low-tech infantry with a warning that the high-tech troops were in the vicinity because of the signals broadcast by the U.S. infantry gear. This is not a guaranteed countermeasure, but a potential and possible one. With the end of the Cold War, the Western nations have something of a monopoly on this stuff and are likely to arrive at a future battlefield with their technical advantages intact.

Tools of the Trade

LIGHT INFANTRY WEAPONS

These are the infantryman's personal weapons. They are called "light" because the weapons and their ammunition are carried by the individual soldier and used without any assistance. These weapons include pistols (generally useless, except during rare instances), bayonets (useful for domestic chores), grenades, and rifles. The most effective weapon is the rifle, now called an assault rifle. These are generally of small caliber (5.56mm), the same as the American .22, but with a high-powered propellant charge. Although capable of fully automatic fire, these weapons carry only 20–40 bullets in a box magazine rather than the 100+ bullet belts used by the heavier machine guns. On full automatic, they fire off 30 rounds in less than three seconds. Also unlike heavier machine guns, the rifles have lighter barrels, which will overheat after 100 rounds are fired in less than a few minutes. This will cause jams, premature firing, or worse. Infantrymen customarily carry no more than a dozen 20-round magazines, each weighing about a pound. The real killing is done with heavier weapons, and firefights rarely last long enough for the infantry to exhaust their ammunition.

The characteristics of grenades, the infantryman's "personal artillery," have been vastly distorted by the media. Fragmentation grenades weigh about a pound, can be thrown a maximum of 40 meters (10–20 meters is more common), and injure about 50 percent of those within six meters of the explosion. Less than 10 percent of the wounded will die, thus making grenades one of the least lethal weapons in the infantryman's arsenal. In theory, grenades have a three-to-five-second fuse. Quality control being what it is, these fuses are sometimes a little longer or shorter, usually longer (for safety reasons). Some grenades use a contact fuse, exploding when they strike something hard. These can be used only if you don't have a lot of soft items the grenade can bounce harmlessly off. Grenades are favored when fighting at night or in cluttered areas (forests, buildings). It is also important to realize that grenades are rarely thrown large distances— the thrower is generally prone or otherwise not in a position to do a proper windup. Therefore, tossing them around corners or over an obstacle is more common. American troops have been using a grenade launcher for over 20 years. Originally, it looked like a large-barrel shotgun, but it gradually evolved into an extra barrel that could be attached to rifles. The 40mm grenade can be propelled over 300 meters, although accurate use is rarely beyond 100 meters. A full range of grenades is available—the weapon also comes as just the barrel, which is attached to an assault rifle. More details are found in the section at the end of this chapter describing infantry weapons.

HEAVY INFANTRY WEAPONS

Any infantry weapon requiring more than one man to operate, although most can be used without assistance in a pinch. Principal weapons of this type are:

- Machine guns, which need an extra man to carry the ammunition.
- Antitank and antiaircraft missiles that require two or more men to carry the system.
- Mortars, whose weight (most are under 200 pounds) of weapon and ammo requires several men. These are small artillery pieces that fire their shells up at a sharp angle.

Ideally, all infantrymen should be adept with these weapons. In practice, everyone specializes. In particular, the mortars and missiles tend to be used only by specialists. All infantrymen are given some training in the use of machine guns, grenade launchers, and antitank rockets. This is called "familiarization training" and is just that. Any real proficiency with these weapons has to be gained in combat.

SPECIAL EQUIPMENT

Some types of equipment are handled by most infantrymen, even if supervision by experts is required. Minefields and booby traps can be installed by experienced infantrymen. These explosive devices can be dangerous to handle, and it is more effective to have a few practiced individuals do the work. If no experienced people are available and the job must be done, you tend to have some accidents.

Other specialist devices, such as sensors and communications equipment (radios, telephones, and flares), are dangerous only if they don't work. This equipment is particularly essential for successful defense, along with mines and booby traps. Sensors warn you of the enemy's approach. Communications equipment coordinates your actions and is the vital link with supporting artillery, commo equipment, and aircraft.

PERSONAL EQUIPMENT

More mundane but essential tools are the vital entrenching tool (folding shovel), a bayonet (used for everything but stabbing someone, for example, opening cans, cutting firewood or rope), a gas mask, and other chemical protectors like ointments, antidotes, and special clothing. The most respected articles of protective clothing are the flak vest and helmet. The latest versions of these vests, which actually extend below the waist, weigh less than 10 pounds and will stop nearly all shell fragments and bullets. They are uncomfortable in warm weather, but combat veterans swear by them. The "flak jacket" reduces casualties about 25 percent. Because of their expense, only a few armies use the vests. These include the United States and most of the industralized nations. Russia began issuing them in the 1980s, first to commando units. In most armies, the helmets are made of steel; the newer ones are of plastic and offer better protection and more comfort. And then there is the first-aid kit, a mini-drugstore with pep pills, aspirin, antibiotics, bandages, painkillers, and other controlled substances. Not everything that goes into the first-aid pouch is official issue, or even legal. Experienced infantrymen learn to equip themselves as best they can. Speaking of unofficial equipment, veteran infantry often obtain a pistol or even a shotgun. The pistol makes the soldier feel a little more secure; the shotgun is very useful in close-range combat. Transistor radios continue to be present, providing another way to find out what is really happening, assuming the stations are still broadcasting. For personal comfort, we find sleeping bags (or just blankets in the low-tech armies), spare clothing (notably socks), sunglasses (good for safely viewing distant nuclear explosions), canteens (more than one in hot climates), mess kits and food (junk food is favored over the official rations). As troops now move around in APCs, the amount of equipment has increased. Losing the APC, therefore, has a greater adverse effect on morale.

Combat Values

This chart assigns a numerical combat value to each weapon, which is a combination of the weapon's destructive power, ease of use, mobility, and reliability.

2-1 Combat Values

	US	Russia
Transport	20	10
Men	1	1
Tank	1,400	1,000
APC	350	250
SP Howitzer	900	500
ATGM	300	200
MG	3	2
Med Mortar	220	150
Hvy Mortar	360	240
AA Gun	200	400
SP SAM	400	300
Lt SAM	200	60
ATRL	40	80

These assessments are used to calculate the overall unit combat values of the charts for U.S. infantry battalions and Russian-type infantry regiments. Actual combat power must also take into account the quality of training and leadership as well as a host of other situational factors. This is generally referred to as the "quality factor." Historically, these training and leadership factors can increase unit effectiveness by several hundred percent. A 20 to 30 percent advantage is normal for most wars, and in some cases the advantage is 200 to 300 percent. Such was the case in the 1991 Gulf War, where U.S. units had a nearly 200 percent quality advantage. Once all the equipment and quality factors have been accounted for, the attacker needs a 3-to-1 advantage in combat power to have a reasonable chance of success. Six-to-one or better is preferred. See Chapter 24, "Attrition," for more details.

Values given are for two major nations' armies: U.S. (United States) and Russia (representing the weapons and doctrine many potential U.S. opponents use). The values show the national differences in weapon design.

TRANSPORT is assigned a value, per vehicle, that represents the ability of the unit's manned vehicles to support the weapons. Fuel, ammunition, and the weapons themselves must be carried. The quantity and quality of the unit's transport determines how effective the weapons will be.

MEN. Each man, with his personal weapons, is assigned a base reference value of 1. In addition, each man is responsible for some other job, either operating a crew-served weapon or providing some form of support. By himself, armed only with his personal weapons, the infantryman is relatively helpless against most other modern weapons.

TANK is a heavily armored, tracked vehicle carrying a large gun in a turret.

APC is an Armored Personnel Carrier (also called IFV).

SP HOWITZER is a self-propelled howitzer (artillery).

ATGM is an Antitank Guided Missile (average of many types from several nations).

MG is a machine gun, not including the infantry's automatic rifles.

MED MORT are medium mortars (81mm and 82mm)—light artillery, often carried in an APC. This also includes 30mm (Russian) and 40mm (U.S.) automatic grenade launchers.

HVY MORT are heavy mortars (120mm) that are mechanically similar to the medium mortars and are typically mounted in APCs.

AA GUN is a self-propelled antiaircraft machine cannon (20mm to 35mm).

SP SAM (Self-Propelled Surface-to-Air Missile) is a vehicle carrying missiles and associated radar and control equipment.

LT (light) SAM is a one-man, shoulder-fired antiaircraft missile.

ATRL (Antitank Rocket Launcher) is portable, carried by individual soldiers.

Infantry Battalions, Companies, and Platoons

Charts 2-2 and 2-3 show the organization, weapons, and combat power of U.S. and Russian-type infantry units. The organization and weaponry of the Russians are used by the vast majority of nations that use Russian equipment. The U.S. system, a variation of Western European systems, uses larger, more heavily armed units. Most nations, including the United States, Germany (in 1945 and the 1970s), Israel, and other major Western military powers have recognized that the leaner organization of the Russians is superior in combat. The Russian type of organization dates from the late 1940s, when the Russians adopted many organizational ideas the Germans had used at the end of World War II. Many Western armies have used the leaner combat-unit organization in conjunction with the more abundant combat-support units typically found in the armies of industrialized nations.

NUMBER OF UNITS is the number of each subordinate unit in the superior unit to the left side of the chart (that is, 3 companies in a battalion, 9 platoons in a battalion). See Combat Values chart for weapons explanations.

COMBAT POWER is the total combat-power rating of the unit divided by 1,000. Based on individual weapon ratings and their quantity in the unit.

% COMBAT POWER, % MANPOWER shows the percentage smaller units have of the next largest unit's combat power or manpower. For example, the 12 infantry platoons of the U.S. infantry battalion possess 61 percent of the battalion's combat power. The remaining combat power is in the battalion and company support units. One immediately obvious fact is that while Russians and Americans put about the same percentage of their manpower in the infantry platoons, Americans place more of their combat power directly in these platoons. The 12 infantry platoons of a U.S. infantry battalion contain 43 percent of the battalion's manpower but 63 percent of its combat power. The Russians have 36 percent of their manpower in the 27 infantry platoons of their infantry regiment, but only 31 percent of the combat power. The Russian system keeps a larger portion of the superior unit's combat under central control. This combat power is applied, typically in large doses, by attaching numerous specialist units to a few of the regiment's nine infantry companies. The advantage of this central control is primarily just that, control. The Russian system does not rely on sophisticated communications as much as Western armies. If the Russian regimental commander wants to get his reserve— over half the regiment's combat power—into action, he sends a messenger down the road to deliver the message. Or leads it himself. This central control is also practical. It eases supply and maintenance problems, with all of the complex gear concentrated in one place instead of dispersed among the numerous infantry units. On the minus side, combat units get fewer opportunities to train with the specialist units. A lot of last-minute "mix and match" places specialist troops next to infantrymen whom they know little about. The infantry tend to be uncomfortable about entrusting their lives to these strangers from the headquarters' reserve. Western units also indulge in this practice in a different form, called "cross attachment." A tank battalion will send one company of its tanks to a neighboring infantry battalion and receive an infantry company in return. The Russians also do this by breaking up their tank units and sending a tank platoon to each infantry company while attaching an infantry platoon or squad to a tank company. However, the Russians prefer to use their specialists as a large mass. This Russian approach has great appeal for Third World armies because they, even more than the Russians, lack the technically competent personnel to provide skilled troops for all combat units.

U.S. INFANTRY UNITS

BATTALION (696 men). The mechanized-infantry battalion contains four infantry companies, one antitank company (69 men, 16 APCs, and 12 TOW launchers), and one headquarters company (356 men, 27 APCs, 6 120mm mortars). The APC (Armored Personnel Carrier) is increasingly replaced by the more elaborate IFV (Infantry Fighting Vehicle).

COMPANY (111 men). The mechanized-infantry company contains three infantry platoons, one headquarters section (12 men, 2 APCs)

PLATOON (33 men). The mechanized-infantry platoon contains a platoon headquarters (six men, one APC, three Dragon ATGMs), three infantry squads (each with nine men, one APC, three machine guns, two grenade launchers). This organization is subject to change every few years, principally because reorganizing infantry platoons is a favorite peacetime activity in many armies. The U.S. Army issues LAW antitank rocket launchers as rounds of ammunition (they are one-shot affairs). Machine guns are distributed, for all practical purposes, on the basis of one for every 12 men in a division, with higher concentrations in combat battalions. Each APC has a machine gun mounted on it. Experienced troops tend to "acquire"

2-2 U.S. Infantry Units

Number of Units>	Battalion 1	Combat Power %	Company 4	Combat Power %	Platoon 12	Combat Power %
Men	696	1%	111	1%	33	1%
Tank	0	0%	0	0%	0	0%
APC	99	48%	14	39%	4	38%
SP How	0	0%	0	0%	0	0%
ATGM	102	42%	23	54%	7	56%
MG	108	0%	27	1%	9	1%
Med Mort	0	0%	0	0%	0	0%
Hvy Mort	6	3%	0	0%	0	0%
AA Gun	0	0%	0	0%	0	0%
SP SAM	0	0%	0	0%	0	0%
Lt SAM	7	2%	0	0%	0	0%
ATRL	72	4%	18	6%	4	4%
Combat Power		73		13		4
% Combat Power		100%		70%		61%
% Manpower		100%		48%		43%

2-3 Russian-Type Infantry Units

No. of Units>	Regiment 1	Combat Power	Battalion 3	Combat Power	Company 9	Combat Power	Platoon 27	Combat Power
Men	2,250	2%	441	2%	103	2%	30	2%
Tank	40	28%	0	0%	0	0%	0	0%
APC	195	35%	47	50%	12	48%	3	46%
SP How	24	9%	0	0%	0	0%	0	0%
ATGM	116	16%	36	31%	12	38%	3	37%
MG	234	0%	73	1%	21	1%	6	1%
Med Mort	24	3%	8	5%	0	0%	0	0%
Hvy Mort	0	0%	0	0%	0	0%	0	0%
AA Gun	4	1%	0	0%	0	0%	0	0%
SP SAM	4	1%	0	0%	0	0%	0	0%
Lt SAM	27	1%	9	2%	0	0%	0	0%
ATRL	81	5%	27	9%	9	11%	3	15%
Combat Power		141		23		6		2
% Combat Power		100%		50%		40%		31%
% Manpower		100%		59%		41%		36%

many more machine guns. Most Western armies follow this same general organization. Practically all armored, and several nonarmored, vehicles have radios. The mechanized-infantry battalion has approximately 60 trucks of various sizes, plus a few armored support vehicles. These, plus over 80 armored combat vehicles, carry most of the noncombat troops, maintenance tools, special equipment, supplies, and special weapons (SAMs, flamethrowers, etc.). Supplies include up to three days or more of food, fuel, and ammunition as well as spare parts.

RUSSIAN-TYPE INFANTRY UNITS

The units described below are but one of several generally similar organization types. The numbers of troops and weapons in regiments vary somewhat within the Russian Army, and vary a bit more in other armies that use Russian equipment and doctrine. The following example gives you a good idea of how the Russian style of unit organization operates.

REGIMENT (2,250 men). In the Russian-type armies, the regiment serves the same function as the battalion in Western armies. Non-Russian armies that use Russian equipment and doctrine often call these regiments "brigades." Whatever the name, these units are capable of supporting themselves in the field. To do this, they must have various support capabilities (signal, maintenance, supply, specialist combat units). Because backing from other specialized units is an all-or-nothing situation in the Russian Army, generally the regiment will have to depend on itself. The Russian mechanized-rifle regiment, for example, contains three mechanized-rifle battalions, a regimental headquarters (65 men, 3 APCs), a tank battalion (165 men, 40 tanks, 2 APCs), an artillery battalion (220 men, 18 122mm self-propelled howitzers), an air-defense battery (60 men, 4 23mm automatic cannon systems, and 4 SA-13 missile systems), a reconnaissance company (57 men, 12 APCs), an antitank battery (55 men, 8 APCs mounting a total of 45 AT-5 ATGMs), an engineer company (70 men with 2 self-propelled bridges), a maintenance company (65 men), a medical company (25 men), a transportation company (70 men with 40 4.5 ton trucks, each with a 10-ton trailer), a chemical-defense company (35 men with 3 decontamination rigs on trucks), a traffic-control platoon (20 men), and a supply-and-service platoon (20 men).

BATTALION (441 men). Contains 3 rifle companies, a mortar battery (51 men, 8 120mm mortars), a weapons-support platoon (16 men, 3 APCs, 8 AGS-17 30mm automatic grenade launchers), an air defense, ground platoon (15 men, 3 APCs, 9 SA-7 or SA-14 portable SAMs), a signal platoon (14 men), a medical section (9 men), a supply-and-maintentance platoon (27 men).

COMPANY (103 men). Contains 3 rifle platoons, a support-weapons platoon (7 men, 2 APCs), and a headquarters section (6 men, 1 APC).

PLATOON (30 men). Contains 3 rifle squads, (each with 10 men), 1 APC, 2 machine guns, and 1 antitank rocket launcher.

The other regimental equipment is similar to that carried by the U.S. battalion. The regiment has 149 trucks and a total of more than 500 vehicles of all types.

Note that most Western armies have field kitchens at the company or battalion level. The Russians have them only at the regimental level. In general, the quality of life for the Russian soldier is lower than for his American counterpart. This puts the Russian closer to the edge of survival on the battlefield. He gets less food, medical care, shelter, and equipment-maintenance support. Compared with those in Western armies, the Russian soldier is less experienced and less capable, at least in the peacetime conscript army. In wartime, he will become as proficient as his Western counterpart. But this method of distributing necessities is wasteful of human life and equipment. Many Third World nations have adopted many aspects of Russian organization, mainly because it is cheaper and more suitable to their needs.

Divisional Equipment and Combat Power

NOTE: See notes on Chart 2-1, Combat Values, for weapons explanations.

Chart 2-4 shows the equipment of the four most common division organizations in the U.S. and Russian armies. Note that both nations have numerous specialized infantry units. The United States also has light-infantry, infantry, air-mobile, and airborne divisions in active service as well as similar units for its reserve and National Guard forces. There are additional reserve and National Guard units that can be organized into other divisions. Adding marine divisions, we have a very diverse force. The differences between the combat power of these divisions is at the bottom of the chart. The basic unit of ground forces is the division, a force of 10,000 to 18,000 men. There are still nearly 1,000 divisions in the world today, a small decline in the wake of the Cold War's end. The Russian-style organization still represents over half of them. Chinese-style infantry divisions, very similar to the Russian type, represent most of the remainder. While the chart shows weapons and their combat power, it does not show the sometimes considerable qualitative differences resulting from:

1. *Quality and quantity of support equipment.* Obvious items enhance combat ability, like engineer, signal, and transportation support, plus more exotic things such as devices for electronic warfare, data processing, and fire control. Also important are procedures for the effective movement of supply and maintenance and repair of equipment before, during, and after combat.
2. *Training and doctrinal differences.* Different nations can use identical organization and equipment, but because of different approaches to the selection and training of troops, or the application of the doctrine, there will be substantial qualitative differences. Take, for example, Bulgaria and Poland. Both use Russian organization and equipment. All things being equal, the Polish unit will be generally superior to the Bulgarian. Other examples are the Argentinean and British ground forces in the 1982 Falkland Wars, where both sides used similar, and sometimes identical, equipment, organization, and doctrine. Another example is the Libyan and Egyptian armies. In 1973, Egypt finally did what no other Arab army was capable of and stood up to the Israeli Army for a while. Finally, the Libyan Army, also

2-4 Divisional Equipment and Combat Power

	Russian Type Motor Rifle	Combat Power %	Tank	Combat Power %	US Mech Inf	Combat Power %	Armored
Transport	2,500	4%	2,500	3%	3,500	6%	3,500
Men	13,498	2%	12,380	2%	16,600	1%	16,300
Tank	266	38%	344	47%	290	35%	348
APC	481	17%	627	21%	727	22%	652
Arty	148	11%	94	6%	143	11%	143
ATGM	486	14%	302	8%	660	17%	523
MG	920	0%	550	0%	1,616	0%	1,360
Med Mort	72	2%	24	0%	0	0%	0
Hvy Mort	0	0%	0	0%	66	2%	66
AA Gun	110	6%	110	6%	24	0%	24
SP SAM	46	2%	46	2%	24	1%	24
Lt SAM	112	1%	112	1%	60	1%	60
ATRL	260	3%	192	2%	1,000	3%	900

equipped with Russian equipment and doctrine, fell to less heavily armed and less numerous Chadian tribesmen in 1987.

3. *Differences within a national army.* Nowhere is this more a consideration than in the Russian Army. See below.

Russian-Style Divisions

Although all Russian divisions use the same organization, they still come in three different grades of readiness. This system will persist for some years despite the collapse of the Soviet Union, so it is still relevant. The number and total combat value of each grade is shown at the bottom of the chart. The highest grade is the "groups of forces" that, until the mid-1990s, were stationed in various Eastern European nations. These comprised 30 divisions (15 tank and 15 infantry). The Russian divisions in the chart are based on these "group of forces" quality divisions. These units were kept at full strength and were the first to receive new equipment, aside from units in western Russia and the Ukraine that tried out new weapons and equipment prior to large-scale distribution. When these divisions returned to Russia, they lost some of their capability. They no longer got the pick of each year's draftees, and the morale of the troops currently is quite low because living conditions in Russia are quite a bit lower than are enjoyed in Eastern Europe. Some of the divisions were also disbanded or officially put on a lower level of readiness. Despite this, the remaining "group of forces" divisions remain among the best that Russia has available.

The next grade are the category 1 and 2 divisions within Russia and the former Soviet Union. These comprised 43 divisions (11 tank, 32 infantry) in the early 1990s (some are due for disbanding or downgrading). They are next in line for new equipment. Generally, they have about 1,500 fewer men, 50–100 fewer tanks,

40–60 fewer artillery pieces, and generally lower equipment levels. Peacetime manning is only 50 to 75 percent, although half a dozen are at full strength. Local reserves, men released from service in the past three years, can bring these units up to strength in a few days and be combat-ready in less than a month.

Overall combat value of these category 1 and 2 units would vary, but would likely average 10–20 percent lower than the group-of-forces divisions. A case can be made that their value would be even lower, as the Russians tend to reward the best officers with assignment in the better (full-strength, group-of-forces) divisions. Those who didn't make the cut would not be expected to do these second-string divisions a lot of good. Moreover, there is a substantial disadvantage when your division is mobilized and you find half your men are strangers to each other, and to the military. One advantage of the end of the Cold War and subsequent disarmament is the newly replaced older equipment. At this point, few of the category 1 and 2 divisions have older hardware than the "group of forces" class divisions.

Last, we have the category 3 divisions (20 tank, 72 infantry). Their equipment levels are similar to category 2 divisions. This equipment is not only the oldest, but also poorly maintained; much has been destroyed and replaced in the wake of treaties signed as the Soviet Union was breaking up. The category 3 divisions will be the first to be disbanded because of the arms reductions and be dispersed among the successor states of the Soviet Union. At least half of these divisions will disappear in the process. Much of the equipment in them is kept in centralized storage areas. It is from this stored equipment that many local militias in the Caucasus (and elsewhere) have gotten their weapons. Manning levels on these divisions range from 10 to 30 percent. Although there are sufficient weapons and combat equipment present or assigned, transport vehicles are to be taken from the civilian economy. Considerable specialist equipment is either obsolete or not present. The reserve troops called to fill out these units will have been out of the service no more than five years, yet most of the equipment will be unfamiliar to them. Requiring three or four months to become combat-ready, these units would have an effectiveness of about 50 percent of the group-of-forces units, if that.

One symptom of the USSR's collapse was the spreading refusal of young men to do their compulsory military service. Reservists also were reluctant to cooperate in maintaining the readiness of category 2 and 3 divisions. Actually, this last phenomenon was seen as early as 1979, when divisions mobilized in Soviet Asia for service in Afghanistan performed with a notable lack of enthusiasm and effectiveness. More problems appeared in 1980, when Russia attempted to mobilize reserve divisions in response to the quickening collapse of communism in Poland. That mobilization had to be called off. Without willing, or at least docile, conscripts and reservists, the 200-division force of the former USSR has crumbled to a fraction of its former size. While Russia and the Ukraine have grabbed the majority of the USSR's armed forces, only Russia is coming away with a significant armed force. The Russian Army now has fewer than 100 divisions, and only about 20 of them are near the level of the former "group of forces" and category 1 divisions. By the end of the decade, the total number of divisions in the successor states of the Soviet Union will probably number less than 100.

In a special category, however, are the over 100,000 airborne, airmobile, commando, and marine troops of the former USSR. These were organized (when the USSR collapsed) into 7 full-strength airborne divisions (6,600 men each), 8 airborne brigades (3,000 men each), 14 airborne battalions (assigned to army headquarters, 400 men each), 3 airmobile brigades (1,800 men each), 1 marine division (8,000 men), and 3 marine brigades (4,000 men each). Two thirds of these troops are light infantry, without APCs or tanks. Finally, we find some 15,000 commandos (Spetsnaz) organized into small units. These troops are trained to operate in squad- or platoon-size units, air-dropped behind enemy lines, and trained to go after key rear-area targets (headquarters, nuclear weapons, industrial plants, etc.). Many of these were used in Afghanistan to fight the Mujhadeen guerrillas on their own terms. The Spetsnaz were fairly successful. These troops are a rough bunch, even though largely conscripts. They are selected carefully from volunteers, rigorously trained, and well rewarded with pay more than 10 times the usual rate plus many privileges. Many of these units were used to keep the peace during the last days of the USSR and, as such, garnered a lot of public ill will. As a result, many have been disbanded, reorganized, or allowed to decline in effectiveness. What remains is still the most effective and reliable troops available to Russia. As reliable as these commandos are, however, they refused to assist reinstituting Communist rule during the August 1991 coup. By the end of the decade, there will still be at least 50,000 of these troops organized into units. Most of them belong to Russia.

Like many other nations, Russia maintains several dozen "paper" divisions that call upon reserve and retired officers and reserve units as well as obsolete weapons and requisitioned civilian equipment. Experience has shown that several months to a year are required to train these units, depending on how desperate the situation is. Russia has long been aware of the weaknesses of its system, but in the post-USSR situation these paper divisions will become more paper and less substance.

The armies of Eastern Europe were, until 1990, auxiliaries of the Soviet Army. These non-Russian divisions were equipped and, to a lesser extent, organized as Russian-type divisions. They were the equivalent to category 1, 2, or 3 Russian divisions. Until 1990, these comprised 45 category 1 and 2 divisions (14 tank, 31 infantry) and 12 category 3 divisions (3 tank, 9 infantry). Many other nations throughout the world use Russian-style organization, notably in the Middle East. Although the manpower levels of these non-Russian clones are close to 100 percent, they usually have less than half the combat effectiveness of top-rated Russian divisions. The Eastern European nations have been reducing their armed forces and reorganizing somewhat. By the mid-1990s, there will probably be only 20–30 divisions among the former Soviet satellites. Middle Eastern and Asian nations that follow the Russian pattern are picking up a lot of inexpensive equipment from the nations of the former Soviet empire, but are looking more to the West for organizational and doctrinal models. The Western success in the 1991 Gulf War has a lot to do with that change of mind.

The armed forces in the nations of the former Soviet Union are undergoing substantial change as Russia and the other nations cleaved from the former USSR set up their own armed forces. Russia plans a professional force, relying much less on conscription. The sheer mass of equipment that characterized the Soviet Army has been sharply reduced by a shortage of money, conscripts, and the various treaties negotiated as the Soviet empire dismantled itself in the late 1980s and early 1990s. Tens of thousands of tanks and other armored vehicles were destroyed or moved into the Ural Mountains east of Moscow. The thousands of armored vehicles in the Urals were allowed by the treaties to be moved so the Russians could defend the Asian portion of their territory. However, as the USSR collapsed, these vehicles were orphaned. Most of them lie, unattended, out in the open. A few Siberian winters and a lack of maintenance will reduce these vehicles to scrap. Aware of this, local governments, as well as the central government, have been selling the newer weapons to other nations and using the older ones for spare parts or scrap metal.

RUSSIAN MOTOR RIFLE DIVISION (often called a Mechanized Infantry Division, which is a more accurate term). These division types will show increasing variation because of the several generations of equipment the Russians keep in service and the different doctrines adopted in the various successor states to the USSR.

A typical organization would be:

A division headquarters (320 men), 3 motor-rifle regiments (2,700 men each), 1 tank regiment (1,101 men, no motor-rifle battalion), an artillery group (1,800 men, 12 100mm guns, 24 122mm rocket launchers, 12 AT-5 ATGM APCs, 4 SS-21 missile launchers, 72 152mm self-propelled howitzers), an air defense, ground regiment (302 men, 20 SA-8B or 6 SA-6 SAM launchers), an independent tank battalion (241 men, 51 tanks), reconnaissance battalion (300 men, 28 APCs, 6 tanks, motorcycles), an engineer battalion (380 men), a signal battalion (294 men), a chemical-defense battalion (150 men), support troops consisting of a maintenance battalion (294 men), a medical battalion (158 men), a transportation battalion (217 men), an aviation company (220 men, 6 Mi-2, 8 Mi-8, and 8 Mi-24 helicopters), and a traffic-control company (60 men).

RUSSIAN TANK DIVISION. Organized identically to the motor-rifle division except for the following changes: 3 tank regiments (1,580 men, 94 tanks, 51 APCs, 4 ZSU-23s, 4 SA-13s, 24 122mm self-propelled howitzers, 6 self-propelled bridges, 1 motor-rifle battalion), 1 motor-rifle regiment, no antitank battalion, no independent tank battalion.

U.S. AND WESTERN DIVISIONS

America and other Western nations have similar divisions in totals of men and equipment. There is one major difference in how they use their divisions. The Germans use their brigades more as independent units. In effect, the brigades become little divisions, much like the Russian regiments. This has a major advantage in that the battalions in the brigade are a permanent part of the brigade and therefore train regularly. In peacetime, the U.S. brigades do keep their battalions together, although combat doctrine stipulates that battalions be freely shifted to other brigades. Another significant difference is the Germans' less lavish use of APCs and ATGMs. The rationale is that, with limited funds, it is better to put the money into fewer and better weapons. Thus, the German APC (the Marder) is far superior to the U.S. M-113 and on a par with the U.S. M-2 IFV. The Germans are also more lavish with artillery and ammunition.

Overall, the similarities are more prominent than the differences. Like the Russians, the Americans and Germans use a "base" system for their divisions; support units are common. Only the mix of combat divisions differentiates between types.

U.S. DIVISIONS. A division headquarters (190 men), 3 brigade headquarters (120 men each), a variable number of tank and mechanized-infantry battalions (6 tank and 5 infantry for an armored division, 4 tank and 6 infantry for a mechanized-infantry division), a divisional artillery brigade (2,500 men, 72 155mm SP howitzers, 12 203mm SP howitzers, 12 SP rocket launchers, two counterbattery radars), an air defense battalion (626 men, 18 cannon vehicles, 18 SAM missile vehicles, 60 Stinger teams), an engineer battalion (890 men, 30 APCs, 8 combat-engineer tanks, 24 Dragon ATGMs), a Combat Aviation Brigade (1,270 men, 60 attack, 50 scout, 54 transport, and 12 electronic-warfare helicopter, 36 M-3 IFV), a signal battalion (582 men), a military-police company (201 men), a chemical-defense company (185 men), a combat electronic-warfare intelligence battalion (465), support troops (2,253). The support troops total varies a bit as unit organizations are modified but is the same for infantry and armored divisions. The combat battalions comprise 6,954 men in the armored division and 7,071 men in the mechanized-infantry division.

The U.S. combat division organization will be undergoing many changes in the 1990s as a result of experiments in the 1980s, the 1991 Gulf War, and the end of the Cold War. For example, in the Gulf War, the engineers were organized into a brigade of three 400-man battalions. This allows one (or two) engineer battalions to be assigned to the division's combat brigades. The Combat Aviation Brigade structure is constantly being rethought, and more heavy truck units are being added to the division.

Germany has tank and infantry battalions similar in size to Russian battalions. Instead of three of these battalions per brigade, there will be five (two tank battalions in the infantry brigade, three in the tank brigade.) The British and French have a "brigade oriented" organization. They have, in effect, 4,000–8,000-man divisions that are slightly larger versions of the German brigades.

Americans and Germans have relatively few reserve and mobilization divisions. The U.S. reserves are identical to the active units. The German reserves are similar but not identical. Any mobilization of reserves depends on trained manpower and usable equipment. The Russians maintain both in a very formal sense. The Western armies have less equipment on hand but a greater capacity to produce it. Depending on how long a war lasts and how many production facilities escape destruction, Western nations like Germany can raise new units similar to those already in existence.

During World War II, Germany raised the equivalent of 50 mechanized and armored divisions, plus more than 200 Chinese-style infantry divisions (see below). This was done with a similar population and a smaller industrial capacity than Germany possesses today. Most Western nations, particularly the United States, France, and Britain, maintain lighter, nonmechanized units suitable for rapid air movement units. These are suitable for intervention in faraway places and rugged terrain.

CHINA

The Chinese divisions are actually closely related to the pre-1950 Russian infantry divisions, before Russia mechanized all of these units. The Chinese system does have several advantages. The majority of the troops are long-term volunteers.

Promotion is still possible from the ranks. Troops tend to remain in one regiment for their entire career. Marriage is allowed only for officers and senior noncommissioned officers. There are now 30 pay grades, from the recruit to the highest officers, who receive better uniforms. Until the late 1980s, there were no formal ranks, only jobs based on positions held (platoon leader, division commander, etc.). Since the early 1980s, China has reduced its troop strength by over a million men, and these reductions continue.

Many of the less efficient infantry divisions in China have now been disbanded. More money has been put into buying modern equipment overseas or building it in China. After the political crackdowns in 1989, the military received even less money, but then the military budget increased. The improvements in Chinese economic performance have also made it more difficult to obtain high-quality volunteers (because of better opportunities in the liberalized civilian economy). This has led to poor morale, lower living conditions, and reduced combat effectiveness. Because the Chinese government looks to the army to protect it from an increasingly restive population, the military budgets were increased in the early 1990s. Much of this increased funding went to higher pay and benefits, but a lot also went to more modern equipment. The Chinese have taken advantage of the collapse of the Soviet Union to purchase Soviet military equipment cheaply, and this has enabled the Chinese to get the most modern Soviet aircraft and technology, which previously they would not have had access to. More infantry divisions are being motorized and mechanized using Chinese-built trucks and armored vehicles.

Moreover, there are obvious disadvantages. In most Chinese divisions, only heavy equipment moves by truck as the infantry walks. There is also a pervasive lack of equipment. Most of what they do have is outdated by Western and Russian standards, and the Chinese are further hampered by a lack of recent combat experience. Senior officers are somewhat debased by the use of political reliability as a promotion criterion. This has produced mediocre performance in border battles with combat-experienced Vietnamese troops. Chinese combat power used to be enhanced by the training, quality, and superior morale of the troops, perhaps an increase of 10 to 30 percent, depending on the unit. But much of this advantage has been dissipated in recent years. Because of its lack of strategic mobility, the Chinese Army is primarily a defensive force. China is trying to change this during the 1990s, and this is making its neighbors justifiably nervous.

Density of Infantry Weapons

Chart 2-5 shows the density of weapons infantry units can muster per 200 meters of front. The U.S. unit is an infantry battalion; the Russian-type unit is an infantry regiment.

FRONTAGE is the size of the unit's frontage (1–5 kilometers for the U.S. battalion, 2–10 kilometers for the Russian regiment). The weapons listed are: MGs (Machine Guns), ATGMs (Antitank Guided Missile launchers), APCs (Armored Personnel Carriers), ATRL (Antitank Rocket Launchers), ARs (Automatic Rifles), MBTs (Main Battle Tanks). Whether the unit is attacking or defending, this would be the density of systems per 200 meters. Normally, only 65 to 90 percent of the

2-5 Density of Infantry Weapons

Major Weapons per 200 Meters of Front
US Mech Infantry Battalion

Battalion Front=	Kilometers Defended				
	1	2	3	4	5
MG	22	11	7	5	4
ATGM	20	10	7	5	4
APC	20	10	7	5	4
ATRL	14	7	5	4	3
AR	70	35	23	17	14

Major Weapons per 200 Meters of Front
Russian Motorized Rifle Regiment

Battalion Front=	Kilometers Defended				
	2	4	6	8	10
MG	23	12	8	6	5
ATGM	12	6	4	3	2
APC	20	10	7	5	4
ATRL	8	4	3	2	2
AR	113	56	38	28	23
MBT	**4**	**2**	**1**	**1**	**1**

items shown are actually facing the enemy; the remainder are held a kilometer or more behind the front as a reserve. Note also that in the defense, systems would be spread out through the depth of the position. This would provide more than one line of resistance for the attacker to overcome. An attacking unit generally takes up only half (or less) of its defensive frontage. For example, a unit that normally defends a four-kilometer front would concentrate its systems into an area two kilometers or less in width for an attack. The idea is to hit the defenders in front of them with overwhelming (hopefully) firepower. The Russians tend toward extremes, using very wide frontages while defending (up to ten kilometers for a regiment) and very narrow frontages when the same unit is attacking (two kilometers or less). As you can see, a Russian-type regiment attacking a defending U.S. battalion (four kilometers' frontage) outnumbers the U.S. troops in the two-kilometers attack sector by 23 to 5 in machine guns, 12 to 5 in ATGMs, 20 to 5 in APCs, 8 to 4 in ATRLs, and 4 to 0 in tanks.

It's an interesting exercise to use this data to calculate who is stronger in such a situation. The Americans are obviously outnumbered. But consider, for each 200 meters of front, the defending ATGMs number five, plus nearly as many shorter-range rocket launchers. Some of these weapons will be destroyed by an enemy artillery bombardment, while friendly artillery might take out some of the attackers. The attacking vehicles will also attempt to mask their approach with smoke, either from friendly artillery smoke shells or the vehicles' own smoke-generating capability. However, the attacking vehicles are out in the open, while the defenders are concealed.

At this point, it all comes down to the "exchange ratio"—how many attackers will be lost for each defender destroyed. During World War II, the ratio averaged as high as 6:1 in favor of the defending (76mm) antitank guns. What the ratio is today is less certain because the ATGM does not operate like a gun. The missile can take up to 30 seconds to reach its target. The ratio is probably now only 4:1. The more lightly armored APCs can be more easily defeated by artillery and heavy machine guns. In addition, mines are typically planted in front of defending positions. All this might put the ratio back up to 6:1. Therefore, the defender needs only five ATGMs per 200 meters to destroy this attack. To stop the attack requires fewer ATGMs, because the attacker will falter before he is completely destroyed. A loss rate of about 50 percent customarily causes the attacker to pull back and reconsider the situation before trying again.

The ATRLs are less effective and serve mainly as a margin of safety. You might lose two or more ATRLs for each enemy vehicle hit. A hit by one of these is rarely a kill when firing at an MBT, although APCs are more vulnerable. This means that one functioning ATGM launcher per 200 meters has a chance of stopping the attack. Of course, while the ATGMs are firing away at the armored vehicles, there is the enemy infantry, who are about 100 meters closer. These foot soldiers are more vulnerable to artillery and machine-gun fire. Two or three machine guns per 200 meters will discourage most infantry.

If the above sounds too simple, it is. The battlefield is a more complex place and is full of uncertainties and ugly surprises. Indeed, surprise of one sort or another tends to be the crucial factor on the battlefield. Consider some of the items that can radically change the balance of combat power. Terrain can help both the attacker and defender. If the terrain is too broken up, the armored vehicles cannot maneuver, and it comes down to an infantry brawl. Fairly flat terrain with a lot of trees and brush helps the attackers by allowing them to get in close before the defenders can shoot at them. Flat, marshy terrain seriously impedes armored vehicles, forcing them to move along only a few routes. This makes it easier for the defenders. Terrain can make or break an attack.

Artillery of some sort will always be part of a battle. Even infantry battalions have their own artillery in the form of mortars. But these units, both attackers and defenders, can call upon larger sources of firepower in the form of additional artillery and air power. It is every attacking soldier's wish that the artillery do all his work for him. It rarely works out that way. The Russians have a reputation for using massed artillery for crucial attacks. But the time required to mass these resources also gives the defender time to prepare. And the defender frequently has significant artillery and air-power resources of his own. Massive use of artillery tends to batter both attacker and defender, leaving the decision to come down to the battle described above. Worst of all, clever and alert defenders have been known to pull back a few kilometers just before a massive artillery preparation is delivered. This forces the attacker to waste precious resources and still leaves the advancing troops to struggle over the decimated terrain.

The Persian Gulf War saw a demonstration of these ratios. The Iraqis were stretched thin, with each infantry battalion defending three to four kilometers of front. They coped with this situation by carving massive triangular (two kilometers on a side) strong points out of the sand. The one-to-two kilometer gaps between these sand walls would be covered by artillery, tank guns, and patrols. The major flaw in this strategy was that Allied air power could easily find these strong points from the air, and over the six weeks of the air campaign the Iraqis were systematically pounded. By the time the Allied ground forces advanced, the Iraqis were no longer in any shape to resist.

The major military powers have backed away from the use of chemical weapons, despite the fact that the use of chemical shells can increase the effectiveness of a bombardment by up to three times. Unfortunately, the attacker will also have to move through these deadly chemicals and take some losses. For this reason, the predominant doctrine is leaning more toward using chemical shells against rear-area targets and letting the troops at the front slug it out with conventional weapons. This assumes that the defender doesn't use chemical weapons, which are more effective in the defense. The defenders only have to stay put and keep their protective gear on.

Technology has also been favoring the defender of late. Small mines, weighing from two to five pounds, can be scattered by defending troops in front of their positions or rapidly delivered by artillery or aircraft. Although these are not buried, they are difficult to spot when you are rushing forward to attack (especially at night). They will kill and injure infantry, and immobilize armored vehicles. The only way to avoid these little "trackbuster" mines is to equip some of the attacking armored vehicles with plows that literally forge a path through these mines (moving them to the side of the path). But these vehicles move more slowly, are prime (and obvious) targets for the defender, and force other attacking vehicles to advance behind the plow vehicles in order to avoid the mines.

And so it goes, not quite as scientific as it first appears. The attacking and defending commanders must use a lot of judgment and guesswork in addition to calculation. And finally, information is spotty on the battlefield. You don't calculate with firm numbers but with estimates. The term "fortunes of war" is well put.

Infantry Weapons

Chart 2-6 shows the most common small arms used worldwide. The various other weapons utilized by the infantry will also be described in this section.

WEAPON is the weapon's official designation.

PRIMARY USER is the nation that is the principal user of the weapon as well as its designer and major manufacturer.

CALIBER is the diameter of the weapon's projectile, in millimeters (1 inch = 25.4mm).

WEAPON WEIGHT (LBS) is the weapon's loaded weight in pounds. This is more meaningful than the empty weight, as the weapon can be used only when loaded with ammunition.

AMMO WEIGHT (LBS/100) is the weight of 100 rounds of ammunition. This includes the magazine, or metal-link weight. Rifles typically have ammunition in

How to Make War

2-6 Infantry Weapons

Weapon	Primary User	Caliber	Weapon Weight (lbs)	Ammo Weight (lbs/100)	Ammo in Weapo	Pract Rate of Fire/RPM	Eff Range (m)	Used For
FN/G3	German	7.62	10.7	5.5	25	75	800	Standard infantry rifle
AK-47/M	Russia	7.62	8.8	6.2	30	90	400	Standard infantry rifle
M-16A1	US	5.56	8.1	3.5	20	80	600	Standard infantry rifle
AK-74	Russia	5.45	8.8	4.7	30	100	500	Standard infantry rifle
MG3	German	7.62	39.6	6.1	200	200	1,200	Standard LMG
M-60 LMG	US	7.62	28.9	6.1	100	200	1,200	Standard LMG
PKM	Russia	7.62	18.4	6.1	250	200	1,200	Standard LMG
RPK	Russia	7.62	13.5	6.1	40	120	800	Standard Squad LMG
RPK-74	Russia	5.45	13.2	6.1	40	120	600	Standard Squad LMG
SAW	US	5.56	19.4	5.6	200	200	800	Standard Squad LMG
SVD	Russia	7.62	10.1	7.3	10	20	800	Standard sniper rifle

magazines; machine-gun rounds are linked together with metal fasteners. Without magazines or links, ammunition has the following weights (rounds per pound): Russian, 5.45mm—43; U.S., 5.56—40; Western, 7.62—19; Russian, 7.62mm (short, AK-47)—42, 7.62mm (long, used in PKM and SVD)—32.

AMMO IN WEAPON is the number of rounds normally loaded in the weapon. Machine guns fire ammo in theoretically endless belts of linked rounds. As a practical matter, the belt is long enough to carry in a box hanging from the weapon (up to 100 rounds). This allows the machine gun to be portable and handled by one man.

PRACT. RATE OF FIRE/RPM is the practical rate of fire per minute. These weapons have theoretical rates of fire between 600 and 1,300 rounds per minute. Several factors make the practical rate lower:

1. *Impaired accuracy at high rates of fire* is the major limitation. As an automatic weapon fires, it recoils. Although modern weapons have reduced this recoil considerably, it still exists and throws off the aim. Bursts of 5 to 10 rounds are generally more effective than a steady stream of bullets. Don't believe what you see in the movies when an actor fires a weapon at full automatic and constantly hits something. In practice, a machine gun with a high rate of fire, used with small bursts, is used as a long-range shotgun. This has proved to be the most effective way of killing people with machine guns.
2. *Barrel overheating* is a more common, and serious, problem. Depending on the weather, especially tropical temperatures and exposure to the sun, a machine-gun barrel quickly overheats if the practical rate of fire is exceeded for a few minutes. The results are that rounds fire without the trigger being pulled ("cooking off") because the excessive heat ignites the propellant without the firing pin hitting the tiny explosive "ignitor" at the base of the

cartridge. Rounds also become jammed due to heat expansion, and the weapon becomes useless. For this reason, water-cooled machine guns were used up through the Korean War (and some nations still use them). The water jacket around the barrel was heavy and prone to failure, but the constant stream of steam escaping from the jacket assured the gunner that he could keep firing. The water cooling also reduced barrel wear and maintained the accuracy of the machine gun. A better solution for the heat problem was removable barrels, a technique the Germans pioneered during World War II and others adopted. However, the overheating problem was most frequently solved by the gunners exercising discipline when using their weapons. Those who did not were frequently found dead next to a jammed machine gun.

3. *Ammunition supply.* Under the best of conditions, it takes a least a few seconds to change magazines. More time is required to load a new belt. Care must be taken during these operations to prevent jams. You can also run out of ammo.

4. *Dirt and fouling.* A machine gun is a precision piece of machinery designed to work under severe stress (a rapid succession of bullets exploding their propellant and forcing a bullet through the barrel at high speed). Dirt can get in any of the moving parts and jam the mechanical parts. Each bullet fired leaves some of its propellant in the barrel, "fouling" it and reducing accuracy. Dust and dirt can also enter the barrel, or other portions of the weapon, also fouling the barrel. You can often tell if troops are well trained by how well they take care of their weapons when not using them. If you see troops marching along with their weapons wrapped in cloth or plastic, or with a condom fitted over the barrel, you are looking at pros. These guys will have cleaner, and more effective, weapons when they have to actually use them. These troops will also take their weapons apart and clean them at every opportunity. Professional troops know that clean weapons can be a matter of life and death.

EFF RANGE (METERS) is the average effective range of the weapon in meters. With any weapon, a superb marksman can obtain hits at twice the average ranges. As a practical matter, there aren't many marksmen in the ranks. Even if there were, the opportunities for accurate shooting are rare in combat. Most firing is done in bursts at fleeting targets. On the battlefield, you keep your head down and move quickly. If you don't, you get killed. Other major factors in the effective range are the design of the weapons and its ammunition as well as troop training. A weapon that is designed to remain steady when fired will produce greater accuracy. This was one of the major reasons for the move to the smaller, but faster, 5.56mm round. Ammunition design can also produce greater accuracy and more lethal results. The latest types of 5.56mm rounds can pierce 15mm (.6 inch) APC armor at 100 meters. Although a larger 7.62mm round can do this at 400 meters, most shooting opportunities are at the shorter range. Aimed fire is possible out to 800 meters (half a mile), and both 5.56mm and 7.62mm rounds are capable of this range. The probability of deliberately hitting anything at that range is quite low. This is where machine guns come in, as they can put dozens of bullets near the target at ranges of 1,000 meters for 5.56mm rounds and 2,000 meters for 7.62mm. Battlefield experience in the last century has shown that 1,000 meters is sufficient range for infantry weapons. Most bullets' strikes cannot be spotted beyond the range of the tracer burnout, which is about 900 meters with most 7.62-mm bullets. Beyond that, you need another fellow with powerful binoculars to spot the landmarks for the gunners to aim for. Note that all the above ranges are for bullets hitting an unprotected man. Flak jackets and some of the newer helmets will make hits beyond a few hundred meters nonfatal, if not harmless. One still finds all those unprotected arms, legs, and faces to be injured. Accuracy is about the same for both calibers. Firing two- or three-round bursts at a six-foot diameter target and using a bipod, the following percentage of hits were obtained with 30 rounds (5.56mm/7.62mm): 300 meters—81%/81%, 400 meters—73/77, 600 meters—55/41. Contrary to popular myth, the lighter 5.56mm rounds are no more likely to be deflected by underbrush than the heavier and slower 7.62mm bullets.

USED FOR is the primary use of the weapon.

Standard infantry rifle is the weapon most commonly used in an army. The FN/ G3 rifle is one of the many variants of the original FN rifle favored by many European armies since the early 1960s. It uses a full-sized 7.62mm round and, although capable of automatic fire, is basically an update of the rifles that have been in use since the late 1800s. The AK-47 is a copy of the German SG-44 assault rifle. The SG-44 saw extensive use during the last year of World War II, and the Soviets wisely adopted it. It uses a shorter 7.62mm round. The M-16 is a high-velocity 22-caliber (5.56mm) weapon that was first proposed in the late 1930s. World War II intervened, and it took 30 years for the idea to be finally accepted. Gradually, nations are converting to this new caliber. The AK-74 is a Soviet version of the M-16, developed about 10 years after the M-16 was first introduced during the Vietnam War. The two AKs are good examples of how the Russians observe the success of military technology and then adopt it themselves. China is still a major manufacturer of AK-47s (and M-16s, also). The Chinese can manufacture an AK-47 for under 20 dollars and are still exporting hundreds of thousands a year in order to obtain hard currency.

Standard LMG (Light Machine Gun) is the most widely used machine-gun type in any army. These weapons are widely used by the infantry and often mounted on vehicles. Although the 5.56mm round was quickly adopted as the infantryman's personal weapon, it took a few years for most armies to accept the fact that this round was adequate for machine-gun use also. Another factor influencing the decision to adopt the smaller-caliber LMG was the problem of supplying two types of ammunition. However, the changeover is not complete in any army. Partially, this is because armies have a large investment in 7.62mm machine guns, which are expensive ($1,000+) and last a long time (easily over 20 years). Another reason for holding on to the 7.62mm LMG is that it is easier to design an effective armor-piercing round for this weapon. Only the light armor of APCs can be defeated, but that can be a significant capability. Most of the current 7.62 LMGs (MG3, M-60, and PKM) are derived from the German World War II MG-42 (the first widely used machine gun with an easily replaceable barrel).

Standard Squad LMG (Light Machine Gun) is a Russian innovation. The Russians solved the problem of having two sizes of ammunition by issuing the infantry squads LMGs that use the same lighter round that the AKs use. These LMGs are heavy-duty versions of the assault rifle with a heavier barrel and capable of using magazine or belted ammunition. The United States eventually adopted this practice, while the Russians came out with a new squad LMG to complement their 5.45mm assault rifle. The United States soon followed with a similar weapon, as have many other nations.

Standard Sniper Rifle is commonly used in a specialized form of combat. In many armies, 2 or 3 percent of the infantry are trained and equipped as snipers. Their weapon is generally a nonautomatic rifle using a full-size (7.62mm) round. In most cases, these weapons are standard rifles that are rebuilt to higher standards of reliability and accuracy and equipped with special sights and other features. A good marksman can also be quite deadly with the standard assault rifle and its lighter round.

Other Infantry Weapons

HEAVY MACHINE GUNS

These are not exactly infantry weapons as they are not portable and are usually mounted on vehicles. Because most infantry now operate with their own APCs, these weapons do qualify as infantry weapons. Except for their larger caliber (12.7mm to 30mm), they operate much like infantry machine guns. These weapons have a longer range and more hitting power and tend to concentrate their fire on vehicles or aircraft. These heavy machine guns are also capable of using more effective armor-piercing projectiles. In a pinch, the infantry do not hesitate to turn such awesome firepower against two-legged targets. In some cases, the heavy machine guns are taken from the vehicles and installed within fortifications.

AUTOMATIC GRENADE LAUNCHERS

To provide heavier firepower for the infantry, the Automatic Grenade Launcher was developed in the 1960s. This was a slower-firing machine gun whose slower-moving high-explosive shells had the effect of covering an area with exploding "grenades" (the shells). This weapon fires a 30mm–40mm shell similar to the one used in the shotgunlike attachment for U.S. and Russian assault rifles. The United States first deployed an automatic version on helicopters during the Vietnam War. In the late 1960s, a ground-based version, the M-19 machine gun, was deployed. Russia came out with a 30mm copy in the early 1970s. The United States ground version weighs 140 pounds and fires a 9-ounce shell as far as 2,000 meters. It takes 17 seconds for shells to travel this distance. An armor-piercing shell can penetrate over 60mm of armor. In other words, APCs and IFVs can be knocked out with the M-19's 40mm shell. During the 1980s, various night sights were added, making the M-19 a powerful weapon for attacking or defending at night. The Russian version, the 30mm AGS-17, weighs only 90 pounds and has a max range of 1,700 meters. Each 30mm round weighs about 6 ounces and is not guaranteed to penetrate APC/IFV armor. Both U.S. and Russian weapons have an effective rate of fire of 100 rounds per minute. The U.S. M-19 jams once every 5,000 rounds or so. The cruder Russian model jams once every 1,000 rounds, and the shell often explodes in the process. These accidents are not always fatal, but must have an adverse effect on users' attitudes toward the weapon. The first major users of the U.S. weapon were the marines, who equip each battalion with 10 weapons. The U.S. Army now uses them nearly as much as the marines, and army troops and commanders were impressed with the weapon's performance in combat during the 1991 Gulf War. Russia deploys eight AGS-17s to each infantry battalion. The grenade launchers have proved more effective than the older, and still widely used, 12–15mm heavy machine guns.

PISTOLS

Generally carried by officers and operators of heavy weapons and equipment, these are rather useless on the battlefield, although handy in tunnels and buildings. Combat officers prefer an assault rifle. The primary problem with pistols is poor accuracy, it being difficult to hit a man-sized target beyond 25 meters. Even if you hit someone, pistols don't have the same stopping power as rifles. Moreover, pistols carry less than half as many rounds as assault rifles. One solution to the shortcomings of pistols was the machine pistol (also known as a "submachine gun.") This is a magazine-fed pistol with a longer barrel. Still not much stopping power, but you can fire more rounds with more accuracy. Out to 100 meters, these weapons are pretty effective. The success of these weapons in World War II (the Sten gun and the MP-40) led to the development of the SG-44, AK-47, and M-16 assault rifles. At present, machine pistols are used primarily by police.

GRENADES

Grenades are small bombs weighing about a pound and, upon detonation, the common fragmentation grenade releases projectiles that can wound exposed personnel out to a radius of up to 15 meters. Most modern fragmentation grenades release hundreds of light, high-speed fragments that are readily stopped by obstacles a bullet would easily pass through. Although movies show a large explosion and bodies flying through the air, real grenades carry a small explosive charge that will throw up dust and knock a man down if he is very close. Noise is the prominent characteristic, plus a drizzle of tiny spent fragments. And don't try to pull the arming pin with your teeth, unless a dentist is handy to repair the damage. The most common grenade is the fragmentation type, good only against people. Other important types are smoke (for some concealment, depending on the wind), high-explosive (for blast effect, to stun someone close by without worrying about fragments), thermite (for burning things up, including metal), illumination (turns night into day), riot-control (tear gas, good for clearing out bunkers or otherwise discomforting the opposition), and marker (colored smoke, to show aircraft where to land or drop, or not drop, something).

The most commonly used grenade is the "defensive grenade," so called because it throws fragments as far as possible and is thus best employed when the user is hiding behind some cover. "Offensive grenades" are largely explosive with few fragments. This is so the user can throw them short distances while they are in the open and not have to worry about getting hit by fragments. The average fragmentation grenade injures nearly everyone within 2 meters of the explosion, 75 percent of those within 4 meters, 50 percent of those within 6 meters, 25 percent of those within 10 meters, 5 to 10 percent of those 15 meters away and less than 1 percent of those 20 meters away. Older grenades, of World War II vintage, were less effective because their fragments were larger, fewer, slower, and much of their destructive effect tended to harmlessly hit the ground. Grenades were first developed several hundred years ago to solve the problem of delivering firepower around or over an obstacle without exposing the user. Fighting in built-up areas would be more costly for the attacker were it not for grenades. The easiest way to clear out a cave, bunker, trench, or roomful of enemy troops is to heave in a grenade. Grenades can be thrown no more than 40 meters, with 20 to 30 meters being a more common extreme range. Most grenades are of the fragmentation type, with four or five ounces of explosive and a three-to-five-second fuse.

Variations on the grenade include rifle-launched grenades. These are not widely used by American or Russian forces but are popular with many other armies. The bullet is used to propel various types of grenades from the barrel of a rifle. Range is over 100 meters, although accuracy is acquired only after practice. Grenade launchers, which are quite different from rifle-launched grenades, are popular with U.S. forces, sending 40mm projectiles ("grenades") out over 300 meters from a shotgunlike weapon, or about 100 meters from a tubelike device fitted under the barrel of an M-16. Rifle-launched grenades are about as effective as thrown grenades, while the 40mm version is about half as powerful.

MORTARS

Mortars are the artillery infantry carry with them. Mortars must be kept light, so the troops can carry them if necessary. Although mortars are capable of high rates of fire (up to 30 rounds a minute), little ammunition can be hauled. The infantry have to maintain their mobility and cannot afford to go into battle weighed down with a lot of extra equipment. With all these restrictions, the chief virtue of mortars is their ability to respond rapidly and accurately to the infantry's need for additional firepower. An additional advantage is the mortar's ability to hit targets behind obstacles. Mortars' shells are fired at a sharp angle (sometimes almost straight up). The most common infantry mortars are 81mm. They weigh about 100 pounds and fire shells weighing 12–15 pounds at maximum ranges of 3,000 to 4,000 meters. The heavier 120mm (U.S. 107mm, being replaced by 120mm) mortar weighs 700 pounds and fires a 33-pound shell out to 6,000 meters. These are almost always mounted inside APCs, as are many of the 81mm types. This allows these mortars to carry more ammo with them, but not as much as the regular artillery units farther back. To alleviate this problem, some armies are using mortar rounds with sensors and maneuver-control mechanisms in them. This allows the mortar round to find armored vehicles and guide themselves to the target. A lot more expensive than the usual high-explosive or ICM mortar round, but the guided round vastly improves the antiarmor capability of mortars. The 60mm mortar continues to be used by nonmechanized infantry. It weighs 50 pounds and, like the 81mm version, can be broken down into two or three components for carrying. Shells weigh less than 10 pounds and can be fired out to 3,500 meters.

MINES AND OTHER SURPRISES

Land mines and their cousins, booby traps, are classic infantry weapons. These are defensive weapons and enable the infantry to more effectively resist larger forces and armored vehicles. In more mobile situations, mines are used to encourage the enemy to move in another direction (where you have set up an ambush). Mines are also used to guard an area when you don't have troops available for the job. The chief limitations of mines are their weight and the time required to emplace them. As a rule of thumb, it takes 1 ton of mines to cover 100 meters of front, and 10 man-hours per ton to emplace them. You can use special machines to plant them, but such equipment is not always available. Mines should be emplaced while the enemy isn't looking, in order to maintain the element of surprise. To overcome these limitations, lightweight "scatterable" mines are becoming more common. Mines are surprise weapons—they are customarily laid in areas covered by the fire of other infantry weapons to prevent the enemy from discovering their presence until it is too late, and then the covering fire makes it more difficult for the attacker to clear the mines. Mines are also laid (dropped on the ground) quickly by artillery shell or aircraft.

Similar to mines are booby traps, which are grenades, mines, or other explosives rigged with trip wires or other devices to make them detonate when the victim stumbles over them. The casualties are bad enough; the effects on troop morale are worse. A land mine planted under an inch or so of dirt is just another form of booby trap. Some mines are meant to be dug up and reused if the enemy never encounters them. This takes three or four times as long as it took to lay them. Many mines are now made of plastic, which makes them much more difficult to clear, as you have to use a portable radar to search under the dirt. Such was the case in the Falklands and (to a lesser extent) Kuwait, where uncleared plastic mines will continue to kill wayward people and animals for many years to come. Considering the dozens of people killed each year in Europe because of uncleared World War I and II mines and shells, we have to assume that any major modern war will keep on killing for a century after the fighting officially stopped.

Mine technology has taken tremendous strides since the 1960s. Microelectronics and other technical advances have spawned new generations of smaller, lighter, and more lethal mines. The first of these were the trackbuster mines. Weighing two to five pounds each, they are not buried but dropped in the path of advancing armored vehicles. The mines can only blow the track off an armored vehicle, but this is enough to temporarily immobilize it. Should this happen in combat, the crippled vehicle is in great peril and usually abandoned by its crew. Another version of the scatterable mine has a magnetic sensor that causes a shaped charge to explode upward when a large metal object passes overhead. This does not blow the track but penetrates the thin bottom armor of tanks and APCs. This will do some damage, and may ignite ammo or fuel and destroy the vehicle. Along with the antitank mines come antipersonnel devices, making a quick exit from crippled tanks on the battlefield, or searching for antitank mines, a risky endeavor. Many Western mines have a self-destruct feature, which takes effect from several hours to several days after they are deployed. This makes them less of a menace to your own troops who later must travel the same ground. As expected (by the troops, not the manufacturers), a large number of the self-destruct devices did not work when first used on a wide scale in Kuwait. About 10 percent of the mines stayed active beyond their self-destruct deadline, causing casualties long after the fighting had been successfully concluded. Worse yet, many of these smaller mines are not laid carefully in the ground, but are scattered from bombs, artillery shells, and dispensers on aircraft and helicopter. This gives the combat troops yet another cause of random mayhem to worry about.

Coming later this decade are robotic mines, with their own sensors and computer, and the ability to sense, track, and fire on armored vehicles. These smaller mines can also be delivered quickly by artillery or aircraft. This makes artillery and air support against an armored attack more efficient than previously, when high-explosive shells were the most common weapon available. Other developments in mine warfare have been more efficient remote-control mines that can be detonated by the defending infantry on command. Some of these smart mines are specifically designed to attack helicopters flying nearby. All of this activity in mine development springs from the historical record. In past wars, mines accounted for up to 50 percent of armored vehicle losses in some battles. The percentage appears to be headed upward, much to the infantryman's relief.

ELECTRONIC AIDS AND OTHER GADGETS

The revolution in electronics has assisted the infantry in many ways. The most useful tools are observation devices. The infantry now has its own radar and, even more useful, passive night-vision equipment. The latter are called "starlight scopes"—vision devices that electronically magnify available light so that night no longer covers enemy movement. These are attached to weapons and vehicles or are used simply to detect troops that can be attacked with mortars or artillery. These devices proved enormously useful in Vietnam and particularly in their first mobile use during the 1991 Gulf War. Other sensors are covered in more detail in Chapter 19, "The Electronic Battlefield."

3

Tanks: The Arm of Decision

TANKS ACCOUNT FOR about a third of a mechanized army's firepower and 20 percent of its equipment cost, yet their crews represent less than 2 percent of its manpower. Tanks usually spend most of their time hiding or looking for a place to hide. They must do this because their considerable firepower makes them a prime target. However, the concentrated combat power of tanks makes them, alone of all the combat arms, capable of forcing a decision quickly and decisively.

The "arm of decision" hasn't always operated this way. Traditionally, there have been three distinct combat forces in land warfare. First, there was the infantry, which took a lot of abuse and was absolutely necessary. Then came the missile troops—spear throwers, slingers, archers, artillery— who were protected by the infantry because the missile troops were better at killing the enemy at a distance than they were at defending themselves. Finally, there was the cavalry: infantry or missile troops on horses. Better armed, trained, and motivated than their footbound associates, the cavalry were the shock troops. Normally, the cavalry was held back either to turn a stalemate into a victory or to mitigate a defeat.

When horse cavalry became obsolete in the early part of this century, its functions and traditions were transferred to the tank troops, with some-times strange results. Initially, particularly during the early stages of World War II, many armor units attempted to storm their way through the op-position. They soon learned that the opposition could shoot back with deadly effect. Sitting behind all that armor, many tank crews feel invulnerable. Experienced tankers know better. They also know that if they are careful, they can avoid getting hurt.

The importance of being careful is a lesson the mounted troops have had to relearn many times over the centuries. The 1991 Gulf War risks giving U.S. tank crews a false sense of invulnerability. In that war, most U.S. tanks were of the latest design and fought against a previous generation of Russian tanks equipped with ineffective Iraqi-made tank shells. Fortunately, U.S. Army tank crews today are the most professional America has ever had in peacetime. The officers and NCOs are already spending a lot of time disabusing the troops of any illusions of invulnerability. The next opponent is likely to be better prepared, and better equipped.

What Tanks Cannot Do

World War II destroyed, at great cost, the various myths about what tanks could do. Each one of the tank "no-no's" in turn defines what a tanker's life is all about. Tanks cannot advance on the enemy without thorough and continuous ground reconnaissance. Tanks are delicate beasts and cannot go just anywhere. Their movements should be planned to take advantage of cover from enemy observation. Tanks are large (25 feet long, 12 feet wide, and 8 to 10 feet high). Tanks can often be heard a long way off, as they sound like a bulldozer, except louder. The tracklaying mechanism is there to move the 40- to-50-ton vehicle over rough terrain without it getting stuck. But armored vehicles can have problems anyway when they encounter excessively steep slopes and overly soft ground. Terrain that is very broken up with rocks and tree stumps will cause the tank's track to pop off. It usually takes several hours to replace the track.

Tanks cannot operate by themselves. When the tank is "buttoned up" with all hatches closed, the crew can see only through slits and periscopes. They cannot see very much, and the crew spends most of its time running the tank, not looking for some foot soldier sneaking up on it. This makes tanks very vulnerable to infantry, especially in close terrain or built-up areas. Tanks may look dangerous, but since they can shoot only at what they can see, a nimble infantryman can usually stay out of harm's way. The infantry know this and strive to defend in broken terrain when facing tanks. One survival technique for tanks facing infantry is the U.S. Army's "overwatch." Half a tank unit gets into a position from which it can observe the advance of the other half. The moving group then moves into positions to observe the movement of the other group. This is actually the ancient "you advance and I'll cover you" technique. This "moving by bounds" is safer, but slower. In combat, time is a luxury. If tanks cannot be accompanied by infantry, which usually slow them down, the only other recourse is for the commander of every tank to keep his head out of the hatch. The Israelis use this technique. You win a lot of battles, but you lose a lot of tank commanders.

Ideally, tanks support infantry. The exception is when the combat is on flat, featureless terrain, where the tank commanders can see any enemy infantry a long way off. In terrain with cover (forests, hills, buildings, etc.), the infantry advance on foot just ahead of the tanks. When opposition is encountered, your infantry keep the enemy infantry from getting at your tanks. The tanks then use their firepower to assist their infantry in clearing out the opposing foot soldiers. The infantry's eyes and ears are thus complemented by the tanks' massive firepower. Against good infantry in "busy" terrain (forested or urban), tanks cannot efficiently operate by themselves. As the U.S. Marines put it, "Hunting tanks is fun and easy," even more so when the tanks charge ahead of their own infantry. Well-trained tank units do not do this. The tanks would prefer to take a shot at the enemy, but can do this only in a fluid battlefield where their speed and long-range weapons can operate to best effect. Most of the time, the tanks creep forward under the infantry's protection. In any case, the infantry will be killed off more easily than the tanks. Even with its own armored personnel carriers, the infantry is more vulnerable. But to be effective, the infantry must dismount and expose itself to enemy fire. Even if infantry and tanks operate together efficiently, tanks will still be around after most of the infantry have been lost. At that point, the tanks advance only at greater risk.

Tanks cannot operate in massed formations. A massed formation is tanks operating closer than 100 meters from each other. Bunched-up tanks only attract fire from artillery and antitank weapons. Artillery will not typically destroy a tank, but can put it out of action by damaging the engine or tracks, not to mention the external components of the tanks' sensors. The tanks' fire-control equipment is particularly vulnerable, as are defensive items like smoke dispensers and the antiaircraft machine gun atop the turret.

No one has perfected a really cost-effective artillery shell that can home in on individual tanks. But even old-fashioned high-explosive shells can wreck a tank unit if enough shells are fired. The shells can't destroy the tanks, but they can damage enough tank equipment to make the tanks ineffective until repaired. The repairs can take days or weeks. Artillery and air strikes attack small areas and will harm only tanks that are in that area. The more the tanks spread out, the less likely they are to get hit. ATGMs also do better if they find a lot of targets close to each other. If one ATGM target momentarily ducks behind some smoke or other cover, the missile operator can quickly shift to another target. Tanks that keep their distance on the battlefield last longer. Not every nation believes this. Russian-type tank units regularly exercise formations with only 25-meter separation betwen armored vehicles. In practice, however, tanks of all nations often find themselves bunched up simply because there is not enough open space available to spread out in.

Tanks cannot survive with untrained crews. An effective tank crew operates as a team. A team is created by allowing a crew to operate with their tank for about six months together. This is not always accomplished, even in peacetime. During a war, the attrition among less capable crews is very high. It's not uncommon for over 50 percent of inadequately trained crews to be lost in their first battle. The slaughter is especially intense if ill-trained crews are attacking. A grim example occurred in the Golan Heights during the 1973 war. Hundreds of poorly trained Syrian armored vehicles advanced against far fewer Israeli tanks. The Israelis were better trained and made few mistakes. The Syrians were advancing in formation and were paying little attention to advantageous terrain or Israeli maneuvers. The Israelis noted this and methodically fell back from one piece of defensive terrain to the next, picking off a few Syrian vehicles between each move. The Syrians lost 10 vehicles for each Israeli one lost. The Israelis knew their terrain, and their crews knew how to move and shoot effectively. The Syrians were deficient in both respects and blindly followed the Soviet doctrine they had been taught. Better-trained Syrian crews would have been more effective at avoiding Israeli fire and more accurate in their own shooting. The Syrians demonstrated the effects of better training in the 1982 Lebanon War, where the ratio of destroyed Israeli and Syrian tanks was not nearly as lopsided as in 1973. History is full of similar examples. Unfortunately, training is expensive. Tank crews using Russian training methods are at a considerable disadvantage because they typically use their vehicles very little in training. Russian vehicles are built inexpensively and wear out quickly. The Russians have observed that combat vehicles don't survive long in battle, so why build them to last? In peacetime, the crews train with crude simulators and spend less time in their vehicles than Western crews. In addition, Western armies have more effective crew simulators and training equipment. As the performance of U.S. tank crews in the Gulf War demonstrated, these differences in training levels were very evident on the battlefield.

Tanks cannot move long distances without running into serious maintenance problems. Long movements require careful planning. If you run tanks too hard, most of them will break down. There have been many tank campaigns since 1939 where most of the losses have come from mechanical failure, not enemy action. Such losses can be reduced considerably by checking the route you plan to send tanks over and making provisions for regular maintenance. Tanks are simply not built to move more than a few hundred kilometers without stopping for maintenance. Weighing 40 to 70 tons and moving on tracks, they are designed for speeds of up to 60 kilometers an hour but not for long periods. Russian tanks break down, on average, every 250 kilometers. Western vehicles last about 300 kilometers.

With adequate maintenance support, most of these breakdowns can be repaired in less than an hour, or a few hours at most. Even so, a division of 300 tanks moving 100 kilometers (three hours' marching) will average 100 or more breakdowns. At the very beginning of a campaign, when all the vehicles are fresh, the rate will be much less, but will increase later to compensate for the initial free ride. In other words, the breakdowns will increase about the same time you make contact with the enemy. Breakdowns will also increase as you stress the vehicles, as you would while maneuvering against the opposition. Depending on the tanks' condition, the crews' maintenance training, and the efficiency of the tank-maintenance units, a division will lose 2 to 20+ percent of its vehicles per hour of movement. Most of these crippled vehicles will get going again and catch up, but the effect will be disorganized units, run-down vehicles and crews, and generally less effective combat divisions. Normally, tanks are moved long distances overland by train or truck. If tanks have to march long distances, there will be a price paid in spare parts and man-hours. Both may not be available, resulting in a lot of broken-down vehicles along the march route. Losses can easily exceed 50 percent. As far as the enemy is concerned, a tank lost to a worn-out transmission is just as advantageous as one hit by an antitank missile. Tanks cannot neglect routine maintenance.

One of the less glamorous aspects of working with tanks is maintenance. Tanks require a lot of it to keep them in top shape. Eight man-hours a day is not unusual if you use the vehicle a lot and want to maintain it in excellent condition. Keeping tanks in such good shape is becoming more difficult. The amount of equipment being added to tanks is increasing, especially electronics. At the same time, there is a trend toward smaller crews (three instead of four). The smaller crew is achieved by installing an automatic gun-loading mechanism. One possible solution is that "ground crews" be made available to tanks, to service them the way aircraft are after each flight. Unfortunately, tanks don't fly back to a relatively secure air base after each combat mission. They are always at risk when in a combat zone. The maintenance problem is worse for Russian-type tank units, as they have more three-man tanks and crews that are less capable and diligent about maintenance in the first place. This was a key factor in the low readiness level of Iraqi tanks in the Gulf War. Tanks cannot operate successfully without adequate recovery and repair units. As pointed out above, armored vehicles are prone to breakdown. During and after battles, tank-repair crews go out to get damaged vehicles running again. Tanks are basically robust but have so many things that can fail and immobilize them. After a battle, it is possible to repair over 50 percent of the vehicles knocked out by enemy action. For noncombat losses, recovery approaches 100 percent. Frequently, damaged vehicles must be hauled back to a repair facility. This is done by recovery vehicles that are turretless, unarmed tanks. The proportion of vehicles returned to service depends on the number, and skill, of your repair and recovery units.

To appreciate the scope of the repair and recovery problem, consider the number of things that can go wrong in a tank. These vehicles have numerous major failure prone systems.

1. First there is the tracklaying mechanism upon which the tank travels. Hit an obstacle at the wrong angle, and the track falls off. This is a common problem with inexperienced, or fatigued, drivers. It can take a few hours to get the track back on. Tracks also wear out. After anywhere from 1,000 to 3,000 kilometers, it's replacement time. All those wheels and rollers associated with the tracks require lubrication and inspection for wear and tear. More so than with an automobile, the driving controls, transmission, brakes, and so on must be inspected frequently and maintained to avoid complete failure. Otherwise, failure tends to come when you can least afford it.
2. The tank engine is also in a class by itself. Typically a diesel, although the U.S. M-1 uses a gas turbine (jet engine), these mechanisms generate 500 to 1,500 horsepower and are under considerable stress.
3. Although there's plenty of work required just to keep the tank moving, it's all for nothing if the vehicle's weapons are not maintained. A tank's weapons are mounted in a 10-ton turret, which is moved about by another complex mechanism of electric motors and bearings. The main gun and machine guns must be cleaned and resighted periodically, usually after much firing or hard movement. Ignore weapons maintenance, and you steadily lose accuracy.
4. Finally, we must deal with the electronics. A fire-control system contains precision optics and frequently one or more computers. Most modern tanks use a laser range finder. Very accurate, but very complex. To assist the main gun, there is an infrared searchlight and/ or a light-amplification system. Most tanks also have smoke-grenade dischargers (small mortars), radios, and an intercom system and sometimes air-conditioning and an automatic fire-extinguishing system. Many Russian tanks are now supplied with shells that are actually guided missiles, which require a separate fire-control system. Supporting all this is an extensive electrical system.

To assist maintenance, crews use checklists, tool kits, manuals, and some test equipment. The complexity of some tanks exceeds that of many aircraft. But it all comes down to the people. If the crew is attentive to maintenance, and is backed up by adequate repair and recovery units, you will have more tanks on the battlefield and recover more once the combat is over. No tank unit is perfect, and some of the above rules will always be broken under the best of conditions. On average, the situation is quite bad.

The urgency of wartime conditions regularly forces commanders and troops to forgo observation of the above maintenance rules. Combat and noncombat losses can be very heavy. World War II and recent experience indicate that tank losses will be five to six times personnel losses during heavy combat. That is, if a unit loses 10 percent of its personnel, it will lose 50 to 60 percent of its tanks and other armored fighting vehicles. However, past experience shows that up to 60 percent of combat tank losses and nearly all noncombat losses can be repaired. Depending on the repair facilities available, a division could return half its disabled vehicles back to service in less than a week. A lot depends on availability of spare parts, even though some vehicles are stripped of usable components. Another critical factor is the mechanical capabilities of the tank crewmen. All this assumes that the wrecked vehicles could be recovered. The side that is driven from the battlefield loses more than the battle.

Tank Units

Tanks almost always operate with infantry, but actually belong to purely tank units. These tank battalions are largely administrative organizations, to make the enormous maintenance load easier to handle. Tanks are organized into platoons of three to five vehicles. A company is three or four platoons plus one or two headquarters tanks. A battalion has three companies, plus a few tanks in a headquarters, for a total of 33 to 60 tanks. Tactical experience has shown that the three-tank platoon is most efficient. In this respect, tanks are used like fighter aircraft, using a "loose deuce" formation where one tank is the lead element supported by one or more "wingmen" behind and off to the side. Tank units rarely remain at full strength long in combat, so two-tank platoons are common. Tank battalions usually have small ATGM, reconnaissance, mortar, headquarters, ammunition, fuel, and maintenance units added, placing the battalion strength 50 to 300 men above the tank crews alone. Russian-type armies add most of these specialist units to the tank regiment.

Tank Tactics

Unlike the infantry, a tank cannot easily sneak up on you, although in some cases it can get within a few hundred meters of enemy infantry undetected. Even during an artillery barrage, a tank tends to announce its imminent arrival with a cacophony of distinctive noises. Tanks produce two noises, the engine and the track squeak. The squeak and squeal of the tracks is louder and easier to pinpoint. The gas turbines on the U.S. M-1 make remarkably little noise.

What a tank can do is survive a lot of punishment and still deliver substantial firepower. And through all this, tanks are able to flit about the battlefield at better than 500 meters a minute. Tanks are not invulnerable, just tough to kill. With all the firepower they attract, the crew tends to hunker down inside, making its view of the outside world somewhat limited. As described elsewhere, the foot soldiers and tanks work with each other. This ordinarily means the tanks spend most of their time moving at speeds closer to 20 to 30 meters a minute. Tanks do not have their own tactics, only procedures for tanks working with infantry. The best way to integrate tanks with infantry has not yet been agreed upon. For over 50 years, a debate has raged over whether it is better for the tanks or infantry to lead the attack. At the moment, a majority of opinion opts for infantry first, but a lot depends on the situation. There are situations where a company or even battalion of tanks can successfully operate independently. Some armies use both methods, depending on the situation, with tanks in front, infantry right behind or beside them, and APCs 100 meters or so to the rear. Because the infantry have their own light armored vehicles (APCs or IFVs) to ride in, it is possible for both tanks and infantry to move quickly when the enemy is not in the immediate vicinity. Under such conditions, the long columns of tanks and APCs (and self-propelled artillery plus antiaircraft and other support vehicles) stand ready to go through a multiphase deployment maneuver if the enemy is detected nearby. Assuming the reconnaissance units are able to find the enemy before your columns get ambushed, the armored columns will first deploy into several smaller columns, moving cross-country.

Just before the enemy comes into sight, these smaller columns will form lines, with tanks in front and APCs directly behind. Artillery will be farther back, and antiaircraft vehicles will be with the APCs. If there are woods or built-up areas involved, at 500 to 1,000 meters from the suspected enemy positions, the infantry will dismount and move forward. Otherwise, the infantry will stay in their vehicles until needed to dig the enemy infantry out of any concealed location. At the same time, the tank guns and artillery may be pounding suspected or confirmed enemy positions. At this point, the attacking units will begin to take fire. Ideally, you are not attacking the front of an enemy position, but the side or rear. The mobility of armored vehicles is supposed to make this possible. But everything depends on accurate information. If you lack precise information of where the enemy is, attacks are always fraught with surprises. If the attack goes right up against the front of a strong enemy position, the attackers may be shot up and forced to withdraw. Because the enemy is also mobile, and capable of reinforcing the position you are attacking, speed is critical. If you wait too long to find out exactly what's in front of you, there is liable to be a lot more opposition once you get the assault going.

Information is the key ingredient in tank tactics. The whole point of putting vulnerable infantry in front of the tanks during the final assault is so the infantry can provide the tanks with better information and keep the equally nimble enemy infantry at bay. Once tanks are committed to an attack, they are exposed to enemy observation and not easily withdrawn from view. Specifically, during the final assault, when the infantry is dismounted, the tanks cannot use their superior mobility to withdraw without risking loss of their infantry. Tanks without infantry are less capable in combat. Tanks can obtain a higher degree of information if the tank commander stands up in the turret, with his head and half his chest exposed. From that vantage point 8 to 10 feet above the ground, much can be seen. Unfortunately, the visibility works both ways, and tank commanders who habitually stand up to see can also be seen, and shot at. The only solution to this problem is to get the battle over with as quickly as possible.

While tanks have problems attacking, they are superb in defense. Especially against other armored vehicles, tanks have the key qualities needed for successful defense. Tanks have firepower, mobility, and protection. The key to defense is surprise. Surprise consists of hitting the enemy when he doesn't expect it, hitting him hard, and then getting out of the way before you get hit. Defense is most efficient when it is successful against a larger force. In this respect, tanks excel. The classic "mobile defense" relies on good planning and reconnaissance. The planning involves picking out several positions for each tank unit to fall back to as it shoots up the advancing enemy. The reconnaissance ensures that you don't lose track of the larger enemy force. If that happens, your tanks are liable to be ambushed themselves.

The favored position for a tank to hide is on the reverse slope of a hill. This is called "defilade." The tank depresses its gun and, while facing the direction of enemy advance, backs down that slope until all the enemy can see is the gun and top of the turret. Even this much need not be shown until the enemy is in range; it takes only a few seconds for the tank to move up the slope and into firing position. It is equally easy to back down and move off to the next firing position when the enemy gets too close. Note that Western tanks can depress their main guns farther than Russian tanks, which means Russian tanks must expose more turret when in defilade. If a defilade position is not available, any other concealment will do. The important thing is to get off the first shot, if not the first few rounds. The defender will have to try to spot you while sitting among burning vehicles and growing panic. Some units may set off their smoke grenades immediately and pull back. This can be done from inside the tank by simply pushing a button. Such protection from observation allows the defender to stay in position, and perhaps call in some artillery fire. Historically, such engagements have resulted in disproportionate losses, with the defender often getting away unharmed. This tactic is ironic in that it cancels the tank's mobility advantage in the attack. As long as the defender does not completely collapse, a handful of tanks, with some infantry and artillery, can delay a larger force (deploying from their road-bound columns). An attacker would have to be some 10 times more numerous and able to maneuver in order to brush aside a tank-based defense.

Tanks are not as efficient in defending against infantry. The 40 to 60 shells carried for the tanks' cannon are primarily (and often exclusively) armor piercing, with only a dozen or so antipersonnel shells (at most). U.S. tanks carry nothing but antitank shells. One or more machine guns, one in the turret alongside the main gun and/or another atop the turret, comprise most of the tank's anti-infantry armament. In the defense, the tanks are always placed behind the infantry. It is frequently tank commanders who are given the task of calling for artillery fire or maintaining communication with support units. There is typically a lot of artillery fire on defending units, and tanks are largely immune to it. The presence of friendly tanks typically provides more confidence than firepower for the infantry, but the positive effects of this morale boost should not be underestimated. The infantry soldiers like the additional firepower potential, not to mention the implied protection from enemy tanks.

Some tanks are equipped with special weapons. A common one is a flamethrower in place of the main gun, or one that works through the main gun's barrel. As noted above, tanks are equipped to generate smoke for concealment. In addition to grenade dischargers, some tanks have a mechanism that sprays diesel oil over a hot engine part and produces a lot of smoke quickly. What an enemy can't see, he has a hard time hitting. But this gets us into some of the more interesting aspects of antitank warfare.

Antitank Tactics

Tanks were originally developed to assist the infantry. This they still do, but primarily as a defense against enemy armored vehicles. Their maneuverability and firepower make them the most effective antitank weapon, but not the most efficient. Tanks are expensive and difficult to maintain. Other antitank weapons are cheaper and nearly as effective. Until the 1960s, the most cost-effective weapon was a tank gun. These were either towed, at one-tenth the cost of a tank, or placed in a lightly armored vehicle, at one-third the cost. Then along came the ATGM (Antitank Guided Missile) and changed the rules for antitank warfare. Cheaper, fairly accurate, potent, long-range, and lightweight, ATGMs did have some shortcomings. They had a slower rate of fire, two or three rounds a minute versus up to a dozen for a gun. A prominent back blast was more likely to give away the crew's position. Although the missiles are slow—taking up to 30 seconds to reach their target—tanks can take evasive action or fire on the missile operator and spoil his aim. Many ATGMs, particularly the early Russian ones, were inaccurate under 500 meters. As this is the average engagement range with tanks, this was a serious deficiency. World War II experience and German Army tests found that, in nondesert areas, you will spot a tank at 500 meters 40 percent of the time, 500 to 1,000 meters 25 percent of the time, 1,000 to 2,000 meters 20 percent, and over 2,000 meters 15 percent. Even in open areas, the longer-range possibilities are compromised by tanks taking advantage of undulations in the ground or cover created by huge dust clouds generated in dry weather.

To better appreciate the problems of using ATGMs, consider the following situation. Armored vehicles are seen approaching 800 meters away. They are moving at 30 kilometers an hour (eight meters a second). Your ATGM crews can get off a maximum of three or four missiles before surviving vehicles are on top of them. The missile crews may not survive that long, as their first shot can easily reveal their position. The tanks' machine-gun fire will not make the missile operators any more efficient, as it will often spoil the missile operators' aim. The tanks can also throw a smoke screen in front of themselves, or call artillery or mortar fire to the exposed missile operators. APCs are vulnerable, as their sighting and tracking equipment is exposed, as are the missiles before they are fired from them. Still, with these deficiencies, ATGMs have proliferated because the missiles are light enough for the infantry to carry and operate. Moreover, 20 years of use and development have made them more effective. Most ATGMs can now hit a tank at short range (under 100 meters). Back blast has been reduced somewhat. Speed is still a problem, however, as it is controlled by the time it takes for wire to be unspooled and the time required for operators to set missiles squarely on the target. Unlike tanks, missile crews are not always as mobile or as well protected. Tanks can pull out under an artillery barrage. Missile crews, in trucks or APCs, are at more risk. Pulling back under enemy pressure is always a tricky maneuver and is made more difficult when you are taking a lot of casualties. The least effective antitank weapon is the light rocket launcher. Carried by the infantry and most other ground troops, these weapons are useful in attacking bunkers and APCs. Against tanks, a lucky hit on the tracks is about the best you can hope for.

The Threat from Below

The most feared antitank weapon is not guns or missiles, but mines. Mines exist for no other purpose than to destroy any vehicle that rolls over them. Mines are cheap and require no crew to make them work. Just place them in or on the ground, and they are ready. Being machines, mines are fearless and unflinching in the performance of their mission. In World War II, over 20 percent of tank losses were due to mines. Since then, mines have become more effective, and the percentage shows signs of increasing with the introduction of robotic mines.

The Threat from Above

Aircraft are generally overrated and overpriced as antitank weapons. The Persian Gulf War was an exception because the enemy was in the desert and not enthusiastic about fighting back. Therefore, helicopters and certain fixed-wing aircraft were more lethal than your average fighter bomber: Helicopters used the same ATGMs as the infantry. Specialized fixed-wing aircraft (the U.S. A-10) used automatic cannons. All aircraft can be exceptionally effective in the antitank role by simply delivering mines. Unless, of course, the enemy tanks are dug in and not moving. Most aircraft, however, do not have the weapons or fire-control systems that are effective enough to hit armored vehicles on the ground. In the Persian Gulf, the Iraqis cooperated by keeping thousands of armored vehicles out in the desert for months. They were easily pinpointed and bombed efficiently by aircraft that normally would not be as effective in going after armored vehicles.

While combat aircraft are expensive to operate, so are effective countermeasures against them. Armies spend considerable sums to maintain antiaircraft weapons for their combat units. Even so, aircraft are difficult to hit—helicopters, perhaps, the most difficult of all. Helicopters lurk, drop down behind trees and hills, or flit around close to the ground at over 100 miles an hour. Those that attack use friendly ground units and scout helicopters to locate the enemy. The attack helicopters then move to an ambush position and try to hit their targets at maximum range (over 3,000 meters) with ATGMs. The helicopters are at greatest risk when they accidentally fly over enemy forces. A modern tank with a laser range finder can quickly destroy a slow-moving helicopter. Battlefields are not neat places, and accidental ambushes happen frequently.

Faster fixed-wing aircraft use speed as a form of protection. Planes come in low and fast, and can speed away at over 400 miles an hour. They make their attack runs at about 100 meters a second, using 20mm to 30mm cannon against the thinner top armor of tanks. If the battlefield is quiet, which it rarely is, you can hear them 20 to 30 seconds away. Unfortunately, you can't always tell what direction the attack is coming from. Ground-attack aircraft are also armored and built to take a lot of abuse, except from enemy interceptors. Tank crews are instructed to stand and slug it out with aircraft. Sometimes this works, but frequently the primordial urge to run the tanks into the woods takes over. The aircraft have an interest in self-preservation and typically make only one or two passes and then depart before their victims can get organized.

Advances in cluster-bomb technology have made aircraft more lethal, but not as much as the air-force people had expected. The most devastating antitank cluster bomb is the one that carries trackbuster mines. A 500-pound cluster bomb carries over 100 of these mines. A fighter bomber can carry over a dozen cluster bombs, enabling it to spread trackbusters over an area 100 meters long with each bomb. A ton of trackbusters (1,200 mines) can cover an area 1,000 by 100 meters. Each tank entering such a minefield would have a 70 percent chance of losing a track. The mines are small, flat, and painted camouflage colors. A tank that loses a track while under fire is likely to be finished off by some other antitank weapon. At night or during combat, armored vehicles don't have an opportunity to check the ground for these small mines. Losses can quickly mount, particularly when antipersonnel mines are mixed in with the trackbusters. A blown track (as with a bulldozer, the part of the tank that touches the ground) under more peaceful circumstances will halt the vehicle for several hours and fatigue the crew. Antipersonnel mines mixed with the trackbusters will make the crew reluctant to move around to repair the tank and will also eliminate the accompanying infantry. The only reliable countermeasure to trackbusters is to equip the lead tanks with plows, which will literally plow any trackbusters out of the way. This slows the advance considerably and makes the advancing tank unit more vulnerable to other antitank weapons.

Another form of cluster bomb deploys bomblets that descend and pierce the thinner top armor of tanks. Such weapons are easier for aircraft to use as they do not require aiming at a single armored vehicle. Unlike the trackbusters, which can be dropped before the enemy arrives, the antitank bomblets have to be dropped on the enemy tank formation.

Individual troops, or even a member of the tank crew, can also eyeball the trackbusters and other cluster bomblets and either avoid them or shoot them up with an assault rifle. The 1991 Gulf War demonstrated that the Iraqi troops, like troops everywhere, use their sense of self-preservation and resourcefulness to overcome much of the anticipated effect of cluster bombs.

Despite their expense, and the battlefield shortcomings of new aircraft weapons, aircraft still have the considerable advantage of being able to concentrate a lot of firepower on a distant battlefield at short notice. They are the antitank weapon of last resort, and this justifies their expense.

Changes in Tank Design

Advances in antitank weapons do not take place without improvements in tank design. Until recently, more powerful antitank weapons resulted in thicker tank armor. You can go only so far making heavier tanks. Once you get over 60 tons, the weight of the vehicle becomes a handicap. Many bridges cannot be used, and the wheels and tracks wear out much more quickly. Armor had to be made better instead of thicker. Composite armor was developed, consisting of layers of metal and other materials. This made solid projectiles break up. Spaced armor can be added, an extra-thin layer of armor mounted a few inches from the hull. This weakened the effect of shaped charges. Spaced armor, and an additional layer bolted on to key parts of the tank, have been in use since World War II.

As projectiles were improved, reactive armor was developed in response. Reactive armor is not really armor but a layer of explosive panels mounted on the tank's armor. When hit by a HEAT (shaped charge) shell, the reactive armor explodes, weakening the effects of impact. All of these new developments have several major problems. No one knows just how well they will work with the various different HEAT warheads. Also, the new armor is more expensive. And the reactive armor, because it is an explosive, cannot be mounted at all times and can be installed only prior to combat or special training sessions. When this armor explodes, it is additionally dangerous to any friendly troops nearby.

Many other measures have been taken to increase the survivability of tanks, such as automatic fire extinguishers, smoke generators, and the like, but the net result has been to make the tanks more expensive and difficult to maintain. The fact is that perfect antitank weapons do not exist, only more or less destructive ones. One trend is certain in antitank warfare: It is becoming increasingly difficult for armored vehicles to survive on the battlefield. But then, it is becoming more difficult for anything to survive on the battlefield.

The Life of a Tanker

Crews spend less than 10 percent of their time inside their tanks or APCs. Moreover, 25 percent of their casualties occur while outside the vehicle. Still, armored vehicles require at least eight hours of maintenance per day. And climate and geography take tolls on the vehicles, often requiring more maintenance. In combat, systems are stressed to the maximum, and if vehicles are not in peak condition, they are more likely to break down. As there is very little space inside any tank, a smaller tank denotes a lighter and cheaper tank. France and Russia, in fact, require their tank crewmen to be less than five feet six inches tall, allowing manufacturers to build smaller vehicles with the same capabilities of tanks a larger crewman would fit into. This means in these countries that the crews can be selected from only 5 percent of the population.

The inside of a tank is not safe. The turret slews around, the main gun recoils, and 50 + -pound shells are in use. Fractures, lacerations, and amputations regularly occur among careless, fatigued, or untrained crewmen. Two or three of them are generally in the turret. The gunner sits in a small seat next to the main gun with his face pressed against a range finder displaying data on the gun's bearing and range of viewing. Connected to the tank's range finder is a computer that adjusts the aim of the gun and tells the gunner when he can fire. The quality of these systems varies, as does the skill of the operators. Skillful gunners operating quality equipment can obtain first-round hits over 90 percent of the time. Poorly trained and unmotivated men can fire only 10 percent (or less) first-round hits. Assisting the gunner is a human or mechanical loader. The human loader is extremely liable to injury, the mechanical loader likely to fail under stress. The latest series of Russian tanks (T-64/72/80) uses a mechanical loader and three-man crews. With so much machinery, you can imagine the readiness problems.

Universally, the third man in the turret is the vehicle commander. His seat is just below a hatch. When all the hatches are closed, visibility is limited to a few small slits and a periscope. If the commander is wounded, which frequently happens—because of his ability to stand with his head and chest outside the hatch—everyone gets upset until the wounded man quiets down or the corpse is allowed to fall to the floor of the tank or is thrown overboard. At that point, the gunner takes over command of the tank from his seat. The result is a tank that can see much less because the gunner cannot work the cannon with his head outside the turret.

Ideally, the tank commander should be able to replace any other crew member, especially the gunner. The current U.S. tank, the M-1, gives the tank commander equal access to the fire-control system, but cross-training to allow crew members to replace each other is an ideal that is rarely achieved. Usually a former gunner, the tank commander is theoretically the most highly skilled member of the crew.

The only crew member not in the turret is the driver. Squeezed into the front part of the tank, the driver sees through a few slits. At best, he can open a small hatch and stick his head out. He takes direction from the commander, who typically has a better view of where they are going. It's no wonder that tanks in combat appear to move blindly. Most of the time, they are doing just that.

Another critical crew skill is the speedy restocking of ammunition and fuel. With some tanks, this can take over an hour. Carrying up to a ton of munitions, and nearly as much fuel, if tanks run low on them during combat, the speed with which they are replenished is critical. The Israelis' war experience led them to design the Merkava tank. This vehicle has large doors in the rear for the rapid loading of larger quantities of ammunition. Defensively, the tank can stay buttoned up with less loss of control. This is because a good crew will have previously checked out the surrounding terrain carefully and be able to manage without the commander exposing himself to enemy artillery and small-arms fire. At this point, the biggest danger often comes from fatigue and nausea caused by engine gases that leak into the crew compartment, as well as gases from the fired shells. This is most often the case with older Western and Russian tanks, which are not well ventilated—the crews suffer accordingly. In hot climates, Russian crews become, for all practical purposes, nonfunctional after an hour of combat because of the lack of ventilation. Western vehicles will last longer because many have some form of air-conditioning. Fortunately, combat normally doesn't last that long. When tanks get into a firefight, they are either hit or they withdraw to a safer position. And they spend a long time waiting for the other fellow to make a false move.

The Russians feel they must win a war quickly, using surprise and shock to overcome their adversaries. This has made night fighting more necessary for them. Using infrared searchlights, thermal sights, and sighting devices that amplify available light, tanks can now see nearly as well as in daylight. These devices favor the defender more than the attacker. The defender can sight his night-viewing devices at the likely avenues of approach.

Infantrymen with APCs live with their armored vehicles in much the same way tank crews do with their tanks. The maintenance load for APCs is lighter because 9 to 12 men are assigned to a mechanically simpler vehicle. Another major difference is that in combat the infantrymen spend most of their time outside their vehicle. It wasn't meant to be that way, as the second generation of APCs (from the 1960s on) were designed so that the infantry could use their weapons from inside them. Subsequent combat experience showed this to be ineffective. This is another example of why you must be wary of new doctrine developed in peacetime.

One final note on APCs: Because they are lighter and less stable than tanks, they cannot move as quickly cross-country without injuring passengers. Tank crews are more securely seated in their heavier and more stable vehicles. A modern tank can move 30 to 40 kilometers an hour, depending on the quality of the suspension system, while APCs can move only about half that speed safely. The heavier APCs, the German Marder and the American M-2 IFV, are better able to keep up with the tanks, but there's one problem after another.

Theory and Practice

Throughout their short history, tanks have struggled to survive in combat. Although the most heavily protected vehicles on the battlefield, tanks are also the most likely to be shot at. Theoretically, they could confront three or four antitank weapons on the battlefield besides other tanks. But the situation gets more complex in peacetime. Tanks and antitank weapons are very high tech. As more gadgets are added, the situation becomes more unpredictable. Experience has shown in the last 50 years that systems rarely work as anticipated in war. On the bright side, however, everyone's systems perform in unexpected ways. The only problem is that peacetime planners have a difficult time calculating what their position on planning should be. Consider the situation in the 1980s, as tanks were equipped with composite and reactive armor. Even though ATGM warheads and tank shells have become more effective, tank partisans now sense a chance to recapture the advantage on the battlefield. To illustrate this situation, the following two tables show armor improvements in the 1980s. Note that the actual thickness of armor is increased by the slope of the armor. Unless an antitank weapon is firing down at a tank, the shell will hit the armor at an angle and have to penetrate more armor to be effective.

This table shows how reactive armor halves the effect of HEAT (High Explosive Antitank) armor piercing shells against T-72 tanks.

Armor or Factor for *T-72*	*Effective Thickness (mm)* *Against HEAT and SHOT Shells*	
	HEAT	SHOT
Steel armor	170	170
With Slope (avg)	238	238
Reactive armor Penetration	Halves	No Effect

Example of how the table above works: A HEAT warhead (TOW 1) with 600mm penetration hits the 170mm armor of a Russian built T-72 tank. The TOW 1 warhead would hit at sloped armor. After blasting through the armor, the warhead would still have over 300mm of penetrating power left to cause mayhem inside the tank. In such cases, it is not unknown for the HEAT warheads' plasma bolt to keep going and come out the other side of the turret. If the T-72 had reactive armor, the total penetrating power of the TOW 1 warhead would be halved from 600mm to 300mm. This would leave only 62mm of penetrating power. In some cases, this might not be enough, because the above data are averages. The SHOT round (also called APDS, etc.) is a solid, rodlike "penetrator" that must be fired from a high-velocity gun. SHOT is generally immune to current reactive armor.

The reactive-armor situation gets worse, as the chart below shows the effect of the composite armor on the Russian T-80.

This table shows how reactive armor halves the effect of HEAT armor piercing shells against T-80 tanks.

Armor or Factor for T-80	*Effective Thickness (mm)* *Against HEAT and SHOT Shells*	
	HEAT	SHOT
Composite armor	400	250
With Slope (avg)	560	350
Reactive armor Penetration	Halves	0

The same 600mm HEAT warhead would have 300mm of penetration encountering 560mm of protection. The latest ATGM warheads (TOW 2 and 3), with penetration in excess of 1,000mm, are apparently effective against current reactive armor. The TOW 3 (or TOW 2A) was specifically designed to defeat reactive armor. Older TOW missiles can be upgraded by replacing the TOW 1 warhead with the TOW 2 or 3 warhead. Not all of the 500,000 TOW missiles built to date will be upgraded. In any event, only about half of these missiles (first built in 1970) are still in use. Most armies do not use reactive armor, and there is not a great deal of faith in the effectiveness of reactive armor, nor will there be until the stuff has gotten an extensive battlefield workout. This did not happen during the 1991 Gulf War, and it may be a while before it does happen. Moreover, the most common antitank weapons were the heavier Hellfire and Maverick missiles, as well as the M-1 tank's 120mm gun.

Normally, a tank would have either steel or composite armor. Russians, however, experimented with adding a thin layer of composite to existing tanks. Spaced armor would not be used with reactive armor. By 1991, most Russian tanks in category 1 and 2 divisions were equipped with reactive armor. Such a vehicle would be invulnerable to most frontal hits from older HEAT warheads. Top-attack HEAT warheads would have a better chance, and these are becoming more popular.

Tanks, however, cannot win battles by themselves, and are not as invincible as the above charts would indicate. Tanks are still vulnerable to attack from the rear, from above and from below. It should be remembered that Western armies deploy massive numbers of new weapons that drop from above. Trackbuster mines may also prove to undo the most robust tank. Meanwhile, the maelstrom of other weapons rips away the accompanying infantry and light armored vehicles. Tanks may be the most powerful system on the battlefield, yet they may not be powerful enough.

The experience of U.S. M-1 tanks rolling, virtually unscathed, right through Iraqi tank units in the 1991 Gulf War, was a result of several unique conditions. The version of the M-1 tank used was the most modern tank in the world and incorporated an advanced type of composite armor. The Iraqis were using armor-piercing shells of their own manufacture. These Iraqi shells were inferior to the ones Russia made for the Russian-built tanks the Iraqis were using. As a result, the U.S. tanks were virtually invulnerable to Iraqi tank fire. As most U.S. tanks were maneuvering around the open flank of the Iraqi positions, there were few mines encountered. Because the battles were in a desert, the long-range guns of the U.S. tanks were able to operate at peak efficiency, and it was rarely necessary to send infantry ahead to clear out enemy infantry and antitank weapons. For the Allied troops, it was an ideal tank battle, fought under ideal conditions and with ideal results. These situations have occurred in previous desert tank battles; they are the exception, and not the rule.

The Future

Armored fighting vehicles have long been caught up in competition between tank protection and tank destruction. At one point in the late 1980s, there was a proposal for new reactive armor with sensors that detected an approaching projectile. It would explode before it was hit. The Soviets went this idea one better by developing and deploying a tank turret mounted system that used a millimeter wave radar to detect incoming missiles and then fire one of eight shotgun-type weapons that would fire a pattern of steel pellets that would damage the missile sufficiently to render the warhead useless. It shows the lengths to which the Soviets were willing to go to save their huge tank investment from the increasing arsenal of Western missiles.

Armor itself is no longer slabs of high-grade steel, but many layers of different materials, designed to better defeat an increasing variety of anti-tank weapons. No one is really sure what will stop a tank anymore; we probably won't find out until there is another major tank battle.

Meanwhile, Western nations have developed missile warheads that can penetrate the new "composite plus reactive armor" on many Russian tanks. Russia has equipped thousands of its older T-62 and T-55 to wear reactive armor, and this technology is being sold to any nation that has the hard currency to pay for it. Many of these older tanks have also been equipped with laser range finders and modern fire-control equipment. The Russians really believe in tanks, and will help equip any other nation that thinks likewise.

Russia and the United States are planning several variants of a new "future technology" tank, one with a very small turret containing the main gun and fire-control sensors. There is no "top" armor in the usual sense, as the frontal armor slopes up and toward the back of the tank, with engine heat vented out the back instead of the top rear. This design adds some protection against conventional weapons that attack the top armor and/or home in on heat. The tank also puts most of the protection to the front. Tank battles in the past 30 years have shown that two thirds of hits are in the front, less than 10 percent in the rear, and the rest on the sides. The future-technology tank is supposed to have a 140mm gun better able to penetrate improved armor designs (more complex, and expensive, composite armor). However, the larger round will reduce the tank's ammunition load and rate of fire. Through the 1980s, work has been under way to develop higher-velocity liquid propellant (which is lighter and safer) and electrically propelled guns for tanks but these are at least 10 years away. Liquid propellant is likely to appear in lower-velocity artillery before a high-velocity liquid-propellant tank gun is introduced. These new technologies are being worked on to ultimately create higher-velocity shells. The higher velocity not only penetrates exotic armor more efficiently but makes countermeasures more difficult. Current high-speed shells move at about 1,500 meters a second. The future-technology shells are expected to achieve 3,000–5,000-meter-a-second speeds. At over 3,500 meters a second, the shells will leave a glowing trail behind them.

Another problem is how the two-man crew will efficiently keep in touch with the outside world. Throughout the tank's history, the commander has been the most effective means of controlling a tank. The future-technology solution appears to be equipping these new tanks with sensors similar to those now found in attack helicopters. This increases the cost enormously and doesn't help much, as attack helicopters are still notoriously blind to what's happening on the ground most of the time. Other features proposed include an armored capsule for the two-man crew and blowout panels for ammunition and fuel storage. Another innovation, previously tried and discarded by Western armies in the early 1970s, is an ATGM fired from the tank's gun tube. An even more immediate problem presents itself: maintenance. A more complex tank with an even smaller crew requires more maintenance personnel. When you have a tank as complex as an aircraft, you need a "ground crew" to keep it going, and more highly skilled "pilots" to operate it. Current Western tank battalions contain about one technician for every tank crewman, and that ratio will eventually be greater than one to one. With all the gadgets proposed for the future-technology tanks, these vehicles will still be vulnerable to mines—something aircraft don't have to worry about. These future-technology tanks have been in development for some time, a common situation as they become increasingly complex and expensive. The end of the Cold War has eliminated most of the enthusiasm for building them, and sharp budget cuts on both sides of the former Iron Curtain have made it impossible to maintain even current stocks of tanks. Future-technology tanks will have to wait for the next arms race.

Most worrisome to all tank-owning nations, and tank crews in general, are the forthcoming "smart" robotic weapons, which use sensors and warheads that can be automatically lobbed 100 yards in any direction to penetrate the thinner top armor of tanks. These weapons have already entered production in Western armies. Several nations are also introducing new features for their ATGMs in addition to modified warheads for penetrating reactive armor. The most popular innovations are top-attack and wireless guidance. These "fire and forget" ATGMs use multiple sensors to home in on armored vehicles. The missile's onboard computer sorts out the battlefield clutter and pinpoints functional tanks, despite countermeasures. The top-attack warhead, first introduced in the Swedish BILL system, passes over the armored vehicle and fires its shaped charge down at the thinner top armor. Reactive armor on the top of the tank can defeat these unless the ATGM warheads are designed to take on reactive armor, which the new ones are. A more brute force approach is embodied in hyper-velocity rockets fired from aircraft or ground vehicles. Also ready for production are electronic weapons that attack the more numerous sensors and electronics of current armored vehicles. If you can't kill them, then blind them or inflict electronic amnesia. Adjusting for inflation, an average tank today costs more than three times what was paid during World War II. Yet it is still a very inefficient system. Only recently have tank tracks been made sturdy enough to last more than 1,000 kilometers. Most Russian-made tanks are still equipped with tracks that wear out after less than 1,000 kilometers of use.

Russia and many of the customers for its tanks have made a large wager on the success of the tank. Western nations have shown greater preference for cheaper countermeasures. It was Western nations that developed and perfected the ATGM, ATRL (bazooka), and trackbuster mine. Ironically, better armor, main guns, and other tank components were also developed in the West, but introduced on a larger scale by the Russians. As history has shown, the defense (antitank weapons) tends to stay in the lead against offensive weapons (tanks). Despite the success of the U.S. M-1 tank in Kuwait, the future holds a horde of cheap, electronics-based "smart" antitank weapons. While it's easy for the United States to control export of its 60-ton M-1 tank, many nations have the electronics technology needed for the new generations of antitank weapons.

Main Battle Tanks

VEHICLE. The official designation of the vehicle.

BUILT BY. The nation that originally built the vehicle. In some cases, the vehicle is also manufactured in other nations. One nation, Russia, accounts for the majority of armored vehicles built annually and to date. This will continue for some years, as it is one item where Russia is the low-cost producer in the global market. Other major manufacturers are the United States, Germany, Britain, France, China, Israel, and Sweden. Several other nations with steel industries and other technological resources also build their own tanks. Original designs are often used. These smaller-scale manufacturers include Japan, South Korea, and Brazil.

FIREPOWER. This is the numerical evaluation of the vehicle's firepower. It is calculated by taking into account the following factors:

The "proving ground" performance of the vehicle's main gun and the various types of ammunition. The type of shell used can have a vastly different effect on the target. Tanks carry various types of shells among the 40 to 50 rounds typically carried. The types carried depend on what opposition they expect to encounter and how large their ammunition budget is. Some shells are more expensive than others. The cheapest shell is HE (High Explosive), useful only against soft targets. Next comes your economy-model armor-piercing APS (Armor Piercing Shot) shell, which is little more than a pointed hunk of high-grade steel. The most expensive "shot" shell is APDS (Armor Piercing Discarding Sabot) and APFSDS (Armor

Piercing Fin Stabilized Discarding Sabot, for smooth-bore guns). The armor-piercing element of discarding sabot rounds is less than half the diameter of the shell and made of very expensive high-density metal. Its smaller size enables it to hit the target at very high speed, up to 1,600 meters a second. This is the most common shell and is constantly being improved. A recent version, using a penetrator of depleted (nonradioactive) uranium, is purchased by the United States. Most armies are installing 120mm tank-gun smooth-bore guns, which have the same penetrating power as the 105mm depleted uranium APDS plus the ability to use future shell designs that require a larger projectile. These would be the "smart" shells with their own sensors and guidance systems. Composite armor was developed to defeat APDS, but it is not always successful. HEAT (High Explosive Antitank) rounds have fallen from favor because their success depends on hitting a flat surface on the tank. Modern tanks have few flat surfaces. On the plus side, HEAT shells must be fired at lower speeds, are good at any range, and many are now built with a fragmentation capability to make them useful for antipersonnel work. The AP-type shells are less effective at longer ranges. Similar to HEAT, more expensive, and still in use, is the HESH (High Explosive Squash Head) shell. This item hits the tank, the explosive warhead squashes, and then it explodes. The force of the explosion goes through the armor and causes things to come loose and fly about the inside of the tank (the spall effect). The vehicle may appear unharmed, but the crew and much of its equipment are not. It works at any range, but is somewhat defeated by spaced and composite armor. The most expensive tank shell is currently used by the Russians in their tanks equipped with 125mm tank guns—namely, the ATGM. The United States tried this in the 1960s and 1970s, but dropped it because of the problems. It's unclear if the Russians will be any more successful. The price range on the above shells goes from several hundred (HE) to several thousand dollars (ATGM) per round.

The fire-control system. This includes the type of range finder (see below) as well as the computing system. The more recent electronic fire-control computers on tanks have proved to be more effective than the older mechanical ones. Unfortunately, the more complex models are usually less reliable, although they are improving.

The internal layout and organization of the tank. This includes how the ammunition is stored and how easily the various crew can reach and operate their equipment. The cramped Russian tanks suffer in this respect. Tanks lacking air-conditioning are also a problem. Tanks that have been upgraded to the point that their interior is crowded also have problems.

Gun stabilization and platform stability are the ability of the tank to provide sufficient stability so that the main gun can be accurately fired while the vehicle is moving or immediately after a halt. This has been something of a Holy Grail for tank builders since World War II. Some of the current systems actually do the deed some of the time.

Ammunition carried. The more you have, the more you can use to hit the other fellow with.

Rate of fire. Notably the ability to get off the first shot accurately and—in these days of voodoo (reactive and composite) armor—the second shot. Experienced crews can fire faster than the number indicated. The chart merely indicates the tank's normal rate of fire that can be maintained without overheating the barrel or wearing the crew out.

PROTECT is the numerical evaluation of the vehicle's ability to defend itself. This is a combination of the following factors:

1. *Quantity and quality of armor.* How thick the armor is and how well it is laid out. Armor that has no sharp edges and that only offers a "slope" for enemy shells to hit is more effective. Antitank shells are just very large bullets. If they hit sloping armor, they have a tendency to ricochet. When hitting four inches of armor at any angle, they will effectively have to go through more metal than if they hit it head-on. This is why modern tanks have such a smooth appearance. Armor thickness counts for less today than what has been used to make it. The armor of the eighties is composite (or Chobham, after the British organization that developed it). This material is an expensive combination of layers of armor, plastics, and ceramics. It absorbs and breaks up shot-type shells before they can penetrate. It is also effective against HEAT and HESH high-explosive shells. Spaced armor has come back into vogue to defeat ATGM HEAT warheads. This is nothing more than thin armor sheets mounted a few inches from the main armor. Basically, it causes the HEAT shell to detonate prematurely and form its penetrating plasma jet inefficiently. Spaced armor can in turn be defeated with a special fuse. And so it goes. The latest wrinkle is reactive armor, which is composed of explosive material. When struck, it explodes and makes HEAT shells' penetration much less efficient. This stuff is only mounted in wartime, for obvious reasons. Most nations can, or do, use spaced armor. The M-1, Leopard II, T-80, and British tanks use composite armor. The Russians and Israelis have installed reactive armor. Composite armor can also be installed as add-on protection, although this increases the weight of the vehicle somewhat.
2. *Speed of the vehicle.* This is a combination of actual top speed, vehicle power (see HP:WT below), ground pressure, and quality of the suspension system and other machinery required to drive the vehicle. Power and speed enable the vehicle to get out of the way quickly. Higher ground pressure makes it more likely that the vehicle will get stuck in soft ground. A better suspension system prevents the crew from being knocked about during high-speed cross-country movement.
3. *Ability to lay smoke.* Some vehicles have smoke-grenade dischargers. Others form smoke by spraying diesel fuel on hot engine parts. Some vehicles cannot produce any smoke, leaving them unable to produce a place to hide when they most need it.
4. *Size.* All armored vehicles are large. Height is the best indicator of a vehicle's ability to remain unseen.
5. *Main gun depression.* The greater this is, the less tank is exposed when it goes into defilade behind a slope, with only its gun and turret visible to the enemy.
6. *Viewing devices from inside the tank.* Ideally, the tank commander should

have his head outside the tank. But this is not always possible. Various arrangements are made in tanks to provide viewing slits protected by bulletproof glass. The quality of the gunner's sight is also considered.

7. *Damage control.* Includes fire-extinguishing system, location of explosive items, and layout of crew compartment to protect the crew in case these items are hit. Chemical-warfare protection system and escape capability also considered.

8. *Communications.* Russian-type tanks typically have many vehicle radios capable of only receiving. It's cheaper and avoids the problem of useless chatter. It does make information gathering more difficult. Quality of internal communication also varies. Timely information can save your life in a tank battle.

RANGE is the unrefueled range of the vehicle in kilometers. Generally, in combat, 100 kilometers of range equals three to five hours of running time (assuming 40 percent off the road, 20 percent on the road, and 40 percent stationary with the engine running). This will vary with the season, more time in the summer when the ground is dry and firm, less when it is very hot (air-conditioning), cold (snow), or muddy. Cruising speed is generally 30 to 40 kilometers per hour.

GRND PRES is the ground pressure in pounds per square inch. The lower this is, the more easily the vehicle can cross soft ground like mud, ice, snow, or sand. An infantryman's weight produces 2 to 10 pounds per square inch.

HP:WT is the horsepower-to-weight ratio (the horsepower of the engine divided by the vehicle weight). The higher this is, the more "lively" the vehicle will move. This is more important for acceleration and moving up slopes than for pure speed.

GUN DPRS is the gun depression in degrees. The greater the depression, the better. A tank defends most effectively from defilade. That is, it backs up behind a hill as far as it can go and still be able to sight its gun over the top of the hill. Depending on how steep the slope is, very little of the vehicle is visible to the enemy. At best, all the enemy sees are the gun and the top of the turret. On gentle slopes, a small depression is adequate. Steeper slopes require more depression, unless you want to expose more of the tank.

WGHT is the full-load weight of the tank in metric tons.

MAX SPD (in kilometers per hour) is the maximum speed of the vehicle on a road. Cross-country speed is limited by vehicle weight and the effectiveness of the suspension system. Heavier vehicles actually have an easier time of it. It's the same difference in rider comfort experienced in a Cadillac and a compact.

RANGE FINDER SYS is the type of range-finder system used. Laser is the easiest to use and most accurate. It's also the most expensive. StadR (stadia reticle) is quite primitive, but cheap. It will do the job at short ranges with an experienced gunner. Coin (coincidence), StroC (stereo coincidence), and OptC (optical coincidence) are based on more elaborate optics and give better results as the gunners' skill and experience increases. LaserT is laser with thermal sight. Newer tanks have an additional thermal sight mounted. This device is used at night and in bad visibility. It displays heat sources, although at shorter ranges. However, what you can see, you can hit. This is an expensive item, but quite devastating in use. Some users report that they could use the thermal sight to see through a heavy white phosphorous cloud, and identify someone urinating from the rear deck of a tank. One more thing to be careful about in combat.

HGHT is the height of the vehicle in meters (one meter equals 3.3 feet). Measured to the top of the turret.

MAIN GUN is the caliber of the main gun in millimeters.

RNDS ON BOARD is the number of main gun rounds of ammunition carried. The more, the better. Normally, a mix of armor-piercing (over 75 percent) and antipersonnel rounds (the rest).

RNDS PER MIN is the nominal number of aimed rounds per minute the main gun can fire. The more, the better. Highly skilled crews can get off as many as 50 percent more rounds per minute. They cannot do this for long, as the barrel will overheat. Less adept crews can manage a high rate of fire, but the aim is often way off.

MAX RANGE is the maximum effective range of the main gun in meters. The farther, the better. As was mentioned elsewhere in this chapter, the average shot is between 500 and 1,000 meters.

MG 1, MG 2 are the machine guns carried in addition to the main gun. The caliber of each machine gun is given in millimeters. One machine gun is customarily mounted next to the main gun and can be fired in its place (using the same viewing system the main gun uses). The second machine gun is mounted on the top of the turret for use against aircraft or ground targets.

IN USE is the number of this type in use as of 1992. The BMP, BMD, M-2, M-3, T-80, T-72, T-64, M-1, and Leopard II are still in production. In the late 1980s, the annual production for each was approximately: BMP—2,500, BMD—200, M-2/M-3—1,400, T-80—400, T-72—1,800, T-64—1,000, M-1—800, Leopard II— 400. By the early 1990s, this production had fallen by more than half, and this decline is expected to continue. There will always be some production of armored vehicles. But the end of the Cold War eliminated the major source of demand for them. By the end of the decade, their production will be at the lowest level since the end of World War II. Western nations, at least, have additional capacity, and can double or triple their production rates quickly.

Armored Personnel Carriers and Infantry Fighting Vehicles

APCs (Armored Personnel Carriers) are also referred to as IFVs (Infantry Fighting Vehicles). An IFV is basically an APC with a turret and a higher price tag. APCs are also used widely as reconnaissance vehicles. In this case, they carry more weapons and fuel and fewer men. Many of the terms used in Chart 3-2 are the same as those used in the tank chart (3-1).

COMFORT is the relative "livability" of the vehicle for passengers. The higher the value, the more livable it is. Low livability tires the passengers and lowers their effectiveness when they must fight.

PASSENGERS is the number of passengers the vehicle was designed to carry. You can crowd a third (or more) additional people in, at substantial loss in livability.

FLOAT indicates if the vehicle can float. The number indicates speed (in kilometers per hour) in the water. These vehicles just barely float and cannot manage in rough water.

GUN PORTS is the number of gun ports in an APC that the passengers can use to engage targets with their rifles. This sort of thing never really worked too well in practice.

WEAP 1, 2, 3 represents the weapons mounted on an APC. Given in caliber (millimeters). All are machine guns except the 73mm guns on the BMP and BMD. The most recent version of the BMP has an automatic cannon (30mm) mounted in place of the 73mm gun.

ATGM is an Antitank Guided Missile that can be fired from the vehicle.

Crew size for tanks is four, except for the S-Tank, T-72/64/80, which is three. These vehicles have an automatic loader that replaces one man, leaving a vehicle commander, gunner, and driver. APCs have a minimal crew of two (commander/gunner and driver). Some have a third man assigned as a gunner if there are more onboard weapons.

VEHICLE NOTES

Each nation tends to have its own philosophy on armored warfare, which carries over to its vehicle designs. Russia has gone for massive numbers of effective yet expendable tanks. Its tanks have had large guns, but incomplete fire-control systems and shoddy ammunition. Armor has been thick, but crude. Externally, the armor is well sloped to deflect hits. Russian tanks are low and wide to present less of a target. The Russians go for a high horsepower-to-weight ratio. Their tanks are cramped, uncomfortable, difficult to maintain, and numerous. In the last 30 years, they have approached Western designs in number and complexity of gadgets. Most of these new items have been copies of similar Western devices. Russia has built over 60,000 tanks since the mid-1960s. Until 1991, most of them were still in use, as they are operated infrequently so as to make the maximum number available for combat. The oldest model is the T-55, a direct descendant of their famous T-34 of World War II fame. Most of these will be scrapped in the 1990s. China still makes a T-55 variant (the T-59). The T-55 caught fire too easily, particularly with fuel tanks in the front of the vehicle. It had a larger, for the time, 100mm

3-1 Main Battle Tanks

Vehicle	Built by	Fire-power	Pro-tect	Range (km)	Grnd Pres	HP: Wt	Gun Dprs	Wght (tons)	Max Spd (km)	Range Finder Sys	Hght (m)	Main Gun	Rnds on Board	Rnds per Min	Max Range	MG 1	MG 2	In Use	Intro-duced
T-80	Russia	10	9	400	11	24	5	42	60	Laser	2.3	125	55	8	3,000	12.7	7.62	2,200	1981
T-64	Russia	10	8	400	11	24	5	42	60	Laser	2.3	125	55	8	3,000	12.7	7.62	10,000	1971
T-72	Russia	9	7	500	12	25	5	40	60	Laser	2.5	125	50	8	2,000	12.7	7.62	16,000	1972
T-62	Russia	8	6	480	11	19	5	37	59	StadR	2.4	115	40	4	1,500		7.62	12,000	1962
T-55	Russia	6	4	300	12	16	5	36	50	StadG	2.4	100	43	3	1,000	12.7	7.62	10,000	1957
PT-76	Russia	3	2	260	7	17	5	14	44	StadG	2.2	76	40	4	1,000	7.62	7.62	2,000	1955
																	Total	52,200	
M-1	US	11	10	560	14	26	10	58	72	Laser	2.4	105	55	6	4,000	12.7	7.62	3,100	1981
M-1A1	US	12	12	560	15	22	10	67	67	Laser	2.4	120	40	6	4,000	12.7	7.62	3,800	1986
M60A3	US	10	7	300	11	19	10	48	48	Laser	3.2	105	63	6	3,000	12.7	7.62	8,000	1977
M48A5	US	10	7	290	13	19	10	47	48	Coin	3.1	105	57	6	2,500	12.7	7.62	1,200	1976
																	Total	16,100	
Leopard II	German	12	10	350	13	30	9	50	68	Laser	2.5	120	60	8	3,500	7.62	7.62	2,100	1978
Leopard I	German	9	7	375	13	23	9	40	65	StroC	2.6	105	60	6	2,500	7.62	7.62	4,500	1965
																	Total	6,600	
AMX-30bis	France	9	6	400	12	19	8	36	65	OptC	2.8	105	50	8	2,500	12.7	7.62	2,000	1967
S-Tank	Sweden	10	7	250	14	6	10	39	50	Laser	2.4	105	50	15	3,000	7.62	7.62 / 7.62	300	1968
Merkava 2	Israel	10	10	320	15	18	10	60	58	Laser	2.7	105	62	6	3,000	7.62	7.62 / 60mm Mortar	200	1978
Type 59	China	6	4	300	12	16	4	36	50	StadG	2.4	105	43	3	1,000	12.7	7.62	6,000	1957
Type 69	China	8	6	430	11	19	4	38	58	Laser	2.8	105	44	6	3,000	12.7	7.62	1,200	1962
																	Total	7,200	

3-2 Armored Personnel Carriers

Vehicle	Built by	Fire-power	Pro-tect	Com-fort	Grnd Pres	HP: Wt	Pass-en-gers	Wght (tons)	Max Spd (km)	Hgh (m)	Float	# Gun Ports	Max Range (km)	Weap 1	Weap 2	Weap 3	In Use	First Used
BMP	Russia	6	3	3	9	21	11	13.5	55	2	8	9	300	73	7.62	ATGM	22,000	1967
BMD	Russia	6	3	4	9	42	9	6.7	55	1.9	6	0	300	73	7.62	7.62	2,400	1969
BRDM	Russia	2	2	5	Wheel	20	3	7	100	2.3	10	0	750	14.5	7.62		9,000	1966
BTR-60	Russia	2	2	5	Wheel	18	16	10	80	2.3	10	6	500	14.5	7.62		5,000	1961
BTR-50	Russia	2	2	5	7	17	16	15	44	2	10	0	260	7.62			6,000	1957
BMP 2/3	Russia	7	3	3	9	19	10	14.5	55	2	8	9	400	20/30	7.62	ATGM	7,000	1967
																Total	51,400	
M-2	US	8	5	6	7	22	9	22.5	68	2.6	7	6	480	25	7.62	ATGM	3,200	1981
M-3	US	8	5	6	7	22	5	22.5	68	2.6	7	0	480	25	7.62	ATGM	1,400	1981
LVTP-7	US	3	3	7	9	17	28	24	60	3.3	13.5	0	480	12.7			940	1972
M-113	US	2	2	6	8	20	13	11	65	2.5	5.8	0	480	12.7	7.62	ATGM	35,000	1960
																Total	40,540	
AMX-10P	France	6	4	6	8	20	11	14	65	2.5	7.9	2	600	20	7.62		2,000	1973
Marder	German	7	5	6	12	21	9	29	75	2.9	No	2	520	20	7.62		2,200	1971

gun and crude fire control. It was fast and simple. Those used in the Middle East and other areas were not popular with their crews. In the early '60s the T-62 came along. This model had a larger gun (115mm), and better armor and fire control. It also had numerous mechanical problems and was replaced earlier than expected in the late '60s by the T64/72. The "64" was a more advanced model used only by the Russian Army, the "72" a cheaper version of the "64," also used for export. Both models had a larger gun (125mm), thicker armor, better fire control, and an automatic loader. This resulted in a three-man crew. A further development is the current T-80, which often sports a laser range finder and ATGM fired from the 125mm smooth-bore gun. The T-80 also had composite armor and is used as a heavy "assault" tank. Reactive armor can be added to all tanks, the primary limitation being expense. On the other extreme, the World War II–era PT-76 light tank persists in service as a reconnaissance vehicle because basically it is an excellent vehicle.

In the late 1940s, the Soviets introduced wheeled APCs for their infantry. In the 1950s they began making tracked APCs that could keep up with their tanks. In the late 1960s came the BMP and phasing out of many of the wheeled APCs for the infantry. The older wheeled models were passed on to combat-support units. The BMP was a mixed success. It was cramped and gave a rough ride. The passengers were in poor shape to do any fighting after a high-speed romp. Its 73mm gun had a weak shell and low rate of fire. The ATGM carried was one of the less effective models. The BMP caught fire easily and was difficult to maintain. The vehicle looks impressive as hell, though. During the 1980s, a new version of the BMP appeared, with an automatic 30mm cannon replacing the 73mm gun. Divisions in the arctic even have a special unarmored tracked vehicle designed to keep going in the snow and cold.

The huge inventory of Russian armored vehicles shrank in the late 1980s when the Soviet Union, facing economic ruin from the arms race and internal misman-agement, signed a series of arms-control treaties. The collapse of the Soviet Union in 1991 rendered still more of its armored vehicles unusable as the units they belonged to shrank or fell apart.

The United States never had a reputation for deploying outstanding armored-vehicle designs. After World War II, tanks were built that tried to have the best of everything: thick armor, heavy firepower, crew comfort, advanced fire control. In most particulars, these objectives were achieved. Although much is made about the larger size of U.S. tanks, this does not appear to have seriously compromised their combat performance. The biggest problem was maintenance. American troops are accustomed to using their vehicles a lot in peacetime, resulting in a heavy maintenance workload. Running a tank is also expensive, making money a limiting factor. Out of this has come electronic devices to enable more realistic training in the field and back at the barracks. In the field, weapons are equipped with lasers and vehicles with sensors so that you can hit targets without hurting anyone. Back in the barracks, one finds elaborate simulators that approximate those of aircraft in their realism and complexity.

The M-48 was developed in the late 1940s from World War II experience, both U.S. and German. The M-60 was basically an upgrade of the M-48. Many M-48s were subsequently upgraded to M-60 standards in terms of gun size, fire control, and engine power. The M-1 is a more radical development in tank design than the

M-60, notably because of its composite armor, propulsion system, and lavish use of electronics.

U.S. APCs were originally built just for transport. The primary stimulus of building the U.S. IFV (M-2/M-3) was the Soviet BMP. The IFV concept, especially fighting from the vehicle, has not been particularly successful in practice. The M-2 is basically an APC with a turret and 25mm cannon. The latest version of the BMP now has a 30mm cannon in its turret. The M-3 is a reconnaissance version of the M-2, and the M-113 continues to be widely used in support roles. Several hundred World War II half-track vehicles are still in use. The LVTP-7 is the U.S. Marine Corps amphibious APC. Other nations adhered to a slightly different tank-design formula. Germany came out with a series of tanks somewhat between those of the United States and Russia in philosophy. The Germans stressed quality, high firepower, and speed. They accepted lower weight and less protection. The French went for an even lighter tank, while the British opted for less speed and more protection. The British designs have been less successful, and for a while they were shopping around in Germany and the United States for their next generation of tanks. The Swedes went for a more defensive system, a low-slung, turretless tank with an automatic loader and a three-man crew. This is well suited to their war policy, although now they are looking for a more conventional design for their next generation of tanks. Israel, after years of using other people's tanks, has designed its own, the Merkava, for defensive warfare. It is heavily protected, and a larger-than-usual storage compartment is easy to resupply through large doors.

Non–U.S./Russian APCs normally follow the Russian model. The French AMX-10P and the German Marder both resemble the BMP. With few exceptions, nations that manufacture tanks do not use those of another nation. Germany still has many U.S. tanks. This is because it has only been a little over 25 years since Germany revived its tank-building capability, and their U.S. tanks are being rapidly retired. Nations that do not produce tanks tend to use more than one type. Purchasing armored vehicles appears to have more to do with political relationships than with technical merit.

Portable Antitank Weapons: Missiles and Rockets

Currently, three broad classes of antitank weapons exist: guns, mines, and the others. These "others" are the more exotic missiles, rockets, and submunitions. Most antitank guns are found on tanks, although some armies, including Russia, still use towed antitank guns (although these may finally disappear in the 1990s). Most guns rely primarily on kinetic (high-velocity) shells, which allow for rapid firing. These shells travel at over 1,000 meters a second. Contrast this with ATGMs' slower 200 meters a second. Mines are one of the more effective antivehicle weapons and are discussed in greater detail in Chapter 20. Mines are passive weapons—they must be placed in the path of enemy vehicles. They are also heavy, particularly in useful quantities. The other antitank weapons are of more recent vintage, and were developed to give troops without tanks and minefields some protection against armored forces. The ATRL (Antitank Rocket Launcher) was an American development during World War II. These weapons were to give the infantry some defense against tanks. Their effectiveness has been overrated, perhaps because unsuccessful users rarely survived to report their failure. An example of this occurred in the early '70s, when an American adviser to South Vietnamese troops survived an encounter with North Vietnamese T-55 tanks. More than a dozen of the latest American ATRL (the LAW) were fired at these older Russian-made tanks to no effect, and a few of the LAW users escaped to report their experience. The LAW had been around for nearly 10 years at that point, and it was only after this incident that attention was paid to the actual (as opposed to announced) effectiveness of these weapons. This was not the first time this happened to the Americans. In 1950, U.S. troops faced Russian-made T-34 tanks with their 60mm bazooka ATRL (of World War II fame). The T-34s were immune. It had been discovered in 1943 that some German tanks were also immune, so the American Army began developing an 88mm (3.5 inch) ATRL and was finally able to send some of these more effective weapons to the front in 1950. The problem was, the 60mm version was thought to be sufficient. The problem with ATRLs is not just their dubious penetrating power, but also their accuracy and ease of use. Their accuracy is dependent on steady nerves and some experience. The rocket-propelled warhead is actually lobbed at the target at low speed. A pretty good marksman is required to hit a moving vehicle at 100 meters. It ain't like the movies at all. Despite these shortcomings, ATRLs are issued in the millions. They do give the infantry a chance, at least against lighter armored vehicles like APCs. The rockets are also quite useful against enemy fortifications, whether in buildings or the field.

The ATRL's deficiencies brought about the development of the Antitank Guided Missile (ATGM). Over 100,000 ATGM launchers are in use, each launcher having up to 10 missiles. These launchers and several million ATRLs are defensive weapons arrayed against nearly 100,000 tanks and several hundred thousand APCs. Naturally, friendly tanks will also be used as antitank weapons. The odds might appear to be against armored vehicles. ATGMs have had mixed success on the battlefield. More than 20 years of use have brought numerous improvements to ATGM design. Yet, for all that, on the battlefield the tank still looms larger than life to the infantryman. ATGMs are no guarantee of survival, just another chance.

MAKER is the country of manufacture.

NAME is the official designation of the weapon. The chart contains the vast majority of weapon types currently in use. For example, nearly 500,000 TOW missiles have been produced since 1970. The improved TOW2 entered production in 1981, with a TOW3 (or TOW 2A) coming on-line in 1987. Each new model was more lethal and reliable than its predecessor. The DRAGON is a smaller and less effective ATGM. About 100,000 of these have been produced, and a replacement is being developed. The Milan, HOT, and Swingfire are all European missiles similar to the U.S. TOW (HOT, Swingfire) and DRAGON (Milan). Only the Milan has been produced in large quantities (over 200,000), mainly because of its superiority to the DRAGON. The TOW is slowly taking over the market in the West for heavy ATGMs. For over 10 years, work has proceeded on a "fire and forget" ATGM that would not require operator guidance to hit its target. The technical problems have proved daunting, and the only system deployed so far is the U.S. Hellfire. This is not a pure fire-and-forget system, as most of the 50,000 missiles deployed use a laser guidance system that requires that the target be illuminated by a laser device on the helicopter or ground. The system can, however, be fitted with a self-contained target seeker once one is perfected. The Sagger was Russia's first widely used ATGM, and more than a quarter-million were probably produced. Although longer made, it is apparently still in use. It has been replaced in manufacture by the Spigot and other models.

Costing $5,000 and up, missile weapons are expensive. The Russians paid a high price for missiles, as these high-tech systems took a lot out of their technology-starved economy. These weapons also degrade with time, especially the solid-fuel rocket motor, batteries, and the warhead explosives. These components must be replaced periodically, otherwise a growing percentage of the missiles are duds. You won't know which ones will fail until you try to use them, and the Russians had a difficult time maintaining inventories of high-tech items. They were also reluctant to fire many for training purposes and tried to rely on simulators, which are not as effective as those used in the West. But here, far more missiles are fired in training. Most of the over 20,000 TOW missiles fired were for training. In the United States, missiles are updated and refurbished regularly to improve their effectiveness. In combat, reliability will be higher, making for significantly more effective weapons.

The LAW is a one-shot rocket launcher that has been manufactured in the hundreds of thousands and is still in wide use. The RPG-18/22 is a similar Russian weapon. All the other RPGs are highly successful copies of a World War II German antitank rocket launcher (the Panzerfaust). This weapon was a small-diameter tube (about two inches) with a 3.5 inch (88mm) HEAT warhead sticking out one end. Behind the warhead was the propelling charge and a longer, narrower extension of the warhead that stabilized the rocket in flight. The German weapon was a one-shot affair. The Russian innovation was to give it a better sight and more powerful rocket, and make it reloadable. The 106mm RR (recoilless rifle) has been included because it is still used by many nations. It is mounted on trucks, jeeps, armored vehicles, or no vehicle at all. A prominent backblast can give away its position, and its warhead is ineffective against the frontal armor of modern tanks, although it will demolish APCs. Still, it's better than nothing. Several other weapons are not shown on the chart, but seem destined to become decisive antitank weapons.

Currently available in increasing quantities are the trackbuster mines. These are small, weigh two to five pounds, and can be scattered about where enemy vehicles will pass. Trackbusters can be delivered by hand, artillery shell, aircraft, or helicopter. These small mines lie on the ground and can be spotted. However, for vehicles moving at night or under enemy fire, these small camouflaged mines are easily missed. They blow the tracks off armored vehicles and immobilize them for several hours at least. Two other weapons are to be deployed by the United States and other Western forces in the next few years. HEAT SM (Submunitions) are submunitions used in bombs and artillery and now in mines also. These fall to the ground and, if there is an armored vehicle beneath them, will strike the thinner top armor and penetrate.

HEAT (High Explosive Antitank) SFW (Self-Forging Warhead) is a more deadly variant now entering use. It uses a high-explosive warhead that forms a thin stream of fast-moving molten metal (the "self-forging warhead"). The advantage of this is that it is effective for several hundred feet from where the warhead detonates. This enables the submunition to descend more slowly by parachute (or other similar device), scan the ground for targets, and then detonate only when it detects something to hit. This weapon is worrisome to the Russians (and Third World nations in general) because it uses existing technology and industrial capabilities the West has and Russia lacks (microcomputer, sensors, precision machining, etc.). Moreover, these weapons are dangerous to the side with the larger number of armored vehicles to hit. There is no easy way to counter the molten-metal HEAT.

ACCURACY is the percentage probability of hitting a target at various ranges. Destroying the target depends on armor penetration. The hit probability is given for each distance under ideal conditions. Many older systems require a few seconds after launch for coordinating the guidance system and the rapidly moving missile. This accounts for the sometimes lengthy minimum range. The maximum range is often a function of the reach of the guidance system. Many systems are wire-guided, with a thin wire fed out from a spool in the launcher to the missile. When you're out of wire, you're out of control. Missiles also run out of momentum. The missile propellant is burned up a few seconds after launch. This, plus visual limitations, limits range and accuracy. Poor visibility and enemy fire will reduce this probability by more than half. To obtain the listed hit probabilities, you need a stationary or slowly moving target in plain sight, in clear weather, and not shooting back. A rapidly maneuvering target (30 to 40 kilometers an hour; that is, 8 to 11 meters a second) heading for cover will be more difficult to hit. At longer ranges, where the missile can spend up to 20 seconds in flight, the tiny speck in the gunner's sight can easily disappear. Fog, smoke, or dust make seeing and hitting the target more difficult. If aware of the situation, the target may shoot back before the gunner can complete guiding the missile to the target. This actually happens, largely because in dry weather the missile launch will throw up a lot of dust. A well-trained tank crew will be on the lookout for such launches, and a lot can be done in 10 seconds when your life depends on it. The missiles can be seen in flight, and firing at the point of launch can easily spoil the gunner's aim.

There are four methods for guiding a missile to its target. The most primitive is used by the rocket launchers (LAW, RPG, Armbrust, Carl Gustav). Since the projectiles have no guidance system, you simply aim the weapon, pull the trigger, and hope for the best. The earliest ATGMs allowed the operator to maneuver the missile to the target with a joystick. Speed could not be controlled, only altitude and direction. If the operator got nervous, or lacked skill, accuracy suffered. Only the Sagger and Swingfire still use this system. The next generation (TOW, DRAGON, Milan, HOT, etc.) required only that the operator keep the target in his sights, and the missile will home in on it. Enemy fire can still make the operator wince and, as the sight shifts, so does the flight of the missile. The newer, not yet perfected, fire-and-forget missiles use a terminal homing system. The missiles are launched in the general direction of the target. The missile has a seeker in it that homes in on the target once the missile is 1,000 to 2,000 meters away. Aside from the expense of these seekers, there is the problem of getting the missiles to hit undamaged targets and not go for burning (or nonburning) wrecks.

Potential targets have several characteristics that a seeker can home in on. Heat sources can be picked up by infrared seekers; images of targets can be picked out of the clutter with the aid of an onboard computer. Large masses of metal can be detected, as can the movement of large objects. For best results, the warhead should have two or more different types of sensor. But this gets very expensive. An example of this is the U.S. Copperhead artillery shell, which has only one sensor. Using a HEAT warhead, it is guided to the target by a seeker that looks for reflected laser light. The laser light is bounced off enemy armored vehicles by front-line troops equipped with laser devices. Unfortunately, the laser is degraded by bad weather. The laser operator is often degraded by enemy fire, as the laser light can be seen by anyone using a special viewing device. Worst of all, the cost of the Copperhead round escalated, preventing more than a few thousand of the shells from being manufactured and distributed. For aircraft, the high cost is less of a factor.

From the air, a larger variety of targets are available, many of them far more valuable than individual armored vehicles. Aircraft are more exposed anyway, so the added visibility of their laser equipment is not as dangerous as it is for the man on the ground. The aircraft are also capable of using the laser farther away and can get out of harm's way more quickly. But for destroying individual armored vehicles, laser-guided missiles from the air are also too expensive. The West does have a considerable advantage in microcomputers, miniature sensors, and the ability to produce these things on a large scale and relatively inexpensively. Fire-and-forget missiles that work at an affordable price will eventually arrive, perhaps in the next 5 or 10 years, depending on how much money the military has in the post–Cold War world. When they do arrive in quantity, a major watershed will have been reached. Man will be fighting very effective robots. Because a desperate sense of self-preservation has nullified new weapons in the past, robotic missiles, whose only function is to seek out and kill, will allow man to encounter a unique adversary.

ARMOR PEN is the number of millimeters the warhead will penetrate if the tank armor is hit directly at a right angle. The angle of hit is then an important consideration. High-velocity solid-shot rounds tend to ricochet off armor if they hit at too radical an angle. HEAT rounds have even more problems dealing with angles. These shaped-charge rounds operate by "focused explosion." The front part of the round is hollow; the rear half is an explosive with a cone-shaped depression (open side facing the front of the shell). When the warhead hits, a detonator is set off at the rear of the explosive. This creates a metal-penetrating stream of superhot gas. This plasma jet burns a small hole in the armor, and once inside the tank will ignite something else like ammunition, fuel, and/or crew. It is not always fatal, as the plasma jet is only 10 to 20 percent the width of the warhead and dissipates quickly. The rule of thumb is that a shaped charge can penetrate armor equal to five times the warhead diameter (a 100mm-wide warhead goes through 500mm of armor). Shaped charges can be defeated in several ways:

1. *Spaced Armor.* The plasma jet exists only for a fraction of a second, burning through whatever is in front of it. If thin armor, or even cyclone fencing as in Vietnam, is placed 300mm from the tank's main armor, the warhead explodes and burns through 300mm of air before it reaches the armor. Shaped-charge warheads also need a fraction of a second for the explosion to form the plasma jet.
2. *Sloped Armor.* This is also used to make high-speed solid-shot round skip off the armor without penetrating it. Shaped-charge rounds may do the same, or they may explode, and the plasma jet will hit the armor at an angle and

end up facing even more armor. Modern tanks have few flat surfaces, so the average slope encountered will degrade shaped charges from 25 to 50 percent. Thus, a normal penetration of 500mm becomes 375mm or 250mm, which is often not sufficient to penetrate the hull or do any serious damage.

3. *Composite Armor.* Instead of just 50mm to 200mm of armor, an equal or greater thickness of lighter, layered materials is used. This combination of metal, plastic, and ceramic layers absorbs the plasma jet's energy without allowing complete penetration. Good composite (or Chobham) armor can degrade a shaped charge's penetration by a factor of 2 or more. It is very expensive.

4. *Reactive Armor.* Blocks of high-speed explosive are mounted on the tank's armor. When a high-energy object strikes one of these blocks, it explodes. This diminishes the effectiveness of HESH and HEAT. Drawbacks are that it's expensive and works only once, as it self-destructs. This is dangerous to any infantry close by. But then a stricken tank, with its ammunition blowing up and fuel catching fire, isn't very safe to be around either. Reactive armor also cannot be used safely on light-armored vehicles. It is normally mounted in wartime, thus giving your opponent another warning that war is on the way.

5. *Soft Layer.* A thin layer of a soft metal, like lead, on the top of the tank is used by some Russian vehicles to defeat the fusing mehanism of HEAT submunitions from cluster bombs. They are calculating that this will not allow munitions to detonate because the detonator will not make hard enough contact. Soft-layer protection is known to have been tested by the Soviets, but not deployed on a large scale.

The above defenses combine to make HEAT shells very ineffective. Tanks like the M-1, with some 600mm of sloped, composite armor and some thin metal skirts, can withstand most hits by warheads capable of penetrating over 1,000mm of normal armor. This does not make a tank invulnerable. Even nonpenetrating hits can damage other components, like running gear, engine, weapons, and sensors. One or more damaging hits can make a tank ineffective without destroying it. For comparison purposes, the maximum armor thickness of other modern tanks is: T-55/62—200mm, M-48/60—250mm, Leopard I—170mm, AMX-30—150mm, Chieftain—400mm. Western tanks have thicker armor on the sides and rear. Russian tanks are thinly armored in these areas and depend on not letting the enemy fire at anything but their front. The above thicknesses should be multiplied by 1.3 to 1.5 to reflect the effect of sloping. Using composite armor adds 40–70 percent to their effective armor protection (or "armor basis") against AP and 200–250 percent against HEAT. The variation depends on whose composite armor is being used. The Western equivalent is much better. There is no additional weight for composite armor, but it takes up more space.

Meanwhile, the technology of shaped-charge warheads goes forward. The latest wrinkle is combining two shaped charges in the same warhead plus a long metal "penetrator" in the front of the projectile. These two charges go off one behind the other, thus increasing the penetration to 10 times the warhead diameter. Still another approach is used by the Swedish BILL system: The warhead flies over the target and detonates downward into the thin top armor of the tank. Other existing

3-3 Antitank Weapons

Maker	Name	Accuracy: % Probability of Hit					Armor Pen (mm)	Effective Range (meters)		Speed (mps)	Back-blast	Missile Weight (lbs)	Launch System Weight (lbs)
		>100m	>500m	>1,000m	>1,500m	>max		Min	Max				
US	TOW	20	90	90	90	90	750	65	3,000	360	Yes	40	184
US	TOW2	80	90	90	90	90	1,200	65	3,750	360	Yes	47	191
US	TOW3	80	90	90	90	90	1,500	65	3,750	360	Yes	50	194
US	DRAGON	0	50	80	0	0	500	300	1,000	100	No	30	32
US	Hellfire	0	20	70	80	80	900	500	6,000	300	No	95	
US	Copperhead	0	0	0	0	70	Top	3,000	17,000	800	No	140	
US	LAW	30	0	0	0	0	200	5	75	100	Yes	5.5	
Russia	AT-3 Sagger	0	0	50	60	70	400	500	3,000	120	No	25	40
Russia	AT-4 Spigot	0	60	70	80	80	500	150	2,000	200	Yes	26	40
Russia	AT-5 Spandrel	0	70	80	90	90	500	150	4,000	200	No	37	50
Russia	AT-6 Spiral	0	0	80	80	80	750	500	6,000	300	No	60	
Russia	AT-7 Saxhorn	0	50	80	0	0	400	300	1,000	100	Yes	34	40
Russia	AT-8 Songster	0	0	80	80	80	750	500	5,000	400	No	80	
Russia	RPG-7V	30	30	0	0	0	320	5	500	200	Yes	5	15.4
Russia	RPG-18	30	0	0	0	0	280	5	200	110	Yes	6	
Russia	RPG-22	30	0	0	0	0	280	5	200	100	Yes	6	
Russia	RPG-16	30	40	0	0	0	500	5	500	200	Yes	16	12
France	Milan 2	70	90	90	90	90	800	25	2,000	180	Yes	32	105
France	HOT 2	80	90	90	90	90	1,100	75	4,000	200	Yes	46	23
Sweden	Bill	0	70	90	90	90	Top	150	2,000	200	Yes	24	
US	106mm RR	90	80	70	0	0	500	10	1,100	300	Yes	37	460
	Averages	21	34	44	37	40	449	236	2,447	192		32	77

ATGMs have been fitted with downward-firing warheads also. The Copperhead shell has a similar effect as it plunges earthward.

EFFECTIVE RANGE is expressed as minimum and maximum. The minimum is necessary to arm the warhead and get the missile under operator control after launch. The control time varies with the sophistication of the missile system. Maximum range is also a matter of control. A HEAT round is effective at any range as long as it hits a target. Although most ATGMs depend on wire for operator control, newer types do not use wire but rather laser or infrared signals to sensors in the rear of the missile. This type of control is less reliable because of atmospheric conditions, but does allow for much faster missiles.

SPEED (meters per second). This is limited primarily by the speed with which wire can be unspooled. That limitation is about 200 meters a second. Another limitation is the reaction time of the operator and the guidance system. HEAT rounds also perform better if they strike their targets at a low speed, although higher-speed rounds can be made. These fast HEAT rounds are more expensive. The long flight time of ATGMs (15 to 20 seconds) has proved sufficient to allow an alert target to react.

BACKBLAST. All missiles have a backblast. In some cases, it is very prominent. These are indicated with a "Yes." The backblast warns an alert opponent that ATGMs are on the way. Even the Sagger, with its relatively small backblast, was spotted by Israeli tankers in their 1973 war. They were able to take evasive action and avoid many missiles.

MISSILE WEIGHT (pounds). This is the missile, rocket, or projectile weight and shows the relative portability of the system.

LAUNCH-SYSTEM WEIGHT (pounds). Many systems have a reusable launcher containing a launch tube and guidance system. This often includes a power supply also. The LAW-type weapons are self-contained. The launcher is thrown away once the rocket is launched. Some systems have different launchers. For example, the DRAGON launcher used for daylight firing weighs only 6.5 pounds, while the more elaborate one for night firing weighs 21 pounds.

4

Artillery:
The Killer

ARTILLERY IS large-caliber guns firing projectiles containing explosive and, increasingly, more diverse implements of destruction. From the user's point of view, artillery is an ideal weapon. It does enormous destruction without exposing the user to much risk. Better still, the users rarely suffer the dismay of seeing their mangled victims. However, artillery is a rich man's weapon. A less wealthy army can be just as destructive, but at greater human cost to itself. Throwing shells instead of infantry at the enemy is preferable, if you can afford it.

When asked which weapons they fear most, soldiers put artillery at the top of the list. Artillery causes the most casualties and is the most unpredictable danger on the battlefield. Worst of all, you can't fight back. Even tanks can be shot at, but artillery is out of sight and always ready to deliver death and mutilation.

During World War II, artillery caused nearly 60 percent of all casualties. That war still holds the record for the most artillery fire thrown at the most troops. It was found during World War II that artillery's effects varied by terrain type. In open plains and deserts, about 75 percent of the casualties were from artillery; in mixed terrain about 60 percent of casualties; and in forests and built-up areas it was 50 percent or less. The trend was clear: Troops will take full advantage of any place to hide. Today's combat troops have armored transport, providing them with more abundant protection from anything but a direct hit. However, artillery has also improved its efficiency. The munitions, in particular, have gotten more deadly. Another crucial change is greater reliance on large supplies of fuel, ammunition, and other items. All of these are carried by unarmored vehicles that are more vulnerable than in the past. Even modern tank divisions consist of over two thirds unarmored vehicles. In fact, the longer range and improved fire control of modern artillery puts combat support at risk almost as much as the infantry.

Artillery Fire and Missions

Modern artillery came of age in the first 20 years of this century. The guns have gotten bigger and acquired more gadgets. Yet the same basic techniques are still used more than 70 years later—artillerymen from 1918 would feel right at home. The big change nearly a century ago was the development of accurate indirect fire—that is, artillery fire that could hit targets the gunners could not see. For 600 years previously, the vast majority of fire was at targets the gunners were looking at. Modern indirect fire is delivered in two forms: barrage and concentration. Beyond this are many variations, but they are of interest only to artillerymen. A barrage is literally a wall of fire—shells exploding in a line—that is employed to screen troops from enemy observation or to prevent enemy movement. A rolling barrage moves forward at a preplanned speed in front of an advance. If this is done properly, the advancing troops will reach the defending positions right behind the exploding shells, leaving the enemy little opportunity to fire back. A concentration is high-density fire for the purpose of destroying a specific target. Barrages and concentrations are fired at three levels of intensity:

1. Harassment—up to 10 percent destruction, enough to keep the troops' heads down
2. Neutralization—about 30 percent destruction, causing a temporary inability of the unit to perform
3. Destruction—50 to 60 percent destruction, resulting in disintegration of the unit or long-term ineffectiveness

"Temporary" means from a few hours to a day. Destruction fire depends on a higher level of casualties breaking the morale of the survivors and completely disrupting the organization of the bombarded unit. More resolute and well-led units will not always break under destruction fire. Indeed, the effects of all three intensities of fire can be compromised by the quality of the defender's fortification as well as the quality of the units. Artillery effects are never a sure thing.

Musical metaphors are often used in describing the use of artillery. One "conducts" or "orchestrates" artillery fire in the hope that the composition will have the desired effect on its victims. The above types of fire are organized into a pattern of missions. Artillery fire requires a lot of expensive equipment plus large supplies of munitions. It is not done in a haphazard manner unless you want to waste it.

Each time a group of guns fires a particular type of fire, they are performing a mission. There are several basic types of missions. Each is either:

- *Preplanned* (guns are assigned to fire a specific number of shells at a specific target according to a schedule), or
- *On Call* (a preplanned mission that is fired as often as called for), or
- *Target of Opportunity* (an observer works out the details on the spot, talking directly to the gunners).

Offensive and defensive barrages are preplanned fires to assist attacking or defending troops by providing a wall of fire. Usually of neutralization or destruction intensity, they may be either stationary or rolling (moving every few minutes). These barrages often use smoke and high-explosive shells together to keep the other side in the dark as much as possible.

A standing barrage is a screen to prevent enemy movement or observation. Done at harassment intensity, it often includes smoke and poison-gas shells. It guards the flank of an advance or cuts the enemy's retreat or route for reinforcements. It is almost always preplanned or on call.

A fire assault concentrates against specific targets in the hope that the defender will be destroyed. It is customarily preplanned, but defenders often use it as on-call fire once the position of the attacker is known. This is the heaviest intensity of fire.

Harassment is usually random fire on enemy positions to keep the enemy from functioning at full efficiency. This type of fire will force the enemy to be careful moving around and prevent him from getting sleep, regular resupply, and so on. It is normally very light fire, a few shells at a time in a small area. Depending on how sloppy, or unlucky, the defender is, there will be little or no damage. When the fire is placed on roads behind the enemy lines, it is more likely to catch some hapless vehicle loaded with fuel or ammunition, with spectacular results.

Interdiction is similar to, but a heavier form of, harassment fire, frequently employed on roads or routes behind enemy lines for the purpose of stopping or slowing down movement. Varying degrees of intensity are used depending on your ammunition supply and how badly you want to interdict.

Counterbattery is fire at enemy artillery to suppress or destroy the enemy guns. This has become more effective of late, as sensors to quickly spot artillery positions become more common and efficient.

Techniques of Artillery Use

Artillery is warfare by the numbers. Even aircraft, for all their technical sophistication, are successful in combat largely because of the skill and talent of a human pilot. Artillery is more a matter of mathematics and formulas. Artillerymen cannot see their targets; all they have are references on a map and perhaps the voice of an observer over the phone. To make this work, surveyors first plot the precise location of the guns. Detailed weather reports, as well as how worn out the gun barrel is, are also taken into account. A computer calculates the precise direction and elevation of the guns, as well as how much propellant to use and what adjustments to make to the fuse. Humans do the less cerebral tasks, like carrying the ammunition and firing the gun. All of this is becoming increasingly auto-mated, including the loading of ammunition and the reports from the front. An observer at the front can now point a laser at a target and have the information automatically radioed back to the guns, which then fire. All of this automation is for a purpose. Gunfire must be accurate; otherwise your own troops will be hit, not to mention the even greater chance of missing the enemy. Losses from friendly fire are all too frequent because of observer error rather than faulty calculations. Automation also solves an increasingly difficult problem with round-the-clock combat. Artillery is often on call 24 hours a day. Gun crews easily make fatal mistakes when suddenly called to provide unplanned fire support at 3:00 A.M. Auto-matic loaders and firing computers can eliminate many of these predawn errors. Development continues on guns that aim, load, and fire automat-ically.

It was during World War I (1914–18) that artillery fire became largely indirect. The gunners could no longer see the effects of their fire. They had to rely on trigonometry, ballistics, maps, electronic communications, observers, and registration by fire to direct the shells to their target. Despite these difficulties, the gunners didn't mind. If they couldn't see the enemy, the enemy couldn't see and shoot back at them. Unlike previous wars, where the artillery was a primary target, the guns now survived longer while their targets perished with greater frequency. When I was in the army, I was in the artillery, and I greatly appreciated the development of indirect fire.

The scientific techniques behind modern artillery are quite simple. First, the flight of shells is fairly predictable if you take into account all of the elements that can alter their path. Items like the minute differences in the composition of different batches of propellant, wear and tear on the gun barrel, humidity, wind direction and speed, and so on. The precise location of guns and targets is taken care of by using accurate maps and surveying equipment. Triangulation is used to determine the direction and elevation the guns will fire. Often a few rounds are fired and adjustments made before unleashing the entire barrage or concentration. During World War II, the United States perfected techniques that allowed one observer to control hundreds of guns: "every gun within range," as the saying went. Before this, each observer talked to, and controlled, one unit of guns. More complex and efficient communications and plotting systems were required to tie in a large number of artillery units and observers. The U.S. Army first developed this system in the 1930s and continues to lead in its development.

Because artillery units themselves are spread over a wide area, determining the bearing (direction) and elevation of the guns is not only a very complex problem but one that must be solved quickly before the target moves or some of the guns are fired upon. Western armies can have shells sent in less than a minute, often in as little as 15 seconds. The major flaw in all this, of course, is the increasing use of electronic jamming. Without reliable communications, the guns might as well go back to direct fire. Good training and imagination can overcome the damage caused by electronic warfare. The common workaround is to do what they did in World War I under similar conditions. You use flares, messengers, and rigidly preplanned fires.

The Russian-trained armies still employ nearly half their artillery in direct fire. This solves the communications problems. It also allows the enemy to shoot back more easily at the artillery. Although direct fire is two to three times as effective as indirect fire, your gun losses go up by a factor of 10. This is not surprising when you consider that direct-fire guns must be used within 1,500 meters of their targets. Although an increasing portion of Russian (and non-Western) artillery is mounted on armored vehicles, the majority is still towed. Non-Western artillery is becoming more sophisticated, but it still does not operate as spontaneously as Western guns. Non-Western artillery also suffers from more problems with defective ammunition. Many Third World nations take pride in producing their own artillery ammunition, but they often do it badly and don't discover their mistakes until they use a lot of their defective shells during a war. The Russians, and their artillery equipment customers, place greater faith in mass than in gadgets and fancy footwork.

Counterbattery fire, shooting at the other fellow's artillery, has always been a tricky business. In the last 20 years, advances in computer and radar technology have given the Western nations very effective counterbattery capability. Previously, one had to estimate gun positions by observing the sound and flash fire and then doing some crude calculations. At best, this technique was not very accurate. Vast quantities of shells were then expended in the hope that some of the enemy guns were where your calculations predicted. Western counterbattery radars, and the use of MLRS rockets with ICM rounds, can quickly eliminate enemy guns. But just as Western technology has come up with an effective counterbattery weapon, it has also developed a solution to it. The U.S. Army has developed a ceramic artillery shell that is invisible to radar. The ceramic shell is more expensive than metal shells and, with the post–Cold War budget cuts, will probably not be produced in significant quantity. Although Third World and Russian counterbattery technology is not up to the Western standard, it is effective enough to encourage frequent changes in firing positions. The age of "shoot and scoot" has arrived, but only if the troops can use and maintain the equipment effectively.

Electronic warfare has also complicated the picture. If the guns are running around shooting and scooting, they are very dependent on radio contact with their front-line observers. If the enemy is blasting away with jammers, communications are unreliable. At best, this slows down the process of requesting fire and getting it. At worst, there is no communication between the users and providers of artillery fire. These problems can be circumvented in a number of ways. Arrangements can be made for the infantry to use certain combinations of colored flares to call for pre-arranged fire. This eliminates targets of opportunity and slows things down in general. But it is preferable to no artillery support at all. If distances are not too great, and time and resources permit, you can lay telephone wire. The wires may get cut, but then you still have your flares. You can also use jamming against the counterbattery radars, or antiradiation rockets to knock them out. Things never become impossible, just more difficult. And accidents happen. The infantry takes a dim view of getting hit by friendly fire, but this is accepted more philosophically in the Russian Army. Russian artillery fire tends to be rigid, preplanned, and massive, and very closely coordinated with the advancing infantry and tanks. Losses from friendly fire are considered preferable to leaving the infantry unprotected as they approach the enemy positions. Most Third World nations have adopted the Russian approach, largely because it allows you to get the most out of poorly trained and inexperienced gun crews.

LIFE ON THE GUN CREW

Like tank crews, gunners have a lot of equipment to maintain. If the guns are self-propelled, as most are, the maintenance load is about the same as a tank. Self-propelled artillery are about the same size as tanks but have light armor like APCs. They normally mount a larger gun (152mm and up) than tanks and have more room inside to accommodate a larger crew and more activity. Self-propelled artillery fire a lot more shells, in less time, than tanks. The other difference from tank guns is that artillery guns fire their shells at a lower velocity. This is done for several good reasons. Low-velocity shells allow the barrel to last longer and fire more shells before overheating. Lower-velocity shells put less stress on the other gun components, allowing them to last longer while making maintenance easier and cheaper. Indeed, the only reason tanks need high-velocity shells is to achieve maximum armor penetration and accuracy.

Gunners have a lot more precombat work than tankers. To avoid counterbattery fire, or simply to support a complex fire plan for a major offensive or defensive operation, they have to prepare a number of alternate firing sites. Teams of gunners and surveyors are sent to positions chosen from a map to mark firing positions for the guns and determine their precise location. Access routes must be checked and storage sites for ammunition laid out. Sometimes ammunition is moved to the firing positions ahead of time. When the firing position is used, the guns drive in and move into their previously marked locations. Each gun's sights are lined up on the surveyor's marker poles, and the guns are rotated and elevated to align them with their distant targets. When the signal is given, it's load, fire, load, fire, etc., until the required number of shells have been sent on their way. Most guns can fire six or more shells a minute. After a few minutes, they have to slow down to two or three shells a minute to avoid overheating the barrel.

Firing a gun takes practice. The gunner keeps it lined up properly, shifting the alignment according to the fire plan so that the proper number of shells fall on the right targets in the right sequence. The loader gets the shells into the gun. The ammo crew, the "gun bunnies," keep the supply of shells moving. These shells weigh 90 pounds for 155mm guns, plus the lighter propellant charge that is loaded separately. The gun chief keeps checking that the right type of shell is being loaded, that the right fuse and setting are being used, and that things are going well in general. He also keeps the gun log, which is important for maintenance and adjusting gun aiming to take account of barrel wear. During a major operation, as many as 500 shells per gun per day may be fired. That could be over four hours of steady firing, but it's rarely all at once. Usually, bursts of a few shells, or a few dozen, are fired interrupted by displacement to new positions, maintenance, and, if the front is close by or the enemy has broken through, defense against ground attack. The crews must always be alert to the danger of air attack and the dreaded counterbattery fire. In a defensive situation, the guns may be on call at all hours. You just wait, day and night, for the call "fire mission." Then you scramble through the drill as quickly as possible. An infantryman's life depends on the gunner's prompt and accurate delivery of the requested fire, but a lot can go wrong.

ORGANIZATION OF ARTILLERY

Almost all artillery units are organized into battalions—typically of 12–24 guns, containing guns of the same type and caliber. The typical battalion has three firing batteries, each with a third of the battalion's guns. A headquarters battery contains the communications and fire-control specialists and their equipment. Some Western armies have a fifth ("detail") battery that takes care of ammunition supply, maintenance, and other details. The actual gun crews of an 18-gun battalion number fewer than

200 men. Ammunition supply troops add another 100, while the fire-control and support troops can be 100 to 200 men. Western armies average some 500 men per battalion, Russian-style battalions about 300, although they place the equivalent of another 100 men per battalion under the control of the next-higher headquarters (divisional artillery, artillery regiment, etc.). These troops perform the same jobs as specialists belonging to Western battalions. Artillery battalions are assigned to combat divisions as "divisional" artillery or to corps and armies as "nondivisional" artillery. Divisional artillery uses lighter guns and usually consists of three to five battalions. Three of these battalions would be some standard caliber (105mm, 122mm, or larger), while the other units would be heavier guns or rockets. Your typical U.S. divisional artillery has 155mm guns and rocket launchers. Russian divisions typically contain 122mm or 152mm guns plus rockets (unlike Western divisions, usually two or more different calibers of launchers). All other armies have variations on the above, and it generally comes down to 80 to 100 large-caliber artillery pieces and rocket launchers per division. These weapons expend some 80 percent of the ammunition used. There are a lot of additional artillery weapons. Everything from an 81mm mortar to a 125mm tank gun is technically artillery. If you count all this other "artillery," you find 400 to 500 pieces for each Western or Russian division. Third World divisions average less than half to three quarters this amount of artillery weapons. Only 100 years ago, few armies had as many as 6 guns per 1,000 men, while today the average is about 30 per 1,000. The standard of dying has gone up along with the standard of living.

The nondivisional artillery is assigned to divisions as needed and contains the heavier-caliber weapons. Few guns are larger than 203mm (eight-inch). Nondivisional artillery units include the long-range (up to 800 kilometers) missiles. These are frequently armed with nuclear or chemical warheads. However, the trend is toward conventional warheads for these missiles, using them to carry submunitions. Eventually, the United States and Russia realized that nuclear and chemical weapons would be more costly for both sides than they are worth.

The rule of thumb is to have one nondivisional gun or rocket launcher for each one in the divisions. This is a wartime standard, using many guns normally manned by reservists during peacetime. For example, in wartime, a corps with 3 divisions and 12 battalions of divisional artillery would have an additional 12 battalions of nondivisional artillery.

Artillery assigned to smaller units in a division have less available ammunition. It is not practical to deliver vast quantities of ammunition to front-line units. Divisional artillery normally operates at least a few kilometers from the fighting. This is to prevent ammunition resupply from being interrupted. Without a substantial and steady supply of ammunition, artillery is much less useful. With adequate supply, a battalion of 155mm guns can fire over 500 tons of munitions a day at the enemy. That tonnage has to reach the guns before it can be sent off to the enemy. Indirect (mortars) and direct (tank guns) fire weapons are used near the front because of the need for quick response to enemy activity. If used properly, the front-line artillery fires only when necessary. Limited ammunition supplies are not an insurmountable problem if the divisional and nondivisional artillery, and their better access to munitions, are available.

SHELLS SMART AND DUMB

Guns use many kinds of artillery shells:

- **High Explosive (HE).** Still the standard artillery shell; basically, a shell container with an explosive charge of 5 to 20+ pounds, depending on the shell's caliber. Despite the introduction of ICM (Improved Conventional Munitions), HE still comprises the vast majority of the world's artillery stocks.
- **Smoke.** Creates a smoke cloud lasting from 10 to 20+ minutes. The most common non-HE type shell, less than 5 percent of all shells.
- **Star Shell.** An illuminating flare, with a parachute to delay its fall so that the light will last 5 to 10 minutes or more. Creates daylight in an area several hundred meters in diameter, depending on climatic conditions (fog, cloud height, humidity).
- **Chemical.** Loaded with one of several poison gases (see Chapter 21, on chemical weapons). Often a variation on the HE shell, with half or more of the explosive replaced with poison.
- **Nuclear.** In guns 152mm and larger. The explosive power is up to five kilotons. About 8,000 of these existed at the end of the Cold War. Over half are supposed to be destroyed during the 1990s. More recent models cost over $2 million each.
- **HEAT.** High Explosive Antitank shell. Generally can penetrate armor equal to five times the shell's diameter (caliber).
- **Beehive.** A large shotgun shell filled with thousands of metal darts. Used to defend against infantry that get too close. Fired directly at target, just like a shotgun.

Each shell can use a variety of fuses, whose function is to make the shell explode. The fuse is a separate component in guns larger than 105mm and is screwed into the tip of the shell. Fuses come in the following varieties:

- **Contact.** The simplest, it ignites the shell when the fuse strikes anything.
- **Delayed action.** Delays ignition for up to a few seconds after contact so that the shell may penetrate first; used for destroying fortifications, creating deep craters, etc.
- **Proximity.** Has a radar range finder that ignites the shell when it is

at a preset distance from a solid object. Good for getting an airburst. This is necessary for improved conventional munitions (ICM) that use submunitions. Also increases the effectiveness of HE, smoke, chemical, and nuclear shells. Most of these shells explode on contact and will promptly bury much of their effectiveness into the ground. The ICM often use smaller submunitions that must be dispersed before they explode. These fuses have been in use for over 40 years and are quite reliable, although still expensive. Originally, they were designed for use against aircraft, for which they are still employed.

- **VT (Variable Time).** A poor man's proximity fuse. Gunners can preset fuse to ignite a certain number of seconds after being fired. If the calculations are correct, this has the same effect as a proximity fuse. Obviously, not as useful against moving targets.

ICMs (Improved Conventional Munitions)

During the 1970s, there was a significant revolution in ammunition design. So dramatic were the performance increases that this new generation was called *improved* conventional munitions. On the downside, the ICMs were also more expensive (over $5,000 for an ICM round, versus a few hundred dollars for a conventional HE shell). This was a minor drawback, as the ability to deliver more destructive power with the same weight of munitions proved an enormous battlefield advantage. Despite the advantages of ICMs, most munitions are of the older type in nearly all armies. ICMs are simply too expensive to become the standard. In the U.S. artillery, however, more than half the shells are of the ICM type, with traditional HE comprising less than a quarter of munitions available and various other specialized types comprising an even smaller fraction. All classes of shells were improved, but only those that showed a dramatic improvement are properly called ICM. The current ICM features include:

- **Cargo Shell.** Hollow shells designed to carry a variety of submunitions (loaded at the factory). The submunitions are either antipersonnel, antiarmor, or DPICM (dual-purpose ICM for use against troops and vehicles). These smaller warheads (about the size of a flashlight battery) are ejected before the shell hits the ground and spread over a wide area before they detonate. Sometimes they don't go off right away, but detonate later or act as mines. Antipersonnel and track-buster mines are often used, and simply lie on the ground until stepped on or passed over by a soldier or vehicle. Other antipersonnel submunitions function like hand grenades, while antitank munitions also come in the form of small HEAT warheads that hit and penetrate the thin top armor of tanks. There is continuous development of deadlier submunitions. The principal current types (and the number of bomblets carried) are 155mm shells (88), 203mm shells (180), MLRS rockets (688), and ATACMS (950).

- **Rocket Boosters.** An add-on for shells that, as the name implies, boosts the range of shells up to 50 percent. There is some loss of accuracy and payload.
- **Guidance Systems.** These have not worked out too well. The only shell in use that has a guidance system is the U.S. Copperhead. It's too expensive, requires someone at the front to bounce a laser off the target, and fog and smoke can interfere with this process. Something like this will work effectively eventually.
- **General Improvements.** Most other types of shell are also being dramatically improved with regard to effectiveness. You can see from this that the number of guns is less important than shell quality and quantity.

Artillery is basically a delivery service. It delivers ammunition in large quantities to targets designated by the combat units.

SELF-PROPELLED VERSUS TOWED

Throughout artillery's history, there has been "foot artillery" and "horse artillery." The more numerous "foot" had the gunners walking and the guns dragged along by horses. In the "horse artillery," everyone rode on a horse or a high-speed wagon. This unit was organized and equipped for speed of movement and action. Modern self-propelled artillery follows that tradition, with a few twists. The first tanks were intended to be self-propelled artillery. The armor was added to give protection against enemy fire. The tracklaying mechanism (like a bulldozer) was used to get this heavy contraption over the torn-up battlefield. The primary purpose of all this was clearing out enemy machine guns so that the friendly foot soldiers could make some headway. Soon both sides had tanks, and the tanks were soon pounding away at each other. This left the infantry in the lurch once more. Some 25 years after the tank was first used, artillery was mounted on a tank chassis and used as mobile artillery. The key was to avoid direct fire and enemy tanks. The new "horse artillery" proved highly successful. Today, the self-propelled (SP) artillery is mounted on a lightly armored chassis of similar size to tanks. Although three or more times as expensive as towed artillery, it has several important advantages.

1. SP artillery can keep up with mechanized units and go places towed artillery cannot.
2. Its armor makes it more resistant to enemy artillery, and more capable of delivering direct fire and surviving.
3. Each SP gun is a self-contained unit, so emplacing the gun is faster. Towed artillery takes about 30 minutes to prepare for firing; SP guns

need about half that time. Most time-consuming is calculating the precise position of the gun relative to its target. Recent developments in electronic navigation systems allow some SP guns to halt and fire within minutes of the order. The GPS (satellite-based navigation system) now allows this to be done even more quickly.

4. SP guns are also faster moving out of a firing position, taking a minute or two. Towed guns have to load gear back onto trucks, hook the guns onto their tractors, and generally stay in one place long enough to get hit by counterbattery fire.

SP guns have their drawbacks.

1. Being tracked vehicles, they are more prone to breakdowns.
2. Traveling along with fast-moving mechanized units exposes them to more enemy fire. Their armor notwithstanding, they take heavier losses.
3. Supply is more difficult for the SP guns. Most of the ammo is carried on trucks, although some armored vehicles are used.
4. These weapons are expensive. While Western armies have had them since World War II, Russian and many Third World nations are still in the process of equipping their divisions with SP guns.

Overall, SP guns are still superior to the towed variety, despite their shortcomings. But SP guns are a wealthy nation's advantage, another example of how you can buy a battlefield advantage.

ROCKETS AND MISSILES

Modern field-artillery rockets were a Soviet innovation during World War II. Western armies have recently begun using these again. The rockets were initially developed to provide a large amount of firepower quickly. Accuracy and range were not critical, just the ability to saturate an area with explosions. These weapons were also relatively cheap. Because the Soviets lost so much conventional artillery in 1941, these rocket launchers were the right weapon at the right time. Rockets had other advantages. Against an opponent with good counterbattery capability, rockets can get into a firing position, fire all their rockets, and get out before enemy counterbattery can hit them. Rockets are inaccurate, but get around this by being launched in large numbers, simultaneously, at the same area. As a result, they are called "area fire weapons." You fire them in the general direction of the target and hit whatever is in the area before the enemy troops have a chance to seek cover.

In the last 40 years, rockets have gained accuracy and range. They are still crude compared to conventional artillery. For example, 50 percent of rockets fired can be expected to land in a 100- to 200-meter circle. Ranges now go up to 40 kilometers. Rockets are still useful in modern warfare and have numerous advantages:

1. They are a surprise weapon. You inflict more casualties when you catch troops outside their tanks, APCs, and fortifications. The first shell to land sends everyone diving for cover. When several dozen rockets arrive all at once, there is little opportunity to duck.
2. When using chemical weapons, rockets are the ideal delivery system. Gas is an area weapon, and surprise is important to prevent troops from putting on their masks.
3. For the Russians and many Third World nations, rockets still compensate for several of their shortcomings. A lack of quality fire-control equipment is overcome with barrages of rockets. This makes rockets an ideal counterbattery weapon for these lower-tech armies.
4. Fear. The sudden and massive firepower delivered by rockets often demoralizes troops on the receiving end. This was the case when rockets were first used against the Germans in 1941, and half a century later Iraqi troops were equally terrified by the U.S.-made MLRS rockets.

As an example of what rockets can do, consider a Russian battalion of 18 BM-21 rocket launchers, with 40 tubes per launcher. The unit can fire 720 rockets in a few seconds to a range of 20 kilometers. The launchers are mounted on trucks and can be on their way in less than 10 minutes. It takes 15 to 30 minutes to occupy a new position, depending on the time of day. A launcher can be reloaded in 10 minutes with three tons of rockets, although an automatic loader is being used in some units, which cuts the reload time to 2 minutes. This makes it possible for a unit to fire two salvos before moving on. Units usually carry only two loads of rockets with them. A 720-round volley of 122mm BM-21 rockets will devastate an area as large as 2,000 by 500 meters. It would take a battalion of guns six minutes of rapid fire to do the same damage. The rocket warheads are no more lethal than equivalent-caliber artillery shells. However, the effect on troop morale is more pronounced. For this reason, rockets are preferred when you want to achieve surprise and overcome the enemy quickly. Western rockets are more accurate, have longer range and carry more exotic warheads (submunitions) than Russian models. The Russians have copied some of these developments, although their less capable manufacturing capabilities prevent them from achieving parity. The U.S.-made MLRS rocket system proved the value of the high-tech Western rocket launchers in the Gulf War. The improved-accuracy, cluster-bomb warhead and longer range of the MLRS had a devastating effect on Iraqi units, particularly artillery units.

The only disadvantages of rockets is their minimum range of a few kilometers and the rather prominent cloud of dust and smoke that pinpoints the launchers' position when the rockets are fired.

Field-artillery missiles are a post–World War II development. These were originally intended for one purpose—delivering nuclear weapons. These weapons have longer ranges and greater accuracy than rockets. Most now have inertial guidance systems, and some have ranges of more than 1,000 kilometers. The shorter-range weapons (less than 200 kilometers) are more often being equipped to deliver chemical or ICM loads. The Western MLRS can fire either 16 conventional artillery rockets or two longer-range missiles (ATACMS).

HELICOPTERS

What has really replaced the fast-moving horse artillery of old is the helicopter. Fixed-wing bombers deliver their bombs while moving along at 200 to 400 miles per hour. Helicopters can hover and deliver their shells with artillerylike accuracy. And they can be equipped with weapons. Most nations build special gunships that can carry rockets, automatic cannons, machine guns, or ATGMs—some now carry air-to-air missiles, and unarmed helicopters often drop mines. Although helicopters are aircraft, armies use them as very mobile artillery, sending them wherever the danger is greatest.

Theory and Practice

Most Western divisions have one or more artillery-spotting radars. Even Russia, and some Third World nations, have begun to deploy them. These devices track mortar and artillery shells in flight and determine where they were fired from. This information is passed back to friendly artillery, which then does a little counterbattery number on the opposition. The Soviets' doctrine long assumed that any of their guns would be targeted and shot at within minutes of firing at a Western unit. These developments have changed the way artillery operates. There is more decentralization: Regiments and brigades have their own artillery. These may be a few batteries or a few battalions. Divisions and armies also have their own artillery groups, which are used to reinforce the brigades and regiments. Forward observers from the artillery units still travel with the infantry and tanks. These observers do not expect to have the kind of good radio communications that they have had in the past.

Many armies still use massed artillery attacks, but only as carefully preplanned operations. These set-piece operations will not require radio; they will go according to the plan. Any armies using these set-piece tactics that are in the wrong place at the wrong time will get smashed by their own guns. Many new developments work against future use of mass fire:

more effective counterbattery fire, electronic warfare, a more fluid battle-field, more effective munitions. The Iraqis received a demonstration of this in 1991.

Artillery was originally developed to tear up unprotected troops—most front-line soldiers are now in or near an armored vehicle. Artillery is not all that cost-effective against armored vehicles. Electronic warfare also makes quick communication between infantry and artillery unreliable. Counterbattery has become so effective that massing guns together is risky. With all combat units on wheels, troops will be spread all over the place. As a result, artillery has been greatly decentralized. A regiment or brigade has its own artillery battalion, while the division retains a few battalions, which often get attached to a brigade anyway. Cargo shells carrying antitank or antipersonnel submunitions are a more effective use of the limited trans-portation resources. The emphasis is on responsiveness and speed.

All industrialized nations now use computers for field-artillery-driven fire-control systems. American forces have a 52-pound laser range finder that also computes the location of the target. Working with this gadget are the GPS receivers that receive signals from navigation satellites—the user always knows their position to within 20 meters or so. These two items had their first major workout in the Gulf War and performed very effec-tively. They were not seriously degraded by Iraqi ECM (Electronic Coun-termeasures), although it was tried.

ICM got their first widespread workout in the 1991 Gulf War, and one ugly side effect was discovered. As reports from Russian use of ICM in Afghanistan confirmed, not all the bomblets in cluster bombs would det-onate when desired. This left the battlefield covered with "dud" bomblets that would still go off if a vehicle, or even a person, came upon them—a nasty surprise for which a solution will have to be found.

While nearly all artillery fired in the vicinity of friendly troops is spotted by artillery observers at the front, some 90 percent of the spotting of targets in the enemy rear is by aircraft. This has been the case since 1917. But now RPVs and satellites are becoming more common.

The Future

After several decades of stagnation, the last 10 years' developments in guns and ammunition have increased artillery's effectiveness considerably. These improvements are only now maturing and spreading to many nations. To date, they include abundant armored self-propelled guns, extended-range ammunition, and more wrinkles in ICM. The most important new development will be sensors and the increased effectiveness of submuni-tions. For example, your average 155mm HE shell creates fires one to two meters from the point of detonation. Some 2,000–4,000 fragments spray out, traveling 500–1,700 meters a second. The average fragment weight is two thirds of an ounce, and most fly harmlessly into the air or ground. ICM can, for the same weight of shell, deliver several times the number of effective fragments and fire-producing capability by using sensors and computers in the shell to determine the optimal position and altitude for detonation.

Of particular interest are the larger weapons, especially improved rockets. These weapons often have the same caliber as artillery, but the projectiles are longer, with thinner walls, and can carry a lot more than artillery shells. This enables rockets to carry larger, and more effective, submunitions. The larger rockets, originally designed for nuclear weapons, are even more effective with ICM, especially as short-range missiles become more accurate because of advances in electronic technology. Other weapons, such as FAE (Fuel Air Explosives), can be used only in rockets with larger warheads. The success of MLRS rockets in the Persian Gulf has confirmed the wisdom of producing longer-range MLRS rockets (up to 50-km range), with the trade-off of a warhead carrying 20 percent fewer munitions.

Artillery-locating radars have existed in theory, with questionable performance, from the 1950s. Since the early 1980s, truly effective artillery-locating radars have been fielded by Western nations. Each U.S. division now has two artillery-locating and three mortar-locating systems. Russia has introduced less capable equipment. The antidote to these radar-directed counterbattery systems is to have artillery battalions fire several hundred rounds and then move on. To facilitate this, Russia introduced thousands of new self-propelled guns during the 1980s, and began organizing them into larger battalions (24 instead of 18 guns) so they can get the required number of rounds off before Western counterbattery found them. Russia has been selling a lot of this equipment, and doctrine, to Third World nations. Another proposed solution to counterbattery fire is to give each gun sufficiently accurate navigation equipment (a GPS) to allow individual guns to fire accurately from widely dispersed locations. This complicates the counterbattery situation immensely, and is also helpful if rounds must be fired within your own rear area to defend against enemy commandos in an increasingly fluid battlefield. Western nations are now fielding such systems. This will make the current chess game between opposing artillery more complex. The edge will go to the side with the more capable electronics and the more efficient guns. Nearly every army has at least first-generation (1960s) computers for plotting and controlling gunfire. A third generation is being introduced into Western armies, as well as proposals for new, highly automated, self-propelled gun designs. These new weapons would use liquid propellant for the shells and three-man crews. All loading and fire control would be automatic. New shell designs and new propellants could extend ranges as far as 50 kilometers. The crew would do little more than drive the vehicle and make whatever repairs it could. Many of these features are being introduced individually and incrementally.

Principal Artillery in Use

The artillery, systems-in-use weapons shown in Chart 4-1 represent over 90 percent of what is currently in use worldwide. The United States and Russia provide much of what is used by other nations, either in the form of experts or designs. Some other Western nations manufacture their own, but these holdings are minor. China manufactures copies of Russian equipment and exports some of it.

CALIBER is the diameter of the projectile in millimeters.

NAME is the designation of the weapon. The 105mm (4.1 inch) guns were standard during World War II but now are used only by Western airborne units. All 122mm weapons are of Russian design. The D-74 is a long-range gun, while the D-30 is the Russians' standard towed howitzer. The SP guns are generally SP versions of towed weapons like the D-30. The BM-21 is the standard, but not the only, rocket launcher. The 130mm M-46 is the most widely used Russian long-range gun. The RPU-14 is the standard rocket launcher in airborne units. The D-20 and the SP version are the standard 152mm artillery and are identical except that one is self-propelled. The M-114A1 is out of production but still widely used. It is being replaced by the (155mm) M-198. The M-110A2 (203mm) is the standard U.S. heavy artillery. The 2S series is the new generation of Russian self-propelled artillery. The Russians use missiles and larger rockets like the BM-24 and BM-27.

ORIGIN is the manufacturing country. NATO indicates a group effort in production by Britain, Germany, and Italy.

RANGE is the extreme range of the gun in kilometers. In practice, the best accuracy is achieved at two-thirds this range. Although the chart does not state it, you can see which artillery are the short-barreled howitzers and which are guns. Howitzers are designed to fire at high angles and hit targets behind obstacles like hills. Guns have longer barrels, a high shell velocity, a flatter trajectory, and a longer range. Although unable to hit targets behind hills, guns have longer ranges. This wears out the barrel more quickly, often after fewer than 500 rounds are fired. Howitzer barrels will last for thousands of rounds. Near the end of the barrel's useful life, wear and tear have an increasingly detrimental effect on accuracy. Range can be increased with RAP (Rocket Assisted Propellant) shells. Although RAP increases range 40 to 50 percent, there is a considerable loss in accuracy. At these extreme ranges, half the shells will fall outside a 150-meter circle. You then have to either fire more shells at the target or use a nuclear warhead to hit the target. The use of submunitions also makes RAP shells more effective, although there is less space in the shell because of the need to make room for the RAP rocket motor itself.

ROF PER MIN is the sustained rate of fire per minute. Guns can fire double to triple that rate for a minute or so. Maintaining a higher rate of fire for any longer will overheat the barrel. For rockets, the number of rockets per reload cycle is given. The rocket launchers fire their projectiles in seconds and take about 10 minutes to reload unless special fast-reload equipment is available. The BM-21 launcher has 40 tubes, the RPU-14 has 16, the BM-24 has 12.

4-1 Artillery

Caliber (mm)	Name	Origin	Range (km)	ROF per min	Radius (m)	Shell (kg)	Protec-tion	AT Cap mm pen	Mobility	Weight (tons)
105	M102	US	11.5	3	175	15	0	102	Towed	1.15
105	M101A1	US	11	3	175	15	0	102	Towed	2.26
122	M55/D74	Russia	24	6	210	22	0	460	Towed	5.50
122	BM-21	Russia	20.5	4	2,000	46	0	0	SP	11.50
122	2S1	Russia	15.3	8	240	26	5	460	SP	16.00
122	M63/D30	Russia	15.3	8	240	26	0	230	Towed	3.20
130	M46	Russia	33	6	280	33	0	230	Towed	7.70
140	RPU-14	Russia	9.8	4	750	40	0	0	Towed	1.20
152	2S5	Russia	28	1	350	44	3	800	SP	21.40
152	2S3	Russia	24	2	350	44	3	800	SP	28.00
152	M55/D20	Russia	24	1	350	44	0	800	Towed	5.70
155	M198	US	30	2	360	44	0	800	Towed	7.20
155	M109A1	US	18	2	360	44	7	800	SP	23.80
155	M114A1	US	14.6	2	360	44	0	800	Towed	5.80
175	M107	US	32.7	0.5	520	67	0	0	SP	28.20
203	2S7	Russia	30	1	470	91	3	0	SP	30.00
203	M110A2	US	29	0.5	470	91	0	0	SP	28.20
220	BM-27	Russia	40	1	750	360	0	0	SP	22.70
227	MLRS	NATO	30	4	750	400	6	0	SP	25.00
240	2S4	Russia	9.7	1	350	100	3	800	SP	32.00

RADIUS (in meters) is the area covered by the battery volley (one shell each from a battery of six guns) of HE (High Explosive). In this area, there is a 50 percent chance of an exposed individual being hit. ICM (Improved Conventional Munitions) used by Western, and increasingly by Russian, armies increases this area by two or three times and the probability of getting hit by up to 90 percent. The ICM customarily use hundreds of smaller bomblets that scatter over a large area before exploding.

SHELL is the weight of the standard HE shell in kilograms (2.2 pounds). A complete round also includes propellant and packing material. This increases total weight 30 to 50 percent. An increasing number of shell types are becoming available. Their weight varies from that of the standard shell for that caliber by no more than 20 percent either way.

PROTECTION is the degree of armored protection. A *0* indicates no protection at all.

AT CAP MM PEN is the armor-piercing capability of the weapon using available armor-piercing shell, in millimeters.

MOBILITY indicates if the gun is towed by a truck or tractor or self-propelled on a tank or APC chassis.

WEIGHT is the weight of the system in tons (without tractor if towed).

Artillery Destruction Table

Chart 4-2 shows how much artillery ammunition must be used to inflict various levels of damage on armored and unarmored units. The casualty figures are averages. Actual losses can be more than doubled or halved depending on the luck and skill of the attackers and defenders. Using conventional HE (High Explosive) shells against armored targets is an expensive and questionable process. Each ton of HE costs about $12,000. Modern armored vehicles (tanks, APCs, and specialized types) cost an average of more than $1 million each. The units in the chart have some $60 million worth of vehicles. To destroy a unit, you must destroy or disable 50 or 60 percent of its vehicles. That comes to about $35 million worth of damage. On the average, you can do this using less than $35 million worth of artillery shells. However, accountants do not determine who wins on the battlefield. The biggest problem with calculations of this sort is how thousands of tons of munitions are to reach their targets. A division in a major attack might have 200 or 300 guns available, with access to large ammunition supplies. Three hundred guns could fire, on a sustained basis, 600 shells a minute. That's about 35 tons a minute. If the division is attacking three battalions, a destruction bombardment will take from one to five hours. Because of the faster reaction times and more accurate counterbattery fire, a gun that fires more than five minutes from the same position is inviting destruction. The other problem is logistical. Providing large quantities of ammunition on the modern battlefield is an uncertain business. All this has not gone unnoticed. Several solutions can be applied. Fewer shells can be fired, using ICM (Improved Conventional Munitions). These were calculated to be 3 to 10 times as effective as HE shells. ICM proved to be slightly less effective after receiving some extensive combat use. Other solutions are more extensive use of rockets, aircraft, and direct fire. Destruction fires will only be used if enemy counterbattery is not a threat. Neutralization fires will be the norm.

ACTIVITY OF DEFENDING UNIT indicates how men and equipment are deployed. The unit represented is a reinforced battalion with 500 to 1,000 men and 50 or 60 combat vehicles if an armored unit.

HASTY ATTACK is a quick movement from column on a road to lines of vehicles moving cross-country to the attack.

4-2 Artillery Destruction Table

Activity of Defending Unit	Area Covered (sq km)	% Casualties per 100 Tons of Ammo		Tons of Ammunition Expended to:			
				Neutralize		Destroy	
		Armor Unit	Soft Unit	Armor Unit	Soft Unit	Armor Unit	Soft Unit
Hasty Attack	1	31	109	96	28	160	46
Prepared Attack	1	21	75	143	40	239	67
Assembly	1.7	30	49	99	61	165	101
Hasty Defense	3.6	9	18	345	169	576	282
Prepared Defense	3.6	3	6	1,043	517	1,739	862
Dispersed Defense	7	1	3	2,029	1,005	3,381	1,676

PREPARED ATTACK is more deliberate, with troops and vehicles taking advantage of terrain to minimize artillery damage.

ASSEMBLY is troops gathered together before engaging in some other activity or simply resting.

HASTY DEFENSE is similar to hasty attack, except that the troops seek cover and prepare to defend.

PREPARED DEFENSE is when troops have time to dig in and prepare to defend.

DISPERSED DEFENSE is similar to prepared defense except that the troops are spread over a wider area.

AREA COVERED is the area occupied by the unit. It is the area into which the artillery falls. It is roughly square shaped and measured in square kilometers.

% CASUALTIES PER 100 TONS OF AMMO is the percentage of the unit's troops and/or vehicles that will be killed, destroyed, or disabled. The two classes of targets are:

- *Armor,* a unit consisting primarily of tanks, APCs, and other armored vehicles.
- *Soft,* a unit consisting only of troops and/or unarmored vehicles.

The traditional rule of thumb for neutralization fire with HE shell is 1 round per 100 square meters for armored units and 1 per 1,000 square meters for soft targets. A Western-type division carries 3,000–5,000 tons of artillery munitions, a Russian or Third World division about half that. These numbers can be increased when transportation and munitions are available. The other problem is time. If you spend too much time blasting away at a unit to soften it up, you give the defender an opportunity to bring up reinforcements. Artillery fires on the modern battlefield will be of short duration—probably no more than 15 minutes.

TONS OF AMMUNITION EXPENDED TO NEUTRALIZE OR DESTROY indicates how much ammunition will be needed to neutralize (destroy one quarter to one third) or destroy (about 50 percent) of the unit. The tonnages shown are for HE shell. About one-fifth that amount will be needed if ICM (Improved Conventional Munitions) are used.

5

Combat Support

THE BATTLEFIELD IS NOT occupied solely by infantry, tank crews, and artillerymen. There are a large number of specialist troops there also. These combat-support troops are not there to fight, but to support those who do. The combat troops need all the support they can get.

The Multiplier Effect of Combat Support

By themselves, combat troops can be quite effective. But in many special situations, their effectiveness can be increased considerably with the addition of specialist troops. Engineer support makes it easier to take enemy fortifications or cross natural and man-made obstacles. Some natural barriers, like rivers, are impassable to tanks without the engineers and their portable bridges. These same bridges will get you across antitank ditches dug by the opposition. Enemy minefields and fortifications can be made less lethal by combat engineers. Signal troops ensure that there is communications between combat troops and their supply sources, headquarters, and support units to the rear. Transportation troops keep the fuel, ammunition, and other supplies coming. Without this, combat troops would be out of necessaries within days. Military police control traffic, guard prisoners, and maintain security just behind the combat zone. Many more combat troops would be required to do what the military police are trained to do. Chemical troops provide assistance in decontaminating vehicles and troops exposed to chemical weapons. Otherwise, chemical-warfare losses would be several times higher. Electronic-warfare troops reduce the effect of enemy jamming and in turn debilitate enemy communications. Headquarters troops coordinate all activity. Without them, there would be more chaos than already exists on the battlefield.

NATIONAL DIFFERENCES

There is a fundamental difference between the way Western and Russian-style armies use combat support. The Russians recognize that support units are expensive and difficult to create and maintain. For this reason, Russian-type armies keep most of the combat-support troops out of the combat divisions to preserve them as much as possible. This makes their combat divisions less efficient, but enables the entire armed forces to stay in combat longer. Nations with larger degrees of industrialization and technology development have an easier time creating support units. Less-developed nations must depend more on pure combat units to fight a short war. An army with slender support resources will not be able to replace combat and noncombat losses as quickly as more technologically advanced states. Without combat support, an army's battlefield losses increase. Western armies are trained and equipped to keep men and machines operational longer. Russian equipment and units are designed and deployed to fight a short, intense war. If they don't, their equipment rapidly breaks down, and they have difficulty rebuilding their shattered arms.

All armies have specialist support units. Each division has them, with others available at the army level, much like divisional and nondivisional artillery. Keep in mind that Western armies have about twice as much combat support as Russian or Third World forces. Below is a description of each unit's function. The size shows the differences between Western and Russian/Third World armies. The larger units are typically Western. Also given is the average percentage each specialist group takes up in a division. Typically, a division is one-third combat troops, the rest combat support. Depending on the type of division and nationality, the infantry comprises 8 to 30 percent of the division's strength; tank crews between 1 and 10 percent; and artillery (including antiaircraft and antitank weapons) between 6 and 12 percent. Combat troops comprise an even smaller portion of nondivisional forces, something like 5 to 10 percent. Because combat divisions account for from 20 to 50 percent of army manpower, combat troops comprise only 10 to 25 percent of all personnel. In all armies, combat-support troops are very much the majority.

ENGINEERS

Engineers comprise between 2 and 10 percent of a division's manpower. Each division has at least a battalion (400 to 1,100 men) of engineers.

Often regiments and brigades have their own engineer company (100 to 300 men). Nondivisional engineer battalions are supplied to armies in a ratio of one or more battalions for each division in the army. Whenever something has to be built or torn down, the engineers are called in. Many of the troops in divisional engineers' battalions are actually combat troops, doing demolition or construction work while under enemy fire. The U.S. Army engineers see their job as twofold: mobility enhancement (keeping things moving) of their own forces and countermobility work to slow down the opposition. The engineers are a hardworking crew, as the following list of their major responsibilities indicates:

1. *Bridges*. Most engineers are builders. About one third of a divisional engineer battalion consists of bridge-building troops. They use various self-propelled and truck-carried bridging equipment. The former are 15- to 20-meter bridges mounted on an unarmored tank chassis or a truck. These can support up to 50 tons or more (one tank). Longer bridge sections, which can also double as ferries, are carried on trucks.

2. *Digging and Minelaying*. Engineers also supervise or control all construction equipment. In a Russian division, sufficient excavation equipment is available to entrench one of the division's four regiments in a day. Each Russian combat regiment has enough engineer equipment to entrench one battalion a day. Minelaying machines (Russian) can lay at least 800 mines (eight tons) per hour. Depending on how many mines are carried, 10 kilometers of minefields are laid down for each regiment. Such a lavish use of mines is generally unlikely in the opening stages of a war, because when on the offensive, a division carries less than 100 tons of mines. Western armies depend more upon trackbuster mines delivered by aircraft and artillery. Stored at the air bases, these weigh less than five pounds each, one tenth as much as conventional mines.

3. *Defensive Positions*. Engineers have found the "speed bump" approach to be effective on the battlefield. Anything that slows the enemy down is an advantage. This entails more than placing mines and trenches. Other engineer chores are constructing road barricades and laying out markers to show were defending units will deploy and where roads will be built and camouflage constructed. This planning and supervisory function is one of the more important ones engineers provide. Many of the earliest military academies, including the United States' West Point, were founded to train engineer officers for this kind of work.

4. *Mine Clearing*. Infantrymen can clear mines, but engineers can do it more quickly and safely. Their training and specialized equipment make engineers critical if you must get through a minefield quickly. Many new plastic mines are very difficult to detect and clear. In this

case, the engineers are responsible for finding and marking these areas. The first large-scale clearing of plastic mines took place after the 1991 Gulf War. There are several such fields remaining in the Falklands, Cambodia, and Afghanistan. Those are gradually being cleared by wayward animals and pedestrians.

5. *Demolition.* What goes up, demolition brings down. Handling tons of explosives to demolish large structures requires expert knowledge and proficiency. Bridges are particularly difficult to bring down. Airfields, roads, rail lines, structures of all kinds, may have to be destroyed by engineer troops. Such jobs take longer if the proper equipment and specialists are not at hand. For example, clearing a 75-meter abatis (large earthen obstacle laden with barbed wire, logs, and booby traps) can take 16 hours with just chain saws and hand tools. The same squad of engineers with a combat engineer vehicle (CEV) can do it in less than four hours.

6. *Construction and Repair.* Aside from field fortifications dug out of the ground, engineers can also quickly put up one-story prefabricated buildings, large tents, and inflatable structures and build roads, runways, and railroads. Special engineer construction battalions do most of the construction, and most other engineer units do the maintenance. For example, repairing a large road crater (30 by 20 by 10 feet deep) takes an hour with a CEV. Air forces maintain special engineer units to quickly repair airfield damage. Navies have their own engineers who specialize in building, maintaining, operating, and repairing port facilities.

7. *Maps.* You can't fight a proper war without a timely supply of accurate maps. Normally, the engineers are responsible for creating, reproducing, and distributing maps.

8. *Utilities.* Engineers are responsible for generating power in the field. Any large plant, such as a field bakery, decontamination equipment, or field baths, is often maintained and operated by them. They simplify the question of whom to call when something breaks down.

Engineers in combat units handle largely combat-related tasks. The non-combat engineer tasks are taken up by nondivisional engineer units.

Signal

Between 3 and 12 percent of a division's personnel are assigned to signal troops. Divisional signal battalions (400 to 1,000 men) are not the only signal units in a division. Every unit down to a company or platoon has some signal troops. Nondivisional signal units exist in a ratio of one per division. Modern armies are held together with electronic-signal equipment. Armored vehicles have an internal intercom system and one or more radios for outside communications. Defensive and noncombat positions make extensive use of telephones. All this equipment is maintained, and often installed and manned, by signal troops. Nondivisional signal battalions take on many aspects and responsibilities of civilian telephone companies. These units set up and maintain long-distance communications, especially statellite links. They set up hundreds of radio and telephone "nets" (party lines) and look after the security and efficiency of these nets. Western armies are making increasing use of satellite and cellular-phone technology as well. Signal troops also assist the intelligence and electronic-warfare troops. The dozens of radio nets in a division can easily lapse into chaos without the efficient efforts of the signal troops. Many units have multiple ones. Typical communication-net types are for combat units (company's battalions, brigades) as well as different types of units (an artillery net, a supply net, an aircraft net, etc.). At headquarters, the nets are connected to one another with multiple radio sets or special equipment. Signal troops assist in maintaining radio and net discipline. That is, no useless chatter, unauthorized breaking in on another net, or transmitting in other than the rigid, authorized format.

Chemical

Chemical troops comprise between 1 and 4 percent of a division's strength. Most divisions now have a chemical company or battalion. Smaller units often have their own chemical unit, such as a chemical platoon for a regiment or brigade. The primary responsibility of the chemical-troops portion in a division is the detection of chemical, nuclear, or biological weapons. The chemical troops also often have decontamination equipment. More information on this is given in Chapter 21.

Transport

Between 8 and 16 percent of a division's troops are involved in transportation, including the drivers of combat-unit supply vehicles. Most divisions have a transport battalion. Otherwise, transport vehicles are scattered through the division and/or the transport units belong to a higher headquarters. Battalions and regiments follow the same pattern. Nondivisional transport units are usually available in a ratio of 2 or 3 transport battalions for each division in an army. No matter how they are organized, there are a lot of trucks running around the battle area with supplies. Transport units move supplies. They are typically equipped with trucks, but some have railroad equipment or even coastal and river boats. A typical medium truck battalion has about 200 five-ton trucks, each capable of pulling a 10-ton trailer. Allowing for out-of-service vehicles and variable load size, this gives the unit a maximum practical carrying capacity of 2,000 tons. A transport company has a 500-ton capacity, a platoon 150 tons. Western armies have introduced a new generation of heavier 10-ton (and up) trucks that are designed to handle pallets and containers while also being able to move more easily off roads. These vehicles got their first wartime workout in the 1991 Gulf War and performed well. This was essential, it turned out, because the older trucks were not able to deliver fuel and supplies fast enough and in adequate quantity across country. The latest generation of tanks uses much more fuel. The Gulf War operations were in the desert, requiring nearly as much water as fuel to be moved. Because of the flat desert terrain, the combat units were able to move more rapidly, putting even more stress on the supply transport units. Without the new generation of trucks, the battle would have proceeded more slowly, and with more coalition losses.

While transport units will carry anything, some specialize. For example, tank-transporter units consist of 30 to 60 heavy tractor-trailers, each with a 50–70-ton capacity. Other heavy units have tanker trucks for carrying fuel. Most divisions and all armies have air-transportation units. These are helicopter and light fixed-wing aircraft. The trend is toward one aviation battalion per division, although this unit is used more as a taxi/delivery/ ambulance/scouting service than as a transportation unit. Army-level aviation units are more likely to be used for transport. For more details, see the chapters on logistics (23), naval transport (26), and air transport (27).

MILITARY POLICE

Between 1 and 2 percent of a division's strength are Military Police (MPs)—traffic control and security troops. Most divisions have at least a company (100 to 200 men). At army level, there is often a battalion or more, usually including criminal investigators (detectives) and lawyers. The main function of MPs in wartime is traffic control. In rear areas, especially just behind the fighting troops, they are also used to maintain order, guard against saboteurs, and handle prisoners.

MEDICAL

Some 2 to 5 percent of a division's strength are medical personnel. In addition to a medical unit (300 to 900 men), all combat units have medical personnel attached. Nondivisional units typically number one battalion per division in an army. At and below division level, the medical troops give first aid and evacuate wounded troops as quickly as possible. Because two thirds of combat casualties can be returned to duty eventually, it is essential to prevent wounds from worsening and evacuate the wounded to rear areas for recuperation as quickly as possible. An equally important task of medical units is the supervision of preventive medicine. In cold climates, this means treating and monitoring exposure casualties. The chief medical officer alerts the unit commanders when these losses get out of hand. In disease-prone locales, like the tropics, the medical troops distribute medicines and eradicate pests. In any area with a lot of civilians, venereal disease will be a major problem, often the number-one cause of losses due to noncombat casualties. At all times, medical troops monitor the purity of food and water and keep an eye on living conditions in general. Because noncombat losses have historically been higher than combat casualties, the medical troops are a critical force in maintaining unit strength.

MAINTENANCE

From 3 to 10 percent of a division's troops are mechanics and technicians who perform equipment repair and maintenance. Most divisions have a maintenance unit (400 to 1,000 men). Depending on the number of vehicles and equipment, smaller units will have up to 20 percent of their personnel specializing in maintenance tasks. Nondivisional units also have 10 percent of their troops engaged in maintenance tasks. Although military equipment is built to take a lot of punishment, the breakdown rate in the field is high. The maintenance units wage, at best, a holding action. See Chapter 24, "Attrition," for more details. Western armies have historically been more proficient at keeping things operational. Russian and Third World armies take a more brute-force approach and abandon broken equipment so that follow-on maintenance units can recover and repair what they find. Like medical units, maintenance troops devote a lot of their efforts to performing and supervising regular and preventive maintenance. This function, in the long run, has more impact than the ability to perform many repairs quickly during combat.

HEADQUARTERS

Between 5 and 15 percent of a division's manpower is assigned to headquarters tasks. Every unit has a headquarters, even if it consists of one man (squad or platoon leader). Larger units have larger headquarters—at the division level the headquarters comprises several hundred men. Nondivisional forces have the same proportion of their manpower devoted to headquarters tasks. Headquarters administer, lead, plan, coordinate, and support. They include intelligence units that often send detachments to combat units to screen prisoners, examine captured equipment, and generally gather information firsthand. Headquarters collect information from subordinate units, analyze it, and issue appropriate orders. Headquarters control the flow of supplies; they also contain the cooks and other personal-service troops, like chaplains or political officers. Without a functioning headquarters, units lose the ability to function effectively and work with other units. Many armies have headquarters that are too large. A dose of combat often indicates how small the headquarters can be to be effective.

ELECTRONICS

Between 1 and 2 percent of a unit's troops perform electronic-warfare, support, and intelligence-gathering tasks. Although these troops could be considered signal troops, their work and equipment is so different as to make them a different category. The trend is toward having one electronic-warfare battalion (400 to 700 men) per division. Each army may have an additional battalion or two. These battalions monitor enemy signal traffic and, where appropriate, jam enemy communications. See Chapter 19, "The Electronic Battlefield," for more details.

Theory and Practice

Anyone entering the armed forces is more likely to become a clerk or technician than a combatant. However, many support personnel, particularly in the navy, are as much at risk in combat as those manning the weapons. During peacetime, the ratio of clerks to fighters tends to grow in favor of the clerks. When the fighting starts, the trend rapidly reverses. Western armies, especially the United States, are criticized for having too many support personnel. Part of the criticism is warranted. But America has developed a style of warfare that uses complex, and often capable, weapons. When working properly, this high-tech war machine is an awesome combat force. To keep it functioning requires prodigious personnel and material support. All nations accept that aircraft require large ground crews and masses of support equipment and supplies. Some ground weapons, like tanks and artillery, are approaching aircraft in complexity and capability. This trend comes from the realization that few troops are injured by hand-to-hand fighting, but rather through massive application of firepower. Although mountains of munitions and spare parts are built up in peacetime, these are rarely sufficient to match the capacity of weapons to consume munitions and spare parts during the initial phases of combat. Running out of ammo and spares adds to the uncertainty of battles. The complexity of current weapons will compound these concerns more so than in the past. Many high-performance weapons require enormous amounts of spare parts when they are used intensively. This has long been accepted for aircraft and ships but is now common with land weapons like tanks and missile systems. Moreover, the higher mobility of current armored vehicles has not been matched by the vehicles that must carry supplies to them. There have not yet been any wars between forces equipped with high-tech weapons. Nor have a sufficient number of technicians been trained to maintain all these new systems. It's quite common in Western armed forces to have civilian technicians from the manufacturer assigned to combat units in order to keep the equipment functioning.

In those wars where a high-tech power went after a lesser power, the initial technical confusion was compensated by the major powers' numerical superiority. The Gulf War of 1991 demonstrated how this works. Iraq quickly exhausted its meager supply of spare parts before the fighting even began. The United States itself only had sufficient spare parts for a few weeks' combat. Many combat units had to resort to cannibalization (taking parts from one vehicle or weapon to repair several others) before the fighting began. The United States had to borrow, buy, or lease hundreds of heavy trucks to keep the troops supplied, and even that was not adequate to support an advance of more than a few hundred miles. What goes around, comes around.

The Future

Maintenance will become more automated—it has to. A shortage of experienced repair people and larger numbers of more complex equipment forces greater use of computer-controlled diagnostic equipment. Russia developed, at great expense to its limited high-tech resources, automatic testing equipment. This was forced on the Russians because most of their troops are teenage conscripts who have less than a year of service left after being trained in some highly technical skill. Much of their complex maintenance work has to be done by officers, who are also in short supply but are at least in for the long haul. In addition to increasing automation, the Russians centralized maintenance as much as possible. Each combat regiment would have its maintenance company perform detailed maintenance on each battalion every five days. This works in peacetime, when the Russians don't use their equipment much anyway, but was inadequate for wartime conditions. Russia exported these techniques to many of the Third World customers for its weapons. The Third World nations have the same problems of limited material and personnel resources and were not able to get any better results from this system than the Russians.

Since the last major war 50 years ago, the quantity of tonnage and different items needed to wage a "modern" war has increased severalfold. The means to physically move the needed supplies to the troops is easily recognized, although the problem itself never seems to be completely solved. A more subtle problem is the mix of items that will be available, or actually needed, when the shooting starts. There are vital expendable items such as hundreds of different batteries, filters, and exotic munitions. Both the combat-support and the fighting troops will have to make a lot of adjustments when a war starts. Things will not be as the planners thought they would be.

Engineer troops are already highly automated in major nations. More countries are adding items like automatic minelayers and combat engineering equipment. Because there is less infantry, automated entrenching equipment is becoming a necessity. What infantrymen remain are kept busy maintaining their own growing inventory of complex gear. Mapmaking is becoming more automated, with major nations maintaining master maps on computers for quick updating and reproduction. Signal equipment will become more capable and more automated. People will be needed primarily to install the automated signal stations and antijamming equipment.

One largely unnoticed but vital function, weather forecasting, will become more accurate as more accurate radars and powerful computers are installed. More accurate and timely weather prediction can have decisive military results. Chemical equipment will see more effective detection and decontamination gear. The most startling new developments will be in the availability and use of computers and similar electronic gear. A lot of this additional computer power is taking over clerical tasks. An unfortunate side effect of this is a growing inability to perform essential tasks without using a computer. More prosaic tasks may become difficult without upcoming technology.

6

Paramilitary Forces
and Reserves

Paramilitary troops do more fighting than regular armed forces, typically against their own people. In a major war, these types often get involved in a major way, although the reserves (partially trained civilians) usually do most of the fighting.

Police Armies

Police forces for keeping the peace and pursuing criminals are a recent development, being practically unknown two centuries ago. Before that, police functions were performed by a combination of semiofficial vigilantes and the armed forces. When a nation is undergoing internal disorder, or the government rules with a heavy hand, special infantry forces are maintained to supplement the police. As the disorder increases, or a major war starts, these police armies grow larger and more active. Many countries organize their national police forces along military lines, making it easier to expand them and go over to more purely military operations. With the glaring exception of the United States, Canada, and several European nations, most countries maintain substantial forces of light infantry whose primary purpose is to protect the government from its own citizens. The Soviet Union was a classic example of the paramilitary police state, as are most dictatorships. Until its collapse, the Soviet Union maintained 200,000 KGB border troops. This "army" had armored units, naval ships, and combat aircraft. These forces served the same functions as the United States Coast Guard and Border Patrol. But in America these forces amount to fewer than 50,000 men and women. In addition, the Soviet Union had 260,000 MVD internal-security troops organized into combat units. There was nothing comparable to this in Western nations, where at most you have a few thousand riot-control troops. The successor states of the Soviet Union did not disband all of these paramilitary troops, and nearly half were retained in some police or military function. The uncertain political situation in these nations may cause the number of paramilitary troops to increase to their previous Soviet Union levels.

Some Western nations do, in fact, use the regular military to wage war against their own citizens, making these troops less capable of performing their traditional role. An example of the effects of this was seen in the Falklands in 1982. The Argentine Army had spent many years waging war against the population. It was in no shape to face the more professional British troops. Paramilitary forces often have little to do but stand around watching people. The existence of such a large group of armed, bored soldiers generally leads to abuse of their police powers and declining military capabilities. The paramilitary police then become part of the problem and use their police and military power to become a self-perpetuating institution. To the government, these troops are basically an expensive insurance policy against the chance of civil disorder. We saw another example of this in Iraq in the wake of the Gulf War, as Iraqi troops spent more time fighting their own people than they did the Kuwaitis or coalition troops. This use of paramilitary and regular troops is one of the heavy costs born by undemocratic governments.

Military Reserves

Some 200 years ago, several major European nations began conscripting civilians for the military on a regular basis. These soldiers served for only two or three years before being released. Shortly thereafter, clever staff officers in several nations came up with the notion of bringing some of these former soldiers back to the army in times of national danger. Thus began the infamous "reserve system," which enabled enormous armies to be created quickly and relatively inexpensively. World Wars I and II would not have been possible without the reserve system. These former soldiers are used in a variety of ways:

1. *To bring skeleton peacetime units up to strength during mobilization.* This is an essential element of the Russian system. The former Soviet Union's army was an extreme application where only a third of the divisions were full strength in peacetime. Even the United States maintains only 55 percent of its divisions at full strength in peacetime.

The Soviets were prepared to mobilize more than 2 million men to fill out their divisions in wartime. America requires a million reservists to bring all units up to strength. About half of all reserves are required for nondivisional (largely support) units. The new Russian Army will probably have a system closer to that of the United States. In any event, the U.S. system worked quite well in the Gulf War, particularly with regard to the noncombat support units. The United States is also reducing its reserve forces with the end of the Cold War. But reserves will remain, as they are too effective a concept to entirely discard.

2. *For maintenance of active units.* The former Soviet Union maintained many of its reserve divisions with but a skeleton crew of active-duty soldiers. The United States maintains its reserve divisions primarily with soldiers who serve full time several days a month and two weeks during the summer. In 1914, the Germans demonstrated to their disbelieving opponents that reserves could be as effective in wartime as regulars. The Germans did this by requiring their reserves to train regularly, much like the current American system does. The Soviet Union could not afford this, although attempts were made to do some training. Most Soviet reservists were assigned to a unit they had never seen, and never would see unless called up. The Soviet Union did activate its reservists in this manner when it invaded Afghanistan in 1979, but quickly removed these reserve troops and replaced them with regulars. The successor states to the Soviet Union are abandoning the traditional Soviet reserve system and trying to emulate the U.S. system. One reason to emulate the U.S. system is that the U.S. system obviously works; the other reason is to eliminate the Soviet Union reserve obligations that were very unpopular with the millions of reservists.

3. *As replacements for combat losses.* During heavy combat, tank and infantry battalions can lose 10 to 20 percent of their men a day. Half these losses will be permanent or long term. Other units in the division will lose smaller amounts. Three weeks of heavy combat with 20 divisions means over 200 battalions losing 40 or 50 men a day. That adds up—in this case it amounts to over 150,000 troops that have to be replaced quickly. The reserve troops are the most readily available source.

4. *For the formation of new units.* Forming a new division requires nondivisional troops as well, for a total of at least 20,000 men per new division. You need troops possessing a variety of technical skills. Some of these specialists have a civilian counterpart and can often be taken directly from the civilian population. Specialists for which there is no civilian equivalent, primarily combat specialists, must come from the reserves. Starting new divisions from scratch, without a pool of trained manpower, can take a year. With sufficient former

soldiers, you can do it in a few months. The former Soviet Union maintained an additional 50 divisions on paper, to be raised in wartime from reserves and obsolete equipment held in storage. These units, with troops in their 30s and 40s using equipment as old as they are, would have been no match for an equal number of active divisions. But such "mobilization" divisions did make a difference during World War II. The successor states to the Soviet Union will probably maintain some paper divisions—if only on paper. There isn't much usable equipment left for these units.

THE FORMER SOVIET UNION

Although the Soviet Union is gone, fragments of its reserve system, the largest in history, still remain in Russia and several other successor states. Just how much of the Soviet reserve system will survive in these successor states will not be known until the end of the decade. The Soviet Union kept track of every veteran until the age of 50. This was its reserve. Most nations, unable to afford the expense of regular reserve training, use the same general concept. The usual source of men with current experience are those discharged in the last few years. This reduced the Soviet Union's effective reserve to a million men times the number of years you want to go back—say, 2–5 million men. This was a major flaw in the Russian system, as it has been found that soldiers lose most of their military skills within a year of leaving the military. It takes several months to get these skills back. If troops are sent into combat before they have been retrained, their units will do very poorly against a better-trained opponent.

The Soviet system, originally developed in 19th-century Germany, is suitable for a nation lacking great wealth. In the Soviet Union, a reservist might not, by law, be called up for more than 90 days a year unless a national emergency was declared. This was not done out of any regard for the reservist, but in recognition of the labor shortage and economic disruptions that would be created. Most reservists were never called up. An example of the problems inherent in this system could be seen in the Soviet mobilization against Poland in 1980. In areas adjacent to Poland, the Soviet Union had 57 divisions. At least 40 would be needed to guarantee a quick pacification of Poland. The Soviets could not afford the political fallout from prolonged fighting in Poland. Of the 57 available divisions, only 28 were fully manned, and 24 of those were occupying East Germany and Czechoslovakia. Because of possible unrest in Eastern Europe, or interference from Western Europe, the divisions in East Germany and Czechoslovakia could probably not be used. This would mean using 36 reserve divisions and bringing most of them in from other areas. Over half a million men would have to be called up. This would have a noticeable effect on the local economy. This strain on the local economy was one of the critical, but not mentioned, factors causing the Soviet Union to halt its attempt to mobilize reserve divisions for use against Poland.

Israel provides another example. Mobilization calls up over 15 percent of the Jewish and Druze population and severely disrupts the economy. Other nations, Sweden and Switzerland, also have reserve armies whose mobilization would shut down their economies. However, these two nations are neutral and depend more on the threat of mobilization. Israel has had to mobilize many times in the past and will probably have to do it again. Economic disruption is not the only problem mobilization armies face. Many of these armies tend to rely heavily on conscripts, to the extent that 75 percent of their manpower are two- or three-year draftees. This is typical in those nations that rely on conscription. In Russian-style armies, most of the noncommissioned officers are senior conscripts of dubious quality. The officers in these armies are generally all volunteers and graduates of military academies. These officers perform the tasks normally assigned to NCOs in Western armed forces.

Supervision, management, and leadership were inadequate in the peacetime Soviet armed forces and would have become even more chaotic if millions of reservists were mobilized. The mobilized army would have been about 85 percent conscript, with the rate going over 90 percent in a third of the divisions. If history is any guide, this third of the old Soviet Army would have been less than half as effective as the top third. The solution to these quality problems is training. Most Western armies train their reserves, or attempt to. Training is critical because an effective soldier is very much a technician. The effective maintenance and use of weapons and military equipment is possible only with constant practice. Reserves that do not regularly practice require one or more months to regain their skills. Personnel with prior military service are easier to whip into shape for combat because of their familiarity with military routine. Because of their prior service, reserve troops have demonstrated an ability to function in a military environment. However, one should not place too much reliance on prior military experience. Unless these troops maintain good physical conditioning and some knowledge of their military skill, they are not a great deal better than raw civilian recruits. The Soviet reserve system provided large numbers of troops, but lower effectiveness. The Russians of the old Soviet Union were aware of this, being diligent students of past experience. Their solution was to prepare for a short war, short enough so their deficiencies will not catch up with them. This is not to say that the Soviets could not have won a long war. They were victorious during World War II, but at a cost of 25 million dead and a ruined economy.

The Soviet Navy and Air Force also used reserves, but not as extensively as the army. They needed skilled personnel to man their more complex equipment. Reserves were used primarily as laborers and support workers, except where civilian skills qualified them for technical tasks. Most of the reserves tabulated in Chapter 29 are counted more as veterans of active service than as trained reserves.

THE U.S. SYSTEM

The U.S. reserve system is generally as misunderstood as the one the former Soviet Union used. Comparing the Soviet Army's 200 divisions with the 21 U.S. Army and Marine units in the late 1980s was comparing apples and oranges. Only a third of the Soviet divisions were at the same level of readiness as the U.S. ones. America had 18 U.S. reserve divisions, or equivalents in smaller units, which were larger and, arguably, more capable than their Soviet counterparts. The ratio was more like 65 to 30 in ready-to-fight divisions, and 200 to 65 in overall division strength. These numbers included marine units but did not take into account the larger borders and number of hostile neighbors the Soviets had to guard against.

The U.S. reserve system grew out of the pre-Revolution militia, now represented by the National Guard System. These units provide 40 percent of the infantry and armor battalions. Although the Guard has a long standing reputation as a social club and fiefdom of local politicians, its performance in this century has demonstrated that it can fight too. Active army units that have "fought" Guard units in maneuvers have learned not to underestimate its skill and effectiveness.

The official reserve units are directly under the control of their respective services. Like the Guard, the reserves use both former active-duty troops and personnel recruited directly into reserve units. Together, the Guard and reserves accounted for more than 50 percent of ground-combat and 60 percent of combat-support units just before the Cold War ended. This militia system is used by several other nations. Britain, for example, has territorial troops who operate much like the U.S. National Guard. Germany has a territorial army whose wartime task is maintaining order and guarding against saboteurs and raids. Most nations have small navy and air-force reserve units. The United States maintains major portions of its naval and air-force strength in the reserves. Hundreds of aircraft, including the most modern combat planes, are manned by reservists. Again, the reserve pilots often show up the regulars. This should not be surprising, as the reserve pilots are former regulars who continue to pile up flying hours as a hobby. The U.S. naval reserve maintains scores of support and escort ships, participating in maneuvers on an equal basis with regular navy units.

The U.S. reserve system is a recent development. Only a wealthy economy can provide enough skilled people with enough leisure time to become effective part-time soldiers. The average reservist spends five weeks a year training. In addition, they can be called up for longer periods in the event of civil or military emergencies. A few nations have gone the United States one better. Sweden, Switzerland, and Israel maintain similar, but proportionately larger, reserve systems. Indeed, Sweden and Switzerland have practically no regular forces to speak of and depend on their huge reserve armies to deter potential aggressors. So far this appears to have worked.

The U.S. system is not without its disadvantages. Although over half of U.S. Army combat strength is from the reserve and National Guard forces, these received only 10 percent of the army's budget at the end of the Cold War. While this might be enough if there were reasonable spending goals, the U.S. Army builds combat units that, in wartime, would have to be supported by reserve units that lack essential equipment. On paper, National Guard brigades are part of regular-army divisions—they would fight together in the event of a war. However, the National Guard units do not have complete sets of equipment like the regular units. In fact, it would take more than 30 days to ship the National Guard units to a war because of the time required to obtain the missing equipment. These discrepancies are regularly glossed over. Indeed, the National Guard officers are told not to report equipment shortages if the discrepancy is major. This approach, therefore, shows minor shortages and simply ignores the major ones. Moreover, during the Gulf War, the regulars simply didn't want the three National Guard brigades that were technically part of divisions sent to the Gulf. There was a considerable scandal over how this was handled, and we haven't heard the last of it.

The only bright spot in this situation is that other nations are probably in a similar situation with regard to their reserve units. Fortunately, the U.S.-style reserve system makes use of fully formed and trained units. The quality of these units, in fact, makes the system work. Training together over many years, these reserve units achieve a degree of cohesion and professionalism that often surpasses that of regular units. It's a rich man's system, which less affluent nations like Russia cannot afford to match.

The Uncounted Reserves

When war breaks out, a lot of civilians find themselves in uniform doing pretty much the same work they performed in peacetime. As warfare becomes more technological, the capabilities of the support soldier become more important. Complex skills are retained only through practice. A soldier who learns a technical job in the service and goes on to another career as a civilian rapidly loses these military skills. The regularly practiced routines of a civilian electronics technician become immediately useful in the military. The ability of a nation to make civilian expertise a military asset depends on the quantity and quality of these skills. The Western nations have a distinct advantage in this respect. These nations have a surplus of these skills because of their higher standard of living. Poor nations live closer to the threshold of survival. Current examples are the many poor colonies that lost their thin reserve of technicians in the post-colonial period. Starvation, economic collapse, and a general inability to make any massive efforts, like industrialization or a major war, resulted. Russia suffered in this fashion during World War II. Much of Russia's industrial base was overrun by the Germans in 1941–42. Most of the aid given to Russia during the war was in terms of industrial goods, raw materials, and other supplies. Because so many Russian technicians were at the front getting killed, the Soviets' industrial and technical resources were not sufficient to keep their armed forces going without external assistance. Russians remember this trauma better than most Westerners realize. Therefore, Russians will continue to implement their traditional solutions. Their equipment will be kept quite simple by Western standards. Russian designers will readily sacrifice performance in order to field a weapon that can be used effectively with minimal training. This is not always possible, but it is pursued diligently enough to make Russian weapons attractive to Third World nations lacking a large pool of technically skilled people.

Theory and Practice

Paramilitary and reserve forces are a case of theory and practice often falling far apart when reality hits. Most of the paramilitary forces in the world, whether they are formally organized or are merely regular armed forces who perform the function, generally perform poorly. Because there is the temptation to substitute quantity for quality in paramilitary forces, troops are usually lightly armed and poorly trained. But when a lot of ill-trained and poorly-paid troops are used to buck up an unpopular government, it's only a matter of time before paramilitary troops become a fertile recruiting ground for rebellious elements. This has become a pattern in Third World nations. Even tightly disciplined and well-trained paramilitary forces, such as those the Communist nations developed, proved more loyal to the population than to the bureaucrats.

Reserves are another case of, "if I don't see anything, it's not happening." Reserves are very difficult to maintain at levels of wartime usefulness. The United States learned this during the Gulf War. Their deficiencies became starkly evident under the pressures of wartime demands. While the performance of U.S. reserves in that war was among the highest of any reserve force in history, they were not always up to what Congress had been promised. But the quantity of the resources available to the United States allowed many of these shortcomings to be shunted into the shadows. Until the next time.

The Future

More nations are training and equipping their reserve troops to better handle civil disorder. Technology is changing the nature and effectiveness of reserve troops. As more complex weapons become the norm, the degree to which reserve troops retain their technical skills after release from active duty becomes more critical. This has been less a problem in the West, where reserves undergo regular training in complex skills. What is becoming more of a problem is creating effective reserves for the increasing number of combat jobs that require technical skills. Less than a century ago, most combat jobs could be quickly taught to physically fit young men. This is no longer the case. Even the infantry must master dozens of unique technical skills to become highly effective fighters. Increasingly, the solution is to use more civilians or uniformed women in combat-support jobs for the active forces while maximizing the number of well-trained men in combat units. The reserve system that developed in the 19th century to provide masses of infantry is now seen as counterproductive. Mass is no longer as effective as it once was in the face of high-tech weapons.

Increasing automation may eventually make it possible to field large armies from reserves, but this development will have to wait for the next century.

Only the United States and Israel have quickly fielded large, modern reserve forces to good effect. But each of these nations exists in special circumstances. While this is seen as a pattern that works, it is one that few nations can afford to emulate.

PART TWO

AIR OPERATIONS

AIR WARFARE is a creature of the 20th century.
Today, it is high-tech, very expensive, and incredibly
destructive.

7

The Air Force: Fighters, Bombers, and Snoopers

AIR FORCES GET very touchy when anyone suggests that their primary purpose is to obtain information. In the beginning, warplanes were used exclusively to gather information for land and naval forces. Despite constant attempts to diversify into other areas, air forces still pay for their keep by getting answers, or preventing the enemy from doing so. Yes, there is a problem with air forces in that they would rather be fighting the war on their own, without getting mixed up in the grubby work of the infantry. This is something of a dirty little secret in the armed forces. Yet you don't have to observe the infighting between the air forces and other services for long to figure out what the flyers would rather be doing. They would rather be fighting other air forces. Air-force people know aircraft; they know less about what goes on in the trenches. It's dirty and dangerous work flying down into the flak zone to support ground troops. Although many pilots prefer this kind of work, the majority don't.

There is also the sense of self-preservation. An air force's most likely enemy is another air force. The air bases are usually far away from the ground fighting, reachable only by enemy aircraft. If they can't stop those enemy planes, their bases will be hit, leaving friendly aircraft cut off from their vital lifeline.

There is a lot not to like when supporting ground forces. In the air, it's either missiles from the ground or aircraft from all over. The missiles are easier to get away from. As the air force attacks ground targets in the combat zone, the hostile fire comes from every direction, in three dimensions.

This ground-support situation varies from air force to air force. In many armed forces, the ground-support aircraft are under army control. In the United States, control of ground-support aircraft was taken away from the army when the independent air force was created after World War II. The U.S. Air Force has had mixed feelings about this move, and the current growth of U.S. Army helicopter forces makes the air force's shrinking number of ground-support aircraft look embarrassing at times. The message from the ground forces seems to be, "If the air force won't give us support, we'll get it any way we can." The U.S. Marine Corps has its own air force and receives superb ground support from it, and the value of this kind of reinforcement is not lost on the army.

Air forces still spend a lot of time snooping around, but satellites have taken some of that work away. Given a free hand, an air force would consist largely of fighters, with some recon and bomber-aircraft flyers. Preferring to pick their own targets, specifically ones deep in the enemy rear, air forces survive by controlling the air and keeping their bases free of enemy attacks. An air force's first priority is to destroy the other fellow's air force. There is never enough in the way of a nation's fighting aircraft because, pound for pound, they are the most expensive weapons available. The air force is also much in demand. Aircraft can be where they are needed quickly and with a lot of firepower. Although they cannot occupy ground or replace ground forces, the air force can give one side a decisive edge by wresting control of the air from its opponents early in the war.

What air forces do has not changed in 80 years. Aircraft take pictures, fight other aircraft, or carry things (bombs or cargo). Their missions are simple; their means are not.

Ground Control and Support

Aircraft give the illusion of freedom to their crews, but they are always very much attached to the ground. Aircraft ultimately answer to someone on the ground, and to the ground all planes must return every few hours to refuel and rearm. Commanders on the ground use radar and radio to maintain control over their airborne subordinates. Ground-based command-and-control radar are increasingly replaced with airborne systems, but these are vulnerable and backed up by ground installations. Russian-style air forces attempt to overcome lower pilot skill and aircraft quality by enforcing more strict ground control on their planes. Western air forces equip their aircraft with more capable radar and electronics, train their pilots more intensively, and expect more initiative in the air.

Early on, and still today, ground observers spot enemy air activity and use that information to guide their own aircraft. Radar now does most of the spotting. Not just a single radar but hundreds of them. Information flows to a small number of headquarters, which then issue orders to their far-flung aircraft. The high speeds and vast range of aircraft mean that the air battlefield covers a far larger area than the ground fighting. Soviet experience developed into a rigid, and much discredited, version of this system. The Soviets' aircraft were told when to take off, what direction, speed, and altitude to fly, and where to release their weapons. They were then guided back to their base. Western aircraft are also given precise directions and instructions, but they are also expected to adapt to unexpected conditions. There is always something unexpected in warfare. Russian pilots are now trained in how to deal with unexpected situations. This was a policy that began in the 1980s and continued past the end of the Soviet Union. But the Russian system still uses the old "positive ground control," and this approach still has a number of critical weaknesses. Everything depends on the continued functioning of the ground-based detection and control centers. Although some airborne radar and control aircraft are available, most of this work is still done from the ground. Ground-control radars cannot afford to be off the air for any length of time without leaving the aircraft or antiaircraft systems impotent. Many nations cling to their positive ground-control system in the face of all its shortcomings because the system helps them cope with an even more imposing array of problems, which include:

1. *Technical Inferiority.* The Russian aircraft industry has never been able to produce machines that are as efficient as Western ones. They compensate by building more aircraft and using them less. Russian aircraft are not as durable or maintainable as Western ones. The Soviets, and then Russia, always made progress, but always lagged behind the West. The collapse of the Soviet Union has greatly decreased work on new combat-aircraft designs. Russia is trying to bring its aircraft up to Western technical standards by rejuvenating its civil aviation first. If the ability to freely import Western technology does result in an upgrading of the Russian aviation industry, the next century may see a resurgence of Russia as a major player in combat-aircraft design. But then, maybe not.

2. *Personnel Inferiority.* With a small number of technically competent personnel, the Russians (and their Third World customers) are unable to man their aircraft or staff their maintenance forces at the same level of performance found in the West. All Third World nations suffer from this problem, but they always have the option of buying Western aircraft and hiring Western technicians to help out. But Russian equipment is cheaper, and often all that slender Third World budgets can afford. Russia's own problems are compounded by its larger number of aircraft and their crude design and components that make them more difficult to maintain. The maintenance

load is kept down by flying them fewer hours, less than half as many as in the West. This leads to less experienced pilots. Russia has ace pilots and crack ground crews. It just has a smaller proportion of them than Western air forces.

Reconnaissance Missions

Reconnaissance has always been the primary mission of air power. The use of satellites has not changed this. Looking at reconnaissance from the viewpoint of the consumer, the ground-forces commander, it appears as follows:

1. *Tactical Reconnaissance.* This is for the troops in a combat division, or the area immediately around a naval task force. Much of this is done by low-performance aircraft, prop-driven planes and helicopters, and, increasingly, RPVs (Remotely Piloted Vehicles). This task involves constant monitoring of the enemy when the bad guys are in contact with friendly forces. Most of the observation is done through various forms of photography. Observers in the aircraft are used less often, largely because of more intense ground fire and the superiority of electromechanical observation devices. Unpiloted aircraft (RPVs) are also gradually replacing manned aircraft. Film is also being replaced by TV cameras and sensors that detect heat, electronic signals, movement, and large metal objects. Infrared cameras, for example, can detect camouflaged positions through the unnatural pattern of heat from inorganic or dead vegetation used as camouflage material and warm, yet hidden, vehicles. Especially in Western air forces, these cameras can obtain accurate pictures even though the aircraft is 50 or more miles away from the target. This is done using a lot of computer power to reconstruct the off-angle image obtained. This technique makes it possible to safely observe heavily defended targets. Most non-Western recon aircraft must still fly over the target. This greatly diminishes recon ability because of the generally more capable Western antiaircraft weapons. Sometimes smaller sensors are dropped in enemy territory. In special situations, recon patrols are dropped, to either make their way back on foot or be picked up later. In all cases, information is often broadcast back to friendly forces from patrols, aircraft, and sensors. Tactical reconnaissance loses its value in a short time, often in hours. Tactical reconnaissance missions are usually flown close to the ground to increase the quality of information and, sometimes, to draw the enemy's fire so as to reveal his positions.

   The major shortcoming of aircraft reconnaissance, as revealed in the Gulf War, was that there was not enough of it. There was more than enough aircraft to fight enemy aircraft, but not enough to keep track of what was on the ground before and after the bombers did their work.

The latest generation of satellites (Improved KH-11) that allow for real-time TV pictures of the battlefield have become an important aspect of tactical reconnaissance. The only drawback is that these birds are enormously expensive, and in peacetime no more than two or three will be up at one time. In wartime, these satellites are prime targets, which may mean that none of them will be available. Moreover, these are not stationary satellites, but orbit around the planet. Although the orbits can be changed, the satellites will make only a few passes over the ground below each day.

The information sought by tactical reconnaissance includes location, strength, identification, and activities of enemy units. It is important to evaluate the results of an air strike, ground attack, or artillery barrage. All of the information is passed back to a headquarters where intelligence people sort it out, give the divisional commander something to chew on, and pass useful material on to the combat units. This frequently prompts requests for more information, which starts the cycle anew. Often, the demands for operational and strategic recon, used by higher-ranking commanders, push aside the requests for tactical recon.

2. *Operational Reconnaissance.* This is longer range and less urgent—it's for army and theater commanders. Tactical reconnaissance extends from right in front of your combat troops to about 20 kilometers behind the enemy lines. Operational reconnaissance may extend hundreds of kilometers into the enemy's rear area, as well as your own, if the situation is fluid. The information required is the same as is needed for tactical recon. Because most of the enemy forces you are scouting are not in contact with your troops, there is less immediacy, at least for friendly ground forces. Such is not the case for your air forces and senior ground commanders. Enemy forces not yet in contact can be attacked from the air, and senior commanders must plan how they will deal with these uncommitted enemy forces. Enemy air forces also fall into this area of reconnaissance. Enemy surface-to-surface missile forces must be constantly watched for signs of imminent use. Operational recon uses specially equipped fighter and strike aircraft to perform these missions deep into enemy territory. Special recon aircraft, like the TR-1, are also sometimes used, as well as satellites. Operational recon flights are considered dangerous combat missions because of the large number of enemy defenses that must be penetrated. These recon aircraft typically carry no weapons but instead load up on fuel (for range, and quick acceleration out of a tight spot), ECM (Electronic Countermeasures), as well as cameras and sensors. Recon aircraft depend

primarily on good planning, speed, ECM, and pilot skill to get in and out in one piece. Sometimes there is a fighter escort, but usually it is solo. Flying is customarily at high speed and low altitude, with radio and radar turned off. Using onboard sensors and computers, to monitor enemy radars and radio, the recon pilot roars low and fast over enemy terrain. More advanced recon aircraft use a terrain-following system that automatically guides them quickly at altitudes of a few hundred feet. A computer chooses the safest path through the thicket of enemy defenses. Recon pilots are often combat veterans, who require superb flying skills and steel nerves to get them through these missions. The only thing a recon pilot fights against is detection. The aircraft must often pop up to a higher altitude to get a better look at its objective, or make an extended high-altitude run over an area to get good photographs. Every enemy fighter pilot in the area would love to bag a recon plane. Pilots know that it requires no little courage to go in alone just to take pictures. These pilots are often the best. They have to be, for without their information the armed forces are blind.

3. *Strategic Reconnaissance.* This covers global information. This includes everything that a nation uses to wage war: armed forces, economic strength and resources, etc. In addition, strategic reconnaissance gathers the same types of information gathered by tactical and operational recon. This is long-term and long-range information. This is the type of reconnaissance that takes place most frequently during peacetime. Major nations use satellites for most of this work (see Chapter 20). More traditional means are still heavily used. These include long-range aircraft and electronic eavesdropping. In wartime, many of the aircraft will be vulnerable and therefore useless unless they have sufficient electronic countermeasures to render them invisible to enemy radars. Peacetime use of these aircraft is intensive, with Russian planes operating throughout the world. Only the United States has high-altitude aircraft (TR-1) that can hope to survive over enemy territory in wartime conditions. The United States retired its high-speed, high-altitude SR-71s in 1990, but there is a secret program to develop a replacement for the SR-71 (which was expensive to operate).

4. *JSTARS.* The E-8 JSTARS (Joint Surveillance and Target Attack Radar System), first used during the 1991 Gulf War, ushered in a new era of air reconnaissance. The "Joint" stems from the fact that it is both a U.S. Air Force and U.S. Army system. This is an Airborne Command and Control aircraft. It was not scheduled for regular troop use until 1993–94. But the two prototype models were undergoing testing at the time of the Iraqi invasion. These two developmental aircraft were quickly brought up to active-service status and sent from Europe (where they were being tested) to the Gulf.

Unlike the AWACS, which handles only air operations, the JSTARS has the primary job of tracking ground activity and was designed to better integrate air and ground operations by quickly locating targets for our aircraft and coordinating those attacks with friendly ground operations. The radar is built into the underbelly of a B-707 aircraft. The radar has two modes: wide area (showing a 25 by 20 kilometer area) and detailed (4,000 by 5,000 meters). Each E-8 had 10 radar displays on board plus 15 more on the ground with army headquarters units. All the radar displays could communicate with each other. The radar simultaneously supported both modes and several different chunks of terrain being watched. While an operator might have to wait a minute or two for an update on his screen, this was not a problem because of the relatively slow pace of ground operations. The radar could see out to several hundred kilometers, and each screenful of information could be saved and brought back later to compare to another view. In this manner, operators could track movement of ground units. Operators could also use the detail mode to pick out specific details of ground units (fortifications, buildings, vehicle deployments, etc). For the first time in history, commanders were able to see and control mechanized forces over a wide area in real time. JSTARS could also pass data directly to radar screens in specially equipped strike aircraft (in this case, F-15Es). This allowed quicker and more accurate air strikes.

During the Persian Gulf War, JSTARS performed its designed mission well and speeded up the development process (and guaranteed the spending of billions of dollars on additional JSTARS aircraft). The two E-8s flew 49 missions during Desert Shield and (mostly) Desert Storm, each lasting about 11 hours.

JSTARS (or J-STARS) is now established as the favored means of controlling large ground operations. Combined with ground-based navigation and communications systems like GPS and PLRS, and linked with friendly strike aircraft, JSTARS allows air and ground forces to work together, everyone sharing the same information. Naturally, the JSTARS picture of the ground situation won't be as clear in forested or mountainous terrain, but the data will still be abundant enough to show commanders where major units are. Eventually, 20 JSTARS are to be built. About one a year will be built through the 1990s.

Interception Missions

Soon after reconnaissance was discovered, air-to-air combat followed. Rifle and pistol fire between passing planes soon escalated to fighter aircraft battling each other to gain control of the air. Control meant access for your own recon forces and exclusion of the enemy's. In other words, the successful air warrior gained an all-seeing eye while rendering his opponents blind. This work was called interception: meeting and defeating enemy aircraft before they could return the favor. The basic rules of this air-to-air combat were established more than 70 years ago and have not changed since. In World War I, pilots soon discovered that the key to success and survival was to gain surprise and get the first shot. Dogfighting—high maneuverability, tighter turning, and greater speed—was a poor second choice and typically ended up in a stalemate or random losses. Today, the same basic tactics apply, with a number of important additions and modifications. While individual pilot skill is important, modern air combat is more a matter of teamwork and technology. Longer-range weapons and better communications enable pilots to detect and attack enemy aircraft at longer distances. Today's 30mm automatic cannon allows 800-meter shots compared to 100 meters with 7.62mm machine guns 70 years ago. Missiles allow kills at ranges of up to 200 km, with highly reliable missile kills at ranges of 10–40 km.

From the beginning of air combat, spotting the other fellow first has remained the key to success. Some 80 percent of air kills are the result of the attacker surprising the defender. The victim usually never even sees his attacker. The cardinal rule of air-to-air combat is, hit the other fellow while he isn't looking. Obtain the favorable position (usually high and behind the enemy) and get in the first shot. The average plane-to-plane combat is over in less than 90 seconds. It's not enough to be good—you must be good in a short space of time. When fighter goes up against fighter, the orderly, planned routine of other air operations goes out the window. Successful interception requires aircraft that are technically capable of staying up with the opposition. Pilot skill often becomes the crucial factor. Superior aircraft and inferior pilots generally equal defeat. You don't need a lot of good pilots to prevail. Historical experience has shown that 5 percent of combat pilots account for the majority of the enemy aircraft destroyed. This is a common pattern in all combat situations. Competence is not enough—you need as many of these exceptional pilots as you can muster in order to win control of the air.

All pilots require a wide range of flying skills. Some are obvious, like knowing how to efficiently take an aircraft through a wide range of maneuvers, from tricky landings and takeoffs under bad weather conditions to reacting to unexpected changes in flying conditions and equipment failures. Other skills are seemingly mundane, such as how to do a thorough preflight check on your aircraft. A loose component or an erratic instrument can lead to flying problems. Such problems during combat can be fatal. A very common combat flying problem is fuel management. As a rule of thumb, a fighter can take its total flying range and divide it into thirds: one third for going out ("operating radius"), one third for coming back, and one third for combat. A typical modern fighter can cruise at 900 kilometers per hour. It might have an extreme range of 2,700 kilometers. That gives it a theoretical flying time of three hours. However, high-performance fighters obtain their speed by having an engine that can increase its fuel consumption enormously for short periods. For example, at cruise speed this fighter burns about .56 percent of its fuel per minute. Kicking in the afterburner can more than triple cruise speed and increase fuel consumption more than 20 times. At full "war power," an F-15 can burn up a third of its fuel in less than three minutes. It can also escape from unfavorable situations because of this sudden increase in speed. A less-experienced pilot will abuse the high performance of his aircraft to get him out of one tight situation after another. Once a fighter reaches BINGO fuel (just enough to get home), combat must cease. Otherwise, the aircraft will likely run out of fuel before reaching its base, and be just as useless as if shot down by the enemy. It's a common tactic to try to force the other guy into more high-fuel-consumption maneuvers. Eventually, he will run low on fuel and try to break away. At this point, he becomes desperate and vulnerable.

Several decisive factors must be considered when you're on an interception mission. Each of these elements multiplies the effectiveness of your aircraft, enabling you to achieve a multiplier effect that makes one of your aircraft equal to two or more of the enemy's.

1. The side with superior detection devices and ECM often gets superior position. This is often in the form of airborne warning radar and control systems (AWACS) and superior electronics in the combat aircraft. This can double or triple aircraft effectiveness.

2. Everything being equal, the side with superior tactics gains an advantage or mitigates the other side's electronic advantages. The opening stages of any war provide numerous examples of tactics surprise. The Gulf War was a good example. Some air forces are better able to figure out how best to use their aircraft in combat before the fighting starts. The ability to quickly adapt to new conditions can be an advantage throughout a war, but especially at the beginning. At the beginning of a war, this can double or triple aircraft effectiveness, although it is less of an advantage later in a war.

3. The side with more skilled and resourceful pilots gains a substantial advantage. This can multiply aircraft effectiveness by a factor of 4 or more.

4. The defender has an advantage in requiring less fuel. The defending interceptor can hang around longer and has more fuel to burn in combat. The defender is closer to his bases and can thus land, refuel, and rearm, and more quickly get back into the battle.

5. And then there is the quantity of aircraft multiplied by aircraft quality. Sheer numbers can prevail if the disparity is too great.

6. Excellence in combat-aircraft design is more important than higher speed. Maneuverability is the key.

If one side has a combination of these factors in its favor giving it a 5 to 10 multiplier effect, it can win a virtually bloodless victory. This has happened quite often in the last 50 years. Examples are the Gulf War and the Arab-Israeli wars. Customarily, the results of one side's superiority are manifested by an exchange ratio: How many aircraft are shot down for each one lost. Western aircraft have nearly always achieved a ratio of 5 to 1 or better against Russian equipment. This is not a guarantee of future success, but an indicator of past performance.

Electronic warfare is becoming an increasingly critical element. In the past, one could get past radar and missiles by coming in "low and fast." During the 1980s, the Soviets and the United States have deployed airborne "look down" radars for waiting interceptors and air warning and control (AWACS) aircraft circling hundreds of kilometers inside friendly territory. Western air forces have the edge in this area because of their general technical lead and the need for substantial computing power to pick aircraft out from everything else seen by the radar. The Soviet Union countered a technical disadvantage with numbers; the Soviets maintained more interceptors than the West and could saturate an area with aircraft if need be. Interceptors that can wait on the ground until they are needed have a substantial advantage. This was first shown when the German Air Force attacked Britain in late 1940. The British had the first large-scale radar warning system in place and were able to conserve their outnumbered interceptors. The British only took off when they knew where the Germans were and thus could mass and outnumber separate groups of German aircraft. The Germans were beaten piecemeal, without being able to effectively use their numerical and qualitative superiority. Western air forces have long planned to do the same thing to Russia, or any other opponent, in any future war. Thus far, it appears the West was able to do what it planned to do—at least as far as the Gulf War was concerned.

Strike Missions

Pilots call these "air-to-mud" missions, and for good reason. Going after ground targets is a dangerous and unpredictable mission. There is danger from enemy interceptors, plus all manner of firepower hidden in the landscape below. Finally, there is the ground itself. Fly too low, and you can make an involuntary fatal contact with the ground. At 400 miles an hour, this is not a pretty sight. Aircraft can't hang around long waiting for someone to request their firepower. Air forces prefer to leave fighting ground units to their own devices. Helicopters have increasingly become the favored ground-attack system for front-line combat support. Therefore, most strike missions by fixed-wing aircraft are arranged in advance by intelligence and planning staffs against objectives behind enemy lines. Targets, in approximate order of priority, are aircraft on the ground (where they can't shoot back), air bases, nuclear-weapons systems, radars, antiaircraft systems, fuel and ammo supplies, transportation systems, combat units, and support units.

Flying into enemy airspace is a risky business. High- and low-altitude antiaircraft defenses are numerous. Radars are all over the place. One approach is to sneak in with small (one to four) groups of planes. When you're coming in low, a few hundred meters high or low enough to singe the treetops, the enemy has little time to react before you are past him. When you're zipping along at 200 meters a second, there is not much for the enemy to see, or shoot at. When you're using electronic mapping and navigation devices, the target is found (most of the time), the munitions released, and an equally rapid exit made. Few aircraft are capable of this approach. The electronics are expensive. However, by designing an aircraft for maximum resistance to detection, you end up with a stealth aircraft. Such an airplane has a reasonable chance of penetrating enemy defenses to hit targets with a high degree of surprise. This is important, as the damage done goes down with the amount of warning the target has. Five minutes of warning can reduce air-base damage 40 to 80 percent, depending on how many concrete aircraft shelters the base has.

Without stealth aircraft, you must send in larger groups of aircraft, led by lavishly equipped electronic-warfare planes. This approach will usually succeed in destroying a lot of enemy ground defenses along the way, which makes it easier for subsequent raids. Such a large operation also attracts enemy attention and is expected to sometimes develop into a major air battle. Surprise is lost, and you end up using up to 10 support aircraft for every 1 going after the primary target. The aircraft that lead such raids are called Wild Weasels. They have radar-detection and jamming equipment that can either hide the group from enemy radar or prevent the enemy from making accurate use of its ground-to-air missiles. You will need fighters to deal with enemy interceptors. Thus, the battle can range from 10,000 meters up down to ground level. The Wild Weasels carry missiles that home in on enemy ground radars. The most dangerous opposition comes from enemy guns, which often can fire without radar in clear weather. For this reason, raids at night and in bad weather are often preferred. If all goes according to plan, the Weasels will protect the electronically less sophisticated strike aircraft to the targets, where they release their loads. Everyone then fights his way home past a thoroughly alerted enemy.

The stealth aircraft are well suited to perform the Wild Weasel role. This would be a common mission, as there will be a lot of nonstealth strike aircraft and a need to suppress antiaircraft defenses. For targets where surprise is not critical, stealth-led raids are the norm. This was the case in the Gulf War. Russia was striving, with some success, until the collapse of the Soviet Union in 1991, to catch up with Western strike aircraft in overall sophistication and effectiveness. None of the Russians' new generation of strike planes has been used under combat conditions, so there is no way of knowing how effective they are. They do not yet have a fully functional AWACS, and their Wild Weasel aircraft are somewhat tame compared to Western models. Russian pilots, by and large, are not as expert, experienced, or audacious as their U.S. counterparts.

Fire Control

The major innovation of the 1980s, validated in the 1991 Gulf War, was the precision fire-control systems on strike aircraft. These systems were pioneered in the U.S. F-111 aircraft, where they were built in. The systems consist of FLIR (Forward Looking Infrared Radar) sensors, laser designators, and guided bombs. The system works like this:

1. The FLIR detects differences in the temperature of objects on the ground and presents a picture of this on a TV screen in the cockpit. These were the black-and-white images you saw from precision-bombing runs during the Gulf War. These images are remarkably sharp. Current FLIR have a range of 10–15 km; by the end of the decade some of these may have twice that range. The pilot uses a joystick to select the target on the TV screen and releases the bomb.
2. When the pilot releases the bomb, a laser light is directed at the spot that the pilot's cross hairs cover. The pilot either manually keeps the cross hairs on the target or more complex systems memorize the target shape and "lock" on to the target.
3. The bomb has a sensor in its nose that can detect laser light reflected from the target. The bomb has a set of controllable fins that keep the bomb heading for the reflected laser light until the bomb hits the target.

The first of these precision-bombing systems cost millions of dollars each. But by the end of the 1980s, the FLIR and laser were packaged into pods the size of small bombs weighing 100–500 pounds. These pods cost $500,000 to $1 million. The price comes down with experience and the general reduction of electronic-component costs. Cheaper pods can be made by using a TV set instead of a FLIR, but these are good only for daylight bombing. The U.S. LANTIRN system is the most famous of these pods, but several European nations have built their own. Future developments will put the targeting information on the pilots' HUD (Head Up Display) or displays mounted in the pilot's helmet. These developments are needed to allow single-seat aircraft to more easily use precision bombing. This is because of the short amount of time available to spot the target, put the cross hairs on it, and release the bomb. With the pilot coming in at 200–300 meters a second, and having to release the bomb at least a few kilometers from the target, the 10–15-km range of the FLIR only gives him 20–50 seconds to do the job. One pilot can do it, as the U.S. F-117A demonstrated. But a very easy-to-use system is required.

RPVs, UAVs, and Drones

RPVs (Remotely Piloted Vehicles, now officially known in the United States as UAVs, or Unmanned Aerial Vehicles) and drones (robot pilots) are increasingly popular for their low cost and inability to get human pilots killed. The lack of a pilot saves a lot of weight, making drones and RPVs cheaper than normal aircraft. Moreover, a lot of the RPVs now work as advertised. This was not always the case in the past. For extremely dangerous missions, they are ideal. RPVs are cheaper, but must be guided by a ground-based pilot and can be jammed. Drones don't need external guidance, but still have a way to go before they can completely take care of themselves in the air. Right now, drones are slowly overtaking RPVs and may soon replace them. During the Vietnam War, some 2,000 drones were used. Overall, each drone survived 5 missions, although by the end of the war this rose to 30 flights. Flak accounted for 12 percent of losses. This is high, but reflects the policy of sending drones into risky areas. Another 10 percent were lost during recovery, which reflects the difficulty of landing any aircraft and especially one without a pilot on board. System failure was 5 percent. Again this was high; a human pilot could have taken care of some of these problems. Israel has improved on this experience throughout the last 20 years.

The Gulf War was the most recent, and most revealing, opportunity for RPVs to strut their stuff. The results were impressive. Here are the experiences of each major RPV deployed in the Gulf:

The *Pioneer RPV* is a small, propeller-driven aircraft carrying either TV or infrared (for night work) cameras and flown by a pilot on the ground by remote control (up to 150–200 kilometers away). Israel has used this RPV for over a decade, and the Pioneer is an adaptation of the Israeli RPV first used by the U.S. Navy on its battleships to spot targets for the big 16-inch guns. As a result of the Pioneer's success with the Israelis and the U.S. Navy, it was adopted by the marines and the U.S. Army. Pioneer weighs only 420 pounds and has a top speed of 180 kilometers an hour and a usual operating range of 160 kilometers. It can stay in the air about four hours and flies as high as 15,000 feet, which takes it out of range of small antiaircraft weapons. It's very difficult to spot on a radar and usually cannot be heard on the ground. During the Gulf War, only about 40 Pioneer RPVs were available for use. Two thirds were used by the ground force, mostly the marines. The Pioneers were used as much as their limited supply of spare parts would allow, flying 533 sorties. Each sortie lasted about three hours. Twenty-six Pioneers were damaged, and twelve were destroyed. Two were lost to enemy fire; the rest were lost to accidents. One ran out of fuel and crashed while shadowing a Scud launcher. Several Pioneers were sent more than 100 kilometers into Iraq to search for aircraft on the ground and Scud launchers. The Pioneers were used principally to look for enemy artillery positions and troop bunkers. The Iraqis soon got wise to this and, although the Pioneer's engine sounded like a chain saw, it couldn't be heard very well when the RPV was flying at altitudes of 2,000 feet or higher. When the Pioneer did come lower for a better look, the Iraqis got their licks as best they could. The Pioneer's advantage was that it was under the control of the ground troops and could thus be sent up quickly when the local ground commander felt he needed to get a look at what was going on over enemy territory. In areas where there are a lot of enemy ground troops who could shoot at helicopters, the RPV can go in, look around, and survive. This proved a significant advantage against Iraqi ground units on the Saudi border. The loss rate of RPVs is high compared to manned aircraft, plus an even higher noncombat-loss rate. But then, no pilots were lost, and each Pioneer cost less than 10 percent as much as the cheapest manned reconnaissance aircraft.

The *Pointer RPV* is a shorter-range RPV under test by U.S. Army troops during the summer of 1990. Although the tests were successful, in the Gulf it was not as effective as expected. This was due to a short operating time of one hour and a maximum range of five kilometers from the operator. Altitude was limited to 500–1,000 feet. The light weight of the Pointer (50 pounds) caused it to be blown around by any but the lightest breeze. In the desert, the troops could often see up to five kilometers, thus obviating the need for the Pointer. However, had the fighting continued into built-up areas, the Pointer would have been very useful. The light weight had some advantages; it can be taken anywhere by the troops. The control unit for the Pointer weighs only 50 pounds, making a complete unit only 100 pounds. The troops called it "a 200-foot-tall observer with binoculars." With only black-and-white TV camera available in the Gulf, it was difficult to pick out distant items in the monochrome desert. In the future, a color-TV model is expected to solve the problem.

Several other RPVs were used in the Gulf, including British and French systems used for artillery fire control. One of the more interesting RPVs deployed was the little-known *ExDrone*. The marines used about 55 of these "Expendable Drones," and they performed somewhat like the Pointer. The system worked well, as another 110 were purchased after the war. The TV-equipped ExDrone was used extensively in scouting the way for the marine advance into Kuwait. The marines attributed their fast advance and low casualty rate to timely information from ExDrones.

Originally, drones and RPVs were used largely as targets to give aircraft and antiaircraft weapons realistic practice. More and more, the primary mission of drones and RPVs is reconnaissance, including electronic warfare. Sensors are lighter than bomb loads, and are reusable. Small, flying low and slow, these aircraft are difficult to detect. Target acquisition is a form of reconnaissance and has become a distinct mission. Advances in electronics have made it possible for the artillery to see what the RPV sees. High flight endurance enables the RPVs to stay over the battle area and give the artillery continuous information on new targets and the effectiveness of fire. Drones and RPVs also have an imporant role in air combat, even without being armed. Electronic gear can be carried that will detect enemy radars. Piloted aircraft can then fire antiradiation missiles, or other munitions, to destroy the enemy radars and missiles. New drones are being developed that will perform the antiradiation mission itself.

While the original research work was done by the United States, Israel has taken the lead in use and development of RPVs. Other nations are now developing their own. This is happening because rapid advances in technology make it possible to build very capable RPVs at relatively low cost. The West appears to have maintained an increasing advantage in this area. There wasn't a lot of drone and RPV activity in the former Soviet Union until the 1980s. During the late 1980s, Russian drones were being used by Syria, but not with a lot of success.

There is still a major problem with drones, and to a lesser extent RPVs. These machines have the potential for taking away pilots' jobs. One man's technological breakthrough is another man's career threat. Few people in the air force will come right out and admit this. Yet half hearted enthusiasm for drones in many air forces can be traced back to pilots' unease over their becoming too effective. This is ironic, as the air forces themselves had to fight similar prejudice from the cavalry, artillery, and navy in the early years of combat aviation.

Theory and Practice

There have been two kinds of air war with modern equipment. The most common is a situation where not a lot of aircraft are available. Operations are sporadic, and often one side does not even have an air force. The Falklands, Lebanon, and the 1980–88 Persian Gulf Wars are examples of sporadic air war. Afghanistan and other counterinsurgency conflicts are typical situations in which only one side has an air force. The other kind of air war is the one most air-force money and energy are spent on. The premier example of this was the effort the Allies put forth in the 1991 Gulf War. That war saw over 2,000 Allied combat aircraft flying over 100,000 sorties in six weeks in the most intense air campaign since World War II. These air forces had been preparing since the late 1940s to fight an even larger air battle in Central Europe, where on either side of a 500-kilometer border were 2,600 NATO and 3,000 Warsaw Pact combat aircraft. In addition, the former Soviet Union had nearly 4,000 additional combat aircraft between Moscow and Russia's western borders. NATO had a smaller number available as reinforcement. This battle was never fought, but the 1991 Gulf War demonstrated how well Western air forces were prepared to fight it.

Another rather murky situation exists with long-range air-to-air missiles. This weapon has existed for over 30 years but has yet to overcome the problem of obtaining positive identification of targets the pilot cannot see with his own eyes. In theory, each aircraft carries an IFF (Identification, Friend or Foe) device that makes it easy to sort out the good guys and bad guys. Until the Gulf War, and the first use of AWACS control aircraft, pilots preferred to trust their eyeballs and get in close with cannon or short-range missiles. In the Gulf War, pilots felt confident to use long-range missiles, and did so with good effect.

The Future

The combat power of bombing is becoming more decisive. In World War II, the British bomber force, attacking mainly at night (without escorts) over a six-year period (1939–45) dropped 955,000 tons of bombs in 199,000 sorties, losing 6,400 aircraft in the process. During Vietnam, a much smaller number of aircraft flew 100,000 sorties and dropped 226,000 tons of bombs with much smaller losses in 1966. In 1991, 2,000 aircraft flew 108,000 sorties to drop 88,000 tons of bombs in six weeks with minuscule losses. Moreover, the accuracy of the bombing has increased dramatically since 1966, after making little progress since World War II. The accuracy of bombing continues to make greater strides during the 1990s as the computerized bombing systems get cheaper, more capable, and equip more aircraft.

Until 1991, the primary focus of future developments was the new generation of U.S. fighters and the "stealth" aircraft. Principal among these is the ATF (Advanced Tactical Fighter), now flying in prototype as the F-22, which will replace the F-14 and F-15 eventually. Before 1991, the F-22 was scheduled for introduction during the mid 1990s, but now it's looking more like the late 1990s or early in the next century. Among the new features of the F-22 are that it is more "stealthy" and easier to maintain and has improved electronics and "supercruise" (allow high cruise speed at relatively low fuel consumption).

The U.S. Navy also planned to have a new attack aircraft to replace the A-6 at that time. The rest of NATO was trying to develop their own ATF. The demise of the Soviet Union in 1989–91 put all these projects in jeopardy. The shrinkage of the former Soviet Air Forces, the collapse of the Soviet R&D effort for new aircraft, and the revelations that new Soviet aircraft weren't so great after all made it impossible to maintain budgets for new Western aircraft developments. The F-22 may not see regular use until the end of the century, if ever. The navy had to cancel its new attack aircraft, largely because of budget problems. The Europeans are slowly killing their own ATF program.

The other big initiative is *stealth* aircraft. The United States has already deployed the F-117A attack aircraft while the more ambitious B-2 stealth bomber may not get beyond a dozen aircraft built. The last stealth aircraft built is the Aurora. Originally conceived as a high-speed, high-altitude replacement for the SR-71, Aurora also has stealth and combat capabilities. Officially announced in 1993, Aurora is one of the last of the U.S. Air Force's series of "Black" (secret) projects. Most of these secret projects were finally revealed to the public in 1993, yet another result of the Cold War's end.

The U.S. Army continues to upgrade its attack helicopter (the AH-64) and will rebuild several hundred of its current models by the end of the decade to include the "Longbow" millimeter-wave radar system and a more powerful fire-control system and "fire and forget" Hellfire missiles to go along with it. This will make the AH-64 an all-weather attack aircraft on a par with anything any air force has. While budget cuts may slow this project down, the R&D has been completed, and all that is required to produce the new AH-64 is the money to rebuild old ones.

Russia began introducing its latest generation of combat aircraft in the late 1980s, about 10–15 years behind the West. As is customary with the Russians, their aircraft are larger, heavier, and less efficient. For example, the Su-27, introduced in 1987 after nine years of flight-testing, is roughly equivalent to the F-15 and F-14. However, the Su-27 is 20 percent heavier than the F-15, much less reliable, and carries missiles heavier than their more effective Western equivalents. The next Russian generation of aircraft, the Su-37, was originally planned for introduction a few years after the ATF (F-22). But new aircraft research has atrophied in the economic upheaval that followed the collapse of the Soviet Union. Russian Air Force officers speak gamely of their next generation of aircraft appearing "sometime early in the next century."

While improvements in combat performance are being stressed in the new generation of aircraft, greater emphasis is being placed on the more mundane areas of maintainability, reliability, and ease of use. There is good reason for emphasis on getting more out of these new planes, as their cost will be almost double that of the current models, so there will be fewer of them. For example, F-15/16–class aircraft must spend 30 minutes on the ground between combat sorties; the ATF is looking to cut that in half. The same applies for the number of aircraft unavailable because of repairs. The current rate is about 15 percent; the ATF is aiming for 2 percent. The speed with which malfunctioning aircraft can be repaired is also critical. Currently, only about 45 percent of malfunctions can be fixed in less than four hours. The ATF hopes to increase this to 75 percent. Compared to aircraft 20 years ago, or current Russian aircraft, improvements like these are not unreasonable. For example, current U.S. carrier aircraft have accidents at a rate giving pilots a 5–10 percent chance of being killed or disabled in a major accident during their flying careers. Twenty years ago, pilots had a better than 50 percent chance of coming to grief. These experiences carry over into combat, where minor accidents often become major during the heat of battle. These improvements also make more aircraft available for combat, and give an often decisive edge in battle.

Ease of use has become a key factor in combat performance. For years, aircraft cockpits have increasingly come to look like video arcades. But as useful as all these displays have become, the pilot still had to be looking forward to use them. The latest wrinkle is to build a CRT inside the helmet's visor. Testing has shown this technique more than doubles the number of air-to-air kills. New sensors that can be built into the skin of aircraft will further multiply the effectiveness of better displays. These trends also show that pilots are gradually being replaced by automation. Aircraft crews have been reduced more than 50 percent in the last 40 years. World War II heavy bombers had a crew of twelve. The 1950s B-52 needs six crewmen, the 1970s B-1 needs four, and the B-2 only a pilot and weapons operator. Advances in computer technology, sensors, robotics, and artificial intelligence have made a pilotless drone interceptor possible, and likely, in the next decade. Meanwhile, Western air forces are beginning to equip aircraft with "pilot associates," computer-based systems that take over the more routine and technical aspects of flying and communicate with the pilot in a spoken language. Many tasks that previously required a button pushed can now be executed with a spoken command. Tests in actual cockpits have demonstrated accuracy of 98 percent, which is higher than many human crews are capable of. Typical tasks for spoken commands and electronic ears are requests for information on aircraft condition or changing the status of a sensor or weapon system. A typical speech system can recognize three dozen commands, including seven in slurred speech common during high-stress maneuvers. Silicon copilots also use computers to constantly collect and examine information from the dozens of sensors on board. These sensors range from the familiar fuel gauge to radar and radar-warning devices. Often overlooked are the numerous calculations and decisions pilots must make in flight. For example, on an interception mission, the pilot must decide how best to approach distant enemy aircraft. Radar will usually spot other aircraft long before weapons can be used or the target can be seen visually. There may also be ground-based missile systems aiming radars at you. These conditions present several options: Should you go after the enemy aircraft with long-range missiles? Or speed up and engage with more accurate cannon and short-range missiles? You also have to worry about your own fuel situation and which of your systems might be malfunctioning. The AI (Artificial Intelligence) computer's memory contains the experiences of many more experienced pilots as well as instant information on the rapidly changing situation. You can ask your electronic assistant what the options are and which one has the best chance of success. The pilot can then make decisions more quickly and accurately. When enemy aircraft are sighted, the electronic assistant can suggest which of the many maneuvers available are likely to work. If the aircraft is damaged, the electronic copilot can rapidly report what the new options are. One becomes quite fond of computers once they have saved your bacon a few times.

Once the robotic copilot is in use, someone will calculate the expense of training human pilots ($5–$10 million) and making space for them in costly aircraft (another $1–$5 million), and decide to go with all-silicon aircrew. More pressing reasons exist for getting rid of human pilots—they restrict the capabilities of the aircraft. When high-performance aircraft twist and turn violently, there is always the possibility that the pilot will black out and lose consciousness from the stress. This "blackout" factor is currently a major limitation in aircraft design. Before robotic combat aircraft come into use, there will be more capable reconnaissance and attack drones. There are now long-range recon drones, using navigation satellites, which enable them to fly in complete electronic silence. Western cruise missiles are the prototypical robotic strike aircraft, while air-to-air homing missiles increasingly contain the needed technology for robotic interceptors. Upcoming antiradar missiles will loiter in the area for up to an hour waiting for enemy radar to come on. The U.S. Navy is particularly keen on robotic aircraft to take the recon load off increasingly expensive manned aircraft. Current trends indicate that robotic pilots will sort of drift casually into use. All of a sudden, they will be all over the place. The first nation to get effective robotic pilots into the air will have a considerable advantage. Such advantages win battles, and wars.

Robots on the ground are also playing a greater role in air warfare. Mission planning has long been the bane of combat operations. This planning consists of working out all the mundane navigation and fuel/weapons load questions before the aircraft take off. This mission planning was in turn driven by the overall strategy the air commander was pursuing, and this in turn was modified by what was known about the enemy capabilities and intentions. During the 1980s, the U.S. Air Force (USAF) took the lead in this area and developed two techniques that have changed the way air campaigns are conducted. These items are:

The Air Tasking Order, which is a computer-supported system that enables the commander to quickly sort out the targets to be hit and the aircraft available. The completed ATO efficiently combined the high command's decisions on what it wanted air power to do on a particular day and the air commander's appraisal of what would be available and how these resources could best be used. Creating the entire ATO by computer and issuing it to the units a day before it is to be used is a recent innovation.

An interconnected system of computers figured out all the tedious (and complex) details such as:

- Where and when each aircraft would fly
- How much fuel it would take off with (and where and when it would refuel in the air with a tanker)
- What weapons would be carried
- What targets would be attacked
- Which aircraft would fly together in a mission package

Details of which pilots would be in the aircraft were left to the air units. The units reported the percentage of their aircraft that were available to fly (usually between 80 and 95 percent), and the ATO computer program would take care of this. Currently, an ATO is transmitted to the air units in electronic form at least 24 hours before the day the ATO was to be used. Most people using the ATO will only see it on a computer screen. The AWACS aircraft will often be the heaviest users of the ATO, as they must make sure aircraft in the air are where they are supposed to be when they are supposed to be there. The ATO controls nearly all U.S. Air Force, Navy, Marine, and (if available) Allied fixed-wing aircraft. Helicopters, with a few exceptions, are not included in the ATO. Some marine aircraft and all attack helicopters are controlled by the ground-combat units they belonged to. The USAF would like to get the attack helicopters and marine fighter bombers under ATO control, but the army and marines insist that the current ATO requires too much time (48 hours) to prepare. This question of ATO control is a quasi-political one, and when the ATO gets its preparation time down to hours, more attack helicopters and marine aircraft will probably make use of it.

The Mission Planning System (MPS) provides pilots with essential mission information before they climb into their aircraft. Current MPS developed, during the 1980s, from a basically manual system to a largely automated one. The basics of mission planning consist of information the pilot needs to find the target, how to attack it, and how to avoid the enemy. Seventy-five years ago, pilots were told roughly what the situation was; then aircraft would go out individually or in small groups to engage enemy air and ground forces. This impromptu approach rapidly escalated over the next 25 years into "mission planning." From the 1950s, the U.S. Air Force used a complex, and largely manual, planning procedure for preparing pilots and aircraft for their increasingly complex missions. This planning includes items like:

- How much fuel can be carried (less fuel means more munitions)
- Where air refueling will take place (if needed)
- The best approach to the target
- The best weapons to carry

- Which aircraft will be in what position to the others during the flight
- Who will do what under different circumstances
- Potential enemy opposition is taken into account.

In the 1980s, the microcomputer revolution entered the process, and in 1986 the air force began installing computer-based MSS ("Mission Support Systems.") Aside from taking a large workload off the pilots, MSS allows for more effective mission planning and execution. For most aircraft, pilots can work out their flight plan on a computer, take a tape of the PC-generated plan, insert the tape into the aircraft computer, and eliminate a lot of the guesswork and rough calculation. Going into the 1990s, the USAF is introducing more powerful microcomputers and workstations, as well as new software, that allow the pilot to simulate flying the combat mission. This looks much like the air-combat simulators you can buy for personal computers. Thus, pilots combine training, practice, and planning on the same machine. The new MSS allows pilots to:

- Graphically see what the target will look like on radar, as well as a computer-generated color "movie" of what the mission will look like from the cockpit. Pilots prefer the movie.
- Make the hundreds of instrument settings (required before takeoff) on the MSS and then insert the MSS tape into the aircraft computer and have all the settings made automatically. This allows for faster takeoff.
- Practice the bomb runs, taking into account the nature of the target and weapons used. For example, the MSS will calculate the safe altitude and speed to avoid damaging the bomber when the target is hit.
- As with the older systems, the data can then be written to a tape for transfer to the aircraft's computer.

By the mid-1990s, the USAF will have several hundred of the new MSS. Some of these will be used by army and navy aviation units. By the end of the decade, all U.S. and some foreign air-force units will have MSS, making these units more effective than those that do not. While pilots have a reputation for being carefree, they are actually the most methodical of warriors. At least the ones that come back in one piece are.

JTIDS (Joint Tactical Integrated Data System) is the glue that will tie together U.S. Air Force, Navy, and Army aircraft control systems. JTIDS is basically a computer workstation and data network that takes data from AWACS, ship radars, ground radars, and combat aircraft systems and passes it to everyone in the network (which can cover over a million square miles). This will enable everyone to have all information available, including the status of friendly aircraft in the air (fuel and weapons available, etc.). JTIDS will be operational by the mid-1990s. Over 1,000

JTIDS systems are to be purchased, at a cost of over half a million dollars each.

A big breakthrough this decade will be in passive radar. This type of system is based on infrared (IR) or passive millimeter-wave technology and fast signal processing. The ability to sense other characteristics besides heat (IR), such as magnetism and sound, are also being developed. For the moment, however, IR "passive radars" are already performing quite well in the laboratory, and the Russians have equipped their MiG-29 fighter with one that apparently works. The current generation of Western IR air-to-air missiles uses a reliable IR radar that can track the heat from an aircraft at any angle and over several kilometers, although problems exist with clouds degrading the heat signal. For this reason, the first passive IR radars will be used in conjunction with conventional radars. There is a great urgency in this area, because missiles that home in on active radars are becoming more common and effective. Passive radars are also an important component of the new generation of air-to-air missiles. A short-range passive sensor, the IR homing device in short-range missiles, has been used for more than 30 years. Longer-range missiles have always required guidance from the aircraft or extremely expensive and space-consuming active radars. Neither of these solutions has been very effective. Progress marches on, however, and smaller components and more powerful microcomputers have made possible missiles like the AMRAAM. Aside from being much lighter than the AIM-7 Sparrow missile it replaces, AMRAAM can find the target on its own without constant guidance from the launching aircraft. AMRAAM has several ways to find its target. In addition to its own search radar, its onboard computer can be told the predicted position of its target. Once launched, the AMRAAM speeds off to this position, and if the target is not immediately found searches for it. This is what torpedoes have been doing for more than 50 years. But then, torpedoes weigh several tons and move a lot more slowly.

Without exception, most air forces see "BVR (Beyond Visual Range) engagements" as the primary means of future victories. Both air-to-air and air-to-ground weapons stress BVR capability. In the air, this requires pilots to trust their sensors to sort out friend from foe. Historically, they have been reluctant to do this. As a fallback, more effective short-range missiles are being developed. The latest version of the U.S. Sidewinder can be fired at a target from any angle and has proven very effective in combat. The longer-range BVR missiles will probably end up being used sporadically for well-planned aerial ambushes. On the ground, the situation is even more dependent on sensors. Hitting ground targets from the air has always been more art than science, and there were never enough artists to go around. In the last 20 years, the technology has come of age, as the 1986 U.S. raid on Tripoli and the 1991 Gulf War demonstrated. These operations also confirmed that accuracy is relative no matter how mature these weapons are. The navigation systems on attack aircraft are becoming quite accurate and reliable. But moving along near the ground at 100–200 meters a second leaves little room for timely pilot action. If the target's position is stationary and known, you can literally program it into the automatic pilot and go along for the ride. This is becoming more common. The "standoff," or BVR, weapons also have their own guidance system, or use other sensors, to actually hit the target. A further acknowledgment of inaccuracy is the common use of cluster weapons, thus ensuring that the target will be hit with something. Easy-to-locate targets like bridges, airfields, and other installations are still the favorite prey of fixed-wing aircraft. On the battlefield itself, helicopters are becoming the air-to-ground weapon of choice. A current innovation is the "look and shoot" helmet, which has a display built into the visor and linked to cannon and rocket pods. When the pilot sees something worth hitting, he just looks and pushes a button and that's it.

Another continuing problem with long-range engagements is making sure you are not firing at your own people. IFF (Identify, Friend or Foe) devices have never really worked as intended, and pilots don't trust them. These gadgets will, on pilot command, send a signal to a suspected target. If the target is a friendly aircraft, its IFF device will respond with the correct code. This system has several serious flaws. If the IFF device fails or malfunctions, you get shot at. The aircraft using IFF is sending out signals that enable the enemy to find you. ECM can be used to deceive IFF devices. All these problems are being addressed, in the laboratory. It may be awhile before an IFF device that pilots will use appears. While long-range engagements are preferred, all previous predictions of long-range ambush taking over the air have proven premature until the first combat use of the AWACS aircraft. These radar-equipped control aircraft can more effectively direct friendly aircraft over enemy territory and give the pilots confidence that their far-distant aerial targets are not friendlies. The Gulf War was the first opportunity to test this system. The system worked, and air combat will never be the same.

Close-range combat continues to be a possibility, however, and success depends on agility. Opposing the streamlined stealth shapes are designs that feature a lot of extra little wings, fins, and other devices that allow unheard-of maneuvers. To give aircraft more agility, microcomputing power is again called upon to control the aircraft flaps and control surfaces more rapidly than any human pilot possibly could. This maneuverability also allows more efficiency in landing, taking off, and flying at high speed with high-fuel efficiency. A fighter that can turn on a dime and tilt up 45 degrees without falling like a rock equals a formidable dogfighter. The key to these designs is that they contain enough computing power to prevent the aircraft from spinning out of control. A major loss of F-4 aircraft in Vietnam was from early model F-4s trying to keep up with more nimble MiGs. Various Western high-maneuverability aircraft designs are in development, and many forms of computer-driven "stability control" are already deployed. The B-2 takes full advantage of this approach, as its flying wing shape is inherently unstable. Other aircraft that make partial use of this technology are the F-16 (in pitch, anyway), EFA, Rafale, ATF, and the Swedish Grippen. An additional advantage of this technology is the ability to operate from shorter, or damaged, airfields. A new generation of engines will allow combat aircraft to fly very high and fast, like the SR-71, without requiring enormous quantities of fuel. Combining this with stealth technology makes these high and fast aircraft more difficult to spot with radar, or hit with radar-guided missiles. The replacement for the SR-71 will basically be a high-altitude and high-speed stealth aircraft. Without an announced replacement, the SR-71 was retired in 1990. It is too expensive to operate, over five times the cost of a fighter, and most of its missions can be undertaken by satellites.

Helicopters have finally arrived, as they are now being used for nearly every task that fixed-wing aircraft perform. Helicopter gunships are being equipped with air-to-air missiles for use against other helicopters as well as fixed-wing fighters. Helicopters loaded with electronics wage electronic warfare. This last task is being complemented in the United States by a new version of the Vietnam-era gunship based on the C-130 transport. This version carries 20mm and 40mm automatic cannon as well as a 105mm howitzer. Soon this gunship will also carry Hellfire missiles. Multiplying the effect of this firepower is a full load of sensors and electronic-warfare equipment. The crew sit in air-conditioned, armored comfort while unleashing all that firepower. There are only going to be 20 of these aircraft, and they will be risky to use in areas where the targets have much anti-aircraft capability. Against poorly armed insurgents, however, they can be devastating. The U.S. Army is also modifying several dozen of its helicopters by adding more sensors and weapons so that they can more effectively support commando operations.

Developing new aircraft is becoming more difficult. An obvious problem is the greater expense needed for increasingly complex technology. The other problem is managing complex technology and equally intricate development projects. Russia has always had problems with the technology, being required to steal or copy most of the cutting-edge stuff from the West. Even after the demise of the Soviet Union, Russian military-intelligence agents continued to go after Western military technology. Western nations are finding that increasingly they can't afford the neat new goodies they are developing.

The number of combat aircraft available has been steadily declining since 1945. The next generation of combat jets will cost over $50 million each, with the number built up to half as much as the current generation. Attack helicopters are also escalating in price. The U.S. Army's current fleet of 9,000 will shrink to less than half that by 1996 and less than a third by 2005. All of this shrinkage is a result of more expensive models. The overall capabilities of aircraft fleets have increased, along with a decline in operational accidents. Indications are that the robotic aircraft will be a natural end product of these trends. Meanwhile, the above new technologies are being integrated into upcoming aircraft. Within 10 years, much of the above will be the norm. The high cost, however, will cause many of these improvements to be built into existing aircraft instead. An effective, although not entirely popular, method of increasing aircraft performance is the installation of new components. Because engines wear out relatively quickly, upgrading these is a favorite exercise. Electronics tend to get smaller and lighter, so new items are not difficult to fit in. Helicopters in particular have always been upgraded over time to the point where they were practically rebuilt. Western firms are having a good time upgrading Third World nations' Russian aircraft, which have sturdy structures but unreliable engines and substandard electronics. Another option increasingly favored by rich and poor nations alike is to use more low-performance aircraft for specific missions. This has been done for several decades, with jet trainers being converted to ground attack or interception aircraft. Another future trend is for many Third World nations to design and build their own low-performance aircraft, thereby depriving the major arms producers of export markets and driving up the cost of the already expensive high-performance aircraft because of smaller production runs.

One thing that will not change is the enormous lead Western aircraft possess over those built in Russia or Third World nations. When Western nations introduced their current generation of high-performance aircraft 10 years ago, Russia decided to attempt matching this technology. The results of these attempts began to appear in the late 1980s. This new generation of Russian aircraft was a mixed success. The most ambitious aircraft, the Blackjack (B-1 bomber clone) and Su-27 (F-14/15 clone) encountered repeated delays as technical problems kept turning up. The Su-27 spent over 10 years in development and was not ready for mass production until 1988. The Blackjack was in development longer and eventually suffered the same fate as the Russian supersonic transport (Tu-144 "Concordski") by being quietly abandoned. When the Russians do get a high-tech weapon into service, they manage to cope using a combination of sturdy, simple, and brute-force equipment, plus willingness to accept high accident rates. Russian technology is not crude, just simple. The Russians possess some very talented scientists and engineers but lack large-scale manufacturing capability for complex equipment. Although their weapons factories turn out a higher proportion of "lemons" than Western ones, the stuff that does work performs surprisingly well. Another characteristic of the Russians that is not well appreciated in the West is their ruthless attitude toward accidents and equipment failures in general. While Western air forces suffer 4 to 10 serious combat aircraft accidents per 100,000 flying hours, the Russian rate is from three to five times higher. That's another reason why they don't use their aircraft as much in peacetime. In wartime, like most other nations, they will send up a lot of aircraft with malfunctioning equipment. But this is why the Russians go for quantity. Their approach may even work in high-tech warfare. With all the Russian aircraft being exported, let's hope we don't have to find out.

There is another new development that may enable us to realistically fight the next war without actually doing so. Dissimilar training and simulation have become an ever more crucial advantage in Western air forces. Flight simulators have been used for more than 50 years, but in the last decade increases in computer power have made possible highly realistic combat-aircraft simulators. Although these machines cost nearly as much as the aircraft they simulate, they are much cheaper to operate. Upcoming are much cheaper simulators, for the same reason microcomputer prices are declining. Already, over a dozen simulators can be electronically linked so that groups of aircraft can fight each other. Of more import is the new ability to operate against accurate aircraft and tactics used by other nations. This works well with a 20-year-old U.S. program to train pilots in the air against "aggressor" aircraft and pilots using the different equipment and tactics pilots can expect in wartime. These training advantages, added to the greater flying time Western pilots get, have proved a critical advantage for Western pilots in recent years.

Fighters, Bombers, and Recon Aircraft

Chart 7-1 shows the capabilities of over 40,000 combat aircraft. These comprise over 90 percent of those available worldwide. Included are helicopters possessing some combat capability. Increasingly, helicopters are taking over ground-support duties. Moreover, helicopters are being armed with air-to-air missiles so they may attack other helicopters and fixed-wing aircraft. Long regarded as little more than flying trucks, helicopters are making the lower altitudes their own exclusive territory. The only helicopter types shown are U.S. and Russian, as these represent over 75 percent of those in use. The remaining machines are manufactured by other Western nations (Britain, France, Italy, etc.) and tend to follow American design practice. The helicopters of these nations have been added to similar types shown in the chart. Not included are training, supply, and reconnaissance aircraft. This gets a bit tricky, as these other aircraft can, and sometimes do, serve as combat vehicles. Indeed, many of the helicopters shown on the chart are primarily transports. However, because they operate so close to the combat zone, transport helicopters are usually armed and frequently have ample opportunities to use their weapons.

COMMON NAME is what people customarily call the aircraft. Often, but not always, the name is officially recognized. Examples of unofficial names are Warthog, Aardvark, and BUFF (Big Ugly Fat Fellow). Russian names are those assigned by NATO. These NATO-assigned names will apparently remain for a while, particularly because the Russians did not always give their aircraft names, and what names they have assigned have never become widely known in the West.

DESIGNATION is an American and Russian convention. European aircraft normally just employ names. American designations indicate primary function of the aircraft (F = Fighter, A = Strike [or Attack], H = Helicopter). Russian designations refer to the design bureau responsible for developing the aircraft. The Russians also use odd numbers to indicate fighters and even numbers for bombers. The designation given here for any aircraft is for the primary model. Several variants are generally produced. Unless a variant is drastically different or produced in large quantities, it is not shown separately. The values shown are usually a composite for all aircraft of that type.

AIRCRAFT TYPES FOUND IN CHART

A-10: U.S. ground-support aircraft. The air force loves to bomb, but not in a combat zone. Enemy troops shoot back, and an aircraft has to be armored to survive. The A-10 was the U.S. Air Force solution to this problem. Although the air force would prefer to sidestep direct support of combat troops, it is reluctant to let the army have fixed-wing combat aircraft. Although the A-10 did exceptionally well in its combat debut during the Gulf War, its slow speed and ground-attack weapons make it different from other air-force combat aircraft. The air force is reluctant to build a replacement and has even expressed a willingness to transfer its A-10s to the army. All this may be moot, as the helicopter is increasingly the primary source of air support for ground troops.

A-4: Predecessor of the A-6. A lightweight carrier bomber. Saw extensive combat in Vietnam and in the Israeli Air Force.

A-6E: Principal U.S. Navy bomber. Heavy reliance on electronics, long range, and carrying capacity contribute to its long-term success.

A-7E: Light bomber originally used by U.S. Air Force and Navy. Being phased out.

AH-1S: Substantially improved version of the AH-1G (the first helicopter gunship, which was, in fact, a heavily modified UH-1). There are still a few AH-1Gs in use, but their number is rapidly declining.

AH-1W: USMC version of the AH-1. A much enhanced AH-1S, particularly the use of two engines instead of one.

AH-64: Second-generation U.S. helicopter gunship.

AV-8B: The original STOL (Short Take Off and Landing) fighter bomber. Can also take off like a helicopter. Saw its first action in the 1982 Falklands War, where it proved even more capable than originally predicted.

Alpha: Inexpensive light bomber.

B-1B: U.S. long-range bomber, designed to use low flying and ECM to penetrate heavy defenses. A very complex system that has had a lot of growing pains.

B-2: The "stealth bomber." The first aircraft to cost more than most warships.

B-52: Basic U.S. long-range bomber since the 1950s. Its electronics have been vastly upgraded, and many now carry cruise missiles.

CH-46E: U.S. Marine Corps helicopter transport.

CH-47: Medium helicopter transport. Being phased out.

CH-53D: Primary U.S. Marine Corps helicopter transport.

CH-53E: Substantially upgraded version of primary U.S. Marine Corps helicopter transport.

F-22: The U.S. ATF (Advanced Tactical Fighter), which is to be the premier fighter by the turn of the century.

F-104: A 1950s design. Contemporary of the MiG-21, but not as successful. Still used by some U.S. allies who have not been able to afford a replacement yet. All will probably be out of service by 2000.

F-111: Principal U.S. medium-range bomber and the model for the larger B-1.

F-117A: Otherwise known as the stealth fighter. This is a rarity in the West, a secret aircraft-development project. The Russians probably knew more about it than the American public, assuming they were able to get a photo satellite into position when these things were flying. This is not really a fighter in the same sense as the F-16, F-18, and F-15. Its function is more akin to the A-6. In addition to a heavy load of electronic devices, largely passive, the F-117A is designed to present a very small target to radar. Like the human eye, radar can see larger targets farther away. A B-52 is the aerial equivalent of an aircraft carrier to a radar; the F-117A appears as a small speedboat. Typical missions for the F-117A are destroying SAM sites or heavily defended targets. Reconnaissance is also an ideal mission. As a fighter, the F-117A would, and probably could, have to get the first shot in if equipped with the right sensors and missiles. This is not a very fast or particularly maneuverable aircraft, so it would have to hit first and then slink away. Veteran fighter pilots prefer this approach anyway, which is why they are veterans.

F-14: Principal U.S. Navy interceptor. Actually designed around its expensive long-range Phoenix missiles. Primary job is defending the fleet and especially the carriers.

F-15: Most effective Western interceptor. Can also be used as a fighter bomber.

F-15E: A new two-seat version of the F-15 was developed primarily for ground attack. The F-15E did very well in the Gulf War.

F-16: The most numerous Western interceptor. Can also function as a bomber and ground-attack aircraft, although not as effectively as the air-force folks would have you believe. Originally designed as a cheaper alternative to the heavier F-15.

F-18: Replaces the A-7 aboard U.S. carriers (as the "F/A-18," with the *A* indicating ground-attack capability). Functions as both an interceptor and bomber. Basically, a two-engine version of the F-16, which is why the navy took the F-18, and the air force the cheaper F-16. The navy prefers two-engine aircraft for carrier operations; it's safer when operating over water.

F-22: The new U.S. ATF (Advanced Tactical Fighter). Not expected to enter service until after 2000. About a dozen will fly in the 1990s for testing and development purposes. With the F-22s costing more than $60 million each, the United States probably won't be able to afford more than a few hundred (less than half what the USAF is asking for). Russia and a consortium of Western European nations are each working on their own version, but because of the cost, neither project is likely to threaten the technical superiority of the F-22. While not invincible, the F-22 is capable enough to dominate any air battle it enters.

F-4: The predecessor of the F-15. The F-4 is an early 1960s design that has been upgraded considerably. Still a capable aircraft and widely used. A classic design that proved very capable in combat.

F-5: Designed and built by the United States as an inexpensive interceptor for nations with tight budgets and insufficient technical manpower to support more complex aircraft. Roughly equal to the MiG-21.

F-6/A-5: A Chinese-built copy of the MiG-19. Comes in ground attack (A-5) and interceptor (F-6) versions. An inexpensive alternative for less wealthy nations, including China.

F-7: A Chinese-built copy of the MiG-21. Many being equipped with Western electronics and engines. This makes it a considerably improved MiG-21.

F-8: Chinese two-engine variant of the MiG-21.

Jaguar: British-French joint effort. Basically a ground-attack bomber.

Ka-50: New Russian attack helicopter. Unique in that it has a crew of one. Western helicopter designers are dubious that the Russians can achieve enough onboard automation to allow one pilot to do it all. Not likely to be produced in large numbers.

Kfir: An upgraded version of the original Mirage III. Designed and manufactured by Israel.

Mi-24: Russian helicopter gunship. Originally designed primarily as an armed transport, but soon modified to emphasize the gunship role.

Mi-6: Russian medium-helicopter transport. An old design but still widely used.

Mi-8: Earliest successful Russian combat helicopter. Although larger, for many years served as Russian version of the UH-1. An improved version is called the Mi-17, and a naval version is the Mi-14.

MiG-21: A 1950s design, the most widely produced post–World War II fighter. Cheap, and easy to maintain. Many nations keep them in service for that reason, and because a wide range of avionics and weapons upgrades are available.

MiG-23: Russian version of F-4 in air-defense role.

MiG-25: Originally designed as a high-altitude interceptor, ended up as a reconnaissance aircraft, with secondary air-defense duties.

MiG-27: Russian version of F-4 in ground-attack role.

MiG-29: Russian version of F-16. A navalized version has been produced to operate Russia's only heavy aircraft carrier.

MiG-31: Upgraded version of MiG-25. Primarily for air defense. Being phased out.

MiG-33: Looks like the MiG-29, but built of different materials, uses a different engine, and has a much improved set of avionics. An attempt to get something into the air to counter the U.S. F-22.

Mirage 2000: Latest in the line of French interceptors. Roughly equivalent to the F-16.

Mirage F1: A major upgrade of the original Mirage interceptor. Basically a fighter bomber in the F-4 class.

Mirage III: Original French lightweight interceptor. Basically a superior Western version of the MiG-21 type. A very capable aircraft in its time. Mirage V and Mirage 50 are ground-attack versions.

OH-58: Current U.S. scout helicopter.

OH-6: Original U.S. scout helicopter. Being phased out.

Rafale: Latest French lightweight interceptor.

Su-17: Older ground-attack aircraft. Exported in less capable versions designated Su-20 and Su-22. Being phased out.

Su-24: Russian version of the F-111 and Tornado.

Su-25: Russian version of the A-10.

Su-27: Russian version of F-15. Primarily for air defense. Also a navalized version for Russia's only heavy aircraft carrier.

Tornado: Multipurpose aircraft, most versions are optimized for medium-range bombing, although the British developed an interceptor variant. It is a British-German-Italian joint effort.

Tu-142: Latest version of Russian heavy bomber that entered service about the same time as the U.S. B-52. Serves as recon aircraft as well as cruise missile carrier.

Tu-16: After nearly 40 years, this bomber still serves. Many are gradually being converted to electronic-warfare duties.

Tu-160 (Blackjack): Russian version of the U.S. B-1. This aircraft has been under development for over 10 years, indicating that the Russians are having a difficult time getting it to perform as they would like. Considering the problems with the B-1, this is understandable. Went into service in 1990.

Tu-22: Older Russian medium bomber, a category that no longer exists in the West.

Tu-22M: Replacement for the Tu-22.

UH-1: The original multipurpose combat helicopter. Most widely used military helicopter.

UH-60: Second generation U.S. helicopter transport. Replaces UH-1.

YAK-38: Russian version of Harrier for use on smaller Russian aircraft carriers. Being withdrawn from service. Not nearly as capable, and the Russians could not afford a more effective replacement.

BY is the nation that designed, and generally manufactures, the aircraft. It is common for widely produced aircraft to be built in several nations. Nation abbreviations used are: US = United States, NT = NATO (consortium of NATO countries), FR = France, RU = Russia, CH = China, UK = United Kingdom.

CAPABILITY RATINGS are numerical evaluations of the aircraft's effectiveness in performing interception and strike missions. Each calls for a different combination of equipment functions. Also included in these calculations are SRT (sortie rate) and AVG AVAIL (Average Availability). These calculations give overall capability of each aircraft type over a week's time. By including sortie rate and availability, we show not just ability in the air but also how capable that aircraft is in performing its mission.

FTR (fighter interception) is the ability to detect and destroy enemy aircraft. This rating is determined by taking into account SRT (sortie rate) CMBT (Combat ability), AVG AVAIL (Average Availability), ECA (Electronics Capability), and the following aircraft features:

1. *Speed* refers primarily to the aircraft engines' ability to reach top speed as quickly as possible. This capability is best used in small doses. This is so for two reasons. First, high speed consumes vast amounts of fuel. Being able to go from slow to fast more quickly than your opponent gives you a position advantage. You can use your high speed only if you have enough fuel. When your fuel is low, you must break off the action and head for home. Second, it is more difficult to maneuver at high speed. Despite the increasing capability of aircraft, pilots cannot physically withstand the stress of twisting and turning at high speed. You can either go fast or you can maneuver. These factors are included in the CMBT (Combat) value shown on the chart.

2. *Weapons.* Superior missiles allow destroying an enemy aircraft fast enough, and far enough away, to avoid any counterattack. The value for this is included in the CMBT (Combat) value shown on the chart. However, air-to-air missiles are more frequently equipped with their own sensors and computers, thus making them "fire and forget" missiles. These new missiles can be put on most aircraft without adding a lot of additional avionics. Thus, less capable aircraft can have their combat value increased substantially by simply adding "fire and forget" missiles. Previously, a more powerful radar and fire-control system had to be added to an aircraft to take advantage of new missiles.

ATK (attack) is the ability to deliver bombs to ground targets. This rating is determined by taking into account SRT (sortie rate) MAX LOAD, ECB (Electronics Capability), AVG AVAIL (Average Availability), and the following aircraft features:

1. *Munitions quality.* The quality of these weapons acts as a multiplier. Guided or self-guided bombs and missiles are more effective than unguided iron bombs, which just drop and explode. The contents of the warheads is also critical. Improved conventional munitions, using more lethal submunitions, are also superior. The maximum weight of bombs is not always carried, as longer range or greater agility may be required for some missions. Quality of munitions is also not shown, as it varies greatly from nation to nation. On average, Western nations will use munitions two or more times as effective as other (mostly Russian) air forces.

2. *Maneuverability.* A particular kind of maneuverability is required for strike aircraft. When the aircraft's coming in low (often less than 100 meters), loaded (more than five tons of bombs), and fast (600 or more kilometers per hour), its ability to maneuver is essential. Moving at 170 meters a second at an altitude of 100 meters is tricky. The target may be an area less, often considerably less, than 100 meters square. Depending on the size and prominence of the target, you often can't find it and begin your final approach until you are less than five kilometers away. This gives you less than 30 seconds to get the bombs on the target before something down there gets you.

3. *Aircraft durability.* Strike aircraft take more sustained punishment than higher-flying interceptors and faster recon aircraft. Strike aircraft often come in too low to get hit by larger antiaircraft missiles. However, there is no shortage of armed opponents on the ground out to bring them down. Every second over a heavily populated combat zone, a strike aircraft passes within range of some 20 to 100 soldiers armed with machine guns. There may also

be half a dozen or more armored vehicles. Every five seconds, the aircraft will pass within range of an antiaircraft gun or portable SAM missile. Normally, none of these weapons will knock you down by themselves. But damage of any sort adds up. Worse yet, damage that would be a minor inconvenience at 2,000 meters looms more ominously when you are down to 100 meters. When you are that low, and moving at 200 meters a second, the consequences of a slight loss of aircraft control or altitude can be catastrophic. Effective ground-attack aircraft cannot be built like tanks because of weight limitations. Instead, the aircraft are built to absorb considerable damage by providing armor for the pilot and a few vital components. Other items are provided in duplicate or triplicate so that you can afford to lose a few. On the U.S. A-10 attack aircraft, the engines are mounted over the rear fuselage to make them more difficult to hit and to reduce the heat source that many infrared missiles home in on. Thus, a combination of some lightweight armor, overbuilding, and clever design gives a strike aircraft the durability to survive more than one pass.

4. *Reconnaissance missions require the ability to take pictures over enemy territory without getting shot down.* A single interceptor-type aircraft operating clean, without weapons load, will often be fast and agile enough to avoid enemy defenses. Recon ability can be estimated by evaluating speed and thrust-to-weight ratio, which allow an aircraft to fly high and fast, or low and fast. Either approach is acceptable. The high approach is good for photographing large areas. If there are not a lot of high-altitude SAM systems, you can get away with flying fast and high. Generally, enemy interceptors will have a difficult time getting at you. American specialized reconnaissance aircraft like the TR-1 (U-2) can avoid even the missiles. If too many SAMs are present, going in low is preferred. Here, thrust is important as the denser atmosphere at low altitudes requires more engine power to attain the same high speeds. The drag from extra fuel tanks, and anything else hanging from the aircraft, is higher at lower altitudes. The result is that you can go about twice as far at high altitude as you can on the deck. And you can't go anywhere unless you go fast.

SRT is the Sortie Rate for one week, assuming two days of surge and five days of sustained sorties. All aircraft have the ability to fly several times a day. But before an aircraft can take off again, it must be checked out visually and electronically to see if all key components are operational or approaching failure. Fuel and munitions are loaded. The pilot must also be briefed on the mission, which can take from a few minutes to over an hour. After a mission, the same cycle must be repeated before another takeoff. You can cut corners in maintenance, which increases the risk of losing the aircraft and/or sending it up with some capabilities crippled. The current record for sorties per day is held by an American F-16 squadron, which used its 20 aircraft and 40 pilots to fly 160 sorties in 12 hours. This was an exceptional performance and not representative of combat conditions, where many aircraft would come back with combat damage. This also points out the need to have more pilots than aircraft, as the pilots are more fragile than the aircraft they fly. Most Western aircraft can fly three or more sorties per day for two or three days and one or two per day indefinitely as long as the spare parts and ground crews hold out. Western air forces practice high-sortie surge tactics far more than their Russian or Third World counterparts. Israel has demonstrated the effectiveness of this practice in all its wars, as did the USAF during the 1991 Gulf War. For this reason, the number of aircraft and the quality of pilots are not the only factors that determine which air force is superior.

CMBT is the ability of an aircraft to engage in air combat with other planes. This takes into account a number of aircraft characteristics, the most important of which is maneuverability. In order to bring weapons to bear on the enemy aircraft, you must be able to get close enough to use them. You must also be able to avoid threatening enemy maneuvers. This maneuverability consists of engine power (thrust-to-weight ratio), wing loading, and general mechanical superiority.

ECA, ECB (Electronic Capability, Air Superiority, and Bombing). Airborne electronics, often just called avionics, is essential for success in air operations. Two separate values are included to show the different sets of avionics needed for air superiority combat (ECA) and bombing (ECB). These are calculated with respect to the following items:

1. Onboard radar is crucial. All aircraft have at least one type, usually search and/or fire-control radar for aiming weapons, primarily missiles. Search radar comes in several levels of capability. The most advanced is "look down" radar that can spot aircraft against the background of all the "clutter" on the ground.

2. Even the classic dogfight is enhanced by electronics. The HUD (Head Up Display) projects a see-through computer display in front of the pilot. On this display are items like air speed, heading, and altitude as well as fire-control information. The HUD can show the position of other aircraft as well as ground contours and location of ground targets. Weapons status, ECM situation, damage status, and radar missile warnings can all be displayed on the HUD and still allow the pilot to keep his eyes up and looking at the air about him. A recent development is a HUD that is attached to the visor on the pilot's helmet. The advantage here is that the head may be turned without losing view of the HUD data. The pilot controls which of many items are to be displayed on the HUD with a switch. The items monitored on the HUD indicate the numerous types of electronic equipment that can enhance an aircraft's capabilities.

3. Ground-attack radars and computers take a lot of the inaccuracy out of bombing. These devices find the target and then assist the pilot in releasing his bombs at the right time. Bombing can be done through pilot skill alone, but such skills take time to develop and even more so when flying modern high-speed jet bombers. This is why electronic navigation and bombing aids have become so essential.

4. Electronic countermeasures (ECM) are needed not only to penetrate enemy detection systems, but also to assist the collection of information. In these days of ever-increasing electronic warfare, aircraft are often sent to take "pictures" of enemy electronic defenses. ECM equipment consists of sensors that detect transmissions and transmitters that broadcast signals that obliterate or confuse enemy reception. The recon aircraft's computers study enemy transmissions and warn the pilot of especially dangerous ones. Some

ECM systems even suggest the safest path through the thicket of enemy defenses. Systems like this are best used in a passive mode. That is, the system does not broadcast radio or radar signals, but simply listens to enemy signals. Recon missions need only add recording devices to capture information on enemy defenses detected by ECM sensors. Not all ECM loads contain all the above gadgets. The minimum load is sensors and transmitters.

5. Navigation equipment is vital, as you can't get from here to there unless you know the way. For all-weather (night and foul weather) operations, more complex navigation gear is required. This would include an inertial navigation system, which keeps track of the aircraft's location at all times without the use of any visual references. Additional items like terrain-avoidance radar and radar mapping of the terrain below enable the aircraft to fly low in conditions of zero visibility (like a moonless night or storm). Often, missions are sent after very small objectives. If you are coming in very low and/or the objective is heavily defended, there may be one approach route that is safer. The safe route is often only usable through precise navigation. Precise navigation is required not only to complete the mission but to survive it.

6. To ensure secrecy, radio silence is typically maintained. This gives the enemy one less transmission to home in on. So you can't call home for directions. You are on your own.

NORMAL COMBAT RADIUS represents the normal maximum distance from the aircraft base to the area where it performs its mission. The usual rule of thumb is that the combat radius is one-third the distance an aircraft can fly in a straight line on a full load of fuel. This allows for the trip out and back plus one third of fuel for combat. All aircraft burn about .5 percent of fuel per minute when cruising at the economical speed (600–800 kilometers an hour). Maximum speed burns up more fuel. Interceptors and recon aircraft will consume 10 to 15 percent of fuel per minute at max speed. Lower speeds consume less, but even strike aircraft will frequently crank it up to 2 or 3 percent of fuel per minute while maneuvering toward or away from their targets. The average aircraft has sufficient fuel for two or three hours of cruising and up to 15 minutes of high-speed maneuvering during combat. Strike aircraft prefer to conserve their fuel so they can circle the battlefield waiting for the opportune moment to go down and hit their targets. Fuel is a weapon. If one aircraft has more fuel, it can force another into a situation where the disadvantaged plane will crash with empty gas tanks. When the low-fuel aircraft realizes that it only has enough to get back to base, it can be more easily outmaneuvered by its opponent, who can be more generous with fuel, and speed. Fuel is also a handy defense. Recon aircraft in particular use bursts of speed to avoid danger from aircraft above or missiles below. Combat aircraft often fly off to their objectives with one or more large fuel tanks hanging from them. These tanks slow the aircraft down and decrease maneuverability. Before entering combat, these tanks are normally dropped. A common tactic is to force the other fellow to jettison his drop tanks before the fuel he carries has been used. This is done by attacking the enemy formation with missiles or interceptors before it has reached its objective. The attack does not have to be serious, just enough to force those partially full tanks to the ground. Note that most U.S. aircraft can be refueled in the air. This aids both fighters and bombers. For fighters, they can travel farther to a combat zone, and refuel just before entering and after leaving the combat area. This enhances their range considerably. Naturally, the United States has the largest fleet of aerial tankers in the world.

YEAR INTRODUCED is the year the aircraft type was first developed to a combat unit. The longer a type is in service, the more it will be improved. Later versions have substantially improved performance. This is not difficult to do, as aircraft must be overhauled frequently. Depending on the type, and country of origin, every 500 to 3,000 flight hours the aircraft must be practically taken apart. During this process, improved components can be installed.

NO. IN USE 1995 is the number of the type of aircraft estimated to be in use during 1995. There may be some small errors due to increased accident/war losses or production changes. Earlier retirement of older planes, as well as the secret nature of most of this information, also make these values approximations. Most air forces plan to shed a lot of older aircraft and order fewer new planes in light of the Cold War's end. Each year, hundreds of military aircraft are lost to accidents and other noncombat causes. Through the remainder of the decade, the number of combat aircraft in use will likely decline, with the older aircraft declining more rapidly than the newer models.

MAINTAINABILITY is the relative ease of maintenance for the aircraft. This is expressed as the number of maintenance man-hours required for each hour in the air. The values shown are for peacetime operations. Wartime standards would be somewhat larger due to the combat damage needing repair. Combat aircraft wear out quickly because they are built to achieve high performance standards, plus a little more. Pilots push the aircraft to their limits and beyond. These planes are built to fail in an orderly fashion, preferably by indicating they're about to go while being tested on the ground, where the spent part can be replaced. Modern aircraft require from 5 to 50 man-hours of maintenance per flight hour. Engines must be replaced every few hundred or few thousand hours. Even without combat damage, the airframe is useless after 2,000–10,000 hours of flying. Obviously, a decrease in maintenance per flight hour makes a big difference in the number of technicians needed. For example, in peacetime if a squadron of 24 aircraft flew 40 hours per month, this would amount to 960 hours a month. At 20 maintenance hours per flight hour, 19,200 man-hours per month would be needed. With a peacetime availability of 118 man-hours per man per month, 163 maintenance troops could keep 24 aircraft flying. In wartime, the number of man-hours available would be tripled by cutting out leave and other duties while following a 12-hour-day, seven-days-a-week schedule. But aircraft use could increase even faster, something on the order of two or three sorties per day, or seven flight hours a day. That's 3,360 maintenance hours per day, nearly twice the man-hours available. What happens? Some maintenance can be deferred, which will eventually produce more frequent failure in the air and more lost aircraft or missions aborted. Lost aircraft will reduce the work load, but repair of damaged aircraft will take up this slack. A lot of battle damage can be taken care of during routine maintenance. More efficient ways will be found to do the maintenance. What all this spotlights is that you cannot keep using combat aircraft intensively day after day. Air-combat activity is either low level over a long period or intense for only a few days. Either way, the maintenance crews will be working their buns off around the clock. Aircraft don't fly if their maintenance needs cannot be attended to. Maintenance needs increase with the complexity of the aircraft. Western planes devote over half their maintenance to electronic components, which continue to proliferate. Even so, aircraft components are constantly made simpler or more easily maintained. Every aircraft has several major systems, each requiring specialists and specific procedures to service them. The key systems are:

1. Airframe (fuselage, wings, etc.)
2. Hydraulics (moves flaps, etc.)
3. Electrical system, electronics (radio, radar, ECM, etc.)
4. Weapons
5. The Engine

The engine(s) are, along with the electronics, the most maintenance-intensive systems. For example, the J-79 engine in the U.S. F-4 has 22,000 parts and requires 1.7 maintenance man-hours per flight hours. The F-4 has two of them. The single (more powerful) F-100 engine in the F-16 has 31,000 parts and requires 4.2 man-hours. The F-101 engine for the F-16 has only 20,000 parts and requires only two maintenance hours per flight hour. All this maintenance and parts replacement has a bright side. Improved parts or entire components are often inserted during routine maintenance. This enables performance to be increased without much additional attention. For example, the most recent combat aircraft have computer-driven "optimization" systems built into the engine. These systems get 5–10 percent higher performance out of the engines and reduce fuel consumption by about the same amount. Military aircraft and helicopters serve for 10 to 20 years, so these gradual improvements are essential to keep capabilities current. Russian equipment generally requires more maintenance. The Russians' manpower pool (and those of most Third World nations) of technicians is smaller and less capable. Russian aircraft fly only one third as many monthly hours as Western planes in peacetime. Still, they have a higher peacetime accident rate, partially as a result of less-qualified pilots, partly because of less-thorough maintenance. In wartime, the Russian equipment's maintenance system will be strained even more than those in Western air forces.

AVG AVAIL is average availability of aircraft for operations. This can be increased or decreased depending on the availability of spare parts and maintenance personnel. The average is a peacetime standard that indicates just how easy it is to keep the aircraft going.

MAX WEIGHT is the maximum takeoff weight in metric tons, ordinarily with a full load of weapons. Aircraft often operate with less than this weight, particularly on intercept missions. Bombers and recon aircraft are more likely to carry a full load.

WING LOADING is the ratio of full-load weight to square meter of wing surface. This is one of the chief factors in an aircraft's maneuverability. An aircraft with high wing loading will be stiffer and less agile. However, wing loading is not the only determinant of maneuverability; it is simply the central one. Equally important are engine power and the general design of the aircraft, encompassing the me-

7-1 Combat Aircraft

Common Name	Designation	By	Ftr	Atk	Srt	Cm	ECA	ECB	Normal Combat Radius (km)	Year Introduced	No. in Use 1995	Maintainability	Avg Avail	Max Wght	Wing Loading	Thrust Loaded	Wght Clean	Max Load	Max Speed (Kph)	Number Built or Planned
Air Superiority																				
Lightning (ATF)	F-22	US	100	31	15	14	11	3	990	2001	0	11	85%	32	0.38	2,188	2,917	8	3,100	650
Eagle	F-15	US	46	21	12	12	8	3	990	1977	1,178	11	80%	25	0.44	2,000	2,809	7.2	2,800	1,500
Rafale	Rafale	FR	40	19	12	12	7	5	700	1998	10	12	80%	14.5	0.31	2,207	3,048	4	1,500	330
Falcon	F-16A	US	39	25	14	11	6	3	900	1980	4,169	10	85%	16	0.57	1,563	2,747	6.9	2,300	4,500
Hornet	F-18A	US	34	35	14	10	6	4	1,000	1982	1,189	12	82%	22	0.59	1,455	2,238	7.7	2,070	1,500
Fulcrum Plus	MiG-33	RU	32	14	12	10	7	4	1,100	1992	0	30	75%	17	0.48	2,153	2,815	4	2,530	3,500
Mirage 2000	Mirage 2000	FR	29	26	12	10	6	4	1,600	1983	547	15	80%	16.5	0.40	1,333	2,268	6.8	2,645	570
Fulcrum	MiG-29	RU	27	7	12	10	6	2	1,100	1984	762	30	75%	17	0.48	2,153	2,815	4	2,530	1,500
Tomcat	F-14A	US	26	10	10	8	8	2	1,000	1970	510	25	80%	34	0.64	1,228	1,522	6.5	2,760	700
Tornado	Tornado	NT	24	22	14	8	8	4	1,300	1980	700	24	75%	24	0.67	1,333	1,905	7.2	2,300	1,400
Kfir C2	Kfir C2	IS	21	20	12	8	4	4	780	1974	143	15	85%	15	0.42	1,218	1,721	4.3	2,645	300
Phantom	F-4E	US	14	21	9	6	5	3	1,100	1963	1,305	15	80%	28	0.57	1,279	1,721	7.2	2,300	5,177
Flanker	SU-27	RU	18	11	10	10	6	3	1,500	1983	220	40	65%	27	0.42	2,176	2,798	6	2,645	800
Flogger-B	MiG-23	RU	15	5	9	8	5	2	960	1971	2,374	25	75%	18	0.66	1,408	1,690	4	2,645	5,000
Mirage F1	Mirage F1	FR	14	14	12	6	5	4	1,000	1973	455	16	80%	15	0.61	1,039	1,411	3	2,530	700
Tiger	F-5E	US	11	12	15	6	3	3	1,000	1972	1,587	8	85%	11	0.61	901	1,250	3.1	1,840	2,500
Mirage III	Mirage III	FR	8	3	11	6	3	2	1,300	1963	668	15	85%	14	0.39	993	1,115	1.5	2,530	1,500
Fishbed	MiG-21J	RU	7	1	9	6	3	1	700	1956	2,159	15	85%	9	0.41	1,548	1,842	1.5	2,415	10,000
Starfighter	F-104	US	6	2	9	5	4	1	1,200	1958	531	25	70%	14	0.77	1,279	1,689	3.4	2,530	2,541
F-8	F-8	CH	6	3	8	6	3	2	800	1969	220	20	85%	18	0.43	1,622	1,825	2	2,800	1,000
Foxhound	MiG-31	RU	6	2	6	6	6	1	1,100	1982	222	50	55%	41	0.73	1,502	1,760	6	2,645	300
F-7	F-7	CH	6	2	9	5	3	2	1,100	1965	192	15	85%	9	0.41	1,426	1,696	1.5	2,415	1,000
F-6/A-5	F-6/A-5	CH	5	1	9	5	3	2	680	1970	4,583	20	70%	9	0.35	1,667	1,768	0.5	1,380	5,000
Foxbat	MiG-25	RU	4	1	6	4	6	1	900	1970	338	40	60%	38	0.67	1,440	1,565	3	3,220	1,200
Forger	Yak-38	RU	2	3	8	3	3	2	300	1975	20	25	55%	11.6	0.63	1,552	2,250	3.6	1,035	100
Bombers																				
B-2	B-2	US	5	200	5	3	8	18	7,200	1992	10	40	75%	181	0.35	420	503	30	1,100	20
B-1B	B-1	US	2	171	4	2	6	12	5,800	1984	95	30	70%	217	1.17	553	723	51	2,530	100
BUFF	B-52	US	1	61	4	1	8	8	16,000	1955	95	65	70%	225	0.60	604	689	27.2	1,025	465

Name	Code	Ctry	(1)	(2)	(3)	(4)	(5)	(6)	(7)	(8)	(9)	(10)	(11)	(12)	(13)	(14)	(15)	(16)	(17)	(18)
Strike Eagle	F-15E	US	38	60	12	10	8	6	990	1988	174	12	80%	32	0.57	1,563	2,315	10.4	2,700	200
Aardvark	F-111F	US	5	58	8	3	6	10	2,000	1967	243	30	72%	45	0.65	871	1,120	10	2,530	501
Stealth	F-117A	US	8	38	9	3	8	14	700	1981	56	15	75%	16	0.67	1,313	1,750	4	1,000	400
Blackjack	TU-160	RU	2	37	4	2	6	9	5,200	1985	40	50	65%	250	0.68	704	752	16	2,415	100
Jaguar	Jaguar	NT	6	35	12	3	4	8	1,300	1972	410	10	80%	18	0.75	811	1,081	4.5	1,725	550
Fencer	SU-24	RU	8	34	8	5	6	6	1,200	1974	632	35	65%	41	0.84	1,237	1,690	11	2,415	1,200
Intruder	A-6E	US	5	33	9	3	6	7	750	1963	488	20	65%	27	0.55	689	984	8.1	1,208	700
Warthog	A-10	US	4	29	16	3	2	3	500	1977	622	7	85%	23	0.49	783	1,139	7.2	644	735
Frogfoot	SU-25	RU	2	21	11	2	3	5	500	1983	445	20	75%	19	0.56	979	1,329	5	690	1,500
Corsair	A-7E	US	6	20	10	4	4	4	550	1966	113	12	75%	19	0.55	789	1,230	6.8	1,035	1,534
Backfire	TU-22M	RU	1	14	4	3	4	5	2,500	1974	300	50	60%	130	0.79	677	746	12	2,312	500
Bear	TU-142	RU	0	14	4	1	1	4	5,000	1955	110	35	55%	188	0.67	309	337	16	800	200
Flogger-C-D	MiG-27	RU	10	14	10	7	4	4	400	1973	855	30	70%	20	0.54	1,268	1,690	5	1,955	1,500
Skyhawk	A-4	US	4	14	11	3	3	4	1,500	1960	386	10	85%	20	0.80	465	571	3.7	1,058	2,960
Harrier	AV-8A	UK	13	11	15	7	3	3	400	1969	249	15	85%	11	0.59	1,818	2,703	3.6	1,035	500
Blinder	TU-22	RU	1	10	4	2	4	6	1,500	1962	125	50	55%	83	0.60	741	820	8	1,610	300
Badger	TU-16	RU	1	7	5	2	2	4	1,500	1955	488	40	55%	75	0.45	560	636	9	886	2,000
Alpha	Alpha	NT	3	7	12	3	2	3	520	1979	566	8	85%	8	0.43	795	1,125	2.2	978	600
Fitter-C	SU-17	RU	1	5	7	3	2	3	600	1972	1,024	20	65%	18	0.44	1,384	1,788	4	2,415	2,500
Helicopters																				
Apache	AH-64	US	8	14	15	4	4	7	300	1985	624	30	65%	9.5	0	358	0	2	300	800
SeaCobra	AH-1W	US	3	11	18	3	2	5	400	1987	256	25	60%	6.6	0	485	0	2.3	350	300
Havoc	Ka-50	RU	11	10	10	6	5	7	400	1992	60	30	70%	10.8	0	407	0	2	350	500
Cobra	AH-1S	US	2	7	15	2	2	4	180	1984	236	20	70%	5	0	360	0	1.6	225	1,200
Hind	Mi-24	RU	2	4	12	2	2	3	160	1972	1,487	20	70%	11	0	400	0	1.3	260	2,500
Kiowa	OH-58	US	0	3	22	0	2	2	200	1969	1,200	15	75%	1.5	0	280	0	1	222	6,000
Hip	Mi-8	RU	0	2	12	0	0	1	150	1962	3,246	25	60%	12	0	283	0	4	250	8,000
Sea Stallion	CH-53E	US	0	1	12	0	1	0	280	1981	60	18	70%	34	0	382	0	17	320	200
Loach	OH-6	US	0	1	16	1	0	1	200	1963	200	15	80%	1.1	0	282	0	1	320	3,000
Chinook	CH-47	US	0	1	14	0	0	0	140	1962	550	30	65%	23	0	326	0	13	300	1,100
Sea Stallion	CH-53D	US	0	1	12	0	0	0	160	1967	250	35	65%	21	0	333	0	9	300	700
Hook	Mi-6	RU	0	1	8	0	0	0	210	1958	440	5	60%	42	0	262	0	12	1,000	1,000
Blackhawk	UH-60A	US	0	0	14	0	0	0	200	1979	1,300	20	75%	4.8	0	625	0	3.6	290	1,500
Huey	UH-1H	US	0	0	18	0	0	0	160	1959	4,900	20	70%	4.7	0	298	0	2	200	11,000
Sea Knight	CH-46E	US	0	0	14	0	0	0	340	1974	280	20	65%	10	0	360	0	2	260	350
Total																				
Total											46,708									110,483

7-2 Aircraft Weapons

Weapon	Made by	Target Detection	Aspect	Range (km)	Weight (lbs)	Speed (mps)	Guidance	Rank	Used On
Air-to-Air Missiles									
Phoenix	US	Active	All	200	1,008	1,600	9	9	F-14
AMRAAM AIM-120	US	Active	All	100	335	1,200	8	9	Most
Sky Flash	Britain	Active	All	55	425	1,000	7	8	F-4, Torn
AA-12 "AMRAAMski"	Russia	Active	All	55	450	1,100	7	7	MiG-29, Su-27
Sparrow AIM-7F	US	Active	All	40	514	1,200	6	7	F-4, F-14, F-5, F-18
Python 3	Israel	Passive	All	15	266	800	7	7	Most
Sidewinder AIM-9M	US	Passive	All	14	190	820	7	7	Most
Magic R550	France	Passive	Rear	10	200	1,000	5	6	Most
Sidewinder AIM-9J	US	Passive	Rear	10	185	820	4	6	Most
AA-9 Amos	Russia	Active	All	100	800	1,100	5	5	MiG-25, MiG-31
AA-11RH Alamo	Russia	Passive	All	40	440	1,000	4	5	MiG-29, Su-27
AA-10IR Alamo	Russia	Active	All	15	350	1,000	6	5	MiG-29, Su-27
AA-6RH Acrid	Russia	Active	All	40	1,700	1,400	3	4	MiG-25
AA-7RH Apex	Russia	Active	All	30	700	1,100	4	4	MiG-23
AA-6IR Acrid	Russia	Passive	Rear	20	1,300	1,400	2	4	MiG-25
AA-7IR Apex	Russia	Passive	Rear	16	600	1,100	3	4	MiG-23
AA-8RH Aphid	Russia	Active	All	15	200	800	4	4	MiG-23
AA-8IR Aphid	Russia	Passive	Rear	7	120	800	3	4	MiG-23, Most
Sidewinder AIM-9B	US	Passive	Rear	4	159	650	2	4	Most
AA-3 Anab	Russia	Passive	Rear	10	500	800	2	3	Su-9, Su-11, Su-15
AA-2 Atoll	Russia	Passive	Rear	7	155	700	1	2	Most
Air-to-Surface Missiles									
AGM-84E SLAM	US	Active	All	100	1,700	280	9	9	S-3, P-3, A-6, A-7
Kormoran	Germany	Both	All	37	1,320	300	7	9	F-104, To
HARM AGM-88A	US	Passive	All	20	807	1,200	7	9	F-4, A-7, Wild Wea
Harpoon	US	Active	All	130	1,498	280	7	9	S-3, P-3, A-6, A-7
Exocet	France	Active	All	60	1,442	300	7	9	F-4
Shrike AGM-45A	US	Passive	All	16	400	650	6	8	F-4, A-6, A-7, Wild Weasel
ALCM AGM-86	US	Active	All	3,200	3,000	240	5	8	B-52

System	Origin	Seeker / Duration (hrs)	Launch / Load (lbs)						Platform
AS-5 Kelt	Russia	Active	All	180	7,700	300	4	8	Tu-16
AS-12 HARM	Russia	Passive	All	100	1,600	330	5	7	Su-24
AS-13	Russia	Passive	All	70	2,500	300	5	7	Su-24
AS-4 Replacement	Russia	Active	All	800	12,100	1,150	5	7	Tu-22M,
AS-6 Kingfish	Russia	Active	All	250	10,600	800	5	7	Tu-22M,
AS-11 HARM	Russia	Passive	All	80	1,100	300	5	6	Su-24
AS-14	Russia	Passive	All	12	1,500	600	3	6	MiG-27, Su-17, Su-24
AS-9 ARM	Russia	Passive	All	80	2,200	260	4	5	Su-24
AS-15	Russia	Active	All	3000	3,500	240	4	5	Tu-95
Maverick AGM-65	US	Passive	All	20	462	670	4	4	Most
AS-4 Kitchen	Russia	Passive	All	300	13,200	400	3	4	Tu-22M, Tu-22
Paveway	US	Passive	All	4	2,100	200	3	4	Most
SRAM AGM-69A	US	Active	All	100	2,240	1,000	3	4	B-52
AS-Vikhr	Russia	Passive	All	20	500	600	3	4	Su-25
Walleye AGM-62A	US	Passive	All	4	2,400	200	2	3	Most
AS-10	Russia	Passive	All	10	600	200	2	2	MiG-27, Su-17
AS-7 Kerry	Russia	Passive	All	10	640	200	1	2	MiG-27, Su-17
AS-3 Kangaroo	Russia	Passive	All	650	24,200	300	1	2	Tu-95
AS-2 Kipper	Russia	Passive	All	210	9,300	550	1	1	Tu-16
Cannon———									
GAU-8 30mm	US	Both	Chase	1	57	1,020	3	9	A-10
M-61A1 20mm	US	Both	Chase	1	28	1,036	3	8	Most
ADEN 30mm	Britain	Both	Chase	1	10	790	2	7	Most
Gsh-23 23mm	Russia	Both	Chase	1	27	950	1	6	Most
NR-30 30mm	Russia	Both	Chase	1	14	780	1	6	Su-17, Su-7
Drones and RPVs———		Duration (hrs)	Load (lbs)						
Pioneer	Israel	9	100	185	430	51	4	4	Does Not Apply
Mastiff	Israel	7.5	81	200	304	51	3	3	Does Not Apply
Scout	Israel	7	84	100	350	50	2	3	Does Not Apply
CL-89	NATO	0.5	37.5	140	343	205	3	3	Does Not Apply

chanical arrangement of the wing, flaps, slats, fences, spoilers, and sundry other mechanical and aerodynamic devices. Look carefully at the wing of a commercial aircraft during landing and takeoff. Combat aircraft have even busier wings. Some aircraft also have swing wings, which can be swept back for faster speed or extended for greater maneuverability. The swing-wing aircraft are B-1, F-111, Tomcat, Tornado, Backfire, MiG-23/27, Blackjack, and Fitter-C.

THRUST:WEIGHT ratio is the pounds of engine thrust per ton of aircraft weight at full (afterburner) power in two configurations: LOADED is at full load (MAX WEIGHT); CLEAN, at full load minus the maximum load, in its most combat-worthy condition. Even at the CLEAN weight, there would still be some internal fuel and weapons. For helicopters, it is the horsepower per ton of weight. This ratio is the best indicator of an aircraft's ability to move. A low ratio indicates a relatively sluggish aircraft. A high ratio value, especially one over 2,200, indicates a highly maneuverable and lively aircraft. Vertical-takeoff aircraft (Harrier and Forger) have a misleadingly high ratio because most of their thrust is dedicated to getting them off the ground straight up like a helicopter.

MAX LOAD is the maximum weapon load (in tons) hung outside the aircraft from the wings and fuselage as well as a smaller amount carried internally. This load is bombs and missiles, as well as fuel tanks or pods (aerodynamically streamlined containers) carrying cannon, rockets, ECM gear, or recon sensors. Anything carried this way can be dropped in flight. Anything hung from the plane impedes maneuverability. Some aircraft also have internal cannon and a few hundred rounds of ammunition. This is reflected in their capability ratings.

MAX SPEED is the maximum speed in kilometers per hour. Mach 1 equals the speed of sound (1,150 kph) at typical combat altitude, which is under 10,000 meters. Supersonic (Mach 1+) speed is attained only by full engine power, often with afterburner. Normal cruise speed is about 900 kilometers an hour at 10,000 meters. Flying at lower altitudes uses more fuel and strains the pilot because the aircraft is more difficult to control in the thicker lower atmosphere. Flying on the deck, 100 meters up, causes even more strain because of the constant need to avoid obstacles. One can use automatic pilot for low-altitude flying, but they are expensive, not every aircraft has them, and the pilot has to keep an eye on things anyway.

NUMBER BUILT OR PLANNED is the estimated figure as of 1995. For Russian aircraft, the figure is the total number built plus an estimate of future production (which is not likely to be a lot). For non-Russian aircraft, it is the number built and on order.

Aircraft Weapons

AIR-TO-AIR MISSILES are of two basic types: infrared homing (IR) and radar homing (RH). The most widely used are the U.S.-made Sidewinder (IR) and Sparrow (RH). Other Western and Russian missiles are derived from these two designs. The Phoenix is ahead of its time in that it has its own radar, which, when the missile is 16 kilometers from the target, seeks it out on its own. The next generation of RH missiles (the AMRAAM) will use the same technique. The new generation is having problems in arriving, partly because each Phoenix costs $3 million, and Sparrow replacement has to be a lot cheaper than that. The Sparrow costs less than $250,000, and the Sidewinder is less than $100,000. Technology can get to the point where you can't afford it.

AIR-TO-SURFACE MISSILES come in four types:

1. *Homing missiles* are launched in the general direction of the target. Thereafter, the missiles' own sensors take over, enabling the launching aircraft to get to safety. These missiles are expensive, most costing around $1 million each. Most air-to-surface missiles are of this type.
2. *Antiradar missiles* (ARM) are specialized to home in on and hit radars. This is an electronic-warfare weapon, with an onboard computer, ARM (Antiradar Missile) and considerable agility. As the radars and their operators become more clever at avoiding these weapons, the ARMs themselves gain more features and capabilities. It's just like everything else in the ECM area. HARM, Strike, and AS-9 are ARMs.
3. *Guided missiles* are controlled by an operator in the aircraft via a TV camera in the missile or simply by eyeballing missile and target. More recent versions require only that you get the target on the TV screen; the missile then remembers that image and homes in on it. As microcomputers become cheaper and more popular, this approach becomes more cost-effective and popular.
4. *Guided bombs* are like the guided missiles (above) except they have no power. A bomb is fitted with wings and fins and a power supply to control these. This was the original air-to-ground guided-weapon concept first used in 1943. Used extensively during the Gulf War because there were more aircraft equipped to handle them. The U.S. GBU series and the Walleye are examples of these systems.

CANNON shown are representative of the more common types. The GAU-8 is the only one of its kind designed solely for destroying armored vehicles. It could be devastating against aircraft except for the fact that it weighs nearly two tons, 10 times as heavy as any other aircraft cannon. Next to the name of each cannon is its caliber in millimeters.

DRONES and RPVS. The former are self-guided aircraft; the latter are controlled by human pilots in the air or on the ground.

MADE BY is the nation that designed the weapon and often the sole source of that weapon.

TARGET DETECTION indicates whether the using aircraft must emit an electronic signal in order to guide the weapon. *Active* means that a radar signal is sent and can be detected and possibly defeated by countermeasures. *Passive* means that no signals are transmitted; the missile sensors just listen or look and the missile is more difficult to defeat with countermeasures. BOTH means that active and passive means are used.

ASPECT shows the direction from which the aircraft may make an attack with that weapon. ALL means that an enemy aircraft, or ground target, may be attacked from any direction. *Rear* means that the enemy aircraft may only be attacked from the rear. *Chase* indicates that although the weapon can be used to attack from all directions, it is far more effective when used from the rear during a chase of the target aircraft. This is the case with cannon.

RANGE (in kilometers) is the maximum effective range. This will be more or less—for exceptionally large or small targets. Longer range is largely a function of the size and efficiency of the propulsion system and the range of the radar. Cannon range is longer when these same cannons are used in ground-based vehicles because of the great loss of accuracy from a rapidly moving platform.

WEIGHT (in pounds) of the missile. Missiles possess four components:

1. Airframe (shell)
2. Propulsion system
3. Guidance system
4. Warhead

The warhead generally comprises 15 percent of missile weight. Propulsion-system weight is a function of range, while airframe weight is a function of missile size. The largest variable is the guidance system, including fins and other control surfaces as well as the flight computer, radio gear, and sensors. Western missiles' more efficient technology allows for lighter and more capable guidance systems. The weight given for cannon is the weight of shell the cannon fires per second.

SPEED (in meters per second). Higher speed is always desirable. It can be obtained only when the guidance system can handle it. Air-to-air missiles have solid-fuel motors that burn out quickly (in 2 to 10+ seconds), leaving only momentum to carry them to the end of their mission. The high initial speed thus accounts for the minimum range of missiles, as the higher speeds are more difficult to control. It also limits the range of highly maneuverable missiles intended for use at close range. Too high a speed and the minimum range will be too long. Ideally, minimum range should be no more than a few hundred meters. Using cannon, aircraft have been brought down at less than 100 meters. This is dangerous with missiles, as the destruction is generally more catastrophic and the debris has been known to take the attacker down with it. The speed given is the highest attained at motor burnout.

GUIDANCE is an evaluation—from 1 (poor) to 9 (excellent)—of the missile's guidance-system quality. The evaluation includes the accuracy and dependability of the system as well as its resistance to countermeasures. Even passive systems, specifically infrared ones, have a number of weaknesses. Because infrared missiles home in on heat, they can be confused by such natural phenomena as the sun or the hot surface of the desert. Also, clouds can mask the heat source, not to mention flares. Radar-guided systems are very sensitive to jamming, especially with chaff. This is often circumvented by having the missiles home in on the jamming source.

RANK indicates comparative effectiveness within the classes, taking all factors discussed into account.

USED ON is the aircraft that uses these weapons. *Most* indicates a simple missile that can be easily mounted on most aircraft. In the West, the majority of aircraft can be equipped to use passive-guidance missiles like the Sidewinder. The pilot using such a weapon need only activate the missile, listen for the audio signal that the missile sensor is "locked on" to something, and then launch it. For missiles dependent on aircraft radar (Sparrow-type radar homing), a more elaborate setup is needed. In this case, a few hundred pounds of equipment must be installed and integrated with the missile's electronics. This equipment must be redesigned to fit each different aircraft it is used with. Russian aircraft are unique in that until recently new planes had a special missile designed just for them. Another Russian habit was equipping these missiles with either a passive (infrared) or active (radar homing) guidance system. The radar homing version is heavier and has a longer range. This solves some inventory problems but is wasteful because the infrared version is larger than necessary and has more range than it can realistically use. Moreover, the flight characteristics of the long-range radar homing missile and the shorter "dogfighting" infrared homing missile are quite different. Thus, Russian short-range infrared missiles are not nearly as agile and lethal as their Western counterparts. Russian aircraft customarily carry two of each version. All Russian missiles have been noticeably unsuccessful in combat. Even when used against civilian airliners, they have not always been very inspiring. In a 1978 incident, a Russian interceptor fired several missiles at a Korean airliner and only managed to damage it. The Korean plane was able to land on a frozen lake. In a 1983 incident, another Korean airliner was not so fortunate, or perhaps the Russian interceptor was the lucky one. Combat use of Russian missiles has been bleak more often than not. It is noteworthy that the Russians still equip their interceptors with cannons.

NOTES ON IRON BOMBS AND UNGUIDED MISSILES

Air-to-ground operations have traditionally used a wide range of gravity bombs and unguided missiles. These have not been eclipsed by guided air-to-ground munitions. During the 1991 Gulf War, only 7 percent of the bomb tonnage consisted of "smart" bombs and missiles. As the list below demonstrates, iron bombs have become a lot smarter and deadlier. Iron bombs are the traditional high-explosive-filled containers dropped by aircraft for the last 75 years. Largely unchanged in the last 50 years, they come in numerous sizes, weighing from a few pounds to over a ton.

CBU (Cluster Bomb Units) saw widespread and effective use during the Vietnam War. First deployed in the 1960s, they are containers of smaller bombs. When the container is dropped, it breaks open and distributes the smaller bombs over a wider area. A typical 600 pound CBU contains 150 smaller (three-pound) bombs, which would fall over an area 50 meters wide and 200 meters long. Often the pilot can select a smaller or larger pattern. Any unprotected people within this 50-by-200-meter area have a better than 50 percent chance of being injured. The CBUs can carry a variety of loads: antitank, incendiary, and chemical. The bomblet weight varies from a few ounces to more than 20 pounds. In addition, the bomblets can be equipped with timers or sensors that turn them into mines and booby traps.

FAE (fuel air explosive) is a variation on the napalm bomb (thickened gasoline). An FAE hits the ground, breaks open, and creates a mist of flammable liquid. A small delayed-action explosive then goes off, causing the cloud to ignite. The pressure of the blast is sufficient to wreck vehicles, ships, and equipment as well as being fatal to personnel. The only other device to produce similar results is nuclear weapons. Pound for pound, FAE weapons are three to five times as destructive as high explosive. For example, a 1,100-pound FAE would destroy most equipment and injure all personnel within 250 meters of the impact point. These devices are also used in CBUs. Because of their area effect, FAE bombs have been successful in clearing mines. In Vietnam, large FAEs were used to clear helicopter landing sites in the jungle. FAEs are effective against entrenched troops, as the blast is severe and will enter any position that is not airtight. Unfortunately, FAEs are not as reliable as other types of bombs. The "explosive mist" must form just so to be effective. Weather conditions can seriously degrade the effect of FAE.

Incendiaries are the familiar napalm bombs plus an assortment of other flammable items. These are being supplanted by more effective and reliable FAEs.

Special-purpose bombs fulfill a variety of specialized needs. Concrete-piercing bombs are used to crater airfields and destroy heavy structures. Also in this category are chemical and nuclear weapons.

Unguided missiles, or free-flight rockets (FFRs), are still used. They have a variety of loads: fragmentation, illumination, smoke, armor piercing. Their range is several kilometers. Usually carried in pods containing 7 to 32 rockets each.

8

Air Defense

WHEN IT WAS first suggested that aircraft be used for military purposes, a common reaction was that these fragile machines would soon be blown out of the sky. They could easily be seen, and shot at, by troops on the ground. The first 25 years of air-combat use demonstrated that they were not that easy to bring down. Even so, in 1939 the Germans thought that only 50 of their 88mm antiaircraft gun shells would be needed to shoot down one enemy aircraft. Allied aircraft turned out to be both elusive and resistant to the vaunted "88." More than 12,000 shells were needed for each aircraft destroyed.

When antiaircraft missiles appeared in the 1950s, it was thought that aircraft were again doomed. Experience over Vietnam and the Middle East in the '60s and '70s, however, saw an average of 50 missiles required to kill one airplane. This was not as large an improvement as might appear, as the 50 missiles cost more than the 12,000 cannon shells needed during World War II. Moreover, the aircraft developed an unpleasant habit of attacking the air-defense units. This only made the task of antiaircraft units more difficult. Air defense has always proved an impediment, at times even a deterrent, to air attacks. But air defense has not been able to stop aerial assaults in the long run. Although aircraft have been touted as the ultimate weapon by many, they too have failed to be overpowering, not because of air defense, but because of limitations in aircraft weapons and the performance limitations of the aircraft themselves. Aircraft are not superweapons, and neither are the antiaircraft systems that attack them.

In light of these limitations, air-defense units learned to strive for attrition and deterrence. Air defense attempts to force aircraft to either abort their missions or take heavy losses. Surface-to-air missiles often force aircraft to fly low enough so they can be shot at by the smaller-caliber but much more numerous machine guns and automatic cannons. At least then the gunners can see what they are shooting at. Indeed, it is at these lower altitudes where most aircraft losses to air-defense forces take place. Over North Vietnam, some 80 percent of aircraft losses were due to low-altitude machine guns, while in the 1973 Arab-Israeli War between 30 and 50 percent of aircraft losses were due to machine guns (Israelis claimed the higher number). On the other hand, over 10,000 small-caliber cannon shells were required for each plane downed. Finally, as in other forms of warfare, the results depended on the quantity and quality of the air defenses and the aircraft they fought.

Detect, Acquire, Track, Destroy

Air defense has learned to go through a four-step drill in its attempts to bring down aircraft. First an aircraft must be detected; then you must acquire a precise idea of where it is. You track the target long enough for your weapons to find it and, hopefully, destroy it. Each of these steps provides ample opportunity for failure. Pilots also have a keen sense of self-preservation and diligently respond to whatever temporary advantage the air-defense crowd might acquire. The four steps are:

1. *Detection.* Aircraft, no matter how large, are small objects in the vastness of the sky. Early air-defense forces learned that the best method for detection was to carefully examine the situation from the enemy pilots' point of view. The always-scarce detection resources were then placed where the enemy planes were likely to come from. There are never enough radars or human observers to cover every possible direction. Pilots are aware of this problem—or opportunity, from their point of view. Electronic warfare and low flying are the favorite ploys to avoid detection. Attacking aircraft have sensors that tell them when they are being "painted" by enemy radars. If their ECM is good enough, they may be able to "play space invaders on the enemy radar screen," as one U.S. pilot put it. ECM can make detection either impossible or dubious. If ECM does not do the trick, the old "on the deck" solution usually works. Flying 100 meters or less from the ground, aircraft can evade most radars, but at the price of considerable pilot fatigue. A third solution to avoiding detection is provided by the "stealth" aircraft, which is designed and equipped to defeat radar as much as possible. The solution to detecting low flyers, and to a lesser extent stealth, has

been airborne radars. During the 1960s, the United States developed the AWACS (Airborne Warning and Control System), a large radar-and-command center in a four-engine commercial jet. The Russians followed with their own version a decade later. AWACS aircraft are only as good as their computer, which caused the Russians enormous problems. Everyone has problems getting enough AWACS to cover everything. The U.S. AWACS can stay on station for only six hours, unless it gets an inflight refueling. Twelve hours in the air is the usual maximum, because of the need for ground maintenance on the aircraft and the complex radars and computers. The Russians had severe problems with reliability. It is no longer as easy as it used to be to avoid detection. Therefore, emphasis has shifted to defeating target acquisition.

2. *Acquisition.* Once an aircraft has been detected, it must be "acquired." That is, you must confirm that it is an enemy aircraft and determine exactly where it is and where it is going. You want to know when the aircraft will be within range of your weapons. The detection and acquisition radar always have a longer range than your weapons so that you can hit the target as far away as possible. This is important for two reasons. First, the air-defense system deploys behind the fighting front. The target aircraft are often attacking targets on the front line or are using long-range missiles. If the aircraft gets too close before being shot at, it may launch its weapons before it can be hit. Second, the aircraft will likely be traveling at high speed, between 200 and 700 meters a second. For a tactical air-defense system with a maximum weapon range of 20,000 meters, every second counts. All of this occurs in an atmosphere of uncertainty. A typical ground radar can spot aircraft up to 550 kilometers out and 30 kilometers high. However, at the 550-kilometers range the probability of making a positive detection is only 50 percent. At 370 kilometers, the probability is still only 90 percent. A daring pilot can take advantage of this uncertainty to fly most of his mission at high altitude before descending to the more dangerous and nerve-racking flying at treetop level for the final approach to target.

3. *Tracking.* Successful target detection and acquisition can take less than a minute; often only seconds are needed. If those two steps are successful, you now go through the white-knuckle phase of the operation. You have to maintain your "track" of the enemy aircraft long enough for your guns or missiles to do their job. Tracking generally commences outside the range of the weapons it serves. Missiles, with their longer range, are fired soon after tracking begins. Missiles without independent guidance systems (that is, most of them) depend on continually successful tracking. Guns, because of their short range, must track the longest before they get a shot off. While all this tracking and shooting is going on, the target is trying

desperately, and often successfully, to "break the track." Violent maneuvers and/or ECM will often succeed. Other countermeasures include diving down to treetop level and dropping flares to draw off heat-seeking missiles and chaff (strips of foil) to befog the radar.

4. *Destruction.* Even if an air-defense weapon manages to succeed in detecting, acquiring, and tracking a target, a hit does not always result in destruction, or even significant damage. Modern aircraft are overbuilt and made to last. They have many duplicate and triplicate systems. The warheads of many missiles are less than 12 pounds. Even a direct hit has to hit a vital component to do the job. Larger warheads explode when they get close, but even here the damage is often not any greater than a direct hit by a smaller warhead.

Air-Defense Weapons

Air-defense weapons range from small-caliber projectiles to nuclear explosives. The size and design of these various warheads combine in different ways to attack their targets.

Small Warheads. It is possible to destroy an aircraft with a small warhead. An aircraft moving along some 100 meters from the ground at 200 meters a second is very susceptible to the slightest damage. When more massive missile damage occurs at the higher altitudes, the aircraft has more distance, and time, to sort things out. Smaller missiles, primarily the low-altitude portable ones, have only five-pound warheads. Half the Israeli A-4 aircraft hit by these warheads in 1973 returned and landed. These missiles are limited by their small size and lack of a proximity fuse, a radar device that allows the warhead to explode in a near-miss situation. The small missiles are heat seekers that, in most cases, can be fired only when behind the target. Their targets tend to fly in low, fast, and unexpectedly. This gives the missile operator about 10 seconds to get off a shot. Many aircraft have sensors that warn of approaching missiles. A sharp pilot will eject flares or zip behind a hill in frequently successful maneuvers to avoid the missile. Often, however, the low-flying pilot never sees the missile. Moreover, newer models of these missiles, like the U.S. Stinger, are more accurate. Under combat conditions in Afghanistan, Stingers were downing Russian aircraft more than 50 percent of the time each missile is fired.

At these low altitudes, under 1,000 meters, guns are still the most effective antiaircraft weapon. Many missiles exist because they are portable, and weapons designers and manufacturers think they are neat. Guns have shells ranging from 20mm to 57mm in size. These shells require a direct hit to do any damage, and one hit is rarely fatal. But these shells are used in large quantities. The damage adds up, if not to a downed aircraft, then to an increased workload on the already overburdened aircraft-maintenance crews. Shell weight varies considerably. A 20mm shell weighs only 3.5 ounces. The 57mm weighs in at 100 ounces, more than 6 pounds. Commonly used are 20mm, 23mm (7 ounces), 35mm (20 ounces), 40mm (30 ounces), and 57mm. These weapons are often used in multiple-barrel turrets. The Swiss-developed Gepard (two 35mm guns) can deliver 18 35mm shells a second for its German users. The Russian ZSU-23 mount four 23mm guns and can deliver 60 shells a second. These are being replaced by 30mm units. These light antiaircraft guns are increasingly deployed primarily against helicopters. And helicopters are being armored and protected so that they can withstand 20mm and 23mm shells. Although calibers are being upgraded, the real damage is being done by larger weapons. The lighter guns can damage, but increasingly they cannot kill.

Larger Warheads. Larger missiles have warheads that are often quite elaborate and weigh hundreds of pounds. The design of these warheads strives for flexibility and the ability to destroy or inflict damage even for misses. Direct hits are difficult to obtain and quite rare. A near miss with the right kind of warhead can cripple or kill. Using shaped charges to direct a flight of high-velocity fragments, these warheads can be fatal to many aircraft 100 or more meters away from the explosion. Proximity fuses calculate the most effective detonation point. Western warheads are the most elaborate and lethal, with Russian ones continually lagging behind. An unexpected form of antiaircraft missile has been found in antitank missiles. Because helicopters fly slowly and close to the ground, it has been found theoretically possible to down them with antitank missiles. There has been no use of this technique yet, but several armies have investigated the possibility. In combat, troops will take advantage of whatever edge is available to them. And in this case it comes full circle, as during World War II the Germans turned their principal antiaircraft weapon, the 88mm gun, into the most deadly antitank weapon of that war.

Larger-caliber (75mm and up) Antiaircraft Guns also use proximity fuses and specially designed fragmentation warheads. These shells are expensive and are used less often than simpler ones. The reason is that a large number of the elaborate shells are still needed to obtain a hit. A new generation of even "smarter" shells is proposed, to give large-caliber antiaircraft guns many of the same capabilities of surface-to-air missiles. However, missiles are more expensive still, but are more flexible and easier to upgrade. Large-caliber guns are still used by Russia and its client states. The guns are used as they were during World War II (1939–45) and in Vietnam (1966–75). A barrage of shells is thrown up where the radar predicts the approaching aircraft will be. In clear weather, when the radars are blinded by ECM, they can still perform well. Navies still make extensive use of large (and small) antiaircraft guns. Part of this is due to the lack of obstacles at sea.

Guns can shoot at what they can see, and on the ocean you can see more. Against high-speed cruise missiles, special small-caliber guns have been developed. Once turned on, these radar-guided weapons will automatically attack any object in the vicinity that resembles a cruise missile. As these missiles come in at up to 1,000 meters a second, there is no time for human intervention.

Very Small-Caliber Antiaircraft Guns. Although not decisive weapons, machine guns and rifles can have an effect. During World War II, the Soviets developed the tactic of having ground troops firing into the air when under attack by aircraft. This not only damaged some aircraft, but also maintained the morale of the troops. Doing something, anything, to fight back is better than simply diving for cover. Most tanks, and many other vehicles, have a heavy-caliber machine gun (12.7mm to 14.5mm) that is effective to an altitude of 1,000 meters. Enough of this small-caliber fire in the air will not discourage aircraft—they usually won't even see it—but damage will be done. In rare instances, aircraft have even been brought down. Normally, however, just more damage is created, and the damage adds up.

Tactical Deployment

Air-defense weapons are deployed according to their range and mobility. The short-range and mobile systems travel with the combat units. The longer-range and less-mobile equipment is set up as far back as 100 kilometers behind the fighting front to protect the rear-area installations and give additional high-altitude protection to front-line units. Ideally, air-defense units should be stationed on high ground to allow the greatest coverage by radar or visually controlled missiles. This is often not practical, especially in a mobile battle, where everyone will be on the road when the aircraft attack. In a defensive situation, or when a rear area is being attacked, the aircraft are more cautious and come in with the primary intention of first destroying air-defense units. As the latter are usually unarmored and full of explosive and flammable materials, they are very vulnerable targets. The new ICM (Improved Conventional Munitions) include bombs that spread dozens of smaller bombs (up to 200 incendiaries from one bomb) over a few hundred thousand square meters. Air-defense systems are fragile things.

The key to successful air defense is layers of defense at multiple depth and altitude. The typical Russian technique, which the Russians export with their weapons, puts ZSU-23 (2-kilometers range) cannon, portable missiles, and SA-9 (8-kilometers range) missiles right up with the combat troops. In addition, the troops have shoulder-fired surface-to-air missiles (SA-7/14, 4-kilometers range). A few kilometers behind the front are SA-8 (12 kilometers), SA-11 (25 kilometers), and SA-6 (30 kilometers).

The SA-4 (75 kilometers) and SA-10 (50 kilometers) systems provide defense farther back, with only some of them extending their coverage beyond the leading units. Western nations use the same general principles. In addition, friendly aircraft are essential for successful air defense. For Western nations, air superiority is seen as the primary air-defense technique. The Russians put more of their air-defense strength on the ground.

The Ultimate Air Defense: Air Superiority

The only sure protection from enemy air attack is to destroy or suppress the enemy air force. In other words, the best air defense is air superiority. While this sounds nice in theory, several potential problems exist in practice. The successful destruction of enemy air forces in World War II has made Western armies slow to realize that they may not always have air superiority. During the last 40 years, America has made belated and desultory attempts to develop air defenses on a par with the Russian-type system. These efforts were dealt a double blow when the Soviet Union collapsed, followed shortly by the triumph of U.S. air power in the Gulf War. It is now, and for the foreseeable future, assumed that U.S. ground forces won't have to worry too much about defending themselves from enemy air attack. With the general demise of the Soviet air forces, there is no air power on the planet to contest Western air forces attaining general air superiority in a future war. But if this air superiority is not obtained, or until it is, the burden of defense will be on the guns and missiles of the antiaircraft units. Even when air superiority is achieved, the enemy may be able to muster sufficient aircraft to obtain temporary air superiority in one area or another.

Air defenses have never been as omnipresent as they are today. In the past, air defenses had shorter ranges and lower altitudes. Today, SAM systems can cover areas more than 100 kilometers from the missiles and over 10,000 meters high. Sufficient systems are available to cover an entire theater of operations containing up to a million square miles of real estate.

One of the more difficult aspects of air defense is keeping your missiles from shooting down your own aircraft. This is attempted by careful planning and trying to maintain control of all the air-defense units. Unfortunately, warfare is a messy process, and confusion is the rule. Whichever side has the initiative will be able to maintain a semblance of order in its SAM and aircraft coordination. However, once things start to get messy, not everyone is going to get his orders in time. Friendly aircraft have been, and will continue to be, shot down by their own air-defense weapons. Unfortunately, the situation will no doubt be worse in the future because of the larger number of air-defense systems on the battlefield. In effect, two quite separate systems exist. One is based on aircraft and has its own radars and control systems. The other is based on missiles and guns and also has its own radars and overall command. No one has put two of these interrelated systems against each other on a large scale. The side most at risk is the one that has air superiority only some of the time. The many ground troops with machine guns and their own portable missiles are difficult to control. It's going to be an interesting mess.

Theory and Practice

One of the curious aspects of air defense is that in the past 45 years most of the action has been between Western aircraft and Soviet-made air-defense systems. This has given the impression that air defense is not very efficient. At least 50 Soviet SAMs were fired for each aircraft hit. The lackadaisical performance of Russian air-defense systems was typical of the low effectiveness of Russian high-tech weapons. Western systems are customarily more effective. In the few instances where Western air-defense systems have been used against Russian aircraft, the SAMs performed better. Israel has used its U.S.-built Hawk antiaircraft missiles against Soviet-built Arab jets and required fewer than five missiles for each aircraft hit. Western portable antiaircraft missiles have proved far more effective in Afghanistan than similar Soviet-built systems. The U.S. Stinger missile has a 90 percent hit rate during testing and over 50 percent on the battle-field. This is a typical pattern between test and combat conditions. The Russian SA-7 and SA-14 results have been less impressive. Historically, air-defense weapons have had to fire enormous quantities of munitions to hit an aircraft. During World War II, between 5,000 and 12,000 88mm or 105mm shells were fired to hit one aircraft. In theory, far fewer shells should be needed. In practice, the aircraft are never that easy to find, and the aircraft are eager to avoid destruction. Even the seeming success of the portable Stinger SAMs in Afghanistan was possible because the Russians have not had time to develop effective defensive measures. During the first year of heavy air combat in World War II, fewer than 2,000 artillery, antiaircraft shells were needed to hit an aircraft. After a year of this, the U.S. and British bombers changed their tactics and raised the shell count three to six times.

Effective air defenses often perform like mines, attacking friendly and enemy aircraft alike. Incorrect identification causes serious problems. During the 1973 Arab-Israeli War, the Arabs fired 2,100 missiles and destroyed 85 aircraft, 45 of which were Arab. This is not supposed to happen. All aircraft carry an electronic gizmo called IFF (Identification, Friend or Foe) that gives a coded electronic response when interrogated by radar. But codes can be broken; responses can be ignored or misinterpreted. The Arab air-defense people and at least 45 Arab pilots know all about this problem. It plagues all air forces in all wars. Target acquisition is no trivial task.

Another important aspect of air defense is the tendency of aircraft to avoid heavily defended areas. Going after air-defense systems, or "flak suppression," is an expensive task. Shutting down air defenses is only undertaken if the target being defended is important enough to warrant such an expensive application of air power. Increasingly, missiles shape up as a more efficient way to go after heavily defended targets. This has spurred development of air-defense systems that can hit missiles. The U.S. Patriot SAMs' ability to intercept Scud missiles was the first combat example of this technique. While crude, the Patriot showed that it could be done. That said, all the Allied aircraft losses in combat during the Gulf War were from low-tech weapons like machine guns and small SAMs. As in the past, air defenses will spend most of their time waiting for targets that never appear.

The Future

Major improvements are coming in missile detection, guidance, and maneuverability capabilities. Detection and guidance improvements are largely electronic, particularly more powerful computers. As with sonar, the big problem with detection is interpreting the returning signals. More powerful computers make it possible to accurately interpret signals from more distant, and less distinct, targets. Accurate "over the horizon" radars with ranges of thousands of kilometers are now coming into use, although current technology only gives an indication that something is out there and an approximate location. Smaller and more powerful electronics make it possible to put powerful radars in missiles and even artillery shells. It is increasingly common for missiles and radars to have guidance computers that can be reprogrammed. Thus, as pilots develop new defensive techniques, the antiaircraft missiles can be quickly reprogrammed.

It is also possible for missile computers to learn on the spot and outthink their prey. High-tech antiaircraft weapons are even coming to the aid of ground troops, as the new generations of shoulder-fired missiles pack a lot more electronic intelligence. Pilots will increasingly have to choose between avoiding heavily defended areas, using massive resources to destroy antiair systems, or accepting high losses to complete their missions.

Naval air defense has additional problems. Over a dozen ships in a task force are spread over several hundred square miles. Each is capable of air defense. But if they coordinate their activities, their defense will be even stronger. The traditional solution has been passive coordination, assigning each ship a sector to defend. Coming into use is active coordination, where computers on each ship talk to other ships and instantly decide who will shoot at what. This rapid coordination is becoming mandatory in the face of massive cruise-missile attacks. The key is not so much the computers, but the communications. If the right types of satellites are available, this coordination becomes even more effective. Electronic-warfare prowess then becomes critical, no matter which side of this battle you are on.

Helicopters have presented air-defense forces with their most elusive targets. However, ground-based antihelicopter mines are in development. These items use acoustic sensors to pick out the sound of a helicopter, plot its course, and, if within range, release a low-flying warhead with its own radar and heat sensor. These items already exist and may be in use by the end of the decade. More advanced models may be able to go after low-flying jets. This will not mean the end of aircraft. It is still questionable just how effective antiaircraft defenses are. A recent example can be found in Angola, where, during the late 1980s, the Soviets constructed the most elaborate air-defense system found outside Europe. Over 70 radars and two dozen missile bases were supported by nearly 100 interceptors. Most of this was maintained by East German mercenaries. Yet South African aircraft regularly penetrated this system. Some things never change, and many potential buyers of Russian weapons took notice. They are apparently not trying to keep up with all the Western advances in stealth and flak suppression. The embarrassments their air-defense forces have suffered over the years are having their effect. With the world's largest investment in air defenses, and a declining growth in industrial technology, we can perceive one more reason why Russia is trying to reform its society.

The collapse of Soviet military power and the 1991 Gulf War both had enormous impact on the future of air-defense weapons. With the enormous Soviet military establishment now a fraction of its former size, there is no longer an easy justification for additional research on more capable air-defense weapons. Yet the Gulf War demonstrated what the low-tech (Iraqi) and high-tech (U.S.) air-defense weapons were capable of. The technological lead the West has in air defense will remain for some time, even without a lot of additional R&D. While military research may not get a lot more money, civilian research on computers and other electronic components will keep the military supplied with affordable upgrades to existing weapons. The only dark spot in all this is that, as high-tech air-defense weapons become cheaper and more dependent on purely civilian technology, these weapons will more easily spread to many different nations. Thus, the next war involving Western air forces may find these aircraft facing more capable weapons that are, in many respects, first cousins to the electronic consumer goods that have always been so abundant.

Air-Defense Weapons

Chart 8-1 shows the characteristics of the world's air-defense weapons. Shown are the most widely used weapons, which are representative of the ones not included. As it is a relatively easy matter for an industrial nation to manufacture most air-defense weapons, a few nations do not have a monopoly on their manufacture, as is the case with aircraft, tanks, and similar weapons.

TYPE gives the designation of the weapon. For Russian weapons, the NATO designation is given. See below for notes on the systems.

NATION indicates the country that originally designed the weapon.

EFFECTIVENESS is a general evaluation of the relative capabilities of the weapon on a 1 to 100 scale. These are estimates, as many of these weapons have not been used in combat. Those that have been used against real targets have since undergone modification. All air-defense weapons constantly undergo upgrading. In addition, the primarily electronic countermeasures of potential targets have a considerable influence on their effectiveness and have been taken into account. The ratings also take into account systems reliability, quality of target-acquisition system, and lethality of warhead.

EFFECTIVE ALTITUDE MAXIMUM is the maximum altitude (in meters) at which the weapon can reasonably be expected to hit a target. This limit is imposed primarily by the weapon's ability to reach that height. Missiles operate best at high altitudes. Guns tend to do better closer to the ground.

EFFECTIVE ALTITUDE MINIMUM indicates the minimum altitude (in meters) at which the weapon can reasonably be expected to hit a target. For missiles, this represents the distance traveled after launch before the warhead is armed and the guidance system can figure out where it is and where the target is. Most missile systems cannot hit targets very near ground level because radar has difficulty spotting a target among the clutter of objects on the ground. The degree to which targets are moving about near the ground also degrades missile-system performance. Because of these problems, the minimum is optimistic and depends on how ideal the situation is for the missile system.

RANGE is the maximum horizontal range of the weapon in kilometers. This limit is dictated largely by the system's target-acquisition ability.

RATE OF FIRE (RPS) indicates the number of projectiles the system can fire per second (rounds per second). Missile systems are indicated. Such systems can normally fire all the missiles on their launchers within a few seconds. It is common to fire two or more missiles at each target in order to improve the chances that the target will be hit. Gun systems similarly rely on a high rate of fire in order to increase chances of a hit.

ALL-WEATHER CAPABILITY is a numerical rating of the system's ability to operate at night and in bad weather. However, even the most sophisticated systems often have manual backups. This is because missile- and radar-guided gun systems are quite complex and subject to failure. The manual backup capability allows the system to be used in clear weather if the all-weather system fails. The higher rating indicates better all-weather capability and higher system reliability.

8-1 Antiaircraft Weapons

Type	Nation	Effectiveness	Effective Minimum	Altitude Maximum (meters)	Range (km)	Rate of Fire (rps)	All Weather Capability	Caliber	Missiles Barrels	Naval Version	Mobility
Patriot	US	100	100	24,000	60	Missile	7	410	4	No	SP
Standard ER RIM67A	US	83	50	25,000	110	Missile	6	343	2	Same	Ship
SA-10b	Russia	71	900	30,000	80	Missile	7	500	2	No	SP
Improved Hawk	US	70	30	18,000	40	Missile	6	370	3	No	Mobile
SA-10a	Russia	67	300	4,500	50	Missile	6	450	4	SA-N-6	Mobile
Standard MR RIM66A	US	62	50	25,000	32	Missile	6	305	2	Same	Ship
Nike-Hercules	US	51	1,000	50,000	150	Missile	6	800	1	No	Mobile
SA-11	Russia	48	30	14,000	30	Missile	6	400	4	SA-N-7	SP
Phalanx	US	47	0	2,000	2	50	7	20	6	Same	Ship
Hawk	US	45	100	11,000	30	Missile	6	350	3	No	Mobile
2S6M	Russia	45	15	3,500	8	Miss/Gun	3	170	9	No	SP
Roland	Germany	39	10	3,000	6	Missile	6	163	4	No	SP
SA-N-3 Improved	Russia	38	150	25,000	55	Missile	6	600	2	Same	Ship
Avenger	US	36	0	4,800	5	Miss/Gun	2	70/12.7	9	No	SP
SA-N-3	Russia	35	150	25,000	30	Missile	6	305	2	Same	Ship
SA-4B	Russia	33	300	20,000	60	Missile	5	800	2	Same	Ship
Tartar RIM24B	US	33	50	20,000	20	Missile	6	300	2	No	Mobile
Sea Sparrow RIM7H	US	32	15	5,000	5	Missile	6	200	8	Same	Ship
Stinger	US	31	0	4,800	5	Missile	0	70	1	No	Portable
SA-6	Russia	30	50	13,000	24	Missile	6	330	3	No	SP
SA-2B	Russia	30	1,000	24,000	100	Missile	4	500	1	SA-N-2	Mobile

Name	Country										
Crotale	France	29	50	3,600	9	Missile	5	156	4	Yes	SP
ADMG-630	Russia	28	0	2,000	2	40	5	30	2	Same	Ship
Rapier	Britain	28	10	3,000	7	Missile	4	133	4	No	SP
AMX-30SA	France	27	0	2,000	4	21	4	30	2	No	SP
SA-3	Russia	26	300	15,000	35	Missile	4	450	2	SA-N-1	SP
SA-8B	Russia	26	10	12,000	15	Missile	4	210	4	SA-N-4	SP
Gepard	Switzer	23	0	2,000	4	18	6	35	2	No	SP
SA-13	Russia	21	20	4,000	8	Missile	0	120	4	No	SP
ZSU-30	Russia	21	0	2,500	4	40	4	30	4	Yes	SP
ZSU-23	Russia	19	0	2,000	3	65	3	23	4	Yes	SP
Chapparral	US	18	100	1,000	5	Missile	0	127	4	No	Portable
SA-14	Russia	16	25	4,500	5	Missile	0	70	1	Yes	SP
ZSU-57	Russia	14	0	4,000	6	4	3	57	2	SA-N-5	SP
SA-7	Russia	11	25	4,200	4	Missile	0	70	1	No	Portable
SA-9	Russia	11	50	4,000	7	Missile	0	110	4	Yes	SP
Vulcan	US	10	0	2,000	2	50	0	20	6	No	SP
M-42	US	10	0	1,500	3	4	0	40	2	Yes	SP
ZPU-4	Russia	10	0	1,400	1	40	0	14.5	4	Yes	SP
.50 Cal	Many	5	0	1,000	1	10	0	12.7	1,2,3,4		

CALIBER is the diameter of the shell or missile in millimeters (25.4mm = 1 inch).

MISSILE BARRELS shows the number of barrels a gun system has or the missile launchers system has. The more, the better.

NAVAL VERSION indicates if the system is also used aboard a ship. If so, this is indicated by "navy" or its navy name. The naval versions generally have the same operating characteristics as the land-based versions.

MOBILITY. *SP* means self-propelled: The entire system moves on one or more vehicles and can be used while equipment is still on the vehicles. *Mobile* means the entire system can be moved on vehicles and put into action after a minimum of unloading and preparation. *Portable* means that the system can be moved but requires extensive setup. *Fixed* means the system operates from permanent sites. *Ship* is a system that is normally mounted on a ship. All naval versions operate from a ship.

THE MISSILE SYSTEMS

.50 Cal (12.7mm) is a machine gun commonly found mounted on armored vehicles and trucks for air defense.

2S6M is a new system that incorporates 30mm guns and SA-19 surface-to-air missiles. Radar and fire-control equipment are available for both weapons.

ADMG-630 is the Russian equivalent of Phalanx. Its capability is somewhat less, which is not very encouraging considering the problems Phalanx has had. There is an earlier version of this weapon that is nothing more than twin 30mm guns. This is basically the small-caliber air-defense cannon developed about 50 years ago. Many navies still use such weapons, although it is unlikely that major-nation aircraft would approach close enough for these to be used. The more advanced air forces use standoff missiles to keep the aircraft away from ship defenses. Unless they're automated, like Phalanx, it is difficult for such weapons to successfully engage missiles coming in at 500+ meters a second.

AMX-30SA is a battlefield air-defense cannon.

Avenger is a U.S. system first deployed in the late 1980s. It consists of a powered turret on a Hummer vehicle. The turret has eight Stinger SAMs and a 12.7mm multibarrel machine gun. There is a FLIR system for spotting targets at night and in bad weather. But normally target acquisition is visual.

Chaparral is an air-to-air missile (the Sidewinder) used as a battlefield air-defense system.

Crotale is similar to the Rapier and Roland systems.

Gepard is a battlefield air-defense cannon developed in Switzerland and used primarily by Germany.

Hawk is the original U.S. missile system for defense against low-flying aircraft. Still used by many nations that cannot afford the upgraded version (see below).

Improved Hawk is an extensively upgraded version of the original Hawk. This is the primary air-defense missile system for the United States and many Western ground forces.

M-42 is a World War II–era battlefield air-defense cannon that is still found in many armies.

Nike-Hercules is the standard long-range air-defense missile system used by nations that cannot afford Patriot and similar systems.

Patriot was introduced in the early 1980s after over 20 years of development. It replaces first Nike-Hercules and eventually Hawk.

Phalanx is a "last chance" automatic defense system against surface-to-surface missiles and low-flying aircraft. Used on ships only.

Rapier is a battlefield missile system. Used extensively for airfield defense against low-flying aircraft.

Roland is a battlefield missile system used by many Western nations.

SA-10a is the standard system for the defense of Russia's borders. Its principal features are quick reaction time of the detection and acquisition systems and high speed of the missiles (2,000 meters a second). Effective against low-flying aircraft and missiles.

SA-11 is a battlefield missile system intended to complement and eventually replace the SA-6. Has increased reliability and accuracy against low-flying aircraft.

SA-10b is the most current Russian long-range system. It uses improved radar and guidance systems. This gives it some capability against small, low-flying targets like cruise missiles. Also has capability against ballistic missiles. This is a mobile system, in effect a mobile version of the older SA-10a.

SA-13 is a replacement for the SA-9 and serves the same purpose.

SA-14 is an improved replacement for the SA-7. This is a clear-weather system with good capability against low-flying aircraft. Considered to be essentially an attempt to clone the U.S. Stinger.

SA-19 is a new, short-range battlefield missile system that is carried by an armored vehicle (2S6M).

SA-2 is an obsolete missile system still used in defense of Russian airspace. It will probably be retired now that the Soviet Union is gone and the successor states can't afford all those obsolete air-defense systems.

SA-3 is an older system, still used because the Russians never throw anything away. Easily defeated but still a lethal nuisance, it will probably go the way of the SA-2.

SA-4 is the Russian heavy battlefield missile. Primarily used for long-range, high-flying aircraft. Russian equivalent of the Nike-Hercules, but not as capable.

SA-6 is the principal Russian battlefield air-defense missile system for which there is no Western equivalent.

SA-7 is the Russian version of the Redeye.

SA-8 is the Russian equivalent of the Roland.

SA-9 is similar in concept to Chaparral, although it uses a missile more similar to the SA-14 than to an air-to-air type.

SA-N-3 Improved is the latest version of the standard heavy naval air-defense missile system and the Russian equivalent of the U.S. Standard.

SA-N-3 is an older version of the improved model (see above).

Sea-Sparrow is an air-to-air missile used in an air-defense system adapted for shipboard use.

Standard ER (extended range) is the standard shipboard missile system for the U.S. Navy.

Standard MR (medium range) is a shorter-range version of the Standard ER (see above).

Stinger is an air-defense missile system carried and fired by one man. It replaces the similar Redeye. Stinger also used as an air-to-air weapon on helicopters (AH-64).

Tartar is an older U.S. Navy missile system that was replaced in the U.S. fleet during the 1980s by the Standard system.

Vulcan is a battlefield air-defense cannon.

ZPU-4 is typical of the multiple machine guns used for air defense. Generally used only by less well equipped armies or reserve formations.

ZSU-23 is a battlefield air-defense cannon. This is a widely used Russian system, many of which have been upgraded to 30mm and improved electronics.

ZSU-30 is a replacement for the ZSU-23, with 30mm guns and better electronics.

ZSU-57 is an older battlefield air-defense cannon that has been replaced by missiles and the ZSU-23.

PART THREE:

NAVAL OPERATIONS

NAVAL WARFARE has always been the least seen, and least understood, form of combat. It is slow, tedious, and expensive warfare. For nations dependent on maritime commerce, naval warfare is almost as important as ground combat.

9

The Navy:
On the Surface

THE ONLY CREDIBLE opponent the U.S. Navy has had since the 1950s is now no more. The Soviet Navy has, since the late 1980s, been wasting away at anchor, starved of the resources that keep a navy viable. One could say that not only is the Soviet Navy history, but it always was more history than substance. However, a lot of the Russian Navy remains, and will continue to exist for some years to come.

If there is a major naval war in the future, two conspicuously different styles of maritime warfare will collide. The two major naval powers are still Russia and the United States. Each has markedly different attitudes toward the use of naval forces. The U.S. Navy (USN) is unquestionably the largest and most powerful navy in the world and has adopted a style of naval warfare that is unique, yet befitting its singular structure and composition. Moreover, the Russian naval doctrine is widely used by many Third World navies. To understand what the Russians and like-minded navies might do, you must understand what the Russians have done.

Lessons from the Past

There is nothing more instructive than defeat. The Russian Navy has taken lessons not only from its own but from those of its enemies. Adopting the submarine doctrine of Germany, which failed in World War I and II, and the kamikaze doctrine of the Japanese, which failed in 1945, the Russians have developed a style of warfare widely regarded as potentially successful. The Russian style has been adopted by most of the smaller navies of the world, including many Western ones. This style depends on the stealth of submarines, sheer numbers of cruise missiles, and vast minefields. This last element, mines, victimized the Russian Navy three times in this century. First there was the Russo-Japanese War (1904–5), then the two World Wars (1914–17 and 1941–45). The Russians have a lot of experience in how not to do it. Out of this experience, they have developed a set of guidelines they trust will change their naval fortunes.

1. *Surprise is essential.* Get in the first shot and make it count. Hit the other fellow before he knows there's a war on. The bulk of the Russian Navy is built and trained for this type of operation and is not organized for a long war. Anything beyond a few months will be beyond its planned capabilities.

2. *Construct ships for maximum "one-shot" capability.* The Russian Navy's targets are, in order of importance, ballistic-missile submarines, aircraft carriers, nuclear-attack submarines, and enemy shipping. The Russian Navy has a lot of small, heavily armed ships so that it can hit as many of these targets as possible in the shortest time.

3. *Learn from the Japanese kamikaze experience.* A multitude of aircraft that crash themselves into ships can overcome massive defense systems. This is reflected in the large number of naval cruise missiles in the Russian Navy.

4. *Learn from the German experience with submarines.* Send enough submarines against the enemy before it can mobilize its forces, and you can deny it use of the oceans. The Germans almost succeeded in 1914–17 and 1939–45. Germany began World War II with only 57 submarines to counter some 16,000 Allied merchant ships. If the third of those ships controlled by Great Britain could have been quickly decimated, victory would have been within sight. If Russia goes into a war today, it could unleash over 100 submarines against 20,000 merchant ships.

The victor in World War II, the United States, also used its experience to develop basic attitudes toward naval war. These can be summarized as follows:

1. *No matter what you thought before the war, new weapon systems will soon assert themselves with superior or unexpected performance.* Before World War II, it was still assumed that the battleship was the decisive naval weapon. The aircraft carrier was seen as just another support system for the big-gun battlewagons, and an untried one at

that. Today, the carriers are seen as the decisive naval weapon, and nuclear submarines are the untried system supporting the carriers. The situation is similar to the pre–World War II one in that the older system (battleships) did prove useful in supporting amphibious landings and protecting task forces from enemy aircraft. The primary function of a capital ship is to go after those of the opponent. So today we have nuclear subs going after each other to decide who rules the seas while carriers support amphibious operations and help protect the fleet from enemy subs. The United States covers its bets by attempting to maintain strength in both areas. Unlike in the 1930s, when the carriers had to scramble for every dollar, nuclear submarines now receive more resources than any other ship type. This is likely to change somewhat in the post–Cold War era, as naval budgets shrink.

2. *Nations that depend on merchant shipping can win a war only if they maintain control of the oceans.* The Western Allies did this during World Wars I and II and were victorious. The Japanese were not able to withstand the onslaught of American submarines in World War II and collapsed when their economy was strangled by this blockade. Merchant-shipping powers like Japan, the United States, and Britain have spent a lot of money on antisubmarine warfare since then. Surprise will not guarantee any future submarine user a victory if its intended victims remain alert and wary. Japan launched a number of surprise attacks in 1941, including Pearl Harbor. Numerous ships and aircraft were destroyed. Yet America recovered. Rather than depending on eventual recovery, the United States and its allies maintain a high degree of vigilance against future surprise attacks. Any future naval aggressor's prime chance for success in a future war depends on surprise.

3. *Superior information-gathering ability is not the same as knowing what the other fellow will do.* Cracking the enemy's codes and keeping him under observation at all times will not allow you to get inside his head. Too much information, incorrectly interpreted, can lead to fatally wrong conclusions. This is one of the most ignored lessons of World War II, Korea, and Vietnam.

Techniques of Modern Surface Warfare

Although fleets continue adding more submarines to their rosters, it is still surface forces that call the shots. There are few independent operations that submarines can undertake. In most cases, subs are a supporting force, albeit a crucial one. The following description of techniques assumes the participation of submarine and antisubmarine forces.

DEPLOYMENT

During peacetime, about 80–90 percent of most Third World navies and 65 percent of those in the West are in port. Ships go to sea to practice, and to keep an eye on potential opponents. Nearly every navy organizes its fleet into task forces of up to a dozen or so ships. The core of these task forces are aircraft carriers or large ships carrying cruise missiles. Normally, there is one major ship (a carrier or large cruiser/battleship) plus 6–10 cruisers, destroyers, and frigates, plus one or more subs. These ships move in a pattern that gets the best effect from their differing capabilities in antiair, antisurface, and antisubmarine warfare. The task forces are based together at naval installations, which contain supply and repair facilities as well as housing for families. When ships go to sea, they are sustained by a network of supply ships. Some travel with the task force, others shuttle back and forth to restore their supplies. These supply ships are always a weak point in naval deployments. Not only are these ships liable to be destroyed, but their detection often gives an indication of where the warships they support are located.

DETECTION

If you want to destroy the other fleet, find it first. The United States uses satellite reconnaissance and a worldwide network of intelligence-collection ships, aircraft, and shore-based observers. In peacetime, some smaller navies shadow major Western task forces with combat and/or surveillance ships. If war comes suddenly, these shadows may be quickly blown away before they can make a suicide attack. A gradual escalation to war would involve attempts to reinforce these shadows, while the Western ships would attempt to elude them. Both these techniques are practiced in peacetime. Generally, Western fleets have the edge in detection with their larger land- and carrier-based air-reconnaissance forces. In addition, the United States maintains a worldwide network of underwater sensors.

ATTACK

The most noticeable change since World War II is the standoff weapons, guided missiles launched from ships and aircraft at distances of nearly 1,000 kilometers. Submarines also carry some versions of these missiles, as well as long-range guided torpedoes (40+ kilometers). Another result of this shift to missiles is a reduction in the striking power of each hit because of the smaller missile warheads compared to those in large-caliber guns and torpedoes.

DEFENSE

Basic techniques vary, depending on the resources of the task force. An aircraft carrier uses a more elaborate defense than a noncarrier force. This defense system is described in the following chapter on naval air operations. Noncarrier task forces use ship-based helicopters to give additional detection capability as well as whatever land-based and satellite reconnaissance resources are available to all naval vessels. Electronic warfare plays a large role in defense, as it is possible to hide oneself by deceiving the enemy's sensors.

DAMAGE CONTROL

Battle damage is inevitable. How quickly ships are able to recover from this becomes a decisive factor, particularly when one side is more capable in this area. Western navies have an edge in damage control. This edge is not absolute, as all navies that have not been in combat for a decade or so lose their edge in this area. The reasons are the usual ones: Situations that do not occur regularly tend to get less attention than those that do. Although accidents occur during peacetime, few are as catastrophic as combat damage. As new equipment and ship designs are introduced during peacetime, there is little opportunity to determine how damage-control equipment and procedures should be changed. Peacetime practice rarely catches up with wartime reality until after there have been several disasters. See also the section below on ship design.

Differences Between Russian and Western Techniques

Most Western navies have long and successful naval traditions. Russia, and most small navies, have had a shorter and less distinguished experience at sea. Neither World War I nor World War II were glorious chapters in Russia's naval history. While Soviet ground forces have regularly come back from initial defeat to gain ultimate victory, the Soviet Navy has begun and ended its wars on equally sour notes. In light of this experience, Russia attempted to rewrite the book on naval practice. Russia began its "new navy" in the 1950s. The Russians have been perceptive, imaginative, resourceful, and desperate. Although the United States had taken the lead in nuclear-attack submarine development, Russia was the first to push ahead in the development of surface-to-surface missiles and electronic warfare. Withal, Russia has clung to its traditional concept of putting all its power up front. Another tradition retained was the building of large numbers of smaller, but heavily armed, ships. The Russians' theory was that this provided more targets and made it more difficult and expensive for their opponents to hunt them all down. All of this was to increase the ability of Russia to more efficiently defend its maritime borders.

Belatedly, the West caught on to the potential of the Soviet innovations. Russia was now faced with two problems. As its fleet grew larger, Russia saw the potential for projecting its naval power beyond its own coastal waters. The second problem was the West's increasing ability to go after the numerous small targets the Soviet fleet provided. This brought about a second shift of Soviet naval planning in the 1960s. The Russians began building larger ships, better able to take punishment and effectively move thousands of miles from their own waters. They now have carriers and battle cruisers, as well as the world's largest cruise-missile submarines. Both sides are becoming more like each other, but for the foreseeable future, fundamental differences remain. These dissimilarities are most prominent in the following areas:

1. *Ship Design.* Russia favors a larger number of smaller, somewhat cheaper, and, ton for ton, less effective ships. These vessels appear to bristle with weapons, especially when compared with Western ships. Indeed, Russian ships do carry more weapons. But they also carry some serious liabilities as well. Work space and equipment access are less than in Western ships. This makes it very difficult to get at anything that breaks down. Russian crews are primarily three-year conscripts, so they are short on skilled technicians. Inaccessibility and unskilled crews mean most repairs must await a return to port. In the meantime, the ship must depend on duplicate systems, if they are available. The multiplicity of weapons and other equipment also serve to ensure that something will be working when the battle begins. Even then, an additional problem exists, as most missile systems have no reloads. One salvo, and that's it. More serious problems are a lack of vibration damping and onboard repair facilities. Electronic systems are very prone to vibration damage. Equipment that would quickly be put right in Western ships would remain broken on Russian vessels. The absence of tools, spares, technicians, or easy access makes command of a Russian warship a struggle against progressive decay. Moreover, combat will reveal that a relative lack of compartmentalization makes damaging hits catastrophic ones. On the plus side, Russian ships tend to have more modern propulsion systems and better sea-keeping capabilities than Western ones. This is just as well, as the crew quarters are cramped and uncomfortable. Keep in mind that the above is suitable for a coastal navy, where ships rarely spend more than a week or so away from port. When the Russian fleet heads for the high seas, the problems multiply.

2. *Command and Control.* Western ships have developed the combat information center (CIC) concept. The CIC is a room, often in the bowels of the ship, where all sensor and fire-control information is centralized. During combat, the captain, or watch officer, commands from the CIC, while the executive officer, the second in command, mans the bridge topside. Computers, CICs and radar displays allow the commander to grasp the entire battle from the CIC. Radars and other ship sensors cover an area beyond what any human being can grasp without electronic assistance. The CIC recognizes this fact, and brings the 100-kilometer range of air and surface radars, as well as underwater sensor data, together where one officer can make sense out of it.

The CIC became essential once ships became dependent on sensors that saw beyond visual range. Commanders could no longer command from the bridge, relying only on their eyes for battle information. Each ship sends data to the task-force flagship, where they are coordinated and analysis is sent back to each ship. All of this takes place at a close to real-time pace. The task-force commander can make more effective decisions for the entire task force. At the same time, the individual ship commanders can still operate independently as needed. In a fast-moving naval situation, the side that is best able to cope with new situations will prevail. Following long-standing practice, Russian operations are carefully planned and executed under centralized control. Little room is left for individual initiative or deviations from the plan. The command layout of Russian ships reflects this. The Russian captain normally commands from the bridge. The navigation, early warning, and fire-control radar sections, sonar antisubmarine warfare, and other sections report to him from a room full of consoles deep within the ship. In contrast to CIC systems, all this information is combined only in the captain's head. The Russian task-force commander issues more detailed orders before an operation, leaving less latitude for individual initiative. This works fine if the previously prepared plan is carried out. Things begin to fall apart when unexpected events occur. Only among some of their submarine captains do the Russians give the individual commanders free rein.

3. *Concept of Mission.* Not all navies have the same purpose and mission. Russia, as a continental nation fighting oceanic powers, has the obvious mission of denying them sea access. The U.S. mission is to maintain sea access. Merely presenting a potential danger to oceanic powers lessens the use of the oceans for moving goods. If, in addition, sufficient quantities of merchant shipping can be destroyed, then the economic and military power of the oceanic nations is diminished. This makes Russia, and any other continental power, like China, relatively stronger. The attacker in this case is similar to a guerrilla

fighter. He doesn't have to be everywhere at once; he can pick and choose his strikes. As Russia's fleet grew more numerous, and its ships larger, it began to look like the navy of an oceanic power. A large fleet must be protected. Trying to be two kinds of fleet does little to concentrate one's attention.

4. *Deployment.* Only 15 percent of Soviet ships were at sea at any time versus 35 percent for Western navies. This reflects a long-standing tradition in the Russian armed forces to not use equipment until war breaks out. This guarantees that there will be somewhat more equipment available and that no one will know how to use it very well. Practical reasons exist for this. With 75 percent of the Russian sailors draftees, there are not enough technicians to maintain heavily used equipment. The ships are cramped and uncomfortable during long cruises. The nuclear-powered ships produce many cases of radiation poisoning. There have been several mutinies on Soviet ships, and the Russians don't want to encourage more. The money saved by not operating ships enabled them to build more ships. Therefore, these Soviet practices allowed them to put more ships to sea when war came. Quantity is preferred to quality because, historically, Russia has been more successful with quantity. There is always the danger that the fleet won't make it very far or won't be able to do much when it gets where it's going. This is another reason why Russia's move toward a high-seas fleet was such a risky undertaking. The Western practice, also based on long experience, is to keep the crews at sea as long as possible. Practice, it has been found, makes for more effective crews. As the majority of sailors are technicians, their skills can be maintained only through constant use. The majority of Western sailors are long-term veterans. There is no substitute for high-seas experience.

5. *Attack Techniques.* Ambush is the preferred technique in all navies. This has become easier to pull off with the growth of electronic warfare and long-range missiles. Beyond this, the major difference is that the smaller navies must stay out of the way of the more powerful Western task forces while preparing their attacks. Western ships are better equipped to come looking for the smaller opponents. In peacetime, ship locations of potential enemies are monitored more accurately by Western forces than the other way around. This is particularly true with submarines. U.S. submariners openly proclaim their ability to detect foreign (particularly Russian) subs at 10 times the range of foreign sensors. This is less true as more recent foreign subs have obtained more effective silencing.

Many navies attempt to overcome their deficiencies by maintaining small surface-combat ships or submarines as "escorts" for all major Western task forces. These ships not only maintain location information for other friendly ships but are expected to get in the first shot themselves. However, these escort ships will likely be destroyed whether they get off any missiles or not. Western task forces are often able to evade these escorts. Once these escorts and their up-to-date information are gone, the location of the enemy task force becomes a mystery very rapidly. For example, in six hours of 30-knot steaming, a task force can travel 320 kilometers in any direction. This search circle includes 320,000 square kilometers. Lacking air-search capability, a noncarrier task force can search only 2,000 square kilometers per hour. A U.S. carrier task force can search over 100,000 square kilometers per hour. Both sides can use helicopters to increase search area when they lack carrier-based fixed-wing aircraft. Under the best conditions, this won't increase the hourly search area beyond 30,000 square kilometers. Satellite and electronic surveillance can work if the satellites remain and/or the enemy task force has sloppy signal discipline. These means are available to both sides, although not continuous (see Chapter 20).

The search capability that really counts is that of the combat ships. Finding the enemy is of little use if you can't attack him. When the non-Western navy has located a U.S. task force, it attempts to launch a saturation attack of cruise missiles launched from land-based aircraft, surface ships, and submarines. First it attempts to hit the carriers with its longest-range cruise missiles. These are launched from whatever platforms can get close enough. But first the targets must be located. This is often left to slow-moving naval aircraft. These aircraft make attractive targets to the enemy and may have a difficult time surviving long enough to do their job.

Once the carriers are crippled, the enemy waits a few hours until all U.S. aircraft aloft are out of fuel. Then he goes in against the remaining ships with all the surface ship and submarine-launched missiles he can muster. Enemy aircraft armed with cruise missiles would not have an easy time of it. The longest-range non-U.S. antiship missiles travel only 550 kilometers. Carriers have early-warning aircraft that can spot air and surface targets 700 kilometers away. They can launch air attacks at targets over 1,000 kilometers distant. Land-based aircraft can attempt to fight their way through if they have friendly interceptors with them. On the high seas, the current Russian solution is enormous cruise-missile submarines, such as the 12,000-ton Oscar class. The subs still have a problem in finding out where the carrier is. Submarines must depend on aircraft and surface ships for most of their reconnaissance information. They rely on stealth to sneak in close enough to launch their 550-kilometer missiles. Other submarines have shorter-range cruise missiles. Cruise missiles from any platform must get to within 30 or 40 kilometers of their targets before they can use their search radar, heat-seeking, or radar-homing systems. The homing radar is ideally turned on as close to the target as possible, a few kilometers at most, to avoid jamming. During its final flight phase, many of them go on the deck and make their attack runs at speeds of 300 meters a second and up. These missiles can be defeated by electronic countermeasures, gunfire, or other missiles. Against a task force, there will be dozens of these defensive systems to get by. Against a noncarrier task force, the attacker will have an easier time of it. The basic attack strategy is the same except for more aggressive air observation. The recon aircraft have to track only the task force's radar emissions. Even helicopters can be used for this, as long as they stay out of surface-to-air missile range. Many navies still use a number of older, shorter-range missiles with more primitive guidance systems. These missiles need all the targeting information they can get. From the attacker's point of view, the more missiles you can send in the direction of the enemy, the more he has to contend with.

Western navies have antiship cruise missiles also, including the longer-range Tomahawk (450 kilometers). They face the same problems of finding out approximately where the target ships are. Their carrier-based strike aircraft carry cruise missiles, so they can avoid going in close enough to face the surface-to-air missiles. Another key question in defense and attack are the Western nuclear-attack submarines. These are quieter and have better sensors than any other nation's. Non-Western antisubmarine capabilities in general are below those of Western navies. Non-Western ships and subs must be wary at all times of Western subs. Most Western shipping routes are close to their potentially hostile naval bases. But several key areas are not. It is for this reason that the West is so dependent on carrier air power to defend these distant links in their economic chain. The carriers are also vital if the hostile naval forces are to be defeated in their sometimes-remote bases. As long as a significant number of hostile ships survive in a future war, they pose a threat to Western commerce and economic survival. The "fleet in being" has long been a viable tactic for a weaker naval power. To guard against the depredations of a less numerous fleet requires substantial effort. The only way to eliminate this burden is to go after the weaker opponent where he will be strongest: his naval bases. This is a risky undertaking but always offers a chance of success for a capable carrier fleet.

The United States maintains 15 attack carriers, of which as many as 12 can be put to sea at any one time. The other Western allies can contribute as many as six smaller carriers. An American aircraft carrier, with its 60 combat and 20 or so support aircraft, is capable of detecting enemy surface ships, submarines, and aircraft over 700 kilometers away. Attack and support aircraft can launch cruise-missile attacks without much risk. A typical attack would include 3 electronic warfare aircraft and 12 strike aircraft carrying 24 cruise missiles, plus other weapons like guided bombs and radar homing missiles. They could, at worst, encounter half a dozen hostile ships mounting about 30 surface-to-air launchers with 500 to 600 functioning missiles. The attacking aircraft don't even have to get within range of these hostile SAMs in order to launch their cruise missiles. The odds are against the defending ships. See Chapter 11 for more details. See Chapter 10 for submarine operations.

The Sailor's Life

Most sailors are technicians. There is little work on a modern warship for the unskilled. Although housekeeping chores still exist, seamen spend most of their time maintaining, repairing, and operating complex equipment. Considerable effort is spent in perfecting combat skills. These consist of practice on weapons and damage-control drills. It is difficult to practice wartime activities in peacetime but the sailors who become proficient at "making believe" will likely survive during the real thing. A sailor's career alternates between sea duty and going ashore for additional schooling. While at sea, a third of the crew is on duty at all times. When combat is possible, half the crew is at work, with the critical combat systems manned. A general quarters (combat) alert puts everyone at battle stations. This can be maintained for only so long before fatigue takes over. Sea duty means being assigned to a ship; it doesn't mean you're going to spend most of your time steaming around some ocean. American ships outside the United States spend about 70 percent of their time at anchor, although not always in a port. Ships in the United States spend over 80 percent of their time stationary. Russian ships spend even less time at sea.

Combat also comes in several flavors. There is active and passive combat. Passive combat is more common, and occurs even in peacetime. This consists of looking for the enemy and/or waiting to be found. Active combat is actually exchanging fire. In peacetime, ships often go looking for those of potential opponents under conditions closely approximating wartime. This is primarily true with submarines, which spend a lot of time stalking surface ships and submarines of potential opponents. In wartime, sailors would spend two thirds to three quarters of their time in passive combat. Active combat would occupy less time, perhaps a few hours a week at most, on the average. When it comes, you wish it hadn't.

Mine Warfare

Mines are the weapon nobody wants, but no one can avoid. Mines are a deadly nuisance. They are considered vaguely unseemly in a violent undertaking that otherwise knows few limits. Perhaps naval officers are uncomfortable commanding warriors who don't salute. Mines are also cheap. They can be employed with relatively little risk to the user. Their effect on their victims is paralyzing. This last item may explain why many navies shun mines. They reduce warfare to the plodding drudgery of a

siege. If you are a fast-moving, dynamic navy, the last thing you want to
think about is mines. But they won't go away. Mines are the weapon of
choice for the little guy. If you are about to get clobbered by a larger navy,
you build and use a lot of mines. You don't have much choice. Russia, no
matter how large its fleet got, always maintained the world's largest stock
of naval mines.

THE HISTORICAL EXPERIENCE

Modern naval mines were widely used for the first time during the
Russo-Japanese War (1904–1905). These were contact mines, floating in
shallow water and kept in place with an anchor and chain. When the tide
was right, they would be just below the surface, ready to explode whenever
struck by a ship. Some 2,000 of these mines were used to destroy 16 ships.
This experience pointed out how important it was to keep track of them.
A number of ships, in fact, were sunk by their own mines, often while
moving through a supposedly clear lane. During and after the war, several
ships were sunk by free-floating mines as well as anchored (moored) ones
that had broken free. Thereafter, more care was taken to reduce the number
of loose mines floating about. This illustrates another unsavory aspect of
mine warfare: The mines are indiscriminate, blowing up friend and foe
alike.

During World War I, modern mine tactics were further developed.
Thousands of mines were laid to provide defensive barriers against enemy
movement. Mines were used offensively by secretly placing them across
known enemy sea routes. More than 1,000 merchant vessels and warships
were lost because of the 230,000 mines used.

Duing World War II, mine warfare came of age. A total of 2,665 ships
were lost or damaged to 100,000 offensive mines. That's a ship for every
37 mines. Some 208,000 mines were used defensively to inhibit enemy
movement and tie up his resources. Most of this went on in the North Sea
between German and British antimine forces, which totaled 2,400 ships
and aircraft operated by 99,000 men. Using mines achieved several striking
successes. In the Pacific, naval mines proved more destructive to the Japanese war effort than the atom bombs. During a 10-week period between
April and August 1945, 12,000 mines were delivered by American bombers.
These accounted for 1,250,000 tons of Japanese shipping (670 hit, 431
destroyed). That's 18 mines for each ship hit. The Americans had air
superiority, so losses during these 1,500 missions amounted to only 15
planes, most of them to accidents. Had these missions been flown against
opposition, losses would have been between 30 and 60 aircraft, plus similar
losses to their fighter escorts. This was siege warfare, and the Japanese
people were starving along with their war industries. Unfortunately, without
the shock of the atomic-bomb attacks, the Japanese government might have
continued resistance throughout the winter of 1945–46. This would have

caused over a million civilian deaths from starvation, disease, and exposure. Mine warfare can win in the long run, but the long run is not pretty when starving civilians are involved. A conventional submarine campaign was also waged against Japanese shipping. Comparisons to the mine campaign are interesting. A hundred submarines were involved in a campaign that ran for 45 months, from December 1941 to August 1945. Some 4.8 million tons of enemy shipping were sunk. For every U.S. submarine sailor lost using submarine-launched torpedoes, 560 tons were sunk. During the mine campaign, 3,500 tons were sunk for each U.S. fatality. On a cost basis, the difference was equally stark. Counting the cost of lost minelaying aircraft (B-29s at $500,000 apiece) or torpedo-armed submarines ($5 million each), we find that each ton of sunk shipping cost $6 when using mines and $55 when using submarines. These data, classified as secret until the 1970s, indicated that mines might have been more effective than torpedoes even if the mines were delivered by submarine.

The Germans waged a minelaying campaign off the eastern coast of the United States between 1942 and 1944. Only 317 mines were used, which sank or damaged 11 ships. This was a ratio of 29 mines used for each ship hit. In addition, eight ports were closed for a total of 40 days. One port, Charleston, South Carolina, was closed for 16 days, tying up not only merchant shipping but the thousands of men, warships, and aircraft dealing with the situation. American submarines also waged a limited mine campaign in the Pacific. For 658 mines used, 54 ships were sunk or damaged (12 mines per ship). No subs were lost. Considerable Japanese resources were tied up dealing with the mines. On the Palau atoll, the port was closed by the mines and not reopened until the war ended. Even surface ships were used to lay mines. Three thousand mines were laid by destroyer. Only 12 ships were hit, but these were barrier fields, not the ambush-type mine-fields that a submarine can create by sneaking into an enemy-held area.

In Korea during the early 1950s, the Soviets provided North Korea with 3,000 mines, many of 1904 vintage. These were used to defend Wonson Harbor. It took several weeks for UN forces to clear these at a loss of a dozen ships hit. Half of them were destroyed. During the Vietnam War, over 300,000 naval mines were used, primarily in rivers. The vast majority were not built as mines but were aerial bombs equipped with magnetic sensors instead of fuses. These bombs/mines used a small parachute to ensure that no damage occurred on landing. In shallow water, these make-shift weapons sat on the bottom and performed as well as mines. Haiphong Harbor was actually mined with 11,000 of these "destructors," as the U.S. Air Force called them, and fewer than 100 conventional mines. A complete tally of the ships destroyed by these mines could not be obtained because neither side was able to keep track of losses. Based on fragmentary reports, the mines performed quite well.

During the 1991 Gulf War, the Iraqis laid more than 1,000 mines off the Iraqi and Kuwaiti coast. The predominantly U.S. naval forces did not have sufficient minesweeping resources to deal with this situation and had a helicopter carrier and cruiser hit and damaged while trying to clear the area. This effectively prevented any U.S. amphibious operations, although the marines were not going to be used for a landing anyway. It took more than a month of mine clearing after the fighting ceased to eliminate all the mines.

NAVAL MINE DESIGN

Currently, naval mines weigh between 1,000 and 2,000 pounds. Normally, a submarine can carry two mines in place of one torpedo. Naval mines have several characteristics that make for different types:

1. *Free-floating mines* are just that, mines that are floating freely. This type was abandoned early on when it was discovered that they would eventually be a danger to friend and foe. The winds and tides are not predictable, leaving these mines to go where you don't want them to. This type is still encountered when moored mines break loose, as they sometimes do. Terrorists also find this approach to their liking. Only Russia is known to maintain a stock of free-floating mines. The Russians have a mechanism that keeps their free-floating mines at a set depth. Once their batteries give out, they probably deactivate.

2. *Moored mines* drop anchor and float either near the surface or up to several hundred feet down (to hit subs). The original ones were detonated by contact. Current models are more sensitive and merely require that a ship pass close by them. These can be deployed in water up to 6,000 feet deep and are called "rising mines" because the mine, or torpedo, that contains the explosive must rise toward the surface to hit its target.

3. *Mobile mines* can move under their own power. They can be either moored or bottom mines. Some simply move a set distance and then settle on the bottom. This makes it safer to lay mines in heavily guarded waterways. The means of delivery is often a modified torpedo. Another type is the U.S. CAPTOR mine. This is a moored mine equipped with an Mk-46 lightweight torpedo. It was developed to provide a quickly deployed (by air) minefield that could cover a very large area. The mine is equipped with a powerful acoustic sensor and is supposed to be able to detect subs at a range of several kilometers. Once detection is confirmed and the course of the target plotted, the torpedo is released to home in on and destroy the sub. These weapons have experienced a lot of problems and may or may not be deployed.

4. *Command mines.* Another distinguishing characteristic of mines is their target-detection system. This area has produced the largest

number of new developments in the last few decades. The earliest system was remote control, where a human observer would detonate the mine when a target came close enough. This is still used, although often just to turn on other sensors in mines or to deactivate mines so your ships can pass. Several nations have remote-control mines in key waterways, ready to be switched on when needed. The most widely used sensor in the early part of this century was the contact fuse. This is the familiar form of mine to most people, a spherical object with long rods protruding from it. These rods are the contact fuses. If a ship hits and breaks one of these rods, the mine detonates. Contact mines are not often used anymore because it is so easy to clear them. They are moored and near the surface. Once they're spotted, you can shoot them up with rifle or machine-gun fire. However, these mines are easy to manufacture and are readily available on the world arms market with no questions asked. These cheap mines can be, and sometimes still are, rigged as command mines.

5. *Influence mines* detect ships over a distance. First came the magnetic-influence mine. A ship is a large hunk of metal that will "influence" a mechanism within the mine that contains small magnets. This was first used as a bottom mine that must lie no more than 100 feet below the surface. Then came the acoustic mine. Ships make noise. A sound detector in the mine will sense this and explode when a ship passes overhead. Acoustic and magnetic mines can also be floating mines held at a certain depth by a cable and anchor. Finally, there is the pressure mine, which senses the change in water pressure as the ship passes overhead. These must lie on the bottom and must also have a sensitive mechanism to account for the pressure generated by the local tides. Some modern mines use two or three of these influences. This makes these mines very difficult to disable. You can't easily fool them into exploding because the mine is programmed to get positive response from all of its sensors before exploding. Microcomputers can now be put into mines to detect ships by weight and even type (warship or merchantman). If you want to destroy only submarines, the mine will be programmed accordingly. The mine can be programmed to let one or more ships pass by before detonating it. Or the mine can activate for a while, then deactivate for a different period of time. This makes clearing mines even more nerve-racking than it has been in the past. When you think you've cleared a channel, you haven't. All you did was get the mines that were active. This deactivation technique also allows for the use of dummy mines—light, empty shells that just lie there. An additional feature of the programmable mine is its ability to self-destruct, either according to a timer or upon command. This saves the hassle of clearing your own mines, particularly if they are a very difficult type.

MINE CLEARING

Mines are at best a deadly nuisance and at worst an impenetrable barrier to ships. Western navies have a greater technical capability to clear them, while other navies simply have more mine-clearing boats. No nation has the resources to clear the number of mines available. Pressure mines, the most difficult to clear, are detected by a minesweeping boat (called, naturally, a "minesweeper") equipped with a special sonar. Then a remote-control miniature submarine goes down to confirm the mine's presence and to plant an explosive to destroy the mine. It's a slow and tedious process, but at least it's a solution. Work goes on to develop quicker methods, but so far mine clearing has resisted assembly-line procedures. Moreover, sweeping techniques are not 100 percent effective. Worse yet, a new minefield typically announces itself by sinking a few ships. The ideal situation for clearing pressure and other bottom mines is to use the sonar to identify all objects underneath a shipping channel. This can be done in peacetime, although it has to be updated periodically depending on how much turnover there is on the bottom. When war, with the possibility of bottom mines, arrives, the sweepers can quickly go over the cleared shipping channel. They only have to stop and send down the minisub if they spot something not seen last time around.

Not all minesweepers have bottom-scanning sonar. Most still use the technique that gave them their name, a cable between two boats that "sweeps" forward looking for the cables of moored mines. The mine-sweeping boats were light and built of nonmetallic material (wood or fiberglass) so as not to detonate magnetic mines. Traveling slowly and posting lookouts to spot contact mines, their light weight and nonmetallic construction protected them from most pressure and magnetic mines. Against magnetic mines, they would sweep with a magnetized cable, or some similar device. To set off acoustic mines, a noisemaker would be towed over the suspect area.

The United States pioneered the use of helicopter-towed "sleds" that could search for magnetic, contact, and acoustic mines at high speed. These sleds had the advantage of being easily sent anywhere in the world by aircraft. They are a lot safer for their crews and cover a larger area more quickly. Despite constant improvements, they are still incapable of clearing out pressure mines. Another disadvantage is that the helicopters can stay in the air only four hours at a time. The only known way to sweep all known mines is a technique developed by the U.S. Navy in the 1960s. An old merchant ship is stripped of all equipment and filled with Styrofoam. The ship moves, slowly, using what are essentially large outboard engines. A minimal crew runs the ship from a shock-mounted pilothouse. Such a rig can take quite a few hits before coming apart. The United States eventually adopted the more practical, second-best, approach to clearing all known mines. In the late 1980s, the United States began building specialized minesweeping boats, as its European allies had been doing for several decades. Going one step further, the United States developed an airborne mini-detector pod ("Magic Lantern") that can be carried on helicopters or jets. This allows a quick sweep of sea areas to detect if mines are present. Then, at least, you know where to send your minesweepers.

As always, the best way to deal with mines is to prevent the enemy from using them. When they do get used, mines announce their general location dramatically. Most will be in shallow water near heavily used naval routes. Bottom mines, the weapon of choice these days, are dropped no deeper than 30 or 40 meters (against surface ships) or 200 meters (against subs) because of sensor limitations. Even then, they will have to rise to the surface before exploding. Otherwise, their explosive force will be smothered by the intervening water. Barriers of moored antisubmarine mines can be placed in waters up to 6,000 feet deep. These barriers are expensive where there is a wide area for subs to maneuver in. Moreover, such a minefield must be three-dimensional. Although you can equip mines with their own passive sensors and nuclear explosives, this is extremely expensive (more than $1 million per mine), and you still need two of them for every kilometer of sea you want to guard. This assumes a 20-kt nuclear charge with a kill range of 700 meters. It can cause varying degrees of damage for about twice that area. Again, when the batteries wear out, the mine becomes useless. The life of such a field would not likely be more than a year at most, and typically only a few months.

Mines are becoming more flexible and reliable as technology, most notably electronics, improves. Western nations have an edge, although it is largely confined to the laboratory. The Russians build more mines; their inventory is currently estimated at 50,000. Western navies have about a third that number.

WHY AREN'T MINES USED MORE?

Mines are not good examples of military discipline and decorum. There's nothing sexy and exciting about them. Mines loiter in dark corners waiting for the unwary victim to wander by. Their fighting habits are more similar to those of muggers than those of trained sailors. They are insubordinate, attacking friend and foe alike. Thus, none of the traditional naval services, surface, submarine, or air, will lay claim to them. Mines are tolerated because they work. Even this is not given full recognition until a war breaks out and the superiority of mine weapons becomes difficult, and dangerous, to ignore. The U.S. Navy is one of the more extreme examples of military loathing of mines. Remember that the reports of mine efficiency against Japan were kept classified until the 1970s. Only recently has the U.S. Navy taken any measures to deal with pressure mines, a type that has been around since the 1940s. Now that many Third World nations see naval mines as a useful way to attack other nations, the United States has finally begun to take mine warfare, and mine clearing, more seriously.

MINES IN THE NEXT WAR

World War II, Korea, Vietnam, and the Gulf War suggest how effective mines can be. These wars demonstrate that the side with control of the air and sea was less exposed to mine damage. Until one side gains the upper hand, mines could be used heavily in a number of critical areas. Indeed, it is quite possible that mines will be put to work even before a future war starts. While they are heavy (1,000 to 2,000 pounds) and bulky (over 10 cubic feet each), numerous techniques are available for planting them. In wartime, mines are delivered by a variety of means: ships, submarines, aircraft, missiles. More worrisome is the laying of mines in peacetime or just before the start of hostilities. Peacetime minefields are quite common. Key harbors or sea passages are routinely mined with devices that can be quickly activated when hostilities are imminent. These are generally bottom mines with a cable connection to a control center. The cable is used for monitoring the mines' readiness as well as for activation. These mines must periodically be retrieved for repair or maintenance.

Another form of prepositioned mines is not talked about. These mines are the ones placed secretly in a potential opponent's harbors or seaways. The Soviets were long suspected of doing this, although it is unlikely that they are guilty of anything more than practicing surreptitious minelaying. Leaving mines in foreign waters is a risky business. The mines must be activated remotely, which is not an easy task for underwater objects. Prolonged submersion may lead to malfunctions, and batteries may last for years but not forever. Finally, these mines may be discovered, causing potentially disastrous diplomatic repercussions. You do not have to place mines in too many places for them to have a dramatic effect. The Western powers have a shortlist of key locations that opponents can mine: the Persian Gulf, the Djakarta and Singapore straits, the east coast Japanese ports, the English Channel ports, the three largest ports in the east and west coasts of North America. Mine the majority of these areas and keep them mined, and you paralyze the Western war and industrial effort.

The most potent minelaying vehicle in the early stages of a war may be merchant vessels. Fitting these ships with mines is not difficult. A coded radio message in a time of imminent conflict could lead to minefields springing up quickly in the wake of these merchant vessels. The world had a taste of this in the summer of 1986, when a Libyan merchant ship secretly dropped a number of Soviet mines in the Red Sea. This was done as an act of terrorism. Multiply this even a few dozen times, and you have a decisive act of war. Missiles, both cruise and ballistic, are another means of placing naval mines in far-distant waters. As the major powers continue to back off from the use of nuclear weapons, their missiles become available for other tasks. Already, many battlefield missiles are having nuclear warheads replaced with ones containing land mines or chemical weapons. Missiles are an expensive way to deliver naval mines, but when one considers the impact these mines can have in the early stages of a war, it is not such a bad bargain.

Theory and Practice

Theory is closer to practice in naval operations than in any other area of warfare. Ships at sea get ample experience just coping with the elements and the complexity of their temperamental equipment. But there have been no major actions between naval forces since 1945. Large American task forces have seen extensive action, but always against land forces, and never against significant air forces. Smaller actions have been instructive, particularly the Falklands battles of 1982. The big lesson has been that antiship missiles have to be respected and that air attacks are still a substantial threat. Unlike fleets of the 1940s, fewer of today's ships are armored. The norm is ill-protected ships crammed with explosive munitions and flammable materials. The "burning aluminum" delusion that came out of the Falklands had some basis in fact. The aluminum did not burn; it did collapse from heat stress more quickly than steel. This also exposed serious deficiencies in damage-control procedures. No one had really given these issues adequate attention until it was too late. Similar surprises are waiting to be found the old-fashioned way: by accident. Among the questions to be resolved only through large-scale combat are: nuclear submarines used on a large scale and in cooperation with other ships; mass use of cruise missiles; viability of attack carriers; impact of electronic warfare; and the effectiveness of ASW against modern submarines. All of these surprises are typical of what happens to navies that go to war with significantly new weapons after decades of peace. The next major battle between naval forces will be noted for its surprises.

The Future

Looking forward, there will be fewer ships, fewer sailors, and a slower development of new technologies. All this is a result of the collapse of the Soviet Navy. Since the 1950s, the primary reason for building warships frequently and abundantly has been the threat of Soviet naval operations in wartime. As the Soviet Navy continued to grow during the 1960s, '70s and '80s, Western navies kept pace. This resulted in the largest peacetime warship building in history. With no more hostile Soviet fleet to contend with, naval budgets, ship-building programs, and R&D are falling, and will continue to decline for the foreseeable future. Attention will now concentrate on the naval threats posed by smaller navies. Most of these will be quite local. This will make the U.S. Navy's job more complex, if smaller in scale. Meanwhile, some technical trends will continue to move forward, if at a slower pace.

Continuing a trend that has been ongoing for centuries, ships are becoming more automated. During World War II, each 1,000 tons of warship required over 80 crewmen. Current ships require a third fewer. On the drawing boards are designs that will again dramatically reduce crew size, taking the men per 1,000 tons down to fewer than 20. This is the result of a number of different technological trends. Sensors are becoming more automated. Missiles are more common, and are often delivered in storage containers from which they are fired and thus require little maintenance. Engines are increasingly automated, just like the industrial machinery from which they are derived. The ships are more frequently built of low-maintenance materials that do not require constant scraping and painting.

In addition, more naval designers are taking into account the advantages of stealth ship-design technology. Submarines have long recognized the need for silence and general unobtrusiveness as a means of avoiding attack. For the past decade, new surface ships have attempted to suppress onboard noise to assist ASW operations. The success of stealth aircraft designs in reducing radar observation has been carried over to warships. The U.S. Navy spent over $1 billion during the 1980s working on stealthy ship design. This will result in ships with lots of smooth corners topside and a lot less clutter. A potentially troublesome side effect of smaller crews will be fewer men available for damage-control duty and greater potential for reduced capability when key personnel are injured.

An understandably unheralded future development is the perfection of many recently installed weapons and systems. Combat technology that has not been used in battle has an alarming tendency not to work very well when it is first made operational. It's more than the unexpected cracks appearing in new aircraft. Systems where performance is more difficult to determine, like missile-guidance systems and ASW equipment, are prime offenders. There are always several examples of these systems being unable to function as designed with the users unaware of it. Eventually, these items get put right, but only at great expense if the flaws are exposed during combat. The expense of these new systems and the shrinking budgets of the post-Soviet era are forcing another practice on navies—upgrading older ships instead of building new ones. The design of warship structures has stabilized in the last 50 years. Meanwhile, weapons and sensors have become smaller as they have also gotten more powerful. If a ship is not heavily stressed, its hull and superstructure are good for 40 or more years of use. New weapons, sensors, and even engines can be added at half the cost of building new ships of equal capability. Even navies that use their ships heavily, like the United States, still get 30 years of use out of their hulls. Extensive upgrades are becoming an accepted practice and can be expected to grow in the future.

The 1991 Gulf War did not give navies as much of a workout as it did the air and ground forces. American carrier aviation was shown to be capable, but behind the regular air forces in using the latest technology. That experience jarred the U.S. Navy into cooperating more energetically with the air force.

The future performance of the former Soviet, now Russian, fleet, and peacetime sailors in general, is a question mark. Long periods of peace have historically been very debilitating for navies. Lacking the incentives provided by a large and energetic potential opponent, the world's larger navies now must struggle to keep the sailors on their toes.

Radical innovations in naval technology will be slow in coming. Meanwhile, the surface navy has yet to come to grips with nuclear submarines. It will take a major naval war to resolve the many unsettling questions raised by these new weapons. Until then, it will be more of the same, along with gradual innovations.

Naval Forces

United States and Russian warships comprise nearly two thirds of all the world's naval forces. These ships and their design are exported to other navies. While the U.S./Russian share of all the world's warships may shrink as smaller navies increase their fleets and the major naval powers cut back from their Cold War levels, the current naval superpowers will retain their hold on the bulk of the planet's naval power.

CLASS TYPE is a code indicating the size and function of the ship. No two navies use the same class names the same way. To bring a little order to this chaos, a single classification criterion has been applied the same way to ships of all nations. More conventional letter designations are given in parentheses. The ship class names are those generally used in the West. Most Russian ships are called "antisubmarine" or "rocket" (antiship) boats of various sizes.

A indicates aircraft carriers (CV, CVA, CVH), which vary in size from 20,000 tons up to over 90,000 displacement tons. These are almost always the centerpiece of a task force. Included in the American section are the helicopter carriers assigned to amphibious operations. Normally, these ships carry helicopters for transporting marines and their equipment ashore. But most of the helicopters have some weapons, and a few are heavily armed. It is also common to base some vertical takeoff fighters (Harriers) on these carriers.

B is battleship (BB), displacing over 20,000 tons of water and capable of independent operation although these are often the primary ships of a task force. This class of ships is likely to finally disappear by the end of the decade, nearly a century after they were first conceived and built.

9-1 U.S. Navy Combat Ships

Class Type	Class Name	# in Class	Combat Values			
			Surf	Sub	Air	Prot
A	Theodore Roosevelt	4	100	24	100	10
A	Nimitz	3	100	24	100	10
A	Enterprise	1	85	24	90	10
A	Kitty Hawk	3	85	24	85	10
A	JFK	1	85	24	85	10
A	Wasp	4	4	0	8	4
A	Tarawa	5	4	0	8	4
A	Iwo Jima	7	2	0	6	3
M	Ohio	17	8	14	0	9
M	Lafayette	6	8	16	0	9
N	Seawolf	1	30	60	0	12
N	Narwhal	1	10	20	0	8
N	Los Angeles II	31	24	48	0	10
N	Sturgeon	10	16	25	0	9
N	Los Angeles I	31	20	40	0	10
C	Arleigh Burke	8	6	16	12	4
C	Ticonderoga	34	30	14	20	3
C	Virginia	4	12	12	8	2
C	California	2	14	9	8	2
C	Belknap	4	4	10	5	2
C	Leahy	4	3	6	5	2
C	Spruance	31	6	16	2	3
C	Long Beach	1	3	8	4	4
C	Kidd	4	4	14	4	2
D	Perry	30	2	12	3	1
D	Knox	15	2	20	3	1
E	Missile Boats	20	2	0	0	1
P	P-3 Squadrons	12	12	40	N/A	1
N/A	Minesweepers	40	0	0	0	1

Class Totals

	Ships	1,000 Tons	% of Total	Avg Class	Averages			
					Surf	Sub	Air	Prot
N	74	438	13%	15	20	39	0	10
M	23	325	10%	12	8	15	0	9
A	28	1,560	48%	4	58	15	60	8
C	92	793	24%	10	9	12	8	3
D	45	167	5%	23	2	16	3	1

Long	Wght	Power Ratio	Speed	Range	Men per Kton	EW	Gun	Air-craft	SAM	SSM	TT DCT	Class End Build
332	96	2.1	56	200	64	9	4	86	3	0	0	1995
327	93	3.0	56	200	66	9	3	86	3	0	0	1982
335	92	3.0	61	200	65	8	3	86	2	0	0	1961
319	81	3.5	54	8	65	8	3	82	3	0	0	1968
326	81	3.5	54	8	65	8	3	82	3	0	0	1968
257	40	1.9	43	18	27	4	3	38	2	0	0	1994
254	39	2.0	43	18	24	4	4	35	2	0	0	1980
183	18	1.3	41	18	38	2	6	25	2	0	0	1970
171	16.6	3.6	45	200	11	6	0	0	0	24	4	1995
130	7.2	2.1	45	200	20	6	0	0	0	16	4	1974
99	8	7.5	80	200	16	12	0	0	0	0	8	1995
96	5.3	3.2	54	200	24	6	0	0	0	0	4	1969
110	6.2	4.8	72	200	21	9	0	0	0	16	4	1995
89	4.3	3.5	63	200	30	7	0	0	0	4	4	1975
110	6.1	4.9	72	200	22	9	0	0	0	4	4	1985
154	8.3	10.8	60	8	37	9	3	1	2	8	0	1995
172	9.1	9.9	58	14	40	8	4	4	4	8	4	1994
178	10	6.0	58	200	57	7	2	2	4	8	4	1980
182	11.1	5.4	54	200	54	6	4	0	2	8	12	1975
167	7.9	10.8	57	14	60	5	5	1	2	8	8	1967
162	7.8	10.9	57	14	54	4	6	0	4	8	14	1964
172	7.8	10.3	59	11	43	7	2	2	1	8	14	1983
220	17.1	4.7	54	200	56	4	4	1	4	8	14	1961
161	8.4	9.5	59	12	43	6	4	0	4	8	10	1982
136	3.6	11.1	52	8	57	6	1	2	1	1	6	1989
134	3.9	9.0	48	8	72	5	1	1	1	1	12	1974
44	0.2	90.0	86	3	105	1	1	0	0	2	0	1982
N/A	N/A	N/A	N/A	2	N/A	6	N/A	10	N/A	N/A	N/A	1992
52	0.7	3.3	25	4	109	0	0	0	0	0	0	1995

Long	Wght	Power Ratio	Speed	Range	Men per Kton	EW	Gun	Air-craft	SAM	SSM	TT DCT	Class End Build
101	6	5	68	200	23	9	0	0	0	5	5	1984
151	12	3	45	200	15	6	0	0	0	20	4	1985
292	68	2.5	51	84	52	7	4	65	3	0	0	1977
174	10	9	57	75	49	6	4	1	3	8	9	1978
135	4	10	50	8	65	6	1	2	1	1	9	1982

9-2 Russian Navy Combat Ships

Class Type	Class Name	# in Class	Combat Values			
			Surf	Sub	Air	Prot
A	Kiev	4	40	22	6	6
A	Kuznetsov	1	54	22	8	8
N	Oscar	3	20	8	0	6
N	Akula	6	10	8	0	6
N	Victor III	24	9	8	0	6
N	Sierra	5	10	8	0	6
N	Charlie II	6	12	7	0	4
N	Alpha	5	10	14	0	8
M	Typhoon	6	0	8	0	6
M	Delta IV	4	2	8	0	6
M	Delta III	0	2	8	0	6
N	Beluga	1	6	12	0	6
N	Foxtrot	6	2	10	0	2
N	Kilo	12	2	9	1	2
B	Kirov	2	30	10	10	5
C	Slava	3	3	10	6	2
C	Udaloy	11	3	12	6	2
C	Sovremenny	12	6	7	5	2
C	Kara	4	3	6	4	2
C	Kresta II	2	3	5	3	2
C	Kynda	0	5	2	1	1
D	Kashin II	6	3	3	2	1
D	Krivak	12	0	1	3	1
E	Tarantul	4	2	0	1	1
E	Pauk	4	0	2	1	1
E	Nanuchka	26	3	0	1	1
E	Grisha II	20	0	1	1	1
E	Mirka II	0	0	2	0	1
E	Petya III	12	0	1	0	1
E	Riga	0	0	2	0	1
E	Missile Boats	40	2	0	0	1
P	ASW Helo. Sqdrn	6	N/A	24	N/A	N/A
P	Tu-22M	2	15	N/A	N/A	N/A
P	Tu-22	1	12	N/A	N/A	N/A
P	Tu-142	1	N/A	20	N/A	N/A
P	Tu-16	0	14	N/A	N/A	N/A
P	Su-17	0	6	N/A	N/A	N/A
P	Il-38	2	N/A	15	N/A	N/A
P	Be-12	2	N/A	12	N/A	N/A
P	Mi-14	2	N/A	12	N/A	N/A
N/A	Minesweepers	40	0	0	0	1

Class Totals

	Ships	1,000 Tons	% of Total	Avg Class	Averages			
					Surf	Sub	Air	Prot
N (N)	49	308	26%	8	12	9	0	6
N (D)	19	43	4%	6	3	10	0	3
M	10	163	14%	3	1	8	0	6
A	5	232	20%	3	47	22	7	7
B	2	46	4%	2	30	10	10	5
C	32	243	21%	5	4	7	4	2
D	18	74	6%	9	2	2	3	1
E	106	74	6%	13	1	1	1	1

Long	Wght	Power Ratio	Speed	Range	Men per Kton	EW	Gun	Aircraft	SAM	SSM	TT DCT	Class End Build
273	43	2.3	61	23	20	7	12	35	4	8	36	1988
321	60	3.0	61	200	28	7	16	60	8	16	24	1991
145	12	5.0	54	200	12	6	0	0	0	24	6	1983
113	9	6.7	63	200	8	6	0	0	0	0	6	1995
145	6	10.0	52	200	14	5	0	0	0	0	4	1992
145	6	10.0	63	200	10	6	0	0	0	0	6	1995
103	4.3	5.1	54	200	21	5	0	0	0	8	6	1985
79	3.6	6.7	72	200	17	2	0	0	0	0	6	1983
170	20	5.0	45	200	8	6	0	0	0	20	6	1990
155	10.8	4.6	43	200	11	6	0	0	0	16	6	1990
155	10.5	4.8	43	200	11	6	0	0	0	16	6	1982
65	2	12.0	40	24	28	2	0	0	0	0	6	1988
92	2	3.0	32	36	38	1	0	0	0	0	10	1973
73	2.4	1.1	36	24	22	2	0	0	2	0	6	1995
247	23	5.2	58	200	48	8	10	2	13	20	14	1992
150	12	10.0	59	12	25	6	10	2	4	0	32	1995
150	5.7	21.1	59	12	53	6	6	2	4	0	32	1995
180	7.5	14.7	54	8	60	5	5	1	4	2	12	1995
174	9.8	12.2	56	14	56	4	8	1	8	0	54	1981
159	7.5	13.3	59	10	53	3	8	1	4	0	54	1978
143	5.6	17.9	63	12	71	2	4	0	2	8	30	1985
146	4.9	19.6	63	8	65	1	8	0	4	4	29	1978
125	3.7	19.5	58	7	68	1	6	0	4	0	36	1986
56	0.8	14.0	63	5	63	1	3	0	1	4	0	1982
56	0.8	13.0	58	5	69	1	2	0	1	0	6	1986
60	0.9	22.2	58	6	67	1	2	0	2	6	0	1985
73	1.1	20.0	61	5	55	1	5	0	2	0	10	1986
82	1.1	38.2	61	9	91	1	4	0	0	0	12	1987
82	1.2	21.7	54	9	83	1	4	0	0	0	14	1972
92	1.3	10.8	50	4	135	1	11	0	0	0	34	1960
40	0.2	50.0	63	2	175	1	4	0	0	4	0	1985
N/A	N/A	N/A	400	4	N/A	5	N/A	24	N/A	N/A	N/A	N/A
N/A	N/A	N/A	400	2	N/A	4	N/A	24	N/A	N/A	N/A	N/A
N/A	N/A	N/A	400	1.5	N/A	3	N/A	24	N/A	N/A	N/A	N/A
N/A	N/A	N/A	400	5	N/A	5	N/A	24	N/A	N/A	N/A	N/A
N/A	N/A	N/A	400	1.5	N/A	3	N/A	24	N/A	N/A	N/A	N/A
N/A	N/A	N/A	400	0.4	N/A	1	N/A	24	N/A	N/A	N/A	N/A
N/A	N/A	N/A	300	2	N/A	4	N/A	24	N/A	N/A	N/A	N/A
N/A	N/A	N/A	300	2	N/A	4	N/A	24	N/A	N/A	N/A	N/A
N/A	N/A	N/A	100	0.5	N/A	3	N/A	24	N/A	N/A	N/A	N/A
60	0.5	12.0	36	3	110	0	4	0	0	0	0	1995

Long	Wght	Power Ratio	Speed	Range	Men per Kton	EW	Gun	Aircraft	SAM	SSM	TT DCT	Class End Build
122	7	7	60	200	14	5	0	0	0	5	6	1989
77	2	5	36	28	29	2	0	0	1	0	7	1985
160	14	5	44	200	10	6	0	0	0	17	6	1987
297	52	3	61	112	24	7	14	48	6	12	30	1990
247	23	5	58	200	48	8	10	2	13	20	14	1992
159	8	15	59	11	53	4	7	1	4	2	36	1985
136	4	20	60	8	66	1	7	0	4	2	33	1982
68	1	24	59	6	92	1	4	0	1	2	10	1978

C is a cruiser-class ship (CA, CG, CL) of 5,000 to 20,000 tons' displacement. Most are between 6,000 and 12,000 tons. Basically, these are smaller battleships with less of everything except speed. Cruisers also tend to specialize in something like antisubmarine, antiair, or surface combat. Cruisers sometimes operate with one or more other cruisers in a small task force.

D are destroyers (DD, DDG, FF, FFG) of 2,000 to 5,000 tons. These are escort ships for task forces and merchant-ship convoys, ordinarily having an orientation toward antiair or antisubmarine work.

E are escort and patrol ships (DE, PH, PT, etc.), less than 2,000 tons and typically found in coastal waters.

M are ballistic-missile boats (SSB, SSBN). These are almost all nuclear, as are an increasing percentage of the attack subs. Indeed, you can always tell if a ship is nuclear-powered by looking at its range. Those with the larger ranges are nuclear. Ms have torpedoes and sensors and can fight other ships but are not intended to do so except in emergencies.

N are nuclear and nonnuclear attack submarines (SS, SSG, SSN, SSGN).

P are land-based naval aircraft that serve the same function as some ships and belong to the navy.

Minesweepers are not heavily armed. They sweep, lay, or hunt mines.

Not included are ships of less than 100 tons. These are little more than seagoing police cars. What antisubmarine gear some of them have is largely ineffective against modern subs. Russia has the largest number of these small boats—several hundred, in fact. Needless to say, Russia's coastline is well patrolled by thousands of very bored sailors.

CLASS NAME is the name of the lead ship of a group of generally identical ships. The ships of that class are normally referred to by the name of the first ship built. For example, "A Spruance-class ship," in reference to a class of U.S. destroyers in which the first one built was called the *Spruance*. Although ships in a class are built according to the same set of plans, modifications occur to individual ships as the class gets larger and/or older. When the differences become too large, a new "class" is created. This is shown on the chart.

IN CLASS is the number in that class as of 1993.

COMBAT VALUES are numerical evaluations of the ship's combat capabilities against surface-ship (SURF), submarine (SUB) and air (AIR) targets. These values take into account the quality and quantity of onboard weapons, equipment, and crew as well as past performance.

PROT is the protection value of that ship against attacks from enemy weapons. For submarines, this includes the difficulty other ships and subs have in detecting it. This is a function of sub quietness, diving depth, displacement, hull arrangement, and countermeasures. For surface ships, these values suggest the number of major weapon hits the ship would have to receive before it was no longer capable of combat.

LONG is the ship's length in meters.

WEIGHT is the ship's full-load displacement in thousands of tons. For submarines, it is surface displacement. The term "displacement" refers to the weight of water the ship displaces when it is floating on the surface. I know it sounds complicated, but it is the common term used. If you want to deal with the navy, learn to speak its language.

POWER RATIO is horsepower per ton, an indicator of agility.

SPEED is top speed in kilometers per hour. Rarely used except in emergencies. Also rarely achieved except when the engines and hull are in top shape. These conditions decline the longer a ship is at sea and/or in action. At that point, top speed declines 10 or 20 percent. Efficient cruising speed tends to be one half to two thirds of top speed.

RANGE is the unrefueled range in thousands of kilometers, at cruise speed of between 20 and 30 kilometers an hour. This is quite slow for wartime activities, and task forces normally cruise at 50 kilometers an hour or even faster. This can reduce RANGE by up to 50 percent. For nuclear ships, the range is shown as 200,000 kilometers. In many cases, it can be up to five times this before the nuclear reactor's fuel must be replaced. The range given is what most nuclear boats would have at the beginning of a war. Note that the navy has its own units of distance (nautical mile, equals 1.8 kilometers) and speed (knot, equal to one nautical mile per hour). Most landlubbers (and some sailors) use kilometers. So will we.

MEN PER KTON is the number of crew per 1,000 tons of ship displacement. This indicates how labor-intensive or automated a ship is. Automated ships tend to be more effective and efficient and require fewer supplies because of the smaller crew.

EW is the effectiveness of the ship's electronics in general and its electronic-warfare capabilities in particular. The higher the number, the better.

GUNS is the number of gun systems in the ship mounts. Multibarrel Gatling types count as one gun. Almost all guns are under 128mm and are used primarily for air defense.

AIRCRAFT is the number of helicopters and fixed-wing aircraft on board. Smaller ships carry only helicopters.

SAM is surface-to-air missile launchers carried.

SSM is surface-to-surface missile launchers. Some SSM missiles carry torpedoes or depth charges for use against submarines. Several ship classes have launchers that can fire both types. In these cases, launchers are shown twice, once under each category.

TT DCT is the number of tubes for launching torpedoes (TT) or depth charges (DCT) against submarines. Modern submarines have 4 to 10 torpedo tubes on board, with twice as many on surface ships armed with torpedoes. The Russians are the largest users of depth-charge throwers, a remarkably ineffective weapon against nuclear subs although quite devastating against Russia's own large fleet of nonnuclear subs. Figure that one out.

CLASS END BUILD is the year in which the last ship of that class was built. This indicates how up-to-date that class is. This is very true with Russian, and non-Western, ships, as Western navies tend to upgrade their ships every 10 years or so. The Russians simply build a new class in most cases. Dates later than 1993 indicate that the class is still being built.

CLASS TOTALS gives the average for each class, making it easier to compare one nation, and/or class, to another. For combat purposes, one should not include ballistic-missile submarines, which exist primarily to carry and launch strategic missiles, not fight other ships.

CLASS DIFFERENCES

While ship classes are a rough guide to different ships' capabilities, national policies give a more accurate appraisal. National policies come in three basic flavors: high-seas Western, Russian, and coast protection. The Western naval tradition stresses control of the high seas wherever the West has commercial interests. Currently, this means the entire world. The U.S. Navy is the best example of this type of sea-control force. The majority of U.S. ships are multipurpose, high-seas, long-range vessels. The principal U.S. combat ship remains the large aircraft carrier. All other ships support the ability of the carriers to carry the war to the enemy homeland. A parallel mission is maintaining the security of the oceans for merchant shipping by sinking enemy subs or confining them to port. Most Western navies no longer maintain more than a few small carriers and comprise mostly antisubmarine ships.

The Russian Navy, in particular, and all navies in general, developed out of a coastal-defense force. Although the Russians now have considerable high-seas capability, this is secondary to their obsession with fighting submarines. This probably won't change much with the disappearance of the Soviet Union. The majority of currently active Russian surface ships are dedicated antisubmarine vessels. Most of the remainder are armed with submarines for attacking carriers. Smaller nations, or those lacking the means or desire for a high-seas fleet, maintain a coast-defense navy.

Over the past 300 years, ship classifications have constantly changed. Many terms are used interchangeably with different meanings. *Capital ships* means vessels capable of engaging anyone else's most powerful ships. In this century, this has been battleships, aircraft carriers, and now nuclear-attack submarines. One has not exactly succeeded the other so much as they have complemented each other. A case can also be made for asserting that long-range surface-to-surface antiship missiles have made smaller ships capable of taking on larger vessels. It's easier to make this case if the missiles have nuclear warheads, for the larger ship can often survive several hits from nonnuclear warheads. Small ships also have problems with not having as many sensors and electronics as their larger opponents. Bigger, it would appear, may still not be automatically superior, but it is certainly safer. *Cruisers* were originally lighter ships used for long-range scouting and maintaining control of areas free of opposing capital ships.

Destroyers were originally "torpedo boat destroyers" at the turn of the century. The torpedo boats turned into submarines, and destroyers evolved into ships that could still go after them.

While Western ships tend to be multipurpose, the Russians have tended more toward specialization. Their 1980s designs have shown more flexibility. Their first big building programs in the 1960s and 1970s saw the expected increases in antisubmarine and antiair capabilities. What shocked the West was the Soviets' novel solution to their lack of attack capability. Lacking carriers, Russia was the first to develop surface-to-surface antiship missiles. Ships with these missiles were, in effect, aircraft carriers. The Soviets also equipped several classes of submarines with these missiles, creating a new type of submarine in the process. Continued Western superiority in antisubmarine warfare and the crude capabilities of these new subs led the Soviets to try building carriers—first small ones and then a 65,000-ton model that finally entered service after the Soviet Union disappeared. After a pause in the late 1970s, the Russians are now also building improved classes of surface ships to protect their carriers. However, it is unlikely that these new ships would last long outside the cover of their land-based interceptors.

Western designs have kept pace with the Russians in air defense and naval and antisubmarine warfare. Western surface-to-surface antiship missiles, introduced a decade after Soviet models, appear to be superior. The ability to fire standard SSMs from a wide variety of launchers also gives the West superiority in numbers. Soviet designs began running into trouble once they got beyond the simple, robust, and effective early designs. No nation is immune to the problems of developing complex weapons.

Western navies are increasingly blurring the traditional differences between cruisers and destroyers. Onboard ASW helicopters give Western cruisers, some of which are called destroyers, a potent weapon against subs. More and more, cruisers are becoming little more than somewhat larger and more powerful destroyers. The class of ships now called *frigates* is, in most cases, comparable to earlier destroyers. These ships' primary function is antisubmarine warfare. The Soviets prefer a larger number of smaller antisubmarine ships. This is another manifestation of their belief in quantity. In any event, most of these Soviet ideas on naval forces are moot. with the Soviet Union gone, along with the communist ideology it supported, the Russians have no need for most of these ships and, in any event, can't support most of them either.

A big problem in keeping ship types consistent is weight/class inflation. For example, the first battleships in World War I were about 20,000 tons. Thirty years later, there were 60,000-ton battlewagons. The same thing happened between World War II (the 1940s) and this decade. In World War II, cruisers ranged from 6,000 to 12,000 tons. Ships in this weight range are today called destroyers. Bigger may be better, but it should not be confusing.

WARSHIP DESIGN

Designing a warship means making compromises. What do you have to spend on what you want to do, and how you want to do it? From a designer's point of view, three classes of ship exist: submarines, aircraft carrier, and surface combat ships. This last class also includes lightly armed supply and amphibious ships. All warships are basically cargo vessels. Weapons replace wheat and iron ore. Aircraft carriers carry tremendous quantities of fuel and munitions (over 10,000 tons), plus up to 100 aircraft. Submarines require a large number of mechanical and hydraulic systems to allow them to operate under water.

As an example of the compromises you must make when designing a warship, let us consider the trade-offs that go into designing your typical surface combat vessel. You must consider:

1. *Weight.* Metal costs money, as does the labor to assemble it. Normally, 40 to 45 percent of the ship's weight goes to the structure: the hull and super-structure. This cost is up to 40 percent more than in merchant ships, largely because of greater compartmentalization and, sometimes, armor.
2. *Power Plant.* Another 20 to 25 percent goes to the main power plant. This is more than twice what a merchant ship requires, as a combat ship requires more speed. Some 15 to 30 percent goes to auxiliary machinery and equipment. Merchant ships have very little of this because combat ships have a lot of additional equipment to support.
3. *Weapons.* From 6 to 14 percent goes to an item merchantmen completely dispense with: weapons. For a warship, this last item is the cargo. For a merchant ship, over 50 percent of the ship weight will be cargo.

The distribution of cost is quite different from weight, primarily because silicon for electronics is more expensive than metal. The structure normally accounts for 15 to 20 percent of the total ship cost. The main power plant takes up 10 to 15 percent. Weapons and sensors amount to between 50 and 65 percent of cost. And that is why a warship will cost three or more times a ton as much as a merchant ship. Ways can be found to save money, if you are willing to sacrifice certain features. The most obvious area is space. Make the ship smaller without reducing the equipment and weapons you want to put in it. The catch is that what is in the ship must be squeezed more closely together. A typical Western ship has 20 percent more internal volume than a comparable Soviet-designed vessel. The Soviets coped by putting more weapons topside, on the deck. They allot less space for equipment access, passageways, internal bulkheads, and work areas. This has serious repercussions in combat as well as during peacetime operations. A U.S. vessel allocates 12 percent of its space to access versus 8 percent for a Soviet ship. Stores occupy 12 percent versus between 2 and 4 percent in Soviet ships. Fifty percent more space (3 versus 2 percent) is allocated to ship control. Ironically, Western ships devote somewhat less space to personnel. Western ships tend to have smaller crews because of greater automation. The Western crew quarters are more comfortable, with amenities like air-conditioning. Even though the Soviets devoted a bit more space to crew quarters, it was less efficiently laid out and less comfortable.

The Western warship-design tradition is based on extensive World War II experience, particularly of the U.S. and British navies. This experience showed what would work and what wouldn't. However, experience is perishable. New technology and conditions intrude. To not change is to court disaster. Yet every change made without combat experience is a risk, a risk that must be taken. Many things have not changed since World War II. Ships still require a lot of space to store spares, test equipment, and tools. While the ship is at sea, even the availability of helicopters to rush in critical parts and supplies is not always adequate. For most of this century, sailors have had to be very resourceful just to keep the increasing amount of equipment functioning.

The Soviets have tried to rewrite the book in this area by cutting out a lot of the space used for workshops and parts storage. This move has to do with the lack of skilled sailors to allow them to operate at the same level as Western navies. Most Russian sailors are short-term draftees; most Western sailors are careerists. As a result, it's a common sight to see a Russian ship riding at anchor in the middle of nowhere because critical systems are broken and incapable of repair with the resources at hand. When it's a submarine, we sometimes hear about it. But it happens just as frequently with the Russians' surface ships and aircraft. But this problem is worse than it appears. The additional space in Western ships is also used in combat to give access to damaged areas. This makes damage control easier and can spell the difference between saving or losing the ship. Some of this "extra" space is also devoted to more watertight compartments, additional pumps, redundant plumbing, and power-control systems.

A major departure from World War II ship design is the near disappearance of armor. This freed up a substantial amount of space on the larger (than destroyer) ships. Western ships took up this space for additional damage-control and maintenance facilities. The Soviets added a few more weapons. All of this gives them what appear to be smaller and more heavily armed ships. On the minus side, these ships are less capable of keeping all their equipment functional in peacetime or recovering from battle damage. All this is in line with the doctrine developed by Russia over the centuries. It is its land forces' doctrine transferred to the sea. It maintains that initial all-out attacks are more important than the ability to carry on a protracted conflict. It is a risky gamble. But then, defeat at sea is less calamitous for a land-based power like Russia. This "risky gamble" approach, however, does have an appeal to many smaller nations that simply cannot afford a protracted war. These countries buy Russian ships because they are cheaper, are built to be run by less skillful sailors, and give the biggest bang for the buck in a short war.

Naval Weapons

Chart 9-3 shows the principal weapons used by naval vessels. Except for missiles, no attempt is made to show every example of each weapon type. This list is adequate because most other naval weapons have very similar characteristics and effects.

WEAPON is the name of the weapon. The weapons are divided into categories for: missiles, torpedoes, depth-charge launchers, and guns. Each category is discussed in greater detail below.

9-3 Naval Weapons

Weapon	Made by	Range (km)	Weight (lbs)	Speed (mps)	Guid-ance	Impact Power	Launch From	Trpdo Tube?	IOC
SSN-2B	Russia	40	5,500	250	2	12	S	No	1958
SSN-2C	Russia	80	6,000	250	3	14	S	No	1967
SSN-3B	Russia	450	12,000	450	3	45	S,U	No	1962
SSN-7	Russia	60	7,700	250	4	38	U	No	1968
SSN-9	Russia	120	6,600	250	5	16	S	No	1969
SSN-12	Russia	500	11,000	800	4	36	U	No	1973
SSN-14	Russia	15	3,500	300	3	10	S	No	1969
SSN-15	Russia	40	4,000	400	3	23	U	Yes	1972
SSN-16	Russia	90	4,000	400	4	23	U	Yes	1972
SSN-19	Russia	500	10,000	800	6	23	S,U	No	1981
SSN-22	Russia	110	6,000	800	6	21	S	No	1981
SSN-25	Russia	50	2,000	300	6	16	S	No	1988
Harpoon	US	110	3,200	280	8	21	A,S,U	Yes	1977
Exocet	France	40	1,620	300	7	15	A,S	No	1981
Tomahawk	US	450	2,700	240	8	30	S,U	Yes	1984
SUBROC	US	55	4,000	400	4	15	U	Yes	1965
ASROC	US	10	959	400	4	15	S	No	1961
Torpedo Mk 48	US	46	3,500	25	8	20	U	Yes	1972
Torpedo Mk 46	US	8	565	25	6	8	S,A	Yes	1965
Torpedo Mk 37	US	12	1,700	12	3	15	S,A	Yes	1957
MBU 1200	Russia	1.2	400	200	2	4	S	No	1964
MBU 6000	Russia	6	500	200	2	5	S	No	1970
Gun 76mm	Various	15	14	900	2	1	S	No	
Gun 127mm	Various	23	70	800	2	5	S	No	

MADE BY gives the country of origin. Most of these weapons are used by allies of the manufacturing country.

RANGE is the effective range of the weapon in kilometers. Anything more than 40 to 50 kilometers is "over the (radar) horizon" and needs to have its target located accurately (by someone closer to the target than the missile launcher) before launching the missile. The "line of sight" from the uppermost part of a ship to the horizon varies with the size of the ship. For smaller ships, it's 10–12 kilometers. For the largest ships, it is 24–30 kilometers. Aircraft and the tops of large ships can be seen farther away because they "pop up" from "below the horizon."

WEIGHT is the launch weight of the weapon in pounds. The lighter it is, the more a ship or aircraft can carry, or the smaller a vehicle can carry it. With the exception of guns, these weapons are launched from a rather light apparatus, either a container or a rail.

SPEED is the average speed of the projectile in meters per second. The faster a weapon, the more difficult it is to evade or destroy. One hundred meters per second equals 360 kilometers an hour, or 225 miles per hour or 330 feet per second. A rifle bullet travels at about 1,000 meters a second.

GUIDANCE is an evaluation of the weapon's guidance system on a 1-to-9 scale. The higher, the better. These evaluations also take into account the sensors of the launch vehicle as well as those in the missile itself (if any).

IMPACT POWER is the destructive power of the weapon, taking into account the accuracy of the guidance system and the destructive power of a nonnuclear, non-chemical warhead. Nuclear warheads will almost always destroy their target, even a near miss. Missiles that always carry a nuclear warhead are indicated with an *N*. Chemical weapons will not destroy a ship, but will make the crew uncomfortable, or dead, if the poison chemicals are not promptly dealt with. Most missile weapons have a warhead containing 100 to 500 pounds of explosives. A 4,000-pound missile causes considerable damage even if its warhead does not explode. Cruise missiles have an additional advantage in that some of them have rocket motors that keep burning over most of the missile's flight. If the missile is fired at a shorter range, and the missile hits a ship while the motor is still burning, the motor acts like a blowtorch inside the target ship and adds incendiary effect to the damage done by the exploding warhead. In some cases, where the cruise missile's warhead failed to explode, the missile's still turning rocket motor caused considerable damage. Even with U.S. cruise missiles, which use small jet engines, there is often unburned fuel remaining when they hit.

LAUNCHED FROM indicates the type of platforms the weapon can be launched from. S = surface ship; U = submarine; A = aircraft. The same weapon launched from an aircraft will have a slightly longer range than a surface launch because it starts at a higher altitude. The air-launched versions are covered in the aircraft weapons chart. Many of these weapons also have coastal-defense versions, which are essentially the naval launcher mounted on land.

TORPEDO TUBE indicates whether a weapon can be launched from a submarine torpedo tube. This is largely a Western concept, which allows a greater variety of weapons to be used in a submarine without additional modification. Most Soviet submarine vessels have special launch facilities in their subs. Often the boat is specially built for a particular missile. Note that American subs can launch tor-pedoes, mines, tactical and strategic cruise missiles, and antisubmarine rockets from their torpedo tubes.

MISSILES

The Soviet Union pioneered the use of antiship missiles. Once the Western nations awoke to the potential of these new weapons, they soon overwhelmed the Soviet models with superior technology. Despite this, the Soviets persisted and left the successor states of the Soviet Union with a wide variety of systems. For example, the SS-N-2 first went to sea in 1958 and is still in use. The follow-on for the SS-N-2 was the SS-N-7 and SS-N-9. These were initially developed for specially designed submarines, although the SS-N-9 replaced the SS-N-2 in new classes of small missile boats since 1969. In 1981, another short-range antishipping missile, the SS-N-22, entered service. In 1988, an Exocet clone, the SS-N-25, appeared. As the Soviets realized the tactical problems of short-range missiles, they devoted most of their efforts to longer-range models. The first long-range missile, the SS-N-3, was first deployed in 1962 as a strategic weapon. It was replaced in this role by ballistic missiles in the 1960s and 1970s. The SS-N-3 continues in use to this day as an antiship missile. In 1973, the SS-N-7 was deployed on Echo-class submarines, and later on Kiev- and Slava-class surface ships. In 1981, the SS-N-19 was deployed on the large Oscar-class submarines and Kirov-class battleship. In 1987, the Soviets began deploying land-attack cruise missiles (SS-N-21) that can be launched from torpedo tubes (26-inch, rather than the U.S. standard 21-inch, tubes). A longer-range cruise missile (SS-N-25) appeared in 1990, but was too large for torpedo tubes. The United States deployed its first antiship missile (Harpoon) in 1977, although it had a superior version of the SS-N-3 out before the SS-N-3. America refrained from producing these missiles for doctrinal reasons. The Americans didn't think they needed antiship missiles. They did produce missiles for going after submarines (ASROC and SUBROC), which the Soviets were not able to duplicate for over 10 years.

Other Western nations produced antiship submarines before the United States. Western antiship missiles quickly surpassed their Soviet counterparts. Aside from being smaller, lighter, and more reliable, Western missiles could be launched from a wider variety of platforms. The Harpoon and Tomahawk can be launched from aircraft, surface ships, and submarines. This keeps the cost of production down and makes training and maintenance easier. By the late 1980s, the U.S. Navy had over 1,500 antiship missile launchers. Allied U.S. navies have nearly as many. Western missiles, in general, are more reliable and have longer range and greater accuracy than Soviet designs.

While most Soviet missiles are inferior to Western models, they are still lethal against a ship that is not well defended. Most Soviet missiles that were exported equip small coastal patrol boats in Third World navies. This can be a lethal combination against unprepared Western warships. The most modern Soviet missiles have long enough range and high enough speed to make an attack on enemy ships a real threat. In the face of such an attack, the best defense is countermeasures. This is accomplished by jamming the three forms of terminal homing missiles used to hit their target. For example, an active radar spots the shape of a ship and homes in on it. Radar can be jammed by sending signals to it that make the target appear somewhere else. A more crude form of jamming simply electronically fuzzes up the signal, or throws up a cloud of metal-foil strips (chaff) for the same effect. The missile may detect this form of jamming and switch to a radar homing system. This in turn can also be confused by turning the ship's radars off or having a helicopter hover near the ship with an electronic "noisemaker" hanging below it. If the missile detects these deceptions, it can use infrared homing, to home in on the heat thrown off by a ship. The ship can fox the infrared by firing off flares. Finally, the target ship can use high-speed cannon to shoot the missile down during its last few seconds of flight. All of this seeking and jamming goes on during the last 5 or 10 seconds of a missile's flight. With so much to be done in so little time, speed, accuracy, miniaturization, and reliability become the arbiters of success. The one item most used on both sides of this contest is the computer. In this area, the West holds a commanding, and increasing, lead. Evidence of this can be seen in smaller Western nations developing credible antiship missiles. Both Norway and Israel have done this. Larger nations like France have created Exocet.

SUBROC (for use by submarines, withdrawn from service in 1990) and ASROC (for surface ships) are really nothing but rockets carrying torpedoes or depth charges. Sensors give an approximate location of the submarine, hopefully out of torpedo range. The missile is programmed to fly to the location, and then, depending on the type of missile, release a nuclear depth charge or a homing torpedo. The depth charge has to be nuclear because a conventional depth charge can damage a sub only within 30 meters of its detonation. A nuclear depth charge is good for 300 meters. Homing torpedoes are even better, as these can run search patterns in a circle several kilometers in diameter. Russia introduced its own version of ASROC and SUBROC in the 1970s and 1980s.

TORPEDOES

These were the first ship-to-ship missiles. Over a century ago, they first sliced through the water, maintaining a steady course toward their typically unaware targets. Eight years later, in 1877, they were first used in combat. Another 16 years were to pass before they actually hit anything in combat. Considering this record, we may consider torpedoes the first high-tech weapon. Nearly 50 years ago, torpedoes acquired the ability to home in on the propeller noise of their targets. Torpedoes have steadily become more capable ever since. The three models shown are all of U.S. manufacture and are representative of most torpedoes in use today. The top of the line is the Mk 48. This is an exceptionally capable weapon, and no other navy is likely to have anything like it. The Mk 48 is the current outer limit of torpedo technology. The Mk 37 is typical of torpedoes found in most navies. The range can be increased, but this is useful only if the torpedoes' sensors can detect the target at that range. This problem is currently solved by a wire extending from the torpedo to the launching ship. The ship guides the torpedo until it is close enough for the torpedo's own sensors to finish the job. This is a common mode of operation for the long-range Mk 48. Against submarines that can travel as fast as a regular torpedo, you need a weapon that is extremely fast, accurate, and quiet.

Although torpedoes are still nominally useful against surface ships, in most cases warships will not allow a submarine close enough to launch. More and more, torpedoes are seen as a weapon against submarines or merchant shipping. Through the 1980s, a troublesome problem with using torpedoes against submarines was the increasing bulk and multiple hulls of recent subs. The Soviets experimented with titanium hulls, strong enough to withstand enormous depths. This strength may also allow a sub to take one or more torpedo hits and keep going. All of this is theoretical and/or speculative. Only actual combat circumstances will reveal what the true situation is, and that is now unlikely for some time to come.

DEPTH-CHARGE LAUNCHERS

These are an elderly but still effective means of destroying submarines, especially diesel-electric boats. They are less effective against nuclear subs. The operation of depth charges is quite simple. A barrel of explosive, set to explode at a certain depth, is dropped from the rear of a ship or fired outward by rocket. The charges are used in quantity, according to a pattern thought likely to hit the sub. These weapons are highly dependent on the ship's sensors locating where the sub is and, more important, where it will be once the charges are launched. Russia and less affluent navies use these weapons extensively. Nuclear subs are rather sturdy creatures and would require a lot more hits by depth charges before they succumbed.

GUNS

With the proliferation of rather bulky missiles, not much space has been left on ships for the more traditional guns. Those that remain are generally 20mm to 40mm, 3-inch (76mm) or 5-inch (127mm) weapons. The smaller ones are often made completely automatic and are actually machine cannon. These weapons are turned on when there is danger of enemy cruise missiles. The automatic cannon will seek out and shoot at any object that moves like a cruise missile. See the chart on air-defense weapons for more details. Otherwise, guns can still be effective if you can get close enough to use them.

10

The Navy:
Run Silent,
Run Deep

IF YOU HAVE THE faith of a true believer and the passion of a zealot, you have the makings of a submariner. Consider the working conditions. You never see, hear, or smell the enemy. Everything is done through instruments. If you make a mistake and the enemy gains an advantage, there's no place to run. Your battlefield is a metal cylinder tapered at both ends. It is 200 to 600 feet long and 20 to 40 feet in diameter. You can move in only one third of this volume—the remainder is crammed with equipment, weapons, supplies, and the rest of the crew. In spite of the above, submarines have become the premier naval weapon in the last 40 years. Why? There are a number of key reasons:

1. *Ability to Hide.* Once submerged, a submarine cannot be easily detected. Even other submarines have a hard time of it. The sea is an excellent place to get lost and stay lost.
2. *Nuclear Power.* Until nuclear power came along, only small-capacity power plants could be crammed into a submarine's limited space. Nuclear power changed that. They were compact and generated enormous power. Nuclear subs could stay submerged as long as they wanted. Power was available to extract air and drinkable water from the sea. Indeed, one of the few drawbacks of nuclear engines was that there was too much power. The noise of the pumps needed to keep the power plant cool made nuclear subs noisier, and easier to

detect, than the older diesel-electric boats. This has changed with some of the more recent nuclear boats, especially British ones.

3. *Improved Sensors.* About the same time combat nuclear-power plants were developed, technology made similar breakthroughs in electronics, computers, and sensors. Submarines were no longer half-blind. Surface ships could now be detected farther away than radar could spot them.

4. *Improved Weapons.* More accurate and longer-range torpedoes, as well as missiles, have extended the submarine's reach. No longer was it necessary to look through a periscope before firing.

Modern Submarine Design

Submarines are seagoing ships capable of moving and fighting under water. They are designed around a pressure hull, a steel tube strong enough to withstand water pressure at depths of from 200 to 1,000 meters or more. Outside the pressure hull are water tanks that are filled and emptied to lower and raise the sub in the water. A metal shell, which is what we usually see when we look at a sub, covers the pressure hull and water tanks. Submarines differ in the following characteristics:

1. *Size.* Size is a disadvantage. Bigger boats are easier to find. When the mission of the sub and the size of the required equipment are large, you end up with a large boat. Larger boats are also harder to kill. The largest Soviet boats have double hulls and wide distance between them. It's not known how effective Western torpedoes will be in getting one-shot kills. Other Soviet subs have been built with titanium hulls to obtain deeper diving performance. These may also provide some invulnerability to lightweight torpedoes. Weights of modern subs range from less than 1,000 tons to more than 16,000 tons' surface displacement. The heaviest subs are nearly 600 feet long and 40 feet in diameter. The smallest are 180 feet long and 20 feet in diameter. Crew sizes range from 30 to 140 men.

2. *Propulsion.* Although nuclear power revolutionized submarine design, it did not completely displace the older diesel-electronic–powered subs. These boats, first introduced at the turn of the century, used a diesel engine for surface cruising and batteries for underwater work. The diesels require a lot of fuel, and the batteries are heavy, dangerous, and require recharging on or near the surface at least six or eight hours a day. Recent models do have the capacity to run silently under water for up to 72 hours. Up through World War II, submarines spent nearly all their time on the surface and could not travel under water for more than a few hours. Diesel-electric boats are not very fast. Nuclear boats can stay at sea longer than diesel-

electric subs, which are cramped and uncomfortable. A nuclear boat can steam over 200,000 kilometers before needing to replenish its nuclear fuel. The chief advantage of diesel-electric boats is that they are cheaper, smaller, and generally superior for coastal defense. They carry the same torpedoes and, if they get off the first shot, can defeat a nuclear boat.

3. *Weapons and Sensors.* Western submarines have the usual technical advantages over Soviet boats. Beyond that, not everyone can afford the best that money can buy. The most modern sensor system on U.S. subs weighs more than 40 tons and costs more than $100 million. Substantial differences exist between the nuclear boats of a nation. New classes often implement vastly improved systems that are too expensive to refit older boats with. A big problem with diesel-electric boats is that they cannot use all their sensors as often as the nuclear subs. Nonnuclear boats can cruise under water for a short time, and that's the only time they can use their more effective underwater sensors. In 1943, the snort (snorkel) was introduced. This allowed subs to cruise at periscope depth. This made the subs harder to spot, but running on the noisy diesels made sensors ineffective and the crew uncomfortable.

A Submarine's Weapons

The earliest subs used torpedoes, mines, and a deck gun as their main weapons. The gun was a practical recognition of the diesel-electric boat's status as a small surface ship that could submerge briefly to sneak up on its victims or evade a more powerful adversary. The introduction of better sensors and torpedoes has eliminated the need for a deck gun. Mines are still carried whenever the situation calls for them. Currently, "torpedoes with brains" and missiles are the principal submarine weapons. Improved technology allows underwater sensors to detect targets more than 100 kilometers away. At ranges of up to 50 kilometers, accuracy is sufficient for wire-guided torpedoes to be driven into a moving target. One reason for the U.S. Mk 48 wire guided torpedo was the longer range of American submarine sensors. Torpedoes that depend on their own sensors, generally acoustic, might find their target gone once they reached the position it had been in when the torpedo was launched. This can be 30 or 40 kilometers from the launching sub.

Torpedo sensors cannot be as powerful as those on a submarine. A partial solution to this problem is to have the torpedo run a search pattern when it arrives where it was supposed to find a target and detects nothing. Russia favors this type of torpedo, mainly because it is cheaper, and Russian long-range sensors are not as accurate. The Western subs are quieter and harder to detect anyway. Submarines always had a problem with the range of their weapons. Until 30 years ago, that range was under 10 kilometers—the extreme range of a torpedo or deck gun. This was not too shabby, as this was the extreme range of battleship guns. Modern torpedoes can't go more than 50 kilometers.

This was all made moot with the widespread introduction of the aircraft carrier 60 years ago. Aircraft could project their firepower for hundreds of kilometers. All of this meant little until subs acquired the capability to detect targets at distances in excess of a few kilometers. Twenty-five years ago, the American Navy deployed a large number of subs with long-range sensors. About the same time, it deployed a rocket-propelled nuclear depth charge (SUBROC) for use by submarines. These SUBROCs were launched from a torpedo tube, surfaced, and took off and flew for 50 kilometers and then released the warhead that sinks to a predetermined depth and detonates. Depending on the size of the charge, any sub within a 300-to-900-meter radius will be destroyed. Total range was only 55 kilometers, about the same as Mk 48. SUBROC was cheaper, and the Mk 48 hadn't come along yet. With the introduction of the Mk 48 in the 1970s and the increasing reluctance to be dependent on nuclear weapons, SUBROC was withdrawn in 1990 except for recently introduced Soviet versions.

The Mk 48 torpedo has a rough equivalent in Russian service, although this system is apparently not yet perfected. Besides, the Russians do not see their subs as primarily antisubmarine weapons. Most Russian submarines are designed for using missiles to attack land or naval targets. This has caused first Russia and then the United States to introduce a number of long-range submarine-launched missiles. There is a significant difference in the way each side uses these missiles. The United States has longer-range underwater sensors and can use its Harpoon missiles to engage surface targets over 100 kilometers away. Tomahawk cruise missiles can be sent more than 2,000 kilometers at land targets or several hundred kilometers at surface ships. Sending submarine missiles at moving targets beyond the range of your sensors is a problem with the Tomahawk, and with all Russian missiles.

For launching missiles beyond the range of the sub's own sensors, the submarine must approach the surface, extend a radio aerial, and receive targeting information from friendly air or surface units. Normally, a nuclear submarine stays away from the surface. The closer it gets to the surface, the easier it is to detect from the air. The U.S. subs have less of a problem because the Russian antisubmarine forces are less of a threat. Russia must use nonsubmarine sensors to give its subs adequate targeting data. This makes Russian missile-firing subs more vulnerable to an already very capable Western submarine-detection system. Under the circumstances, the Russians don't have a lot of choice.

Sensors

The key to combat success or survival in underwater warfare is the ability to detect other ships before they detect you. This is done with sensors. Submarines of different classes vary enormously in their sensor capability. American submariners openly proclaim their ability to detect most Russian submarines at 10 times the range that U.S. subs can be detected. There is ample opportunity in peacetime to test this claim. Although the Soviets made vigorous efforts to close the gap, they never quite made it and remain at a grave disadvantage to this day. Technical inferiority in electronics and computers was the primary reason for the Soviet shortfall. But no one yet has equipment that can make the sea transparent. Although sonar (underwater sound-detection equipment) has made great strides in the last 80 years, it still has a lot of problems sorting out the multitude of underwater sounds.

SONAR INTERFERENCE

Sonar equipment is similar to radar in that it broadcasts a signal, in this case sound, and listens for that signal as it bounces off distant objects. Because water is thicker and "busier" than air, long-range sonar requires a computer to sort out the returning signals. Depending on the quality and power of the sonar equipment, accurate detection can take place at ranges from 1 to more than 50 kilometers. The biggest problem is that there are so many other factors that can affect range. In deep water, varying temperatures and salinity in different layers of water distort and misdirect signals. Water tends to form layers of different temperatures, and these layers fluctuate. The deeper the water, the greater the number of layers encountered. Each layer is a potential hiding place. Submarines detect the different layers by dropping a long cable with water-analysis sensors attached to it. This gives the sonar some idea of the temperature "geography" in the area and allows adjustments to be made to returning signals.

Another method of dealing with layers is to lower a sonar transmitter and receiver so that the conditions of different layers can be measured and a more accurate picture of the area formed. Sound tends to travel through a layer, even if the layer has a lot of ups and downs. Very few layers are straight. Moreover, several layers normally exist between you and your target. The signals will bend and slow down as each layer is encountered. Unless you know the nature of the layers, your sonar information will be inaccurate at best and misleading at worst. Noise caused by your own vessel also causes problems. This is also taken care of by surface ships and submarines towing a sonar array behind you on a cable. The local sea noises of fish and whales are taken care of with signal processing. The level of noise given off by the target must also be considered. If the target is making enough noise, he will have a harder time hiding in thermal layers. All of this noise and interference makes accurate information a sometime and uncertain thing.

SIGNAL PROCESSING

Sorting out all the noise your sonar hears is a data-processing job best handled by a computer. Many nations cannot afford this approach and still rely on human operators. But trained and effective operators are difficult to come by. Some people have the ears and mind for it; most don't. It's a bit of an art, because the sounds are often so subtle. Even with computers, the operator still has decisions to make. But a powerful computer and a library of sounds enable you to classify sounds quickly and accurately most of the time. The simplest sonar puts a blip on a TV screen to show the contact. The more powerful your sonar transmitter is, the farther away you will detect targets. Because of all the interference, the farther away the target, the less accurate its indicated location.

Without signal processing, your best approach to solving the problem is to use more than one sonar set in ships a few kilometers from each other. Triangulation will then provide a more accurate fix. This method is widely used by Russian surface ships. They attempt to use as many sonar-equipped ships as possible when hunting enemy subs. However, this method is not possible for submarines. The sonar ships and aircraft must constantly communicate, and subs cannot do this. A more accurate approach and one usable by submarines is to collect as much data as possible on temperature layers, salinity, and other aspects of the underwater geography, as well as recordings of sea noises and other ships. Identify and classify as many of these as possible. Take into account whatever noise your own ship makes. Put all of this on a tape that can be loaded into the sonar-sets computer. When you use the sonar, it compares the signals it received with its signal library and makes a more accurate estimate of what is out there and where it is. This will only work instantaneously with very powerful computers. Western nations have them; the Russians and non-Western nations do not. The Soviets tried to catch up but never quite made it. Finally, these data libraries are updated periodically and new tapes distributed to the submarines and surface ships. Apparently, individual ships and submarines can be identified by their noise "signature"—at least until they undergo some modification that changes their sound. This brings us to the most effective use of sonar: passive mode.

ACTIVE VERSUS PASSIVE SONAR

If your opponent is noisy enough, you can use your sonar in the passive mode and gain an enormous advantage. Passive means not broadcasting any signals (as in active mode), just listening. One major disadvantage of sonar is that you can hear someone else using it, even without a receiver. With your reception equipment, you can locate the other fellow quite accurately. A powerful passive sonar can detect a noisy ship or submarine three to five times farther away than with active sonar. Passive sonar works best with a fast computer, signal processing, and a large library of ocean sounds. This is called a signal processor. The least capable passive sonar can pick up loud targets, like fast-moving ships, at ranges of over 300 kilometers, or quiet submarines at up to 5 or 10 kilometers. More capable equipment can triple these ranges. Some targets are almost impossible to detect. A motionless diesel-electric submarine is almost soundless. Such a target can be picked up only with active sonar. Unfortunately, a motionless diesel-electric boat is sitting there with its passive sonar on waiting for just such an opportunity. Sensor superiority is the key to survival. Active sonars vary enormously according to type. Some can be very effective under the right conditions.

Sonars come in a number of different forms:

1. *Towed Arrays.* Ships and subs tow a sonar set behind them. This gets it away from ship noise. These can also be sent down to a different thermal layer for better results (variable depth sonar). Again, the world's most capable sonar boat, the U.S. Los Angeles class, has a towed array that can detect targets more than 100 kilometers away.
2. *Sonobuoys.* These are small, portable sonars that are dropped from aircraft. In active mode, they have a range of up to two kilometers. In passive mode, they have a range of from 10 to 20 kilometers.
3. *Dunking Sonar.* Helicopters hover and "dunk" a sonar into the water. In passive mode, these are good out to eight kilometers. Also has an active mode, but this lets the sub know it is being tracked.
4. *Hull-mounted Sonar.* The most common form. Ships and submarines use it. The best of these, in modern U.S. subs, are good out to 50 kilometers. Less effective rigs, poorly maintained and used by inexperienced operators, are only effective out to 5 or 10 kilometers at best.

Run Silent, Run Deep

Active sonar range can vary from 1 to 100 kilometers. In passive mode, the spread is from 5 to more than 1,000 kilometers. Differences are attributable to equipment and operator quality. But the nature of the target plays a large role, particularly the amount of noise your prey throws off. To take advantage of the noise factor, submarines and ships engage in as much silencing as they can. Silencing is the art of making your boat as quiet as possible. The old submariner's expression, "Run silent, run deep," pays homage to this lifesaving practice. The deeper you are, the less sound gets to searching surface ships. Many things can create noise in a sub, e.g., the water rushing past the hull, either from movement or currents. The less streamlined hull of a diesel-electric hull creates more potential for this kind of noise. Inside and outside the boat, soundproofing materials are used extensively. Vibration-damping mounts for propellers and other machinery eliminates telltale sounds. Nuclear subs require constantly operating pumps to cool their nuclear power plants (except at low power levels, when some subs can use convection cooling). For this reason, diesel-electric boats, when operating on batteries and stationary, are inherently quieter. Even the crew moving around can make noise. Everyone wears rubber-soled shoes and practices "noise discipline" at all times, just so they don't develop bad habits. Active sonar isn't the only thing that produces dangerous sound. A coughing crewman can give you away to a sensitive passive sonar.

ANTISUBMARINE WARFARE (ASW)

Although friendly submarines are the best defense against hostile subs, surface ships cannot always depend on having one handy. This problem is solved with a mixture of surface ships and aircraft equipped with sensors and antisubmarine weapons. Surface ships and aircraft wage antisubmarine warfare using a large number of tools. Already mentioned are the *tactical sensors,* which are similar to those used by submarines. Added to these are *strategic sensors.*

STRATEGIC SENSORS

The United States has a system of passive sonars in key ocean areas. SOSUS (SOund SUrveillance System) is on the continental-shelf areas bordering the North Atlantic (the CAESAR network) and the North Pacific (COLOSSUS), plus a few in the Indian Ocean. They listen to everything and send their data via cable to land stations. There it is sent back to a central processing facility, often via satellite link. Currently, this system is accurate enough to locate a submarine within a circle no wider than 100 kilometers. That's a large area, but depending on the quality of the contact, the circle may be reduced up to one tenth of that size. The major drawback of the system is that it does not cover deep-water areas more than 500 kilometers from the edge of the continental shelf. The Soviets knew this and tried to stay in the deep water as much as possible.

The deep-water zones are covered intermittently with SURTASS (SURveillance Towed Array SyStem). This system is a large "sled" containing passive sonar and towed by tugs in areas needing coverage. Data is sent via satellite to the signal-processing centers. The only other potential worldwide sensor system would use low-flying satellites with special sensors linked to powerful signal processors on the ground. These would cover all ocean regions, including deep-water areas.

Both the United States and Russia have been working on these systems for nearly 20 years, although Russia's work has slowed appreciably in the 1990s. The sensors look for large metal objects and heat and water disturbances caused by ships passing through the water, or under it. These systems have had some success finding surface ships and may eventually be able to track submarines. However, to a greater degree than SOSUS, these systems are subject to prompt destruction during the opening stages of a major war. A further complication is that these satellites orbit the earth, preventing them from maintaining the steady surveillance provided by SOSUS. Both the satellite and SOSUS systems are very expensive to maintain, and given the shrinking naval budgets and Russian submarine fleet of the post–Cold War world, both systems are likely to be heavily cut back or eliminated.

Once the strategic sensors detect a likely target, surface ships, subs, and aircraft can be sent within hours. These use a variety of tactical sensors. Sonar is the principal sensor for surface ships and aircraft. In addition, radar is used against surfaced submarines, and fixed-wing aircraft (and some helicopters) can use magnetic anomaly detectors (MAD). These devices sense disturbances in the magnetic field caused by the subs' large metal hull passing through the water. Helicopters use a dunking sonar that is lowered into the sea on a cable. All aircraft use sonobuoys, miniature sonar sets that are dropped into the water and float around transmitting whatever they have detected. Ships and aircraft have their own signal-processing equipment; helicopters pass data to a ship for complex signal processing. Russian sensors lack the degree of computer and signal-processing support of Western equipment.

The Crew

More so than with any other type of ship, the quality and attitudes of the crew are essential to making a modern submarine an effective weapon. In most navies, submariners (or "squids") are volunteers. They are highly trained, especially on nuclear boats. The crews are small, usually 100–150 men on nuclear boats and half that on diesel-electric boats. The majority of the crew have a college education or equivalent in years of technical training. Over half the sub crews are career sailors; the remainder are usually in on long (six-year) enlistments. The long enlistments are necessary to provide sufficient time to train the sailors before they join their boat.

The duty is the hardest part of the job. When nuclear subs go on patrol, they are out for from one to three months. Normally, they are under water the entire time. The crew members work 12-hour shifts much of the time. They work and live in a crowded environment, affording little privacy.

There is constant low-level noise from machinery, plumbing, and fans. The odors of 100 men and tons of operating machinery confined to a small area soon dull the taste buds. Many squids note a sensory shock when they first encounter the surface world after 30–90 days under water.

These long absences from family and friends on shore put additional strains on the squids. The navies with nuclear boats have a difficult time retaining crews for this silent, and arduous, service.

Tactics

Destroying a submarine is not impossible, just difficult. First you've got to find it. This is usually accomplished in two ways, either through strategic sensors or because the sub attacked you. Either way, you rarely get a precise fix on the sub's location. Antisubmarine tactics consist largely of converting a general location into a precise one and then attacking.

A general location for a sub may be a circular area over 100 kilometers in diameter, or as small as a few kilometers. The first task is to prevent the sub from escaping by setting up lines of sonar detectors. Naturally, you will never have enough ships or aircraft to cover the entire area quickly. In this case, you use probability theory to lay out a search pattern that will give you the highest potential for pinpointing the sub's location. Western nations have an enormous advantage with their hundreds of long-range ASW aircraft. The aircraft can be concentrated quickly before a sub escapes. Of course, escape is a relative matter. If the sub speeds up, it will generate more noise, thus making it easier to track. If it slows down or stops, the searching ASW units will get a crack at finding it. In many cases, the class the sub belongs to determines what it will do. Older nuclear boats are noisy even when stationary. However, they are still fast. So running for it makes sense. The newer Russian boats are quieter, dive deeper, and are just as fast. They come close to Western boats in overall capability, and many are now for sale to whoever has hard currency.

Sometimes strategic sensors or intelligence can identify the type of sub being pursued. This will cause more resources to be directed against the more capable boats. The first units on the scene are frequently aircraft. They drop lines of sonobuoys and listen for a contact. The sonobuoys use their sonar in passive mode initially. They will go to active mode only when a sub has been located and a more precise fix is needed for torpedo launch. Surface ASW units will proceed to an assigned area where they will stop or slow down to use their passive sonar. ASW ships also have helicopters with dunking sonar, radar, sonobuoys, and MAD. These will take off and move off up to 50 or more kilometers from their ship and lay down sonobuoys. The helicopters enable the ship to spread its sonar net around without moving the ship. A moving surface ship makes a lot of noise to a sub. A missile or long-range torpedo from the sub can quickly turn the tables. Once the sub passes close enough to a sonobuoy, the aircraft rush to that spot. A helicopter deploys a dunking sonar to confirm the sub's location. MAD gear is also used to pinpoint the sub's location. At this point, one or more homing torpedoes are dropped, and the sub is in big trouble. If the sonobuoys do not detect an explosion but still indicate a sub, more torpedoes are used and reinforcements called for.

Subs are not defenseless. Against sonar and MAD, they can go deep and take advantage of the underwater terrain to evade their hunters. The MAD is only effective for about a kilometer, and an aircraft must be lower than 200 meters to use it. When dunking sonar is used, a sub can hear the noise of a helicopter's rotors. During the 1980s, navies were moving toward equipping their subs with antiaircraft missiles. These could be encapsulated in a torpedo, launched, and take off and run a search pattern for nearby helicopters or fixed-wing aircraft. Other devices were more similar to Stinger or Redeye missiles.

Some subs, largely Russian and British ones, have insulating tiles on their hulls to make the limited passive sonar of homing torpedoes less effective. These tiles reduce the accuracy of other sonars somewhat less. Subs also can deceive homing torpedoes by ejecting noisemakers when they hear a torpedo approach. Surface ships use the same type of decoy. Recent Russian subs can, under some circumstances, outdive and outrun many types of torpedoes. Moreover, some of the larger Russian subs may be of sufficiently massive construction to survive one or more torpedo hits. All the hunter can do is try to keep the torpedoes up to the task through constant upgrades. This cat-and-mouse game may go into several rounds. The aircraft do not have inexhaustible resources. They can stay on station for several hours, depending on how far they had to travel to the search area. Aircraft carry over 100 sonobuoys and four or more torpedoes. The sonobuoys themselves last about eight hours. Carriers have 10 smaller fixed-wing aircraft that can replenish ship supplies and equipment by flying them in, as can the shorter-range helicopters. The larger P-3 aircraft must return to a land base. Longer-term weapons can be left behind to harry the subs. Antisubmarine mines can be dropped. These are too far down to detect or harm surface ships. They can be set to deactivate after a certain time so that friendly subs can also use the area. If the search is abandoned, it can be turned over to friendly subs. This, however, raises a number of additional problems. It is difficult to tell friendly from enemy subs when they are under water. It is not unlikely that there will be cases where friendly subs will be hit.

The above description of hypothetical antisubmarine combat is a unique situation because there has not yet been a major naval war involving nuclear subs. In the past, subs spent most of their time on the surface, where positive identification was easier. This is just another complication in what is shaping up to be a unique and nerve-racking new form of naval warfare.

There have been some antisubmarine operations in the past 30 years.

American and Soviet nuclear subs have been stalking each other, for practice and bragging rights, since the 1960s. Sweden and Norway have found Soviet nuclear and diesel subs lurking in their coastal waters and have had a hard time nailing these interlopers. This highlights the most likely antisubmarine warfare of the future. Many nations have diesel subs and will most likely use them close to shore. This is the worst possible situation for antisubmarine warfare. Diesel boats are quieter under water, and the closer to land you get, the more chaotic the underwater landscape is for sonar and other ASW sensors.

WHO IS HUNTING WHOM?

Before nuclear submarines came along, it was rare for submarines to successfully turn on pursuing ASW forces. Nuclear submarines are different. They never have to surface. They are as fast, and often faster, than ASW ships. Equipped with missiles and long-range torpedoes, they can attack as decisively as surface ships. Submarines have superior sensors. Surface ships cannot hide as easily as subs, nor can they find their underwater opponents as easily. Nuclear subs are seen as solitary predators. They must operate independently because of the lack of communications under water, not to mention the need for silence to maintain their cover. Submarines have inertial guidance systems that enable them to keep precise track of their position. To avoid fatal contact with friendly ASW forces, the subs will follow a precise route and schedule to their area of operations. Then, like a lion stalking a herd of antelope, the submarine slowly patrols its sector until it detects enemy ships or submarines. The sub then moves close enough to use one of its weapons, fires, and then dives quietly to avoid retribution. Run silent, run deep.

No one knows just how easy it will be to detect submarine weapons being fired under combat conditions. Peacetime exercises in the West assume the worst—that detection of submarine weapons being launched will be difficult. Under these conditions, the SSNs have done great damage, even to the point of putting carriers out of action during wargame exercises. This is one reason why every major fleet has some nuclear-attack submarines. A late-model Russian cruise-missile sub has yet to go up against a U.S. carrier group, and probably never will in our time, so no one knows for sure what will happen. Meanwhile, each U.S. carrier group has 10 fixed-wing and a dozen helicopter ASW aircraft. Every escort ship has its own ASW gear. Everyone has a strong urge to not get hit by a Russian, or any other, sub. Nonnuclear subs could, and probably would, operate in groups because they must be on or near the surface most of the time. At the very least, they could have their periscope, breathing apparatus, and radio antennae on the surface. These boats are easier to find and sink and would be effectively used close to shore in largely defensive operations. Until better sensors come along, the tables appear to have been turned.

It is now the surface warships that must always steam in fear of the superior threat beneath the waves.

Theory and Practice

Ever since World War II, the United States and the Soviet Union were the principal potential adversaries in any submarine war. The virtual disintegration of the Soviet fleet makes any of those potential battles of historical interest only. But if there were another arms race in the next century, the situation the United States and USSR found themselves in would still apply in many of its particulars. Moreover, if there is a right-wing revival in Russia, the old Cold War scenarios would regain some vitality.

The USSR and the United States had submarines that were designed differently and intended for markedly different uses. At its peak in the late 1980s, the Soviet Union had some 350 submarines. Half of them were stationed near Murmansk in northern Russia (close by the Norwegian border). Another third were in the Pacific, in Vladivostok or Petropavlosk. The remainder were split between the Baltic and Black seas fleets. In terms of submarine quality, the Northern and Pacific fleets possessed over 90 percent of what was available. The Soviets had nearly 200 nuclear submarines (61 ballistic-missile boats, 50 cruise-missile boats, and 80 attack boats), plus more than 160 diesel-electric boats (12 ballistic-missile boats, 12 cruise-missile boats, and 140 attack boats). The quality and capabilities of these boats varied enormously, more so than with Western subs. Only 10 percent of the nuclear boats approached Western standards in quietness and combat ability. About half the diesel-electric attack boats were of a modern standard; all the rest are virtually obsolete. Partially because of the large number of elderly subs and partially because of tradition, no more than 15 percent of the Russian subs were at sea at any one time. The remaining subs were cooped up in out-of-the-way bases, one near the Arctic Circle and another west of Japan (in the Sea of Japan). Two smaller fleets were bottled up in the Baltic and Black seas. Going to war with this submarine force meant getting a lot of these subs out onto the high seas. The necessity of running a gauntlet of mines, aircraft, and SSNs while observed by SOSUS made this a questionable enterprise. Moving the subs out to sea before war was declared could easily have been one of those events that actually kicked off large-scale hostilities. Should a sufficient number of subs have made it to the high seas, attempts would have been made to coordinate their attacks through the use of long-range reconnaissance aircraft. The subs could communicate only when on or near the surface, and this made them easier to detect.

All of this was a dubious proposition, as it assumed there would be no Western air power around to bash the Soviet recon aircraft. But sending "wolfpacks" against Western shipping was never high on Soviets' list of naval priorities. The premier task of the Soviet fleet was the protection of its ballistic-missile submarines. The Soviets considered the SSBNs their key nuclear-retaliation force. This is one reason why so many Soviet ships specialized in antisubmarine warfare or attacks on large aircraft carriers. Since the late 1970s, all of the Soviets' SSBNs were built with missiles that could reach their targets without leaving port or their base areas. This produced a "bastion"-type defense that still required some SSNs for defense. This was because some of the older SSBNs still had to be submerged to launch their missiles. In addition, Western SSNs were able to launch land-attack cruise missiles at these bases. This made launching from dockside a questionable idea as it exposed these SSBNs to cruise-missile hits. These long-range (more than 1,000 kilometers) Tomahawk cruise missiles, plus any carrier aircraft fortunate enough to make it, discouraged leaving any subs at their bases during the opening stages of hostilities.

Up to 20 percent of the subs would not have been able to put to sea because they were being repaired or overhauled. This left about 290 subs.

The SSBNs would have been protected by an equal number of attack subs, most of them nuclear. That took care of 100 submarines. They still had 190 left. All of the cruise-missile boats would have gone to sea to engage carriers. This was what these subs were designed for. That took care of another 40 boats, leaving 150. The nonnuclear ballistic-missile and cruise-missile boats would not last long on the high seas and normally operated in the more congested waters of the Baltic and Black seas. The older nonnuclear-attack boats would also have been nearly worthless on the high seas, and would thus have been kept back for coastal defense at all four major base areas. This took care of another 80 submarines. Some 70 attack boats were left, most of them nuclear. These remaining subs could have been used against shipping or Western SSBNs. According to the Soviets' published doctrine, the destruction of enemy SSBNs was considered more important. Experience has shown that the Western SSBNs were difficult to find and attack. There would have been about 40 Western SSBNs at sea during an alert situation. If one attack boat were sent after each SSBN, 40 would have been left for merchant shipping. These subs would have been going up against escorted convoys. The escorts would include surface ships and ASW aircraft and, in some cases, SSNs.

The above scenario was based on published Soviet doctrine and a bit of interpolation. The real world is rarely as well laid out as the above deployments. Looming over all these likely plans is the need to maintain operating bases. Nuclear subs can cruise for years without refueling, but they require food for the crews, spare parts, and ammunition reloads. After six months or so, the surviving boats have to come back or the crews will starve. This leads us to the Western version of how a global submarine war would be fought.

The U.S. Navy was not alone in confronting the Soviet fleet. Many other nations, particularly those of the NATO alliance, plus Japan and to a lesser extent China, had a vested interest in suppressing Soviet submarines. The massed antisubmarine forces of this coalition could muster more subs than the Soviets—more than 1,000 ASW aircraft, more than 500 surface warships and SOSUS. These forces were deployed roughly in proportion to the Soviet forces present in each ocean area. From a historical perspective, the Soviet prospects were not good. Their sailors were largely conscripts. Western crews were composed of volunteers serving far longer than the Soviet three years of compulsory service. Western ships were generally technologically superior. In every area, the West was superior to Soviet-controlled forces, with the exception of the Baltic Sea, where there was a rough parity.

What it came down to was, who would attack whom? In either case, the attacker would have been at a grave disadvantage. The West has made extensive preparations to blunt a Soviet submarine campaign. This effort began with peacetime operations, where SOSUS, SSNs, and ASW aircraft constantly "practiced" by tracking Soviet subs. ASW aircraft were stationed in locations where they could easily cover the narrow straits the Soviet subs would have had to transit before reaching the open sea. The critical area was (and still is) the Britain-Iceland-Greenland (BIG) gap. These three islands forced Soviet subs to travel through areas covered with SOSUS and antisubmarine mines. The narrowness of these areas makes it easy for Western SSNs to wait in ambush. Any subs surviving this gauntlet would then face Western surface warships, including carriers. Going in the other direction, the attack would be led by carrier groups. Five or six groups could have been mustered for an assault on the largest Soviet base around Murmansk. This would have added up to about 50 surface ships. Twenty or 30 SSNs could have used their ability to launch cruise missiles, but each sub can only carry about a dozen of them. The carriers could put up to 300 combat aircraft into the air. The Soviet defenders could muster 200 interceptors and 120 bombers. Given sufficient warning, these could be reinforced and their numbers nearly doubled. The area possessed 100 SAM sites, plus naval mines and more than 100 attack and cruise-missile submarines. Finally, you had 90 surface warships. Western forces could be further increased by stripping other areas. This can be dangerous, as there would be much to defend against if any Soviet subs were still at large. Even if this attack force were increased 50 percent, it would still have a stiff fight on its hands.

Both navies were aware of this imbalance of power. The Soviets stood in more fear of a Western offensive than the other way around. The Soviets realized that if they must go to war, they must do it in a way that gave their ships a chance to reach the high seas. Being in an inferior position, they had to be innovative. Their options for innovation were limited. One obvious target was the ASW aircraft bases, notably the ones in Britain, Iceland, Norway, Japan, and elsewhere. Nuclear weapons were risky, because of the possible escalation. Commando operations were a possibility, although less reliable than missiles. Chemical weapons could do the job, although still with some potential for nuclear escalation. There was always the possibility that Western forces would retaliate with chemical weapons. Cruise missiles from subs, using conventional warheads, could do substantial damage to these facilities. Such attacks would, because of some destroyed aircraft, ultimately save some subs from destruction. The Soviets might have counted this as a reasonable trade-off. Another target is the SOSUS system. Cables can be cut; underwater equipment can be attacked with torpedoes or frogmen. Land stations could have been hit with missiles. Countermeasures could also be developed for use against SOSUS detection, as is done in the air against radar detection. It is also possible that, despite all the current and historical evidence, Soviet submarine forces would not have been so inferior. The Soviets continually increased the technical quality of their boats through the 1970s and 1980s. Short of a war, there was no way of knowing precisely how much the quality gap had been closed. All indications from peacetime operations were that the gap was still quite wide in 1991.

OPERATIONAL REALITIES

The underwater world is dark, murky, and full of distracting sounds. U.S. submarine wargames have shown that up to 40 percent of potential targets were not even detected, and 20 percent of those that were cannot be successfully tracked and attacked. Experience with Soviet subs indicates that their record was (and still is) even worse. The large number of Soviet cruise-missile submarines would have been highly dependent on this blind-man's-bluff atmosphere in order to have had a chance to get close enough to U.S. ships to fire missiles. But then, Soviet subs may have had a hard time even finding surface ships. The weapons always have problems. Wire-guided torpedoes can be very effective because they have at their disposal all the sub's sensors as they were steered toward their target. However, the wire must remain intact, and the tube cannot be reloaded until the torpedo has hit something or run out of fuel. This means that the firing sub cannot move around violently lest the wire be broken. Depending on how far the torpedo has to go, it will spend 10 to 20 minutes running. Meanwhile, the target may detect the torpedo launch and fire off one of its own. Or the target may dive fast and deep and escape. Definitely a nail-biting exercise.

The Future

The future is moving backward somewhat. With the former Soviet sub fleet in disarray and disintegration, the focus of undersea warfare shifts back to the nearly 200 diesel-electric submarines held by unstable Third

World nations. While this is a formidable technical challenge, the extent of the threat is small, with fewer than a dozen nations possessing these subs. This has not prevented a lot of anxious talk about the new submarine "threat."

Whatever excitement the Third World submarine threat generates will not balance the rapid decline of the former Soviet submarine fleet. Even before the collapse of the Soviet Union in 1991, the Soviet submarine fleet was suffering from a shrinking pool of resources. Less money was allocated for maintaining and operating the Soviets' existing subs. This led to an accelerated retirement of the older boats, both diesel and nuclear. But this wasn't enough. Qualified sailors for sub crews became more difficult to obtain. Budgets shrank and, after the Soviet Union collapsed in 1991, the navy's budget shrank even further.

Moreover, the introduction of market pricing in Russia took away the ability of the military to grab resources at bargain prices. Since the mid-1980s, the combat value of the former Soviet submarine fleet has shrunk by more than half. There is no relief in sight for the Russian sub fleet. The Russians have taken over most of the Soviet submarines and simply can't support them. This has turned out to be a debilitating prospect for Western, and particularly U.S., submariners. The U.S. sub fleet was created in response to the perceived Soviet sub threat. With that threat now rapidly wasting away, it is difficult to justify the tens of billions of dollars spent each year on U.S. subs. However, even after drastic cuts in the U.S. submarine and ASW forces, it will be a while before any other nation comes up with a credible submarine threat to the U.S. Navy.

Underwater "threats" have always been with us. Consider the last one. During the early 1980s, a Soviet spy ring (the Walkers) learned details on how the Americans were finding Soviet subs. Even with that knowledge, many deficiencies of Soviet subs could not be fixed, especially in older boats. However, the Soviets found that by paying more attention to the details of propeller construction, they could substantially reduce the noise their boats generated. They managed to obtain the equipment and software from Japan and Norway. American sensors quickly noticed the quieter Soviet subs. Despite the outcry in Western naval circles, this situation did not seriously tip the balance of power at sea. For one thing, only a few Soviet subs had the new propellers and other improvements. The Soviets' other subs had several additional sources of noise that would have taken many years to replace. Moreover, the technical, psychological, and training advantages of U.S. subs over their Soviet counterparts was so large that it would have taken a decade or more for a substantial change in the naval balance to occur. This shift could have happened only if the United States Navy did nothing in response.

History has shown that change comes quickly when there is a substantial incentive. Quieter Soviet subs provided this. In a final irony, it turned out that the "propeller incident" was but one aspect of the Soviets' effort to quiet their subs. Indeed, the first quieter subs noticed were the result of Soviet silencing work done before the new propeller technology was obtained.

Noise also has a lot to do with who will be attacking or defending. As with air combat, underwater warfare consists largely of ambush. Whoever gets the first shot in usually wins. A submarine that is stationary or moving at minimum speed is less likely to be detected by a faster-moving sub. It comes down to who must move. Until the mid-1980s, Soviet subs had the choice of moving out of their isolated sanctuaries or staying put and not contributing to the fighting. Western subs would simply wait and ambush oncoming Soviet boats. But then the U.S. Navy decided to change its strategy, which now had U.S. subs and surface ships attacking heavily defended Soviet naval bases. This would give Soviet subs the opportunity to sit around waiting for targets to move into torpedo range. Noisier and less efficient Soviet subs would still be at a disadvantage, with an exchange ratio of perhaps two or three to one U.S. sub destroyed. But the previous situation, with Western subs doing the waiting, provided opportunities for exchange ratios of up to 10 Soviet subs for each Western one lost. The chatter about the threat of Third World diesel-electric subs is real, in that these boats are quieter and would normally be waiting for U.S. nuclear subs to come wandering by. The solution will probably be to go after these diesel boats with ASW aircraft and surface ships.

The weapons of submarine warfare are changing. Research is being done on using nuclear or nonnuclear warheads in submarine and land-based ballistic missiles for attacking surface ships. The trend toward non-nuclear weapons has spurred work on warheads using their own sensors to seek out surface targets. Sensor technology also seems ready for a major leap forward. Part of this may be propelled by the recent breakthroughs in superconductivity. Meanwhile, large increases in computing power make for more efficient analysis of data already being collected. More computing power also makes some types of sensors more practical. Sensors that detect neutrinos, heat, color, and other subtle submarine characteristics may indeed make the oceans transparent. Just installing state-of-the-art computers can increase detection probability by several times. More prosaic changes include putting sonars into towed arrays. This eliminates one problem with active sonar, that it gives the users' position away. Many Western nuclear subs have towed passive arrays, which are wormlike devices linked to the sub with a cable. Western technology has made it possible to get the more complex electronics needed by active sonar into the "worm." Better communications also allows for greater use of multistatic sensors. This system depends on one or more active sensors working in coordination with many more passive sensors. Communications coordinates all the information, sorts it out, and more rapidly pinpoints the location of enemy subs. Once more, computer signal-processing power is the key to making this work.

This research will lose a lot of steam, as the major rationale for it—finding the numerous subs of the former Soviet Union—has disappeared.

New classes of nuclear submarines were in development up until the collapse of the Soviet Union. Russia, at great expense, had introduced a new class of submarine every two or three years through the 1980s. These had been largely evolutionary in design, and most underwent severe development problems. The United States has regularly modified the design of its Los Angeles–class attack subs as well as upgrading its ballistic-missile boats. The next class of U.S. attack subs, the Sea Wolf, will incorporate a number of major changes. For one thing, it will displace nearly 10,000 tons (submerged) and be of a somewhat different shape than previous nuclear subs. It will have more, and probably larger, torpedo tubes, as well as enough bunks for all crew members. It will carry more than 50 torpedoes and cruise missiles, be quieter and more capable of operating under ice, and have better sensors. These boats will also cost up to $2 billion each. It looks probable that only one, or a few, Sea Wolfs will be built. Many other nations were planning to join the nuclear-submarine club. These included Canada, India, and Brazil. Britain, Russia, and France are ready to sell smaller, cheaper, and most likely secondhand nuclear subs to these nations. These nations are in for a rude surprise once the bills come in. Nuclear ships, it turns out, are twice as expensive to operate as conventional ships. Despite the fuel savings, it turns out that anything involved with nuclear power comes with gold-plated expenses. Submarines of all types have another problem. As good as their sensors are, even the best submarines have trouble finding anything. The future holds forth little prospect of this changing soon. Little is said about this problem, yet it will be the major factor in any major naval war involving submarines.

Until recently, Russian subs were so noisy when moving that they provided about as good a "noise beacon" as one could want. Although their boats are still not nearly as quiet as Western ones, and probably never will be, they are quiet enough to make consistent detection difficult. The problem is so bad that even when you are pretty sure they are in a particular area, you may have no more than a 50 percent chance of getting an accurate enough fix to fire a long-range torpedo. The torpedo-guidance system may also fail to find the target. These problems have been demonstrated in simulated combat in ocean exercise areas. Proposed solutions are larger subs with more powerful sensors and remote-control minisubs that would act as scouts and also be useful for finding a path through minefields. More discriminating active and passive sonars are also in the works for navigation through minefields and other tricky underwater landscapes.

The task of finding enemy subs was to be aided by upgrading the SOSUS network. This will go forward to some degree by Japan's work on its own SOSUS net in the waters facing Russian territory. Another solution is special satellites to constantly monitor the shifting currents that make up the ocean's geography. The Soviet Union had long been sending ocean-survey ships out to chart the ocean bottom and to seek suitable hiding places for its subs. The Soviets had some ocean-surveillance satellites in orbit, but their sensors were quite primitive and limited. The first U.S. satellite was to go up in 1988, but the *Challenger* disaster delayed this until 1991. Even with the new boats and the satellites, submarine combat will be more a game of blindman's bluff than most people would like to admit. Attacks on surface ships are similarly handicapped by the relative blindness of subs. Three lines of research are being pursued to solve this. One aims to increase the power of onboard sensors. Another seeks to increase the ability to communicate with other submarines, aircraft, and satellites. Finally, there are continuing attempts to provide subs with their own recon RPVs. No breakthroughs in any of these areas are expected anytime soon. However, the U.S. Navy continues to openly proclaim the combat superiority of U.S. subs over anything anyone else can muster now or for the next 10 years.

11

The Navy:
In the Air

AIRCRAFT HAVE REVOLUTIONIZED naval operations and become the central item of equipment in all major fleets. The navy first used aircraft for reconnaissance. It still does. This started before World War I (1914–18). During that war and the 1920s, it was realized that aircraft could be used for naval combat. Once planes became powerful enough to lift a torpedo or large bomb, they could sink the largest warship. Shortly after that revelation, aircraft carriers started appearing in significant numbers. Combat experience in World War II confirmed the predictions, as carriers replaced the large-gun battleship as the "capital ship." The nuclear submarine is touted by some as the replacement for the aircraft carrier. That may be so, but it will not replace aircraft. Indeed, the most potent new weapon on submarines is the cruise missile, which is little more than an aircraft flown by a robot. Subs can't carry more than two dozen cruise missiles, and, unlike carriers, they cannot reuse missiles or obtain reconnaissance from them. Moreover, a submarine's persistent enemies are the various types of ASW aircraft that hound them constantly. Submarines may supplant or replace various types of surface ships. Nothing on the horizon will replace aircraft in their various forms.

Carrier-Task-Force Defense System

The modern (U.S.) aircraft carrier may yet prove to be a dinosaur overstaying its welcome. But for the moment it is one of the more lethal and flexible weapons systems available. The key to carrier operations is the ability of the carrier to defend itself. It does this by putting up a multizone defense extending out for more than 700 kilometers from the carrier and its escorts.

THE INNER ZONE

The primary, or vital, zone extends 10 to 20 kilometers from the carrier and is monitored by shipboard sensors. This zone is defended primarily by electronic weapons, naval missiles, and guns. Electronic jammers blind cruise-missile homing systems. "Blip" enhancers make low-flying helicopters appear like carriers to the missiles and decoy the missiles from their intended targets. Electronic pulses can even detonate the missile warhead prematurely. Nonelectronic defenses include chaff—a cloud of metal foil blinds a radar. Last-ditch defenses are fully automatic machine cannon that shoot automatically at anything that looks like an approaching missile.

THE MIDDLE ZONE

Covering the area 10–160 kilometers from the carrier, this zone is monitored by the carrier task force's AEGIS cruiser and antisubmarine ships. The AEGIS ships are built around a powerful radar system and hundreds of surface-to-air-missiles (SAMs) carried by the AEGIS cruiser and the other escort ships. The AEGIS radar and fire-control systems can coordinate the use of hundreds of SAMs fired at incoming aircraft and cruise missiles. Other escorts will monitor the ocean for the telltale sounds of approaching enemy subs.

THE OUTER ZONE

This zone is for threats more than 160 kilometers away and is monitored by patrol aircraft from the carrier. They can spot surface ships nearly 400 kilometers away and aircraft more than 700 kilometers distant. This zone is defended by aircraft and detachments of surface ships and submarines. These detachments of one to four ships use the same techniques as the ships in the primary and middle zone. In addition, these ships may get an opportunity to use their antiship missiles against enemy vessels that come into range. The major drawback is that these ships cannot always take up their positions fast enough. The carriers' F-14 aircraft also have missiles with a range of 200 kilometers that are effective against cruise missiles and aircraft. Their primary targets are enemy aircraft carrying cruise missiles. Other aircraft have air-to-surface antiship missiles with a range of nearly 200 kilometers. Six to 12 F-14s with six Phoenix missiles each should be able to stop most cruise-missile attacks, or at least chop them up so that the primary- and middle-zone defenses are not overwhelmed. Timing is a critical consideration. U.S. carrier aircraft normally spend about 100 minutes in the air. Few aerial tankers are available for refueling, and you still have to land to rearm. The only alternative is to put up the aircraft in shifts, leaving yourself with a less than maximum defense.

THE STRATEGIC ZONE

Beyond the 700 kilometers from the carrier is the strategic zone. This zone is monitored by satellites, land-based aircraft, and SOSUS. This demonstrates how vulnerable fleets are to having their satellites destroyed. Not only do the satellites provide some of the reconnaissance, they are vital for passing all information between the fleet and far-distant land and naval units. Once something is spotted, strike aircraft are sent after targets in this zone. The maximum range of aircraft strikes is about 2,000 kilometers. This is the zone in which enemy recon aircraft are hit.

Many navies model their long-range naval-aviation doctrine after the one developed by the former Soviet Navy. That has more than 100 long-range bombers used as naval recon aircraft. In addition to a heavy load of EW and ECM equipment, the Soviets could also carry one or more long-range cruise missiles. These aircraft were also responsible for providing targeting information for less well equipped aircraft. This is critical, as cruise missiles need accurate target-location updates if they are fired over the horizon, as most are. Without the assistance of the recon planes, many cruise missiles will miss their targets. Indeed, without a current and precise location of the enemy ships, other aircraft and ships will often not even fire at targets they cannot see. Because of all the electronic warfare used, it is critical that the autopilots on the cruise missiles get their missiles as close to the targets as possible before turning on their terminal homing radar or sensors. This requirement will not soon be eliminated. The sensors needed to enable a missile to find an over-the-horizon target by itself are extremely complex.

This strategic zone is quite possibly the most important. It presents the best opportunities for destroying cruise-missile carriers before they can launch. Russian-built Tu-16 and Tu-22 aircraft carry one or two missiles each. Each Russian-built surface warship or submarine carries up to 10 or more cruise missiles. Once these missiles are launched, they provide a greater number of targets to shoot down. A cruise missile is more difficult to detect and hit than an aircraft or ship. This was one reason the Soviets built over 50 cruise-missile submarines.

The carrier-defense system has two modes, passive and active. The passive mode is used in peacetime and in wartime when an attack is not imminent. In this mode, most of the escort ships are within a few kilometers of each other and the task-force carrier. The one or two nuclear-attack subs attached to the task force generally travel out in front of the task force, using their sensors to detect other submarines the task force may encounter.

Active mode is used when an attack is expected. The escort ships spread out, with several taking up position in the middle zone. The carrier's aircraft fly more frequently and are kept ready to concentrate in the direction an attack comes from. The task force's nuclear subs take up position in the rear of the task force, to watch for enemy subs coming from that direction. You don't want your own subs maneuvering in the direction of an enemy attack as that is also the direction enemy subs may come from and there is no way to sort out the enemy and friendly subs when your antisubmarine forces go into action.

ANTISUBMARINE WARFARE

Helicopters are the most common ASW aircraft. Ships of over 3,000 tons can usually carry at least one, and often two. Helicopters can extend a ship's ASW capabilities more than 100 kilometers. Helicopters can pursue a submarine contact diligently and enable surface ships to keep up with swifter SSNs. Many navies have small aircraft carriers that use nothing but helicopters. The U.S. Navy also maintains a large fleet of P-3 four-engine maritime patrol/ASW aircraft. Other nations have similar aircraft. These planes enable large ocean areas to be patrolled and subs to be attacked wherever they are found.

ORGANIZATION OF CARRIER AIRCRAFT

Large U.S. carriers have between 85 and 90 aircraft. These consist of 24 fighters (F-14s), 34 strike (F-18s for the most part, plus some A-6s), 10 ASW aircraft (S-3s), 6 ASW helicopters, 4 ECM (A-6s), 4 radar (E-2Cs) and 4 tankers (KA-6Ds). A few of the F-14s are equipped as recon aircraft. The S-3s can stay aloft for six hours and carry sonobuoys, torpedoes, and air-to-surface missiles. The E-2C radar aircraft can search out to 700 kilometers. No other nation has anything quite like these carriers. The Soviets built one and scrapped two others before they could be finished. The Soviet carrier was not capable as the U.S. CVs and, because of economic problems, will unlikely develop into much of a capable naval force. France has two smaller carriers, each with 39 aircraft, including four or more helicopters. The U.S. Navy also has 12 smaller helicopter carriers. These carry a combination of vertical takeoff jets and helicopters. These are used by the marines for amphibious operations. Other nations, like Britain, France,

Italy, and Russia, use these vessels for antisubmarine and surface combat operations.

Land-Based Naval Aircraft Operations

Few navies have aircraft carriers; nearly all have land-based aircraft. These planes are used for patrolling one's own coastline and, in most cases, to attack hostile ships. Western nations have more than 1,000 multi-engine, long-range patrol aircraft. These are primarily U.S. P-3 Orion aircraft, which can also carry cruise missiles. In addition, the U.S. Air Force has trained some of its B-52 bomber crews to drop naval mines (CAPTORs) and use Harpoon antiship missiles. A substantial number of naval aircraft are interceptors. As was learned in World War II, naval patrol aircraft are vulnerable to interceptors. Russia is a strong proponent of defending its coastline and naval bases with interceptors. Against a defended shore, patrol aircraft are increasingly at risk if they approach closer than 500 kilometers to the enemy coast.

Worldwide, navies have more than 3,000 fixed-wing and 2,000 helicopter aircraft operating from land bases. The majority are equipped to hunt submarines. Many of the antisubmarine weapons on these aircraft can also be used against surface ships. It's becoming more common to see ASW aircraft with long-range cruise missiles. This allows the slow patrol planes to get out of harm's way after launching an attack. If a nation has access to enough land bases, these long-range aircraft can be nearly as flexible as carrier-based patrol planes. Carrying an impressive array of sensors and weapons and moving at more than 400 kilometers an hour, these aircraft form a fast-moving reserve of naval power. They are able to detect and attack ships far more rapidly than any other vessel can. So why have ships at all? Patrol aircraft eventually have to land; ships can sit where they wish for as long as they want. Although some aircraft can stay aloft for more than 12 hours, they must eventually land to rearm, refuel, and perform maintenance. Depending on the skill and efficiency of the ground crews, a patrol aircraft can fly one sortie a day for several weeks. After that, things will start to fall apart. Aircraft would replace ships if only they were as durable.

PATROL-AIRCRAFT MISSIONS

Surface Ship Search. This is the simplest form of patrol and is normally performed with radar-equipped aircraft. The most capable of these aircraft, the P-3, can spot large aircraft carriers or tankers 350 kilometers away. Smaller ships must be closer to be spotted—200 kilometers for cruisers, 100 kilometers for destroyers, and 50 kilometers for trawlers and surfaced submarines. The cheaper E-2s can spot large ships 180 kilometers away while the aircraft moves along at a speed of 400 kilometers an hour. Other aircraft surface-search radars have shorter ranges—up to 200 kilometers for fixed-wing aircraft and up to 100 kilometers for helicopters. By comparison, human observers can see 20 to 30 kilometers during clear weather. Searches are performed offensively or defensively. That is, the aircraft can either establish a barrier of observation to prevent the undetected intrusion of enemy ships or scour an area looking for something to shoot at. Whenever enemy ships are found, strike aircraft or warships are directed toward the target.

Antisubmarine Search. Not as efficient as searching for surface ships. Aircraft are used to pinpoint a sub that has been reported in an area. These reports come either from an attack by the sub or a SOSUS detection. See previous chapter for details.

Strike. Most aircraft can carry at least one air-to-surface missile. Only the long-range cruise missiles on U.S. (and some Western) aircraft are likely to be used against enemy task forces lacking air cover. Russian patrol aircraft with missiles are actually bombers modified for naval patrol and attack. These Tu-16s and Tu-22s would have a rough time of it against carrier-based interceptors.

Theory and Practice

Cruise missiles, because they are the cheapest and most widely available antiship weapon, are likely to be the biggest threat to ships for some time to come. Although cruise missiles have not been used on a mass scale yet, there was a parallel experience during World War II. American task forces encountered massive kamikaze attacks by Japanese aircraft crewed by hastily trained suicide pilots. The Okinawa Campaign saw 1,900 aircraft attacking over a period of 100 days (March–June 1945). Under attack were 587 ships, of which 320 were warships. Each attack averaged 150 aircraft. One had as many as 350 planes. Defending were carrier-based interceptors and antiaircraft guns. Only 7 percent of the suicide aircraft scored hits. Eighteen percent of the ships hit were sunk or put out of action. Although the kamikaze tactic was unexpected, the defending fleet had the usual strong sense of self-preservation. The Americans were also heavily armed. The kamikazes were, in effect, cruise missiles. Because they initially had the element of surprise, they were more successful during this first use.

Twenty-two years later, electronic pilots were developed to replace human ones, and Israel lost a destroyer to Egyptian cruise missiles. Over the next five years, the cruise missile was used a number of times, severely damaging more than a dozen ships. During the 1973 Arab-Israeli War, Israel demonstrated that the cruise missile could be stopped cold with a combination of electronic warfare, gunfire, and evasive maneuvers. More than 50 Arab cruise missiles were fired without scoring a hit. Fifty percent of the Israeli cruise missiles scored hits. It would appear that an unsuspecting target has a 90 percent chance of being hit by a modern cruise missile. Various defensive measures—guns, missiles, electronics, maneuvers—can bring this hit probability down close to zero percent. The crucial question is, what would be the percentage of hits by future attackers on defending ships? Based on historical experience, between 0 and 10 percent. This assumes an alert defender. Considering the previously demonstrated ineffectiveness of non-Western nations' antiaircraft and cruise missiles, 1 to 3 percent is more likely. If the attackers achieve surprise, the probability can easily increase by a factor of 3 or more. Western cruise missiles will probably hit 3 to 10 times as often (3 to 30 percent) if they are the attacker against a non-Western defender.

What, then, would be the outcome of a large-scale use of cruise missiles? It depends on what type of missile is used and against what kind of target. Russia has several kinds of cruise missiles that may end up on the arms market. Its most formidable system is the Oscar-class submarine, armed with 24 SS-N-19 missiles. These missiles have a range of 550 kilometers and home in on the target's radars. The missiles travel close to the water at over 800 meters a second. The tricky part is the sub discovering the precise position of the defending task force and then getting close enough to launch.

Let us assume that the Oscar does get within 100 kilometers of a task force without being discovered, perhaps by sitting in the right place until the task force steamed into range. Suppose it got off 20 missiles. In two minutes, they will hit the task force. The task force, if it is American, has at least six ships, most with their sensors turned on. An SSN with the task force would likely hear the missiles launch but would not have enough time to give warning. There might be time to activate all the Phalanx gun systems, chaff, and flares. The task force might even be practiced in turning off all radars quickly. There might still be one or more radar aircraft in the air that could keep their radars on. This would deny the missiles any surface targets to home in on. If these SS-N-19s also had heat-seeking or active radar guidance, they could be deceived by the chaff and flares. There would be perhaps 10 operational Phalanx units. Some of the missiles would malfunction before they reached their targets. Between all of these defensive measures, and making allowances for human error, perhaps one or two missiles would hit a ship. This might not include the carrier. This is in line with the World War II kamikaze experience and might be too high considering that such are not a surprise this time around. Meanwhile, the Oscar could be in big trouble if it was attacking a U.S. carrier task force. Spotted when its missiles were launched, it now has an SSN stalking it. It's possible that an Oscar could evade all the SOSUS, aircraft, and ships looking for subs making for the open sea. It is less likely that two or more of these subs would be able to coordinate an ambush like the one described above.

A more likely scenario is some Third World nation (like Iran or Iraq) using a combination of air- and land-based cruise missiles, plus some launched from small ships, delivering something resembling a coordinated attack. If the naval task force was caught napping, this kind of attack could cause serious damage. If the task force was alert, a few of the missiles would still get through. Argentina demonstrated this in 1982, as did Iraq in 1986. We won't know who will try it in the 1990s, but someone probably will.

The last major naval war saw aircraft carriers dominate the action, with a strong assist from shore-based aircraft, submarines, and mines. It's uncertain which mix of weapons will be decisive in a future major naval war. It would appear that aircraft will continue to dominate, mines will be as effective as in the past, and submarines will be more effective. Where does that leave aircraft carriers? The United States, with 15 large and 12 smaller carriers, has the largest investment in this ship type. American carriers outnumber those of all other fleets combined, even if budget cuts reduce this force by nearly half in the 1990s. This points out that U.S. carriers will not be needed primarily for anticarrier operations, as in World War II. With their large complement of long-range aircraft, U.S. carriers would be lethal against enemy surface ships and, to a lesser extent, against land-based aircraft. Any ship equipped with cruise missiles is also something of an aircraft carrier, but the shorter range and/or need for targeting data make cruise missiles decidedly second-rate.

Submarines and mines are the biggest question mark. No navy has ever had to deploy over 100 nuclear subs, or defend against such a force. Although nuclear subs are larger and more robust because of it, they are not very well protected. Although much is made of their sturdy waterproof hulls, the least amount of damage can ruin this underwater capability. On the surface, nuclear subs are extremely vulnerable, especially against aircraft. Moreover, when under water, subs have a very difficult time communicating. When they do, they come near the surface. Again, this makes them vulnerable to aircraft detection. Communications problems make coordinated operations difficult to the point of impossibility. While the Germans used large "wolfpacks" of subs during World War II, these boats were operating on the surface most of the time. Modern aircraft and electronic monitoring devices make it risky for current subs to spend too much time on the surface or communicating openly. Operating individually, nuclear subs will close off their operating areas to friendly forces. This will create a killing zone where any ships are considered hostile.

Mines are another increasing danger. The current models are very difficult to find. They often remain on the ocean floor and require diligent and time-consuming searches. Moreover, mines lying on the bottom cannot be cleared easily using helicopters. The problem with mines is getting them to where they can threaten enemy shipping. Aircraft can be effective, if they have sufficient range and air superiority. More likely is the use of submarines to deliver mines, if the subs can survive the gauntlet of anti-submarine aircraft.

The question of whether aircraft carriers are worthwhile rests on their ability to stay afloat. Submarines may or may not be able to get after them. Whatever the case, air-delivered weapons will continue to dominate naval warfare. Even submarines depend on cruise missiles for most of their firepower against surface ships.

The Future

During the 1980s, the U.S. Air Force and U.S. Navy took different paths in developing bombing systems. The air force's "smart bomb" approach proved to be superior. The navy found itself embarrassed by the superior performance of air-force bombers and in the wake of the Gulf War agreed to work with the air force on future generations of smart bombs and bombing systems.

In 1990, Russia put to sea its first Western-style aircraft carrier, capable of launching fixed-wing aircraft. Even before this, there were indications that the Russians are having second thoughts about trying to catch up with America's three generations of experience in this area. The collapse of the Soviet Union cut out the funding for further work on this class of ships, and the Russians will either embark a large number of helicopters, vertical takeoff jets, and a few Su-27 fixed-wing aircraft on this ship, or try to sell it off. Meanwhile, the United States is still trying to deploy the V-22 Osprey, a vertical takeoff turboprop that can also fly like a normal fixed-wing aircraft. It does this by rotating its two engines for takeoff and landing. The U.S. Navy and Marines were to have received 900 of these for transport, rescue, and ASW work. These are basically superior helicopters. Top speed of 460 kph with a range of more than 1,000 kilometers and in-flight refueling capability. They can carry 24 troops or three tons of internal cargo, as well as external loads. With an unrefueled ferry range of 3,900 kilometers, these aircraft can be deployed worldwide in a short time. Their primary purpose is to move marines inland quickly and farther than now possible with helicopters. The fleet can always use their longer range to deliver spare parts and other essential supplies to any ship at sea.

For carrier operations, V-22s can operate from a fleet tanker's helicopter pad and take fuel direct from the tanker to waiting carrier aircraft. This is especially useful during combat operations, when valuable carrier-deck space would have to be taken up by conventional aerial tankers. As ASW aircraft, the V-22 provides the potential for a much more lethal weapon. Its high speed and ability to hover with dunking sonar enables rapid concentration of ASW capability. Larger and more powerful sonobuoys can be carried, and recovered, over longer distances. These advantages are not without cost, as the V-22 is more than twice the cost of the current helicopters and the S-3 ASW jet. The ever-present question has always been whether the increased cost will bring with it sufficiently greater capability. One factor in its favor was the U.S. Navy's increasing fleet of 40,000-ton amphibious carriers. Although primarily designed to carry and support marines, these ships can handle more than 40 helicopters and vertical take-off aircraft like the AV-8 and V-22. With the proper mix of aircraft, these ships can perform most of the missions now handled by the 90,000-ton attack carriers. But the disappearance of the Soviet armed forces and the ensuing budget cuts have just about killed the V-22. What has kept the project going is pure politics. The legislators with V-22 work in their districts are reluctant to be accused of losing jobs for their constituents if the V-22 is canceled. So now we have the not-uncommon situation where the military says it cannot afford the V-22 and, given the current military situation, doesn't need it. But the politicians need it, and the struggle continues.

Naval aviation is also threatened by longer-range air-force planes. The B-2 bomber, also fighting for its fiscal life, is touted as a cheaper way to put bombs on far-distant targets without the expense of a carrier group. The new budget pressures will probably reduce the U.S. carrier inventory by as much as half. Naval aircraft have already felt the heat. Budget problems have destroyed the U.S. Navy's plans for replacing its A-6 attack aircraft and the P-3 recon aircraft. More such damage will be felt through the 1990s.

Patrol Aircraft in Service

Chart 11-1 shows the distribution of patrol aircraft and helicopters among the major maritime powers in the world. This includes AWACS-type planes, as their function is basically one of surveillance. Most of the world's surface is water, and these areas are largely unobserved most of the time. Understandably, navies have taken the lead in developing reconnaissance and patrol aircraft. The United States represents more than a third of the total. The top three nations account for more than 70 percent of all patrol aircraft. There is somewhat less concentration of aircraft types—the three most numerous types account for less than 40 percent of all aircraft. However, when adjustments are made for aircraft capability, the top three aircraft account for more than 50 percent of what is available. The P-3 Orion is used as the aircraft all others are compared to.

The P-3 is one of the more capable patrol aircraft and the single most widely available type. The nations most dependent on seaborne trade possess more than 80 percent of the world's patrol-aircraft capability. Three navies possess two thirds of the world's naval helicopters, and six types account for more than 70 percent of those in service. If the relative capabilities of the different helicopters are taken into account, the three top naval powers own nearly 80 percent of the world's

11-1 Patrol Aircraft in Use

	Total	US	RU	JAP	Ger	FR	BRIT	CAN	AUS	TAI	NETH	BRAZ	SA	IND	SWE	INDO	TURK	SK	ITAL
	1,948	696	472	189	26	60	32	66	20	18	36	27	8	65	21	27	30	59	96
P-3 Orion	286	200		50				12	12		12								
P-2H Neptune	24			24															
E-3A AWACS	42	40					2												
1150 Atlantic	50				14	20													16
S-3A Viking	100	100																	
Tu-142	58		50											8					
Il-38 May	35		30											5					
Tu-22M Backfire	25		25																
Il-76 Mainstay	12		12																
S-2E	67							19				6					18	24	
SH-60B LAMPS 3	120	120																	
Ka-27 Helix	45		45																
SH-3 Sea King	163	90					35		8										30
Tu-16 Badger	15		15																
M-12 Mail	55		55																
Nimrod	30						30												
SH-2F LAMPS 2	50	50																	
Mi-14 Haze	105		105																
E-8 JSTARS	4	4																	
Ka-25 Hormone	117		110											7					
E-2	70	70																	
TR-1 (U-2)	22	22																	
Other	453		25	115	12	40				18	24	21	8	45	21	27	12	35	50

helicopter capability. The six most numerous types actually account for nearly 90 percent of the total. Other nations usually have a naval helicopter capability that is more form than substance. The primary reason for this investment in the equivalent of nearly 1,000 P-3s was their fear of many of former Soviet Union's 300+ submarines being unleashed on their warships and seaborne commerce. With the Soviet sub fleet out of the picture, we can expect the number of naval patrol aircraft to shrink with it.

The first row gives the nation possessing the patrol aircraft indicated in the rows below. Abbreviations for nations are: US—United States, RU—Russia, JAP—Japan, GER—Germany, FR—France, BRIT—Great Britain, CAN—Canada, AUS—Australia, TAI—Taiwan, NETH—Netherlands, BRAZ—Brazil, SA—South Africa, IND—India, SWE—Sweden, INDO—Indonesia, TURK—Turkey, SK—South Korea, ITAL—Italy. The second row gives the aircraft total for each nation.

The first column gives the name of the aircraft. The second column gives the total aircraft for that type. The nation with the largest number is normally the manufacturer. The subsequent columns show quantity of each type of aircraft possessed by each nation.

Patrol Aircraft Characteristics

Chart 11-2 shows the characteristics and capabilities of more than 75 percent of the patrol aircraft in service today. Reconnaissance, especially for fleets, is a critical capability. The navy that has the edge in this area is considered to possess a force multiplier, or the equivalent of additional combat ships. In practical terms, the multiplier can often come to a 50 or 100 percent increase in combat capability. Patrol aircraft in navies became even more efficient when they received radar in the early 1940s. This made these aircraft effective when the weather was bad and fog or mist covered the water's surface. Equipped with bombs, depth charges, and rockets, these aircraft could not only find, but also attack, submarines and light surface ships. You no longer required ships to control large portions of the ocean. Except where the larger warships or interceptors held sway, the armed patrol aircraft ruled the waves. This search capability was eventually extended to land operations, where the complex jumble of objects on the ground required a more intelligent radar. Being able to pick out aircraft flying close to the ground beneath you was an important breakthrough for Western armed forces in the 1970s. Russian technology is still trying to catch up with this development.

The U.S. E-2 and E-3 are the principal aircraft with this feature. Russian Il-76 Mainstay aircraft also have it, although in a less reliable form. The development of exotic metals and engine technologies led to the development of the TR-1 (U-2) in the 1950s, the SR-71 in the 1960s, and a new aircraft in the 1980s. These aircraft fly so high (30,000 meters) and fast that most antiaircraft weapons cannot reach them. Because they are constantly improved and upgraded, no one has been able to match these strategic patrol aircraft. Naval helicopters are used for search missions and for transport from sea to land. Except for transport helicopters of the U.S. Marine Corps, most of the world's naval helicopters are used primarily for search. Often flying from ships at sea, these helicopters look for surface ships or submarines.

11-2 Patrol Aircraft Characteristics

Aircraft	% of To	Index	Total	Search Surf	Search Sub	Search Air	Attack Surf	Attack Sub	Attack Air	From	Cruise	Rng	Time	IFR	Wght	Crew	Len	Wpns
P-3 Orion	38%	100	286	6	10	2	8	10	0	US	600	7,600	13	N	64	12	36	9
P-2H Neptune	2%	61	24	4	6	1	5	8	0	US	400	4,500	11	N	34	7	28	3
E-3A AWACS	3%	62	42	8	2	10	0	0	10	US	800	8,000	10	Y	147	17	47	0
1150 Atlantic	4%	55	50	5	6	1	3	6	1	FR	550	6,400	12	N	43	14	32	3
S-3A Viking	7%	54	100	4	7	2	6	8	0	US	680	5,500	8	Y	25	4	16	1.4
Tu-142	4%	54	58	4	0	2	7	0	2	RU	800	12,500	16	Y	188	10	50	11
Il-38 May	2%	39	35	3	4	1	2	6	0	RU	645	7,200	11	N	61	12	40	5
Tu-22M Backfire	1%	37	25	3	0	3	8	0	2	RU	900	8,000	9	Y	130	7	43	7.5
Il-76 Mainstay	1%	32	12	5	0	8	0	0	5	RU	750	4,000	8	N	190	12	47	0
S-2E	3%	31	67	4	5	2	3	6	0	US	440	2,100	5	N	13	4	13	3
SH-60B LAMPS 3	5%	28	120	6	6	0	4	9	0	US	240	250	2.5	N	9	3	20	2
Ka-27 Helix	2%	28	45	5	5	0	3	6	0	RU	230	250	4.5	N	11	3	11	4
SH-3 Sea King	6%	27	163	4	5	0	3	8	0	US	220	350	4	N	8	4	22	1.5
Tu-16 Badger	0%	24	15	3	0	2	7	0	2	RU	900	5,700	6	Y	72	6	35	4.5
M-12 Mail	2%	22	55	1	4	1	2	4	0	RU	550	4,000	7	N	29	5	30	3
NIMROD	1%	22	30	6	10	2	8	10	0	UK	800	8,000	12	Y	87	12	39	8
SH-2F LAMPS 2	1%	21	50	4	5	0	2	6	0	US	210	300	3	N	5.8	3	16	1.8
Mi-14 Haze	3%	21	105	4	3	0	3	5	0	RU	180	300	4	N	14	5	25	2
E-9 JSTARS	0%	18	4	12	0	0	0	0	0	US	800	8,000	12	Y	145	18	47	0
Ka-26 Hormone	2%	15	117	3	4	0	2	5	0	RU	120	250	2	N	8	4	10	1.5
E-2	1%	12	70	8	0	0	0	0	0	US	500	4,000	8	N	23	5	18	1
TR-1 (U-2)	0%	12	22	8	0	0	0	0	0	US	650	4,800	8	N	13	1	19	0
Other	11%	19	453															

In peacetime, many search helicopters do a lot of patrol and rescue work. When going after surface ships, the purpose is not just to find the enemy ship, but often to keep it in sight to help guide missiles from the launching ship. This type of mission allows ships to fire missiles over the horizon. The helicopter remains out of antiaircraft range of the target ships, if possible.

Against a navy with carriers, the "spotter" helicopter has a more difficult time avoiding destruction. The most common combat use of naval helicopters is antisubmarine work. In this role, helicopters are quite effective. The sensors and weapons required cost more than the helicopter, but provide the ability to easily convert just about any cargo-carrying helicopter into an effective antisubmarine system. The equipment needed includes sonobuoys, dunking sonar, MAD, computers, radios, and lightweight torpedoes. Search radar can also be added to track surfaced subs or other warships. Most of these weapons and sensors weigh less than 600 pounds each. This is important, as helicopters do not possess great lifting power. The adaptability of helicopters through the installation of specialized equipment provides a wide variety of capabilities for the same model. This is very true of the UH-1 and Sea King types.

How to Read the Chart of Patrol Aircraft Characteristics

% OF TOTAL gives the percentage of the total P-3 equivalents each type now comprises. As imperfect as this method is, it does indicate relative capabilities. All patrol aircraft are not created equal.

INDEX is an evaluation of each aircraft. The chart shows to what extent each aircraft varies in capability. Most of these aircraft specialize in antisubmarine operations. The remainder either have, or can be equipped to have, attack capability against surface shipping. All these aircraft have search capability. In an attempt to show the general qualitative differences among all these types, a value has been assigned to each. The highest value ("100") has been given to the P-3. This aircraft is generally considered the most capable all-round patrol aircraft, despite the fact that it was designed primarily as an antisubmarine aircraft. Note that several different versions of the P-3 exist, largely newer models or rebuilds of older aircraft. The P-3 value given is an average.

TOTAL is the number of each aircraft type.

CAPABILITY RATINGS are the various capabilities of the aircraft expressed on a scale of 0 (nonexistent) to 10 (best available). Where a certain capability on this chart does not have a 10 rating, it means that some other type of aircraft is the best available. Improvements in aircraft weapons and equipment can increase an aircraft's rating by a point or two. Sometimes improvements have a negative effect for a time because they are markedly less reliable than whatever they replaced. The skill and training of the aircraft and ground crews can modify these ratings by more than half.

SURFACE SEARCH is the ability to detect objects on the land or water. Generally, this means radar search. Other sensors can detect heat, engine exhaust (diesel-electric subs), electronic transmissions, etc. Visual search is also used, but is limited by the need for clear weather. Special viewing devices that can see at night are available.

SUBMARINE SEARCH is the ability to detect submerged subs through MAD (Magnetic Anomaly Detector) and sonobuoys. See Chapter 10 for more details.

AIR SEARCH is the ability to detect aircraft, especially those flying close to the ground. This is done primarily with radar.

SURFACE ATTACK is the ability to attack surface targets. The most effective weapon is the air-to-surface missile. Other weapons include torpedoes, rockets, bombs, and cannon. Also taken into account in this evaluation is the quality of the aircraft's fire-control system.

SUBMARINE ATTACK is the ability to attack submerged subs with homing torpedoes or depth charges. Therefore, submarine attack ability is highly dependent on submarine search ability.

AIR ATTACK is the ability to attack, not just defend against, other aircraft. This is a rare quality in patrol aircraft. These planes are designed for long periods of relatively slow cruising. The fast, violent maneuvers of air-to-air combat are not possible with most of these aircraft. However, aircraft equipped to control other aircraft (AWACS) do obtain high ratings in this category because of their ability to spot potential attackers and direct defending fighters to these attackers as a means of protection.

FROM. Primary nation of manufacture.

CRUISE (speed in kilometers per hour) is the most fuel-efficient flying speed (for maximum time in the air). Often the aircraft must move slower to use certain equipment, like MAD. The TR-1 is essentially a powered glider that can shut off its jet engine and glide if the situation permits.

RNG (range in kilometers) is the maximum distance the aircraft can fly in one trip without refueling.

TIME (in hours) is the maximum flying time at cruising speed. For antisubmarine work, this will be 10 to 20 percent less to account for time spent on maneuvering during attacks on subs.

IFR (In-Flight Refueling) If the aircraft can be refueled in flight, it can greatly increase its range. At this point, the limiting factor becomes crew endurance. If two crews are carried, as is the case in some large aircraft, endurance can be extended to 24 hours.

WGHT (tons) is the aircraft's maximum takeoff weight. This is an indicator of size.

CREW is the number of crew carried. This number will sometimes vary with the mission. Generally, the crew is divided into two sections: flight (to operate the aircraft) and operations (to take care of the sensors and weapons).

LEN (in meters) is the length of the aircraft. This is another indicator of the aircraft size.

WPNS (tons) is the amount of weapons that can be dropped or launched against their targets. It indicates the aircraft's destructive potential. The value of weapons is heavily modified by the quality of fire-control and sensor systems.

ONE FINAL NOTE: thousands of other aircraft are used for reconnaissance, largely over land. These are usually fighters without weapons and often equipped with a large array of sensors and electronic countermeasures. Indeed, this special equipment typically comes in the form of pods. They are in the shape of bombs and hang from the aircraft just as a bomb would. Western air forces are quite advanced in this area.

THE AIRCRAFT

The aircraft are arranged in order of ability. At the top of each column in Chart 11-1 is the nation owning the aircraft (see notes on chart for nation abbreviations). The first column shows the aircraft designation. The second column is the total of each type. The second row gives the total aircraft for each nation. Unless otherwise noted, all are primarily antisubmarine aircraft. Listing below is in alphabetical order.

1150 Atlantic (France) is similar to, but smaller than, the P-2.

E-2 (U.S.) is a patrol version of the S-2.

E-3A AWACS (U.S.) is a more powerful version of the E-2. The E-3 is a Boeing 707 crammed with electronics. It can track more than 1,000 enemy aircraft at once while controlling more than 100 friendly aircraft. Capable of tracking land traffic and ships.

E-9 JSTARS is similar to E-3, but for tracking ground forces.

Il-38 (Russia) is similar to the P-2.

Il-76 Mainstay (Russia) is second Russian version of AWACS. Much better than the Il-38, but not up to standard of U.S. AWACS.

Ka-26 Hormone is the standard Russian shipboard antisubmarine helicopter.

Ka-27 Helix is the "heavy" Russian shipboard antisubmarine helicopter.

M-12 (Russia) is an amphibious patrol aircraft.

Mi-14 Haze is a naval version of the Russian Mi-8 Hip helicopter.

Nimrod is a British version of the U.S. P-3.

P-2H (U.S.) was the predecessor of the P-3 and is still in use.

P-3 Orion (U.S.) is the most powerful patrol aircraft currently in service. Excellent as a surface-search patrol aircraft as well as for antisubmarine work.

S-2E (U.S.) was the predecessor of the S-3 and is still used by many nations as a land-based aircraft.

S-3A (U.S.) is a carrier-based antisubmarine aircraft.

SH-2F LAMPS 2 (U.S.) are antisubmarine helicopters operating from ships.

SH-3 Sea King is a U.S. helicopter design manufactured by many other Western nations (Italy, Britain, Japan, etc.). Primarily used for search and patrol as well as ASW.

SH-60B LAMPS 3 is a naval version of the U.S. Army UH-60 helicopter. The 3 model is replacing the earlier II model.

TR-1 (U.S.) is an updated version of the 1950s U-2. Capable of staying aloft for 12 hours. Max altitude is 27,000 meters. Flies along edge of battle area looking for enemy electronic installations and other data.

Tu-142 (Russia) is a long-range bomber used as a naval patrol aircraft. The bomber version is called the Tu-95.

Tu-16 (Russia) was originally designed as a bomber. Many are now used for naval patrol and attack work. Some also serve as aerial tankers.

Tu-22M (Russia) is a long-range bomber that does double duty as a naval patrol aircraft.

12

The Navy:
On the Ground

A NAVY EXISTS to settle disputes between nations. As these difficulties escalate toward more extensive forms of warfare, ships are not sufficient to force a decision. The final arbiter of armed conflicts is the infantry, and the ultimate form of naval warfare is landing infantry on your opponent's territory. The current term for this is "power projection." Until this century, power projection meant landing army troops. During the 1920s and 1930s, the U.S. Marines developed theories, and equipment, for a new form of war. This was what we think of as amphibious warfare today: specialized troops storming ashore in the face of stiff opposition. War would never be the same.

During World War II, the United States rewrote the book by raising a specialized army-size amphibious force, the U.S. Marine Corps. The marines provided training for the U.S. Army, which eventually performed more amphibious operations and itself invented many key amphibious techniques. After World War II, the U.S. Marines retained their relatively large size and, more important, maintained their specialized skills as amphibious troops. Like most other maritime powers, the United States always had a Marine Corps.

Marines were originally organized as shipboard close-combat specialists at a time when ship crews still boarded each other to decide naval battles. When landing parties of infantry were infrequently needed, they were largely sailors led by marines. During the last 100 years, most navies use their marines as onboard police, gun crews, and, occasionally, landing parties. World War II brought forth the capability to move hundreds of thousands of heavily armed troops long distances quickly by sea and land them on an enemy shore.

Currently, more than half the world's officially designated marines are American. More than half the marine reserve troops are also in the United States. In addition, only the U.S. Marine Corps maintains its own air force as well as a fleet of specialized amphibious ships and equipment. Although all the ships and aircraft, as well as the Marine Corps itself, are nominally under U.S. Navy control, the USMC manages to maintain an individual identity.

Capabilities

By definition, all marine forces mentioned here have some amphibious capability. With that, they can perform three types of combat functions:

1. *Raiding.* These are commando-type operations. The British Royal Marines excel at this and have largely written the book of how to do it. Such employment requires troops with above-average combat skills and high training levels. Although all marine forces are highly trained and somewhat elite, when used in raiding, they must be even more so. Raids often involve parachuting or descending from helicopters. The United States even modified two of its older nuclear subs as high-speed transports for raiding parties.
2. *Spearheading amphibious operations for army troops.* Like a raid, except you don't always have to fight your way out. If the job is done right, the nonmarine troops coming ashore behind you will bail you out. Marines are often called upon to make the initial beachhead on an enemy-held shore. Functioning like assault troops, they use a variety of special skills and equipment so that the army troops can get ashore with a minimum of trouble. At that point, the marines can be withdrawn. Often they have to stick around. After all, marines are very capable infantry.
3. *Getting there first with the most.* Often military action is needed, and regular ground forces are either not available or cannot get there fast enough. The marines are often trained, equipped, and used as a rapid intervention force. They are basically light infantry. Although normally moved by ship, they can be, and sometimes are, put into aircraft. During the 1982 Falklands War, the first British ground forces on the scene were marines. The U.S. Marine Corps has a long list of areas they train to move into during an emergency. These include Europe, Japan, Korea, the Persian Gulf, Iceland, and several others.

Tactics and Techniques of an Amphibious Landing

The following description uses an American Marine Amphibious Force (MAF) in its example. Any other nation's amphibious operations would follow the same pattern for a large-scale division-level operation against opposition. Most other nations cannot muster a force larger than a brigade, however. Most marine forces prefer to go in with one to three battalions against areas empty of enemy forces. In preparation for this, the United States maintains battalion-size marine assault units that are already loaded on their amphibious ships and prepared for landings about as quickly as they can steam to their objectives. However, you cannot always expect to find your landing area undefended. The most difficult amphibious operation is storming an occupied shore. This is what the following explanation describes.

PREPARATIONS

The fleet first approaches to 40 kilometers off the enemy shore. Friendly naval forces have established control over the local sea areas, swept mines, and cleared underwater beach obstacles. Naval aircraft—land-based if within 600 kilometers of the beach—have established air superiority. Intensive air, electronic, and naval reconnaissance is imperative. If possible, Navy SEAL commando teams and Marine reconnaissance patrol units are landed. Undetected underwater or beach obstacles, minefields, and gun emplacements and entrenchments can easily wreck the entire operation. All this takes place within five days of the actual landing. Even though detailed plans may be drawn up far in advance, it is necessary to double-check all information. Planning is a highly perishable item; it must be constantly refreshed to be effective. Surprise, although not always complete, must be achieved to prevent the enemy from reinforcing the landing area to an invulnerable level.

Detection is riskiest while the MAF (Marine Amphibious Force) is at sea. The MAF can steam 800 kilometers a day and often uses this speed to evade notice or deceive the enemy about where the landing will take place. The most favored situation is to assemble the MAF convoy as close as possible to the target area while still out of range of enemy land-based aircraft. One or two days' steaming to the landing area would be ideal, providing opportunities to deceive the enemy yet minimizing time at sea. An MAF is a division-size ground unit, plus support units, carried by over 60 ships and escorted by over a dozen warships. The USMC also uses brigade-size forces that are one third to one half the size of the division-size force. Before departing from the United States or overseas bases, there will be a frantic period of planning and organizing. Time will likely be critical. Ships and the units they are to carry will arrive in a random sequence, but will have to be loaded properly for the landing. Once under way, the MAF will hold onboard exercises to keep the troops in shape. If possible, a rehearsal landing will be held. Because a division rarely practices together, this rehearsal can prevent costly errors in the presence of the enemy. While the MAF convoy is making its way toward the landing area, the several dozen ships of the carrier task forces apply their firepower to the defender. They pay particular attention to the transportation system, and any units moving toward positions that could threaten the landing. If the enemy intelligence service is up to snuff, it suspects something is likely to happen. It has probably alerted its forces and is looking for the oncoming amphibious force. At this point, the work of a few dozen intelligence analysts can have a decisive effect on the outcome of the coming battle. If the enemy correctly deduces where the landing will be, and causes rein- forcements to be sent there, the prospects of the amphibious forces decline considerably.

In theory, only a few hours after the MAF steams into their holding pattern 40 kilometers off the enemy coast, the marines will be ashore. Two thirds of the marines will move over the beach; the rest of the battalions will descend inland by helicopter. The minesweepers have cleared a series of one-kilometer-wide lanes to the landing area, usually about four kilo- meters wide and deep, marked by two primary control ships. One of these ships contains the primary control officer and his staff. The four-kilometers depth of the landing area keeps the large ships out of machine-gun range, although not artillery range. The larger ships carrying the landing craft take about an hour to enter the landing area plus another half hour to launch their landing craft. These amphibious boats line up at the line of departure, 3 to 3.5 kilometers from the shore, from which the waveguide commander, on the primary control ship, directs them to their landing beaches.

THE BEACH ASSAULT

The two regiments assigned to beach assault land two of their three battalions in the first wave. Each of these two battalions lands two of its companies initially. The success of the entire 54,000-man MAF hinges on the two dozen LVTP-7 assault vehicles and their 700 passengers getting ashore in one piece. The first wave takes 25 minutes to hit the shore. At two-minute intervals, the next three waves arrive. The second wave contains the other infantry and heavy-weapons units of each battalion. The third wave contains a tank company (in LCUs) and battalion support units (in LVTs and LCMs). The fourth wave contains more support units. In eight minutes, more than 3,000 men and more than 150 armored vehicles and artillery pieces are ashore. In support, four kilometers offshore, are six destroyers and two cruisers. Overhead, up to 400 navy and marine aircraft are on call.

THE HELICOPTER ASSAULT

The third marine regiment of the division goes in by helicopter. It is landed 10 to 30 kilometers inland before the landing force reaches the beach. Reconnaissance aircraft constantly patrol the air-landing area, while helicopter gunships and strike aircraft clean out the helicopter flight paths of any enemy antiaircraft forces. Sixty-five helicopters carrying an infantry battalion and a battery of artillery form the first wave. Once this landing zone is clear of enemy resistance, the remainder of the regiment is brought in. Ideally, you land in places where the enemy is not around. Sometimes more than one landing zone is established.

CONSOLIDATION

Once the beaches have been cleared and linkup has been achieved with the helicopter-landed marines inland, combat proceeds until a tenable beachhead is taken. This must be an area large enough to hold an airfield and supply dumps. These installations should be out of range of enemy artillery. An area 30 kilometers deep and 50 kilometers wide will ordinarily suffice. At this point, two or three days after the initial landing, airfields are built, and available army troops should be coming ashore. The carrier task forces will withdraw as soon as airfields are capable of supporting land-based aircraft. This naval withdrawal is a high-priority task so as to avoid any land-based enemy aircraft and submarines. Supply will continue to come over the beach until a port is taken or engineers build a temporary one. Landing craft and marine helicopters can bring supplies, but only at great cost. Every time an amphibious ship runs up on a beach, it suffers wear and tear. Helicopters require many man-hours of maintenance for each hour flown. Sustained operations, even without enemy fire, wear down the machines and their maintenance crews. Losses resulting from wear and tear are missed just as much as those caused by enemy fire.

How to Stop an Amphibious Landing

From the enemy's point of view, the situation is grim. Within the space of a few hours, over 20,000 combative marines have been landed and are carving out a beachhead. Ideally, an amphibious landing will be made in the vicinity of an enemy port and/or airfield. A landing is made across a beach only because nearby ports and airfields are too heavily defended to be taken by amphibious assault. Once a port is captured and repaired, whole armies can be brought ashore quickly. The closer the attacker lands to a port, the stronger the initial resistance is likely to be. But the farther away from the port a landing is made, the more time and space the defender has to organize an effective resistance. Also, the number of suitable landing sites on the coast is limited. The defender can calculate approximately which beaches the marines will choose. He must also gamble on which areas to defend heavily. The attacker relies on good reconnaissance to come ashore where the defender is not. The enemy, given sufficient time and resources, can prepare substantial passive defenses: naval and land minefields, beach obstacles, roadblocks, etc. Active measures include stationing naval and air forces near likely landing sites. The attacker must neutralize, if not destroy, these defenses before the MAF can land. Any surviving naval and air forces can make desperate attacks, which, in the early stages of the landing, can have a devastating effect. Taking care of these potential threats prevents air and naval support forces from providing direct support to the marine infantry. Many likely defenders against amphibious operations are capable of using chemical weapons delivered by ballistic missiles. Chemical weapons can be dealt with; nuclear weapons are a more difficult threat. Current amphibious doctrine spreads ships out to mitigate the effects of nuclear explosions. But enough nukes will cripple the MAF. The marines can also use nuclear weapons. See the chapters on chemical and nuclear weapons.

Different Approaches

The United States' amphibious doctrine is often quoted because the U.S. Marine Corps (USMC) is the foremost practitioner of amphibious warfare. Many Western marine forces follow USMC practice out of convenience if not always conviction. Many Asian marine forces were trained by USMC advisers and are organized along USMC lines. The only major amphibious forces other than the USMC and its allies are the Russians and Chinese.

Only in the last quarter-century has Russia developed an amphibious capability. Before the Soviet Union collapsed in 1991, each of its three European fleets (Northern, Baltic, and Black Sea) had a marine brigade (four infantry battalions plus combat support) of 4,000 men. The Soviet Pacific Fleet had a marine division (nine infantry battalions, plus combat support) of 8,000 men. These troops did not function as a division but were to be used for raids against crucial targets or as spearheads for larger nonmarine infantry forces. Soviet marines had less distant objectives than the USMC. For example, the Northern Fleet marines were needed to help secure northern Norway. Smaller groups could be sent against Iceland, which has no formal armed forces of its own. The Baltic Fleet marines had the same mission against Germany, Denmark, and Sweden. Here, the Soviets were to be aided by more than a division of Polish and East German marines. In the Black Sea, marines would have been used to seize key Turkish areas. In the Pacific, Soviet marines were to be used against Japan.

Soviet marines were meant for short-range operations, almost always within range of land-based air power. Their amphibious transport was in short supply, and the follow-up army forces would have required a functioning port. Despite these limitations, the Soviets did possess amphibious capability in all of their fleet areas, and this threat had to be guarded against. The only positive aspect to this was that the Soviet marine forces were fragmented among the four fleet areas, while the larger U.S. Marine force could be concentrated. With the collapse of the Soviet Union, its marine forces began to atrophy. The amphibious shipping deteriorated from lack of use and maintenance. The Polish and East German marines disappeared, and economic pressures will probably cause the current Russian marine units to evolve into an organization only a third the size of the earlier Soviet marines.

Other nations with marine capability are in the same situation as the Soviets and Russians: a local force with limited offensive power. China, for example, has few amphibious ships for the many troops it designates marines. Many of the world's marines are more so by designation than by performance. This is especially true when you compare many of them to the U.S. Marines.

Theory and Practice

Two distinct types of amphibious capability exist: long-range and local. Only the United States has any significant long-range amphibious capability. All the other major amphibious forces are equipped for local operations. One reason for the long-range U.S. capability is that most of the potential invasion sites are outside the Western Hemisphere. At the moment, no nation is ready to launch the multidivision type of amphibious invasion that we traditionally think of as an amphibious operation. The reason for the lack of this capability is simple: Such large operations are needed only during a major war. Only the United States has sufficient amphibious shipping to lift an entire division, and these specialized ships are spread all over the world.

At the moment, amphibious forces are most useful for their ability to swiftly put a few thousand marines ashore in some hot spot. America, Britain, and France are very keen on this. Other significant amphibious powers merely want the capability to either land troops quickly somewhere down their own coast or on a hostile neighbor's.

Although ground forces can be moved farther and faster by aircraft, amphibious shipping maintains a considerable cost advantage. It's cheaper to float than to fly. Besides, with amphibious ships you don't have to find the naval equivalent of an airfield. Keep in mind, though, that amphibious shipping cannot land on any coast. Some shore areas are too rough for landing. Some areas are better than others. That less than 20 percent of most shorelines lend themselves to amphibious landings is a major reason why the U.S. Marines are provided with a dozen helicopter carriers by the U.S. Navy. More so than other military operations, amphibious assaults are very susceptible to things going wrong, with the worst possible results. Speed is imperative, both in planning and execution. It is likely that marines will have to undertake operations with fewer amphibious ships than they would like. Ships are always being lost or kept in other operations longer than expected. A marine's greatest asset is an ability to improvise. It is not enough to possess uncommon courage in the face of the enemy. Equally important is the ability to make do in the face of your own side's short-comings. Things will go wrong, often very wrong. The USMC is accustomed to taking heavy losses, heavier than those of normal combat, in order to compensate for the uncertainties of amphibious operations. While it's easier to avoid, or improvise around, the mistakes in the first place, there is often neither the time nor the opportunity.

The Future

Most marine infantry forces will continue to emphasize raiding and commando-type operations. Only 5 nations can muster a division-size force of marines, although about 10 others have a sufficient number to spearhead a force of nonmarine army troops. While commando operations will nominally operate from ships against shore targets, the increasing availability of helicopters tends to make marines into airmobile troops who can swim, tolerate seasickness, and call the toilet the "head." These airborne amphibious operations enable raids far inland, up to 200 kilometers or more. This gives the United States a devastating raiding capability against nations with long coasts or low defensive capability. Third World nations are particularly vulnerable. The U.S. Marines have been traditionally used for these small-scale conflicts, over 80 times since 1945. The U.S. Marines haven't conducted an amphibious assault since 1950, although they continue to prepare for one.

In many smaller nations, the local marines will also increasingly be political pawns, to either give the navy its own ground troops or to provide the government with a palace guard.

One trend to be watched is the increasing number of large merchant ships available. For example, there are now many large civilian ferries, some of which can carry over 100 armored vehicles per trip. Assault troops on helicopters can seize a port, and these large ships can bring ashore an armored division in hours. Future amphibious operations may not look at all like those we have seen in the past.

The only high-seas marine force remains that of the United States, which is larger than many national armed forces. The USMC continues to receive newer and larger amphibious ships as well as more helicopters. Budget cuts will slow this down, but the older equipment will be demobilized first, leaving a smaller and, man for man, more lethal force. Recognizing the need for speed, and the limitations of even the swiftest naval transports, the USMC has increasingly chosen to preposition heavy equipment in likely areas of conflict. This is an expensive and controversial program for the marines, although the U.S. Army has been doing it for years. More money buys more speed in other areas. Using hovercraft instead of small landing craft, you can put men and material across the beach three times as fast. The cost is more than three times as much, and it is still uncertain that the military budget will support it. A similar situation exists with USMC air support. In the interest of economy, marine pilots fly the same aircraft as the navy. Sometimes this is of marginal utility, as with the F-18 interceptor being turned into a fighter bomber for the marines, who would rather have the more expensive AV-8 Harrier. The future of marine troops will be shaped more by fiscal constraints than technological achievements.

The 1991 Gulf War, and Somalia in 1992, showed the utility of the MPF (Maritime Prepositioned Force). This concept was developed in the late 1970s. There are currently three MPF prepositioned squadrons that contain the equipment and logistic support to sustain a USMC expeditionary brigade for 30 days of combat. One of these was on the island of Diego Garcia, several thousand miles south of Saudi Arabia, and proved its worth during Desert Shield. That MPF was restored to its peacetime condition at the conclusion of Desert Storm. MPF was the reason that within 30 days of the invasion of Kuwait, the 7th Marine Brigade was the only fully armed and equipped ground force in the country. This could not have been done as quickly by aircraft (not enough aircraft) or by sea (North American bases are too far away). The 7th Marine Brigade used airlift to bring in its 15,000 troops and some equipment. This required about 250 C-141 sorties (or equivalents). A U.S. Army light-infantry division, with about the same number of troops, requires twice as much airlift and puts a more lightly armed, equipped, and supplied force on the ground.

The World's Amphibious Forces

The 24 nations' marine forces shown on Chart 12-1 represent over 98 percent of the world's amphibious capability. Many nations with small amphibious forces that are used primarily for local transport or police functions are not included. Most marine forces are capable of conducting only raids or short-range landings against light opposition. The official (primary) function of the U.S. Marine Corps is to seize advanced naval bases for its parent organization, the U.S. Navy. As a practical matter, the USMC is ready to go anywhere and do just about anything.

AMPHIBIOUS ABILITY. This rating represents the overall quantity and quality of the nation's amphibious forces. This is calculated by taking into account the number of marines, their quality, and the amphibious shipping available to them.

12-1 Amphibious Forces as of 1992

Rank	Nation	Amphibious Ability	Troops	Units Available		Displacement Tons Amphib Ships	Troop Lift	Quality Rating
1	United States	1,000	203,000	4	Divisions, 4 Air Wings	901,887	48,840	100
2	Taiwan	103	30,000	2	Divisions	102,000	8,500	75
3	South Korea	80	24,000	1	Division, 1 Brigade	36,000	3,273	85
4	Russia	50	8,000	4	Brigades	147,620	11,200	65
5	Great Britain	43	7,200	2	Brigades	53,000	3,533	100
6	China	34	6,000	1	Brigade	160,000	14,545	45
7	Thailand	32	20,000	7	Regiments	32,000	2,667	40
8	Spain	30	7,500	6	Regiments	52,000	4,333	70
9	Brazil	27	15,000	1	Division	26,000	2,167	45
10	Philippines	24	8,500	10	Battalions	88,000	8,000	40
11	France	17	2,600	1	Brigade	32,000	2,286	85
12	Greece	15	2,000	1	Brigade	62,000	5,167	55
13	Indonesia	15	12,000	2	Brigades	60,000	5,000	25
14	Turkey	14	4,000	1	Brigade	34,000	2,833	55
15	Venezuela	11	6,000	6	Battalions	20,000	1,667	40
16	Netherlands	8	2,700	2	Battalions, 1 Company	2,000	154	85
17	Argentina	8	5,000	6	Battalions	9,000	750	40
18	Chile	8	5,000	4	Regiments	6,000	500	40
19	Iran	6	1,800	3	Battalions	22,000	2,000	45
20	Portugal	6	2,400	3	Battalions	1,000	83	65
21	Italy	5	800	1	Battalions	11,000	786	75
	Totals	1,535	373,500			1,857,507	128,283	

Russian marine forces, often thought to be second only to the Americans, are one of several second-place amphibious forces. The Russian marines are not as numerous as several others. Russian amphibious ships are second only to the Americans in tonnage, but not that far ahead of several other nations.

TROOPS represents the number of men organized for amphibious operations. Not all of these belong to the navy or even to an organization called "marines." The primary criteria are training and ability to perform amphibious operations. Another important consideration is reserves. Only the United States has a significant number of them. The U.S. Marine Corps can quickly expand its force by over 30 percent when the reserves are called up. No other nation comes even close to this.

UNITS AVAILABLE gives the designations of the marine units referred to under TROOPS. Not all nations organize their marines the same way. Most have several small units, the better to support small amphibious operations, units, and organization. Marines are generally considered more reliable and effective than other troops. For this reason, they are generally used as elite ground troops, and not in their theoretical role as amphibious troops.

DISPLACEMENT TONS AMPHIB. SHIPS gives the displacement tonnage at full load of that nation's seagoing amphibious ships. See amphibious shipping chart for more details.

TROOP LIFT is the number of troops that the nation's amphibious ships can lift for an amphibious operation. This is calculated by dividing total amphibious tonnage by the average number of tons normally needed to carry out an operation. You can get by with less amphibious shipping by using a greater proportion of conventional vessels. Passenger ships can be used if you are willing to spend more time transferring troops to landing craft. In this case, you would also have fewer landing craft, as these are carried by larger amphibious ships. Overcrowding can also increase capacity, but this works only for short voyages. Otherwise, your troops are not going to be in very good shape for combat. Without overcrowding or using nonamphibious ships, you can increase your lift capacity by simply shuttling back and forth to your land base to pick up more troops, which can be loaded in a few hours. The success of this depends on how close your base is to the landing area. Another problem with amphibious vessels is that this same specialized shipping is used to resupply the troops. This often requires 100 pounds per man per day (see Chapter 23, "Logistics"). The first day of the landing you will be lucky to get one day's supply ashore. Fortunately, the landed units typically carry with them three days' supplies. After the first few days of a successful landing, you can build up two to five days of supplies per day. It's preferable to build up a reserve of 30 days' supply. The speed of this depends on how many additional combat and support troops are brought ashore and the loss of landing craft to enemy action or wear and tear.

QUALITY RATING. This quality rating reflects the quality of that nation's marine forces as well as its overall ability to conduct amphibious warfare. There is no formula for this qualitative rating. An examination of each nation's abilities and resources should not vary from this rating. Each nation's abilities and past performance speak for themselves.

Amphibious Shipping

Chart 12-2 shows the capabilities of amphibious ships by the United States and Russia, the two major amphibious powers. Most other nations use amphibious ships manufactured by the United States or Russia. Other nations build their own, either to the same designs or very similar ones. A further source of amphibious shipping is specialized peacetime vessels. Examples are air-cushion vehicles, ferries, and RoRo (Roll on, Roll off) ships (see Chapter 26 on naval shipping).

TYPES

HELO. Helicopters. Various types carried on some amphibious ships. Used for carrying cargo, passengers, and light vehicles. Their weight is full-load weight. Surface Effect Ships (hovercraft) are used for high-speed amphibious assaults and resupply, whole heavy-lift helicopters still do most of the work because they are much cheaper than hovercraft. Russian LPDs carry helicopters, which are ASW models modified for carrying troops.

12-2 Amphibious Shipping

Type	Class Name	No. in Class	Last Built	Disp (tons)	Len (M)	Crew	Passengers	Cargo	Gun	Miss	Landing Craft & Aircraft Carried
United States											
LCC	Blue Ridge	2	1970	19,000	189	720	700		2	2	5 LCVP
LHD	Wasp	2	1995	40,500	257	1,080	2,000		11	2	3 LCAC, 48 AC
LHA	Tarawa	5	1980	39,300	254	940	2,000		10	2	4 LCU, 2 LCM, 30 AC
LPH	Iwo Jima	7	1970	18,300	183	685	2,100		4	2	24 AC
LKA	Charleston	5	1970	18,600	176	370	220	6,000	6		Cargo and Vehicles
LPD	Austin	11	1971	17,000	173	490	930	3,900	4		6 AC
LPD	Raleigh	2	1964	13,900	159	490	930	2,000	8		6 AC
LSD	Anchorage	5	1972	13,700	163	400	380		6		20 LCVP, 4 AC
LSD	Thomaston	3	1957	11,300	155	400	350		6		3 LCVP, 2 AC
LSD	Whidbey	2	1988	15,700	186	400	340		2		4 LCAC, 4 AC
LST	Newport	18	1972	8,300	159	225	390	500	6		AC
LCA	Hover Craft		1988	100	30	10	80	55			Cargo Only or 1 Tank
LCU	Landing Craft	60	1976	390	41	12	400	180	1		Cargo Only or 4 Tanks
LCU	Landing Craft	31	1957	347	36	12	400	180	2		Cargo Only or 4 Tanks
LCU	Landing Craft	23	1945	310	37	12	80	140	2		Cargo Only or 3 Tanks
LCM(	Mod 1			107	22	4	80	65			
LCM(	Mod 2			130	22	4	80	65			
LCM(	Mod 2			62	17	4	80	34			
LVT				26		2		5			
LVTP	APC			13	11	3	25	5			
Helo	CH-46F	224				2	20	2.9			
	CH-53	132				3	38	3.6			
	CH-53E	58				3	38	14.5			
	UH-1	112				2	7	1.0			
Russia											
LPD	Ivan Rogov	2	1982	13,000	158	200	550		10	9	3 SES4, 10 MBT, 30 APC, 4 A
LST	Ropucha	20	1985	3,200	113	70	230	450	4	16	Cargo or 25 APC
LST	Alligator	8	1977	4,700	113	75	300	1,500	6	13	Cargo or 25 APC
LSM	Polvocny	20	1973	800	74	40	100	200	8	18	Cargo or 8 APC
LCU	Vydra	5	1969	600	55	20	100	250			Cargo
SES5	Pomornik	2	1988	360	59	30	220	140	2	1	Troops or 3 MBT or Cargo
SES4	Lebed	12	1988	85	25	20	120	45	1		Troops or 2 APC
SES3	Tsaplya	2	1988	90	25	20	80	25			Troops or Cargo
SES2	Utenok	2	1988	60	26	15		40	4		Cargo or 1 MBT
SES1	Aist	20	1988	250	47	18	220	120	4	8	Troops or 4 APC or Cargo
SES	Gus	30	1974	27	21	14	25	5			Troops or Cargo
LCM	Ondatra	12	1988	90	24	4	80	40			Troops or Cargo or 2 APC
Helo	Ka-26	8	1988			3	12	4			Cargo or Troops

LCC. The command-and-control ship has extensive communication and other facilities to enable it to handle all the control functions of a major amphibious operation.

LCM. Landing craft, mechanized. This is the standard landing craft of carrying men and cargo.

LCU. Landing craft, utility. They are carried on larger amphibious ships, although large enough for limited seagoing movement. Many smaller nations use LCUs by themselves. They also run up on beaches to discharge vehicles or cargo.

LHA. Helicopter assault ship. Internal loading dock for landing craft. Best amphibious assault ship available.

LPD, LSD. Landing ships with internal loading docks for landing craft. LPD also have a helicopter platform, but usually no onboard helicopters, for launching air assaults.

LPH. Helicopter assault ship without loading dock or landing craft. This prohibits use for landing of APCs and heavy trucks. Does have extensive medical facilities. Excellent for raids.

LST. Landing ship, tank. Originally designed during World War II, it lands tanks and other vehicles directly onto beach. Prone to damage as a result of this. Some have helicopter platforms or landing craft for offshore delivery of cargo.

LVT. Landing vehicle, tracked. A boat with tracks (like a tank). Moves off beach under its own power. Typically for carrying cargo.

LVTP-7. An amphibious APC for carrying combat troops from the ship right into combat. See chart for APCs in Chapter 3 for more details.

SES. Surface Effect Ship, also known as Air Cushion Vehicle or hovercraft. Floats on a cushion of air and can travel over water or land at speeds of up to 70 kilometers per hour.

SSN. Several of the older U.S. SSBNs have been converted to other uses (training, transport, rescue, etc.). These subs also have most of the capabilities of SSNs.

CLASS NAME is the name given to the first ship built in a series. It is a convenient way to identify a ship type.

NO. IN CLASS is the number in use as of 1993.

LAST BUILT is the year in which the last ship of that class was put in service. The term "building" indicates that, as of 1993, ships of that class were still being built.

DISP TONS is the weight of water the ship displaces under full load.

LEN. Length in meters—gives you an idea of ship's relative size. Amphibious ships tend to be broad. Those that run up on the beach (LSTs, landing craft) have a shallow draft.

CREW is the number of personnel needed to run the ship in wartime. In peacetime, some navies run these ships with 80 percent or less of the wartime crew.

PASSENGERS are usually troops. Onboard facilities to eat and sleep are available in the larger ships.

CARGO carried, in metric tons.

AA is antiaircraft defense—G = gun, M = missile launcher. Amphibious ships depend on the protection of other combat ships. Amphibious ships of the major navies are being equipped with automatic guns for cruise-missile defense.

LC & AC are the usual vehicles carried. LC are landing craft and AC are aircraft for getting the passengers and/or cargo to the landing zone. Most ships can carry a combination of landing craft, cargo, and troops.

THE ORGANIZATION OF A MARINE AMPHIBIOUS FORCE

Through the 1980s, the U.S. Marines developed a modular organization for amphibious operations. The traditional marine division is basically an administrative one in peacetime. In wartime, the division headquarters controls a division or two worth of units, depending on what got to the battlefield. The typical combat unit in peacetime is a brigade, which will often land and fight as a brigade unless there is sufficient time to bring in enough units to form a division. Such was the case in the 1991 Gulf War, where there was sufficient time to organize two marine divisions.

The following description refers to a division-size "Amphibious Force," one of many organizations that the marines are prepared to use in wartime. The 60- to 65-ship American MAF (marine amphibious force) consists of a marine division and a marine air wing (MAW). A MAW (17,000 men) has 159 aircraft, including 48 F-18s, 40 AV-8s, 8 EA-6s, 9 OV-4s, 12 OV-10s, 8 RF-4Bs, 20 A-6s, and 12 KC-130s. Also, 156 helicopters, including 60 CH-46s, 48 CH-53s, 24 UH-1s, and 24 AH-1s. One SAM battalion with 24 Hawk launchers and 75 Stinger teams. Most of the MAW can operate from carriers initially but will shift to land operation as soon as a field is captured or prepared. The 18,000-man marine division consists of 9 infantry battalions, each with 1,041 men, 32 ATGMs, 8 81mm mortars, 30 machine guns; one tank battalion (72 M-60A3 tanks, 72 ATGMs); four artillery battalions (54 towed and 18 self-propelled 155mm howitzers); one amphibious tractor battalion (208 LVTP-7s, each carrying 25 marines or five tons of supplies). Plus the usual support units. There is a total of 72 tanks, 72 81mm mortars, 81 60mm mortars, 288 Dragon ATGMs and 144 TOWs, 208 APCs, 147 armored cars, 90 towed and 18 SP 155mm howitzers, 601 machine guns, and 345 40mm grenade launchers. There are some variations depending on where each of the four marine divisions is expected to fight. Some have more or fewer tanks and other equipment. All of the ships are "combat loaded." That is, men and equipment (especially equipment) are spread among many ships so that the loss of one vessel will not result in the loss of all of a particular unit, like an engineer battalion. All equipment goes into the ships so that it may be quickly unloaded in the order needed. Total: 54,000 men, up to 330 armored vehicles, more than 250 aircraft, 1.2 million tons of shipping.

The U.S. Marine Corps force operating in the 1991 Gulf War comprised two divisions that were assembled from units that could be moved to the Gulf. Note that the LAI battalion is "light armor," equipped with armored cars.

1st Marine Expeditionary Force was, in effect, the corps headquarters for the two marine divisions formed for the liberation of Kuwait. Assigned to Force headquarters was the Marine Raider Battalion, intelligence units, and four naval construction battalions (Seabees).

1st Marine Division: 1st LAI Battalion (Task Force Shepherd), 3rd Assault Amphib Battalion, 1st Recon Battalion. There were four regiments in the division: 1st Marine Regiment (Task Force Papa Bear)—1st Battalion. 1st Marine Infantry Regiment (or 1-1 Marines), 3-9 Marines, 1st Tank Battalion (2 companies), 3rd Assault Amphib Battalion. 3rd Marine Regiment (Task Force Taro)—1-3 Marines, 2-3 Marines, 3-3 Marines. 4th Marine Regiment (Task Force Grizzly)—2-7 Marines, 3-7 Marines. 7th Marine Regiment (Task Force Ripper)—1-7 Marines, 1-5 Marines, 1st Combat Engineer Battalion, 3rd Tank Battalion. 11th Marine Regiment (Artillery)—1-11 Marines, 3-1 Marines, 5-11 Marines, 1-12 Marines, 3-12 Marines.

2nd Marine Division: 2nd LAI Battalion, 2nd Tank Battalion, 8th Tank Battalion, 2nd Assault Amphibian Battalion, 2 Combat Engineer Battalion, 2nd Recon Battalion. There were three marine regiments and one army armored brigade in the second division. 6th Marine Regiment—1-6 Marines, 3-6 Marines, 1-8 Marines, 2-2 Marines, Task Force Breach Alpha. 8th Marine Regiment—2-4 Marines, 3-23 Marines, Task Force Breach Bravo, Co. B, 4 Assault Amphib Battalion Co. F, 2nd LAI Battalion. 10th Marine Regiment (Artillery)—2-10 Marines, 3-10 Marines, 5-10 Marines, 2-12 Marines. 1st ("Tiger") Brigade, 2nd Armored Div (U.S. Army)—1/67 Armor, 3/67 Armor, 3/41 Infantry (Mech), 1/3 Artillery, Air Defense Artillery platoon, Engineer Platoon.

3rd Marine Air Wing—MAG-11, MAG-13, MAG-16, MAG-26, MACG-38, MWSG-37.

Rear Area Security: 24th Marine Regiment—2-24 Marines, 3-24 Marines.

Forces Afloat (not under I MEF command): 4th Marine Expeditionary Brigade. Regimental Landing Team 2. HQ, 2 Marine Regiment—1-2 Marines, 3-2 Marines, 1-10 Marines (artillery), 2nd LAI Battalion Co. A, 2nd Assault Amphib Battalion Co. A, 2nd Tank Battalion Co. A, 2nd Recon Battalion. MAG-40, Bty A, 2 LAAD Battalion. 5th Marine Expeditionary Brigade, Regimental Landing Team-5. HQ, 5 Marine Regiment—2-5 Marines, 3-5 Marines, 3-1 Marines, 2-11 Marines (artillery), 1 LAI Battalion Co. B, 1 Cmbt Eng Battalion Co. A, 4th Tank Battalion, 4th Assault Amphib Battalion Co. B, 1st Recon Battalion, MAG-50. 13th Marine Expeditionary Unit—1-4 Marines.

PART FOUR
HUMAN FACTORS

OFTEN OVERLOOKED, frequently underestimated, but never ignored for long. When it comes to the fighting, warfare is not waged by the numbers, but through the courage, determination, skill, and leadership of individuals.

13

Getting Psyched: Why Soldiers Fight

Convincing people to fight, and getting them to do it well, is one of the more essential and less noticed aspects of maintaining an armed force. Illusions must be created, and maintained, often unto death. Few individuals, once aware what combat is all about, want to spend any time at it.

It Won't Happen to Me

Anyone introduced or forced into combat service is not told how dangerous it is. If potential recruits knew their chances, it would be more difficult to get anyone into the infantry. During this century, the odds of serving in the infantry during combat and escaping injury have been less than one in three. And given a choice, most new soldiers will volunteer for any other branch of the armed forces to avoid it. Most other military jobs are no more dangerous than civilian occupations. Even troops in combat support units like armor and artillery have better than even chances of seeing the war's end uninjured. To get people into the infantry, first convince them that they have a good chance of surviving in one piece. Better yet, ignore the concept of surviving, or not surviving. Modern combat, however, doesn't work that way. It's always a deadly business for at least one side.

Indoctrination

Those selected for the infantry are customarily subjected to an ancient indoctrination routine that stresses the following points:

1. *Pride.* The recruit is told that the infantry is the premier branch of the armed forces, the most noble calling, and the most respected and patriotic service one can render one's country. This is all true, particularly if getting killed or injured for one's fellow citizens is recognized as the highest form of patriotism. The pride taken in the dangerous business of infantry fighting is reinforced by the respect given to combat veterans. As with many other bad experiences, the memories lose their hard edges over time. Hearing the veterans' stories, the potential recruits tend to fixate on the glory instead of the death and terror. This is human nature, and it is drawn on generously to get troops into the fighting without losing them to panic. During times of international tension, when journalists interview combat troops about their eagerness to get to it, the young troops are eager, while the older veterans long for a diplomatic solution to the conflict. No one who's been shot at retains the enthusiasm of the uninitiated.

2. *Effective Preparation.* The combat soldiers are constantly told that they have the best equipment, training, and leadership available. The message is that these advantages will allow the troops to carry out their admittedly dangerous tasks as effectively and safely as possible. This is only rarely true. These tales are often believed by many infantry recruits, who tend to have less education and a more accepting attitude than your average college grad. Moreover, if a nation has a winning tradition, one has reason to believe that it will turn out all right. In peacetime, when there is no contradictory evidence like body bags and maimed veterans, the official line gets accepted. It is far more comfortable to believe that you will survive. A nation without a military tradition, or one noted for defeat, will have problems from the start. There will be a feeling of inferiority among the troops. The 1982 Argentine infantry collapsing in the face of the highly regarded British troops was a typical example. Another is the attitudes of the various combat forces during the 1979–89 Afghanistan War. The rebels had their track record of no defeats and a zealous religious belief. The Russian troops' attitudes ranged from a well-founded fear among the regular troops to a sense of cocky superiority within the small contingents of Spetsnaz commandos. On the positive side, a reluctant attitude is more realistic than blind optimism. Such unfounded optimism can lead to rashly aggressive action in combat. The opening stages of World War I were

infamous for this. Hundreds of thousands of troops were needlessly killed charging into machine-gun and artillery fire. A latter-day example is the reckless courage of the Iranian Revolutionary Guards. Raw, unthinking courage is no match for firepower.

3. *Friends.* A vastly underestimated influence in combat performance is the "primary group." This is nothing more than the smallest unit of soldiers, 5 to 40 men, organized for mutual support. Not all armies see to it that effective primary groups are formed. The primary group must be well trained and well led and, most important, must know and trust one another personally and professionally. The troops must believe in their own skills and the abilities of their leaders. The members of the group must serve together for at least a few months before entering combat. New members should not be brought in until the unit is taken out of combat. Experienced troops do not want to be introduced to replacements while being shot at. In life-and-death situations, you want to know the people you work with pretty well. The transformation from green troops to battle-hardened ones is nothing more than the creation of these primary groups among trained soldiers. Just getting men in and out of combat does not form primary groups; leaders make it happen. Some armies are more effective at producing combat leaders. The Germans may have lost World War II, but they were more successful at the troop level. They consistently inflicted more casualties per man than their opponents. This occurred because they took good care of their combat soldiers and paid attention to preparing troop leaders. During World War II, the Germans gave their NCOs more training (six months) than the U.S. Army gave junior officers (the "90-day wonders"). Right up until the end of the war, German officers received a one-year training course before being let loose with troops. The Germans found it was preferable to have a shortage of leaders than to have ones that were not well prepared. The logic of this was that troops knew that any officer or NCO was qualified, not someone who was hastily appointed to a position he could not handle. Studies after the war demonstrated the universal validity of this system. This is not to say that the United States did not have any well-prepared combat units. However, this occurred only because exceptional senior leaders made it happen. One U.S. infantry division had a commander who set up training schools for officers and NCOs and basically duplicated the German system. The results were noticeable, especially to the Germans. It was only in the last 10 years that the high command of the U.S. Army has picked up on this wisdom.

4. *Fight or Else.* A very ancient, and still effective, motivating tool is fear. As one general put it, "My soldiers will fight well because they are more afraid of their officers than they are of the enemy." This fear takes many forms. Most cultures apply great social pressure to

get out there and fight. Many armies use even more severe measures. Russian officers have long had the authority to shoot their men on the spot for slack discipline in a combat zone. Other measures include posting a line of military police behind advancing units to discourage any reluctant troops moving in the wrong direction. This approach was used by the U.S. Army in Korea and was a standard practice for the Soviets during many World War II battles. A U.S. innovation in Vietnam was landing troops by helicopter in hostile territory. They had a choice of fighting their way out or getting killed by the enemy. This unofficial policy was very effective as a motivator. The troops, however, were not fooled; some would refuse to board the helicopters.

What Works

1. *Superior motivation, leadership, and training* have consistently proved the formula that produces victorious armies. Leaders who are willing to get out front and get shot at, and often killed, are respected and followed. Officers who stay to the rear find their troops following them in that direction also. Training that draws from experience, not untried theories, produces the most competent troops. Equipment that works most of the time, and does what needs to be done, is the most effective. Men will start fighting for any number of reasons, but will continue fighting, and do so successfully, only if they have confidence in their leaders, equipment, training, and themselves.

2. *Conviction.* When a soldier believes he should be fighting, he has conviction. Such an attitude is not easily acquired. Too often, men are simply put in uniform, armed, and called a military force. As Napoleon put it, "The moral is to the physical as two is to one." Moral force, morale, conviction—they are all interrelated and serve as the most powerful motivator a soldier can possess. There are three sources for this motivation: loyalty, personal gain, and desire for adventure. This last one is a chronic defect among the young. Loyalty is more commonly a form of patriotism. Patriotism can come in many forms. The loyalty can be to nation, region, ethnic group, family, organization, or group of friends. Often, loyalty is owed to several of these groups. Patriotism tends to be a group endeavor. If enough individuals are so motivated, they will inspire each other as well as the less motivated members of the group. History has shown that patriotism propels people into situations of almost certain death or injury. The opening stages of wars between patriotic groups are always bloodier than the later stages. As the fighting grinds on, convictions begin to waver. Taken away from the good things one is

fighting for, soldiers justify the fight by the prospect of victory and the end of combat. Eventually, one side senses its own weakness and looming defeat. The less determined individuals begin to shrink from further combat. This defeatism spreads until the losing side's armed forces fall apart. For this reason, few wars or battles are fought to the death. Some groups have such a high degree of conviction that they will continue until all are dead or incapacitated.

The 1979–89 Afghanistan War showed how a tradition of warlike behavior plus multiple loyalties (tribe, ethnic group, nation) can produce an extremely high degree of conviction. It was the main reason the Afghans have never been subdued. Belonging to the planet's poorest nation did not substantially diminish this intense conviction in the face of the world's largest army. Less frequently, personal gain and a thirst for adventure propel people into combat. Patriotism plus a dash of adventure have been the traditional lure to get young men to volunteer in the early stages of a war. The adventure rapidly dissipates when the survivors straggle back with tales of how it really is. The bloody horrors of war are not going to prompt many to enlist, so duty and adventure are stressed during recruitment and training.

Once under fire, most soldiers fight well enough because it seems a reasonable thing to do in order to survive. Mercenaries are still quite common. Some do it as much for adventure as for money, but for most it's a living. The majority of today's mercenaries are government employees. More than 100,000 Cubans have served in Africa as paid representatives of Soviet interests. Cuba, East Germany, North Korea, Pakistan, Nepal, Britain, etc., export mercenaries under government contract. Several other nations, like Israel, the United States, Russia, and South Africa, do it unofficially. One can make a case that anyone who volunteers for military service is a mercenary. The dividing line appears to be whose interests you are defending. If you are bearing arms for your own government, you are not a mercenary. If you do it for someone else's, you are. Perhaps the true dividing line is whether or not you are getting shot at. Few of today's mercenaries take up their work with the idea that the job will be fatal. Mercenaries have a bad reputation because they are essentially guns for hire. Whoever hires them tends to use the mercenaries in an abusive manner. Folks with guns doing the dirty work for people with money. Money still motivates.

3. *Magic Bullets*. Many politicians, and military leaders, are misled by the performance of weapons. Troop leadership and motivation are slippery subjects. Buying the latest high-tech instruments of death and destruction appears as a more certain way to obtain combat power. This is not the way the world really works. The best weapons available in the hands of poorly led, ill-trained, and unmotivated

troops will lead to defeat. This is historical experience. The arms merchants' sales brochures will not mention these unpleasant facts. Weapon performance is more capable of measurement in peacetime than motivation, leadership, and competence.

Throughout history, peacetime armies have tended to rely more on technical superiority than on the more slippery factors. Many examples exist. The Soviet Army in 1941 was one of the most lavishly equipped in history. Poorly led and poorly trained, and not very well motivated, the Soviets melted before the onslaught of the Germans. The Wehrmacht was not only outnumbered, but also had inferior weapons. Another example was the fighting between Israel and Syria in 1982. The Syrians took a beating. Yet Israelis insist that if each side used the other's weapons, the outcome would have been the same. Past experience shows that this is probably true. The most recent example was the Gulf War of 1991. Despite many years of recent combat experience and lavish amounts of weapons and equipment, the Iraqis were overrun by the better trained and better led American troops. Yet much of the media coverage of the war emphasized the technology. With more wealth and technology available today than ever before, there is still a tendency to rely on gadgets as an expression of combat power. The preference for hardware over human values in magnificently equipped armies manned by the incompetent and led by people who believe their own press releases is all too common. The historical record tells a quite different story. Again and again, ill-trained troops get their hands on high-tech weapons and make a mess of it. Most of the wars in the Middle East had numerous examples of this. Even the industrialized nations have their shaky moments with their wonder weapons. It's difficult to keep all these wonder weapons in perspective. If you don't, unexpected losses and unpredictable performance will focus your attention.

Theory and Practice

In modern warfare, the vast majority of troops are never in combat. Even as long ago as World War II, no more than 25 percent of those who served in the U.S. Army ever came under enemy fire of any sort. Today, troops in combat units comprise less than 10 percent of army strength. The infantry, who take most of the punishment, account for less than half of all "combat" troops. The air force and navy expose even fewer of their personnel to the dangers of combat. In the Russian Army, the infantry account for less than 20 percent of total manpower. For every infantryman, there is another soldier who gets shot at but is still at less risk than the infantry. Although there is a lot more firepower today, the troops are spread out more. This is a trend that has been going on for the last few centuries. As weapons increase in lethality, the troops take more energetic measures to avoid injury. In theory, the rear-area troops have always been liable to air or long-range artillery attack, and yet they have managed to avoid injury. The use of nuclear weapons can change all that, but in the meantime wearing a uniform is not as dangerous as it used to be.

With a small fraction of uniformed personnel now assigned to fighting, it becomes more difficult to motivate the combat troops. There is a feeling of unfairness when one is thrust into danger while so many others serve in essentially civilian jobs. This corrosive attitude tends to grow as the combat lengthens and the casualties increase. The classic approach to this problem is to shower the combat troops, and their surviving families, with material and spiritual attention. Cash and praise go a long way toward stiffening the embattled troops' resolve. When these measures are not taken, your combat power fades away. Many nations realize this only when it is too late.

A recent example of this can be found in Iraq, where substantial payments were made to the survivors of troops killed in combat during the 1980–88 war with Iran. Combat is an activity for which populations rapidly lose their enthusiasm. American commanders in the Persian Gulf were told during the summer of 1990 that keeping U.S. casualties low was a very high priority. As a result, operations likely to result in high casualties were avoided, which was why there were no amphibious or airborne assaults. One comment heard from several senior officers in the wake of the U.S. Gulf War victory was that no one wanted to be in charge in a future war when more than 200 Americans were killed. No one relished having to explain to Congress why this was so, and why the Gulf War was an exceptional situation that could not be expected to occur in future wars.

The Future

The trend is toward increasingly violent combat that is more debilitating. The faster tempo and increased firepower of modern warfare increases demoralization and combat fatigue. Experience in World War I with chemical warfare and large-scale artillery barrages demonstrated that the troops on the receiving end of this punishment can quickly be shocked into a state of apathy. Current weapons can generate sufficient firepower more easily and quickly, to do in days or hours what weeks of punishment in World War I required. Nuclear weapons are also expected to have a devastating effect on the morale and motivation of survivors. Sustaining mental health looms as an increasingly crucial task for leaders at all levels. Warfare in the '80s (Afghanistan, Iraq, Lebanon, the Falklands, and the Gulf War) all revealed higher rates of combat fatigue. This problem is exacerbated by the increasing presence of portable radios among the troops. Friendly and enemy news broadcasts make it more difficult for commanders to "control" troop morale. Psychological warfare against enemy morale and motivation has had scant success in the past. But the psywar crowd keeps trying and is getting better. A new form of demoralization is looming, and the first example of it was demonstrated during the 1991 Gulf War, where the Iraqi Army was completely demoralized by air bombardment, psywar, and an overwhelming ground offensive.

The increasing dependence on electronic sensors finds a larger number of troops staring at computer terminals. While this is sometimes akin to playing a video game, the results can often be fatal for the player. The troops know this, and their nervous faith in their instruments' reliability creates a new form of stress. Expect to see more combat fatigue among the silicon warriors. The only exception to this are those troops, particularly in the West, who spent many youthful hours playing electronic arcade games. It seems that this experience makes them very facile dealing with the intimidating arrays of screens and buttons found in modern military equipment.

Of more interest to military commanders is the capability of film and video to realistically portray the horrors of war. The pervasive presence of the media makes it important for the government to control information and ensure that the bad news is kept from damaging morale. Most people don't want to fight in the first place and are easily discouraged when confronted with the realities of war. Too much reality too fast turns the most stouthearted troops, and their families, into reluctant warriors. Again the Gulf War revealed how seriously the U.S. military considered this problem, and how strenuously the military dealt with it.

Peacetime armies tend to lose sight of the need for unit cohesion. Some nations are more successful at maintaining effective unit organization and cohesion in peacetime than others. It is always a problem, so you should expect some surprises when troops go into combat for the first time.

14

Leadership

GOOD LEADERSHIP IS the glue that keeps a military organization together during the stresses of combat. But it is a fragile thing. It tends to shrivel up and disappear in peacetime. Incompetent wartime military leaders are often highly regarded peacetime commanders. This has been a common pattern throughout history, and for good reason. You can prepare for war, but you can't actually practice the real thing. This places a premium on leaders who can prepare seemingly adequate military forces under peacetime conditions. A lot of their efforts will go toward convincing their superiors that all their efforts and expenditures will have the desired effect when the shooting stars. Fighting a war, it turns out, requires a quite different mind-set than preparing for one.

Another problem of military leaders, especially in peacetime, is their tendency to prefer hardware over less tangible items like training and creating effective troops. Hardware you can see and feel. The troops? The goal is often to have the troops smartly turned out. Never mind that effective armies often look like a bunch of bandits. Perfectly aligned and attired formations of soldiers are easier to comprehend than their ability to inflict devastation upon the enemy.

Some nations avoid these peacetime traps to a greater degree than others. A country with a long and systematically preserved military tradition develops better wartime leaders. These military traditions are usually preserved with wars each generation to ensure that memories do not grow dim. The habits and customs of war are bizarre to a nation at peace. The armed forces must maintain these attitudes blindly between wars. They can do this only by establishing generation after generation of soldiers who will accept certain practices blindly and accurately. This is military tradition. It is sniggered at in peacetime, but saves lives in battle.

Not all nations have such traditions. Germany has a military tradition, even though it has not won a war in more than a century. Winning wars is actually not what a military tradition is about, but fighting them efficiently is. Political leaders start wars and set the stage for eventual victory or defeat. Soldiers fight the battles as best they can under the conditions laid down by the politicians. Other nations with military traditions are Britain, France, Russia, and Japan. The United States has a military tradition for its navy and marines, but less so with its air force and especially its army. This underwent a profound change between the end of the Vietnam War (1975) and the late 1980s. The U.S. Army and Air Force radically reformed the way they prepared their leaders and troops for combat. The results were vividly demonstrated in the "Hundred Hour War."

In peacetime, air forces and navies do much the same tasks as they would in wartime. Just moving all their machines around comes very close to wartime conditions. Armies attempt the same thing, but it is too expensive to move large masses of troops around in peacetime. Armies are normally less ready for war than navies and air forces. Human nature being what it is, most leaders, military or otherwise, seek the easy way out. Unless feedback corrects ineffective procedures, bad habits become standards. Flying and navigating the oceans are unforgiving exercises; mistakes are painfully apparent. Pilots and sailors tend to get buried with their mistakes. As a result, navy and air-force leaders are forced to get to know their subordinates' strengths and weaknesses. Armies are larger and more expensive, and there is a great deal of pressure to keep costs down. Army leaders have to rock the boat to smoke out officers who may be ineffective in wartime. Making a commotion is dangerous in any large organization, so the incompetents tend to remain. A leader who knows either from experience or intuition that a subordinate will be ineffective in combat cannot normally take any action. The victim of this dismissal can insist that no grounds exist for the charge. Unless commanders are supported by a widely accepted military tradition, they will be forced to retain a large number of ineffective combat-unit commanders. This is the factor that makes some armed forces more effective than others of the same size and composition.

Even experienced and tradition-minded armies find 50 percent or more of the leaders ineffective in wartime. Many will get themselves killed or captured. Unfortunately, the same fate will befall the troops in their charge. How quickly these inadequate leaders can be replaced once the shooting starts is a key ingredient for ultimate success in a war. Meaningful reform of military leadership is no easy task. It can be carried out only by a truly exceptional leader or after a traumatic national defeat. It hardly ever occurs in a nation that has won its previous wars. A rare exception was the reform of the Russian (Soviet) Navy under Admiral Gorshkov. But then, one can make a case for the Russian Navy having "lost" most of its battles during World War II. Although Russia defeated Germany, the Soviets diligently copied many German techniques and weapons after that war. They knew that, man for man, the Germans outfought them.

Scientific Leadership

Leadership is a nebulous quality. While science has conquered many irksome aspects of human frailty, attempts to develop a "scientific" approach to leadership have been difficult. Russia has provided one of the more interesting attempts with this form of leadership development. Before the 1917 revolution, Russian armies were not much worse than any others. A significant defect was that the highest commands were given to Russian nobles without regard to merit. Other nations did this, but they managed to screen their candidates more carefully. Russian troops, whose training, equipment, and leadership were fairly good, were often misused. After the revolution, three major changes were made. First, officers were appointed on the basis of merit. Second, a scientific approach was embraced for all training and leadership. Third, technically advanced weapons and techniques were sought. All of this affected leadership profoundly. Initiative, resourcefulness, and imagination in combat were to be replaced with scientific planning and precision. During World War II, it was modified by a very large dose of combat experience. Combat experience is highly perishable. The doctrine of scientific leadership was made of more durable stuff. Toward the end of the Soviet period (the 1980s), the Soviet armed forces had become similar to their pre–World War II predecessor. The "Red Army" looked splendidly equipped and scientifically led, but neither the splendid equipment nor the scientific doctrine and leadership have been thoroughly tested. Whenever their armed-forces doctrine has been tested, as during the Afghanistan or Arab-Israeli wars, the Russian approach has been found wanting. Even the noncombat experience of Czechoslovakia in 1968 exposed glaring leadership and control problems.

The Russians have an advantage in that if their training works, their troops will perform their duties according to set procedures. This will give commanders a degree of control and knowledge of who is doing what, even if what the troops are doing is ineffective. Russian officer training emphasizes knowing the "correct" procedure and keeping your wits about you long enough to carry out your orders. To assist this process, every Soviet unit commander had a deputy representing the Communist party. This fellow also went to officer-training school but selected a decidedly different specialty. The political officer was responsible for the ideological purity of the troops and reported to the party, not his unit commander. This *"Zam-*

polit" recruited informers among the troops and used these agents to keep an eye on everyone and everything. If the unit did not perform well, both the military commander and the political officer were in big trouble. The political officer typically covered his ass by sending in a lot of reports to the party. If things got hairy, he could at least say he warned the party authorities. In practice, the political officer and unit commander normally worked well together. Both had the same goals of military effectiveness. However, if there was any dissidence among the troops, or any incident that smacked of "antiparty" attitudes, the harsh hand of party discipline came down hard and fast. In this case, military effectiveness took a backseat to ideological purity. The military commander had to constantly look over his shoulder at his *Zampolit* political officer. This was not a very efficient system, and its inefficiency was demonstrated frequently. During World War II, the political officers lost some of their power, and got it all back as soon as the Germans were defeated. Variations on the *Zampolit* system are common in the armies of dictatorships.

Western armies often place too much responsibility on the individual leaders and less on the system. This is fine if the leaders are up to the demands. But the only substitute for combat experience is some form of system. The Germans were good at developing both system and leadership. The German Army entered World War II with a tactical doctrine based upon a careful analysis of its World War I experience. This doctrine was put into a manual that was regarded as a bible by combat officers. The procedures found in *Tante Friede* ("Aunt Friede," the nickname for the manual) got officers through enough combat to give them experience. At that point, they could use their resourcefulness and imagination to stay one jump ahead of the enemy. This German approach was at once purposeful and pragmatic. It helped the slow learner to survive and allowed the talented combat officer to achieve great success.

Operating Within the Cycle

Combat is generally a series of intentional or accidental ambushes. Self-preservation and the obvious appeal of hitting the other fellow when he can't fight back make ambush the most sought-after situation. To pull this off, you must practice another skill: operating within the other guy's cycle. A person's or unit's "cycle" is nothing more than his or its limitations in reacting to events. In sports, athletes outperform less skillful opponents by moving or reacting first. A superior boxer, as an example of maneuver warfare, doesn't just parry his opponent's punch, he gets in one of his own. A superior fighter operates within his opponent's ability to respond. Skillful soldiers operate the same way. Even if a defender seems to have every advantage, a more skillful attack can uncover and exploit the defender's weaknesses. An attacker's superior ability to move, conceal himself, and use his weapons can negate a defender's advantages and enable the attack to succeed with minimal losses. Leadership makes this work. But it takes a particular kind of leader, one that not every nation can produce—he must know the techniques of his craft, whether it be air force, army, or navy. These leaders must know their troops well, and be actively involved in their training and well-being. Finally, they must lead. This often involves getting out front where it is quite dangerous. One indicator of a well-led army is that officers have a higher casualty rate than their troops. History has demonstrated, through the ages, that any troops can be turned into competent soldiers if they have competent officers. Leadership is always the key.

Push-Button Leadership

A hundred and fifty years ago, leaders had to command through shouting, messengers, or signal flags. They still got the job done. Today, leaders are often helpless without radios, telephones, and other electronic gadgets. Leaders can now command far beyond what they can see. Extreme examples were seen during the Vietnam War, when platoon leaders in the bush sometimes got tactical advice direct from the White House. Micromanagement was rarely that extreme, but it was pervasive. Senior commanders tend to want more control and information. Only exceptional ones can resist this temptation. During World War II, the Germans went out of their way to keep senior commanders from running small-level operations they could not see. The Soviets and Japanese didn't have sufficient communications equipment. The other Western armies did start a trend that eventually turned the American president into a platoon commander. This problem is now recognized by all armies. Everyone assumes at least a lip-service attitude toward a solution. However, there is a positive side. The information flows both ways. Commanders of larger units can get a more accurate picture of how their entire organization is doing. The hundreds of reports that move up the chain of command help to dissipate the fog of war. Computers are increasingly used to quickly sort out this data. This has gotten to the point where "artificial intelligence" programs help the commander to make effective decisions with these increasing masses of information. Some items, like artillery, logistical planning, and intelligence analysis, are ideally suited to this approach.

If the electronic tools are not working, the effects on leadership can be devastating. This is why we have electronic warfare (EW). Communications are the primary target of EW. Without fresh supplies of data, the computers no longer have much to do. Exclusive reliance on electronic tools, without adequate backup systems and procedures, can prove fatal in wartime. Western armies have tried to solve this problem with more technology, while Russian-style armies go back to simpler manual methods for backups.

Facing up to such problems and developing effective solutions is another characteristic of superior leadership. Something as simple as using EW frequently during exercises can give the troops invaluable experience in coping with these problems. Attention to this has been spotty. One more of the more embarrassing aspects of a major future war would be the general inability to cope with the loss of communication because of Electronic Warfare. For more details on EW, see Chapter 19.

Creating Leaders

There are only a few basic approaches to selecting and training military leaders.

1. *The gentleman officer* is the oldest approach. Get an overeducated fellow with a lust for blood and adventure, and give him a pretty uniform and some authority. The United States inherited this terrible system from the British during the Revolution and still uses it. This is sometimes called "Burgoyne's revenge," after the remarkably inept British general "Gentleman Johnny" Burgoyne. Note that Britain's long combat experience produced customs that negated many of the bad effects of this system. For example, British NCOs tend to be superb. The officers are expected, if nothing else, to provide a good example for the troops. If this means little more than standing up, leading the attack, and being quickly killed, the officer has done his duty. Unfortunately, not all nations that adopt this system have good NCOs, or inept officers who will get out in front. The gentleman-officer approach, still widely used in Third World nations, generally leads to a credibility gap between the troops and the leaders appointed to lead them.
2. *The aspirant system* is a more effective one. This is a "trial-by-experience" method of selection and promotion. It can be traced back to the Romans, and earlier. This really works best during a war, although it has advantages even in peacetime. Potential officers are selected from the troops and systematically put into higher and higher positions of responsibility. The theory is that a man who can't lead a squad isn't going to do any better with a platoon, company, battalion, or army. Germany and Israel, an odd pair, both use this system. In peacetime, the officer candidate is also given a technical and scholarly education, if he isn't already a university graduate. Education is considered a nice touch, but the cut is made ruthlessly at each level of command. At worst, you will end up with good small-unit commanders. Troops and subordinate leaders respond well to this system, as they know that their leaders have been where they

are and know what it's like. Most nations fall back on this system in wartime to a certain extent.

3. *Trial by examination* is a pervasive curse of educated cultures. Academics are obsessed by the thought that you can evaluate a person's abilities through a written examination. It is true that people who excel at examinations are often bright, but what has that got to do with leadership? Particularly leadership in combat? Very little. The examination process does select leaders who at least have book knowledge of their profession. Russia uses this method extensively, as do, to a lesser extent, other industrialized nations. Its major drawback is that it tends to depend on the examination process to rate qualities that are not easily evaluated by written exercises. In particular, promotions are often dependent on examination performance. This path of least resistance becomes a fatal flaw when the shooting starts.

4. *Trial by fire,* in wartime, is often the system that just naturally emerges. In the hazardous atmosphere of combat, only the competent survive. This is a new system in peacetime, however, and it was pioneered by the United States. The American version arose from the proliferation of electronic substitutes for weapons and the ancient (but rarely used) technique of training against people operating like potential enemies. The air force and the navy were the first to introduce this system during the 1970s. The navy's "Top Gun" school for training carrier pilots was adopted by the air force. The navy used similar technology to train its submarine and surface-ship crews. In the early 1980s, the army applied the use of electronic scoring and a realistic opposing force to train units. All of these techniques were initially used simply to train the troops more effectively and to make them more capable of dealing with the often quite different techniques potential enemies might use. But after Vietnam, the U.S. Army also took a hard look at its use of the gentleman-officer system and made some key changes. The principal one was a result of the use of more realistic combat training. The use of electronic scoring of weapons "fired" led to the evaluation of officers on their performance under these realistic conditions. Many officers were found wanting, and the presence of such a screening device profoundly changed the attitudes of the officers and their troops. Since battlefield competence could now be measured more accurately in peacetime than ever before, the officers adopted a much more professional attitude toward their jobs. At base, the U.S. system was still the "gentleman officer," but now the gentlemen were much more effective combat leaders, as was vividly demonstrated during the Gulf War.

Variations. Each nation selects its military leaders on the basis of its military traditions, experience, and perceived needs. Nations that have been defeated are prone to change their systems. Similarly, nations that have not suffered a traumatic defeat, or have not fought a war for a long time, will not change. Resistance to change often occurs after a dramatic victory, resting on one's laurels, as it were. This is how obviously inefficient systems have persisted. It is unlikely that change will occur any other way. Vietnam was the "defeat" that spurred reform in the U.S. military, and the Gulf War looms as the "victory" that may cause a lapse into bad habits.

Chapter 29, "The Armed Forces of the World," gives a quality value for each nation's armed forces. This is an indicator of leadership quality. It shows who is ahead in this area and who needs improvement. A common problem in many nations is the ability to attract good candidates. It is easier to create superior leaders if your raw material is superior to begin with. This happens only if the military attracts superior candidates. Social attitudes toward the military profession in peacetime vary from nation to nation. Most societies view the military profession with some disdain. At the very least, several other professions that engender more respect and career prospects will attract much of the talent the military needs to be effective. After all, the military absorbs considerable sums of money in return for an intangible, and often debatable, degree of national security. There is no way, short of war, for the military to prove that it is doing its job adequately.

Marketing the Product

To obtain additional funds from unenthusiastic taxpayers, the military tends to downplay its abilities relative to its potential enemies. The average citizen wonders where all the money is going when the armed forces always protest that they are not up to doing their job without seemingly endless additional funds. The situation is different in nations bordered by obviously belligerent and historically hostile forces. Here, the average citizen regards the military in a different light. Service in the military is seen as a high calling, a true public service that can attract superior manpower. In a situation like this, the military gains further credibility because it possesses superior officers. This is especially true in nations that fill the ranks by universal conscription. Israel, Switzerland, and Germany are examples of this type. Germany has a long tradition of threatened borders and a need for strong and effective military forces. Even the traumas of World Wars I and II have not shaken this tradition.

Another method of attracting superior talent is by having less competition from the civilian economy. Less developed nations lack enough suitable jobs for young, talented, ambitious, and educated youngsters. The result is a highly professional, often well led, although usually poorly equipped military. This is not the case if the military is simply a police force for the party in power. In this case, these bright young lads become the leaders of heavily armed cops. India, China, and even Russia have superior candidates for their officer openings because of a lack of opportunity in the civilian sector. As China loosened up its economic controls in the 1980s, it had to demobilize more than a million soldiers to save money for development and modernization, and to avoid a labor shortage. In this way, the Chinese got rid of a lot of deadwood that had accumulated during more than 20 years of little military, but considerable political, activity in the armed forces. At the other extreme are the United States and Western nations. Except in countries where the military has a modicum of respect, recruiting the best leadership talent is an uphill struggle.

THE OBVIOUS EFFECTS OF SUPERIOR LEADERSHIP

Consider the numerous examples of the impact of excellent leadership. World War II revealed many. In 1950, the American counteroffensive against North Korea was a brilliant illustration. Shortly thereafter, the Chinese provided another example when they moved into Korea. The Arab-Israeli wars are a continuous chain of combat successes caused by superior leadership. Most of these events were the result of Israeli leadership. But in 1973, the Egyptian commanders outdid the Israelis in the opening stages of that war. Superior leadership need not be of earthshaking dimensions in order to be effective. As long as one side's leaders are demonstrably better than the other's, speedy victory will usually result. All other things being equal, if a war breaks out and does not come to a rapid conclusion, you can be fairly certain that neither side has a marked leadership advantage. If one side is larger than the other, you can assume that the smaller force, by avoiding rapid defeat, has superior leaders.

In peacetime, the effects of superior leadership are more difficult to detect. Success does not manifest itself until the improvements are put to the test of combat. However, some examples are so extraordinary in their results that they spotlight superior peacetime leadership. Admiral Rickover's role in the development of American nuclear submarines is one example. There was a counterpart in the Soviet Navy, Admiral Gorshkov. The army and air-force officers who reformed the U.S. military after Vietnam have yet to get the recognition they deserve. Many other peacetime leaders exist who almost singlehandedly introduced reforms or the development of radically effective new weapons or equipment. Unfortunately, it is more difficult to determine beforehand who the effective future combat leaders are. And on that issue, the potential outcomes of these wars become murky.

THE TROOPS

Although the old truism "There are no bad troops, only bad officers" still applies, there are significant differences in the intrinsic quality of troops. Let's start with the basic distribution of skill and intelligence in any population. Tests have shown that troops drawn from the more intelligent 20 percent of the population can perform tasks about twice as efficiently as those in the lower 20 percent. This applies particularly to such things as hitting another tank with a missile or gun. A cross section of tests on infantry skills yields the same results. There are also very real cultural differences. The Ghurka soldiers from Nepal have served as highly valued mercenary infantry for several centuries. Many other cultures are noted for their skill and enthusiasm for combat. There is another problem found in mercenary troops that applies to many national armies. In the former Soviet Union, for example, nearly half the population was not fluent in Russian, and recruits had to be first taught a sparse "military" vocabulary before they could be trained in military skills. Russia, today, still has a substantial minority of recruits who do not speak Russian, and has to continue the old Soviet practice. Age also plays a role, with men in their 20s much more efficient than teenage soldiers. An effective officer must be aware of the nature of his troops and the proven remedies for whatever shortcomings these recruits may have. Military history is littered with unsuccessful officers who lacked insight and forethought. It's not enough to lead; you have to know where you're coming from and where you're going.

RANK AND ORGANIZATION

Worldwide, military organizations tend to use the same patterns and rank structure. Ranks are divided into three groups: troops, noncommissioned officers, and commissioned officers. The "ordinary" soldiers have ranks for recruits and one or two ranks for trained soldiers. Terms in English-speaking countries for these lowest-ranking troops are: private, soldier, marine, seaman, and airman. Noncommissioned officers are the traditional professional long-term soldiers with sufficient experience and talent to lead or supervise soldiers. British-derived terms are "sergeant" and "petty officer" (navy).

Several grades of NCO ranks exist, corresponding to the size of the unit. NCOs command units from fire team (4–5 men) to platoon size. At the platoon level, NCOs sometimes share command with the lowest rank of commissioned officer.

Commissioned officers are so called because they are "commissioned" by their government to lead the combat forces. Three levels of officers exist:

1. *Company grade* (lieutenants and captains in the army/air force, ensigns and lieutenants in the navy). These are the apprentice officers and rarely command more than a company or a very small ship.
2. *Field grade* (majors and colonels in the army/air force, commanders and captain in the navy). Field-grade officers command battalions, regiments, and brigades, as well as ships of all sizes.
3. *Flag officers* (generals in army and air force, admirals in the navy).

Staff officers serve in staffs of units one level higher than they would normally command. More officers serve in staff than in command positions. This is because each unit of battalion size and larger has but one commander but four or more staff officers. Each unit from company size up also has one or more "assistant commanders" who help the commander out and take his place if he becomes a casualty. These assistants are customarily one rank lower than the commander. Significant variations can be found, particularly in the organization of staffs. Nearly all nations organize their staffs along these functional areas:

1. *Personnel.* Keeping track of the troops, and maintaining performance records for officers (and often NCOs) to determine who should be promoted and when. Dictatorships often use the "personnel" staff officer as the local spy, to keep an eye on officer and troop loyalty.
2. *Intelligence.* Collects and analyzes information about the enemy. A cushy job in peacetime, but a real career killer when the shooting starts and you have to perform against a hostile and secretive enemy.
3. *Operations.* Planned and supervised operations of the unit. The head of this section was often also the "chief of staff" and was the first among equals among the staff section commanders. Good performance in this job was generally a prerequisite for promotion to command of the unit.
4. *Logistics.* Taking care of supply and maintenance of equipment. Another job that is often much more difficult in wartime than in peacetime.
5. *Other.* Most common is a section dealing with civilian affairs in enemy territory. Some nations also have a separate "political" section.

Several nations have adapted to the need for recognizing technically expert troops who do not perform supervisory functions by providing a separate set of ranks for "technical experts." Most of the time, this is done by expanding the number of NCOs to provide the needed monetary and social incentives. Only those NCOs occupying leadership jobs have the traditional authority and rank of NCOs. The specialists have the same pay scales as the NCOs, but sometimes are given different titles. For many years, the U.S. Army used a parallel rank structure for enlisted troops. Instead of a lot more NCOs, you had troops with the rank of Specialist 4, 5, 6, etc. (the numbers representing pay grade). This caused problems with the older troops in the senior grades to the point that in the early 1980s all grades but Specialist 4 were eliminated. For the older and more experienced technical people, use was made of four grades of Warrant Officer. This rank was given all the privileges of officers, but, in theory, none of the leadership responsibility. The "warrant" approach is quite common as the need for uniformed technicians increases. This has been another case of making people something that is neither fish nor fowl. Many nations use warrant officers and then eliminate them, and then bring them back again. Russia's inability to develop effective NCOs caused it to introduce its version of warrant officers in the 1970s. It was unable to attract a large number of candidates, partially because of resistance from regular officers.

Theory and Practice

Peacetime soldiers lack practical experience with combat activities. Most troops have not actually used many combat techniques or have not used them in cooperation with other combat units. The knowledge of these procedures and the ability to use them determines who will prevail in a war. Peacetime leadership comes down to whether or not leaders can maintain a knowledge of efficient combat activities and effectively pass this knowledge on to their troops. The patterns of a combat officer's daily routine differs considerably in peacetime and wartime. Wartime conditions are hellish and not fondly remembered or re-created in peacetime. Peacetime habits tend toward bureaucratic routine and avoiding unpleasantness. Officers who push their troops toward more rigorous, and inevitably dangerous, training activities are often tolerated and accepted by the troops. Such officers can, however, get in trouble with the civilians and the press. In democracies, more troop-training injuries can attract unpleasant attention from the press and elected officials.

Dictatorships are often in worse shape in wartime because officers are chosen first (in peacetime) on the basis of their political reliability. Such individuals have shown themselves more comfortable behind a desk than thrashing about in the bush with a bunch of lowlife enlisted scum. Some nations rise above the tendency to be unprepared for combat. They do this by blindly following military "traditions" and/or having a good supply of clearheaded and persistent officers who never shut up about the importance of keeping the troops in shape for combat. But these groups are the minority. Military leaders tend to be bureaucrats in uniform.

Another problem with military leadership is that there tends to be a relationship between the ratio of leaders to troops and the effectiveness of those leaders. It is easier to create additional officers than it is to ensure that those you have are up to their jobs. This is one area where quantity does not compensate for quality. Various reasons are put forward for this officer explosion. One is that more complex technology requires more officers who tend to be better educated. This, however, clouds the issue of what a military officer is. Originally, officers were government officials who performed a dangerous job—they led soldiers in combat. That description today fits less than 10 percent of officers. While all officers are thought of as soldiers, only a small percentage are. Some armies solve this problem by creating new classes of officials, who are paid more and given officerlike privileges, but are not considered officers. In most armies, there is little obvious distinction between combat and noncombat officers. The net result of all this is to diminish the stature of the real combat leaders, the ones who actually direct the fighting. This weakens the armed forces in order to give the noncombat officers a vicarious thrill.

Normally, it is nearly impossible to give leaders of combat units realistic training during peacetime. In the past, this was only overcome during the 1800s when the Germans introduced detailed wargames. These games required time and diligence to use, and were only as good as the historical experience that was built into them. Such games could not easily represent new developments in weapons, equipment, and other factors. Few officers had the devotion necessary to make these games work. In the 1980s, the United States began using a new training system that used nonlethal lasers to represent real weapons. All participating troops and vehicles have sensors so that hits can be recorded. The entire battle area is wired with sensors so that all the action can be recorded and reviewed later. At first, only direct-fire weapons were wired into the system. But now mines and some forms of artillery are incorporated. At the U.S. National Training Center (NTC), U.S. battalions go up against a U.S. version of a Russian infantry regiment. The "Russian" unit is quite good, as it gets a lot of practice. This unit is said to be the best Russian infantry regiment in the world. The American units get very realistic training, as can be seen from the similarity of the results with what is encountered during combat. The good news is that this is a source of combat experience without massive loss of life. The bad news is that each U.S. combat battalion can get only two weeks of this training every two years. This program has been expanded, especially after the demonstrated success of the program's training effect in the Gulf War. No other nation has anything quite like it, although many are trying to set up their own versions. If history is any guide, those nations with a predilection for routine drills will prove debilitated if they ever encounter American units possessed of realistic training. This is precisely what happened in the Persian Gulf. These same training practices are applied in the U.S. Air Force and Navy.

During the Vietnam War, both the air force and naval combat pilots discovered how inadequate their peacetime training had been. The Top Gun training programs begun in the late 1960s have been continued and expanded. The navy has used similar training for its ship crews, although it has been unable to provide realistic training for the most dangerous, unpredictable, and chaotic of its combat operations: damage control.

The quality and quantity of leadership varies quite a lot between the Western and Russian-style systems. American armed forces have a core group of 600,000 NCOs and officers to lead a force of only 1.5 million troops. U.S. forces have some 200,000 officers versus the former Soviet Union's 1.3 million. The United States also has more than 400,000 well-trained NCOs, while the Soviet Union had fewer than half that amount. Thus, the extensive use of conscripts and harsh service conditions that discourage NCO retention left the Soviets with a less favorable ratio of troops to leaders. The post-Soviet armed forces are led by officers who want a more realistic (and "Western") attitude toward developing officer and noncommissioned-officer development. But there may not be money available to do it for some time.

The U.S. system was developed from European models and has gone through a number of radical transitions in this century before settling down in the last 10 years. Until the late 1940s, the U.S. officers were a very small group, as were the armed forces they commanded. During the Civil War, World War I, and World War II, these forces were greatly expanded and staffed with officers from the National Guard and hastily trained civilians. Only a few of these new officers were willing, or able, to stay in the service after the wars were over and the armed forces demobilized. U.S. Korean War forces were largely led by World War II veterans. In the late 1950s, there was a major RIF (Reduction in Force) that discharged many World War II–era officers or reduced them to NCO rank so they could qualify for pensions in the early 1960s. Then came Vietnam and a large infusion of hastily trained officers. Another fallout from Vietnam, and the continuing boom in the post–World War II economy, was an inability to attract quality candidates for officer posts.

By the 1980s, military service became attractive once more, and the Vietnam-era duds had been discarded. The American NCO was also in the European mold of a long-term professional who stayed in his job longer than officers and identified with the officer class. NCO quality suffered during Vietnam, as the last of the World War II–era people retired and the quality of enlisted recruits fell. This problem was also largely overcome by the 1980s. Another persistent problem with U.S. NCOs, lack of training, was also addressed during the 1970s and '80s.

The Future

During peacetime, armed forces endure a constant struggle between the "warrior" and "manager" mentality, and it's getting worse. Peacetime soldiers have always grumbled about "political generals" and officers, more concerned with their careers than their ability to succeed in combat. This debate has taken on new meaning as armed forces become more mechanized and automated. An increasing proportion of officers will never lead troops in combat. Their jobs, even in wartime, consist of keeping a lot of machines operational. That group of hard-charging and ruthless characters known as "warrior officers" becomes increasingly smaller. When it comes to a shouting contest over policy, numbers still count. Although combat officers are usually given priority when it comes to promotions to general and admiral, there is increasing pressure to give the technician officers more of the goodies.

An additional complication is the admission by many experienced combat generals that few among them really have a talent for combat. Solutions to this problem vary. The Russians have always crossed their fingers and hoped that a "Suvarov" (a legendary 18th-century combat genius) will pop up from their general ranks when a war breaks out. A "technical" breakthrough of enormous import would be a technique that would effectively identify which peacetime generals can really get the job done in wartime. This would still not be a panacea, as good wartime leaders are often inept at surviving in the more political atmosphere of the peacetime military. Moreover, the armed forces also have a more difficult time attracting and keeping larger numbers of technically competent people. This can be done in peacetime only with volunteers. If the conditions of service turn worse, your volunteers begin to leave, or not volunteer in the first place. The best example of this is in navies, particularly those with nuclear ships. If these crews must spend too much time at sea, the skilled volunteers will decide to get out. This is becoming a critical factor. In the U.S. Navy, there are more lucrative and less arduous career temptations in the civilian world. Every additional month the U.S. fleet spends on emergency duty in far-distant waters costs it several hundred skilled officers and sailors who decide not to continue service because of the additional duty and separation from families. Many peacetime armed forces carry this nine-to-five attitude to extremes. Swedish antisubmarine efforts against Soviet subs in the 1980s were hampered because active-duty sailors work an eight-hour day and must be paid overtime pay if more time is required. As a result, searches had to be called off if there was not enough overtime pay left in the unit's budget. Strange, but true.

Future wars hold still other terrors for leaders. Armed forces develop different ways of doing things, and different equipment to do it with. It's not enough to know what your own forces are capable of, and often you don't. It's not enough to know what your opponent's forces are capable of, and frequently you don't. What is important is to know what will happen when these two forces of unknown capability meet in combat. In the past, wargaming and other forms of simulation and historical research were used to gain a sense of where everyone stood in peacetime. Unfortunately, the two superpowers corrupted these tools. The Soviet Union permeated its historical research with dogmatic restrictions. All past events had to be interpreted according to Communist scripture. This often got in the way of seeing the world as it is. In the United States, history-based models were replaced by purely quantitative ones from 1945 until the 1980s. These were adequate for modeling individual equipment in the laboratory. On the larger and more complex battlefield, these models were less successful. In both the former Soviet Union and the United States, models had to conform to political requirements. Battlefield truths are often not popular with peacetime politicians. And some of the politicians are in uniform, with the military being the largest pool of government employees in many nations. This is quite true with the United States. Some worthwhile modeling projects are started, but interest is rarely sustained from one administration to another, and inertia and expertise are squandered. An important future development is that there is unlikely to be much change in this situation.

Training simulators are a different story, particularly for pilots, ship crews, and leaders in general. As computers become more powerful, aircraft simulators are reaching the point where they can simulate everything except the very real death faced by careless pilots. In the United States, these "reality" simulations are being carried several steps further. Computer-supported simulators are already available for ships in port. Future shipboard equipment is to include simulation capability, and the computers needed to run realistic exercises. The U.S. Army is creating equally realistic simulators for armored fighting vehicles and ground-to-air missiles. These training simulators are a significant development in training, and the edge they give the Western troops that use them is considerable. This is particularly important in light of the expense of exercising modern equipment. Maintaining top form as a combat pilot requires 300 or more hours of flying a year. Even without the cost of using expensive weapons, this can cost over $10,000 an hour. Minimal weapons use can more than triple this. The current cost for training a top-notch pilot is $5–$7 million. Even an infantry officer can cost several hundred thousand dollars to train if he is to be made competent at commanding a wide range of expensive weapons systems. Poor nations cannot even afford to let their artillery crews fire the 200 or so rounds a year required to maintain proficiency. Experience is expensive, but lack of same is more costly in combat.

15

Intelligence

OBTAINING TIMELY and accurate information about your opponent, and preventing him from doing the same, is what military intelligence is all about. Three distinct layers of intelligence exist, each with its own characteristic needs and methods:

Strategic Intelligence. This covers everything the enemy is capable of doing. The sheer mass of information available at this level must be simplified and generalized for the senior officials who must use it. Information obtained at other levels is passed on to be analyzed for strategic implications. Satellites and large computers have made strategic intelligence less a matter of cosmic guesswork. Strategic intelligence must be updated monthly, although computers enable more frequent updates.

Operational Intelligence. This level goes into more detail as it covers smaller areas: a continent like Europe, or the Pacific Ocean. It is often further divided by activity: land, naval, air operations, economic, political, etc. Commanders of armies and fleets use operational intelligence. The means of gathering this information are the same as for the strategic level. The data is studied and analyzed in greater detail, as users at this level are dealing in more specific operations. Hence the use of the term "operational." Must be updated weekly, daily, or more frequently depending on whether a war is going on. The strategic-level people keep in touch with the operational-level crew to let them know when a strategic development affects the lower level.

Tactical Intelligence. Also known as battlefield intelligence. Very detailed and usually needed immediately. Updates are required at least a few times a day to be useful. Units down to battalion, or major warships, assign people to collect and analyze data. The analyzed data is passed on as quickly as possible to the operational- and strategic-level people. In turn, the other levels pass down the implications of their analysis on each tactical situation. The increased use of computers and more capable sensors allows tactical intelligence to be collected and used in real time. In other words, a radar not only detects objects but uses its analysis capabilities to determine what has been spotted and what it may be up to. See Chapter 10 for more on signal processing.

Electronic sensors collect the majority of information, and computers play a large role in analyzing what information is obtained. The only place where people still do most of the work is in ground combat. The infantry must still patrol. No one has come up with a way of automating this bloody exercise. Reconnaissance resources are always limited. It takes time to get a good picture of what the other fellow is up to. During battles, or when a lot of combat units are moving, it is very difficult to get a detailed picture of the enemy situation. As a rule of thumb, when everyone settles down, you can reveal 10 to 20 percent (or more) of the enemy's situation per day. A week or so of this leaves you with a good idea of the enemy's strength, dispositions, and capabilities. This assumes the two sides have equal information-gathering ability. If one antagonist has inferior intelligence-gathering capabilities, he will be in the dark longer, perhaps indefinitely. A nation with superior counterintelligence abilities, like Russia, can conceal its situation longer. This is a necessary skill for the Russians, as their intelligence-gathering capabilities are not up to Western levels.

The West has taken a long-standing skill at intelligence gathering and made it even more formidable through the use of technology. Satellites, electronic sensors, high-resolution cameras, and powerful computers give the West a considerable edge. This advantage is not always decisive. The pursuit of technology often overlooks the insights of a human analyst. It is possible to become overly dependent on technology. This is more likely when you consider that intelligence work does not have a terribly high status within the military. While some very bright people are attracted to this kind of work, they are not ordinarily the ones who become generals in great numbers. The combat arms are where the action is promotion-wise. Some armies habitually send their marginal officers into intelligence work. In Russia, the analysis of intelligence data is considered something good only "for women and lieutenants." The effects of this policy are not usually felt until the shooting starts.

Recent Developments

Things have become considerably more complex in the last 40 years, more complicated than people realize. At the beginning of this century, intelligence work was much as it had been for thousands of years. Spies, diplomats, and diligent trivia seekers collected strategic intelligence, often of dubious value. The same crew collected operational-level intelligence, although combat units often contributed. Tactical intelligence was normally as fresh and accurate as the enemy fire coming in your direction. Intelligence work began to change during World War I (1914–18). Aircraft reconnaissance was introduced on a wide scale and provided a good look at enemy territories. You were no longer dependent on groups of hard-riding horsemen to find out what was going on in the enemy rear area. Radio also came into general use. This brought forth electronic intelligence, otherwise known as eavesdropping. Shortly thereafter, the cryptographers were called in to devise codes for radio messages and the means to break the enemy's codes. World War II generally refined World War I developments. Air photography and photoanalysis became more effective. The big breakthrough came on the Allied side as many German and Japanese codes were broken continually throughout the war. We still live in the shadow of this achievement.

The Data Explosion

In the past, intelligence analysts could never get enough information. This is no longer the case. Electronic collection provides an avalanche of data. The problem now is separating useful information from the noise. This glut of intelligence comes from a variety of distinct sources.

1. *Electronic Reconnaissance.* Originally, this was just listening in on enemy radio transmissions. Currently, anything that is transmitted electronically can be plucked from the ether for later examination. This includes some emissions people aren't aware of—for example, infrared (heat) images and disturbances in the magnetic field. This last item is created whenever a large metal object moves around. Sound is also becoming a popular transmission to monitor, especially when it travels through the earth or water. The sensors to pick up all this information are found at all levels. Infantrymen have sensors for detecting sound and electronic emissions. Aircraft carry just about every sensor imaginable, as do satellites. Helicopters 25 kilometers behind the front, hovering at 1,000 meters, can monitor transmissions hundreds of kilometers away. Any transmitter broadcasting continuously for more than 30 seconds can be located to

within one or two kilometers. More powerful computers are making these locating devices even more accurate.

2. *Photo Reconnaissance.* More precise locations of any object can be obtained by photo reconnaissance. Satellites and aircraft do most of this work. Photographs taken from a U.S. satellite 128 kilometers up can show objects as small as one foot in diameter. It can distinguish between civilian clothes and uniforms. The cameras are no longer just cameras; "sensors" would be a more apt term. Traditional photographs are still taken. Other images are also taken showing patterns of heat, radiation, magnetic fields, and any other items that imaginative scientists can dream up. All of these sensors are quite accurate. These other images get around the problems cameras have, such as darkness, clouds, and camouflage on the ground.

3. *Spies, Informants, and Prisoners.* "Human intelligence" is still potentially the most valuable. However, people are more difficult to deal with and interpret than photography and electronic data. It is easier to favor the more "precise" information. But the photos and sensor data, as tangible as they are, can also be misleading. A sufficient amount of human intelligence can determine what is likely true and what is not. A lot of information from human informants (spies) can clarify all the stuff the satellites and other sensors pick up. During peacetime, you don't get many prisoners of war (POWs), a copious source of human intelligence. With POWs, you can also cross-check their stories to find out who is telling the truth. Spies and informants in foreign countries often provide data that is difficult to verify. Spies are expensive to train and support, particularly in peacetime. Informants in the enemy camp are erratic. In peacetime, many of the military plans you attempt to uncover are just that, plans. You may never know if they are real, or would even work. The same problem applies to enemy weapons and military units. Worst of all, without human intelligence, there is less appreciation of what is going on behind the photo and sensor images. The United States, because of its lead in photo and electronic sensors, tends to slight the use of spies and informants. It's easier to peruse masses of sensor data that won't contradict whatever you are looking for. Those nations with less sensor capability must use human sources more heavily. Given a choice, most nations would opt for more sensors. However, slighting the human element provides the risk that the image seen is not the image that is there.

4. *Technical Intelligence.* Most nations have similar weapons; at least appearances indicate equivalence. Reality is quite different, but this is not known until you can examine the other fellow's stuff as carefully as your own. In wartime, you expect that a lot of everyone's material will be captured and examined. In peacetime, the situation is somewhat different. Several ways exist to gather technical intel-

ligence on forces you are not at war with. For superpowers, there are satellite photos. but these are limited in their detail and rarely show you the inner workings of tanks, aircraft, and ships. Spies can be useful, especially in the West, where enough cash will often obtain technical manuals. Better than documentation is the equipment itself. In this case, the Soviet Union was always at a disadvantage. A steady flow of Soviet equipment came across its borders and into the hands of Western analysts. Some of this came directly from the former Soviet Union; a lot of it comes from nations that have purchased Soviet equipment. Buyers of Western equipment, such as Third World nations, were prone to give Soviet agents access to their high-tech ordnance. Money usually changes hands, but rarely did major items end up in the Soviet Union. Enough Soviet equipment ended up in Western hands that it could be used in training. The Israelis modified captured Soviet equipment and used it in their own units. The Soviets got their hands on enough Western equipment to keep them properly respectful and eager to obtain as much of this technology as they possibly could. Because of the more open nature of Western societies, it is relatively easy for considerable data to be collected by subscribing to technical journals, buying books, and attending trade shows. While diplomats openly collect printed material, foreign intelligence agents approach technical specialists with offers to pick up some fast money for a little photocopying or the loan of some technical manuals for a few hours. More elaborate operations strive to illegally export powerful computers or manufacturing equipment unavailable in nations unfriendly to the West.

Analysis

The cutting edge of intelligence work is no longer the collection of information, but the sorting out of all that data and making some sense of it. In other words, analysis. This task is further complicated by the ever-present problem of figuring out what the enemy intends to do. Moreover, people do not think alike, and people from different cultures even less so. Analysis is not easy. In fact, it's nearly impossible. Success is how much better you do it than analysts in opposing nations. It is relatively easy to count rifles, tanks, ships, or missiles. It is more difficult to answer questions like:

- What is a particular piece of equipment really capable of?
- What does the enemy believe his equipment is capable of?
- What is the enemy equipment capable of in relation to your own equipment? For example, what can the Russian T-80 tank really accomplish on the battlefield, and what do the Russians believe this

tank can do? More important, what can this tank do versus Western models like the U.S. M-1? And then you must ask yourself the big question: What do they intend to do with all this equipment? For example, the Iranians purchased several thousand Russian armored vehicles in the early 1990s. Does this mean they think they can successfully overrun Iraq, or the Gulf States? And if they tried it, how successful would they be? And that's not all. Suppose the Iranian leadership changed its military plans for defending Iran, or attacking Iraq. What could the Iranians reasonably expect to do? All of these questions must be applied across the full spectrum of military equipment, troop capabilities, and anything else that has a bearing on the subject. Lots of ground to cover, and many opportunities to get it wrong.

- What should we report back to our own troops and when? This is the major problem with the United States. There is so much data coming in from so many sources, and the analysis bureaucracy is so large, that a disproportionately small amount of analysis gets back to the troops who need it. And when the data does arrive, it is often too late.

Current examples of insufficient analysis abound:

- During the Vietnam War, U.S. pilots discovered that the air-combat techniques they had developed since the Korean War 15 years earlier were not effective. Although the United States had a considerable amount of intelligence on Soviet aircraft, tactics, and pilot training, American pilots were going to war trained to fight American pilots in American aircraft. Intelligence had not gotten across the point that the Soviets, who supplied and trained the North Vietnamese Air Force, used markedly different aircraft and tactics. It took several years before American pilots could be retrained and achieve decisive success.

- During the 1973 Arab-Israeli War, the Israeli Air Force ignored intelligence data on the upgrading of Arab air-defense systems. In particular, Israeli commanders thought they could counter new radar-controlled cannon and missiles with pilot skill. This was considered cheaper than buying expensive electronic countermeasures (ECM) equipment from the Americans. Heavy aircraft losses taught them a hard lesson. The information was not lacking; the proper analysis was.

- Ground forces also have their problems. During the Soviet invasion of Afghanistan in 1980, initial analysis was that the Soviets had pulled off a masterful land operation. Soon afterward, reports from inside Afghanistan indicated that the Soviets had grossly misinterpreted their intelligence data on the Afghans. Overoptimism, a common problem with intelligence analysis, caused the Soviets to go charging into numerous combat situations where they found themselves more disadvantaged than their analysts had predicted.

- During the Gulf War, U.S. battlefield commanders were open in their criticism of the vast U.S. intelligence bureaucracies and the inability of these bureaucracies to deliver useful information in a timely manner. "Muscle-bound" is probably the most succinct way to describe the U.S. intelligence organizations. Too much of a good thing can have unfavorable results.

Every war reveals examples of faulty analysis or intelligence gathering. Some mistakes are understandable. Too many mistakes can threaten the success of the operation and the survival of the nation that undertakes it.

One of the more frequent reasons for bad analysis is the multiplicity of intelligence agencies in many nations. This makes it difficult to determine which of the many, and often contradictory, analyses is correct. It's often not just a matter of different analysts coming to different conclusions. Each intelligence group represents a different interest. Often each branch of the armed forces, foreign office, national intelligence group, and other organizations have their own institutional requirements when gathering and interpreting information. One of the more extreme examples is the United States. Each branch of the armed forces has its own intelligence group, as does the Department of Defense. On top of that, the secretary of defense has his own personal group of analysts. In addition, there are the CIA, the State Department, the National Reconnaissance Office, and many more. Who's where on the playing field? It depends on which team you belong to and whose game you are in.

GOOD ANALYSIS IS ONLY HALF THE JOB

The mass of annual data, billions of words plus pictures, collected by a major nation's intelligence agencies is too enormous for any individual to handle. Even the summaries are millions of words. The problem is compounded by the dynamics of secrecy; much information cannot even be looked at by all analysts available. The reason analysts exist is to somehow make sense out of all this information. The analyst's client, the decision maker, is typically not involved in intelligence work. Normally, this person is a political leader, senior civil servant, or military commander. An analyst's job consists of more than simply going through masses of information and deriving conclusions. First, he must find the data. This is a never-ending process. Analysts are forever saying things like, "Hey, I didn't know that." It is the nature of the analysis process to turn over stones and find unexpected items crawling out. This makes the analyst's product tentative, always subject to revision and reissue. This disturbs decision makers. What antagonizes them even more are analyst conclusions that conflict with policymakers' view of the world. The analyst must take this situation into account. A good intelligence analyst makes many enemies. A good analyst has the misfortune to spot new military developments before others do. This is especially vexing in peacetime, when there is no clear-cut way to prove yourself right, or wrong. A good analyst survives in such a situation by becoming very persuasive. The analysts must also be able to defend their conclusions effectively. To achieve all the above, a good analyst does the job in three phases.

Phase 1 is accurately determining what the client wants and finding the raw data.

Phase 2 is doing the analysis, including smoking out the client decision maker's biases and preconceived ideas.

Phase 3 is following up the analysis with effective rebuttals of decision-maker objections. There is always the possibility that the decision maker will find valid flaws in the analysis. A good analyst must be capable of dealing effectively with these also.

A competent analyst is part detective, part evaluator, part diplomat, and part politician. The analyst is up for election every time the work goes out the door.

THE GREAT GAME

Intelligence is more than collecting and analyzing data. There is also ample opportunity for deceiving the enemy. Keeping your secrets is counterintelligence. Making the other fellow believe what you want him to is deception. Deception is better; it is also more difficult. It is called the Great Game, and indeed it is. The Soviet Union was the premier practitioner of counterintelligence and deception. It had several large organizations devoted to counterintelligence, including the KGB (a combined CIA, FBI, Coast Guard, Border Patrol), GRU (military intelligence), and MVD (national police). The U.S. counterparts are noted in parenthesis, although American has no real equivalent to the MVD. There was another organization that has no equal in the West, the Principal Directorate of Strategic Deception. This organization coordinated nationwide activities designed to deceive foreign analysts as to the Soviet Union's true capabilities and intentions. It was led by a marshal of the army. This organization had the power to order any military or civilian operation to change its activities. For example, a factory could have been ordered, on a certain day and certain time, to have all of its workers leave their buildings and return exactly an hour later. This would deceive a recon satellite as to when a work shift began, or perhaps imply that additional shifts were being used. At other times, combat units were ordered to maintain radio silence or to make moves at odd hours. Sometimes these drills were for satellites, to get an idea of just what can be seen from way up there. American satellite photo reconnaissance often caught the Soviets in the acts of setting up deceptions. Because U.S. KH series spy satellites are so maneuverable, they can quickly shift orbits and show up where the Soviets didn't expect them to be. In these situations, formerly unknown units, facilities, and equipment were revealed. What this has shown is that the Soviets were quite good at hiding things. They took full advantage of their closed society, and many of these attitudes, capabilities, and security organizations survived the collapse of the Soviet Union in one form or another.

Several distinct skills and activities are involved in counterintelligence and deception. All must be used and done well in order to succeed. The margin between success and failure is very thin in this business.

1. *Camouflage.* This is the oldest technique. You physically conceal troops, equipment, and structures with camouflage nets, natural cover, special paints, smoke, and anything else you can dream up. Special paints that resist infrared (heat) or radar detection are a popular item at the moment. Equipment can also be designed to be more difficult to detect, either physically or electronically. Nuclear submarines have been doing this for years. The U.S. stealth series of aircraft are another example.

2. *Electronic Deception.* Turning the enemy's collection of electronic emissions against him has been a popular and successful technique for over 40 years. Radar and sonar can be detected simply because they are broadcasting a signal. You can deceive the enemy by changing the arrangement and schedule of use for radios, radars, and sonars to make the other fellow believe you are what you are not. You can have a small number of troops operating a large number of transmitters falsely representing a larger unit. Another effective technique is silence: Simply turn all the equipment off. This can be very effective. An example of this would be a naval task force that turns all its transmitters off and then steams in one direction while sending one or two ships off in another direction with their electronics blasting. If this works, the enemy tracks the one or two loud ships, and the silent task force takes up position in a more favorable location without being detected. This has been a popular and successful technique in the past but may prove more difficult if you don't have powerful computers and signal-processing equipment.

3. *Plants.* An ancient, and still effective, technique. You "plant" false or misleading information. This usually refers to documents or some other physical evidence. Similar to electronic deception, except that you are working with more tangible items. This also includes use of dummy equipment, weapons, or even building. Inflatable items are popular. These techniques are easily exposed by advanced sensors, such as those looking for heat or metal. Some nations will take extreme measures to deceive U.S. satellite reconnaissance. These techniques are popularly known in peacetime as Disinformation.

4. *Double Agents.* Nonelectronic intelligence still plays a role, and the

ability to have one of your agents pretending to work for the other side is one of the most sought-after goals. A double agent not only obtains information, but lets you know what the other side knows about your own operations.

Playing the Great Game involves using all the above techniques to present a puzzle for the enemy. When the puzzle is figured out, it presents a convincing, but false, picture of what you want the enemy to believe. With all the loose ends, deceptions, preconceived ideas, and general murkiness of intelligence operations, you must be careful not to get sidetracked yourself. When playing the Great Game, you are exploiting the nature of intelligence analysts. All is not what it appears to be, and it is too easy to create an illusion where none is intended.

Another problem is the different ways each culture, or organization, will interpret the same events. Americans and Chinese don't think alike. But then, naval officers and army officers have quite different views of how the world operates. Most analysts are never able to fully perceive the unique mind-set of their opposite numbers. Scattered individuals do possess the ability to correctly fathom how other cultures think. In most nations, especially totalitarian ones, group mentality and party solidarity work against such rare perceptions. In wartime, false perceptions are quickly brought up short by reality. This is an expensive way to obtain insight. It also does not help prevent a war in the first place. Ideally, the Great Game is played to protect, not to incite, warfare. Too often, there is more incitement than protection. All of this is not helped by the secrecy that plagues these operations. The Great Game goes on.

Theory and Practice

Often, all that stands between war and peace in times of crisis is an intelligence officer's analysis of what the other fellow is really up to. It is easy to forget in peacetime how crucial good intelligence is during wartime. In a pattern ongoing over many centuries, intelligence work is not seen as a fast-track assignment and does not attract the best people. Thus, the reputation of peacetime intelligence people is so low that this carefully crafted analysis often has little impact on the decision maker. Analysts are often seen as similar to economists, always saying, "On the other hand. . . ." Decision makers under the gun don't care what's on the other hand—they are simply desperate to know where they stand relative to the other fellow. This dismal state of affairs arises from the tendency of government officials to believe what they want to believe. In peacetime, there is little to divert them from this course.

Ongoing efforts are made by the intelligence community to systematically probe the future. Gaming and simulation are used, with varying degrees of success, to forecast difficult situations in time for solutions to be devised. These techniques are useful in technical areas. Wind tunnels are used to test aircraft designs. Computer simulations check out electronic-equipment designs. Flying simulators help train pilots and later teach them new skills. When it comes to actual warfare, and the political conditions that bring it about, most nations, their governments, and their armed forces play another game. What passes for wargaming is often a predetermined confirmation of policies already decided upon. Although this attitude is not always present, it is pervasive enough to poison nearly all the military uses of modeling and gaming. What happens is that this form of research has very little credibility. Partially, this is human nature. Unlike with wind-tunnel tests, you rarely get a chance to see if the results of a wargame will reproduce themselves on the battlefield. But mostly, it is a self-inflicted wound. Fortunately, gaming and simulation are even more widely used outside the intelligence community, particularly in the United States. The availability of different groups gaming the same future has led to some realistic consensus on what the future holds, and this knowledge gets to the commanders, even if it doesn't come from the intelligence crowd.

The Great Game of deception and counterdeception is played with great intensity in peacetime. This is quite true with the many totalitarian governments on the planet, where a closed society and frenzied attitude toward secrecy and deception keep Western analysts constantly off balance. In the West, weapons systems are hustled to foreign buyers along with substantial, and quite open, operational data. Even though many key characteristics of systems are kept secret, it's not difficult for a diligent amateur to fill in the blanks. The Soviet Union played upon this situation to introduce weapons and equipment either unknown to the West or at least imperfectly understood. Two examples were its first rocket-propelled torpedoes in the 1970s and its laser weapons during the 1980s. In the early 1960s, the United States introduced ASROC, a nuclear depth charge that was fired by rocket from a surface ship. Later, a submarine version (SUBROC) was introduced that used a torpedo instead of a depth charge. In the late 1970s, the Soviets introduced a new shipboard rocket that for several years was thought to be another surface-to-surface missile. Eventually, it was determined that this was their version of ASROC. A device appearing in the 1980s was a laser weapon. What exactly it could do was unclear for some years. Eventually, it was determined that it was used to blind aircraft sensors. This points up the difficulty of analyzing secret-weapons projects without access to all the information collected by Western intelligence agencies. All of this work is secret, especially its failures and misjudgments. In peacetime, the reverse side of intelligence, deception, is regularly overlooked, especially in the West. The Soviets were more diligent about deception, it being habitual with them. One of the greatest dangers to Western nations is a lapse in attention toward deception efforts. Iraq gave a recent demonstration of how even a Third World nation can run a successful deception program. Iraq managed to keep details of the extent of its nuclear-weapons program from Western intelligence agencies until UN inspectors were inside Iraq itself.

In wartime, competent military units use deception and are more successful because of it. Often the very survival of smaller units depends on their skill at deception. Most losses occur during the short period of time spent in combat. At lower levels of combat, it is not unusual for entire units (squads, platoons, companies) to be destroyed due to their own errors, particularly in the use of deception. This does not always show up in the histories. So we rarely get clear examples of how poor use of deception can have catastrophic results. Further, deception favors the defense. In theory, deception should be an offensive tool, but in practice it works better in the defense because the attacker is up and about looking for defenders. Successful deception is difficult. Soldiers will often concentrate on more attainable, but less beneficial in the long term, goals.

Wars also have a way of revealing faults in even the best-prepared and best-equipped intelligence organizations. The 1991 Gulf War was no exception. Numerous details of the Iraqi nuclear weapons program were unknown or vastly underestimated. On the battlefield, the U.S. intelligence found itself muscle-bound in some respects and underequipped in others. There were so many strategic intelligence organizations, and so much capability to collect information, that the intel bureaucracies back in Washington were unable to sort out and forward information to the Gulf in time to be useful. There was also a major underestimation of how much air reconnaissance would be needed to support the air campaign. Without timely "Battle Damage Assessment" (BDA), targets that needed more attention didn't get it, while targets that had been destroyed the first time around got revisited. The ground troops were a little better off, mainly because the JSTARS aircraft (an AWACS for ground forces) was far enough along in its R&D to be quickly sent in for its first battlefield use. These problems are not new—they happen in every war. If nothing else, they will keep the intel crowd on their toes for a few years.

The Future

Computers and other electronic aids are transforming intelligence work. For the past 30 years, increasing masses of information were collected electronically, but the means to analyze this flood of data lagged way behind. Microcomputers have been infiltrating intelligence work throughout the 1980s. As these machines become more powerful, they enable individual analysts to effectively process enormous amounts of data. More so than in other branches of the military, individual initiative is more critical in modern intelligence work in order to use limited resources to ferret useful information out of the masses of data collected. The right details are not always selected for closer scrutiny. Larger and more powerful computers have long been applied to this problem at the highest levels, but the real work gets done further down.

The United States is in the process of introducing a joint army/air force intelligence collection and analysis system for divisions and brigades. This system takes advantage of the power and portability of microcomputers. Digitized maps, a growing number of sensors, and better communications make this system possible. Another capability for field units is immediate access to data collected by satellites and other high-flying sensors. The images, and other data, are collected and processed in minutes. This provides a tremendous advantage in combat, where in the past it has taken hours or days to get this information to the field commanders. While some are dubious of it working, the same criticisms were made when similarly "advanced" systems were introduced during World Wars I and II. New technology is not always perfect, but it is usually better. Eventually. In this case, parts of this system were available in the Gulf War; most was not. The missing parts were truly missed.

Signal processing is maturing more rapidly and acquiring the capability to efficiently find the right needle in the information haystack. This is another offshoot of the rapid increase in computing power. Unfortunately, programs must still be written to tell the computers what to do. The lack of efficient software is still one of the most significant choke points for automated intelligence work. This becomes more crucial as advances in technology make it more difficult to find what you are looking for. An example is decoys representing tanks and aircraft on the ground designed to respond correctly to the several different sensors carried by recon aircraft and satellites. You've got to figure out what pattern of signals to look for in order to separate the decoys from the real thing. Deception is becoming more a war of computers. It has even spawned MASINT (measurement and signature intelligence).

In the American armed forces, one of the unrecognized positive side effects of women in the service academies is that many of these women go into intelligence work. They do so because they are barred from the combat arms, the traditional route to higher ranks. Many of the fast-track females opt for intelligence, one of the more challenging noncombat branches of the service. Intelligence work puts a premium on diligence, perception, attention to nuance, and good communication skills. These are just the traits in which females tend to have an edge over males. There's also no premium on physical strength for intel work, as is the case in most combat jobs. This trend will have an increasingly beneficial effect as these women work their way up the promotion ladder.

16

The Primary Law
of Warfare: Murphy's

"ANYTHING THAT CAN GO WRONG, will go wrong. And at the worst possible moment." Engineers love this one, and refer to it as Murphy's Law. Soldiers have good reason to add to this O'Niel's Law: "Murphy was an optimist." Warfare is, by its very nature, a chaotic and unpredictable undertaking. Combat and the endless preparations for it are fraught with unanticipated problems. This becomes acute during the opening stages of a conflict, when all the differences in weapons characteristics, tactics, doctrine, and quality become concrete. Once the war settles down to a steady grind of mutual destruction, it is possible to get a fix on many of the interactions. More precise planning is then possible. Before that occurs, key factors are largely unknown.

Infantrymen have always been the most frequent victims of Murphy's Law and, as one would expect, gradually codified their collective observations in a list of "Murphy's Laws of Combat." I've seen variations of this list in different infantry units, as well as in several foreign armies. Bad news travels fast. Below is a composite of several of these lists. They are a telling testimony to the vagaries of ground combat.

Murphy's Laws of Combat

You are not Superman.

Recoilless rifles aren't.

Suppressive fire won't.

If it's stupid but works, it's not stupid.

Don't look conspicuous. It draws fire.

Never draw fire. It makes everyone around you nervous.

When in doubt, empty the magazine.

Never share a foxhole with anyone braver than you.

Always keep in mind that your weapon was made by the lowest bidder.

If your attack is going well, it's an ambush.

If you can't remember . . . the claymore is pointed at you. (The claymore is a flat mine that is set up and pointed at the enemy, unless you set it up the wrong way.)

All five-second grenade fuses are three seconds.

Try to look unimportant. The enemy may be low on ammo.

If you are forward of your position, the artillery will be short.

The enemy diversion you're ignoring is the main attack.

The easy way is always mined.

The important things are always simple.

The simple things are always hard.

When you have secured an area, don't forget to tell the enemy.

Incoming fire has the right of way.

No combat-ready unit has ever passed inspection.

No inspection-ready unit has ever passed combat.

Teamwork is essential. It gives the enemy other people to shoot at.

If the enemy is in range, so are you.

Friendly fire isn't.

Anything you can do can get you shot . . . including doing nothing.

Make it too tough for the enemy to get in . . . and you can't get out.

Tracers work both ways.

The only thing more accurate than incoming enemy fire is incoming friendly fire.

Radios will fail as soon as you need something desperately.

When both sides are convinced they are about to lose . . . they are both right.

Professionals are predictable, but the world is full of amateurs.

All-weather close support doesn't work in bad weather.

The bursting radius of a grenade is always one foot greater than your jumping range.

The only terrain that is truly controlled is the terrain upon which you're standing.

The law of the bayonet says the man with the bullet wins.

REMF (rear echelon motherfuckers, or noncombat troops) are everywhere.

The best tank killer is another tank. Therefore tanks are always fighting each other . . . and have no time to help the infantry.

Precision bombing is normally accurate within plus/minus one mile.

Cluster bombing from B-52s and C-130s is very, very accurate. The bombs always hit the ground.

Murphy was an eleven bush (11B is the U.S. Army job code for basic rifleman).

Perfect plans aren't.

The easy way generally gets you killed.

The side with the fanciest uniforms loses.

Armored vehicles are bullet magnets, a moving foxhole that attracts attention.

If you are short of everything except the enemy, you're in combat.

No plan survives the first few seconds of combat.

Ammo is cheap; your life isn't.

It's easier to expend material in combat than to fill out the forms for Graves Registration.

If you can't see the enemy, he still may be able to see you.

Final protective fire doesn't.

You can win without fighting, but it's a lot tougher to do. And the enemy may not cooperate.

Weapon Effectiveness

High-tech weapons provide numerous examples of things that not only don't work, but often don't even let you know they don't work. A recent example was the U.S. Navy's S-3 antisubmarine aircraft. Introduced in the mid-'70s to operate from carriers, it had a new electronics system to control the data coming from the sonobuoys it dropped. The rough carrier landings jarred the delicate equipment to the extent that the operators often did not get the information the sonobuoys were broadcasting. For some years, it was not realized that this was happening. Only when several highly experienced operators began to suspect a malfunction and complained was the situation carefully looked into. It took quite a while to get things working right. At least one hopes the system was fixed.

The only weapons you can really depend on to perform as expected are those that were used in the last war. Even improved, as opposed to radically new, weapons are suspect. Another example occurred just before World War II when the U.S. Navy introduced a new torpedo. One of the improvements in this model was that it exploded under the target ship instead of hitting it, thus causing more damage. Testing demonstrated this. This helped the chances of destroying the ship. Soon after the war began, reports about dud torpedoes came back from subs in the Pacific. The naval weapons-development people did not believe it and resisted change for a year. Finally, more tests were performed, and it was found that the temperature of the water influenced the operation of the torpedo. The water temperature in the Pacific was different, just different enough to make the torpedo fail. Peacetime testing had not revealed this. There were many other examples during World War II. Every nation had problems with this, some more than others. In 1987, Britain deployed a new class of destroyer. While the new ship was being tested, it was discovered that unanticipated engine noises made the sonar nearly useless. The Soviets had similar problems on many of their ships, and in many cases never really eliminated this flaw. During the 1973 Arab-Israeli War, the U.S. TOW antitank missile often became unstable when fired across the Suez Canal. The TOW missile was controlled through a thin wire between the missile and the operator's guidance system. Electrical signals went through the wire, keeping it on target. The canal was full of salt water, which had different electrical properties from fresh water. This problem had not been detected during testing and was soon fixed. In the meantime, Israeli troops became quite wary of the TOW.

Also during the 1973 war, it was discovered that the hydraulic fluid used in the M-60 tank was too readily ignited when the tank was hit. Minor, or at least nonfatal, damage was turned into a major problem. The fluid was thought to be safe and was soon replaced by a less flammable type. Speaking of hydraulic fluid, Russian tanks use alcohol. If the troops lack anything to drink, they have been known to consume this fluid. The Russians still have problems with this, in that sometimes tanks are made inoperable due to fluid consumed by the troops.

Even more bizarre examples can be found. At the start of World War I in 1914, there were two types of artillery shells. One was high explosive. The other, more expensive to build and theoretically more effective, was shrapnel. This type was like a shotgun shell—it exploded in the air and sprayed the ground below with metal balls. Tests had shown that these balls would penetrate wood boards set up to represent troops. Because of the expense, fewer than half the shells used were shrapnel. In the 1930s, a group of American technicians were setting up some shells for a test, and the shell exploded prematurely, peppering some of the people with the "lethal" metal balls. They all survived. Further investigation revealed that human skin, muscle, and bone were far more resistant to the metal balls than wood boards. Combat surgeons, when questioned, remembered that they had never seen a penetration wound caused by shrapnel balls. There has never been much official note made of this very humane weapon.

Other weapons lethal more in appearance than reality are bayonets and sabers. U.S. Civil War medical records (of dead and wounded) noted that less than one percent of all wounds were caused by these weapons. Sabers were dropped from most arsenals 50 years ago. Recently, armies have designed bayonets better suited for cutting wood and wire than enemy soldiers. This could also have been deduced from American Civil War experience, where officers noted that bayonet attacks rarely resulted in anyone being stabbed by a bayonet.

High-technology weapons are the most common types to suffer multiple flaws. The numerous MiG-21 fighters suffered a number of serious short-comings that were only discovered when a large number of users could be interviewed by Western intelligence analysts. The most serious flaws in this aircraft occurred during the violent maneuvering that accompanied com-bat. The gunsight was easily thrown out of alignment. This gave the pilot false information as to what his guns might hit. In effect, the cannon became useless. Add to this the crude nature of the MiG-21's air-to-air missiles, and you have a relatively harmless fighter. Except to the pilot. The other problem had to do with the fuel tanks. When more than half the fuel was gone and the aircraft was violently maneuvered, fuel stopped going into the engine, and the aircraft lost power. Very embarrassing. Things have not changed a lot in the aircraft industry. In 1987, there were published reports in the Soviet Union about continuing design and quality-control problems with the new AN-28 light transport. This corroborates the reports of recurring crashes and groundings of MiG-23/27 aircraft. Western aircraft also have these problems, but not to the same extent. Part of the problem is the quality of the ground crews. In the West, they are largely volunteers, with technicians having many years' experience.

Like the Americans, the Russians also have their problems with tanks. Their T-62 model had a host of problems, some minor and some serious. One of the more vexing ones was its tendency to throw the tracks off the road wheels when the vehicle was violently maneuvered. This would not happen frequently in training, but would be a common occurrence during combat. A Czech civilian technician eventually came up with a simple modification that eliminated the problem. Meanwhile, the T-62 was replaced earlier than usual. The remaining vehicles still have a bad reputation among their users. In most cases, the simplicity and robustness of Russian weapons appeal to the Third World. However, this low-tech approach can backfire. Iraq, like many buyers of Soviet tanks, found that it could make tank ammunition itself. The simple construction of Soviet tank guns allowed this. However, tank ammunition is a key component of a tank. You can't cut corners in its manufacture. The Iraqis did, and their use of low-grade materials in their T-72 tank gun ammunition resulted in shells that bounced off U.S. M-1 tanks even at point-blank range.

Superior Western technology is not immune to embarrassing flaws. There was the case of the harmless ballistic missile. During the early 1960s, the warhead of the U.S. Polaris missile would not detonate. The error was not detected for a while. When it was, the problem proved immune to numerous solutions. Meanwhile, the missiles might as well have carried rocks in their warheads. Most of the embarrassing failures of weapons in combat are a result of poor testing. Antitank missiles that cost $10,000 and antiaircraft missiles that cost $2 million make extensive live-fire training risky for the budget. Equally frightening from a fiscal point of view is destruction testing of increasingly expensive vehicles. This involves firing enemy weapons, or something close, at your stuff to see how robust your vehicles are under combat conditions. As a practical matter, this destruction testing is rarely done, particularly with expensive systems like aircraft. Instead, some parts of the vehicles are shot at. This helps, but it does not expose those embarrassing vulnerabilities that show up when the shooting starts. Lack of adequate testing goes against the ancient combat wisdom: "The more you sweat in peace, the less you bleed in war." One bright spot in this situation is that many weapons developed in peacetime are "overbuilt." This accounts for a lot of the high cost of weapons. But this makes them more flexible when facing uncertain wartime conditions. Weapons developed and built in wartime can zero in on precisely what they know they have to do. But it's nice to have halfway decent weapons for those first few battles of a war.

Another problem with perfecting weapons in peacetime is unimaginative and unenergetic leaders. Efficiently re-creating the chaos of combat is the stage director's art, and military leaders are not selected for their theatrical abilities. Those armies that have more successfully gone from peacetime theory to wartime practice have done so on the backs of effective training exercises. Each nation's doctrine and standard operating procedures also play significant roles in combat readiness. Weapons and equipment are used as little as possible to preserve them for war. No armed force is immune to this idea. But it's also a historical fact that the troops do well in war in direct proportion to how long and hard they have trained with their equipment. The dangers of waiting until the shooting starts before discovering the weapons and troops are not up to it is a lesson that is never really learned.

Tactical Principles

The same weapons are often used quite differently by nations. This creates problems in cooperating with allies and recognizing different tactics of opponents. Chauvinism, inertia, and sundry other factors lead armies to view potential enemies as clones of themselves. The results are interesting history and ugly battlefield incidents. In the opening stages of World War I, the French were so obsessed with retaking their two lost provinces on the lower Rhine River that they paid little attention to the Germans marching through Belgium. The French nearly lost Paris, and the war, as a result. On a tactical level, all combatants misunderstood the impact of machine guns and rapid-fire artillery. The French in particular thought that energetic and persistent attacks could overcome anything. They were wrong, and hundreds of thousands of French soldiers died in futile attacks before the end of 1914. World War I was full of technicians unwilling to perceive the differences between their own tactics and those of their opponents. The Germans were the first to pick up on these differences and exploit them. This brought them close to victory again in 1918, even though they were outnumbered. World War II was equally embarrassing in its repetition of many of the perception errors of World War I. The Germans had developed a new set of tactics, blitzkrieg, based on motorized units led by armored vehicles. Germany's opponents had the same, and in some cases superior, equipment. German tactics were developed from the writings of British theorists, so there was no secrecy involved. Even though German doctrine was widely known, it came as a nasty shock when confronted in practice. Granted, German success was largely due to superior training and leadership. Yet without these dynamic tactics, and their enemies' lack of the same, Germany's early success would not have been nearly as complete. After World War II, tactical blindness continued unabated. In Korea, Chinese infantry tactics smothered enemy units unaccustomed to opponents running up and down hills without benefit of abundant supply lines. The American forces quickly adapted to this, but not before many friendly troops were lost in the confusion. The 1973 Arab-Israeli War held surprises for all parties. Israel did not anticipate Egypt blasting its way across the Suez Canal and just digging in. Israeli disdain for Egyptian tactical competence led to one very embarrassing incident in which a well-prepared Egyptian defense destroyed an Israeli armored brigade. In Syria, another illuminating example unfolded. Syrian armored units, well drilled in Soviet tactics, found themselves defeated by a moving ambush. Outnumbered Israeli tanks refused to stand and be overrun. Leapfrogging backward, Israeli tanks destroyed the advancing Syrian divisions piecemeal. The Soviet Union immediately reconsidered its tactics, and Israel designed a tank with a larger ammunition capacity and better protection. This included development of reactive armor. The Soviets obtained some of this when the Syrians captured some Israeli tanks in the 1982 war. Manufacturing a crude version of its own, Russia now looks to reactive armor as a partial solution to the Israeli leapfrog-ambush tactics. Since reactive armor does little to deflect tank shells, the Russians still have not overcome the tactical embarrassment of Syria. The Soviets were similarly surprised at the one-sided air battle over southern Lebanon in 1982 between Israeli and Syrian aircraft. In one battle, the Syrians lost dozens of aircraft and the Israelis none. This operation was carefully analyzed by the Soviets and, according to the articles published in their military journals, they were more intent on finding excuses than reasons. They did little to change the weapons, equipment, and training of their air force. This reaction is not uncommon. Tactical myopia is frighteningly persistent.

Lurching Forward

Solving problems in the military is further hampered by the contending "unions." Between and within each branch of the armed forces, sundry factions battle over limited resources. The U.S. Navy has five major career groups: surface ships, the marines, aviation, submarines, and strategic missiles. The U.S. Defense Department is probably the worst example of office politics. The U.S. defense budget contains over 5,000 separate line items and more than 1,500 different programs. Each has an interest group of contractors and military personnel pulling for it. To confuse the issue totally, more than 100 different accounting systems are used in the U.S. military. Comparisons are difficult, cooperation is rare, duplication is rampant, and delays are interminable. It's a Darwinian system where the political performance counts for more than combat capability. Pragmatic military men soon adopt the attitude that they'll attempt to get what they think they'll need. Get what they can. Do what they can with what they've got. Hope they've guessed right.

How does one analyze the experience of the past and predict how new techniques will work in the future? Over the past 50 years, a debate has gone on between the historians and the technocrats. Before World War II, history, not science, was more frequently invoked to settle disputes over what direction to take in military planning. The avalanche of new gadgets produced during World War II gave the technocrats the edge after 1945. Since then, experience has shown that warfare is ill suited to effective analysis with current scientific tools. At the same time, history-minded planners got a bad reputation from their frequent resistance to, and ignorance about, new technology. In the last 10 years, the historians have made a comeback, and the technical types have come round to accepting a hybrid modeling process using historical experience. Ironically, Russia has always stayed with historical analysis, even though it worships science in military affairs. European armies are also less mesmerized by technology, although the United States has forced its technology approach on its allies whenever it has had the chance. The study and analysis of historical experience has returned to favor. A synergy is growing between historical experience and rapidly changing technology. Although planning still lurches forward into the unknown, it is less frequently lurching forward from the unknown. The results of this synergy could be seen in the number of times U.S. military planners were right on the money during the 1991 Gulf War.

Theory and Practice

The most effective work on re-creating combat conditions under peacetime conditions has been done in the West. This began in the 1960s with increasingly realistic aircraft simulators. Work on these devices began with the commercial market, to train airline pilots at less cost. Air combat is more complex, and it wasn't until the late 1970s that fighter pilots had realistic simulators. The U.S. Navy has kept pace with the air force, training in the development of realistic training simulators for its ship crews. By the early 1980s, the U.S. Army had developed the first realistic ground-combat training system. Not a simulator exactly, it worked by fitting troops and equipment with sensors that could detect lasers fired from mechanisms attached to infantry and vehicle weapons. For the first time in history, ground troops could exercise under something approximating combat conditions. This has had a significant effect on improving combat skills. Other Western nations also adopted the aircraft and naval simulators. Lacking the technology, Soviet forces were stuck with less effective simulators and significantly lower skill levels. This was one reason why Russian officers demanded a professional volunteer army even while the Soviet Union was collapsing.

Western forces, notably the United States, have also maintained their use of dissimilar forces training. In other words, their opponents in the simulators and training exercises operate as in combat. In other words, the opposing force uses Russian weapons and tactics. The Soviets paid less attention to this type of training. The net result of all of this is that Western forces are better prepared to fight than their potential Soviet-equipped and Soviet-trained enemies. In Soviet military circles, there was extensive debate during the 1980s on how to overcome this, but the Soviets were never able to get far in solving the problem. This bodes ill for all those Third World nations that use Russian equipment and doctrine. As Iraq painfully discovered, the American troops were better prepared to fight Russian-equipped armies than the other way around.

While great strides have been made with training, serious problems persist with equipment performance and reliability. The British had considerable firsthand experience with damage control in modern warships during the 1982 Falklands campaign. But five years later, the U.S. Navy had an embarrassing experience when the *Stark* was hit by an Exocet missile in the Persian Gulf. What is unnerving is that this type of situation constantly repeats itself. Before new systems enter combat, all manner of studies and estimates are made about what they need and what they can do. This is usually off the mark somewhat—that's only human. But sometimes the performance estimates are way off. And even in wartime, remedial action often comes too slowly or inaccurately. Peacetime situations, like those that led to the *Stark*'s problems, are typically worse.

The Future

"Battle management" is one of the latest military buzzwords. For decades, the Soviets were working on "cybernetic" combat-control systems. Their theory was that if information could be passed efficiently enough between troops and commanders, decisions could be made more easily with the help of an optimal solution suggested by a computer. This would have the effect of making your troops more lethal while lowering your losses. The Western approach is basically the same. All of this battle management depends on two technical items: effective communications and efficient computers to quickly sort out all the data. Because of the energetic efforts to jam communications and the relative inexperience in developing computerized "expert systems," there is a lot of uncertainty on how effective these systems would be. Historically, getting the hang of effective combat leadership is a skill largely acquired on the battlefield. Extensive changing of the rules during peacetime creates more chaos in the initial battles.

A more modest, but more likely successful, American approach to sorting out battlefield chaos was first used by the U.S. Marines in 1987, and an enhanced version (the EPLRS) is scheduled for use by the U.S. Army in the early 1990s. This is the PLRS (Position Locator Reporting System), which tackles one of the premier problems of modern warfare: Where is everybody? Platoons tend to stick fairly close together, but individual platoons quickly become scattered all over the battlefield. A battalion has about 20 platoons, a division more than 250. There are actually twice as many separate entities running around, if you include antiaircraft and antitank missile teams, aircraft, individual vehicles, patrols, and so on. PLRS equips the division with 600–900 PLRS user units and up to a dozen base units. The user units are about the same size and weight as portable radios and broadcast a secure (difficult to jam or intercept) signal that base units can use to precisely locate all nearby user units. The system is not perfect; there are several limitations to its use. But even in its present state, and assuming the usual performance degradation in action, it will be a big step forward in clearing out the fog of war. During meeting engagements or surprise attacks, PLRS would quickly give commanders a picture of who is doing what to whom. Reports of enemy contact, particularly approaching aircraft, would enable friendly artillery, sensors, and missiles to be quickly brought to bear.

PLRS would also cut down on losses from friendly fire, particularly since the U.S. Air Force will be able to read the army's PLRS signals. Portable radios were unsung heroes in World War II; PLRS looks capable of doing an even better job in a future war.

There is historical precedent for this. Before World War II, the U.S. Army developed an integrated artillery fire-control system that enabled a forward observer to call in fire from "every gun within range." Since artillery provides most of an army's firepower, this system was a preview of how powerful electronic control systems could be. During the 1991 Gulf War, PLRS got a limited workout with the marines, and another related system, the hand-held, satellite-supported GPS navigation unit, was a big success. The GPS gave users their location to within 25 meters. This allowed for unprecedented accuracy in keeping track of where the troops were. This was particularly crucial in the desert, where there are few landmarks. While PLRS is automatic, the GPS-equipped troops didn't mind using the new "eavesdropping proof" radios to call in their positions. Above (literally) and beyond this is the JSTARS aircraft, which uses a ground-mapping radar that shows vehicles moving on the ground for hundreds of kilometers from the aircraft. JSTARS data can be sent to the ground commanders, who are also using PLRS data. Thus JSTARS and GPS, combined with PLRS, will revolutionize battlefield operations in the coming decades.

However, as more distance separates the major armed forces from their last sizable battles, the opportunities increase for more things to go wrong. The very success of Western forces in the Gulf War puts them under a lot of pressure to not misinterpret the factors contributing to their victory. This effect is compounded by the vast changes in technology. If there is another major war between large, modernized armed forces, there will be a lot of sorting out to do. A lot of needless deaths will occur before everyone gets a good idea of how things are supposed to work.

17

Who Wins

NOBODY WINS, but this is often forgotten. Wars are easy to start, expensive to continue, and difficult to stop. Wars often begin when someone feels that victory is assured. The fighting continues largely because of national and personal pride. Wars end when one or both sides are devastated, demoralized, or, rarely, suddenly enlightened by the absurdity of it all.

Starting Wars

Armed forces are almost always raised for defense. But once you have all this armed strength, there is the temptation to use it. A large dollop of military force encourages nations to be more aggressive in their dealings with others. Military and diplomatic adventures become more common. This causes some wars to start by accident, the result of playing with fire. At other times, the situation becomes quite depraved, with nations doing the "grab what we can and sue for peace" drill. The illusion of military power is not easily given up because of a few battlefield setbacks. Political leaders have followers who are killed and injured in these defeats and demand revenge. Even though leaders know how bad the situation often is, they preach optimism. Otherwise, they could be replaced by less defeatist politicians. Wars acquire a life of their own and just keep going. They are a triumph of hope over experience. Defenders are extremely resilient. Defeat rarely settles anything except the certainty of another round of fighting.

Attitudes are different on the battlefield. For one thing, it's difficult to tell who's winning. This is especially true during combat in this century. Previously, battles rarely lasted more than a day. Larger 20th-century armies faced each other continually, engaging in a lower-level but endless violence that now passes for combat. Results of this carnage are reported by publicity professionals. The endless stream of press releases gives the impression that no one ever loses a battle. Back on the battlefield, if one side really got the worst of it, the troops would decide who won, and the losers would move smartly to the rear, perhaps overrunning their publicity people in the process. Even so, it was usually possible for noncombatants to maintain a reasonable belief in continuing victory. Without knowledge of the big picture, a local disaster could be explained away as an exception to the favorable prospects everywhere else. What soldiers see as victory or defeat varies with where the troops are and what they are doing. Perceptions also vary greatly with one's rank and situation.

Perceptions of Victory in the Foxhole

Troops in modern combat often find themselves in situations where they are forced to fight for survival. Heroism is not always a voluntary act: "A hero is a coward who got cornered." Individuals and small groups fight to survive. More frequently, they avoid fighting to survive. Fire teams, squads, and aircraft crews require a combination of discipline, effective leadership, fear of reprisal, self-delusion, and peer pressure to generate an effective fighting attitude. Ship crews operate in a more controlled situation, where training and technical skill are decisive. These are the conditions that enable one side to prevail. Soldiers recognize that the war will not end until one side or the other can no longer put up any resistance. Individual soldiers know little of the war's progress beyond their immediate vicinity. Combat troops attempt to survive from one day to the next. When there is combat, a soldier's objectives become even more immediate. The troops who do the fighting operate in a very small battlefield. The more dangerous the activity, the more each minor part of that activity becomes an occasion for victory or defeat. Crossing an area possibly covered by enemy fire, sticking your head around a corner, firing a weapon, calculating where the enemy is, and a multitude of other actions constitute the hundreds of little battles the soldier fights. In combat, a participant's concept of victory is very short range. There isn't much choice.

Victory in the Middle

Combat leaders who are not in the middle of the fighting themselves, or command troops they can't see and supervise, have a different perspective. Commanders of platoons, companies, battalions, ships, or aircraft squadrons are primarily concerned with the contributions of their unit to the success of a larger operation. The commander views the unit's contribution to an operation as more important than the survival of any individual. This seemingly callous attitude is one aspect of military operations that is distasteful but necessary. The unavoidable death and destruction of warfare makes for an impersonal attitude in commanders. To grieve for each death or mutilation would quickly make leaders ineffective. A successful combat commander is a strange bird, and normally difficult to spot in peacetime. While individual soldiers consider survival a victory, unit leaders consider success a group activity that often crushes men beneath it.

Historians play down what middle-level commanders do with their time. Studying the brief moments makes for more exciting reading. Correct moves in combat are more clear in hindsight. During the battle, the usual chaos is made worse by inept, unreliable, or incompetent subordinates. Issuing orders for the obvious solution to a combat situation is a futile exercise if those orders cannot be effectively carried out. A common problem is commanders of platoons and companies not knowing their troops very well. A ship captain cannot succeed if he is ignorant of who his sailors are and what they can do. Air forces come to grief when pilots do not develop a bond with their ground crews. Commanders of aircraft units succeed or fail in proportion to how well they know their aircraft and their pilots' capabilities. Ignorance of the capability of one's troops and equipment can be overlooked in peacetime, but becomes painfully apparent during the stress of combat. Commanders at this level are truly middlemen. They are not privy to all the highest-level decisions, nor do they participate in the daily routine of the fighting troops. Yet these officers are directly responsible for carrying out the nation's military policy. Commanders at this level fight a two-front war. They fight the enemy, if somewhat abstractly. They also fight their peers and superiors for scarce resources. Rarely do these commanders have to face the enemy personally. They do regularly confront their own subordinates. If they cannot motivate these subordinate leaders to perform well, they cannot defeat the enemy.

Winning at the Top

At the moment, not many generals and admirals exist who have been in combat *as* generals and admirals. Many saw action as junior officers, which is some help if war comes. But the number of serving officers with combat experience as generals is, at any time, less than one percent of those available. This is a serious problem that is usually overlooked. But it is an issue when a war starts, as a majority of the peacetime generals are found wanting when commanding troops in battle. This has been the experience throughout history. Generals and admirals have fairly substantial egos. The system encourages them. A person in this situation tends to believe he knows what he's doing. Who's going to contradict him? Certainly not some civilian who happens to be the head of state. Competent military leaders at the senior levels prefer to avoid wars. They know the history of people in their position. They also prefer to retire with their honor and reputation intact. They know well the risks of war and that history is unkind to losers. Leaders most effective in command are also aware of their limitations. They know that it is easier to defend than to attack, and want to let some other miscalculating egomaniac start the fight. Inescapably involved in a political activity, generals learn along the way the importance of good public relations. These usually strong-willed men with considerable self-confidence must constantly contend with their military and civilian peers for limited resources. This does not make them venal or any less public-spirited. It does make for a lively exchange of views on what is really needed for defense. Senior commanders fight a war in the shadows, where goals and methods are often lost in a fog of political decision making. In peacetime, they are directed to plan and prepare for a number of potential wars. Sometimes the war they have to fight is one of these; often it is not.

In wartime, generals have a difficult time staying in touch with the results of their orders. Their concept of victory is often more political than military. The general's concept of winning is far removed from that of the soldier in combat. Sometimes a general maintains the goodwill of his troops, sometimes not. The more successful ones do, but no general can succeed if he cannot generate enthusiasm from his subordinate commanders.

Nationalism and War

America has generally been reluctant to get involved in wars. This has been so for several reasons:

1. America is a nation descended from draft dodgers. Most immigrants to America are from nations where war, or the threat of war, made emigration a promising option. So off they went to America, and they brought their distaste for military affairs with them. This is the source of the isolationism still prominent in America.
2. As a democracy, America has a hard time making the decisions necessary to get a country into a war. It took German U-boats killing

U.S. citizens to get America into World War I (at the very end of the war) and Pearl Harbor to bring the United States into World War II (after everyone else had been at it for a year or two). Korea and Vietnam caused such a political ruckus that presidents now think twice about sending off the troops, even for minor events like Grenada and Panama. The Gulf War required a formidable public-relations effort on the part of the government, and there was a lot of pressure on the generals to win and win big.

3. America has less to go to war about than most nations. Protected by two vast oceans and bereft of any significant military threats in their part of the world, few Americans see anything worth fighting for. The Persian Gulf with its oil was one of the few exceptions. Attacks on major U.S. allies such as Japan, Korea, or Europe would also qualify.

Vietnam provided most Americans with a vivid lesson of what happens when the troops are sent to fight a war without most of the population behind them. While one can get the population excited at the beginning of just about any war, if things go badly and there is not a very compelling reason to continue fighting, the population quickly loses enthusiasm. Even during World War II, popular support was beginning to decrease in 1945. One reason for dropping the A-bombs on Japan was because the government did not want to risk the huge casualties an invasion of Japan might have entailed.

This need for popular enthusiasm cuts both ways. During the 1991 Gulf War, the Iraqi people, and most of the Iraqi troops, were not excited about invading an Arab neighbor. Months of sitting in the desert, weeks of U.S. bombing, and a few days of ground fighting were all it took for the vast majority of Iraqi troops to throw their hands up and surrender.

It's much easier to get into a war than it is to keep the troops, and the people, at it.

Winning in the News

Secrecy is a goal governments pursue at all times. During a war, secrecy is a veritable article of faith. The temptation to manipulate the news during a war is frequently overwhelming. The farther away you get from the slaughter, the more optimism replaces reality. Reality is often nonexistent at the highest decision-making levels. This is especially true when you are losing a war. News of what is happening at the fighting front comes down from on high. Some of the most fantastic fiction ever written appears in a nation's media the day before surrender. Correspondents at the front see only a small portion of what is going on, even if they are allowed to wander around. Optimism can easily prevail over any unpleasant reality, especially because "defeatist" journalists are typically quickly replaced. War is such a discouraging process that media manipulation is often the margin of victory. Populations are making many sacrifices, and without encouragement, defeat will soon appear preferable to continued fighting. A common example occurs when the winning side calls upon the loser to surrender, sometimes on favorable terms. A government recognizes that its war effort will not survive long after negotiations are announced. Thus, news of a possible settlement or negotiations is kept secret or disguised. Since Vietnam, governments have come to realize how powerful an effect on public opinion TV coverage can have. The Iraqis certainly recognized this in 1990–91. TV journalists will probably never again have as much of a free hand as they had during the 1960s, and this was borne out in Grenada, Panama, and the Persian Gulf. The proliferation of radios has made it more difficult for governments to completely hide the true nature of the war's progress. Enemy broadcasts can be jammed, or the truth can be mangled by your own media, but enough of the truth always gets through. Despite the energetic, and generally successful, efforts of the United States to keep a lid on the media during the Gulf War, the public still had access to accurate information about what was going on. Military security was kept intact, the reporters were ticked off, and the public was not left in the dark. Managing the news may have become more difficult, but it has become no less important.

Winning After Winning

One generally unrecognized aspect of military affairs that got some exposure in the 1991 Gulf War was the Civil Affairs troops. This military specialty is a 20th-century development and came of age during World War II. The Civil Affairs units deal with civilians in the combat zone and take over government functions in areas recently conquered, or liberated. During World War II, major population areas were rapidly occupied by Allied troops. Naturally, the existing governmental institutions were either destroyed or severely damaged in the process. All those leaderless civilians, many of them refugees or injured, had to be dealt with before they got in the way of the military operations. The Civil Affairs troops were created to do this. Basically, these units were trained to take over the government in battle-torn areas and quickly restore order and relief for the battered civilian population. They also proved to be a key element in a lasting victory. In the immediate aftermath of war, a lot can go wrong, and the population generally blames the winners. Between World War II and the Gulf War, U.S. Civil Affairs units managed to rapidly restore economic and social order in the fought-over areas. The civilians did not forget, and this memory has contributed to the lasting peace since World War II.

Theory and Practice

The psychological distance between troops and generals reached a peak during World War I. During that war, especially between 1915 and 1918, most leaders were unaware of how wretched a time the troops were having in the trenches. Since then, generals have attempted to eliminate this distance, if only because of the unrest and rebellion the World War I situation brought about in 1917. Not every general has a knack for keeping his wits about him under fire. Since 1918, combat has become more spread out, although this has largely been overcome by the use of helicopters to get up to the front. Reconnaissance aircraft and satellites can now send back detailed television pictures in real time. Commanders who avail themselves of opportunities to get up front and see things firsthand also expose themselves to somewhat more danger. Future wars will see long-range rockets and aircraft looking for headquarters to obliterate. This will ensure that life in the rear is not nearly as secure as it once was. Long-range weapons and the more diffuse nature of the battlefield has increased the degree of constant insecurity all troops must endure. The absence of a well-defined front line makes everyone more nervous: Current wars still have a "front," but tend to be more fluid and densely populated by helicopters and robotic weapons. Weapons may have limitless possibilities, but the troops don't. Exhausted and reluctant soldiers slow things down to a more tolerable pace.

Nuclear and chemical weapons were not enthusiastically received by combat troops. These weapons are not directed against the enemy so much as they are unleashed on the enemy. Such indiscriminate destruction causes uncertainty in an already ambiguous effort. As the implications of this have sunk in, there has been a move away from using nuclear and chemical weapons. These munitions will never disappear, but the owners are increasingly less disposed to use them.

The Future

Micromanagement and media management are the future trends that will determine who thinks he is winning. Micromanagement, most notable when the chief of state directs the actions of a platoon, first became possible during the Vietnam War. This meddlesome custom was most noticeable in the United States, where the technology and lack of military tradition combined to make presidents into platoon leaders. Most other major nations know enough to leave battlefield leadership to the commanders on the scene. In light of the Vietnam experience, the United States also backed away from micromanagement. However, current and future communications capabilities make the temptation real, and a severe case of anxiety at the highest levels can now be sated by picking up the phone and calling the fighting troops directly. These same communications capabilities also serve the useful purpose of giving battlefield commanders more control. The current generation of U.S. recon satellites has the capability of showing moving and still pictures in real time. Woe be it to any platoon commander who screws up on camera. As the technology becomes cheaper and more reliable, micromanagement will spread, or at least the temptation. During the 1991 Gulf War, U.S. commanders, many the victims of micromanagement while junior officers in Vietnam, refrained from returning the favor. But the temptation remains. Even guerrilla units are often equipped with portable radios.

Innovations in training have improved the attitudes toward who can win, and to what degree, on the battlefield. The American "wired battlefield," where troops, weapons, and equipment carry sensors that allow for "hits" and "damage" quickly drive home how easily one can become a statistic on the battlefield. Some commanders, however, have still not fully accepted the fact that when something is lost on the battlefield, it is gone, and it isn't coming back. The tendency during training is to quickly resurrect casualties and reintroduce them as "replacements." Real combat doesn't work that way, and if you don't learn to cope with the losses in peacetime, you'll have to learn the hard way on the battlefield.

The art and science of promoting one's beliefs and ideas through the media continues to grow in power and effectiveness. In warfare, these media campaigns increasingly decide whether or not there will be a war, and if there is one, how long it will last. The "will to fight" can be sold like cornflakes, and increasingly it is and very effectively at that. You can look forward to this year's wars being promoted as effectively as the latest consumer products.

18

What Armed Forces Do in Peacetime

MOST SOLDIERS SPEND their entire careers without seeing combat. Even if there is a major war, most people in the military do not have a combat job. In other words, for most people in uniform, their job is little different than a civilian occupation. There is a lot of work in the military that has no exact counterpart in the civilian world. And military people will often pull more overtime, have to salute their superiors, and be subject to a more rigid code of conduct than civilians. The American military is also unique in that it moves its people around the world every few years. In most nations, troops are assigned to a unit and rarely leave one location for their entire career. On the positive side, military jobs are generally more secure, being a form of civil service.

Combat and combat-support troops will spend a lot of their time running about the countryside practicing violence. All troops will devote most of their time to maintaining equipment and learning new skills. Noncombat troops follow a workday routine little different from civilians'. Less wealthy armies will put the troops to work on nonmilitary tasks: public works, farming, and the like.

The Daily Routine

Unmarried troops customarily live in barracks. Depending on the nation's wealth, these range from crudely heated barns with no plumbing to

Western college-style dormitories. Married troops, usually NCOs and officers, live with their families in government housing or private homes near the military base. Troops serving overseas often do so without families. In this case, the officer and NCO barracks are more plush than troop accommodations. Quality of housing varies with rank, as one would expect. Some navies have additional housing ashore for unmarried sailors; a few put the troops up in ships even when they are in port. The day normally begins at an early hour, 5:00 to 6:00 A.M. There is at least one assembly of each company-size unit each day where announcements are made or a head count taken. Some units do this several times a day. The daily routine is set by a long-established schedule. Meals, taken in large dining halls, are at fixed times.

Sailors at sea run a different routine, customarily one to four hours of work ("on watch") followed by eight hours to themselves. Often much of their personal time is usurped for other vital activities. When a ship is practicing for combat, its sailors are lucky to get four hours' sleep a day. Western armies tend to require five or six eight-hour workdays a week. Russian-style forces schedule every waking hour for six or seven days a week. The more restrictive the schedule, the more it tends to be abused. The stricter armies tend to have more troops ending up in prisoner units. In the West, workdays are generally nine to five (or 8:00 A.M. to 4:00 P.M.). In Russian-style armed forces, only the officers are given any leeway to come and go as they please.

The regular schedule is often by "alerts" and field exercises, primarily in combat units. Here, the entire unit must quickly turn out as if for combat. Some noncombat units will also go on field exercises or otherwise work longer hours in support of the combat troops. The alerts merely test a unit's ability to be ready for combat on short notice. Field exercises range from a day to a week or more. This is as close as peacetime units get to combat conditions. Night training also disrupts the regular routine. Perhaps once a year, entire divisions might operate in the field as they would in wartime. This is very expensive; thus, there is a temptation to avoid it or to cut corners. One of the advantages of the six months U.S. forces were in the desert before the 1991 Gulf War ground offensive was the opportunity for the divisions to practice together under wartime conditions. Armed forces in less wealthy nations do fewer field exercises and send their ships to sea and fly their aircraft less frequently. All these activities are expensive. Armies in these countries, including Russia, will often send the troops out to help with economic emergencies. Helping with the harvest, tending vegetable gardens, or helping to repair the damage wrought by natural disasters is common. This last task is performed by nearly every nation's troops. Poor nations tend to have more devastating natural calamities and thus rely on troops more.

Armed-forces routines vary from country to country. Western nations are the most easygoing. The Russian system, often adopted by Third World nations, is severe and regimented. When you are in a Russian-style army, there's no mistaking where you are.

Keeping Score

Armed forces exist to make war, yet they cannot do this in peacetime. This presents a problem in evaluating a force's capabilities in peacetime. The problem is an ancient one. The enduring solution, inspection, is almost as old as organized combat itself. The Inspector General system is only a few hundred years old and is currently used by most armed forces. A separate bureaucracy, the Inspector General (IG), conducts regular and surprise inspections on all units. The IG inspection is generally an annual affair, and the careers of commanders rise or fall based on their unit's performance. In between these annual horrors, daily, weekly, and monthly inspections of varying severity occur. Inspections don't just evaluate the completeness and readiness of unit personnel, weapons, and equipment, but also attempt to assess potential unit combat performance. Inspections are also held during field exercises. Units are rated on how well they perform battlefield tasks. Some of the mundane matters examined are how quickly a unit can move from one location to another, how well they camouflage their vehicles, and whether field fortifications are prepared adequately. Hundreds of skills and procedures must be checked.

The IG system does not always work at peak efficiency for two reasons. First, the items to be checked are an ever-changing list. Part of this is to be expected—new equipment and tactics require new inspection criteria. It takes a while before an efficient inspection procedure is found for new items. This begets the second problem: the urge to cheat. Inspectors tend to set standards that the troops and their limited budget cannot meet consistently. Because everyone's promotions depend on looking good, there is an irresistible urge to fudge a bit. Actually, there tends to be a lot of hanky-panky. The only incentive to be honest is a potential advantage in combat. But battle may never come, while peacetime promotions are right around the corner for the creative scorekeeper.

Characteristics of Peacetime Armed Forces

All peacetime armed forces share certain key characteristics. What is interesting about these traits is that they are now widely known outside the uniformed services.

1. *Short Memories.* Armed forces tend to remember no more of their past than their oldest members. History presents an endless cycle of armies sinking into peacetime routine that prepares them less for

war than for the establishment of another bureaucracy. War comes, and the bureaucracy is transformed into a fighting organization through a bloody and expensive process. The war ends, and the combat veterans, as long as they remain, maintain a sense of what must be done. The veterans age and depart, and the cycle begins again. There is also a generation gap in many armed forces, especially those that depend on conscription. Conscript armies generally consist of only 15–30 percent long-term professionals. Volunteer armies comprise 40–70 percent personnel who stay beyond their initial three-to-six-year term. New recruits will be 18–21 years old. The average of the long-term professionals (lifers) will be 10 to 15 years older than that. Volunteer forces will narrow that gap quite a bit, and create a greater sense of shared values. This is an important, but frequently underestimated, advantage.

2. *Fear of Flying.* Several things that ought to be done in peacetime are avoided for various reasons. Exercises using live ammunition provide more realistic training, but they do cause more casualties. This is often unpalatable in peacetime. Russian-style armies do a lot of live-fire work, but they are less subject to adverse public opinion, and the casualties are not reported in the press.

3. *Draftees Versus Regulars.* Conscription is preferable if you must have (or simply want to have) a large armed force. This has several advantages. It is cheaper, as you don't have to pay salaries competitive with the civilian job market. It exposes all classes of society to military service, and to each other. This doesn't work if the wealthy are allowed to buy their way out. High-performance standards are nice in theory but difficult to maintain in practice. You need a strong tradition concerning what warfare is all about and the ability to attract top people as officers.

4. *Quality Versus Quantity.* Even the wealthiest nations are torn between buying more equipment or investing in maintaining and using what they already have. The size of the armed forces and their actual combat power are not the same thing. However, size is more visible than power. Buy more tanks; put more men in uniform. These you can see and count. Training is expensive, especially firing those expensive weapons frequently. The results cannot be seen in peacetime, although this type of expenditure pays off in combat. Nations tend to have a lot of troops and equipment that are not being used together. Training on the cheap makes it easier to get troops killed when the shooting starts.

5. *Who Is the Enemy?* Without a war to settle the arguments, solutions to doctrine and equipment-design debates must be found elsewhere. Often there is no elsewhere, and the debates wander aimlessly. Equipment design and doctrine development also wander, to everyone's detriment. It's not entirely the intelligence agency's fault for

not coming up with a convincing evaluation of what the enemy forces are all about. The military is an instrument of the political process, and must periodically change course in response to political trends. The military budget is often a political football, largely because there is no way of shutting down the paranoid legislators with unequivocal information on what the potential opponents are up to. All of this is an ancient problem. Some nations deal with it more effectively than others. The United States is not one of them, and the Soviet Union was not much better.

6. *Paper Bullets and Ticket Punching.* The paper bullets of peacetime administrative combat tend to make cowards of officers who would more bravely face the metal variety. Death in battle provides recognition for valiant service; dismissal during a bureaucratic dispute is rather more ignominious and just as fatal to one's career. It's a case of the pen, indeed, being mightier than the sword. Making waves is not the key to peacetime promotion; getting the right assignments and not rocking the boat is. This is similar to combat, where some jobs are deemed more important than others. Unlike combat, values placed on choice peacetime assignments are often more political than practical. In combat, what doesn't work becomes painfully evident rather quickly. In peacetime, combat effectiveness is something more talked about than acted upon. If you want to get ahead, go along. The warrior mentality is usually out of place, and often out of a job as well.

National Differences

More than 100 nations have significant armed forces. There are only three general models for running these combat organizations: Russian, Western, and Third World. The Russian style is characterized by the use of conscription, few real NCOs, and an officer class that holds it all together. Other habits include the reluctance to use equipment. Soviet doctrine insists on having the maximum amount of weapons and equipment available for combat. Because of the enormous turnover in troops, nearly 40 percent each year, most training time is devoted to basics. Crude simulators are used more than actual equipment. Discipline is strict, and amenities are few. Except for the privileged officers, service is boring and physically demanding. Low morale, theft, abuse of recruits, and alcoholism are major problems. Much of the stealing goes to purchase vodka. The dedication of the officers and strict discipline enable Russian forces to get moving in short order. However, spotty training and strict adherence to drills and regulations create a rather wooden battlefield manner. Ironically, these are the patterns that have persisted in the Russian armed forces for centuries. Communism has had little effect on them, although the end of the Cold

War and the perceived superiority of the Western style have caused many Russian officers to demand wide-ranging reforms.

Western-style armies are characterized by more volunteers, competent NCOs, and extensive use of equipment in peacetime. Conscription is still used by many nations, but is not nearly as disruptive as in the Russian armed forces. Western nations also go for more technology and wider use of it. Western doctrine is also less bloody-minded, trying to minimize friendly casualties.

Third World nations fall into two broad groups—those with a long military tradition and those without. Nations like China and India have had organized armed forces far longer than Western nations and have maintained these traditions. Another divider among Third World nations is wealth. A few oil-rich nations can afford all the high-tech weapons they desire. Most Third World nations have to get along with what little they can afford. Those nations with a military tradition can attract qualified recruits and turn them into excellent soldiers. The more technical services, air forces and navies, suffer somewhat because the nations cannot afford the expense of using aircraft and ships enough to give their crews experience.

The Bad Drive Out the Good

People join the military because of patriotism, adventure, a desire to render public service, careerism, a need to accomplish something. People of vastly differing abilities join. Too many of the best, especially the "warriors," leave in peacetime. The "warrior" and the "manager" are two distinct types. The warrior tends to be uncompromising, always striving for unambiguous results. A warrior searching for trial by combat leaves the peacetime military for the "real" world. Battles conducted with balance sheets and market shares are unambiguous indicators. Those left behind are the ones who pay more attention to career than combat. The end result of this careerism is a decline in the quality of leadership.

When the real conflict comes, the pinstripe soldiers often return, many from reserve units. Fortunately, many with uncommon determination and patience remain in the military. Their critical leadership staves off defeat until the nation's strength can be militarized. The pool of good combat leadership in the active military varies for each service and nation. Navies and air forces retain more warriors. Flying and working a warship are essentially the same in peace or war. Sailors and pilots can test many of their wartime skills without a war. Some nations give greater status to the military than others. If a country takes its military very seriously, then the military has an easier time attracting high-quality leaders. Also, political considerations carry less weight than professional military judgment under these conditions.

Theory and Practice

Most soldiers are young males, frequently teenagers. They are generally away from their families for the first time. When not being shouted at or shot at, these guys tend to horniness and boredom. Playing with weapons and chasing the local women are looked upon as both fun and exciting. Venereal disease is a common affliction of soldiers and often accounts for the majority of noncombat casualties. When women are not available, the troops will go after alcohol or drugs, or each other. Managing armed teenagers recently liberated from parental supervision has never been easy. During the 20th century, with its largely more indulged and aware adolescents, the control problem has gotten worse. Armies that can afford it try to use as few teenagers as possible in peacetime. In wartime, it's a different story, because you're either working them round the clock or getting them killed off before they can cause too much trouble. However, armed forces are at peace most of the time. Those that still depend on conscripts therefore have serious problems. The Soviets essentially turned their military bases into prison camps, with very low pay, constant activity, and negligible access to the outside world. Still, their troops manage to get alcohol, either from vehicle systems or by secretly trading equipment to civilians for it. In one glaring example, a Soviet tank crew in Czechoslovakia got lost on a field exercise, stumbled across a country inn, and traded their tank to the innkeeper for all the vodka they could drink and carry. The drunken troops were found and the innkeeper caught before he was able to cut the tank up for scrap and parts.

The successful approach to these problems is to develop good NCOs and officers and keep the troops busy. This combination is rarely achieved. Combat troops in particular are hard to handle. The noncombat forces generally skim off the brightest and most able recruits, leaving the infantry with a higher proportion of problem cases. The noncombat troops also have more useful and interesting work to do than infantry without a war to fight. Volunteer forces handle this problem by filling the combat ranks with a lot of people who want to be there. The Soviets handled this problem by putting all real and potential troublemakers in labor battalions. Undergoing six days a week of manual labor takes the mischief out of most youngsters. Unfortunately for the Soviets, they had the most manpower-intensive armed forces in the world and not enough need for labor battalions to take care of all the slackers. Reports coming across from immigrants and the Soviet military press indicated that the personnel problems in the Soviet armed forces constantly went from bad to worse and eventually contributed to the collapse of the Soviet Union.

Western nations that still rely on the draft cope by keeping the period of service short, between 12 and 24 months, and paying close attention to troop morale. If this means a lot of long-haired Dutch infantrymen wearing earrings, it doesn't matter as long as they can perform (and they usually do). The Dutch issued hairnets to the mechanics and banned jewelry on the job. The nations with volunteer forces have the age-old tool for troop control: Do the job or become unemployed. This works wonders to stimulate performance in peacetime. Volunteer forces are not without their problems. Long-term troops mean wives and families. This tends to divide the attention of the troops, even though their primary loyalty is, in theory, to the armed forces. In practice, there is an above-average divorce rate and a lot of alcoholism. It's not generosity that causes volunteer forces to offer retirement after 20 years. Although many troops stay beyond 20, this practice does serve as a safety valve. Navies have particular problems with the long periods of sea duty. Especially in Western navies, sailors can be away for up to a year at a time. The situation is worst in the American Navy. This is especially difficult with the ballistic-missile subs and their crews of highly skilled technicians. Serious problems are encountered trying to keep these people in the service. The original idea was to have two crews per sub, but even with that, you still have six-month cruises to contend with. This, however, is nothing compared to the Soviet (and now Russian) problems with radiation poisoning and naval bases in arctic areas. Moreover, Russia must use some conscripts and generally less skilled crews for its nuclear ships.

Russia is also a prime example of another problem with armed forces: the military looking on itself as a separate society. Even though over two thirds of Russia's personnel are conscripts, the other third are officers and senior NCOs who make up a distinct social class. Many of these people come from families that have been in the military for many generations. The Soviets attacked the problem with large numbers of political officers representing the Communist party. Currently, Russia appeals to the patriotism and professionalism of its ex-Soviet officers and hopes for the best. Other nations cope as best they can and hope the soldiers will not get too many ideas about running the country.

The Future

One major trend is reducing the size of armed forces in order to make them more professional and combat-capable. Another growing trend is the use of troops for nonmilitary tasks. As one would suspect, few nations follow both of these trends at once. The Chinese, in an effort to modernize their armed forces and economy, discharged nearly a million troops in the early 1980s and several hundred thousand more in the early 1990s. The Soviets began a similar excision in 1990, and this was carried further after the demise of the Soviet Union. Also, despite their drive toward professionalism and combat capability, Russian and Chinese troops also spend much of their time on nonmilitary tasks like tending vegetable gardens and helping out civilian industries.

A problem common in nations with bustling economies is a shortage of people willing to put up with military service unless suitable financial inducements are made. Weapons and equipment cost is growing even faster. When the cuts must be made, they tend to be of people. While there may be more troops worldwide because of all the low-cost light infantry running around in less affluent nations, the industrialized powers are headed toward fewer people in uniform. Indeed, another variation on this trend is the tendency to use civilians for skilled technical posts. Even large warships tend to go to sea with several dozen civilian technicians performing jobs no uniformed personnel can be trained and/or retained for. Another tendency is that the further we get from the last major war, the more unreal peacetime conditions in the military become. As civilian living standards increase, troops expect better living conditions during military service, and in combat. This is raising the cost of war, and troop morale, throughout the world.

PART FIVE

SPECIAL
WEAPONS

MODERN TECHNOLOGY HAS created entire new classes of weapons. Most of these high-tech wonders never see combat before they are "improved" and replaced with new models. These new devices are potentially the most decisive contrivances ever sent into combat. Some are thought too lethal to be unleashed. Only time will tell.

19

The Electronic Battlefield

COMMUNICATIONS, AND the control of information, are the glue that holds armed forces together, that turns a potential mob into an organized fighting force. During the U.S. Civil War (1861–65), electronic communications first came into wide military use. Initially, only telegraph was used. But this allowed forces hundreds of miles apart to communicate almost instantly. In some cases, wire was strung throughout a battle area so that a commander could instantly receive reports and issue orders instead of relying on messengers. Fifty years later, World War I saw smaller units and some aircraft using wireless telegraph. Less than 20 years after that, during World War II, infantry units were manpacking their own wireless telephones. Most aircraft and tanks had radios. Today, more than 10 percent of all soldiers operate some sort of electronic device. Not all are radios; some are sensors. And some are computers. A lot has happened since the battlefield was first electrified in the 1860s.

Command, Control, Communications, and Intelligence (C³I)

Warfare is a complicated business, and the introduction of electronics didn't simplify things. In the decades since World War II, there evolved a concept known as C³I. This implied that if a commander had sufficient quantities of communications and intelligence fed to him electronically, he could communicate with his subordinate units electronically and control them with heretofore-unknown efficiency. The theory has not held up well in practice through most of this century. Indeed, it has not been attempted in a war with both sides using a lot of the latest electronic gear. The Arab-Israeli War and the 1991 Gulf War came pretty close, and things got gummed up pretty bad in the first week or so. Jamming and using everything at once under combat conditions introduced unanticipated traumas to the undertaking. Undismayed, commanders have redoubled their efforts to make C³I work. This is little different from attempts in the past to make new technologies work in wartime. Success comes eventually. It did in the Gulf War, as Iraqi jamming had limited effect and U.S. C³I capabilities finally delivered the degree of control generals have sought for centuries.

The original use of military electronic communications was nothing more than adaption of existing civilian telegraph resources. The military had made no effort to prepare "militarized" systems beforehand. World War I was also largely an improvise-as-you-go situation. Going into World War II, there were more custom military systems, especially for the control of artillery and aircraft. Both these systems required considerable debugging and refining before they became practical on the battlefield.

The latest systems have three major problems:

First, they are complex and in a constant state of flux as new features are added and existing ones are repaired.

Second, the commanders and staff who will use these systems don't have experience with them, particularly under the chaotic and uncertain conditions of combat. Many portions of these systems will be randomly destroyed in combat. Unanticipated technical problems will crop up. The results of all these problems, and their solutions, will not be known until the battle is fought. Finally, there is the false security one obtains from seeing the situation neatly displayed on a computer terminal. The real world is not that neat, and the users will have to learn how to relate the electronic version of the battle with what is really happening.

Commanders had good reason to be nervous about what would happen when they tried to run a war with all these C³I goodies. This happened in the 1991 Gulf War when the U.S. JSTARS aircraft gave commanders the last link in the electronic chain of control that had been building for more than a century. For the first time in history, the commanders could see units moving, in real time, across an area hundreds of square miles in size. The catch was that the images on the computer screen didn't positively identify whose units they were. There were some anxious moments as U.S. and British divisions almost collided with guns blazing. This happened before, but some frantic radio conversations sorted out who was who and prevented a repetition of a common 20th-century occurrence of friendly-fire losses. The next major war will see wider use of this technology, and the danger that the next opponent will have an electronic means to muddy the picture once more.

Electronic Warfare

Shortly after the first military messages went over the wire, other soldiers saw ways to use this dependence to their advantage. Electronic warfare was initially crude. Cutting the wire or listening in were effective. Later attempts were made to send false messages. During World War I, codes were used, and regularly broken. Radio direction finders were used, and microphones were planted on the battlefield to detect enemy activity. Dummy radio traffic was used to deceive enemy intelligence analysts.

By the end of World War II, electronic warfare had become a major factor in combat planning. Major offensives were not planned without drawing up a communications deception plan. It wasn't enough to declare radio silence; the enemy would know something was up. Dummy radio traffic was established. Enemy radars and navigation devices were jammed or deceived. Since World War II, electronic warfare has matured into a decisive weapon. Tests have shown that units become aimless and unresponsive when hit with effective jamming and electronic deception. Oddly enough, none of the major armed forces have yet had an opportunity to use current electronic-warfare techniques on each other. These imposing systems have been used on minor countries with devastating effect. American aircraft over Vietnam and Israel in the Middle East wars were extensive and devastating examples. In 1991, the Iraqis were able to use some of their EW equipment, but not enough to have any effective impact. Peacetime applications of EW to field exercises have often been catastrophic in their effectiveness. When both sides can use electronic warfare on each other at full blast, it is expected that the effect will be similar to chemical or nuclear weapons. Not so much in terms of direct casualties, of course. But the confusion and disorientation are expected to be massive. Given the various good reasons for not using chemical or nuclear weapons in a major power war, electronic warfare may well be the most overwhelming new entry to the battlefield of the future.

Russia takes electronic warfare seriously. In theory, it is less dependent on continuous radio communication than Western forces. Soviet ground forces' doctrine was to point their combat divisions in a certain direction and turn them loose. They were expected to keep going until they reached their objectives or burned out in the attempt. The Soviets continued to place great emphasis on nonelectronic communications like flares, flags, and messengers. They also favored field telephones when in static positions. Their air-force and naval units were arguably more dependent on radio than Western counterparts. Moreover, throughout the Soviet armed forces there was a tradition of not doing anything untoward without detailed instructions from the high command. Soviet units practiced operating without radio in field exercises. However, their own military writers criticized these same field exercises for being stage-managed and not representative of an actual battlefield. In the future, the greatest danger from Russian-built, and exported, EW gear and doctrine is its use by Third World nations against Western forces. The Soviet Union may be gone, but its EW legacy will be with us for some time to come.

While all armed forces may find their dependence on electronic equipment threatened by electronic warfare, there are also electronic solutions. Again, computers come into play. One of the more common solutions to jamming is the use of computer-controlled frequency hopping. This has the transmitter constantly switch frequencies at high speed. As it is very difficult to jam all frequencies, a frequency hopper will generally get the message delivered.

The problem with defending against electronic warfare is that the solutions are implemented on paper and frequently never get any further. Russia turns out a lot of crude EW equipment. Most Western EW gear stays in the laboratory. Only in the air and at sea is Western EW equipment getting into the field in quantity. A future major ground war could be very interesting. Even ground wars against Third World armies will be fraught with unforeseen consequences.

Components of Electronic Warfare

Electronic warfare is not a simple matter. It consists of several distinct activities. Each of these is quite complex in itself, and understanding some of this complexity gives you an idea of how vast a subject electronic warfare is.

ESM (ELECTRONIC SURVEILLANCE MEASURES)

Just keeping track of the enemy's electronic devices has become a major operation, especially since no one knows exactly how everyone's electronic equipment will interact until there is a sustained period of use. Such use does not occur in peacetime, when the EW equipment is used infrequently for training and testing. All electronic equipment has a unique electronic signature. Even equipment that is not broadcasting will appear a certain way to various sensors like radar or sonar. Thus, a critical peacetime function is to determine what these signatures are. For this reason, navies and air forces devote a significant amount of their time to tracking other nations' capabilities. As a counter to ESM, equipment is disguised where possible. Signals can be varied in some circumstances. For equipment that is detected by shape and composition, like aircraft and ships, their shape and substance can be designed to minimize detection. This is the essence of the stealth technology that the United States is applying to a number of vehicles, especially aircraft. Small ships, aircraft, helicopters, and vehicles loaded with sensors do most of the collecting. Low-flying satellites are useful for catching signals deep inside a nation's territory. Drones and RPV aircraft are used also, plus robotic sensors that are left on the ground or sea bottom.

Collection involves more than sensors. Recording devices, foreign-language interpreters, and signal-processing equipment also come into play. Computers are increasingly crucial in sifting through the ocean of data swept up. Huge libraries of signals are collected, analyzed, and boiled down to manageable amounts of data friendly troops and weapons can use. ESM has been so successful that one entire class of sensors, active sensors, has become endangered. Active sensors detect things by broadcasting a signal. When this signal bounces off something, the sensor detects the bounce-back and knows something is out there. This is the basis of radar, which broadcasts microwaves, and sonar, which broadcasts sound. Because of the signal being broadcast, a passive sensor can detect it. Passive sensors just listen. Because active sensor signals must reach an object in sufficient force to bounce something back, a vehicle carrying a passive sensor will detect a vehicle carrying an active sensor first. This is what happens when you use a radar detector in your car to detect police speed-trap radars. You usually have time to slow down before your illegal speed is detected by the police radar. As users of these devices well know, there is constant competition to come up with better radars and countermeasures. Passive sensors are the hot item in research and development these days, and for obvious reasons. Passive sensors are nearly impossible to detect. Passive sensors can also pick up a wide variety of signals. Infrared sensors can detect heat, including something as faint as body heat or the hot skin of an approaching jet aircraft.

Photography is also an increasingly effective passive sensor. Using a TV camera-type device to capture images and heat, and applying a lot of computer-processing muscle, these sensors can see at night, through fog and smoke. Satellites and aircraft are major users of these image sensors. As image sensors get smaller, they are found more in ground vehicles. Modern Western tanks use such devices.

Sonar is not the only form of sound sensor. Indeed, the earliest application of this technology was known as *sound ranging,* which detected the range of distant artillery by counting the seconds between the flash of the gun firing and when the sound reached you. Sound travels though the air at a fairly standard rate (the "speed of sound"). This century-old technique has been coupled with signal processing to create passive sensors for ground troops. In the same circumstance, often within the same unit, seismic sensors are also used. These listen to sound transmitted through the earth by approaching vehicles. Sound and seismic sensors are often packaged together with a radio transmitter and dropped behind enemy lines. They can be delivered by aircraft, artillery, shell, or by hand. There they wait for some activity. When something is detected, a short, high-intensity burst of compressed data is radioed back. This method of transmission is used in order to avoid enemy detection of the sensor. These sensors are frequently designed to resemble local vegetation. Sometimes these sensors are easier to find. During the Vietnam War, an early form of this sensor was designed to resemble a bamboo plant. The ones that were not used in Vietnam were shipped to Germany. These were eventually replaced before we could find out if Soviet troops would recognize bamboo plants as out of place in a pine forest.

In the last 10 years, sensors have been combined more frequently with weapons. Naval mines have been using these techniques for over 40 years. Now, miniaturized electronics have enabled land mines to have their own sensors. Vehicles, especially heavy ones like tanks, make a lot of noise. Some mines currently available can detect when a tank is moving over it and fire a small armor-piercing charge through the thin bottom armor of the vehicle. Other systems actually fire a mortarlike projectile, which in turn detects an armored vehicle and fires a projectile through the thinner top armor. Where previously you would use several tons of mines to destroy one tank, you now need only several hundred pounds' worth. This is a twentyfold increase in efficiency. Although the new mines are 10 times as expensive, weight is the critical factor on the battlefield. You can't carry a lot onto the battlefield; every pound counts.

Passive sensors are becoming the dominant form. They are limited in their range compared to active sensors. But they have the invaluable advantage of concealing their presence from the enemy. Sensor projects in the West are capitalizing on technological advantages in electronics and computers to give passive sensors greater range. Moreover, computer-controlled weapons can be radically changed more quickly by reprogramming the instructions. Change will come even faster on the current and future battlefield.

ECM (ELECTRONIC COUNTERMEASURES)

Electronic weapons begat electronic defenses. This wide range of techniques deceives or disrupts electronic devices. Jamming is one of the more obvious forms of ECM. This consists of broadcasting a loud signal on the same frequency the enemy is using for communications, or whatever. More sophisticated jamming makes the enemy equipment appear defective or makes it show erroneous data. Chaff jamming is done with a cloud of metallic strips. This makes radar think the chaff cloud is the target. Flares do the same for heat-seeking (infrared) sensors. Electronic noisemakers draw missiles with passive sensors that home in on active sensors.

ECCM (ELECTRONIC COUNTER COUNTERMEASURES)

There are various techniques for dealing with ECM. One of the unsophisticated forms is to simply crank up the transmitter and burn through the enemy jamming. A more practical variation is burst transmission: The message is compressed and transmitted in a very powerful but brief burst of energy. Automated frequency hopping has become a standard high-tech solution to jamming and signal homing. Two radios with the same built-in computer rapidly switch frequencies as they transmit and receive. Computer software can also be used to reconstruct any portions of the messages that do get jammed. To jam a frequency hopper requires jamming a large number of frequencies. This takes a lot of equipment and power, two things in short supply on the battlefield.

Another straightforward form of ECCM is to give missiles more than one type of homing system. It's expensive, but some missiles have radar, radar homing, and heat-seeking devices. Of course, all three can be jammed.

SIGNAL PROCESSING

This has become a large and crucial component of electronic warfare. "Signal processing" is a ten-dollar word for a computer doing what humans have been doing for many years. For example, a photo-interpreter recognizes patterns representing certain types of enemy fortifications or installations. Thousands of years ago, scouts learned to recognize whose army a horse belonged to by the shape of the tracks left behind. You can still do this with tanks, by examining the thread marks they make in the ground. And so on. You get the idea. When computers came along, it was possible to let the machine keep track of the patterns. In addition, more complex patterns could be identified and remembered. The sounds made by ships or the signals broadcast by radars all are as unique as finger-prints. And computers now take care of identifying fingerprints, as well as thumb and palm prints and even retina (eye) patterns, for security systems. As the computers get smaller, it is possible to do signal processing where previously there wasn't sufficient space, like the guidance systems of missiles or the fire-control mechanism of tanks and ships.

The first dramatic use of computer signal processing was in passive sonar. The ocean is a noisy place, further confused by layers of water with different temperatures, which makes sound bounce around and become distorted. Sorting out the sound of a submarine from the mackerel gossip and merchant ships was first accomplished by signal processing. Vast libraries of sounds are kept in the computers' memories, and updated periodically, so that individual ships can be identified, as well as their course and speed. Similar libraries for aircraft and ground combat allow the identification of signals quickly and accurately. The air force uses signal processing to identify radar and radio signals and enable aircraft to avoid antiaircraft weapons and interceptors. Targets can also be found more easily, as well as areas covered by friendly radars. Ground units use signal processing for air defense and intelligence gathering.

A variation on signal processing is traffic analysis, the study of past patterns of enemy messages and sensor use. For different operations, like preparations for attack or defense, different patterns are watched for.

One final aspect of signal processing is that the substantial advantage of Western nations' lead over other nations in computer technology makes this weapon largely a Western one.

EDM (ELECTRONIC DECEPTION MEASURES)

These are an assortment of techniques to deceive the enemy. Transmitters can be set up solely to divert the enemy's attention or simulate the presence of one of your units. Simulated message traffic can indicate a unit is going to attack, when it is really going to move elsewhere. The oldest deception technique is sending messages in code. This field, cryptography, is almost entirely dependent on electronic devices. Computers devise the codes and attempt to break them. Sensors continually monitor enemy codes looking for new variations to be broken. Simpler, cheaper, and often more effective methods exist based on how long you broadcast. The more modern radars are accurate enough to stay on for a few seconds and then use that "snapshot" for up to a minute or more before turning the radar on again. These short bursts of radar usage can be powerful enough to overcome most jamming. This is another example of how simplicity is often the most effective solution.

Offensive Electronic Warfare

When a force is attacking, electronic warfare provides a number of critical functions:

Target Acquisition. Sensors, ESM, and signal processing aid the attempt to identify the activity, strength, and position of enemy units. From this list, critical targets are selected for attack.

Disruption of C^3 (Command, Control, and Communications). Jamming of enemy communications, sending of false messages, and destruction of enemy communications' equipment prevent your opponent from effectively opposing your attack.

Deception. EDM deceives the enemy about your real intentions before you lower the boom.

Defensive Electronic Warfare

In electronic warfare, defense is far more important than offense. Because everyone is so dependent on radios and sensors, disruption of these devices can be devastating. Fortunately, EW does not disrupt radio and sensor use continually. Jamming equipment is expensive and attracts a lot of unwanted attention when it is used. Antiradiation missiles have an easy time homing in on jammers that broadcast continually. Jammers are generally used when crucial operations are under way, primarily offensives. Defenders have several remedies available.

Alternative Communications. Alternatives to radios are available: messengers, field and regular telephones, flares, etc. All of these are either slower or less flexible than radio. To plan for their use, you must be prepared to adjust your operations accordingly. Alternative sensors are also less powerful. These include more lookouts, trip flares, minefields, and so on. The important thing is to be prepared for the loss of normal radio and sensor capability. Being caught by surprise is the worst possible situation for the defender.

Communications Discipline. Because ESM is the one electronic-warfare activity carried out continually, it is the one you must fear the most. If your troops get into the habit of using radio and sensors in the same predictable way all the time, your opponent will soon know about it. The enemy will be able to pinpoint your key installations and units and hit or jam them effectively in the opening stages of an attack.

ESM. Electronic surveillance is critical because if you do it right, you will know what your opponent is up to. Not being surprised is more than half of an effective electronic defense.

Equipment Hardening. Nuclear weapons release a pulse of electromagnetic energy (EMP, or Electromagnetic Pulse) that will disable or destroy electronic equipment. A one-megaton nuclear explosion high in the atmosphere will disable electronic components thousands of kilometers away. There are now available nonnuclear explosive devices that deliver an EMP pulse over a much shorter distance (a few kilometers), but with the same lethal effects to electronics. Some of this equipment can be used again in minutes or hours; other equipment will be permanently crippled. Closer explosions will destroy more equipment. Most of this can be avoided by shielding and/or redesigning solid-state equipment to resist this surge of energy. Such measures increase the cost of equipment 5 percent or so. This hardening is becoming a common practice.

Theory and Practice

Electronic-warfare devices account for only about one percent of world defense spending. Still, that's nearly $10 billion a year, and rising. Other electronics spending pushes the overall spending to more than 10 percent. The complexity of electronics devices, and their development, has spawned a number of problems somewhat unique to this type of equipment:

1. *Specifications.* The potential user of electronic weapons is far removed in terms of knowledge and expertise from the people who develop and build these devices. This causes an uncommon amount of confusion, as the user and developer frequently misunderstand each other. The developer, working on the leading edge of technology, tends to overestimate what can be done in a certain amount of time and budget, thus overestimating performance. The user often never fully understands what he is getting. Often, user uncertainty will cause seemingly arbitrary changes in specifications before and after the equipment is fielded. It's all somewhat akin to a blind man buying a horse without ever having seen one. He might just end up with an elephant, or worse.

2. *Soggy Software.* Computer software is present in nearly all electronic systems. Creating software is more akin to art than science, but few people in electronics R&D are ready to accept this fact. The hardware can be more readily completed to a certain specification. Software is more prone to unpredictable results. When the software and hardware are merged, the result frequently leaves the performance flaws in never-never land. It becomes hideously expensive to discover if the problems are hardware- or software-related. Compounding this is a shortage of skilled software developers. The typical institutional solution is to put more people on the software-development work. Yet experience has shown that the more people involved in software development, especially when it's behind schedule, the longer and more complex successful completion of the project will be. All of this becomes a very complex trial-and-error exercise. Equipment that works erratically often ends up in the hands of the troops. The users become understandably shy about relying too much on these devices until they have "matured."

3. *Budget Panic.* Electronics are very expensive. As the user sees costs climbing out of sight, there is a tendency to put a cap on expenditures and thereby put the developers in a no-win situation. Something will often be produced, but the result is usually a device no one is satisfied with.

4. *Turf Battles.* Several different technical organizations will customarily be involved in developing electronic devices. Office politics frequently crop up, over shares for both credit and blame. Even the Soviet Union, with a seemingly monolithic organizational structure, used a number of "design bureaus" and institutes to develop electronics. The arrangement does not appear to have changed much, except for a lot of shrinkage, in the current Russian state. Bureaucrats and ambitious scientists are the same the world over.

5. *Hype.* It's easier to say what some new device will do before it actually exists. Looking good is more important, and attainable, than doing it right. There is tremendous pressure to justify all the expense and effort. Because most of these devices will not be truly proven effective or otherwise until the shooting starts, there is ample opportunity to make believe. This is less true with devices that must perform in peacetime, like navigation equipment. The uncertain performance of these devices, compounded by differences between potential opponents' equipment, will create confusion during the opening stages of a conflict. The winner will be who can first adapt to what his own gear can actually do and counter his opponents' capabilities.

Western nations have a pronounced lead in electronic technology and computers. This should translate into a strong position in electronic warfare. Such is not always the case, and you never know which situation will find you in a superior position. Russia, and less technically endowed nations in general, compensate with several clever strategies:

1. *Barrage Jamming.* Lacking the sophisticated jamming Western nations are capable of producing, many countries opt for barrage jamming of many frequencies. They can build lots of simple jammers and generators to power them. They also put a lot more radio direction-location equipment into the field.

2. *Concealed Equipment.* Many potential enemies are closed societies with a mania for secrecy and deception. The Soviet Union habitually kept some new equipment from its own troops. The idea being that the troops could learn to use it quickly enough, and the enemy would be in the dark longer. The Soviets used this technique successfully for more than half a century. You can be assured that not all the electronic warfare equipment of many nations is known to their potential opponents.

3. *Redundant Systems.* Soviet ships, aircraft, and ground units often appeared to have more equipment than Western counterparts. They did, and it was partly because they couldn't maintain their equipment

as well as Western troops and also because this gave them more options in combat. If one system was defeated by Western countermeasures, perhaps a different one would do the trick. Crude, but effective.

4. *Spies.* Traditionally more inclined to use spies than the United States, many nations find that a handicap in the fancy electronic-espionage department can be made up with more human agents. To counter many of these practices, the West still has more flexible equipment. Computer-controlled EW gear can be quickly reconfigured. Western forces increasingly capitalize on this.

Finally, remember that for all its apparent efficiency, electronic-equipment performance is a now-and-again thing. Anyone who has experienced the occasionally unstable performance of radio and TV equipment has experienced this. Any electronic gear that sends signals through the atmosphere must contend with natural interference. As a result, equipment specifications are misleadingly deceptive. A radar with a quoted range of 100 kilometers will not spot every target every time at that range. More detailed equipment specs will show that at 100 kilometers targets of a certain (usually large) size can be spotted 90 percent of the time, and at 50 kilometers 99 percent of the time. In practice, spotting probability may be less than 10 percent at 100 kilometers and only 50 percent at 50 kilometers. This is the idea behind stealth technology. Not to make something *invisible* to radar, but simply harder to detect. Since detection must be continuous to be useful, a target that blinks on and off upon the radar screen is less likely to be tracked and hit by a missile. The electronic battlefield is one of probabilities, not certainties. Victory will go to the side that can best cope when the gadgets don't perform according to the spec sheet.

The Future

Weapons costs comprise nearly 50 percent of military spending, and more than a third of the weapons' expense goes to electronics. Overall military spending is rapidly approaching the point where 20 percent of all costs will be for electronics. For all this expense, military electronics are cursed with two major problems: instant obsolescence and unreliability.

One of the ironies of high technology is that much research valuable for civilian uses is paid for as part of weapons development, yet military equipment is generally the last to benefit. This is largely because of the torpid pace of getting workable weapons approved and into production. An example is the P-3 antisubmarine aircraft. Heavily dependent on electronics, many of these planes are still using 20-year-old technology. Thus, we have two futures for electronics: the latest breakthroughs in the laboratory and 10- or 20-year-old developments in current weapons.

In one area of electronics, there is hope for change. The continuing development of microcomputers has introduced some revolutionary opportunities in weapons design and fabrication. To appreciate the scope of these developments, consider the costs of microcomputers versus previous devices. One standard measurement of computing power is the MIPS (million instructions per second that a computer can perform). In the mid-1970s, the most powerful mainframe computers available could generate 1 MIPS. At that time, a few thousand instructions per second powered the most advanced missiles and less than a MIPS was used to perform signal processing for advanced radar and sonar systems. Today, the largest mainframe computers possess hundreds of MIPS at a cost of $50,000 per MIPS. Minicomputers and workstations generate under 100 MIPS at a cost of $1,000 per MIPS. Most important, microcomputers put out over 20 MIPS at a cost of less than $500 per MIPS. Rugged militarized microcomputers can pump out 5 MIPS for less than $10,000 per system. The most recent U.S. submarine signal-processing computers can produce more than 700 MIPS, nearly tripling search range in the process. The American military has subsidized research into even faster microcomputers for immediate use in new and existing sensors and weapons. Now, a tremendous amount of calculation can be performed quickly and cheaply. By itself, this is an important capability. It is made even more revolutionary by the ability of troops and civilian contractors to quickly and easily develop new software (instructions) for the microcomputer-powered machines. In the vanguard is the American military, which has purchased hundreds of thousands of the latest civilian microcomputers and spread them around liberally. Just as American and Canadian troops had an advantage in World War II because most could drive vehicles, a similar edge is now held because so many U.S. troops can use and/or program microcomputers. This process has been going on since the late 1970s, when troops bought the first microcomputers with their own money and automated their military duties. The military in the West has taken advantage of this situation by short-circuiting its own procurement system. Civilian microcomputers have shielding and shockproofing added to them, producing computers at one-fourth the cost and five years earlier than equipment developed expressly for the military. In some cases, they were able to replace military equipment that was much less powerful and cost 10 times as much as the militarized civilian equipment.

Computers can be reprogrammed. Computer programs are not easily created, but in a pinch they can be gotten together faster than anything that requires bending metal. Increasingly, computers and their programs are driving other electronic equipment. The Western lead in computer technology appears as a decisive advantage in the full spectrum of electronic equipment. A current example is ECM systems that store the characteristics of enemy radars and then can recognize and jam them quickly. Radars and sonars are benefiting the most from cheaper and more powerful computers. This is because the key problem with radars has not been sending the signal out, but correctly interpreting the fainter signal that bounces back from the target. Much of the Western stealth technology is still based on the weakness of Soviet radar technology. It is possible to build radars that can spot stealth aircraft, but you must have powerful enough computers to correctly interpret the signals, and transmit the right signals in the first place. This computer power also makes over the horizon radars practical for ships and mobile antiaircraft units. The United States is pushing many new electronic items.

Even the army, traditionally well behind the navy and air force, is increasingly going electronic. A major attempt to integrate communications between U.S. Army and Air Force units is the JTIDS (Joint Tactical Information Distribution System), which was delivered to troop units in the early 1990s. Ever since the U.S. Air Force became a separate service in the late 1940s, the army has had problems with ground units communicating directly with aircraft. This was much less of a problem when the air force was part of the army, or with many armed forces where the army still calls all the shots.

You now find computers all over the place; even infantry battalions have several. Like all new technology, there will be a period of uncertainty and confusion when all these new items are used in combat for the first time.

The Soviet Union was always struggling to catch up. Each year during the 1980s, they spent over $2 billion of their scarce hard currency to buy or steal military equipment and production techniques that they were legally barred from. They were quite successful in this, and saved tens of billions of dollars in research costs. But because they lacked high-quality production capacity, in most cases they ended up with second-rate clones of the Western gear.

Everyone has severe problems with reliability. Hardware unreliability is endemic in Third World equipment. This problem becomes worse when you try to field technology requiring more sophistication than you are capable of maintaining. One good example was the Soviet LASAR device of the late 1980s. This was a laser radar that looks for highly reflective surfaces, such as lenses for optical devices, and then blasts them with a high-energy laser. Lacking sufficient precision-manufacturing capabilities, the Soviet LASAR devices continually displayed a high level of false alarms in field tests and was never perfected for troop use despite enormous amounts of investment. But weapons using electronic transmissions have succeeded in the past. The Israelis used electronic broadcasts to prematurely detonate the warheads of Soviet missiles as early as 1973. Electronic equipment can be damaged or destroyed, as can people, with the right kind of transmissions. Not to be outdone, the United States is working on a device that will generate an EMP (Electromagnetic Pulse) similar to the one created by nuclear explosions and capable of destroying unshielded electronic equipment.

Quality control is the key, and some nations are better at it than others.

The Japanese learned about quality control from the United States in the 1950s, about the same time Americans were forgetting it. While American civilian industries hustled to recapture their quality-control skills in the 1980s, the military's supplier firms were a little slower. There is not always superior civilian equipment to fall back on as with microcomputers. There are always several military R&D disasters under way. The future indicates slow increases in quality control among Western military manufacturers. Software quality control will loom as a larger problem, as the military comes to grips with increasingly ambitious programming projects. The primary problem here is the inexperience of managers on the military side of the contract. Civilian firms that create software consider military work much less favorably than commercial projects for this reason. How well these reliability and software problems are solved will determine how successful electronics are in a future war.

20

The War in Space

THE UPPER REACHES OF earth's atmosphere will be a battlefield in any future war. The reasons are the same as in the past; everyone wants reconnaissance. Space has been used for surveillance since the 1960s. Space war will occur when there is a war involving the nations that use space. More nations are capable of this, even Third World nations. In addition, there will be more at stake. Space is not used just for reconnaissance; it has also become a crucial link for communications. A growing space-based capability is the potential for attacking missiles as they take off and arc toward their targets thousands of kilometers away. Called Star Wars or SDI (Strategic Defense Initiative), this system also threatens other nations' satellites and their ability to launch new ones. Currently, about 1,500 satellites remain in orbit, of which nearly 400 are still functioning. Some 40 percent are Russian (CIS, Soviet, or whatever), 40 percent American, and the remainder largely belong to other Western nations. Nearly 50 percent of these birds are military. The space battlefield extends from 150 to 36,000 kilometers above the earth's surface. The upper limits of conventional aircraft are about 36 kilometers. Although air forces would prefer human pilots taking care of things, it's cheaper to put unmanned satellites up. A war in space will be largely a robot war, a truly automated battlefield.

Military Uses of Space

While an increasing number of civilian satellites are put up, most of the money still goes into military birds. These cover a number of specifically military uses. These are:

PHOTO RECONNAISSANCE

This is perhaps the most important military use of space. These satellites use cameras as well as infrared and passive electronic sensors. Electronic data is transmitted to ground stations for further processing and analysis. High-resolution camera photographs are sent back in canisters. Western technology increasingly uses digital photographs, of the same high resolution, that can be transmitted back. The U.S. technology allows for objects less than a foot in diameter to be distinguished. These satellites are of low altitude and short endurance because they must carry fuel for maneuvering and, in many cases, film. U.S. models have always been on the cutting edge of this technology. The KH series (for Key Hole) began in 1961 with a primitive KH-1s and KH-4s. These took pictures and sent the film back in canisters. Comparable Soviet models had to bring the entire satellite back. The next generation, KH-5s and KH-6s, lifted off in 1963. These birds were able to transmit some of their pictures back. This was a major advance, as it allowed satellites to remain useful for more than a few weeks. The major limitation now became fuel, which allowed the KH birds to maneuver over the area to be searched.

The next generation, KH-7 and KH-8, went up in 1966 and were notable for their wider variety of sensors. Infrared sensors could detect heat, making it more difficult to conceal things. Multispectral scanning can detect different materials and gives satellite data another dimension as well as making deception more difficult. More capable cameras were also carried, producing photographs that identified objects two or three inches small. This allowed detailed technical analysis of troop units in the bases and on maneuvers, airfields, missile sites, warships, ports, and potential landing beaches, bridges, roads, railways, and terrain in general. The next jump in resolution, to an inch or less, allowed detailed analysis of supply dumps, rockets and artillery, aircraft, headquarters, nuclear weapons, and vehicles.

All of this was not without problems. High-resolution photos still had to come back in canisters. The KH-8s were still used into the late 1980s, partially because they were relatively lightweight (at less than four tons). The next generation, the KH-9, was a major advance. First launched in 1971, these birds were large, nearly 15 tons. Their nickname was Big Bird. This larger size was needed to support larger sensors. The KH-9 was meant for wide-area surveillance. Although it could detect items only 12 inches in size, it could take pictures of thousands of square miles in minutes. This resolution allowed precise identification of all classes of objects, although not detailed analysis. It also allowed technical intelligence on transportation networks and urban areas. These photos still had to come down in canisters. Data from the other sensors could be transmitted. With the KH-9, you could keep an eye on continents and even do it at night. This required larger sensors and a lot of fuel. The KH-9 was a thirsty bird, as it had to frequently use fuel to change orbits. Initially, KH-9s lasted 52 days, but this was increased to nine months by the early 1980s.

Through the 1970s, the United States depended on the KH-8 for close-in photo work and the KH-9 for covering larger areas. In 1977, the fifth generation dawned with the launch of the KH-11. This was a major break-through, as canisters were no longer needed and resolution was such that objects a few inches in size could be identified from more than 100 miles up. The KH-11 telescopic cameras operated like a high-resolution TV camera. Images were captured continuously and transmitted to earth stations. Computers were used to finish the process and produce photos identical to those taken by a conventional camera. You could even have motion pictures, as well as indications of heat and the nature of the various items. KH-11 could often tell what kind of metal an object on the ground was made of. This did not come cheap—these birds cost more than $400 million each and lasted three or four years, depending on fuel usage. Moreover, you needed two of them up at the same time in order to guarantee coverage and save the birds from having to change orbit too frequently. Nineteen eighty-seven was to have been the year the next generation went up, the KH-12. Because of the space-shuttle problems, only a belated KH-11 was launched in October 1987. The KH-12 has several advantages over the KH-11. Along with improvements in ground data-processing equipment, the KH-12 could send back data in real time. You could watch events on a large high-resolution screen as they were happening. This would also allow military headquarters and other users to get their satellite information directly, without going through a CIA or NRO (National Reconnaissance Office) processing center. Data from the more esoteric sensors would still have to be studied by the specialists elsewhere. The KH-12 was expected to make users even more enthusiastic about satellite reconnaissance. Such enthusiasm may be needed when shrinking defense budgets have to decide between birds in the sky and weapons in hand.

Normally, the number of types of satellites available for use is a military secret. But during the 1991 Gulf War, a lot more information got out for one reason or another. The U.S. satellites available in early 1991 comprised the following:

KH-11 series reconnaissance satellite. There were three KH-11 satellites in orbit. These were launched December 1984, October 1987, and November 1988. There were also four advanced KH-11s, sometimes referred to as KH-12s. These were launched August 1989, February 1990, June 1990, and November 1990. These advanced models had the standard KH-11 equipment, but were also capable of photographing objects at night using infrared scanner, plus a sensor package capable of detecting some materials used in camouflage. The December 1984 KH-11 was apparently no longer fully operational in early 1991, because of lack of fuel or multiple-system breakdowns. One of the advanced KH-11s apparently failed in orbit, although no one would confirm it. This left five KH-11s available for observing the Gulf by early 1991. The KH-11 birds move about in orbit and can observe an area for about two hours while passing over. The detailed photos are transmitted via relay satellites to a ground station in Maryland and then retransmitted to people who need the information quickly, or further analyzed. These images could be shown within minutes to U.S. analysts and commanders in Saudi Arabia, but often were not. The analysts in the United States usually hung on to the data for further analysis and then forwarded their report to the Gulf.

One Lacrosse radar satellite (launched December 1988), which can see through clouds and other atmospheric obstructions. This satellite can detect items buried up to 10 feet underground to pinpoint missiles and other equipment hidden in trenches and bunkers. Only available a few hours a day.

Two Mentor SIGINT (Signal Intelligence) satellites (launched January 1985 and November 1989) that sit in fixed orbit and eavesdropped on Iraqi transmissions (communications, radars, etc.). This supported photo recon by giving an indication something was down there because of the electronic emissions from a well-hidden enemy facility.

One Vortex SIGINT satellite (launched May 1989), which is like the Mentor but more specialized.

The Defense Support Program satellites (exact number classified, but an advanced model was launched November 1990 to increase Scud missile launch coverage). Use large infrared telescope to locate the hot plumes of missile launches. Were used to spot Scud missiles being fired and provided warning to target areas. Only able to give a few minutes' warning, but that was enough and a good example of real-time satellite recon.

GPS (Global Positioning Satellite) System. Provides precise location information (to within 25 meters or less) via a hand-held satellite signal receiver. Not all 24 satellites were in orbit when war began, but there were enough up there to give coverage over most of the Gulf except for a few hours in the late afternoon. While not a recon-satellite system, the GPS proved crucial in supporting ground-based recon in the desert.

The Soviets were always at a major disadvantage in the recon-satellite area. They were at least two generations behind the United States. However, they had one large advantage in that they have more birds in the air and a large stockpile of ready-to-go launchers. The Soviets could get a new bird in orbit with a few days' notice. In America, it takes at least a few weeks, and usually a few months, to do an unscheduled launch. The Soviets did at least one launch a week and kept stockpiles of satellites and launchers in readiness for emergencies. In wartime, with satellites being shot down, the Soviets hoped their birds would be the only ones left in orbit. At least until they ran out of fuel and film.

Because of the expense of U.S. birds, more than $500 million for the KH-12 and $100 million for many of the smaller ones, fewer of them are used. American satellites last longer than Soviet ones, so the failure of one of them is more of a problem. If there is trouble getting replacements into orbit, the situation becomes acute. This is what happened to the United States in 1987. The shuttle *Challenger* disaster in 1986, plus the loss of an expendable launcher several months later, left the United States with only one aging KH-11, with dwindling fuel and limited mobility, to supply all its quality photo reconnaissance. This situation began when the United States decided to use the shuttle for all recon-satellite launches.

The new KH-12 birds are too heavy for anything but the shuttle. The KH-12 is heavier largely because of its large fuel load. Indeed, items were continually added until even the carrying capacity of the shuttle was reached. At that point, a new type of solid-fuel booster was introduced in order to provide additional lifting capacity, and to replace an existing type that was causing problems. After shuttle flights were halted in 1986, a contract was quickly issued for a rocket that could lift a lighter KH-12. The bird would go up with half a fuel load, to be refueled in orbit by a later shuttle tanker. In addition to refueling, shuttles could also perform repairs, by replacing the largely modular components. In this way, the KH-12 could be kept up indefinitely.

Before the end of the century, the KH-13 may go up, probably in sections. The KH-13 is basically an unmanned space station, capable of covering more of the earth on a constant basis. In effect, most of the capabilities planned for the KH-13 are being folded into the Star Wars antimissile system. While satellite reconnaissance has always strived for continual observation, this was rarely achieved, as it requires many satellites in orbit and working order simultaneously. As sensors become more capable, and expensive, fewer of them can be bought and kept operational. But to provide antimissile defense, detailed coverage must be continuous. If Star Wars ever gets off the ground, the KH-13 probably will also. Otherwise, a system of four KH-12s, serviced and upgraded by shuttle flights, may be up there for quite a while.

The KH-12 points out an important facet of satellites: They don't wear out but dry up. Fuel is needed to position the birds over targets. Because of the low orbits, fuel is also needed to make frequent adjustments to an orbit that is constantly slipping closer to a fiery plunge through that atmosphere. With a larger fuel supply, satellites can quickly move to new locations. This is very useful for the bird's more discriminating sensors. Soviet satellites took a different development course than U.S. birds. Unable to match U.S. technology, the Russians paid more attention to signal collection and radar observation. There were several reasons for this, all of them typical of Soviet pragmatism. Aside from the Soviets' inability to match American capabilities in photo reconnaissance, there was the fact that in the more open U.S. society, it was easier to send people over with cameras to take pictures from the ground or commercial aircraft. Soviet photo-recon birds were used primarily for emergency photo work. Their photo satellites rarely stayed up for more than a few weeks before returning with their photos. Before the Soviet Union collapsed in 1991, the Soviets were beginning to use birds approaching the KH-11 in capability, but they still have reliability problems. The "Soviet" satellites could stay up for up to six or eight months. Russia inherited the Soviet Union's satellite program and promptly cut it back because of the enormous expense. The Russians still have satellites up there, just not as many as before.

COMMUNICATIONS

Satellites are excellent relay stations for ground communications. They are cheaper than equivalent facilities on the ground and are more flexible and relatively immune to interference. Western nations maintain about a dozen communications satellites. The Soviets kept three times as many in space. This disparity in numbers was caused by geography, technology, and doctrine. Soviet launch sites were too far from the equator, making it difficult to launch satellites into efficient orbits. They needed more satellites in space to ensure that one is always in position to relay data. The Soviets' electronic technology was not as advanced, giving them less reliable and capable satellites. Finally, there is doctrine. The Soviets simply felt safer with a larger number of satellites in orbit. Russia inherited the Soviet Union's communications satellites and is trying to maintain most of them for largely commercial reasons. Russia is still a vast country, and satellites are still the most efficient way to maintain effective communications over such a large area.

OCEAN RECONNAISSANCE

Radar and other sensors track surface ships. Strategic radar satellites cover large areas by radar. Smaller birds use electronic sensors. The radar models, at least the Russian ones, are powered by a special short-life nuclear reactor. These birds are heavy, weighing between 10 and 20 tons. These satellites are broken apart once they wear out so that the radioactive components are vaporized on reentry. The United States keeps three in orbit. Soviet naval recon satellites gave the location of most Western task forces every four days. The Soviets planned to put up more capable birds, so that they could bring this down to every three days. Soviet ocean recon birds worked in pairs, one with radar and another just listening for electronic emissions. The Soviets used a more powerful radar than Western models, getting better coverage.

Radar satellites were important to the Soviets because the larger Western naval forces had to be tracked. These birds required a lot of power and got it from a small nuclear reactor. Since they lasted only about three months, their constant replacement contributed to the 100 or so satellites a year that the Soviets launched. An example of the new attitude of the new Russian government was its quite eager offer to sell this nuclear-reactor technology to the United States at a very attractive price. With the Russians backing off from supporting extensive satellite activity, U.S. recon birds will rule the orbital roost for some years to come.

ELECTRONIC INTELLIGENCE

These birds fly low over the ground and pick up transmissions. Called "ferrets," they carry a variety of sensors. The Soviets launched about six a year, the United States half that number. Russia currently launches one very rarely and is apparently holding those birds it has for any future emergency.

Ferrets are small, and often piggyback with a larger satellite.

EARLY WARNING

These reconnaissance satellites are specially designed to detect missile launches. They also collect information on missile performance during tests. They use infrared sensors to spot the missile's rockets on takeoff. Electronic sensors pick up test missiles' transmissions of performance data. The Soviet Union launched about four a year. American versions have virtually unlimited endurance, but one or two new ones are launched each year containing improved sensors and other equipment.

NAVIGATION

These satellites maintain stable, fixed orbits in order to give reliable position data to vehicles on earth with a receiver. America has spent years installing a system of 24 GPS satellites. It costs over $600 million a year just to maintain. The Soviet Union has a similar GLONAS system that Russia is still trying to get operational. These systems are needed for highly accurate missiles, which correct their position using the satellite transmissions.

WEATHER SURVEILLANCE

Image and heat sensors plot weather movements. The United States has four in orbit, and must launch one or two a year to keep them operational. Russia also has four in orbit, and must launch two or three a year to maintain that number. These are for civilian use, but a few special military weather satellites are up there also.

SCIENTIFIC

These conduct a wide range of experiments for civilian and military research. A variable number are launched each year. Many are not announced. One with some military use is the VELA, which can detect the characteristic double flash of an atmospheric nuclear explosion.

ANTISATELLITE

These destroy other satellites. The Soviet Union was suspected of having several in orbit, but they never came clean, and Russia is unlikely to further support these efforts. They have had mixed success on testing these. The Soviet versions were basically space mines—they move close to their victim and explode. A more pragmatic and effective approach has been developed by the United States. Here, a high-altitude fighter carries a special missile and releases it. This has proved a very inexpensive way to hit low-altitude reconnaissance satellites, just the kind you would want to destroy in wartime.

FOBS (FRACTIONAL ORBITING BOMBARDMENT SATELLITE)

They carry reentry vehicles similar to the warheads of ballistic missiles. By launching their warheads in orbit, they gain the element of surprise that ICBMs find difficult to achieve. These are illegal, and probably unwanted because of the risk of accidental launch of warheads. They could be put up with existing technology.

BATTLE STATIONS

Very large manned or unmanned satellites carrying a wide variety of sensors, communications gear, power supplies, and weapons. Such systems are an essential component of Star Wars antimissile defense systems. None built yet, but lots of planning activity.

GETTING INTO ORBIT

Getting a workable satellite into orbit requires three things:

1. Sufficient thrust to overcome the earth's gravity and get the satellite high enough so gravity is very weak.
2. Accurate control to place the satellite in a proper orbit.
3. Effective communications with and control of the satellite so that it can perform whatever tasks it was sent up there for.

In the late 1950s, the first satellites had little beyond minimum thrust and imperfect control when achieving precarious orbits. Through the 1960s, thrust increased enormously, allowing larger satellites to be sent up. Control became more precise, allowing for more efficient orbits. Expense is now a greater limitation than technology. The cost of putting a satellite up varies from $500 to $10,000 a pound. The primary purpose of the U.S. space shuttle was to bring this cost down. This did not happen, primarily because the American space program became obsessed with high technology to the point where it was costing the Americans 10 times more per pound than the Soviets to put a satellite into orbit. The cheaper Soviet launches were partially a result of more launches. Soviet technology was of a lower standard, and the Soviets' satellites did not last as long, so they had to launch more of them. The Soviets launched 8 to 10 times as many satellites each year as the United States but had only 10–15 percent more birds in orbit at any one time. Thus, they achieved economies of scale in mass-producing vehicles, which are often basically ICBM rockets modified for satellite launching. The Soviets' biggest cost advantage was that they stayed with a basic design of low-potency fuels and simple motors. The Soviet launchers were less reliable, but this could be attributed to the lower reliability of Soviet technology in general. However, even taking into account the cost of lost satellites from less reliable launchers, the Soviet system still cost less than one fifth as much as the U.S. approach. One justification of the more reliable U.S. high-tech rockets is the need for more safety in launching manned missions. This did not stop the Soviets from pursuing a more ambitious manned-spaceflight program. Moreover, this ignored the fact that space missions can be more cheaply and safely done using robots. It's easier to get money for manned spaceflight than for robotic missions. Post–Cold War budget cutbacks may force the United States and Russia to give the robots more opportunities.

Improvements in technology have made satellites more capable on a pound-for-pound basis. This is crucial, as the cost of putting them up there has not come down in the West. Costs of over $5,000 a pound for low orbits (LEO = Low Earth Orbit) and twice or more of that for high orbits (GTO = Geosynchronous Transit Orbit) make lighter satellites very valuable. The higher (36,000 kilometers) orbits are for the stationary satellites used for communications. The lower orbits are not stationary and tend to degrade over time, until the satellite plows into the thicker atmosphere and burns up from the friction.

Limits of Satellite Endurance

If placed in a stable orbit, a satellite can stay up indefinitely. But a number of other factors limit a satellite's useful life besides how long it can maintain its orbit.

1. *Stability of Orbit.* Satellites stay up longer in higher orbits. Coming in closer brings the satellite in contact with more of the earth's atmosphere, which extends over 100 kilometers out. That far out, it is pretty thin, but not so sparse that a fast-moving satellite will not be influenced. Not all launches are perfect, and sometimes the satellite is positioned in a less than optimum orbit.

2. *Endurance of Maneuvering System.* Although most satellites have some propulsion capability, it is intended for minor adjustments, not repairing a bad orbit. These small rockets are to turn the satellite around to catch more sunlight or to position another instrument. In some satellites, such as those used for electronic reconnaissance, a substantial amount of fuel is carried so the orbit can be adjusted. When this maneuvering fuel is gone, the satellite loses a lot of its capability. Low-orbit satellites often move lower and burn up. Larger satellites take up more than five tons of fuel with them.

3. *Power Supply.* Power is needed to transmit data back to earth. Other equipment can have varying power loads, ranging from low for some sensors to high for powerful radars. The power source is typically a combination of solar panels to batteries. Batteries are needed for those times when the satellite is in the earth's shadow. Russia uses a special nuclear reactor, not the same type used in power plants, that generates a lot of energy in a few months and then runs down. If the satellite has low power requirements, solar panels can keep it going for hundreds of years.

4. *Expendables.* Pre KH-11 U.S. recon satellites used film cameras and sent the film back to earth in canisters. When the film was gone, the satellite was no longer useful. KH-11 and later models took electronic pictures. All Soviet photo satellites had to return to earth for film to be recovered.

5. *Fatigue.* Any complex electromechanical device will eventually have one or more parts wear out and fail. Although built with many redundant systems, satellites operate in a harsh environment. Constant use, extremes of heat and cold, plus the occasional damage

from a piece of high-speed dust will wear it down. Extensive self-test equipment allows ground controllers to repair some damage, or work around it. One of the advantages of the space shuttle is its ability to repair satellites, or recover them for overhaul on the ground.

6. *Obsolescence.* Technological improvements are relentless. A satellite built to last for 10 years might find itself so outclassed by new models that it is not worth using anymore. Again, this is where the space shuttle comes into play, being capable of bringing down older satellites for rebuilding.

Vulnerability

Destroying satellites in wartime is a high-priority task. It would make enemy surveillance, communications, and navigation more difficult. Various methods exist to accomplish this destruction:

1. *Destroy the ground stations.* This is the simplest method, but it becomes more difficult as the stations multiply. The saucer-shaped send/receive antennae are becoming cheaper and more numerous. However, a few of these stations also contain extensive computers, as well as retransmission and satellite-control facilities. If this equipment is destroyed, the satellites they support become less useful.

2. *Destroy satellite ground bases.* Few of these exist. The United States and Russia have two major bases each, which account for the vast majority of launches. For example, the first use of the Soviet *Energia* rocket so damaged the launch site that it was nearly two years before repairs were made and another could be sent up. A few minor bases were available. The United States and the former Soviet Union were developing the ability to send up small satellites using military ballistic missiles. These could even be launched from submarines. The U.S. program is still alive; the Russian one is probably defunct.

3. *Prevent additional launches.* Star Wars–type weapons have the capability to destroy satellites as they are being sent up. This was worrisome to the Soviets, who had to launch three or four satellites to each one sent up by the United States to achieve the same effect.

4. *Jam, blind, or otherwise disable enemy satellites.* Electronic jammers on the ground, in aircraft, or in other satellites can do this. Blinding visual sensors with high-powered lasers is possible. A low-flying satellite can receive temporary or long-term damage from lasers. The electromagnetic pulse from a nuclear explosion will also disable satellites that are not hardened against this. Reducing a satellite's effectiveness is the next-best thing to destroying it.

5. *Destroy the satellite.* This is no easy task, as it currently involves sending up a "killer" satellite to attack another. It is also dangerous:

Attacking satellites may be easily considered an act of war, given their importance in the strategic scheme of things. The Soviets had their space-mine satellites, which had to come up close to their victims and then destroy both in a large explosion. The advantage of this approach is that you can use a nuclear warhead. This will not only guarantee the destruction of the nearby enemy satellite, but will disable any other satellites within a few hundred kilometers (depending on the size of the nuke). The primary system available in the West is ASAT, a satellite-homing missile that is launched from a high-flying fighter against low-orbit recon satellites. However, this system is cheap, fast, and difficult for the defender to detect. This leaves midrange satellites safe for the moment. The only current way to get at the communication satellites in their 36,000-kilometers orbits is to send out a nuclear-bomb satellite to their vicinity. You don't have to get real close, just near enough for the powerful electromagnetic pulse to scramble the satellite's innards. Unfortunately, only a few positions exist for these satellites to orbit; thus, such an explosion might get one of your birds also. In addition, no one has tried to send a killer satellite out this far, with or without a nuke. Moreover, a future enemy may see an advantage in leaving Western navigation satellites up, as many of its ships, aircraft, and missiles can use Western satellite signals. Also keep in mind that satellites are small objects in a large space. Only the high-communications satellites stay in one place. Those in orbit usually have some capability to shift orbits. Tracking your own and others' satellites has become a big business.

American capabilities are extensive, and include the ability to make detailed films of satellites in action, including detailed examination of what space-shuttle or satellite crews do when outside their vehicles. American capabilities are such that a baseball-size object can be detected nearly 40,000 kilometers out. The West has more mobile satellites and a greater capability at tracking them. In addition, there is the little-discussed effort to employ electronic warfare in space. Satellites are controlled via radio link by ground stations. If these control messages can be jammed or mimicked, the satellite in question will be neutralized or destroyed. Who is ahead in this area will not be revealed until hostilities begin. To tip your hand earlier allows the enemy to develop countermeasures. The opening of major hostilities will reveal very strange events in the orbital arena.

Satellite Defense

Aside from small size and ability to shift position somewhat, several other aspects can be achieved to increase a satellite's survivability.

1. Components can be shielded from the electromagnetic pulse of a nuclear weapon. Some hardening is also possible as a defense against laser attack.

2. Defensive missiles can be carried to home in on a killer satellite's tracking radar. Large and important satellites could be equipped with radar and missiles for killer satellites that use passive sensors to home with.

3. Satellites can be equipped with more fuel so that they can move about more. Antisatellite warfare will probably come to resemble a high-speed chess game played on a very large, and spherical, playing surface.

4. The foremost defensive advantage the Soviets had was a higher rate of launches, about 100 a year. This gave them about 150 useful satellites in orbit. The higher launch rate gave the Soviets a better capability to replace war losses quickly, assuming their launch facilities were not damaged or that Star Wars did not become operational. They were also thought to be looking into using land-based ICBMs as emergency-launch vehicles. The United States investigated the same technique, although with an emphasis on using submarine-launched ICBMs. Neither nation went very far with this idea, mainly because of the cost of developing satellites for the different shape of combat-missile warheads. The testing expense would also have been high.

5. The least-talked-about defensive technique is deception. Most satellites can be easily identified as to purpose. Land-based U.S. cameras can count the rivets on low-flying satellites. Many satellites collect electronic intelligence on other birds. Satellites that broadcast data earthward often disguise these transmissions by routing them through another satellite. Existing models often have additional capabilities added without changing the external appearance of the satellite. Typically, a photo-recon bird is given electronic eavesdropping capabilities. Radar and photo-recon capabilities are difficult to hide as they require large mirrors or radar receivers. All is not what it appears to be in the heavens.

Star Wars

This is also known as SDI (Strategic Defense Initiative), a system that would, in theory, defend against attack by long-range ballistic missiles. The proposal to build an orbital antiballistic missile system by the United States became an instant controversy when first proposed in the early 1980s. This is a system that does not exist at this moment and may never be built. The reasons for this are manifold:

1. *Public opposition.* SDI is expensive, and the taxpayers can see more immediate things to do with the money.
2. *Technical problems.* These are detailed below.
3. *The opposition of other nations that use space,* because of the threat to non-American satellites and the militarization of space.
4. *The Anti-Ballistic Missile treaty between the United States and the USSR,* which prohibits SDI (depending on whose lawyers you talk to). This treaty was brought about at the insistence of U.S. negotiators who argued that antimissile systems would encourage the building of more strategic nuclear weapons.

The Soviets had been working on SDI–type systems since the 1960s. What worried them was that they quickly found themselves in over their heads with technology that the West repeatedly excels at. The Soviets felt they could not afford to fall behind. Given the state of their industry and technology, they couldn't really afford to compete in this area either. But they knew that if the United States went forward with Star Wars, they would have to follow. This plunged Soviet technological capabilities even farther behind the West, and it was a price the Soviets were traditionally willing to pay. Besides, they have always had the fear that anything the West did might just work.

The reasoning behind SDI was based on the increasing accuracy of ICBMs and their eventual ability to destroy another nation's ICBMs before they could be used. The first ICBMs were quite inaccurate and effective only against large targets. Over 30 years, accuracy increased to the point where a warhead could hit the other fellow's missile silos. This also made it theoretically possible to strike first and leave the enemy with nothing to strike back with. As a defense against enemy nuclear weapons, this first-strike approach appears too risky. Indeed, any defense against ballistic missiles has been elusive. Initial attempts at missile defense were oriented toward ground-based defenses. The problem here was the high speed with which warheads approach the ground and the short amount of time available to the defender. Ground-based defenses have to struggle against time, gravity, and a thick atmosphere to get at the warheads plunging toward them. Worse yet, ground-based defenses could protect an area only 100 or so miles from the ground-based antimissile missiles. This made it prohibitively expensive to protect the entire nation. The Soviet Union could get away with just protecting Moscow, but a democracy had to protect enough voters to get the legislature to agree to a program.

Before long, the idea of placing missile defenses in orbit was proposed. This solved the problem of gravity, atmosphere, and, to a lesser extent, time. It gets more complicated than that. Unanticipated countermeasures are available to the missile user that can make the orbiting defense system less effective. An unplanned-for countermeasure could cause catastrophic leakage (warheads getting through). When the warheads' penetration rate ("leakage") rises over 10 percent, the losses become devastating. Despite the inherent weaknesses of an orbital antimissile system, it poses another threat to an opponent that is even more worrisome. Instead of attacking ICBMs, these same defensive systems can go after enemy satellites. This would deny the enemy reconnaissance capability, cripple communication, and degrade navigation on ships and aircraft.

The task of suppressing ballistic missiles using orbiting weapons is daunting, but not impossible. The debate comes down to three issues:

1. Can one afford it?
2. Will it be cheaper to shoot down enemy missiles than it will be for the enemy to simply build additional missiles?
3. How many warheads will get through anyway? No system is perfect.

There's no doubt that SDI would be expensive, several hundred billion dollars at least, and quite likely more than a trillion dollars. There's also general agreement that some warheads will get through no matter how good the system is. To understand these two issues, consider what such a defensive system is up against. First, there is the target. Intercontinental ballistic missiles, whether from land-based or sea-based launchers, follow the same routine. After launch, it takes from 90 seconds to five minutes for the ICBM to rise through the atmosphere. At that point, the warhead separates from the rocket and spends another minute or two moving into orbit and, in most cases, dispensing several reentry vehicles. Each contains a nuclear weapon and/or several decoys. These reentry vehicles then spend 5 to 20 minutes skimming along the upper reaches of the atmosphere on their way to their targets. The last stage takes a minute or so as the atmosphere is entered and the weapon detonates over the target. The Star Wars concept accepts the fact that no single system can stop all incoming missiles. Several different types of weapons are used to attack the missiles at the different stages of their journey. Each stage of the defensive battle is termed a "layer," and each layer is expected to destroy a percentage of the attacking warheads. The big question mark is what percentage of the warheads will be destroyed within each layer. No one expects 100 percent of the warheads will be destroyed. If 5,000 warheads are launched and one percent get through, 50 nuclear explosions occur, each killing or injuring several hundred thousand people and causing several hundred million dollars' worth of damage. A nuclear counterattack, probable in order to "even up" the damage done by the warheads that got through Star Wars, will do an equal or greater amount of damage.

One could make a case that 100 nuclear explosions and 25 million dead and injured is preferable to an unlimited nuclear holocaust. The problem is that there is no way of knowing what the "leakage" of warheads through Star Wars will be. It might be 10 percent or more. Untested weapons systems tend to perform unpredictably. In other words, you cannot just wish for 99 of 100 percent destruction of incoming missiles—you must test for it.

The end of the Cold War has eliminated, for the moment, the threat from the Soviet Union's ICBM fleet. Thus, the need to protect North America from several thousand incoming ICBMs is gone. The remaining threat is from the growing number of nations with a few ICBMs. France has ICBMs, but these pose no threat. China has ICBMs, and China is also unlikely to be a threat. Russia will still have several thousand ICBM warheads even after all the current disarmament agreements are fulfilled. But the Russians have publicly proclaimed that they are not pointing them at North America anymore. That leaves the new members of the ICBM club. By the end of the decade, ICBM technology will have proliferated sufficiently to allow a dozen or more nations to, in theory, arm themselves with ICBMs. How much of a threat any of these nations will be is hard to say. This is a unique situation in world history. The question then becomes one of, does one spend hundreds of billions of dollars on a technologically risky system to offset a nebulous threat? Good question. Wish I had a definitive answer.

All current nuclear systems have been tested, although the United States has not tested launching a ballistic missile with a live nuclear warhead. Indeed, there have been cases where the warhead-detonation system of some missiles was found to be defective after deployment. There may still be some defective systems. However, most components of the ballistic-missile systems have been tested. With Star Wars, most systems will not be tested under anything approaching combat conditions. Combat conditions for SDI means several thousand missiles coming off the planet at once. Try to fit that into the SDI budget.

Another serious problem with Star Wars is that it involves an extraordinary amount of technology that doesn't exist yet. This is not unusual for weapons-development projects. What is different here is the sheer volume of uninvented components. This, plus the lack of testing, does not bode well for success.

The projected components of the system consist of:

1. *Sensors.* There is already an impressive array of sensors looking for missiles. On the ground, we find over-the-horizon radars. Orbiting early-warning satellites use passive sensors and some radar. Infrared (heat) sensors are favored, as missiles use a lot of heat to get where they are going. To shut down a ballistic-missile attack, you need a sensor system that can detect and track up to 10,000 missiles being launched within a few minutes of each other. As not all of these missiles will be destroyed before they disperse their multiple warheads, the system must also be able to track up to 10,000 or more warheads. This is more difficult than tracking rockets climbing up into the sky on a column of flame. This problem is complicated by the presence of dummy warheads. These are lighter than the real

thing, but otherwise look the same. These fake warheads will not survive reentry, but you can't wait that long.

2. *Beam Weapons.* Once you've spotted a missile or warhead, you've got to destroy it. Several types of beam weapons are proposed. There is little time, so speed-of-light beam weapons are the only alternative. Lasers are the first choice, but only one type of laser will do, the X-ray laser. This is a high-powered beam that will destroy rockets and warheads instantly. Unfortunately, you need a prodigious power supply in orbit to do this. You can't use lasers from the ground because they burn up passing through the atmosphere. They can work, but need still higher energy levels. They are more efficient in the vacuum of space. The only way to get the required power in orbit is to explode a small nuclear bomb and focus the resulting rays in such a way that the X-ray laser light is produced. In a very theoretical sense, it works, but it's a one-shot weapon. It can be built in such a way that several targets can be taken out with each explosion. Using lower-powered lasers or particle beam weapons eliminates some of the power problems but interjects another control problem. You must to be able to detect when the rocket or warhead has been "burned" sufficiently to be nonoperational. This problem can be solved only by a sensor system that can detect when a target has been damaged sufficiently to be worthless. That's a tough one to do in a few seconds.

3. *Kinetic Weapons.* An alternative, if only because of their relative simplicity and cheapness, are weapons that destroy things by running into them. These projectile weapons are inherently slower than beam weapons, but under some circumstances can provide useful service. Because Star Wars intends to defeat missiles by making them run through several "layers" of defenses, kinetic weapons can be used in some of the later layers. In space, rockets or high-speed projectiles can chase after warheads as they cruise in a semiorbit toward their targets. Also, on the ground, last-chance rockets can be launched to cover the atmosphere over the target area with dust or similar small particles. The warhead reentering the atmosphere could be destroyed or deflected by striking these small particles. There are also rail guns, which fire high-velocity projectiles using magnetism instead of gunpowder.

4. *Control Software.* Someone, or in this case, something, has to orchestrate this immense defense system. Because of the very quick responses needed for the system to succeed, it will have to be activated and run by a computerized system. It is estimated that a Star Wars system would have from four to seven layers of defense. Each layer is a different set of weapons with different capabilities and shortcomings. The computer system must know who is doing what on both sides of the battle and at all times. We are talking about

several hundred satellites, as many sensors plus installations on the earth's surface. Computer programs are complex and unpredictable beasts. This is quite true with large programs, or in this case *very* large programs. The one needed to run Star Wars will be one of the largest ever written. Again, the big problem is that it can never be tested under actual conditions. The military and government track record in developing software is less successful than in the civilian sector, which makes probable success in this area even lower.

5. *Moving Targets.* As Star Wars comes closer to deployment, other nations will become more energetic in creating ploys to deceive the system. This is a problem massive research and development projects in the past had to face. For example, the World War II Manhattan Project, which developed the atomic bomb, did not have to concern itself with the victim's coming up with countermeasures. The Manhattan Project scientists figured out how to make a bomb, built one, tested it, and then dropped two of them on Japan. Another project, to land men on the moon in the 1960s, was in a similar situation. The team working on the project did not have to worry about the moon running away or fighting back. An essential component of developing Star Wars will be an awareness of real and potential countermeasures. Given past experience in this area, potential attackers cannot be expected to cooperate. The SDI satellites will have to either forcibly exclude other nations' satellites from their vicinity or accept the possibility of sabotage. A seemingly innocent commercial or military recon satellite can be commanded to shift its orbit slightly and detonate a nuclear weapon that could severely damage key SDI systems. The sabotage need not be nuclear; simply launching golf-ball-size projectiles at the SDI satellites could be fatal. There is always the probability that a stray piece of debris or micrometeorite could hit any satellite. An opponent could easily fabricate such incidents. A satellite-based defense system has a higher priority than defeating earth-based missiles. First it must defend itself. The orbiting battle stations of SDI must be, first of all, superb destroyers of other satellites. It is this function that frightens other nations more than anything else. For even if the SDI system proves less effective at stopping ballistic missiles, it will have abundant firepower for wiping anyone's satellites from space. Without these satellites, other nations are blind, and their communications are crippled. This probably worries the other nations more than the possibility of SDI neutralizing their strategic rockets.

Defending against nuclear attack presents several problems. First, one can deliver nuclear weapons without using missiles. The world's merchant fleet consists of tens of thousands of oceangoing vessels. A few dozen of these ships could be equipped to release a high-yield nuclear weapon onto the bottom of numerous major harbors. Equipped with timers or very low-frequency radio receivers, they would demolish a significant number of the West's major cities. As outlandish as this might appear, a nation faced with a seemingly successful Star Wars defense system will look for other ways to use its nuclear power. The Star Wars system itself is susceptible to similar sabotage. Many satellites could be equipped with nuclear explosives. Although Star Wars satellites would be hardened against nuclear explosions, they would not be immune. Several multimegaton explosions in areas near the Star Wars orbits would seriously degrade the system. This brings us to other problems with Star Wars.

The concept of detonating nuclear weapons in the high atmosphere raises a lot of questions. For example, what effect will these explosions have on missiles moving upward into the clouds of radiation and ionized matter the explosions left behind? There have been a few nuclear explosions high in the atmosphere and one that occurred in the Pacific during the 1950s that zapped a lot of electrical equipment in Hawaii. Computer models and underground tests attempt to discover the exact impact of such explosions. However, short of an actual test, there is no way of knowing the precise effect. This uncertainty makes Star Wars less reliable.

Theory and Practice

Satellites are notoriously unreliable and unpredictable beasts. Despite all the money and skill poured into them, they have to be used carefully to prevent catastrophic failure. This situation is understandable when you realize what these birds have to go through. First of all, they carry extremely delicate instruments into one of the harshest environments known to man. The trip itself is a trauma, rising from the earth on a pillar of flame, accelerating quickly to several times the speed of sound. When the satellite launcher has done its job, the bird is in a vacuum, exposed to temperature differences ranging from very cold to very hot depending on which part of the satellite is facing the sun.

Once in orbit, the satellite systems must perform precision maneuvers with exacting instruments. They are built with double and triple redundancy. You cannot test the satellite in its operating environment, but must simulate it as best you can on the ground. The birds are made with two and three copies of critical components. Elaborate procedures are worked out to reconfigure how a bird can maintain some form of functionality as components fail. The space shuttle is a partial solution to this, but it will take time. Existing satellites must be brought down for repairs. Newer satellites are designed for modular replacement while in orbit, as well as in-flight refueling. All of this increases the cost of the birds. The maintenance trips are not cheap either. Each major satellite launch costs over $300 million. Cost was one area where the Soviets came out ahead. Their low technical capabilities forced them to stick with simple, and cheaper, boosters. The United States gambled that its high-tech approach would eventually be cheaper. It was wrong, and ended up paying six times more to get a pound of anything into orbit. Currently, it costs Russia between $500 and $1,000 per pound and the United States between $4,000 and $8,000 per pound to get into low orbit. A further complication of satellite operations is the more than 40,000 manmade objects in orbit. These are just the ones the size of a pea or larger. Moving at over 5,000 meters a second, even these tiny objects can wreck a critical satellite component. Right now, a large satellite has to be in orbit 10 years to get hit, with the chance of destruction being nearly one percent. But as more litter is left in orbit, the odds of a collision increase. Hardening to provide protection will raise cost and weight still more.

New satellites always perform better on paper than in orbit. The big problem with photo and infrared reconnaissance is atmospheric cover, which cloaks much of the earth's surface at frequent and unpredictable intervals. The 1982 Falklands War, for example, was shielded from space surveillance most of the time by fog and cloud cover. More exotic sensors can penetrate this cover to some degree, but the fact remains that a bird overhead does not always guarantee a picture. Experiments have already been conducted to blind or deceive satellite sensors with lasers, or something as mundane as a gigantic smoke screen. The new KH-12 birds are intended to operate as a four-satellite system, providing continuous coverage over the entire planet. With spares and maintenance flights, that's a billion dollars a year of satellites. In addition, you need radar models and lower-flying electronic birds and higher communications ones. Then there is the cost of ground-processing and support equipment as well as research and development. The total cost comes to some $30 billion a year. And you are still not guaranteed to get a picture of what you want when you need it. You pays your money and takes your chances.

The Future

The Soviet Union, and its successor, Russia, are still moving forward with their dual policy of many expendable satellites as well as permanent manned space stations. The Russians tested a very heavy lift booster in 1987 that could put more than 100 tons into low orbit, but it had worse reliability problems than their earlier heavy-lift rockets. Indeed, Soviet launcher reliability did not improve much during the 1980s, with its rate of launch failures running at two to three times the U.S. rate. The Soviets tested a reusable shuttle to better service their space stations and recon satellites, but dropped the project because of cost at about the time the Soviet Union collapsed. The United States will probably get a permanent space station into orbit in the next decade, especially since the project has become something of a "make work" effort for those technicians put out of work by post–Cold War cuts in the military budget.

The most ambitious space program currently is SDI. Technical and cost problems will probably prevent SDI from ever being built as planned. Some components of SDI will continue to be put into use and will provide some protection from hostile missiles, and better space reconnaissance.

Chinese, European, and Third World satellite-launch capabilities will continue to grow. Even more capable Western satellites will be launched. China is also becoming a major player in space. Its first recon satellite was launched in 1975, returning film capsules after a few weeks. A shortage of launchers prevented sending up more than one bird a year. In the next year or so, the Chinese plan to put up a recon bird that can broadcast images back to Earth while staying in orbit for months or years. Other nations, such as Japan, will develop a lesser launch capacity. The problems with the space-shuttle program are causing a major revision in U.S. satellite-launch organization. In the late 1980s and early 1990s, demobilized *Titan II* ICBMs provided over a dozen launch vehicles. A larger model of the Titan series, the *Titan IV,* will provide another 50 launchers for use well into the 1990s. The collapse of the Soviet Union put many of the (now-Russian) military satellite launchers onto the international market. For a while, this will make it cheaper for many nations to get into space.

Major improvements are being sought by the major satellite-launching nations. These improvements are sought in several areas. Several, however, are likely to suffer from post–Cold War budget cuts.

1. Increased satellite maneuverability by carrying more fuel, or refuel capability.
2. More accurate navigation satellites enable air and ground units to locate themselves more accurately. This is the GPS system, which will be complete by the mid-1990s and will no doubt be upgraded thereafter. The current GPS system provides 10–20 meter accuracy, but upgrades are planned that will do even better than that.
3. Better satellite self-defense through the use of onboard protection and self-defense weapons. A likely Cold War victim, until a hostile nation starts launching antisatellite systems.
4. Better attack systems to disable enemy satellites. Another Cold War victim, although the United States may press for this to stave off "orbital terrorism."
5. Improved resistance to jamming and more powerful transmitters are also high-priority items. A possible victim of budget cuts.
6. Better satellite repair and replacement capability. This is a major reason for the U.S. space shuttle.
7. More secure ground-control facilities, which are currently one of the more vulnerable portions of satellite systems. Less likely in the post–Cold War world.

8. More relay satellites, making it easier to transmit data to and from birds no matter where they are in orbit.

9. Minisatellites to replace birds knocked out in combat. Numerous small satellites also have an advantage in that the enemy needs one or two orbits to detect a new satellite. While a satellite is undetected, it can observe activities that would normally be hidden from orbital observation. These smaller satellites perform only one or two of the functions of the standard, much larger systems. These minibirds would weigh under a ton and be launchable by ICBMs or missiles carried by high-flying bombers. Such satellites could also be put in groups of two or more in current commercial launch vehicles. This concept is still being pursued after the Cold War because it provides some peaceful use for a lot of ICBMs tagged for demobilization.

Satellite Launch Vehicles

DESIGNATION is the name of the vehicle. These are the most common vehicles. Many were originally designed as ICBMs. The U.S. space shuttle is supposed to replace all other U.S. and Western vehicles. This seems unlikely in light of reliability and cost problems with the shuttle.

SATELLITE LIFT is the amount of weight in tons each vehicle can put into LEO (Low Earth Orbit—150 to 1,000 kilometers) or GTO (Geosynchronous Transfer Orbit—36,000 kilometers). The latter is the orbit in which the satellite stays over one spot on Earth and can cover about half the planet.

LAUNCH WEIGHT (tons) is the total weight of the vehicle with payload. Most of the weight consists of fuel.

STAGES is the number of sections the vehicle is divided into. Most of the fuel is burning during the first few kilometers of climbing. Rather than drag huge, empty fuel tanks into orbit, vehicles are separated into different sections, or "stages." Each consists of a motor and fuel tanks. The final stage, containing the payload, comprises less than 10 percent of the total vehicle weight.

USER. Nation that manufactures and uses spacecraft.

COST. The approximate cost of sending this launcher up.

Satellites

TYPE is the function of the satellite.

TYPICAL WEIGHT (tons) is the weight of most satellites of each type. Most could be larger if there were a cheap enough way to get them into orbit. Inflation will have its way with satellite weights as it does with everything else.

TYPICAL ORBIT (kilometers) is the height at which each type normally operates. Most orbits are not circular but elliptical. The work is usually done at the lower phase of the orbit.

TYPICAL ENDURANCE (days) is the typical useful life of the satellite. Endurance is largely a function of supplies and other expendable items. Often the spent satellite is sent toward earth, where it burns up while reentering the atmosphere. This is to prevent useless objects from clogging up valuable orbit space.

NOTE: A Ferret is a low-altitude recon satellite.

20-1 Satellite Launch Vehicles

Designation	Satellite Lift LEO (tons)	GTO	Launch Weight (tons)	Stages	User	Cost (Mil)
Delta	10	2.2	200	3	US	$80
Titan 34D	13	1.8	682	3	US	$150
Titan 4	20	4.5	864	2	US	$250
Shuttle	24	2	1,984	2	US	$450
SL-4 (Soyuz)	7.5	1.1	310	3	Russia	$30
SL-13 (Salyut)	21	2	670	4	Russia	$45
Energia	130	12	2,300	3	Russia	$90
Ariane 3	8	2.6	241	3	France	$110
FB-1	7	2	191	3	China	$35

20-2 Satellites

Type	Typical Weight (tons)	Typical Orbit (km)	Typical Endurance (days)
Navigation	0.3	1,000	2,400
Communications	1	36,000	Unlimited
Ferret	0.3	200	100
Surveillance	12	12	200
Weather	0.7	800	100,000
Early Warning	1	36,000	1,000

21

Chemical, Biological, and Nuclear Weapons

THESE ARE THE WEAPONS no one wants to use. Yet the major nations have them, many minor nations are close to having them, and the user countries train their troops on how to use them and survive an opponent's doing the same. These weapons are unpredictable and cause disorder among the user troops as well. Warfare is unpredictable enough; none of the practitioners want it any more so.

The Specter of Nuclear Escalation

The chief reason for avoiding the use of CBN (chemical, biological, and nuclear weapons, sometimes called NBC) is the possibility of escalation to a worldwide nuclear holocaust. Escalation is easily accomplished with CBN weapons because they are all wide-area weapons. The effect of their use is not only unpredictable, but also takes a larger toll among local civilians than the troops. Soldiers are trained to deal with these horrors; civilians are not. Large civilian losses put nations in a position where they want to make retribution. This is especially true in places like Asia, where an increasing quantity of the world's CBN weapons are available. While the threat of a NATO/Warsaw Pact chemical and nuclear war in Europe is gone, the weapons still exist. A global nuclear holocaust is less of a threat, but the potential still exists.

The current concept behind using CBN is to do so only when you are on the ropes militarily and have no other option. If it comes down to a choice between CBN and defeat, you choose CBN. This is where it starts to get complicated. Many Third World nations have, or will soon have, one or more CBN weapons, and many of these nations have shown little hesitation to use these weapons. Western nations have shown themselves reluctant to reply in kind, preferring to threaten severe retribution with conventional weapons. However, if Western forces found themselves in danger of defeat or severe damage because of another nation's use of chemical or nuclear warfare, the option of using chemical or nuclear weapons first, or in retaliation, is a real possibility. The basic problem is that no one wants to lose a war, thus no nation wants to get rid of its chemical weapons. These weapons are increasingly seen as "the poor man's nuclear weapons." Chemical weapons are relatively easy to make and use. And smaller nations have been doing just that for the past 30 years.

Chemical and nuclear weapons have been used before. Military planners do confront the conditions under which these weapons would be employed. The extensive past experience with chemical weapons offers mixed signals on what might happen in the future. First used in 1915, these weapons were quickly made more lethal with developmental work. By 1917, 15 percent of British casualties were caused by chemical weapons. Moreover, chemical weapons tended to be less fatal than conventional arms like artillery and machine guns. While 30 percent of conventional-weapon casualties were fatal, only half as many chemical casualties died.

For fear of retaliation in kind, during World War II the adversaries did not use chemical weapons. There were a few isolated cases of use, but always against an opponent who could not respond with chemicals. The same pattern has persisted to the present. Even during the 1991 Gulf War, Iraq refrained from using its chemical weapons against coalition forces that had them and implied a threat to use them in retaliation.

After World War I, the effectiveness of chemical weapons was increased. The Germans developed nerve gas during the 1930s. Here was a weapon of mass destruction, at least against dense, unprotected populations. Nerve gases killed within minutes and could enter the body through the skin or inhalation. Minute quantities of nerve gas were needed to be effective, much less than with previous poison gases. Although only the Germans had large quantities of nerve gas during World War II, they never used it because they feared the Allies had these easily manufactured nerve agents also. German nerve gas was developed from research done in the United States and Russia on insect killers. This was one of the earliest "balance of terror" situations. Nerve gas would cause such massive casualties in urban areas that the Germans refrained from using it for fear that the Allies would do the same, especially after the Allied bombing of German cities got in gear. They assumed that the Allies were following the same logic about non-use. This was a situation remarkably similar to current attitudes toward nuclear weapons. Moreover, the World War II situation involved one of the more bloody-minded dictators of recent memory, Adolf Hitler.

Here is a historical precedent for restraint with a weapon similar to nuclear weapons. Does this historical lesson still apply? Available evidence is mixed. After all, Hitler himself was gassed during World War I, while no current world leaders have experienced nuclear war. The Soviets equipped their troops with chemical weapons on a lavish scale. They published procedures for the extensive and immediate use of these weapons. They trained their troops, and their allies, accordingly. However, Soviet chemical doctrine underwent a gradual softening during the 1980s. The Russians eventually adopted a doctrine in which they would use chemical weapons, if they used them at all, largely against rear-area targets only. They eventually recognized that using chemical weapons in the midst of the fast-moving combat units would be counterproductive. But their backing away from chemical weapons also constituted recognition that Western armies were increasingly capable of retaliating in kind. The Soviets recognized that chemical weapons, if they do nothing else, slow things down. As they expected Soviet troops to be doing most of the moving, chemical weapons would have been a net disadvantage. This was a curious turnabout, as the Soviets turned to chemical weapons initially to overcome their tactical disadvantage in Europe. This was not widely recognized. Without chemical weapons, Soviet armies formerly in Eastern Europe were not likely to have great success when attempting to march west. After 30 years of threatening and posturing with chemical weapons, both Soviet and Western armies in the 1980s began pulling back from any chance of using these horrors in combat. Meanwhile, Third World nations like Iraq were demonstrating that desperate nations could still resort to chemical weapons.

Despite all the nonuse of chemical weapons, their mere existence has had a serious effect on military operations. Troops are still equipped with protective gear and often lug this equipment with them into combat. Beyond the physical burden of taking the chemical-protection stuff into combat, the troops have yet another battlefield terror to worry about. These worries are not trivial, as all battles have mental-stress casualties. These stress losses are frequently a major portion of combat losses.

The Nuclear Battlefield

Nuclear weapons are easy to use on the battlefield. Put simply, they are tremendous multipliers of the firepower in existing weapons. A single 100-pound nuclear artillery shell more than equals the destructive effect of at least 8,000 conventional shells. This saves 350 tons of conventional shells, plus the wear and tear on the guns, time, transportation, etc. Beyond equaling the blast effects of conventional shells, nuclear explosives also produce radiation. Armies try to manufacture nuclear weapons that release a minimum amount of radiation. These "clean" weapons are not developed for humanitarian reasons, but because the radiation lingers and attacks friend and foe indiscriminately.

It doesn't take too many small nuclear weapons to make a difference on the battlefield. The mathematics of this mutual slaughter are straightforward. It takes only two or three nuclear weapons per enemy battalion to assure destruction. A combat division averages about a dozen combat battalions. Smaller nations would likely have only a few nuclear weapons and would be disposed to use them to greater effect against enemy cities. Each nuclear weapon used would kill several thousand civilians even if it missed an enemy city and simply landed on a nearby densely populated area. But as nuclear weapons continue to proliferate, nations would have ample nukes to throw at a wide variety of targets. This brings us to another grim aspect of tactical nuclear weapons in warfare. The targeting strategies for these weapons almost guarantees that, if enough are available, their use will quickly spread beyond the fighting front.

For example, most nuclear weapons are delivered by aircraft or missile. Therefore, a primary target of each side is the airfields of nuclear bomb-carrying aircraft and wherever you think the missile launchers might be. As all these nuclear bombs and missiles rain down, it won't take too much paranoia to make one believe that the other side is going a little too far, and maybe we should up the ante a little bit. Before long, the number of targets being hit grows to the point where the local nuclear war is causing destruction about equal to a general one. Partially in response to the ease of escalation, nuclear-bomb designers have come up with some new twists to the traditional mushroom-shaped cloud. These "designer nukes" have less blast and long-term radioactivity and put more emphasis on short-term radioactive effects. The best example is the neutron bomb, which has been around on paper for 20 years—it has been touted as "the bomb that kills people but leaves property unharmed." The effect of these weapons is mainly short term radioactivity, with much less blast effect. Other designer nukes could focus their short-term radioactivity to hit an even smaller area. These weapons make sense only if everyone uses them. Newly minted nuclear powers don't have the technology to immediately (or even eventually) equip their nuclear arsenal with designer nukes. The only positive aspect of this is that if the industrialized nuclear powers find they have to meet a first use of nukes with their own nuclear weapons, they can at least do it with relatively "clean" nukes. Scant satisfaction, that.

The Chemical Battlefield

Like nuclear weapons, chemical warheads multiply the firepower of conventional artillery and air power. Moreover, chemical weapons are generally used only against troops and, in any event, are less lethal than nuclear weapons. Chemical weapons can be designed to have immediate effects, and then dissipate. Or, if the formula is changed slightly, the effects can linger for hours, days, weeks, or even decades. Troops can more easily protect themselves from chemicals than from nukes. If properly equipped, well trained, and given warning, troops who make these preparations can reduce the effect of a large-scale chemical attack to less than 2 percent losses per day. On the other extreme, casualties can range between 70 and 90 percent, with a quarter of these being fatal. This is also a war of material. Protective equipment must be replaced frequently as it becomes contaminated. Gas masks require new filters, protective garments must be replaced, antidotes and protective ointments must be replenished. The troops have every incentive to use this equipment, and there is a lot to use, as different items are needed for protection against different chemicals.

Prolonged injury from chemical weapons is very unpleasant; to die from these weapons even more so. Like nuclear weapons, chemical weapons are best used against targets far from your own troops. Enemy airfields are a favorite target. Other choice targets are supply dumps and rear-area combat support facilities. When front-line units are hit with chemicals, it is often over a several-day period. This wears down the troops as they continually struggle to avoid injury from the toxic chemicals. Chemical weapons can be used defensively. This was done in 1917–18, when large areas were sprayed with chemicals to prevent enemy troops from moving rapidly through. This is still considered a viable tactic for chemical weapons today. Indeed, the primary effect of chemical weapons seems to be slowing down operations on the battlefield. The protective clothing is cumbersome. In warm weather, this clothing also becomes unbearably hot if the wearer moves about too quickly or too much. Specially equipped vehicles also offer some protection. But under the stress of combat use, these chemical-proof systems can be expected to leak a bit. Troop morale would be devastated if chemical casualties began to occur in supposedly secure vehicles. Because the trooops know there is a defense against chemical weapons, they will attempt to protect themselves. No matter how well trained and disciplined, troops will slow down in a chemical environment. During the initial use of chemical weapons, operations will be slow because of unfamiliarity. This slowdown in operations is one of the least talked about, yet most arresting, effects of chemical weapons' use.

Nerve gas has long been touted as the most common chemical weapon to be used. It hasn't been used that much because, in practice, it is tricky to manufacture in truly effective forms, difficult to store and deliver, and often not as effective as predicted.

Still, nerve gas is something to be very wary of. Despite masks and special suits, there is still a chance of getting a touch of this nasty stuff. When this happens, there is a minute or so to apply the antidote. This consists of sticking a syringe into a large muscle; the thigh is preferred. If you inject this stuff when you are not ill from nerve agent, you get sick from the antidote. Perhaps in recognition of all these problems, armies would prefer to stay out of contaminated areas as much as possible.

When attacking, only nonpersistent chemicals are used on defending troops. Chemical-monitoring teams travel with all units to give maximum warning about entering an unanticipated contaminated area. These "dirty" areas must be crossed as quickly as possible. If a unit assembly area is hit with chemical weapons, the area is evacuated as quickly as possible. It comes down to this: When chemicals are in the area, you either move on or stay in place and slow down a lot. You also start losing people and enthusiasm real quick.

Actual holdings of chemical weapons are still well-kept secrets. Western forces, mainly the United States, held some 40,000 tons of the stuff through the end of the Cold War. At least 16 nations currently possess chemical weapons, including several in the Middle East. Not all the chemical agents are loaded into artillery shells or bombs, because once loaded, the shells and bombs will become subject to leakage and degradation. The stock immediately available to troops was probably no more than few thousand shells, plus a smaller number of bombs and still fewer warheads for missiles. It would take a month or more to load the remaining stocks into weapons. Until the early 1990s, about half of all U.S. chemicals were stored in Europe. These have largely been withdrawn and destroyed. Soviet stocks were also larger, probably amounting to tens of thousands of shells, bombs, and missile warheads. The Soviets' doctrine was to use these weapons on a massive scale at the very beginning of a war. Most of their chemical munitions were stored close to troop units. Ideally, chemical weapons should be used in the opening stages of a surprise attack. In this way, the shock of encountering chemical weapons for the first time would be compounded by the trauma of the unexpected attack. The Russians have withdrawn all the Soviet chemical weapons from Eastern Europe and destroyed most of them, as well as much of what was stored in the former Soviet territories.

Western armed forces were slow to realize the seriousness of the Soviet chemical-warfare capability. It was only during the 1980s that Western forces became serious about preparing their troops for the strong likelihood of chemical warfare. Western intelligence forces have labored mightily to avoid surprise attacks. But there's no escaping the shock troops will get when they encounter chemical weapons on the battlefield for the first time. Prepared troops hit with an artillery barrage of chemical and nonchemical shells would suffer 10 to 30 percent casualties, one quarter of them fatal. Anyone with overhead cover would suffer half the casualty rate. If the troops are fatigued and off guard, the rate would rise to between 40 to 50 percent. If the troops are untrained, 80 percent could be killed or permanently out of action, while 20 percent would be temporarily incapacitated. This rate would also apply to civilians, of whom there might be more than 100 per square kilometer in European areas. Surprise can also be achieved away from the fighting line. Aircraft and helicopters can spray lines of gas many kilometers long. If the wind is blowing the right way, a wall of gas rolls over the unsuspecting troops. Although the gas alarms will go off, a 10-kilometers-per-hour wind can catch more than half the troops before they can put on their masks and protective clothing. Time-delay chemical bombs and mines can be dropped near enemy positions. Set to go off at night, they can have devastating effects.

Despite all the exotic methods developed for using chemical weapons in the last 50 years, the actual methods used in combat have been more prosaic. The largest use of chemical weapons recently was during the 1980–88 Iran-Iraq war. Iraq used chemical weapons, and the favorite method of delivery was via artillery shell or canisters dropped from aircraft or helicopters. Not very exotic, but effective enough. The threat that Iraq might use chemicals again in the 1991 Gulf War was very real. Again, the threat of retaliation in kind worked its magic. But the threat of retaliation cannot guarantee a chemical-free battlefield every time.

Casualties: Physical and Mental

The chief characteristic of the chemical/nuclear battlefield is the increased number of wounded casualties. During the long wars of this century, there have been 20 or more nonbattle casualties for each man killed or wounded in combat. Chemical and nuclear weapons will increase the number of both combat and noncombat casualties. Calculating the effect of nuclear and/or chemical weapons in a future war is part of the peacetime planners' art. World War I losses were 10 to 15 percent when troops advanced into a gassed enemy position. Under these conditions, the defender's losses exceeded 60 percent, thus justifying the attacker's losses to chemical weapons.

Soviet planners, who expected widespread use of chemical weapons, envisioned daily loss rates of 20 percent under chemical-warfare conditions. After five days of such operations, they assumed that a unit, now reduced to one third of its original strength, would have to be withdrawn and replaced.

The most terrifying effect of nuclear weapons is radiation. While the blast effects of nuclear weapons are formidable, they are at least somewhat familiar to anyone who has experienced shellfire. Radiation has long-term effects. It's common knowledge that radiation, if not taken in large enough doses to be immediately fatal, will do you in within hours, days, weeks, or months. Beyond that, the long-term effects can be sterility, birth defects, cancer, and general unpleasantness. Radioactivity is odorless, tasteless, and colorless.

The effects of chemical weapons are less insidious. Nerve gas has its immediate effects and then either kills you or wears off, although some long-term damage is suspected. While there is quite a lot known about nuclear weapons' effects on humans because of their actual use during World War II, there is little comparable data on the effects of nerve gas. Other chemical agents take effect immediately and also have long-term effects, as seen from their use in the Iran-Iraq War. Blister gases leave wounds and scars; blindness and damaged lungs are common. Blood agents damage internal organs such as kidneys and liver. The constant danger of injury from chemicals has greatly increased the potential for stress casualties, otherwise known as combat fatigue. Consider the symptoms of radiation and some chemical sickness: listlessness, upset stomach, headaches, fatigue. These same symptoms can also result from stress. What could be more stressful than the knowledge that you might accidentally, and unknowingly, pass through a contaminated zone? Regular doses of tranquilizers have been seriously considered as a means of calming everyone's nerves.

The fighting on a chemical and/or nuclear battlefield may quickly evolve into an exhausted stalemate or a series of duels between the scattered survivors. Historical experience reveals that survivors of high-attrition combat either give up completely or fight only to survive. It will be difficult to carry on a war if the soldiers are either immobilized by shock or ready to fight only in self-defense.

Navy and Air Force

Naval forces have fewer problems with chemical weapons. Seawater quickly absorbs chemicals, there is usually more wind at sea to blow the stuff away, and ships can more easily wash themselves down. Also, when you fight ships, you want to destroy them, not just their crews. Air forces have a more complex problem. At higher altitudes, pilots have little to fear from chemicals. However, they are at risk when they fly close to the ground. Low-level flight is very common, either on strike missions or simply to evade detection. Ultimately, all aircraft have to land, and their bases may have been gassed. Ground crews have a more difficult time of it. Their work is strenuous and must often be done quickly to get aircraft refueled and rearmed for another mission. Working inside masks and protective clothing makes you tire more easily. Fatigued ground crews are also more likely to make errors, which can be fatal for the pilots later on. The ground crews will wear out more quickly, and in some cases aircraft won't get into the air because of it. Another problem that will plague the air-force pilots and ground crews is the marginal effects of nerve gas. In diluted concentrations, nerve gas still has an effect, typically blurred vision or disorientation. These symptoms can be quite fatal for a pilot and potentially dangerous for ground crews handling fuel and munitions. Of the three services, air forces will quite likely have the worst time of it with chemical warfare.

The effects of nuclear weapons on naval targets and airfields are much the same as on army targets. In addition, it has been widely believed that nuclear weapons may be used more freely at sea. As the saying goes, "Nukes don't leave holes in the water." Neither do dead fish prompt escalation in the same way that dead civilians do. Despite this, there is a growing reluctance to automatically use nuclear weapons at sea. New antisubmarine weapons rarely have only nuclear warheads. They either have a choice of conventional or nuclear warheads or only conventional. It has been recognized that even nuclear weapons used at sea can trigger a general holocaust. Several thousand tactical nuclear weapons are still at sea, down from over 6,000 at the end of the Cold War. These were, and are, largely with the United States and Russian fleets.

Biological Warfare

Biological warfare is nothing new. For thousands of years, spreading disease throughout the enemy's army was considered a practical tactic. Even in the last century, disease killed more soldiers than battle in wartime. Disease has always been so endemic in Russian forces that as recently as World War I it was said to be more dangerous to shake a Russian soldier's hand than to be shot at by him.

For all the work that has been done on biological weapons in this century, no one seems to have used them. It appears that the balance of terror is at work here also. To use biological warfare, you first invent a new disease, usually a variant of an existing one that will spread rapidly and be fatal or very debilitating. Then you immunize your own troops. However, because these diseases cannot easily be controlled, you may have to immunize your entire population. Therefore, this approach is viewed with some circumspection. Another approach is to develop a fatal disease that will not spread from each victim. You can catch it only from the powder or spray dispersed from the bomb or artillery shell. However, none of these appears to be much more flexible or fatal than the various nerve gases around. What makes biological warfare so frightful is that no one has actually tried it yet in modern times. And there is a primordial memory in all soldiers of the depredations of disease among their ancient (and not so ancient) comrades.

Another use of biological warfare is strategic warfare. New plant diseases can be inflicted on the enemy's cropland. Herds of domestic animals can be decimated by diseases that work only on a particular species. Whatever the possibilities, no one seems eager to unleash biological warfare. There appears to be too many risks with this potentially uncontrollable form of combat.

Offensive Strategies

The data shown on the four nuclear-weapons charts has caused military planners to develop the following tactics for the nuclear battlefield. Even a minor nuclear power with only a few nukes has to pay attention to these tactical guidelines.

1. *Attack key targets that can best be destroyed with tactical nuclear weapons.* The primary targets are headquarters and units that deliver nuclear weapons. Headquarters are ideal targets because they co-ordinate subordinate units, including the ones that fire nuclear weapons. They also use a lot of communications equipment and make a lot of electronic noise. Headquarters tend to be lax in concealing themselves and maintaining a low electronic profile. Headquarters tend to sit in one place long enough to be located. After several of them disappear in a cloud of radioactive static, the surviving head-quarters will no doubt tighten up. Even so, they are always prime targets. Often more than one nuclear weapon would be thrown at a suspected headquarters site to ensure destruction.

2. *Take advantage of the wide-area effect of nuclear weapons.* Artillery, missiles, and rockets are often quite inaccurate. Artillery, firing by the map without visual observation of the target, can be off by more than 200 meters when firing at ranges over 20 kilometers. This makes it very difficult to hit hard targets like bunkers or bridges. Rockets and missiles are often off by 300 to 500 meters at these ranges. Nuclear weapons mitigate these inaccuracies. In the 1980s, battlefield missiles have gotten more accurate, particularly Western ones. This simply allows the use of smaller nuclear warheads, or more than one warhead per missile.

3. *Beware the pulse.* The growing use of electronics in combat units makes the use of nuclear weapons near your own troops very risky. Even though the troops may be a safe distance from the explosion, their electronics are still at risk. Gamma rays, produced in abundance by nuclear explosions, create large, although brief, electrical charges. This electrical disturbance looms large to tiny electronic components. The excessive electrical charge causes microcomputer components to go "tilt" or "crash." The damage can be temporary or permanent. Although many components receive special protec-tion against this electromagnetic pulse, the protection is not perfect. And not all electronics are shielded. The effect of the pulse dimin-ishes with distance, but can still be felt hundreds of kilometers away. The general lack of knowledge of the precise effects of the pulse on specific pieces of equipment is another reason for the growing re-luctance to use nuclear weapons. Soon after the first few explosions

take place, a lot more will be known about the pulse. At that point, there will probably be a lot of changes in the way nuclear weapons are used.

4. *Each nuclear weapon has to count.* At the end of the Cold War, NATO forces had about 5,000 tactical nukes available; Soviet forces have about two thirds that number. The newer ones each cost over a million dollars. Not many replacements would have been available once a war got under way. If nukes were used, there would be no replacements for a century or more, if ever. Current use of tactical nuclear weapons still calls for a certain number to be allocated to an operation. This group of weapons is called a "package." This package of weapons must be distributed among a number of targets behind the fighting line. Let us assume that a nuclear army has allocated a package of 100 nuclear weapons for an attack on an enemy corps (two divisions, several brigades, plus support units). Reconnaissance units must not only locate the targets, but keep them located until the moment of attack. Weapons would be used in such a way that some surprise would be achieved and so that the after-effects of the explosions would not hinder advancing friendly units. In practice, there are only two nations that possess sufficient quantities of nuclear weapons to fight this way: the United States and Russia. Both nations are demobilizing many (if not eventually most) of their tactical nuclear weapons and are not really interested in fighting each other. A more likely nuclear war would be some Third World nation like Iraq or Iran trying to deal with a Western army. In this case, either side would not want to use more than a few nukes. The Western army would not want to take too much political heat for nuking the neighborhood, even in the interest of preventing a wider use of nuclear weapons. The smaller nation would not have many nukes to use in the first place.

But, for historical (past and possibly future) purposes, the aforementioned package of 100 nuclear weapons would likely be distributed in the following fashion:

- *Units that fire nuclear weapons.* These are primarily missile, artillery, and air force nuclear-weapons units. Probably some 30 targets. Most of the air-force targets and some of the missile units will be outside the corps area of operations. These attacks may have to be coordinated with other attacking units that also consider a particular air base a legitimate target. Missile and artillery units are another matter. These would ideally comprise 90 percent of the targets. These units are highly mobile. The artillery units often use armored, self-propelled guns. These units know they are prime targets and pay a lot of attention to not being found. If the war lasts long enough, the word will get around that it's not safe to be where a missile unit was. That is often where the nuclear weapon will explode. Not only are these units mobile, they tend to spread out. Artillery battalions have 12 or 18 guns; missile battalions have four or more launchers. Guns and launchers often operate several kilometers from each other. Getting a fix on these units is a targeting nightmare.

- *Headquarters.* There will be about 30 of these, including corps, division, brigade, and major support-unit headquarters. Each is spread out over a few square kilometers and will attempt to avoid detection by such subterfuges as camouflage and dummy transmitters. So important are these targets that nuclear weapons will be targeted at possible locations. This is a common practice carried over from conventional artillery.
- *Supply installations.* Includes supply dumps and transportation facilities. Perhaps two dozen units. Except for preattack buildups, there should not be any large dumps. Most of the supplies should be either in transit or in small dumps near the using units. This is done on purpose to deny the enemy any good targets. More lucrative targets are found in the transportation network: railroad yards, ports, airfields, bridges, tunnels, and maintenance facilities. Those that are within the corps sector can be hit.
- *Combat units.* At least half will not be in contact with the enemy. They furnish another 20 targets.

The Results. The hundred weapons available would not cover all the targets listed above with individual attention. Because of the enormous explosive force of nuclear weapons, in many cases there will be opportunities to destroy two or more targets with one weapon. These weapons might average 20 kilotons per weapon. Assume a division-level density of troops and equipment about 50 percent of the density used on the Density of Troops, Vehicles, and Weapons on the Battlefield chart on the following pages. The 100 weapons would produce the following losses: 30,200 troops (55 percent of corps troops, 20,250 caught in the open, the remainder under cover), 1,050 nonarmored vehicles (10 percent of corps strength), 600 armored vehicles (18 percent of corps strength). In addition, if the nukes were used in a built-up area, there would be 141,800 civilian casualties plus 567,100 homeless civilians. Nearly 200,000 dwellings would be destroyed or damaged.

This sort of attack leaves the front-line combat units largely intact while severely injuring the combat support units behind the front. A conventional attack has an easier time piercing the now feebly supported combat units. Once this conventional attack gets past the front-line combat troops, there is less available to stop the attackers. The antidote for this grim scenario is good intelligence on the enemy's resources, movements, and probable intentions. If both sides were able to keep an accurate eye on each other, there would likely be sporadic use of nuclear weapons to forestall a massive attack by their opponents.

During the height of the Cold War, it was estimated that if half of the tactical nuclear weapons in Europe were used, they would cause the following losses:

Troops—1.2 million (70 percent of total)

Nonarmored vehicles—43,000 (17 percent)

Armored vehicles—15,000 (29 percent)

Proportionately more armored than nonarmored vehicles would be destroyed because these tend to be concentrated, while most trucks are on the road. Most casualties will be among support troops. Combat units would still be battling away with conventional weapons. Additional losses would include 5.6 million civilians, 23 million civilians made homeless, and 8 million dwellings destroyed. One third of Germany's economy would be laid waste. These conservative estimates include only immediate casualties. Lack of medical, support, and maintenance facilities would eventually double all the personnel losses. Similar lack of support will increase vehicle losses four or five times.

There was a lot to be grateful for when the Cold War ended, particularly among Europeans.

Theory and Practice

This area of warfare is far more theory than practice. Indeed, the practical experience has been so scanty and discouraging that most armies have been gradually edging further and further away from using chemical, biological, or nuclear weapons. After many years of studying the use of CBN and practicing and simulating it in exercises, professional soldiers seem reluctant to unleash weapons that appear ever more capable of upsetting their carefully honed visions of what war should be. As soldiers practice defending against ever more capable nuclear and chemical weapons, they realize that they would have little time or energy for anything else. They have come to fear, in effect, that nuclear and chemical theory would become practice. Soldiers are traditionalists—they would rather practice their craft with the familiar.

The Future

Nuclear weapons will continue to get smaller, cheaper, more reliable, and more versatile. The proliferation of more efficient nuclear weapons has created smaller, less powerful, and more accurate weapons among the major nuclear powers. But with the end of the Cold War, these weapons are no longer the principal problem. Each decade since the 1960s, one or more additional nations have acquired nukes, and the momentum of this proliferation is increasing. Third World nations see nuclear weapons as the great equalizer. If not against the nuclear-armed West, than against some hated neighbor. In these circumstances, the newly minted nuclear power is adopting the attitude that when it comes to firepower, too much is better than just enough. Or not enough.

Nevertheless, most nations would like to forgo nuclear and chemical weapons. Proposals are constantly put forward to do just that. Verification is always a problem because these weapons can be quickly manufactured and easily hidden. More worrisome is the prospect of more, and less stable, nations getting nuclear weapons. Many nations would like to have nukes. Those that already do, like Israel, South Africa, India, Pakistan, and China, have caused their neighbors to push nuclear-weapons development programs. The original technology is more than 50 years old and widely known and understood. It's only a matter of time before two antagonists get them. At that point, there are many more opportunities for nuclear showdowns. There is also the threat of internal disorder releasing nuclear weapons. But irrational national leaders are not unknown—look at Saddam Hussein. When one of them gets some nuclear weapons, we may see nukes used as readily as some, like Saddam, have already used chemical weapons.

Chemical weapons possession is even more widespread. Besides the United States and Russia, China, Egypt, France, Iraq, Israel, North Korea, South Africa, Syria, Taiwan, Vietnam, and Libya have them. Most other industrialized nations could develop them in less than a year. While aircraft are the easiest way to deliver these home-brew chemical weapons, many Third World nations now have access to a wider array of short-range ballistic missiles. These weapons are widely sold by Russia, North Korea, and China. They are usually older models, and are often sold at bargain prices. The buyers were getting them largely for prestige, as they are inaccurate and effective only if you have modern, lightweight nuclear warheads— although Iraq demonstrated the largely political impact Scuds fired into the Saudi and Israeli deserts could have. Iraq also threatened to use chemical warheads. Many people quickly realized during the Gulf War how easily one could use these missiles with locally produced chemical warheads. To make matters worse, Third World nations like India, Brazil, and Taiwan have also developed arms industries capable of producing these missiles and are planning to sell all they can produce in the 1990s. While Russia, and to a lesser extent China, can be restrained from selling missiles by the threat to withhold economic aid, there are still more, and better, missiles coming on the open market.

In response to this proliferation, there has been a lot of growth in the chemical-protection business, with a growing variety of chemical detector systems, masks, suits and antidotes coming onto the market. Unlike chemical weapons, the chemical defensive gear is much easier to sell, although more difficult and expensive to manufacture than chemical weapons. In fact, more is spent on chemical protection than on the chemical weapons themselves.

Up until the end of the Cold War, the two superpowers had not completely sworn off chemicals. In the late 1980s, the Soviets announced a new generation of chemical and biological bomblets that could be used down to the infantry-battalion level. Their new tactics stressed the use of chemicals at the fighting line only when resistance could not be quickly overcome with conventional weapons. Orders to "go chemical" were still to come from the highest headquarters. All of this disappeared with the end of the Cold War, although Russia retained a chemical capability, as did most of the other new nations that emerged from the ashes of the Soviet Union.

Future use of chemical weapons will be deep in the enemy rear against military and civilian targets. Attacks against major population areas with less lethal chemicals would panic civilians and cause traffic jams, and are considered a useful tactic. New biological weapons that can attack civilians and infrastructure electronic components are also in the works. Chemical warfare isn't going away, it's just getting more complicated.

Tactical Nuclear Weapons' Effects on Ground Forces

TYPE OF TARGET. Down the left side of the chart are listed various situations troops may find themselves in when a nuclear weapon goes off nearby.

TROOPS IN THE OPEN. It is assumed that most troops in the field will be in this situation when a nuclear weapon detonates. Because most of a nuclear weapon's energy goes into creating blast and heat (or flash), it is more successful if it surprises troops outside shelter or vehicles. The flash/heat travels at the speed of light and is nearly instantaneous. It burns exposed skin and blinds those looking at it. Flash will be diminished by clouds or fog. Clothing will also absorb a lot of this damage. Bad weather will not only provide more protection with clouds and fog, but more troops will be inside some form of shelter and wearing more clothing. This can reduce flash casualties by more than half. Under most conditions, the majority of injuries will be from this. In addition, there will be blast injuries. Blast travels at the speed of sound, about 325 meters a second. Nuclear-weapon blast arrives as a high-speed wind. For each weapon size shown on the chart, the wind is about 130 kilometers per hour at the maximum distance and about 380 kilometers per hour at half that distance. A hurricane generates winds of from 120 to 200 kilometers per hour, a tornado up to 480 kilometers per hour. The flying objects tossed about by these winds cause additional losses, although troops have a few seconds to seek shelter. Troops at the greatest risk are those away from the fighting, where at least half may be in the open during daytime.

21-1 Nuclear Weapons' Effects on Ground Forces

Meters from Point of Explosion Where 50% Casualties Will Occur

Type of Target		1	10	20	100	200	500	1000
		Numbers above indicate yield of weapon in kilotons.						
Troops in the Open		1,000	2,154	2,714	4,642	5,848	7,937	10,000
	Sq Km	3	15	23	68	107	198	314
Protected in Open Earthworks		700	1,508	1,900	3,249	4,094	5,556	7,000
	Sq Km	1.54	7	11	33	53	97	154
Nonarmored Vehicles & Aircraft		600	1,293	1,629	2,785	3,509	4,762	6,000
	Sq Km	1.13	5	8	24	39	71	113
Armored Vehicles		450	969	1,221	2,089	2,632	3,572	4,500
	Sq Km	0.64	3	5	14	22	40	64
Heavy Structures of Concrete, etc		200	431	543	928	1,170	1,587	2,000
	Sq Km	0.13	0.58	0.93	3	4	8	13

TROOPS PROTECTED IN OPEN EARTHWORKS represents troops in fox-holes, trenches, vehicles, and other light structures that shield them from much of the flash and blast. There would still be significant losses from fire and falling debris.

NONARMORED VEHICLES AND AIRCRAFT ON GROUND would have enough components damaged to be unusable. The primary cause of damage will be blast. Winds of more than 400 kilometers per hour (240 mph) will do terrible things to trucks and parked aircraft.

ARMORED VEHICLES are generally too heavy to be severely damaged by high winds. Antennae, searchlights, and other protrusions can be damaged. Heat will also damage nonmetallic items like fire-control and sighting gear. At the ranges shown, radiation will kill or injure crew members inside vehicles. Any crew outside the vehicles at the ranges shown will certainly be lost. Crews spend 85 percent of their time outside their vehicles. Without trained crews, the armored vehicles are useless.

HEAVY STRUCTURES OF CONCRETE, ETC. This represents substantial com-mercial buildings as well as military bunkers. Personnel inside will be protected from most radiation effects.

Weapons size is represented across the top of the chart in equivalent kilotons (thousand tons) of TNT explosive. The common sizes for tactical nuclear weapons are from 1 to 1,000 kilotons, with the preferred range less than 100 kilotons. Larger ones (more than 1,000) are used in strategic missiles, although these systems are also tending toward the 100–500 kiloton range. Note that 14-kiloton weapons were dropped on Japan in 1945. The effects of the weapon is by the two numbers within the chart. The top figure is the distance from the explosion at which 50 percent of troops or vehicles will become casualties. One third of the casualties will be fatal immediately. Another third may be fatal eventually without adequate treatment. Casualties may increase a further 50 percent if radioactive fallout is not avoided or decontamination does not take place. The range of effect is measured from the explosion. An airburst is assumed. The height of the airburst varies with the size of the weapon. The only reason for using a ground burst is to increase radioactivity or to ensure destruction of hard targets.

Tactical nukes want to avoid radioactivity as much as possible. The second figure for each type of target is the area covered (in square kilometers) by the effects of various weapons under the conditions shown. This is convenient when comparing effects that depend on the density of troops or equipment in the area.

Tactical Nuclear Weapons' Effects on Ships

SINK OR PERMANENTLY DISABLE indicates sufficient damage to either sink the ship outright or disable it to the extent that repairs at sea are impossible. Immediate radiation casualties at this range will also be high, putting up to 50 percent of the crew out of action. This is also the range for damage to modern submarines from an underwater explosion of a nuclear weapon. Older subs would be damaged or destroyed even at these ranges, perhaps 25 percent longer.

TEMPORARILY DISABLE MOBILITY indicates sufficient damage to the ship's power plant to impair or completely shut down. On aircraft carriers, any aircraft on the flight deck would be destroyed. Landing and takeoff operations would probably be impossible for at least a few hours. Many aircraft in the air would have to find an alternative landing field, as most U.S. carrier aircraft are launched on the assumption that they will land within two hours. Repairs on ship power

21-2 Nuclear Weapons' Effects on Ships

Type of Effect on Ship		Range of Effect in Meters			
		20 Kiloton	200	2,000 Kiloton	20,000
Sink or Permanently Disable	Sq Km	800 2	1,724 9	3,714 43	8,001 201
Temporarily Disable Mobility	Sq Km	1,500 7	3,232 33	6,962 152	15,000 707
Temporarily Disable Sensors and Weapons	Sq Km	2,000 13	4,309 58	9,284 271	20,001 1,257

systems could take from hours to days. Meanwhile, these ships would be more vulnerable to additional enemy attacks. This range is also the extreme range at which underwater nuclear explosions can cause any damage to modern nuclear submarines. Older, nonnuclear subs could still be hurt at 25 percent longer ranges. Surface ships could also receive some damage from underwater nuclear explosions within this range.

TEMPORARILY DISABLE SENSORS AND WEAPONS. Physical damage to antennae and viewing devices as well as light deck structures, especially missile launchers, would be significant. Within this range, any aircraft in the way would also suffer severe, often fatal, damage. Ships without sufficient onboard repair capability would have permanent damage. The electromagnetic pulse of the explosion would also extend for hundreds of kilometers. This would be very dangerous to aircraft in the air within the range of the pulse. Submerged submarines would be unaffected by underwater nuclear explosions at this range.

Across the top of the chart is shown the weapon size (in kilotons). Naval nuclear weapons tend to be larger than land versions. The 2,000-kiloton weapon would be found only in strategic missiles, which may be used at sea if satellite surveillance becomes efficient enough. The 20,000-kiloton weapon exists in small quantities, but is likely to disappear during post–Cold War disarmament. However, such weapons can be produced again by any nation so inclined.

THE EFFECTS. The top figure gives the range of that effect. The bottom figure is the area covered in square kilometers. An average task force of 8 to 12 ships would occupy an area up to 1,000 square kilometers. A merchant convoy of 30 to 50 ships, plus 8 or more escorts, would cover the same area. The more important ships occupy the center of such an area.

Number of Losses Assuming Indicated Densities

Chart 21-3 shows the losses in troops, vehicles, or structures, depending on the nuclear weapon's size and posture of the target. Across the top of the chart are the various sizes of nuclear weapons, and below each is number of personnel, vehicles, or structures that would be injured, depending on their situation.

DENSITY PER SQUARE KILOMETER is the assumed density of personnel for calculating casualties. The targets are assumed to be battalion size, the basic combat unit in all armies. Each contains from 400 to 1,000 men, and the battalions would be distributed throughout their assigned areas. A battalion normally deploys in an area covering 5 to 12 square kilometers. Some battalion-deployment areas overlap others to a minor extent. Support units also frequently occupy the same area. In the chart, we are only showing losses from single battalions. There is some "empty" space between battalions, occupied only by any civilians who have not fled the area. Smaller nuclear weapons are more effective, as larger ones waste much of their effect on areas not occupied by combat troops. These larger weapons will injure one half to one third the number shown on the chart because of the "empty space" they will hit.

21-3 Losses to Nuclear Weapons

	Density per Square Km	1	10	20	100	200	500	1,000
		Number above indicates yield of weapon in kilotons. Numbers below represent the losses in each category as shown in the first column.						
Troops in the Open	35	55	255	405	1,185	1,881	3,465	5,500
Protected in Open Earthworks	35	27	125	199	581	922	1,698	2,695
Nonarmored Vehicles & Aircraft	5	3	13	21	61	97	178	283
Armored Vehicles	5	2	7	12	34	54	100	159
Heavy Structures of Concrete, etc.	20	0	1	2	7	11	20	31
Civilian Losses	250	193	894	1,418	4,147	6,583	12,127	19,250
Dwellings Rendered Uninhabitable	85	262	1,215	1,929	5,640	8,953	16,492	26,180
Civilians Made Homeless		770	3,573	5,671	16,583	26,323	48,488	76,969
Distance at Which Housing Is Rendered Uninhabitable (in meters from bomb)		1,400	3,016	3,800	6,498	8,187	11,112	14,000

TROOPS IN THE OPEN. Normally, half the troops are outside, half are under cover in open earthworks or some other shelter. If the weather is bad, or it is night, more are under cover. The more troops that are in the open, the more will get hit.

NONARMORED VEHICLES. Density is for an entire division area. These are largely trucks.

ARMORED VEHICLES density is for a combat battalion (average).

HEAVY STRUCTURES density is of a heavily urbanized area. This is where most of the critical fighting would take place in Western Europe.

CIVILIAN LOSSES represent population losses for population density in Germany (which has a population density typical of places that might get nuked). Belgium and the Netherlands have a higher density. The rest of Europe (East and West) has about half the density of Germany. Civilian casualties will vary considerably throughout a country. The heavily built-up areas have densities of more than 5,000 people per square kilometer, which is typical for cities and urban areas worldwide. Even agricultural areas will have densities of more than 400. Nonagricultural rural areas will have densities of less than 100, all the way down to 10. If dirty nuclear weapons are used, eventual casualties will be more than doubled due to delayed radiation effects. The magnitude of civilian casualties will overwhelm medical facilities, and otherwise nonfatal injuries will kill. Fifty percent of all casualties will be fatal under these conditions. Many of the civilians will have fled the combat area, or attempted to do so. However, they have to go somewhere. Because nuclear weapons will be used largely against rear-area targets, the density of civilians may be greater in these areas because of refugees. It will be difficult for civilians to stay away from military targets, as the troops will be widely dispersed to lessen the effects of nuclear weapons.

DWELLINGS RENDERED UNINHABITABLE. Given the density of population, this is the number of dwellings rendered uninhabitable by each size weapon.

CIVILIANS MADE HOMELESS is the average number of civilians whose residences are no longer livable. Up to a point, these civilians can be accommodated in other homes. The average dwelling in Europe has four or five rooms, with less than one inhabitant per room. Other parts of the world typically average two or more people per room and fewer rooms per dwelling. Each dwelling lost is a significant loss for the inhabitants.

DISTANCE AT WHICH HOUSING IS RENDERED UNINHABITABLE (IN METERS FROM BOMB). This is heavy damage. It includes broken windows, minor fires, roof-tile damage, and the like. Without repairs, this housing is only marginally habitable. Still, it's better than staying outside.

Density of Troops, Vehicles, and Weapons on the Battlefield

Chart 21-4 shows the average density of troops and vehicles in units of the United States Army (or armies of other Western nations) and Russian/Third World–style armies.

UNIT DESIGNATION represents the most common units of both armies. The U.S. Corps and the Russian Army are roughly equivalent in combat power and manpower. The U.S. Corps contains two divisions, an armored cavalry regiment and support units. The Russian Army contains four divisions and support units. The figures for both armies are averages for combat, combat support, and supply units. Each division contains 12 to 16 battalions.

LOCAL CIVILIANS gives the average density of civilians, dwellings, and vehicles located in the combat-unit deployment area.

AREA is the area in which the combat units are dispersed, in square kilometers. Generally, this is an irregular area roughly resembling a rectangle. The corps/army occupies an area 50 by 50 kilometers, divisions 25 by 24 or 20 by 17. The battalion area is three by four kilometers. These are averages; they are often half as large when a unit is attacking.

TROOPS TOTAL are the total number of troops assigned to that unit. The divisions usually are in contact with the enemy and thus occupy most of the forward portion of the corps/army area. The empty space at the front line is covered by corps/army reconnaissance troops. The corps/army rear area has the lowest concentration of troops.

ARMORED VEHICLES TOTAL is the total number of armored vehicles in the unit. This includes tanks, APCs and self-propelled artillery.

TRUCKS TOTAL is the total number of nonarmored vehicles in the unit. This includes aircraft.

TROOPS PER KM is the average number of troops per square kilometer in the unit's area.

ARMORED VEHICLES PER KM is the average number of armored vehicles per square kilometer in the unit's area.

TRUCKS PER KM is the average number of nonarmored vehicles per square kilometer in the unit's area.

21-4 Density of Troops, Vehicles, and Weapons on the Battlefield

Unit Designation	Area (sq km)	Troops Total	Armored Vehcls Total	Trucks Total	Troops per km	Armored Vehcls per km	Trucks per km
US Corps	3,000	55,000	5,085	10,000	18	2	3
Russian Army	3,000	61,000	5,826	9,000	20	2	3
US Division	600	20,000	1,220	3,500	33	2	6
Russian Division	350	14,000	1,068	1,500	40	3	4
US Battalion Team	12	900	60	10	75	5	1
Russ Battalion Team	10	600	50	2	60	5	0
Local Civilians	All				250 Civilians	85 Dwellings	90 Cars and Trucks

Chemical Weapons

"GAS" NAME, the common name of the chemical agent. Derived from its effects on troops.

- Tear gas, commonly used by police and military forces. Has been produced in many variants. Other names are CS, CN, etc. Because of its generally nonlethal nature, tear gas has been accepted as not being a chemical agent in the common sense of the word. In other words, tear gas is widely used. However, it can be lethal. Some of the more powerful variants induce severe coughing, involuntary defecation, and vomiting. These effects can render a victim quite helpless. Tear gas is also used in a powder form, to serve as a persistent harassing agent on the battlefield.
- Vomiting gas is a super tear gas. Also known as Adamsite. It was a favorite with the Soviets and probably still exists in Russia. Like tear gas, it is ideal for clearing out enemy troops, or anyone else, in built-up areas, caves, and fortifications. While tear gas will often cause vomiting, this stuff will practically guarantee it.
- Blister gas was a Soviet development, an improvement on World War I mustard gas. Also known as Phosgine Oxime. It acts more quickly than mustard gas and completely destroys skin tissue. Very ugly stuff.
- Mustard gas is an updated version of the harassment agent used extensively during World War I. Not really a gas, but a liquid spray. It takes a while to act, but once it gets going, it leaves ugly blisters. Many victims still carry scars, not to mention blindness and lung injuries, from this gas. Used by Iraq in the 1980s Persian Gulf War. Some of this mustard used in the Persian Gulf was said to be a powder that burned deep into the skin. Very nasty stuff.
- Choking gas is one of the first modern chemical agents. Also known as Phosgene. Caused 80 percent of the gas fatalities during World War I. Still available, but being replaced by still more effective agents.
- Blood gas also had its origins in World War I. It was valued for its ability to act quickly by causing suffocation. This made it the ideal surprise agent. The original was called cyanogen chloride (CK). Modern versions are prussic acid and hydrogen cyanide. Even the names have a grotesque ring to them. This one was another favorite of the Soviets.
- Nerve gas was first developed during the 1930s as a variation of an insecticide. Has gone through many reformulations and is known by a variety of names: Tabun (GA), Sarin (GB), Soman (GD), CMPF (GP), VR-55, VX, etc. It comes in persistent and nonpersistent forms. Can be used in lethal and harassing concentrations. Perhaps the most widely stockpiled agents, and would probably be the most widely used. Shuts down the body's nervous system, causing suffocation, etc. Light doses cause blindness or blurred vision, severe headaches, and disorientation. Germans used a nerve gas in their extermination camps. Very ugly.

CODE NAMES are the two-letter U.S. Army code names.

PHYSICAL EFFECT on victims. Most chemical agents are fairly simple elements that primarily irritate tissues, like the skin and eyes. Any that gets into the lungs

21-5 Chemical Weapons

Gas Name	Code Name	Physical Effect	Used to	Persistence (hours)	Inhaled Agents		Skin Contact Agents		Can It Be Smelled?	Tons to Cover (sq km)
					Time to Take Effect (minutes)	Minimum Dosage Level	Time to Take Effect (minutes)	Minimum Dosage Level		
Tear	CS	Irritation, tears, nausea	Harass	0.5	1	1,157	NA	NA	Yes	NA
Vomiting	DM	Headache, cough, nausea	Harass	0.5	1	4,080	NA	NA	No	NA
Blister	CX	Severe skin blisters	Harass	36-1,300	NA	NA	100	5	No	NA
Mustard	HD	Severe skin blisters	Harass	36-1,300	NA	NA	300	6	Yes	10
Choking	CG	Cough, suffocation	Kill	0.1	600	89	NA	NA	Yes	NA
Blood	AC	Convulsions, suffocation	Kill	0.1	8	139	NA	NA	Yes	NA
Nerve	GD	Convulsions, suffocation	Kill	.2-50	8	2	8	143	No	1
Nerve	VX	Convulsions, suffocation	Kill	1-2,700	6	1	6	28	No	0

has a more pronounced effect. The only chemical agents that go beyond these simplistic effects are blood and nerve gases. Blood gases interfere with the absorption of oxygen by the blood in the lungs. This causes a form of suffocation. Nerve gases interfere with the transmission of messages in the body's nervous system. All these agents are potentially fatal. The fatal ones will not kill in smaller doses. This phenomenon exacerbates any hypochondriac tendencies among victims. Sickness in general tends to be higher among troops in the field. Less than 5 percent of the casualties in an army are the direct result of combat; the remainder come from a variety of accidents and common illnesses. Chemical agents and their ability to make troops slightly ill will combine with the troops' fear of gas fatalities to produce some very nervous and unwell soldiers.

USED TO indicates whether the chemical agent is intended primarily for harassment or killing. Harassment agents are popular because they can be used more aggressively without endangering your own troops. A harassment agent that is nonpersistent (see next column) can be used without fear of causing significant injury to your own troops. This makes an ideal weapon for use at the front, where friendly troops are nearby. Harassment agents are customarily fired on troops about to be attacked by your own troops. In the short term, this forces the defenders to put on their protective gear. This makes them less effective. Sometimes harassment agents are fired at defending troops over a period of days. This can substantially wear down the enemy's willingness to fight. Harassment agents are also used to create large areas that are difficult for the enemy to pass through. Lethal chemical agents are principally used on enemy targets far to the rear, where your own troops are unlikely to be affected. Dead and wounded soldiers do have an impact on the survivors' morale and willingness to go on. Consider, for example, the effect on a soldier's fighting spirit after he has been gassed once, or more than once. A harassment agent is not used to be humane; it is an attempt to discourage troops from fighting by forcing them to wear cumbersome protective gear and by inflicting painful injuries. Surviving an encounter with chemical injuries can be more damaging to an army than fatalities. The victims, instead of being buried with their pain and horror, live to tell others about it.

PERSISTENCE (hours) is the length of time the chemical agents remain effective after they are released. The least persistent form of chemical is gas or vapor. Like common smoke, this quickly dissipates in the atmosphere. Depending on the concentration of the chemical, wind speed, and humidity, the potency of the agent may disappear in minutes. Other factors affect chemical persistence. Persistent agents will last longer in vegetation. Porous soil will retain them longer. Nonporous soil allows water or wind to carry the chemicals away quickly. Sunlight causes most agents to degrade quickly, with nerve-gas effectiveness diminished by more than 60 percent. Temperature also affects chemicals. It does so in two ways. Cold decreases the speed of dispersal. This keeps the chemicals in a smaller area and in higher concentrations. A high temperature gradient, cold air near the ground and warm air just above it, holds the chemical agents to the ground. This makes inhalation less likely. Moisture washes the agents away. A bad side effect is the contamination of any nearby water supplies until the agent is diluted enough to become ineffective. With gas, it's one damn thing after another.

Wind both aids and hinders the gases. It dilutes them to an impotent level more quickly. A 20-kilometers-per-hour wind reduces area coverage over a 4-kilometers-per-hour wind by more than 60 percent. Wind also creates a downwind hazard. Depending on the time of day and wind speed, nerve agents can cause nonfatal injuries 120 kilometers away. A high wind, at any time of day, can carry effective concentrations of nerve agents up to 75 kilometers. On a sunny day, with winds of less than 10 kilometers per hour, the agent will travel no farther than 1 kilometer. At dawn, dusk, or on a heavily overcast day, the range will be 10 kilometers. The worst conditions are a calm night. Even with only a four-to-five-kilometers-per-hour wind, the nerve agents will travel from 45 kilometers to 120 kilometers. Any troops in the path of these agents will be manning sensors, on guard duty, asleep, or driving. The damage caused by impaired vision, dizziness, and other nonfatal effects could be considerable, especially drivers having accidents. Gases tend to flow along the contour of the ground, collecting in low areas. One bright young officer, while on a training exercise, set off some tear-gas grenades on the high ground overlooking an "enemy" headquarters. As the cloud charged down the hill, the lieutenant and his troops advanced behind it to mop up. Altogether, the above climate factors decrease the area effectively covered by chemical agents by more than 90 percent. For example, in most cases a 155mm artillery chemical shell would spread a lethal dose (to 50 percent of unprotected troops) of nerve gas over a 13-meter radius from the shell burst. Winds faster than 38 kilometers per hour disperse the chemical so quickly that you have to be four meters from the shell burst to get a fatal dose. With a 28-kilometers wind, it's only six meters. With a sunny day and a 4-kilometers breeze, the distance is 7.5 meters. In subzero temperatures, this would go up to eight meters. Best conditions for chemicals are cold, windless evenings in terrain with porous soil and lush vegetation (northern Russia in the summer). Worst conditions are hot, windy daylight in an area with nonporous soil, little foliage, and lots of rain (Persian Gulf coast during the rainy season). Persistent agents work best in winter, except for the fact that potential victims are bundled up. Mustard gas will last up to eight weeks in the winter, seven days during the summer, and only two days during a rainy period. VX, a liquid persistent nerve agent, will last 16 weeks in winter, 3 weeks in summer, but only 12 hours in the rain.

INHALED TIME TO TAKE EFFECT (min.) is the shortest average time for the agents to take effect through inhalation, in minutes. This assumes a sufficient concentration. The quickest agents are those that work on the nervous or respiratory systems. Nerve gas is by far the fastest, at least in theory. If inhaled, its effect can be within seconds. Even exposure to nerve agents through the skin often take effect in minutes. Blood gases act quickly to block the absorption of oxygen by the body, producing the equivalent of suffocation. Tear gases act upon the sensitive eye tissues and to a lesser extent on the skin. Blister and mustard gases can be inhaled. In less lethal doses, which will be quite common, agents will take longer to have an effect. Normally, the gases will continue to diminish and dissipate, and their effects will not get worse.

MINIMUM DOSAGE LEVEL is the relative amount of agent in milligrams that must be present in a cubic meter of atmosphere, during a one-minute period, to kill 50 percent of unprotected personnel. Multiply by 36 to get the actual lethal dose.

SKIN CONTACT TIME TO TAKE EFFECT (min.) is the shortest average time for the agent to take effect through skin contact, in minutes. For mustard and blister gases, this is the time required to cause blindness. The eyes are the most sensitive external part of the body; mustard and blister gases attack the eyes first. The substance can enter the eyes if a soldier gets some of the agent on his hands and then rubs his eyes. Over 10 times more of the chemical agents is required to blister the skin. To inflict fatal casualties, 50 times as much is required.

MINIMUM DOSAGE LEVEL is the minimum amount required to have the desired effect on 50 percent of unprotected personnel. A higher dosage is required for skin transmission than for inhalation. The skin is designed to repel foreign substances; the lungs are constructed to absorb things quickly. A mask cannot provide sufficient protection because so many agents can enter through the skin. Many agents need not even be fatal in order to put a soldier out of action. Nonfatal doses of nerve gas, either inhaled or absorbed through the skin, have a very debilitating and demoralizing effect. Nonfatal doses of blister agents are equally unpleasant.

CAN IT BE SMELLED? This is an important consideration. If the agent cannot be smelled, its presence will be announced either by scarce and sometimes unreliable "chemical warning instruments" or by troops becoming casualties. Gases that can be smelled can often be seen also. However, many of the more modern agents are odorless and invisible. This makes detection instruments all the more important. These devices usually detect agents in sublethal doses or even before they are concentrated enough to do much damage at all. This gives troops a chance to put on protective equipment or stay away from the contaminated areas.

TONS TO COVER SQ KM indicates the tonnage of the chemical agents required to cover a square kilometer. Method of delivery is spraying the agent from aircraft. This is not only the most effective method of delivering chemical agents, but likely to be the most widely used in the opening stages of a future war. Spraying is likely to be favored because of the emphasis on surprise and the use of aircraft to deliver chemicals. A typical fighter-bomber aircraft can spray four tons of GD over a six-kilometer frontage in less than a minute's flying time. One kilometer downwind, this six-kilometer wall of gas will cause 50 percent fatalities. Five kilometers downwind (in open terrain, with a light wind, etc.), unwarned but gas-trained and equipped troops will likely suffer 20 percent fatalities and 70 percent nonfatal casualties. GD nerve gas is a vapor and travels with the wind. VX is a "drizzle" agent. Its large droplets will not travel far before hitting the ground and staying there. An aircraft laying down a line of VX two kilometers wide and 130 kilometers long will kill 50 percent of any unprepared troops entering this nerve-gas zone. Why bother with anything but nerve gas? The main problem is decontamination. Nerve agents are potent, persistent, and unable to tell friend from foe. Protective clothing and masks cause a significant loss of efficiency. For example, voice communication and vision are reduced 25 to 50 percent when masks are worn. When the temperature rises above 60 degrees, troops cannot be active for more than a few hours without risk of heat prostration. Prolonged wearing of full protective gear causes additional problems, as it is difficult to sleep, eat, or drink. The only way out of this mess is to decontaminate. Even leaving the contaminated area will do you no good, as you take the gas along. Decontamination of nerve agents means washing everything down with a lot of water, or a lot less of a special decontamination solution. Even when you use the special solution, 320 pounds of liquid are required to clean up one vehicle. Other methods, faster and using less liquid, are available but are not 100 percent effective. What will happen to troop morale and effectiveness if casualties are caused by chemical agents on previously "decontaminated" vehicles?

22

Strategic Nuclear Weapons

Nuclear weapons are instruments of mass destruction. They are a much-feared, never-before-used weapon. No one knows how leaders will react when confronted with actually using them. Even with restraint employment, the destruction will be enormous. Worse yet, military planners have, since the late 1970s, seriously looked into the mechanics of fighting and winning a nuclear war. Nuclear wars are unlikely to have any recognizable winners.

Proliferation

The nuclear war everyone fears is between superpowers and involves thousands of warheads. With the end of the Cold War and the collapse of one of the world's two superpowers, a major nuclear war becomes less likely. The first use of nuclear missiles will more likely occur between two smaller nations. There is another form of proliferation among the major nuclear powers. We're not talking about the steady increase in the number of nuclear weapons throughout the Cold War. More than 50,000 of them are in the hands of the United States, Russia, Britain, France, China, India, Pakistan, Israel, and South Africa by the late 1980s. The two nuclear superpowers have 95 percent of them, and the United States has the majority of these. The "proliferation" came from these nations having become accustomed to having these weapons. Many military units have carried and trained with nuclear weapons for over 30 years. People have become used to them. The novelty factor is gone, and the weapons are just another piece of equipment. People still are in awe of the possible use of these weapons. While the awe remains, so does a certain familiarity. Familiarity breeds attempt. While the end of the Cold War brought about a welcome cutback in the number of weapons (to perhaps fewer than 10,000 by the end of the decade), many will remain ready for use.

Ah, But Will They Work?

Yes and no. As the charts indicate, serviceability and reliability vary from missile to missile. Like complex machinery everywhere, missiles will work only some of the time. Consider satellite launchers, which are coddled far more than combat missiles. The U.S. success rate is over 90 percent. The Soviet success rate was closer to 75 percent. The success rate of satellites functioning as designed after surviving the launch process is somewhat better. No one wants to admit it, but combat missiles will probably perform less well than satellite launchers. In addition, several other problems with combat missiles must be dealt with.

1. *Navigation.* Several factors can degrade the accuracy of missile-guidance systems. The most prominent one is called bias. This arises from most missile tests being from east to west or west to east. In combat, most of the missiles will be going north, over the pole. This makes a big difference, as vagaries in gravity, magnetic fields, and weather are quite dissimilar going over the pole. Although guidance specialists insist these problems have been solved, we'll never know until many missiles go flying over the North Pole. As that would be considered an act of war, we are at an impasse on this problem. Then again, it may be something of a nonproblem. The effect of bias would be to degrade the accuracy of the warheads. The CEP (Circular Error Probable) may increase by hundreds or thousands of meters. This will only diminish the accuracy of missiles attempting to destroy other missiles in their armored, underground silos. No one admits to any desire to achieve such a capability. An attempt is moot because the missiles from invulnerable submarines would survive to destroy everyone's industry and population. When you are city bashing, such inaccuracies mean little. However, whenever anyone talks about first-strike capability and silo busting, remind them of bias and reliability in general. The Soviets were always worried that Western technology would do them in once more. American engineers have developed terminal homing devices for ballistic missiles that allow a warhead to make fine adjustments as it hustles earthward. This generally involves an image-processing capability, a

technology more highly developed in the West. The same sort of thing is used in cruise missiles. Another approach is a warhead navigation system that can take positional information from navigation satellites (GPS). This assumes that these satellites have not yet been destroyed.

2. *Fratricide.* This is what happens when the explosion of one nuclear weapon causes problems for other warheads that are still burning through the atmosphere toward their targets. Nukes going for urban areas explode in the atmosphere. They suck up a lot of dirt and debris, blasting it all upward some 20,000 meters. Warheads going after silos explode near the ground, throwing even more crap skyward. Any warhead following the first one into the same target area gets a blast of radiation and, worst of all, lots of more substantial garbage thrown into its path. Zipping along at thousands of meters per second, little grains of sand can destroy or disrupt incoming warheads.

3. *Reliability.* This is taken for granted. This is easy to do, as these weapons are rarely tested and have never been used in action. Ballistic missiles consist of several complex systems, each of which must function individually and with the other systems. The simplest system is the rocket motors. Most are solid fuel, which is actually a slow-burning explosive. Manufacturing these solid fuels is an exacting process, one very few nations are really adept at. However, the process is not perfect. Like flashbulbs, solid-fuel rockets can't be tested. You can poke and probe them and double-check them. Ultimately, you play the percentages and hope your numbers are high enough. The Soviets were still using liquid-fuel motors in many of their ICBMs right up until the collapse of the USSR. As these liquid-fuel motors are mechanical devices, there is a heavy maintenance load and even higher probability of system failure. Holding the rocket motor, and everything else, is the rocket structure. This is the shell into which all components are fitted. This is quite a complex piece of work, as missiles consist of two or three stages. That is, you actually have two or three rockets piled on top of each other.

The first section, or stage, is the largest and contains a large rocket motor. The second stage is another motor, and the third stage is the warhead, guidance system, and smaller rocket. Thus, there is not one structure but three. Modern missiles use MIRV (Multiple Independent Reentry Vehicle) warheads. This is a final stage, now renamed a "bus," that releases warheads like passengers getting off at different times. This requires another mechanical device linked to the guidance system to ensure that the warheads are let go at the proper time. Another time-critical event in the separation of a lower stage during flight. This is done with explosive bolts. Should one or more of these fail, the entire missile is lost.

The entire process is intolerant to any failure. There is much that can go wrong and ample opportunity for failure to occur. The rocket motor and missile structure are simple items compared to the guidance system and warheads. The guidance system is a particularly complex piece of electromechanical precision. It is responsible for guiding the missile and its warheads over a course of up to 10,000 kilometers and hitting within 100 to 2,000 meters of the target. Not only are these systems subject to frequent failure, they are also at the mercy of their computer programs. Undiscovered errors on these programs have previously caused many embarrassing breakdowns. Frequently, flaws in the system are not discovered until after months or years of supposedly combat-ready deployment. The warheads are subject to many of the same ills experienced by the guidance system. A nuclear weapon is not a simple device. Basically, it is a bit of radioactive material surrounded by high explosives and other elements needed to produce the desired explosive effect. Extraordinary measures are taken to ensure that these weapons do not go off except when intended. These safety devices are complex and numerous. Should any one of them fail, the weapon will not go off.

4. *Readiness.* As complex as these missiles are, they have one more obstacle to overcome before they have a chance to complete their mission. Years of inactivity are spent buried within underground silos or aboard submarines. The dozens of major electronic and mechanical systems are constantly monitored. Periodically, a missile is taken out of service for repairs or maintenance. Overshadowing all this effort is the realization that there has never been a mass attack with these weapons. What the exact readiness level will be is unknown. One can only estimate from related equipment. The closest parallel is combat aircraft. Readiness levels here vary between 50 to 90 percent. This is the result of decades of testing and preparation. Alas, missiles just don't get used that much. Currently, a few percent of all missiles are test-fired each year. But the testing is not pure; it cannot be. The guidance systems have to be reprogrammed to hit a location in a testing area, not an enemy target. Moreover, the missiles are often moved from their silos to special test silos. There is lots of opportunity to cook the books in this sort of testing. The peacetime military environment being what it is, the tests do not always reveal the problems they are meant to seek out. Military history is replete with large organizations that spent decades preparing for battles in which their initial performance was deplorable. Strategic rockets seem quite capable of falling into this trap.

Political Distortions

Doctrinal requirements—what the missiles are required to do and how they are to do it—have become an increasing burden. Initially, users were grateful to see the missiles lift off and go in the general direction of the target. Success begat excess, and before long the strategy of the first strike appeared. This notion sprang from the theoretical accuracy of multiple warheads launched from MIRV missiles. With more than one warhead coming from each missile, it was theoretically possible to launch enough warheads to destroy all the enemy missiles in their silos. Enemy missiles left at sea in their submarines would presumably submit to some equally devastating technological breakthrough. These tantalizing technological possibilities put the missile people in an embarrassing position during the 1970s and 1980s. To admit that their weapons are not capable of such feats was not politically prudent. A vicious circle developed as each side suspected the other of superior technological capabilities. Lacking any means to prove the other fellow actually had these capabilities, each side made claims that became ever more outrageous and expensive to counter. More pressure was put on the commanders of the missile forces.

In the Soviet Union, where the spirit and practice of the Potemkin village, a motion picture–like false front, survived for many years, the national mania for secrecy only made the validation problem worse. The possibilities were endless, as was the expense. Even more dangerous was, and still is, a national leader believing the illusions and attempting to use them. The arms race turned into an illusions race. Various missile, bomber, nuclear-weapon, and Star Wars gaps appeared and eventually melted away. All of these gaps turned out to exist in the imagination, not reality. This did not, until the collapse of the Soviet Union in 1991, give any of the participants pause. The untried weapons continued to proliferate, unfettered by reality. What was real was that enough of these weapons would work well enough to essentially wreck most of the economies and societies on the planet if there is a nuclear war. How such a nuclear war would occur was open to vivid speculation. No one wants to use nuclear weapons, because nearly every world leader recognizes the no-win aspect of a nuclear war. A nuclear war could start by accident. A missile could be fired by a submarine commander even though he was not authorized to do so. A technical failure could cause a missile to launch and attack its targets.

Finally, and least likely, a national leader could deliberately order the missiles launched. It is always least likely that a national leader would launch a major war. Yet this has happened twice in this century. In 1914, it was an overconfident leader of Russia forcing his will on the Austrians, and overconfident Austrians expecting German support to make the Russians back down. In 1939, it was an overconfident German leader invading Poland, with the cooperation of the Soviets. What was different between 1945 and 1991 was that only two major powers existed; all other industrialized nations were secondary military powers.

For nearly half a century, only the Soviet Union and the United States could start a world war, and could also stop nearly any war they wanted terminated. Smaller nations are already obtaining nuclear weapons. It's almost inevitable that some of these weapons will eventually be used. What will happen then?

The Post-Holocaust World

The worst case is a massive exchange of nuclear weapons. Several thousand warheads are all that is needed. Even after all the post–Cold War nuclear-weapons cuts take place, there will still be several thousand nuclear weapons left. Still enough to fry the planet.

If such a holocaust occurs, tens, if not hundreds, of millions of people will be dead on the first day. Most of the survivors will perish during the following few years from disease, starvation, exposure, radiation poisoning, and the violence of civil disorder. The "nuclear winter" problem is still largely theoretical.

Depending on the type of nuclear war fought, and the amount of dirt thrown up into the upper atmosphere, some areas will hardly notice any climate change. At worst, interior areas in northern latitudes will suffer one or more lost growing seasons. Coastal areas will be less affected. The 20 to 30 percent of the prewar population that survives will have a functioning technology similar to the 19th century. What type of society emerges from all this will be interesting to contemplate. Previous social holocausts have seen similar, but different, societies emerge from the ashes of their predecessors. This should not change. People seem not to care if their killers are barbarians, disease, or political miscalculation. The primary goal is survival.

The cause of most death and destruction from a nuclear war is the elimination of the intricate web of interdependent industries and their transportation nets that produce enormously wealthy modern societies. Even Third World nations are dependent on the major industrial societies for key technologies and emergency food supplies. Take away these items, and several nations will be in big trouble.

The global realignment of power will be interesting. Basically, there will be a lot less global power for several decades at least. Every nation will be largely concerned with survival for quite some time.

The Radiation Problem

Radiation will not be a major problem in a post-holocaust world. To understand this, you must consider the role radiation plays in our lives under normal conditions. Radiation is a natural occurrence. Until recently, it was thought that we were all exposed, on the average, to 160 mrem per year. An mrem (milliroentgen equivalent to man) is a standard measure for radiation absorbed by humans. This exposure causes the following annual health problems per 100 million population: 4,100 fatal cancers, 2,500 nonfatal cancers, 4,600 genetic defects (not all of which are obvious). For every additional mrem per person per year, the above rates will increase .67 percent (75 cancers and genetic defects per 100 million population). About a fifth of the average natural radiation (30 mrem) is received from the sun, which is an ongoing thermonuclear explosion. About 25 mrem comes from proximity to building materials, stone being the most radio-active. Living inside a stone building will add 50 mrem a year. The things we eat and drink add another 40 mrem. The remaining 65 mrem come from such manmade sources as: X rays and medical treatments (50 mrem), air travel (1 mrem per 1,500 miles), watching TV (1 mrem if you watch 6.67 hours a day), fallout from previous atmospheric nuclear-weapons tests (4 mrem), and the remainder from various consumer products. Spending all your time next to a nuclear-power plant adds 5 mrem (less than 1 mrem if you live two kilometers away and zero mrem if you are eight or more kilometers distant). If a nuclear-power plant does blow, like Chernobyl, you get doses similar to those received from nuclear weapons.

During the 1980s, another major cause of radiation was discovered: radon. This stuff is a gas produced from the natural breakdown of uranium in the earth. The gas seeps into houses and concentrates to the point where it gives the inhabitants an average of 200 mrem per year. The problem with radon is that its concentration varies from one area to another. In a few places, inhabitants of well-insulated houses sitting atop large uranium deposits can receive more than the safety limit of 5,000 mrem per year. The key factor here is modern, well-insulated housing. People living in more primitive shelter have little to fear from radon gas.

Nuclear weapons are noted for longer-lasting radioactivity as well as instant blast and heat damage. The unit of radiation for nuclear weapons is the rad, which is equal, for our purposes, to 1,000 mrem. Radiation kills over time. If enough radiation is received in a short period, it can kill immediately or within days, weeks, or months, depending on the dose. Six hundred or more rads can kill within hours and disable immediately; 500 to 600 rads are always fatal, often within days. About 50 percent will die with 200 to 500 rads. At levels of 100 to 200 rads, 5 percent will die, although long-term effects (cancer) become a major factor. A 50-rad dose will induce nearly 2 percent early deaths from cancer and genetic defects.

These high levels of radiation exist very briefly, seconds in some cases. In the area closest to a ground-level explosion, which is preferred for destroying missile silos, there will be hot spots of intense, longer-lasting radiation. One year after the explosion of a one-megaton bomb on the surface, the 100-rad zone will be a circular area of 46 square kilometers (7.6 kilometers in diameter). Nearly 4 percent of the population in that area will die prematurely. Many others will suffer radiation sickness. This area should be a forbidden zone, even though it will be teeming with vegetation and small animals. The point of highest radiation in this zone will be the explosion crater, 360 meters wide and 120 meters deep. The next zone has an average of 50 rads and covers 67 square kilometers (9 kilometers in diameter). There will not be as much radiation sickness, but 2 percent of inhabitants will die early. The 10-rad zone covers 300 square kilometers (20 kilometers in diameter.) This could be lived in, although there would be three or four early deaths per thousand population. Within a few years, even the crater will be under the 10-rad level. However, because of the blast and fire damage to the area from the initial explosion, most people would have died from starvation, exposure, or disease. Small groups of survivors are not going to live off canned goods in supermarkets. Most canned food goes bad within a year or so. You can also forget about giant spiders and two-headed mutants. Insects are far more resistant to radiation than mammals. Mutations are generally either fatal or unnoticeable. Natural radiation has been responsible for more mutation than any nuclear war could ever produce.

HERE COMES THE SUN

One of the theoretical side effects of a massive nuclear exchange is the partial destruction of the ozone layer of the upper atmosphere, which screens the earth's surface from most of the sun's harmful radiation. This destruction could subject all inhabitants of earth to perhaps hundreds of additional mrem per year. Worse, additional ultraviolet radiation could blind land animals. In theory, a major nuclear war could destroy the ozone layer in the Northern Hemisphere, and somewhat less in the Southern Hemisphere.

Potentially disastrous side effects can result from large-scale nuclear war. The enormous quantities of dirt thrown up into the atmosphere by the explosions, plus the smoke generated by numerous fires, will block the sunlight for many months. This is not theory; it has happened in the past as a result of large volcanic explosions. Recorded instances of demonstrably lower temperatures and visible reduction in sunlight have resulted from these explosions. A nuclear war would throw more material into the upper atmosphere and cause longer periods of cold weather. That's the short-term effect. A possible long-term effect is preventing heat from leaving the planet. This, over decades and centuries, causes an increase in average temperature, a meltdown of the polar ice caps, and a rise in sea level. Coastal areas would soon be under water. This has happened regularly in the past, and is followed by a cold age of thousands of years' duration. A nuclear war could speed up the process. Radiation, it would appear, is one of the lesser worries.

PUTTING IT ALL IN CONTEXT

The industrialized nations are highly dependent on the efficient functioning of their technology. Even agriculture and food processing require enormous quantities of fuel, machinery, and electrical power to function. Several hundred nuclear weapons aimed at industrial targets can destroy this web of support. Food production would collapse. Less than a week's supply of food is kept on shelves, warehouses, and in transit. Most of this food is perishable. Without refrigeration, it quickly spoils.

The electrical power grid and sources of gas and oil can easily be destroyed with a few dozen nuclear weapons. Water supplies and waste disposal require fuel to run the pumps and other machinery. Without food, fresh water, and waste disposal, the huge urban populations not directly affected by the nuclear explosions are nevertheless quickly subjected to epidemic diseases. In the absence of a large supply of antibiotics, even pneumonia would again become the major killer it was only 50 years ago. There is not much speculation required for this forecast; social breakdowns have occurred frequently even in this century.

Humans are a resilient lot. Despite the huge devastation, there will be survivors. Moreover, knowledge will survive. Individuals will possess some, surviving libraries the rest. The 20 to 30 percent of the population that survives nuclear explosions, radiation, starvation, disease, and general disorder will go on to create a new culture. Nuclear war won't be the end of the world, just the end of most people reading this.

The Conventional Option

Because of the "no win" aspect of nuclear weapons, there is an increasingly popular trend toward arming strategic and tactical missiles with nonnuclear warheads. This gets rid of the doomsday aspect of nuclear weapons and makes it possible to use these 10-million-to-100-million-dollar one-shot weapons without destroying the world as we know it. This also recognizes the historical fact that nations are more interested in winning an advantage and not gambling with their very national existence. There are three choices of nonnuclear warheads: biological, chemical, and conventional.

The biological warhead would be least likely used. Partially, this is because biological weapons take a while to get going. Your enemy has time to retaliate. This puts biological weapons in the same class as nukes: massive destruction and high probability of retaliation in kind. However, biological warheads cannot be completely dismissed; it is possible.

Chemicals would not be as devastating as biological or nuclear weapons. However, great damage can be done with nerve gas. A ton or more of persistent nerve agent spread over a few hundred square kilometers could kill tens of thousands of people. More devastating would be the civil disorder. Panic, and the resources needed to deal with casualties and the cleanup, would shut down the area for weeks or months. Imagine the effect of one of these nerve-gas warheads on a major metropolitan area. An ICBM warhead releasing several hundred pounds of persistent nerve gas over New York, Washington, London, or Moscow would disable these cities for weeks or months. It was the threat of such an attack by Iraqi Scud missiles on Israel that caused such a commotion during the 1991 Gulf War.

Conventional warheads have become more significant because of Western developments in terminal guidance. The United States has developed a ballistic-missile guidance system that has a picture of the target in its computer memory and uses sensors to make a precision final approach. This allows the warhead to literally "land in a pickle barrel." American cruise missiles have a similar guidance system. As an example of what can happen when you replace a nuclear warhead with a conventional one in a strategic weapon, consider the carbon-fiber warhead of the cruise missiles used in the 1991 Gulf War. The first weapons fired in the Gulf War were cruise missiles launched from U.S. Navy ships and submarines. Many of these were equipped with warheads that dispensed thousands of rolls of carbon-fiber thread over Iraqi power lines. The carbon-fiber thread shorted out most of Iraq's national electrical power grid. This was a major factor in the rapid destruction of Iraq's air-defense system. Most nations are heavily dependent on their electrical power system, and this kind of non-nuclear attack by strategic weapons (cruise missiles or ICBMs) can have a devastating effect.

Improved conventional munitions also made ballistic-missile and cruise-missile warheads more productive in hitting high-value targets without using nukes. Satellite-launch facilities, early-warning radars, ships in port, and crucial bridges and transportation facilities were now at risk. The crucial difference between these conventional alternatives is the lack of massive damage. Nuclear retaliation would be difficult to justify. The attacker would have to be careful to launch only a few missiles, if not one at a time, so as not to provoke a nuclear response. Nonnuclear ballistic-missile warheads are a growing trend. You don't hear about them because they are considered a touchy subject. Anything having to do with missiles and nukes gets people agitated. However, under wartime or crisis conditions, nuclear warheads could be converted rather quickly. What is worrisome is that many nations already have many nonnuclear battlefield ballistic missiles deployed. Armed with chemical weapons, or ICM, they were used by Iraq during the 1991 war. It is for this reason that work is being rushed on defenses against these tactical ballistic missiles. A miniature version of Star Wars, so to speak. This defense would also be useful against ICBMs. And ICBMs could easily join this cascade of nonnuclear warheads. Both superpowers have more nuclear ballistic missiles than are needed to destroy their opponent. The temptation to divert some to conventional warfare will be strong. The missiles are a difficult weapon to defend against. When a target must be hit, missiles are the most effective way to do it.

Any use of ballistic missiles with nonnuclear warheads would take place amid a continuing fear of nuclear escalation. The fear element implicit in nuclear weapons is something major powers at war have never had to deal with before. There is no sure way of knowing how leaders would deal with such a situation. Further complicating the situation is the fact that many nations now have missile-production facilities. While the threat of a nuclear holocaust declines, the proliferation of nuclear and missile technology spreads. For these smaller nuclear powers, their shorter-range missiles are strategic weapons because, unlike the Soviet Union and America, the enemy is usually right across the border. But the danger is greater than that. The technology for long-range ballistic missiles continues to proliferate. The Cold War may be over, but the nuclear-arms race is not.

Theory and Practice

Although the missiles don't get much practice, aircraft and defensive systems do. The first nuclear weapons were dropped by aircraft, and today a large proportion of the available weapons are still carried by numerous aircraft types. We think of large B-52 bombers as the primary aircraft delivery system. This is not the case. In fact, most B-52s, and other large bombers, merely carry cruise missiles. It is the cruise missiles that actually find the target and deliver the nuclear weapon. Smaller aircraft would be used to deliver thousands of nuclear bombs. Many nations are especially concerned about American naval aircraft, and their ability to take off from a roving carrier and slip through antiaircraft defenses. These smaller aircraft practice their skills regularly. For many nations, American bombers in far-flung bases that can reach their heartland are considered as dangerous as ICBMs in their American midwestern silos. Fortunately, the United States and Russian navies have withdrawn nukes from their ships, and the U.S. Army has withdrawn all its tactical nukes from Europe. But the capability remains.

Another system regularly exercised is the warning radars and satellites. These sensors are constantly turned toward other nations' missile launch sites. This includes ocean areas from which submarines or aircraft carriers can launch missiles or aircraft. These systems give at least 15 minutes' warning that an attack is on the way. During the 1991 Persian Gulf War, these early-warning systems were used to warn of Iraqi Scud missile launches. These systems are not perfect. Occasionally, false reports are given, indicating one or a few missiles coming in. Each of these incidents spurs the users to greater efforts at improving system reliability.

In the future, it is more likely that only a few missiles might be fired. A high-altitude nuke could release the dreaded electromagnetic pulse (EMP) and blind radars and ruin a like proportion of electronics. However, given the number of false alarms, it is not likely that anyone would start a nuclear exchange on the basis of one false alarm. Besides, these false alarms often disappear after a few minutes. Missile-carrying submarines are another matter, as are satellites carrying nuclear weapons. Subs are closer to their targets and allow for only about 10 minutes or less of warning. Worse yet is a satellite with a nuke. One of these going off in low orbit would give no warning while unleashing an EMP. With the enemy blinded by the EMP, the full-scale attack has a better chance of succeeding. Often overlooked in the nuclear equation is the tremendous number of nuclear weapons ready for delivery by systems other than ballistic and cruise missiles. All nations with nuclear weapons have aircraft of all sizes ready to deliver nuclear weapons. All it takes is a nuclear weapon in the same container as a conventional bomb and some additional wiring to allow control over activating the nuke. As the missile and nuclear arsenals of America and the former Soviet Union are dismantled, similar weapons in the hands of many other nations continue to proliferate. There was a time when you had to look in only two directions to keep an eye on the prospects of a nuclear war. Now, you must look in many directions, with new ones appearing every year.

The popularity of cruise missiles can be traced to their relatively low cost and flexibility. A cruise missile costs less than 10 percent as much as a ballistic missile and is more accurate. This makes it cheap enough to effectively deliver nonnuclear warheads. Another crucial advantage of cruise missiles is that they are difficult to detect and likely to become more difficult as future models are equipped with design features and gadgets making them even harder to spot. A somewhat unspoken additional advantage of cruise missiles is that they drive the many potentially hostile nations up the wall. Cruise missiles expose the weakest aspect of any air-defense system, which generally has a hard time spotting small, low-flying aircraft. Like cruise missiles, for example.

A further irritation is that to produce cruise missiles requires mastery of technologies most nations have always had a difficult time with. Miniature jet engines of great reliability and microcomputer-based terrain-scanning guidance systems are two items that very few nations besides America can manufacture. Other nations can produce cruise missiles, but not at a price that makes military sense. Cruise missiles also bring out another dirty little secret of high tech: It doesn't always work. From the beginning, the terrain-following system in cruise missiles has proved troublesome. New quirks continually turn up. With America's several-decade head start, hostile cruise missiles are one thing the friends of the United States won't have to worry about for a while.

By the end of the 1980s, both the Soviet Union and the United States had more than 10 times the number of nuclear weapons needed to devastate each other. At the same time, both attempted to develop antiballistic missile (ABM) systems. Rockets, killer satellites, lasers, and beam weapons have all been tried or are still in development. Some of these systems have successfully intercepted missiles. The crucial problem is developing the control system to run such a defense. The collapse of the Soviet Union put an end to antiballistic-missiles system development in that part of the world, while the United States has continued its program in the face of post–Cold War budget cuts. Both the United States and Russia are still working on weapons that will stop short-range missiles. This is a threat that increases as missile technology continues to spread.

Star Wars defense systems also provide an early-warning capability. The benefit of this is that there is less chance of war by accident. The existing early-warning systems proved useful by giving advance warning of Iraqi Scud missile launches in the 1991 war.

The Future

With the Cold War over, strategic nuclear weapons are being destroyed, R&D stopped, and the manufacture of new weapons is at a standstill. Russia is retaining hundreds of former Soviet land- and submarine-based ICBMs while the United States is retaining an even larger portion of its Cold War ICBM inventory. The capability still exists to destroy the planet's civilization several times over, but the intentions have become much more peaceful.

While the threat of a global nuclear holocaust is greatly diminished in the short term, it still remains for the long term. And any use of nuclear weapons is undiminished by the end of the Cold War. The collapse of the Soviet Union put a lot of Soviet strategic weapons technology on the auction block, officially and unofficially. Despite protests from Western nations, the successor states of the Soviet Union have sold strategic-weapons technology or allowed illegal transfers.

Currently, only five nations have a strategic nuclear weapons capability: the United States, Russia, France, Britain, and China. In the wake of the Soviet Union's breakup, several of the successor states, such as Belarus, Ukraine, and Kazakstan found themselves in possession of strategic missiles. However, these missiles were not under the operational control of the new governments, and in return for foreign economic aid, they agreed to have the ICBMs on their territory dismantled.

Because of the post–Cold War technology transfers, several more are on the verge of obtaining this capability, including India, Israel, and several others. China has found it very profitable to sell missile technology to whoever can pay for it, and this will probably continue until a democratic government takes over in China. This will likely happen before the end of the decade, but not before more nations develop ICBM capability because of Chinese weapons and technology sales.

The prospect of more nations having ICBMs has kept the U.S. SDI antiballistic-missile program alive. The future ICBM threat will come from many directions and not just over the North Pole as it did during the Cold War.

Strategic Weapons

WEAPON. This is the designation. For former Soviet weapons (now Russian), the NATO designations are used. Often a missile is modified over the years, resulting in variants with very different capabilities. ALCM are air-launched cruise missiles launched from bombers. Some bombers carry SRAM (Short-Range Attack Missiles), described in the aircraft weapons chart. Some Russian bombers can be equipped with a variety of ALCM, also described in the aircraft weapons chart. Surface ships and submarines carry SLCM (Sea-Launched Cruise Missiles.) Weapons listed for bombers are gravity bombs; they are simply dropped. Other nations with known delivery systems are also listed.

MISSILES DEP. This is the number of missiles ready for use in underground concrete silos, on board submarines and aircraft, or otherwise deployed for action. This last category would include mobile missiles, a category now being dismantled by Russia. Missiles with a "0" in this category are weapons that have recently been withdrawn from service (or soon will be) because of the series of nuclear-disarmament treaties agreed to in the wake of the Cold War's end.

WARHEADS. The number of warheads per missile.

ON TARGET. Nothing is perfect. A certain number of missiles will be out of service for repairs or maintenance. Once launched, some missiles and/or warheads will not perform as planned. The On Target value is obtained by multiplying the number of warheads by the serviceability and reliability levels. For example: The *Minuteman II* could have 442 warheads available, but only 90 percent would be serviceable, and only 80 percent of the remainder would perform reliably (442 × .9 × .8 = 318).

EQUIVALENT MEGATONS (EMT). Compares the destructive effects of nuclear weapons on all targets except hardened ones, namely underground missile silos. The formula is the number of weapons times yield of each in megatons, to the two-third power. Thus, a 9-megaton weapon is equal to a 4.34 EMT, a 1-megaton weapon is equal to 1 EMT, a 170-kiloton weapon is equal to .31 EMT, and a 40-

22-1 Strategic Weapons

Weapon	Miss-iles Deployed	War-heads	Total War-heads	On Tar-get	Equiv. Mega-tons	"K" Fac-tor	Total "K"	Silo "K" Def	Total "K" Def	CEP meter	Range (km)	head Yield (kt)	Raw MT	% Ser-vice-able	% Re-li-able	Throw Wght tons	Year De-ploy-ed
US Totals	5,561		14,070	6,051	2,150		355,414		636,290				1,424				
Russia Total	2,664		10,500	5,709	3,069		111,164		521,700				2,359				
United States																	
Land Based																	
Minute Man IIIB	300	3	900	689	332	34	23,560	108	32,400	220	12,800	335	231	90	85	2.4	1980
Minute Man II	450	1	450	324	324	25	8,126	108	48,600	370	12,800	1,000	324	90	80	1.6	1965
Minute Man IIIA	200	3	600	459	141	22	9,993	108	21,600	220	14,800	170	78	90	85	2.2	1970
ALCM AGM-86B	1,600	1	1,600	384	131	145	55,670	200	NA	90	3,000	200	77	60	40	0.03	1985
SRAM AGM-69A	1,100	1	1,400	252	77	5	1,311	200	NA	450	150	170	43	30	60	0.02	1974
B-1B	95	8	760	285	97	145	41,318	50	4,750	90	14,000	200	57	75	50	4.0	1986
B-52H	84	8	672	176	60	145	25,573	50	4,200	90	12,000	200	35	75	35	2.0	1959
B-52G	70	8	560	127	44	145	18,470	50	3,500	90	10,000	200	25	65	35	2.0	1959
FB-111A	48	2	96	31	11	145	4,454	80	3,840	90	4,000	200	6	80	40	2.0	1969
DF-4 (China)	6	1	6	3	5	3	8	0	0	1,500	7,000	3,000	8	65	65	4.0	1979
Peacekeeper	50	10	500	405	201	171	69,064	108	5,400	100	11,000	350	142	90	90	7.0	1986
DF-5 (China)	2	1	2	1	3	7	7	80	160	1,200	15,000	5,000	5	65	75	4.0	1981
Total	4,005		7,546	3,136	1,427		257,554		124,450				1,030				
Submarine Based																	
Poseidon C3	160	10	1,600	768	90	2	1,523	500	80,000	450	4,600	40	31	60	80	1.2	1971
MSBS M-4 (Fr)	64	3	192	86	24	3	233	500	32,000	600	5,000	150	13	60	75	0.5	1985
MSBS M-20 (Fr)	0	1	0	0	0	4	0	500	0	926	3,100	1,000	0	60	75	1.0	1977
Polaris A3 (UK)	64	1	64	29	10	1	39	500	32,000	926	4,600	200	6	60	75	1.5	1967
Trident C4	384	8	3,072	1,475	318	4	5,387	500	192,000	450	7,400	100	147	60	80	1.6	1979
JL-1 (China)	12	1	12	4	4	1	2	300	3,600	2,400	2,500	1,000	4	50	65	0.5	1984

SLCM BGM-109A	900	1	900	216	74	145	31,314	200	180,000	90	2,400	200	43	60	40	0.0	1985
Trident II D5	120	8	960	461	250	129	59,650	500	60,000	120	12,000	400	184	60	80	2.6	1989
Total	1,704		6,800	3,038	770		98,149		579,600				428				
Russia (all former USSR weapons, pre-START reductions)																	
Land Based																	
SS-19 Mod 3	300	6	1,800	1,224	822	26	31,347	150	45,000	300	10,000	550	673	85	80	7.5	1982
SS-17 Mod 3	50	4	200	113	71	14	1,521	150	7,500	400	10,000	500	56	75	75	6.0	1982
SS-18 Mod 4	308	10	3,080	1,733	1,091	35	59,960	150	46,200	250	11,000	500	866	75	75	16.7	1982
Tu-95	140	2	280	31	19	54	1,666	20	2,800	200	8,000	500	15	55	20	9.0	1955
ALCM AS-15	200	1	200	30	10	7	220	200	NA	400	1,500	200	6	50	30	0.03	1985
Tu-160	0	4	0	0	0	0	0	20	0	200	7,000	0	0	50	20	0.0	1989
SS-25	300	1	300	217	171	30	6,519	150	45,000	300	10,000	700	152	85	85	1.6	1986
SS-11 Mod 3	300	3	900	540	242	1	577	150	45,000	1,200	12,000	300	162	80	75	2.2	1975
SS-13 Mod 2	40	1	40	27	17	1	16	110	4,400	1,900	9,000	500	14	80	85	1.3	1969
SS-24	90	10	900	650	140	12	7,696	500	45,000	250	10,000	100	65	85	85	8.0	1988
Total	1,728		7,700	4,564	2,584		109,523		240,900				2,009				
Submarine Based																	
SS-N-18	224	3	672	328	206	2	586	300	67,200	1,100	7,200	500	164	65	75	2.6	1978
SS-N-6	176	1	176	40	25	1	51	300	52,800	1,300	2,500	500	20	35	65	0.8	1974
SS-N-8	280	1	280	118	98	3	335	300	84,000	1,000	7,700	750	89	65	65	2.4	1973
SS-N-23	112	4	448	110	38	1	159	300	33,600	900	8,300	200	22	35	70	0.8	1985
SS-N-24 (SLCM)	24	1	24	4	1	29	106	300	7,200	200	2,400	200	1	50	30	0.3	1992
SS-N-20	120	10	1,200	546	118	1	404	300	36,000	1,000	9,000	100	55	65	70	2.2	1981
Total	936		2,800	1,145	486		1,641		280,800				350				

kiloton weapon is equal to .12 EMT. EMT expresses the fact that larger explosions are less efficient than smaller ones. The effects of a one-megaton weapon are as follows. If detonated as an airburst at 2,000 meters up, nearly every building within seven kilometers of the explosion will be destroyed or damaged beyond repair. Virtually everyone within this area will be killed or severely injured, without hope of medical aid. How large an area is this 14-kilometers-diameter zone? Pick a ground zero, the point on the ground directly under the blast. Drive about 6.5 minutes in any direction at 40 mph. Or walk for an hour and a half. That's 7 kilometers, or a total area of 154 square kilometers. Population densities go from 3,000–4,000 people in "sprawl"-type cities to more than 100,000 (New York City) per square kilometer. A single EMT would put any area back into the Stone Age. See discussion earlier in this chapter on the effects of post-explosion radiation in this area.

"K" FACTOR. This is the warhead's silo attack value. To destroy an enemy missile silo, the attacking warhead must explode as close as possible. The K factor is derived using the formula K = weapons yield (to the two-thirds power) divided by CEP (to the second power). As you can see from the yields and CEPs of various weapons, accuracy is far more important than yield. Note the difference between U.S. MX and cruise missiles and older missiles. See also the section below on SILO "K" DEFENSE.

TOTAL "K." Warheads reaching target times each warhead's "K" factor.

SILO "K" defense, ICBMs. This is the missile "K" factor needed to disable a missile silo with 97 percent probability. Thus a 100-psi (pounds per square inch) silo requires 20 "K"; 300 requires 45; 1,000 requires 108; 3,000 requires 200. The higher the "K" value over the one shown for each missile, the more likely the silo will be rendered unusable. Hardening these silos to withstand greater explosive force is expensive. Building a 3,000-psi silo costs over $15 million. Just hardening a bare-bones 100-psi silo to 1,000 psi costs over $3 million. It has become cheaper to make attacking missiles more accurate, so the trend is away from silos. Mobile land-based missiles were deployed by the Soviet Union but demobilized in the early 1990s. The United States places more warhead power in its submarine-launched ICBMs. Submarine-based missiles, and others not in fixed locations, have been given estimated K factors to reflect the possibility that some of them will be discovered and attacked. No basing system is invulnerable, so this value strives to put this situation into perspective.

TOTAL "K" DEFENSE. Missiles deployed times silo "K" defense. For one side to defeat the other in a nuclear war without suffering unacceptable damage, the attacker would have to be able to destroy the defender's nuclear forces before the defender could use them. At the moment, this is impossible, because no one has developed a way to quickly destroy the SSBNs (missile-carrying submarines). Also, no matter how high an individual missile's "K" factor is, it does not absolutely guarantee destruction, because of reliability and other problems.

CEP (Circular Error Probable). This is the measure of a missile's accuracy. The CEP is measured in meters from the intended point of warhead impact. This circle represents the area into which 50 percent of the warheads with that CEP will fall. Farther out, the circle eventually covers an area in which more than 99 percent of the warheads will fall. The CEP represents a convenient midpoint for measurement. If you are attacking industrial or population targets, CEPs of 1,000 or 2,000 meters are no big deal. For example, over 30 warheads were thought to be targeted at the New York City metropolitan area. More than half would hit close enough to their targets. The rest of the warheads were going to do substantial unintended and unpredictable damage to suburban communities and the local fish population. Hitting hardened targets, like command centers and missile silos, accuracy and small CEPs become crucial. There is a limit to how small CEPs can go just using the missile-guidance system—a CEP of 150 meters for land-based missiles and 400 for submarine-launched missiles is acceptable. To get smaller CEPs, you need some form of terminal guidance in the warhead, either radar or pattern recognition. Some American missiles already have this capability (cruise missiles). Finally, keep in mind that many CEP figures have to be taken with a grain of salt. It is often prudent to add a few hundred meters to CEPs. This has a significant effect on the "K" factor. See the chart for examples.

RANGE. The maximum range of the missile. There is also a minimum range of up to a few hundred kilometers for any missile.

WARHEAD YIELD. The destructive power of nuclear weapons is expressed in terms of kilotons (thousand tons) of conventional high-explosive TNT.

RAW MT. As opposed to equivalent megatons, raw megatons are just that, the number of arriving warheads times the yields of each.

% SERVICEABLE. This is the percentage of missiles that will be available for launch at any given time. Each missile is a very complex piece of machinery. This figure includes planned downtime for maintenance and expected repairs.

% RELIABLE. Once launched, a certain percentage of the systems will not work as planned. This often occurs during testing. In combat, the unreliability will probably be higher. In addition, an estimate has been made for defects that will not be discovered until the systems are used. These defects are often caught during peacetime. Some of them were so bad that entire classes of missiles were rendered useless for combat. For cruise missiles, an estimate was made for the number shot down on the way to their targets. Being shot down en route is not yet a problem for ballistic missiles.

THROW WEIGHT. The total weight of the missile that can be delivered to the target. In the beginning, all this weight was devoted to a nuclear weapon and the heat-resistant structure that enabled the weapon to survive its fiery final plunge to earth. A MIRV warhead is called a bus. The bus carries a mechanism for deploying several smaller warheads, each equipped with a nuclear weapon. The bus also contains a computer to calculate when to deploy the nuclear-armed warheads so that they will continue on the proper trajectory to hit their assigned targets. The bus sometimes contain decoys and electronic devices to deceive enemy warning systems. These "penetration aids" take up still more space. The warheads must become smaller without losing too much of their explosive power. This is the primary reason for ongoing nuclear testing. It's getting crowded inside these warheads, and more components provide more things that can fail to perform.

YEAR DEPLOYED. The year in which the missile was first available for use. A new type of missile is built for several years, and then its assembly line is taken over by a newer model. The older missiles stay in service for many years after the last one is built. Like any complex piece of equipment, a missile can be made to last forever by replacing worn parts. Although the missile is used only once, it is alive while sitting around waiting. The guidance system is always active whenever the missile is available for use. The electrohydraulic systems that work the mechanical controls—fins, flaps, and air brakes—must be exercised periodically. This exercise will eventually fatigue them, as the guidance system will wear out from constant use. The fuel, even if solid, deteriorates over time. The warhead components, especially the electronic ones, also degrade over time. Russian warheads have to be rebuilt every 10–15 years, while Western warheads are replaced every 10–20 years as improved components become available. The longer a missile sits around waiting, the lower its reliability and serviceability rates.

Missile Construction Techniques

The basic principles of ballistic-missile construction were developed and tested more than 50 years ago. The first practical applications were during World War II, the German V-2 rocket. Technology has become more refined, but not radically different. A rocket must attain speeds of 6,000 to 7,000 meters per second to escape earth's gravity. This is achieved by stacking a series of rockets on top of each other. The first "stage" comprises more than 75 percent of the total vehicle weight. Once in the upper atmosphere, this rocket is dropped, and a second stage (15 to 20 percent of vehicle weight) puts the warhead into an orbit that will take it 10,000 kilometers or more to its target. The third stage is the unpowered warhead, typically less than 3 percent of vehicle weight. The warhead is equipped with a thermal shield to prevent burnup on plunging through the earth's atmosphere at speeds in excess of 13,000 meters per second.

The first rocket motors used liquid fuel. This was a reliability nightmare, plus you had to go through a several-hour fueling process just prior to launch. The big breakthrough was solid-fuel rockets. The United States was the first to develop and perfect these items.

Meanwhile, the Soviet Union came up with a less reliable and more manageable low-tech approach with storable liquid fuel. Many Soviet (now Russian) rockets still use storable liquid fuel. The liquid is not as stable as solid fuel, and there's still all that damn plumbing. Solid fuel had additional benefits: smaller rockets and more stages.

The U.S. approach also developed smaller warheads, although 15 to 20 percent heavier in relation to total missile weight than liquid fuel rockets.

Along with more efficient warheads and guidance systems, the United States was able to build missiles one-fifth the weight of their Soviet counterparts, but with equal range, greater accuracy, and equivalent destructive power. No less critical was the lower cost of these solid-fuel systems. Higher manufacturing and maintenance costs led the Soviets to spend three times as much per missile. Their earliest missiles for submarines (SS-N-4 and SS-N-5) were liquid-fueled. Their first attempt at solid fuel for land-based missiles was the SS-13, which they never were able to get working right. They chopped it down to a two-stage, shorter-range system, the SS-20. Everyone still uses liquid-fuel rockets, as they are still the best method for lifting very heavy loads into space. For this reason, the large number of oversize, liquid-fuel Soviet rockets used for strategic combat gave them an additional source of satellite lift.

National Differences

As is obvious from the chart, Soviet-designed missiles are larger and less accurate than their U.S. counterparts. While the larger size was forced on the Soviets because of their problems with mastering solid-fuel technology, they used the greater throw weight to install larger nuclear weapons. This enabled them to compensate for the less capable guidance systems they were stuck with. This is the technological path many of the new ICBM-armed nations will follow. Many of these nations are obtaining their technology from Russia (officially or otherwise) and China.

The Soviets stockpiled missiles, with more than 1,000 spare missiles available. Many of these were intended as replacements for silo missiles that break down beyond the point where they're worth repairing.

A more recent addition to the strategic arsenal has been the cruise missile. These weapons are low and slow jets that are very difficult to detect with radar. They carry a nuclear weapon and are very accurate because of their terrain-pattern matching guidance system. This type of guidance requires quite a bit of computing and pattern-recognition capability. Cruise missiles can be launched from submarines, surface ships, land vehicles, and aircraft. Although hardly fast enough to be a first-strike weapon, they make the success of a first strike less likely.

In 1987, the first modern Soviet cruise missile, the SS-N-21, was deployed. This type of system was pioneered by the United States 10 years earlier. Although the Soviets may have stolen or copied much of the technology in this type of weapon, they continued to have problems with it. The American version went through considerable teething problems, and the precision technology required for this type of equipment is just the thing the Soviets were short of. This type of technology is not likely to spread as quickly as the older ballistic-missile stuff. In any event, the United States demonstrated in the 1991 Gulf War that cruise missiles are excellent

22-2 Theater Weapons

Weapon	System	Warheads per Sys.	Total	On Target	Equiv. Mega-tons	Raw Mega-tons	Warhead Yield (kt)	Range (km)	Service-ability	Surviva-bility	First De-ployed
NATO Totals	2,632		1,845	960	299	168					
Russia Totals	7,790		6,200	3,056	699	398					
NATO											
Aircraft											
F-16	920	0.5	460	294	101	59	200	1,250	80	80	1979
F-4	800	0.5	400	150	51	30	200	750	75	50	1962
F-111E/F	290	2.0	580	348	119	70	200	2,400	80	75	1967
F-104 (NATO)	260	0.3	87	21	7	4	200	800	70	35	1958
A-6E (CV based)	280	1.0	280	137	47	27	200	1,000	75	65	1963
F-16 (Israel)	36	1.0	36	23	5	2	100	1,250	80	80	1978
Mirage F 1 (S Afr)	12	1.0	12	7	1	1	100	600	80	70	1980
F-16 (Pakistan)	2	1.0	2	1	0	0	50	1,250	75	70	1988
Jaguar (India)	6	1.0	6	3	1	0	100	720	80	70	1982
Jaguar (Fr)	40	0.5	20	10	4	2	100	720	80	65	1974
Mirage IVA (Fr)	30	1.0	30	10	2	11	200	1,600	65	50	1964
H-6 (China)	100	2.0	51	11	11	11	1,000	2,100	60	35	1968
Mirage III (Fr)	30	0.2	6	2	1	0	200	600	75	40	1964
Aircraft Total	2,806		1,970	1,017	349	217					
Missiles/Artillery											
DF-3 (China)	60	1.0	60	38	38	38	1,000	2,500	70	90	1971
Prithvi (India)	6	1.0	6	4	0	0	20	250	80	90	1988
Hatf (Pakistan)	0	1.0	0	0	0	0	20	80	80	90	1998
Prithvi 150 (India)	0	1.0	0	0	0	0	20	150	80	90	1996
MB/EE (Brazil)	0	1.0	0	0	0	0	20	150	80	90	1997
Mushak (Iran)	0	1.0	0	0	0	0	20	200	80	90	1998
SS 300 (Brazil)	0	1.0	0	0	0	0	20	300	80	90	2000

Hatf 2 (Pakistan)	0	1.0	0	0	0	0	20	300	80	90	2000
Vector (Egypt)	0	1.0	0	0	0	0	20	600	80	90	2000
Al Fatah (Libya)	0	1.0	0	0	0	0	20	600	80	90	2000
Tien Ma (Taiwan)	0	1.0	0	0	0	0	20	950	80	90	2000
Agni (India)	0	1.0	0	0	0	3	20	2,500	90	90	2000
203mm How (NATO)	400	2.0	800	648	19	2	5	16	80	90	1962
Jerico (Israel)	24	2.0	48	35	5	7	50	900	80	90	1988
Lance (NATO)	50	4.0	200	144	20	1	50	110	80	90	1976
155mm How (NATO)	1,800	0.5	900	729	12	1	2	16	90	90	1964
Pluton (Fr)	40	2.0	80	54	4	2	20	120	75	90	1974
SSBS S-3 (Fr)	18	1.0	18	14	4		150	3,500	90	85	1980
Missiles/Artillery	**2,398**		**2,112**	**1,665**	**101**	**55**					
Russia											
Aircraft											
SU-24	700	1	700	319	109	64	200	1,600	65	70	1974
SU-17	500	1	500	206	71	41	200	600	75	55	1974
TU-22M (Backfire)	260	4	1,040	546	187	109	200	4,000	70	75	1974
MiG-27	800	2	1,600	676	231	135	200	720	65	65	1973
TU-22 (Blinder)	100	2	200	72	25	14	200	750	60	60	1962
TU-16	250	1	250	73	25	15	200	2,100	65	45	1955
Aircraft Total	**2,610**		**4,290**	**1,892**	**647**	**378**					
Missiles/Artillery											
FROG-7	200	0.2	40	23	3	1	50	70	65	90	1967
SS-21	300	0.5	150	95	20	9	100	120	70	90	1971
SS-1C (SCUD B)	200	0.3	60	38	8	4	100	300	70	90	1962
152mm Gun	1,500	0.3	450	236	7	1	5	27	70	75	1980
152mm Howitzer	2,500	0.1	250	131	4	1	5	17	70	75	1980
203mm Howitzer	240	2	480	252	7	1	5	18	70	75	1980
240mm Mortar	240	2	480	389	2	2	5	10	90	90	1980
Missiles/Artillery	**5,180**		**1,910**	**1,164**	**52**	**19**					

weapons for attacking heavily defended targets successfully. That alone will give many rambunctious dictators pause.

Aircraft, Tactical Missiles, and Artillery

These shorter-range nuclear weapons are frequently called Theater Nuclear Weapons. In addition to the nuclear warheads listed below, over 10,000 additional warheads are used by surface-to-air missile systems and on warships. Most of these have been withdrawn to be destroyed or put in storage as a result of the Cold War ending.

WEAPON is the system designation. Weapons are listed in order of their equivalent megatonnage. More destructive systems are ranked higher. Most of the nonsuperpower systems show up on this Chart: UK = United Kingdom; FR = France; NATO = NATO countries that possess vehicles to carry nuclear weapons but not the weapons themselves (Germany, in particular); China = People's Republic of China; CV-based indicates U.S. aircraft flying from aircraft carriers.

SYSTEMS are the number of aircraft or missiles in use. The "0" next to a weapon indicates it has not yet been deployed as of 1993 or has been withdrawn recently.

WARHEADS PER SYS. For aircraft and missiles that can use nuclear or conventional warheads, it is the average number of nuclear weapons available for each system. For larger missiles, those with a range of more than 1,400 kilometers, it indicates the number of warheads carried by each missile.

TOTAL WARHEADS, WARHEADS REACHING TARGET, EQUIVALENT MEGATONNAGE, RAW MEGATONNAGE, and WARHEAD YIELD are described under the strategic-missiles chart notes.

RANGE is the maximum distance a missile or artillery shell will travel (in kilometers). For aircraft, it is the outbound leg of a round-trip mission.

SERVICEABILITY. See strategic-missiles chart notes.

SURVIVABILITY is the percentage of serviceable systems that will make it to the target and deliver their nuclear weapons. The survivability figure also includes losses taken before missiles can even be launched, as well as reload missiles and artillery shells destroyed before they can be used.

FIRST DEPLOYED is the year the system was first available for use.

PART SIX
WARFARE BY THE NUMBERS

BEHIND EVERY INFANTRYMAN, pilot, or sailor we find many other troops moving supplies, pushing paper, and operating computers. The warriors and the clerks have a symbiotic relationship. You can't wage war unless both groups do their jobs well. The numbers war demonstrates how important calculation has always been in warfare.

23

Logistics

IF THE TROOPS have no ammunition, they can't do much damage to their opponents. Without food and medical supplies, your soldiers will melt away without ever fighting a battle. Without spare parts and fuel, vehicles and equipment quickly become inoperable. The task of supplying ammunition, food, fuel, spares, and other items to the troops is called "logistics." It's not a very glamorous task, and is often neglected. Such lack of dedication normally leads to disasters. It's an ancient military maxim that "amateurs study strategy and tactics, professionals study logistics."

Grim Numbers

Problems with logistics are quite common in military history. These disasters occur not just because commanders ignore logistical matters. Astute opponents remain very aware of logistics and go out of their way to protect their own and disrupt their opponents' supply arrangements. Much of the military effort in the Vietnam War was directed at disrupting North Vietnamese supply efforts. The results of the largest bombing campaign in history were mixed, although the bombing did cause the North Vietnamese and Viet Cong enormous casualties and considerable trouble. A similar campaign against Chinese forces in Korea (1950–53) met with equal lack of success. The same thing happened in the campaign against German forces in Italy during 1943–44. The problem was primarily that the supply requirements of military forces are relatively small in comparison to the ability to transport material. It is rarely possible to stop all supply movement. What does get through is usually enough to keep the fighting going. Consider the following situation. A double-line railroad can, under wartime conditions, move at least 50 or more trains (400 tons each) a day. That's 20,000 tons a day. A two-lane hard-surface road can handle at least as much traffic, although at greater expense. Trains are cheaper to operate than trucks. A dirt road can handle half as much traffic and requires even more expense (more trucks, more breakdowns, etc.). With no roads at all, you have to create some kind of road, and such roads are generally no better than a single dirt road and often much worse.

A nonmechanized army requires only 15 to 30 pounds of supply per man per day. Every 1,000 tons of supply keeps 100,000 men in combat for a day. If one rail line or road enters an area occupied by 100,000 troops, it must be cut for more than 95 percent of the time to have any effect. And it must be cut for a sustained period, because military forces stockpile supplies when they have a chance. Even if you get supply below the minimum levels, combat capability won't be reduced until more than one third of the requirement is denied. Once that level is reached, for every percentage point of supply denied, one percent of the unit's combat power is lost. Even when completely cut off from supply, the average unit still retains one third of its combat power.

Mechanized units have more vehicles and weapons and require more than 10 times as much supply per man. Unit mobility in mechanized units is the first thing to go when supply is shut off, because of the weight of fuel. Such units have to choose between staying in place or moving and abandoning some vehicles.

Units without supplies can still fight, but at greater cost in casualties. As the Chinese in Korea and the North Vietnamese in Vietnam demonstrated, it is possible to take more casualties in lieu of using ammunition and still stand off a better-supplied force. In Korea, it was found that with twice the manpower taking twice the casualties, the Chinese were able to match better-armed and better-supplied UN units. Lack of food and medical supplies gradually wears down the troops.

The key point is that the adverse effects of reduced or no supply are gradual. Troops can continue to operate under these conditions for weeks or months. How is this so? Call it the "Use What You Got" rule of supply. When troops are well supplied, they are profligate. When times are lean, so are expenditures. Necessity is the mother of efficient supply use. When supply dries up for any reason, expedient methods are found to get by with less. History is full of examples.

Logistics can become very expensive when your opponent deliberately attacks your supply forces. Supplies and their transport are destroyed, to be replaced at no small cost. This exercise becomes a battle of wealth and material. A single sortie by a fighter bomber can cost $500,000. A truck is about $50,000, plus the cost of its cargo. A train and its cargo will cost tens of millions of dollars and up. Bridges, tunnels, and railroad yards are equally expensive. To replace these items is also costly in time. While portions of the transportation network are being rebuilt, additional expense is incurred in detouring around blown bridges or tunnels. Because most of this damage is outside the combat area, civilian resources can be used for the repairs. This makes it difficult to destroy transportation paraphernalia and keep it destroyed. Worse yet, the defender soon learns the advantages of camouflage and deception, making it difficult for the attacker to find out if a line has been cut, is still cut, or has been repaired.

There are two situations where logistics becomes the overwhelming factor: wilderness (deserts, jungles, mountains, etc.) and small islands. The 1991 Gulf War showed what dire straights an army (the Iraqis') is in if caught in the desert without supply. The same thing happened in the Arab-Israeli wars in the Sinai Desert and during World War II in the North African desert. The perils of having troops on an isolated island were vividly demonstrated during World War II in the Pacific. While the islands that U.S. Army and Marine infantry assaulted were costly in lives, many more enemy-occupied islands were simply bypassed, with many of the enemy troops starving to death before the war ended. Even the islands attacked were not as stoutly defended as they could have been, because the U.S. blockade prevented a lot of troops and material from reaching the islands before the U.S. assault.

It's easier to move troops than to move the supplies needed to keep the troops fighting effectively. If you want to determine who is going to win a future war, examine the supply situation first.

The Modern Major General's Dilemma

Anyone who has been involved with moving household goods several hundred or thousand miles has an inkling of what soldiers are up against. Few of us have any logistical experience beyond getting the groceries from the supermarket to the kitchen. Contemporary soldiers deal with numbers that quickly grow to immense proportions. Each trooper needs 6 pounds of food daily plus 20 pounds of water. The water often has to be delivered, and not just taken from a nearby lake. The food weight includes packaging, which is somewhat more copious than the wrappings found in your local fast-food outlet. Such basic necessities are the least of the supply officers' worries.

In typical operations, over 60 percent of the weight of supplies moved is fuel. The next largest category, ammunition, takes up some 20 percent of the weight transported. This is in sharp contrast to the World War II supply needs. The German Army, somewhat of a cross between the largely motorized Western armies and the generally unmotorized Soviet Army, required an average of 28 pounds per day per man. Some 40 percent was ammunition, 38 percent fuel (one quarter being fodder for horses), and the remainder rations and spares, etc. American units required 55 pounds per man per day. About half was ammo and 36 percent fuel. Current U.S. divisions require between 100 and 500 pounds per man per day, depending on the type of operation. Fuel and ammo still comprise more than three quarters of the requirements. Air-force logistics requirements have increased along the same lines as the army. Navy requirements have grown little. Smaller crews (automation), less fuel (nuclear power), and less ammo (more missiles) are the cause.

Although modern armed forces are burning more fuel and firing more ammo, this does not mean an equal increase in combat performance. All that extra fuel is needed to move heavier and more numerous vehicles around. Many of the armored vehicles are for transport, not combat. Ammunition does not represent combat power, but its ability to destroy enemy combat forces. More capable ammunition has been countered by better-protected troops and vehicles. Thus, the vast increase of ammunition weight available since World War II is not meaningful unless you are fighting a World War II–type force. One of the major differences between World War II weapons and current ones is that the logistics people have to move more than five times more material to support the current arms.

Rules of Thumb

The easiest way to comprehend logistical calculations is to start with the large numbers and work your way down into the detail. Taking the American situation today, every soldier operating outside the United States needs at least 100 pounds of supply per day. Each sailor needs four to six times that amount, and each airman up to 1,000 pounds a day. Troops on land can be cut down to less than 50 pounds a day if they are not doing anything. Sailors at sea require 300 pounds each just to keep the ships operational. When supply is moved by sea or rail, the fuel required is not a significant factor. To move a ton of material 100 kilometers by train uses 14 ounces of fuel. A large ship uses about half that. When material is moved by truck or air, it's a different story. By truck, one percent of the weight moved will be consumed as fuel for each 100 kilometers traveled. By air, the cost will be from 2 to 5 percent, depending on the type of aircraft. Large commercial cargo jets are the most efficient. Helicopters are notorious fuel hogs and can consume 10 percent of their cargo weight for each 100 kilometers traveled. Moving supply by animal, including humans, will have the same fuel cost as aircraft because of the food required. A recent innovation is the portable fuel pipeline, quickly laid alongside existing roads. It is twice as efficient as trucks, but more vulnerable to attack. A lot of supply will be in transit at any given time. You always encounter problems with keeping things moving, and some types of operations require larger amounts of logistical support. To cope with these conditions, forces strive to keep reserves, 30 to 90 days' worth of supply, on hand in locations around the combat area. For land operations, this would amount to 10 tons of supplies for each man in the area. For an army of 250,000 men, this will be a fairly large quantity of supply to store and keep track of—about 2.5 million tons. The half-million coalition troops massed for the liberation of Kuwait in 1991 piled up over 7 million tons of supply to support their efforts. The dimensions of the problem are becoming clearer.

Running the Store

Modern military commanders don't get to practice fighting, but they do get a lot of practice at logistics. Even in peacetime, large quantities of war material must be moved. Valuable experience is thus gained for the more massive demands of wartime. Peacetime logistics officers are primarily concerned with maintaining war-reserve stocks and the regular flow of spare parts, fuel, and food. War-reserve stocks are stockpiles of supply that, it is hoped, will get units through the first 30 or more days of combat. These stocks are absolutely essential for a units' wartime effectiveness. Immediate resupply from the civilian economy is unlikely, and these reserves are all the combat units will have initially. The war reserve stocks include everything needed: ammunition, fuel, food, spares, and supplies of every description. A three-to-five-day supply of all items is carried by each division at all times. Air force and naval units have similar reserves. The remainder is stockpiled in the rear areas, away from the expected battle areas. "Getting into the enemy's rear" and destroying these supplies often means that the enemy is soon immobile, going hungry, and fighting with empty weapons.

The placement of war reserve stocks is critical. Ammunition is preferably stored in bunkers. This affords some protection from enemy attack and decreases the possibility of one exploding bunker igniting another. These bunkers have to be located where they are unlikely to be quickly overrun by an advancing enemy. Bunkers must also be placed close to roads, rail lines, and perhaps water access. These bunkers witness a fair amount of activity as munitions are moved in and out.

Ammunition, as well as fuel, is perishable. Fuel cannot be stored for more than a year. Fuel and munitions must be rotated regularly. This is no problem with fuel, as vehicles use it constantly. Munitions are another problem. Peacetime use for training is much less than wartime use. At peacetime rates of use, munitions would last for decades. Unfortunately, munitions eventually begin to deteriorate and become unreliable. The explosives and propellants in munitions will begin to degrade after several years. This is a vexing problem. Nations take two different approaches to the problem. NATO nations tend not to maintain large stocks of munitions. They also use a lot more in peacetime and keep their stocks current. On the downside, these nations often have less than 30 days' of munitions available for combat. The other approach, followed by many Third World nations and Russia, keeps munitions until they are obviously useless. This produces a lot of munitions that do not work in combat. An example was the large number of Argentinean bombs that did not explode during the 1982 Falklands War. The Soviet Union maintained large stocks, up to 90 days' worth in some categories. However, their munitions were frequently unreliable due to their age. Even the new stuff suffered from above average manufacturing defects. Overall, this degraded the effectiveness of Soviet munitions up to 50 percent. With the demise of the Soviet Union, many of these older ammunition stocks were destroyed, so the successor states have less, but marginally more reliable, munitions on hand.

Another growing problem is spare parts, and replacements for lost equipment. Weapons, equipment, and munitions have all become more complex. Armies now have more technicians than infantrymen. All this to keep all this complex gear functioning. This is a difficult task even in peacetime. This process is complicated by the design of military equipment. To make repair possible using hastily trained repairmen, military gear tends to be modular. Entire assemblies are taken out and replaced, even if only a single component of the assembly is defective. It is often possible to repair assemblies, if skilled technicians are available. Otherwise, it is sent back to the factory, if possible, and a working one brought forward. The cost of spares to keep an F-15 going in combat average $300,000 a day if assemblies are used. If the technicians can make more detailed repairs themselves, the cost is reduced more than 70 percent. The weight of these spare parts is not great, just their value. We are talking about a lot of electronics and precision components. Complications proliferate as we are talking about millions of different parts. Each component in an aircraft comes under different types of stress depending on what the aircraft does. Different types of missions wear out different components at a different rate. Not knowing exactly how the aircraft will be used in wartime, peacetime planners have to make educated guesses as to how many of what spares to stock. There really is no easy way around this. Aircraft usage depends a lot on how the enemy operates, and one can only make estimates about this. Not only is there likely to be the wrong mix of spares, there will also be too few of them. Money is always short in military budgets.

When push comes to shove, more effort is put into producing weapons and less emphasis is placed on spares procurement. One might say this is another reason why professional soldiers wish to avoid war. If widespread combat occurred, complex weapons systems would quickly, too quickly, run out of spares. This would not shut them all down. Some aircraft, for example, can still fly and fight with a number of complex systems inoperative. The aircraft is less capable and more at risk, but it is still out there swinging. In addition, some aircraft can be cannibalized for parts to keep others going. The net result is that low spares inventories means weapons work less well and are destroyed sooner in combat. Spare parts are as essential as fuel and ammunition to keep a modern armed force functioning.

Some forms of supply can be obtained locally. Food, water, and fuel are commonly foraged. Unlike the good old days when the troops were instructed to grab whatever wasn't nailed down, today living off the local population must be conducted in an organized manner for the best results. Planning for this foraging is done in peacetime and often practiced as well. A strong local economy is a vital wartime asset. American forces in Europe obtained many needed items locally in peacetime and expected to continue if war came. An example of how this worked occurred during the Korean War (1950–53), where Japan was able to produce many items UN forces needed. Indeed, this business gave Japan a start on the way to reconstruction from the economic devastation of World War II. During the 1991 Gulf War, much of what the troops needed was obtained locally. Ironically, because of a shortage of refinery capacity, oil-rich Saudi Arabia had to import millions of tons of refined petroleum products to support the coalition forces. But even in this case, the abundance of oil-shipping facilities in the area was a big help.

The increasing use of computers has made the logistics planners' task somewhat more manageable. Yet the very complexity of modern logistic arrangements has made them more vulnerable to disruption. There has been only one experience in maintaining such technically sophisticated armies in a major war, the 1991 Gulf War. The experience served as a wake-up call for the generally blasé attitude toward logistics in peacetime. Not only do logistics planners face unprecedented problems, they also have to fight the ever-present general attitude that the supply situation will somehow take care of itself. It won't.

Us Versus Them

The Soviets developed a different attitude toward logistics, one that they passed on to many of their Third World clients and one that these generally poor nations would have been forced to adopt even without Soviet advisers. This system doesn't worry as much about spare parts. This system treats everything as expendable, including large units like divisions. If it breaks, bring up another. As Lenin put it, "Quantity has a quality all its own." Obviously, we have here at least two different styles in logistics. Western nations in general, and the United States in particular, prefer quality in their equipment, troops, and combat units. A constant stream of replacements, spares, and other essentials keep the combat units constantly in action. In the Soviet-type armed forces, the priorities are munitions, fuel, and little else. As equipment is disabled, it is allowed to fall by the wayside, to be picked over and repaired if possible by technical units that follow the fighting. Especially during combat, logistics is stripped down to the basics. Food, sleep, and maintenance can wait. The Soviet approach was, and is, pragmatic. They could not keep track of huge parts inventories or move massive tonnages of different supplies as efficiently as Western nations. To overcome these problems, Soviet units were to begin combat operations loaded with several days' worth of fuel and munitions. Food and other "nonessential" items might never reach the troops. Soldiers were encouraged, by hunger, if nothing else, to live off the land. Units were to advance for a few days or a week and then halt to rest and resupply. Western units attempt to maintain continuous operations. Whichever supply method is used, supplies are maintained at several different levels. The lowest level is the munitions carried with the weapon. This is commonly called a "unit of fire." An infantryman carries up to 300 rounds of assault-rifle ammunition with him. An artillery piece carries 50 to 100+ rounds depending on caliber. A tank carries 40+ rounds for its main gun, about a ton of all munitions, and up to a ton of fuel. Artillery units carry several tons of munitions with each gun. The next-higher unit, usually a division, will carry additional units of fire. At army and theater level, a dozen or more units of fire are held, typically immobile in supply dumps. Now you know where that term came from—they dump the stuff anywhere in the expectation that it will be moved and used shortly. A Soviet division tried to carry into battle five units of fire (1,000 tons each) and three or four refills for its vehicles' fuel tanks (1,000 tons each). American and Western divisions are larger. American divisional fuel refills and units of fire weigh about 1,100 tons each. Western divisions carry fewer of each, closer to two of fuel and three of munitions. Western units expect supply to keep moving; the Soviets were more pessimistic, or pragmatic.

Soviet and Western supply delivery systems differed in who was responsible for moving supplies. In Soviet practice, senior units were responsible for moving supplies forward to their subordinate units. In Western units, it works both ways, primarily because there is more transport and because subordinate units have more leeway in how they operate. The Soviet system was more straightforward and pragmatic; it was also more easily disrupted and prone to collapse. The Western system requires a lot more on-the-spot decision making. It is a more flexible system and more likely to survive a fluid battlefield. This was demonstrated during the 1991 Gulf War, and even before that Soviet officers were agitating for adopting a more "Western" style of warfare. After the Soviet empire collapsed later in 1991, this movement went into high gear. While the current successor states to the Soviet Union possess very "Soviet" armed forces, many of the officers in charge look to Desert Storm as an example of how it should be done.

On one point, both Western and Soviet-style armies were converging:

the overriding dependence on firepower. Soviet armies always used a lot of firepower, but largely in fixed situations. For examples, Soviet armies were legendary for their prodigious artillery preparations. Fewer opportunities are expected for this use of artillery. Everyone is expected to move around a lot, and artillery preparations will have to be hastily delivered before the opportunity passes. Unstable battlefields and unpredictable supply deliveries will be the norm. The future is a logistical nightmare.

Looting and pillaging will become more common. Soviet planners always kept an eye on civilian fuel-storage areas. Whether planned or not, troops will grab whatever they require in times of need. In the best of times, arming a man still seems to change his concepts of property rights. Iraqi troops in Kuwait gave a rather vivid demonstration of this in 1990.

Fists of Iron, Feet of Clay

Failures in the logistical system are quickly recognized. The absence of food or fuel is noticed even if no one is shooting at you. Logistics people are aware of this and expend considerable effort in contingency planning. Although planning is ordinarily done around logistical constraints, the planners are never aware of all the new twists in overall military plans. Worse, you never know exactly what your potential opponent has in mind for your efforts. If your own people decide to pursue a new tactic for using artillery and, perhaps, order the armored vehicles not to move around as much, this is going to change supply demands. The supply people will be informed of these changes, but no one knows exactly how this will impact ammo and fuel expenditure on the battlefield. Despite its dour reputation, keeping the supplies moving can be very exciting.

An intelligent and perceptive commander will always attempt to deny his opponent supply while preventing the enemy from doing the same to his side. Most combat sorties are flown against enemy supply lines and dumps. If one side gains air superiority for any length of time, his opponent can generally forget about victory. With an enemy air force overhead, supplies are constantly being hunted down and delayed or destroyed. As in the past, it is possible to hide your supplies and their transports from enemy air power. Some supply will always get through. That is sufficient if you are a guerrilla force fighting a regular army. If you are a mechanized army, these troublesome air attacks can be fatal. This was first seen in the summer of 1944. Allied airpower shut down all rail and most road movement within several hundred miles of the D-Day invasion beaches at Normandy. The Germans fought at a severe handicap. This was just as well—it took the Allies over a month to break through the German resistance. A motorized and heavily armed army is in worse shape today. The aircraft have better sensors, can fly in any weather, and carry more lethal warloads. Although antiaircraft weapons are also more powerful and numerous, the aircraft still have the advantage of choosing where they will go and when. Enormous quantities of supply are required to equip a combat division. It takes more than 200 tons of fuel to move a division 100 kilometers. A single U.S. M-1A1 tank battalion in the 1991 Gulf War could consume nearly 500 tons of supply (mostly fuel and water) in 24 hours of constant movement and fighting. Worse, it takes five tons of conventional artillery shells to inflict one casualty on the enemy. Not having the degree of supply you are used to creates a cascade of unwelcome events. Well, they are unwelcome to some. Lack of supply slows down the tempo of combat and results in fewer casualties. Lack of mobility prevents units from getting to the fighting, or avoiding being bypassed. Combat units often begin abandoning vehicles and equipment in order to move some of their strength. This abandonment diminishes combat power, if not immediately then eventually. Support vehicles, such as repair and supply resources, will be needed soon. Lacking this support, combat vehicles will be lost where they could normally be saved. The impact of poor supply is more acutely felt when attacking. A defender can more effectively stretch diminished resources. A shovel needs no fuel or spare parts. Mechanized combat divisions, with all their high-tech weapons, are very fragile units. When their constant and copious supply of fuel, munitions, and spares are interrupted, they are revealed to have fists of iron but feet of clay.

Air Force and Navy Logistics

Air forces, including naval air forces, concentrate on one thing: generating sorties. A sortie is one flight by one aircraft on some kind of mission. Hundreds of man-hours and 10 to 20 tons of supplies are needed to launch one sortie. The cost is over half a million dollars if it is a combat mission. For each ground combat division in a battle area, there would be about 100 combat aircraft. In the first few days of an operation, each aircraft could fly about three sorties. Three hundred sorties equals about 4,000 tons of supplies, over twice the daily rate for a division. Fortunately, air bases are not as mobile as combat divisions and are typically at least 50 to 100 kilometers away from the fighting. An air unit's primary problem is just getting the supply to the aircraft. At sea, the major consumer of supply is the aircraft carrier. A large carrier carries sufficient supplies to support about 1,000 sorties. With about 80 aircraft, most of these sorties will be flown by support aircraft, or combat aircraft on patrol missions. Like land-based combat aircraft, their naval counterparts will consume the same prodigious amounts of material on strike missions. A carrier task force can easily consume 5,000 tons of supply a day while at sea. A non-carrier task force will need less than a third that amount. Navies prefer to keep their supply mobile, with dozens of tankers and dry cargo ships chasing after or accompanying the task forces. These combat-support naval ships are constantly at risk from enemy submarines. Even at sea, the people who move supplies are eagerly sought targets. Wartime demands require that civilian merchant ships be pressed into service to supply the fleet. Navy technicians and some special equipment is required to perform at-sea re-supply. Sometimes naval personnel are put aboard merchant ships to make them capable of at-sea replenishment. More often, merchant ships move supplies to forward naval bases, where the specialized naval-supply ships pick it up for transport into the combat zone.

Few nations have any at-sea replenishment capability at all, and none have the ability to supply so many ships so far from their home port as the United States.

Theory and Practice

The Soviet system was based on past experience and a pragmatic appraisal of the Soviets' own circumstances. However, they were done in by technology and ambition. More complex weapons require far more spare parts and items in general. Lacking experience with managing large, complex inventories, not to mention primitive computers, the Soviets had little hope of maintaining their more recent, and more complex, systems in wartime. Soviet inventory disasters were common in peacetime, and some hair-raising stories of logistical problems emerged after the Soviet Union collapsed and former Soviet officers were able to speak more freely. More complex technology could not be avoided by the Soviets, and attempts to emulate Western solutions (computerization, free-market suppliers) proved impossible. This logistical chaos in post-Soviet Russia has made it difficult for the Russians to sell their weapons, even at fire-sale prices. For truly desperate customers, additional weapons were bought to serve as a source of replacement parts. It was well known that adequate parts and supply support has not been reliable in the past from Russia, and no one expected it to get better with the Russian armed forces no longer having first pick of economic resources.

The magnitude of unrepairable breakdowns of high-tech equipment in wartime will be shocking only to those who ignored the trends. The Western nations have similar problems, but at least they see them coming and are better equipped to overcome the shortages. During the 1990 buildup for the Gulf War, U.S. forces quickly discovered which items had not been stocked in sufficient quantity in peacetime to support a wartime level of operations. A strong and resourceful market economy back in the United States made it possible to manufacture (sometimes after quickly designing the item first) the needed parts and equipment.

More so than in past wars, supply movements will face greater danger than ever before. Missiles and a more fluid battlefield will eliminate the relative reliability of past supply movements. Western nations have a more serious problem in their reluctance to stockpile spares and munitions for the opening stages of a war. The combat-unit commanders plan to use thousands of tons of munitions per day in the opening battles. Many smaller Western nations have stocks to last less than a week at this rate. Nations like the United States aren't much better off.

One of the recurring issues in the last century has been commanders who have underestimated supply requirements during the early stages of a war. America had the problem during Korea and Vietnam and even in the 1991 Gulf War. The Soviet Union was similarly caught short in Afghanistan. The wisdom gained in these wars proved to have a short shelf life. Face it, logistics is not the sort of thing that gets the attention of leaders and their budgets in peacetime. It is too easy to ignore it or simply study the problem to death without undertaking a solution.

Another problem unique to the United States is the level of additional goodies peacetime planners add to what is "required" for troops overseas. The army is the biggest offender in this area because army troops do not normally train at moving large units overseas for extended periods. The navy is constantly overseas, and its marines regularly land units up to brigade strength on distant shores. Fortunately, most potential wars involving the United States require small numbers of troops. American planners, however, live in fear of being asked to move several divisions quickly to a distant battlefield, and keeping them there for months under combat conditions. This happened in 1990–91. What prevented a logistical disaster was a six-month period of no enemy activity to allow for a supply buildup and the construction of a supply system. The army general in charge of logistics was promoted during the operation. He received this honor because he was able to improvise solutions for many of the logistical nightmares U.S. forces brought with them to the Gulf. Some of these improvisations were directly a result of civilian technology that Western nations have in abundance. For example, it was discovered that it was taking too long (several weeks) to get parts requests back to the United States using the normal "system." So, a laptop computer and satellite-communications link were rigged together, and a parts clerk was able to sit in the desert and get parts requests transmitted to America and confirmations on availablity sent back to the desert in less than an hour. You need that kind of resourcefulness, and resources, to avoid logistical disasters in modern wars.

The Future

Commercial methods of handling and moving materials have made tremendous advances during the last few decades, even if many of these developments were not adopted by the military. The Gulf War saw an extensive adoption of commercial materials handling techniques and equipment. Modern weapons are built to fire a lot more ammunition in a shorter time than in the past. Current armored fighting vehicles are faster and more agile than equipment 20 or 30 years ago. Logistics vehicle mobility has not improved as rapidly. Slowly, some nations are producing resupply vehicles that can keep up with the fast-moving armored fighting vehicles. The biggest question mark is whether enough of these vehicle will be available during a major operation. During the Gulf War, sufficient heavy-lift vehicles had to be begged, borrowed, leased, and, in a few cases, stolen, to meet the troops' needs. The United States did, in the 1980s, begin to build specialized cross-country military transports. Several thousand of these 10-ton cross-country HEMTT trucks were available in the Gulf, and they were a vital part of the success of the campaign. The United States also had about 1,000 HET tank transporters available. More of both classes of vehicles are being built.

On the positive side, the increasing use of private automobiles provides enormous stocks of gasoline for military vehicles that do not require special fuel. This was a valuable asset in Saudi Arabia, as it would be in major industrial areas like Europe. But in too many potential hot spots, there's not much of anything to sustain a major mechanized force. In most parts of the world, all the logistician will find are headaches and aggravation.

Divisional Daily Supply Requirements

Chart 23-1 shows divisional supply requirements for each day of operations. For logistics purposes, we have four types: offense, defense, pursuit, and reserve. Reality is not as neat as this chart. Offensive operations will generally use all the supply they can get. Defensive operations try to adapt their supply needs to the intensity of their attacker's efforts. Sometimes a unit will use enormous quantities of supply on the defense if the material is available and the position must be held. At other times, the defender will be parsimonious with supplies while sacrificing men and ground instead. A pursuit is similar to simply moving around a lot. Reserve is sitting in one place, sometimes in contact with the enemy, using as little supply as possible. The last category is the average of all the above operations, in a mixture typical of future combat. This is the average amount of supplies given an assumed mix of the different types of operations. Troops don't spend all their time doing any of the four types of combat, but a mix. The supply norms for Soviet-type and U.S. divisions were estimated from each nation's policies. Divisions can easily consume three or four times more ammunition in a day. Often this is the case. For planning purposes, norms are established so that operations can be planned without exceeding available supplies.

SUPPLY TYPE is the class of supply. The official NATO terms for the various classes of supply are: Class 1—Food; Class 2/7/9—Individual equipment/ Medical/ Spares; Class 3—Fuel; Class 4—Barrier and Construction Material; Class 5—Ammunition.

23-1 Divisional Logistics

Supp Type	Type of Division							
	Russian Tank Division (tons)		Russian Rifle Division (tons)		US Armor Division (tons)		US Infantry Division (tons)	
Offense								
Amm	1,500	39%	1,200	31%	2,300	64%	2,500	66%
Fuel	2,216	58%	2,480	65%	1,133	31%	1,210	32%
Food	26	1%	31	1%	40	1%	51	1%
Spar	70	2%	110	3%	137	4%	55	1%
Total	3,812	100%	3,821	100%	3,610	100%	3,816	100%
Lbs/	799		672		481		525	
Defense								
Amm	2,000	61%	2,200	61%	3,000	81%	3,500	82%
Fuel	1,212	37%	1,320	36%	616	17%	671	16%
Food	29	1%	33	1%	41	1%	49	1%
Spar	60	2%	83	2%	40	1%	50	1%
Total	3,301	100%	3,636	100%	3,697	100%	4,270	100%
Lbs/	692		640		493		587	
Pursuit								
Amm	300	8%	150	4%	400	17%	410	21%
Fuel	3,432	91%	3,748	94%	1,914	80%	1,496	75%
Food	17	0%	21	1%	42	2%	50	3%
Spar	40	1%	55	1%	46	2%	44	2%
Total	3,789	100%	3,974	100%	2,402	100%	2,000	100%
Lbs/	794		699		320		275	
Reserve								
Amm	132	13%	145	13%	390	41%	438	46%
Fuel	844	82%	948	82%	484	50%	440	47%
Food	23	2%	26	2%	41	4%	48	5%
Spar	28	3%	39	3%	44	5%	20	2%
Total	1,027	100%	1,158	100%	959	100%	946	100%
Lbs/	215		204		128		130	
Average								
Amm	846	37%	773	42%	1,135	65%	1,309	68%
Fuel	1,350	60%	910	50%	467	27%	461	24%
Food	25	1%	63	3%	73	4%	79	4%
Spar	43	2%	84	5%	74	4%	65	3%
	2,264	100%	1,830	100%	1,749	100%	1,914	100%

AMMO is munitions, primarily artillery ammunition.

FUEL is all types of fuel, for vehicles, aircraft, and power generators. Usage is highest in pursuit operations because every vehicle is moving. In combat operations, combat vehicles do most of their moving as they maneuver about the battlefield. In reserve operations, most movement is by noncombat support vehicles.

FOOD includes canned and other long-shelf-life combat rations as well as fresh provisions for units in stable situations.

SPARES is all the spare parts to keep equipment going and the troops in good health. Also includes medical supplies, normal replacements for clothing and equipment, and so on.

TONS is the number of tons of supply for each class and type of operation.

% shows the percentage of each class of supply for each type of operation.

LBS/MAN is the pounds per man of supply for each type of operation. Armies other than those of the United States and Russia have similar supply norms. Other Western armies use, if anything, somewhat higher norms than the United States, especially for ammunition. Armies using Soviet equipment generally use somewhat lower norms than their former Soviet mentors. Less wealthy nations also use lower norms. Norms will always be modified by the quantities of men, weapons, and equipment in divisions, as well as the tempo of operations.

It is still possible to fight a low-budget war. It depends on whom you are fighting and where. An ill-armed and ill-equipped opponent requires less ammunition to fight. More fuel may be required for running around a lot, as in antiguerrilla actions. Modern armies fighting guerrillas also use a lot of munitions trying to keep the little buggers out of mischief.

Ground-Transport Characteristics

This chart shows the characteristics of the combat and noncombat vehicles most frequently found in divisions. The noncombat vehicles are largely trucks, many of them civilian models repainted for military use. Special military trucks are, despite their somewhat different appearance, basically modified civilian versions, with items such as four-wheel drive (for off-road travel), multifuel engines (so they can burn whatever is available), convertible cabs (so someone can stand up and watch out for aircraft or ambush), and open cargo area (so that a variety of loads can be carried).

VEHICLE USER is the nation using that vehicle, typically also the manufacturer.

NAME is the designation of the vehicle.

VEHICLE WEIGHT is the empty weight in tons.

VEHICLE LOAD is the average load carried on roads. Off roads, capacity is reduced about 50 percent. Many trucks also pull small trailers.

VEHICLE RANGE is how far a vehicle can go, on road, with one tank of fuel.

LITERS OF FUEL CARRIED in the vehicle tank. One gallon equals 3.79 liters.

TONS OF FUEL PER 1,000 KM is the tonnage of fuel the vehicle will need to travel 1,000 kilometers on roads. Up to twice the fuel is needed to travel off roads, depending on the roughness of terrain and the adaptability of the vehicle to cross-country travel.

IN DIVISION is the number of each vehicle found in the average division.

TONS OF FUEL PER 100 KM is the tonnage of fuel required to move all the vehicles of each type in the division 100 kilometers. The armored vehicles account for the bulk of the fuel.

TONS OF LIFT TOTAL is the tonnage the division's transports can move. American and Western divisions possess more transport than Soviet-style divisions. The Soviets made strenuous attempts to close this gap, but economic considerations and a shortage of manufacturing capacity prevented dramatic progress.

Classification of Vehicles

Transports carry supplies and equipment. Light transports like jeeps also carry commanders and light weapons or run errands. Combat vehicles carry weapons and fight.

Combat vehicles also include APCs, which carry infantry or a wide range of specialized combat-support vehicles' equipment, like communications gear, mobile headquarters, and artillery. Not all vehicles are covered in this chart. For example, the Soviets had, and Russia still has, a wide variety of tracked transports with the same general load capacities and fuel requirements as wheeled vehicles. These are used in northern areas where snow cover or mud is the common ground condition. Track-laying vehicles are more complex mechanisms and require more maintenance and spares. These vehicles are almost as difficult to keep going as their heavier cousins, the tanks and APCs. The fuel situation is not likely to improve in the future. The new U.S. M-1 and Russian T-80 have engines that consume more fuel. An M-1's turbine engine uses about as much fuel standing still as it does moving. Larger APCs and more trucks to accommodate growing munitions requirements constantly push fuel usage higher.

Supply Requirements for Aircraft

Aircraft logistics is complicated by the spares situation and unused munitions. High-performance aircraft literally burn up many of their components. Engines are the biggest item. These must be replaced every few hundred or few thousand

23-2 Typical Ground Combat Vehicles

Vehicle User	Name	Weight (tons)	Load (tons)	Range (km)	Liters Fuel Carried	Tons Fuel per 1,000 km	# in Division	Tons Fuel 100 km	Tons Lift Total
	Trucks								
US	M-54 (truck)	11.6	9	563	380	0.61	600	37	5,400
US	M-34 (truck)	5.5	4.7	563	189	0.31	1,500	46	7,050
US	M-37 (3/4)	2.6	0.9	362	91	0.23	400	9	360
US	Hummer	2.8	1.1	565	83	0.13	800	11	880
US	M-151 (jeep)	1.1	0.45	482	56	0.11	200	2	90
	Transport Tot Tons	16,470			569 tons		3,500	105	13,780
	Armored Fighting Vehicles								
US	M-113	11.5	0	480	310	0.59	400	23	
US	M-1	52	0	440	1,900	3.93	290	114	
US	M-2	21.4	0	480	570	1.08	320	35	
	AFV Total	11,448			779 tons		1,010	172	
	Division Tot	27,918			1,348 tons		4,510	276	
	Trucks								
Russia	Ural-375	8.4	6	750	360	0.44	400	17	2,400
Russia	Zil-131	6.7	5	850	340	0.36	700	25	3,500
Russia	Zil-157K	5.8	4.5	510	215	0.38	600	23	2,700
Russia	Gaz-69	1.5	0.4	430	60	0.13	300	4	120
	Transport Tot Tons	12,006			481		2,000	70	8,720
	Armored Fighting Vehicles								
Russia	BMP(& Others)	12.5		455	400	0.80	1,000	80	
Russia	T-64	38		500	1,000	1.82	300	55	
	AFV Total Tot Tons	23,900			636		1,300	134	
	Division Tot Tons	35,906			1,117		3,300	204	8,720
	Other Armored Fighting Vehicles								
France	AMX-30b	36	0	500	970	1.76	150	26	
Germany	Leopard I	40	0	600	955	1.45	300	43	
US	M1	52	0	440	1,900	3.93	351	138	
US	M-2	21.4	0	480	570	1.08	515	56	
US	M60A3	52	0	480	950	1.80	351	63	

hours, depending on the aircraft and the amount of stressful maneuvering. The weight of a new engine won't add that much to each sortie, but the expense will be noticeable. On the bright side, many aircraft return from missions with expensive weapons they did not have to use. This is common with interceptors; they don't always have to fire all the expensive missiles they carry. Bombers no longer jettison their loads if targets cannot be found. The downside of this is that you have a lot of aircraft landing with live ordnance dangling from them. This adds a little more excitement to landing accidents.

AIRCRAFT is the aircraft designation, although more than one variant of an aircraft often exists. These variants sometimes differ significantly in characteristics. An average is used here.

PRINCIPAL USER is the nation of manufacture and the principal user. West is many Western nations (including Israel and South Africa). The Chinese F-6 is a copy of the Soviet MiG-19. They also have a MiG-21 clone called the F-7.

FUEL is the average tonnage of fuel used on one sortie.

WARLOAD is the average load of disposable weapons carried on one sortie. It is assumed that some of the air-to-air missiles will be brought back unused. Unused bombs are sometimes dropped to avoid landing accidents.

AVERAGE SORTIES PER DAY can vary quite a lot depending on the situation and the skill of the ground crews. Number used here is the average.

TONS/100 SORTIES is the total tonnage of supply required for 100 sorties. This includes an allowance for maintenance supplies and supply needed to maintain personnel.

TONS/100 AIRCRAFT is the total tonnage of supply for 100 aircraft of each type per day if they are flying the average number of sorties per day.

PERCENT OF SUPPLY WARLOAD is the percentage of the total supply requirements that is disposable weapons (bombs, bullets, missiles, etc.). You can see significant differences in carrying capacity, particularly between Western and Russian aircraft.

WARLOAD/100 AIRCRAFT is the warload carried by 100 aircraft of each type per day if they are flying the average number of sorties per day.

23-3 Supply Requirements for Aircraft

Aircraft	Principal User	Tons Carried Fuel	War Load	Avg Sortie Day	Tons /100 Sorties	Tons /100 Aircraft	Percent Warload	Warload /100 Aircraft
Russian Land Based								
MiG-21	Third World	2.1	1.5	1	360	360	42%	150
MiG-23	Third World	4.7	1.5	1	620	620	24%	150
MiG-27	Third World	4.7	4.5	1	920	920	49%	450
MiG-25	Third World	15.1	2	0.5	1,710	855	12%	100
MiG-29	Russia	4	4.5	2	850	1,700	53%	900
Su-17	Third World	3.3	4.5	1	780	780	58%	450
Su-24	Russia	24	4.5	1	2,850	2,850	16%	450
Su-25	Third World	3.5	6.5	2	1,000	2,000	65%	1,300
Su-27	Russia	5	2	2	700	1,400	29%	400
Tu-22M	Third World	13.4	8	1	2,140	2,140	37%	800
Mi-8	Third World	2	4	4	600	2,400	67%	1,600
Mi-24	Third World	1.5	1.7	4	320	1,280	53%	680
Western Land Based								
F-4	West	5.7	7.2	2	1,290	2,580	56%	1,440
F-16	West	3.2	6.9	3	1,010	3,030	68%	2,070
F-15	West	6.1	7.2	3	1,330	3,990	54%	2,160
A-10	U.S.	6.1	7.2	5	1,330	6,650	54%	3,600
Mirage 3	West	2.7	1.5	2	420	840	36%	300
F-104	West	2.8	3.4	1	620	620	55%	340
Harrier	West	3.5	3.6	5	710	3,550	51%	1,800
Tornado	West	5.2	7.2	2	1,240	2,480	58%	1,440
Alpha	West	1.5	2.2	3	370	1,110	59%	660
F-6	China	1.8	0.5	1	230	230	22%	50
F-111	U.S.	15.4	10	1	2,540	2,540	39%	1,000
UH-1	West	1	2	5	300	1,500	67%	1,000
AH-1S	West	1	0.5	4	150	600	33%	200
UH-60	U.S.	2	3	5	500	2,500	60%	1,500
AH-64	U.S.	7	1.7	4	870	3,480	20%	680
US Carrier Aircraft								
F-14	U.S.	7.5	6.5	2	1,400	2,800	46%	1,300
A-7	West	4.5	6.8	3	1,130	3,390	60%	2,040
A-6	U.S.	7.2	8.1	3	1,530	4,590	53%	2,430
F-18	West	5.1	7.7	3	1,280	3,840	60%	2,310

24

Attrition

Combat does not destroy armed forces, it merely hastens the process. The real killer is day-to-day wear and tear. Armies die by inches, not yards. Attrition is people and their equipment wearing out. Even in peacetime, up to 2 percent of combat aircraft can be lost to accidents and deterioration each year. In wartime, up to 50 percent of aircraft will be lost each year to noncombat wear and tear. Rarely will more than 90 percent of armored vehicles be in running condition at any one time. Those vehicles that are running will likely break down after going less than 500 kilometers. More important, people wear out too. Without enough people to tend them, the machines wear out even faster.

What Really Destroys Armies

Annually, disease and noncombat injuries often cause far more loss than the dangers of combat. Most major wars go on for years. Battles are relatively infrequent. As long as the troops are living in primitive field conditions, they are more prone to disease and injury. The annual loss rates in the wars of this century, expressed in terms of average daily losses per 100,000 men, bear this out. Battle losses, killed and wounded but not prisoners, varied from a low of 6 per day in World War II theaters such as North Africa to more than 200 Germans a day on the Soviet front. Soviet casualties were sometimes double the German rate. World War I had battles where the rate exceeded several thousand per day. Nuclear war could easily exceed even these horrendous rates.

The World War I casualty rates, and the numerous mutinies they eventually caused, were not forgotten. The butchery of World War I made an impression, and the casualty rates were consistently lower in World War II. Since World War II, still more efforts have been made to protect the troops. Armored vehicles and protective gear have become more commonplace. Daily loss rates of 40 per 100,000, similar to the Western allies of World War II, can be expected in the future. Nuclear or chemical weapons may push this up, but high loss rates in a short time may also cause disintegration of military units. This is likely because these wide-area weapons are intended for use against combat-support and supply units. The combat forces cannot advance with empty weapons and stomachs.

Nonbattle casualties, primarily from disease and especially in tropical and winter conditions, regularly reach 200 to 500 men per day per 100,000 strength. Malaria alone can cause nearly 200 casualties a day. Another constant menace in populated areas is venereal disease, which can render ineffective as many as 40 men per day. Injuries often exceed battle losses. The troops tend to get careless in the combat zone. Vehicle and weapons accidents were so common in the past that they often reached 20 men per day per 100,000 troops.

The Forms of Combat Losses

Losses as a direct result of combat—the effects of enemy weapons as opposed to indirect effects such as trench foot, malaria, or pneumonia contracted from sleeping in a wet trench—fall into four categories.

1. *Fatal:* The victim is dead.
2. *Wounded:* The victim is injured but not fatally and has a good chance of returning to combat.
3. *Mental:* The victim suffers a mental breakdown from the stresses of combat.
4. *Absence:* The victim is captured or deserts.

FATAL/WOUNDED RATIOS

The rate and lethality of combat casualties vary with such factors as the amount of enemy artillery fire versus machine-gun fire. Artillery will cause more, but less lethal, casualties than bullets. Closed terrain like forests and towns allows proportionately more bullet wounds by reducing the effects of artillery. Fast-moving operations prevent treatment of wounded troops; many more die or take longer to recover. Better-prepared and better-led troops avoid casualties. Armored vehicles, fortifications, and protective clothing all reduce casualties and their severity. Finally, the availability and efficiency of medical care make a difference. Leaving out the absent prisoners and deserters and assuming the usual heavy use of fragmentation weapons (shells and bombs), historical experience suggests there will be one fatality for every three wounded troops. About 80 percent of these casualties will be caused by fragments. About 12 percent of these wounds will occur in the head (43 percent immediately fatal), 16 percent in the chest (25 percent fatal), 11 percent in the abdomen (17 percent fatal), 22 percent in arms and legs (5 percent fatal). In the past, 20 percent of all wounds were multiple, and over half of those combinations were fatal. Modern lightweight plastic armor in the form of Kevlar cloth or rigid plate will reduce fatalities and injuries up to 25 percent. This material does cause heat buildup in warm weather, sometimes leading to heat-exhaustion injuries. If it is used selectively for troops in exposed situations, its beneficial aspects are retained without injurious side effects. Although the jackets cost over $300, the savings in troops, not to mention the morale boost, are well worth it. In addition to the armored jackets, improved helmets, boots, and protective curtains for vehicle interiors are available. Many of these items were first widely used during World War II by U.S. bomber crews. The U.S. Army is now the leading proponent of these protective measures, followed by other Western nations and, lately, even some Third World nations.

MENTAL CASUALTIES

Combat is an extremely stressful activity that causes a number of nervous breakdowns and related disabilities. These disabling maladies are commonly called "combat fatigue." The rate of breakdown is highest in poorly trained and badly led armed forces. During World War II, the U.S. Army had three combat-fatigue cases for every two troops wounded in combat. For every 100 men killed, 125 were discharged from service because of mental breakdown. The average combat-fatigue victim was out of action half as long as men who were physically wounded. The German Army, in contrast, had only 13 combat-fatigue cases for every 100 wounded. This was primarily a result of better training and leadership. Other armies fell somewhere in between these extremes. A contemporary war may well produce higher levels of combat fatigue because of the higher intensity of fighting and lower levels of training and experience. The Germans did better handling combat fatigue in World War II because they carefully studied their World War I experience and planned accordingly.

PRISONERS AND DESERTERS

Losses are not always due to death and injury. Soldiers are taken prisoner, and others decide to pursue more peaceful endeavors and desert.

The number of prisoners and deserters varies considerably depending on how badly you are losing. Even a victorious force lists a few percent of its total losses as MIA (Missing in Action). About 50 percent of MIAs are KIA (Killed in Action) or badly wounded and dead before they can be identified. Many of the rest turn out to be deserters (who sometimes surface years later) or prisoners (who die in captivity). In the U.S. Army, it has sometimes happened that men who were killed in combat were reported as missing by friends so that the dead man's family could continue to receive his pay. Eventually, MIAs are declared dead, their pay stopped, and death benefits paid.

Deserters will often come forward after the war and throw themselves on the mercy of the courts. In wartime, desertion is punishable by death or a long prison sentence. Waiting for the war to end thus improves a deserter's chances of getting away with it. Most deserters are actually combat-fatigue cases who simply broke and ran for it. A substantial minority of deserters are criminals, who calculate their prospects are better by leaving their units and continuing their black-market or other criminal activities out of uniform.

Historically, many men who surrender are not captured alive by the enemy. Up to 50 percent of those surrendering do not survive the process. They are either killed on the spot or die in captivity. Troops in combat quickly learn this, which explains why surrender is not more common. When survivable surrenders do occur, they tend to be in large numbers or by negotiation.

WASTING AWAY

It's not unusual for armies to waste away to nothing without ever having come in contact with the enemy. Historically, natural causes have killed or disabled far more soldiers than combat. Many wars are won by the side best able to maintain the health of their troops. Perceptive military commanders have long recognized the substantial assistance of General Winter, Colonel Mud, and the carnage wrought by pestilence, poor climate, thirst, and starvation. An armed force may be an impressive sight, yet people have to live. They must eat, sleep, and escape the elements. Disease and injury are ever present. Adequate medical care prevents minor afflictions from becoming major ones. More important is public sanitation. Many diseases thrive in careless accumulations of human waste. Public sanitation, even within an army on the move, eliminates the cause of most disease. For example, from 1900 to 1940 in the United States, the average life expectancy of males increased 12 years (a 31 percent increase) as a result of improved sanitation. Since 1940, the introduction of many wonder drugs and medical procedures have lifted life expectancy another nine years (15 percent increase). During World War II, sanitation was so bad in the Japanese Army, and disease so widespread, that infantry battalions in tropical areas would lose more than 10 percent of their strength per month just to disease and privation.

The American Army's history of disease deaths is illustrative. In 1846 (Mexican American War), 10 percent of troops died from disease. In the 1860s (Civil War), 7.2 percent. In 1918 (World War I), 1.3 percent. In the 1940s (World War II), .6 percent. Although the deaths due to disease have declined markedly, the incidence of disease has not. As the chart on noncombat losses demonstrates, armies are never far from a disaster of uncontrolled disease. The Gulf War was unique in that for the first time this century, an American Army suffered more noncombat than combat casualties. This was an aberration because of the overwhelming combat power brought to bear on the enemy. Most battles are more evenly matched, and not fought in as disease-ridden an area as the Persian Gulf.

Useful Combat Life

Warfare produces many bizarre situations. For example, a dead soldier is less of a loss than a wounded one. While a dead soldier is no longer useful, neither is a wounded one. In addition, a wounded trooper requires the attention of others and is not always returned to action. Some armies actually do follow the cold-blooded policy, either officially or due to circumstances, of killing the badly wounded. A "shoot the wounded" policy soon demoralizes troops to the point where they will desert or violently resist their leaders. Some armies enforce such bloody-minded systems with ruthless efficiency. In the Soviet Army, a division had a hospital with only 60 beds. Medical facilities throughout the division were slight. Wounded men were to make their way to the rear as best they could. Those who couldn't generally perished. Draconian methods were used to ensure acceptance of this system. As Joseph Stalin put it, "It takes a very brave man to not be a hero in the Red Army."

Commanders must still take into account the mathematics of combat casualties. Combat wears a man down and out, particularly infantry fighting. Experience has shown that the average soldier can be effective for about 200 days of combat. After that, you generally have a case of combat fatigue—someone dangerous to himself and those around him. At that point, these veterans are best removed to noncombat jobs or civilian occupations. Let us assume that this will provide another 400 days of useful service. If a soldier is killed after 100 days of combat, the armed forces loses 500 days of service. During World War II, 65 percent of all incidents of lost time in the U.S. Army were from noncombat injuries. These resulted in very few deaths. Still, each case put a soldier out of action for 10 days. The average combat injury put a soldier out of action for 100 days. Twenty percent of combat injuries resulted in death. For each day a soldier is out of action due to wounds or disease, one or more additional soldiers is assigned to taking care of him. For this reason, nonfatal casualties comprise two thirds of the days lost due to injury or illness. Therefore, taking 100 injured soldiers, we have the following pattern of lost days:

Combat Deaths—one. Five hundred days lost or 21 percent of total days lost for injuries. This is only 13 percent of days lost if time of medical personnel is included.

Combat Wounded—four. Four hundred days lost or 17 percent of days lost although 22 percent if medical-personnel time is included.

Noncombat Deaths (mostly accidents)—one. Same as combat deaths.

Noncombat Illness and Injuries—94. Nine hundred forty days lost or 41 percent of time lost; some 52 percent if medical-personnel time is included.

Chemical and nuclear casualties (nonfatal) tend to be more severe than the usual noncombat "illness," but not as devastating as combat wounds from shot and shell. Perhaps only 50 days lost per chemical/nuclear casualty. With medical-personnel time added, this comes to more than 100 days lost per incident. Since each soldier may be wounded by chemical agents several times, the total time lost approaches that of a combat death. Moreover, chemical and nuclear injuries are expected to have a severe psychological effect, probably resulting in higher combat-fatigue losses. This is another reason why commanders are reluctant to use these weapons. They risk losing control of their troops.

The Rate of Return

Depending on the quality of training and leadership, the rate of troops returning to duty after combat injury will vary. During World War II, the German Army achieved an 80 percent return rate, while the U.S. Army returned 64 percent. The higher German rate was partially the result of returning slightly disabled troops to less physically demanding duty, and partially attributable to better administration. Generally, 60 percent of the combat wounded who eventually recover return to duty within three months, 85 percent within six months, and more than 95 percent within a year. Fifty percent of the noncombat casualties return within a month, 85 percent within three months, and nearly all by six months.

Since World War II, the United States has pioneered rapid evacuation of wounded troops, usually by helicopter. This is a major advantage, as the treatment a wounded soldier receives within an hour of being wounded often determines survival or how rapid eventual recovery will be. The high quality of U.S. medical care has saved many troops who previously would have died. The return-to-duty rate has not gone up because of this.

Naval and Air Casualties

Navies and air forces suffer far fewer casualties, in absolute and relative terms, than armies. Exceptions to this are not uncommon. Aircraft crews and submarine personnel take a pounding, often proportionately worse than the infantry. But there are a lot more infantry getting shot at. In a large-scale war, when naval and air bases are attacked, the naval and air-force personnel casualty rate can be expected to be one quarter to one half the army's rate.

Most naval casualties are suffered at sea. About a third of the deaths are from noncombat injuries. Combat deaths generally equal combat injuries. This is because ships suffer catastrophic damage—being blown up or sinking quickly and killing or injuring nearly all the crew. Modern ships are heavily armed and unarmored, which makes them prime candidates for massive losses from smoke and fire.

During World War II, the loss rate—dead, wounded, and captured—for long-range bombers averaged nearly four men per aircraft lost, and one aircraft was lost for every 100 sorties (66 sorties for bombers, 145 sorties for fighters). Altogether, 40,000 aircraft were lost during the three-year strategic bombing campaign in Europe. Current aircraft fly one or two sorties a day and would probably last less than three months in constant combat unless one side quickly obtained air superiority. Most modern aircraft have a crew of one, which will lower the rate of air-crew losses. Modern aircraft are also more reliable, lowering noncombat losses and increasing chances of surviving battle damage. Air bases are likely to take a greater pounding than in past wars, largely because of more capable aircraft, weapons, and ballistic missiles.

Theory and Practice

Casualties in wartime are taken for granted and accepted. What to do about it is less clear. Casualties have several effects. The victim feels it first, and longest. But the victim's companions also get hit with a bit of stress and dismay. The unit suffering casualties undergoes instant reorganization, whether it is ready or not. Some armed forces cope with the psychological problems accompanying losses better than others. Combat units rarely have the number of troops they are supposed to have. Noncombat losses and administrative requirements will keep between 3 and 10 percent of a unit's strength unavailable at any time. Combat losses simply increase the organizational disruption. During the opening stages of a major and protracted war, not all attempts to cope with these losses will be successful. Aside from the problems of anticipating what equipment and types of troops will be lost and in what quantities, you have better and worse ways to send the replacements in. Generally, it is more effective to pull battered units out of combat, rest them, introduce new men and equipment, and put the revived unit through some training. The temptation is strong to keep units in action and feed in the replacements. This rarely gives good results, but is often done anyway.

Firepower has increased since World War II, even without taking nuclear weapons into account. Armies have equipped themselves with more potent weapons in nearly every category. For example:

1. *Infantry Weapons.* At the end of World War II, the Germans began to arm their infantry with the SG-44, which the Soviets copied as the AK-47. The United States responded with the M-16 (first proposed in the 1930s). It has long been noted that a machine gun generates firepower equal to 10 or more rifle-armed troops. Now, nearly every soldier has a machine gun, albeit a lightweight one. Still, infantry firepower has more than tripled since 1945.

2. *Artillery.* The bigger-is-better concept applies to artillery, increasing size development. The average artillery shell in World War II weighed about 33 pounds (105mm); today, it is close to 100 pounds (155mm). Armies plan on firing more shells per day per gun, something on the order of three to five times more weight of shell per day. The design of artillery munitions has changed. Shells are now two to three times more lethal for those nations that can afford these ICM (Improved Conventional Munitions). Improved fire control, and the use of rockets, provides the most devastating artillery ever available. The introduction of ICM with robotic submunitions will make artillery even more lethal.

3. *Armored Vehicles.* Armies have a lot more of them. In 1945, the average Western division had about 10 AFV (Armored Fighting Vehicles) per thousand troops. Today, we find nearly 100 AFV per 1,000 troops in the armies of industrialized nations. The quality of AFVs available to different armies also varies much more. The United States and other Western nations have very capable tanks like the M-1, while many Third World nations have T-55s and T-72s, which are far outclassed by the M-1–type vehicles.

4. *Air Power.* This has never been a significant source of injury to combat troops, although it is the scourge of support units behind the fighting line. The introduction of the helicopter produced an air weapon that caused the combat troops a lot of grief. Air forces have also produced special fixed-wing aircraft for support of front-line troops. Until the 1980s, helicopters provide the majority of the air power for use against combat troops. But during the 1980s, fighter bombers received much more accurate bombing systems, enabling them to literally take out one target with one bomb more than half

the time. AFVs in particular have more to worry about from air weapons than ever before.

5. *Electronics.* Most new weapons depend on electronic controls and sensors for their efficient operation. This increases the accuracy of weapons, even though electronic warfare is more common. However, the electronic warfare is largely directed against communications, not weapons sensors and controls.

6. *Chemical and Nuclear Weapons.* Considerable inhibitions exist against using these weapons, especially against someone who can return the favor. If they are used, all previous norms for casualty rates go out the window. Losses would be four, five, or more times the rates with conventional weapons. This is very true if nuclear weapons are used. Chemical weapons, based on past experience, would increase casualties but may well slow operations to a crawl.

Considering these developments, what is to prevent casualty rates from doubling, tripling, or worse? Several other defensive measures are now available. Many troops have flak jackets and better helmets. This provides good protection against artillery fragments and some bullets. In addition, nearly every combat soldier rides in an armored vehicle. Recent experience has shown that more armored vehicles have not reduced the casualty rate appreciably, although vehicle losses are increasing enormously. What may decrease losses in a major war is the peculiar relationship between personnel and AFV losses. For all their apparent robustness, AFVs are more fragile than troops. Experience shows that the percentage of AFV losses will be 4 to 10 times personnel casualties. If troops suffer 5 percent losses, the unit's AFV losses would be 20 to 50 percent. Many of the AFV losses are not combat-related, but the result of breakdowns. AFV casualties can usually be repaired quickly, more than 10 times as fast as wounded troops are returned. If the troops continue fighting without their disabled AFVs, their losses will increase. This will have a more debilitating effect on the staying power of assaults than most commanders would like to admit. Once troops have tasted the security of armored vehicles, they are less enthusiastic about advancing on foot.

Navies have paralleled the increasing lethality of ground-force weapons. Most naval firepower now comes from missiles, which may be carried by ships of all sizes, and submarines. Those navies with aircraft carriers have increased their firepower through more capable aircraft and more lethal aircraft weapons and sensors.

The Future

Current weapons are more lethal, making it possible to increase historical daily loss rates by a factor of 2 or more for as long as the expensive munitions hold out. The other side of this is that an army that achieves surprise and attacks with overwhelming force can reduce its own casualties to historical lows. This is what the coalition forces did in the Gulf War and why they achieved a historically low loss rate among their own troops. This has been the trend among industrialized nations. For example, in the 1860s, during the American Civil War, 1 of every 16 soldiers died in battle. A century later, 1 in every 184 soldiers died in Vietnam. In the 1991 Gulf War, 1 in every 3,300 was killed in combat. Noncombat deaths have been reduced even more. For nonindustrialized nations, losses are still similar to those in the American Civil War.

After the ammo is gone, things settle down quite a bit, and this still happens quite a lot in wars we generally don't hear much about. The greater mobility of modern armies is also likely to expose more troops to combat, particularly support units that are not as adept at it. Traditionally, a 2 percent daily casualty rate for a 15,000-man division translated into a 10–20 percent rate for the 1,000 or 2,000 troops actually in contact with the enemy. Better sensors and ICM, plus breakthroughs by the more numerous armored vehicles, can easily increase the daily losses.

Armed forces are better prepared to take care of and prevent noncombat casualties than ever before. Not so mental fatigue, which is likely to be a lot more common during increasingly hyperactive combat. The Germans, during World War II, developed pragmatic techniques for treating combat fatigue that were widely adopted by other nations. During the Korean War, and until the last few years of Vietnam, American troops had combat fatigue losses at less than a quarter of the World War II rate. However, Israel had increasing levels of combat fatigue in the 1973 and 1982 wars. In 1982, its rate was similar to the U.S. experience of World War II. Part of the 1982 experience can be attributed to the unpopularity of the Lebanon invasion. The same thing happened when combat troops were sent to put down Arab riots in 1987–88. Any future wars featuring increased firepower, lower public support, and sustained combat can be expected to produce above-average combat-fatigue losses.

Equipment attrition can be expected to be higher in future wars. This arises from a combination of new, un-battle-tested equipment made of high-tech, low-reliability components.

Basic Daily Loss Rate

Chart 24-1 shows the basic daily personnel-loss rates of modern armies as well as the factors that will increase or decrease these rates.

ATTACKER is the basic daily combat loss rate (3 percent of personnel) for the attacking division-size force. This is a daily loss rate derived from historical experience since 1940. It includes losses from all combat-related sources—dead, wounded, combat fatigue, prisoners, desertion, etc.

DEFENDER is the basic daily loss rate (1.5 percent) for the defending force.

Each factor can increase or decrease casualties, depending on the situation. The examples following these notes explain this phenomenon.

MAX EFFECT, maximizing effect, is the most that a particular factor can increase casualties. A 2 means that casualties can be doubled.

MIN EFFECT, minimizing effect, is the most that a particular factor can decrease casualties. A .3 means that casualties can be reduced 70 percent (from 100 to 30).

CUMULATIVE MAX/MIN EFFECT. The cumulative maximum effect for each factor for both attackers and defenders. Shows extent of growth or decline of casualties if all factors going for or against you.

SIZE OF FORCE takes into account that larger forces devote a smaller proportion of their total manpower to combat troops. Minimum-size force here is a regiment/brigade task force of 3,000–5,000 men, which has double the loss rate. Maximum-size force would be an army of up to 250,000 men, which halves the loss rate. Another example of the inefficiency of large organizations.

POSTURE indicates type of operation the unit is engaged in. Normal attack or defense posture is a 1. Various degrees of retreat cut the basic daily loss rate by up to 70 percent (.3). A retreat, in most cases, is trading space for casualties. These movements can be tricky. If mishandled the enemy will catch the defenders in the open and inflict even greater losses. Some forms of attack can modify losses. A well-prepared and -executed attack will be easier on the attacker and harder on the defender than a hasty advance in the direction of entrenched defenders.

FORCE RATIO. All other things being equal, 10,000 troops of one army are equal in combat power to 10,000 troops of another army. The force ratio, the ratio of one side's troops to another, increases the basic daily loss rate for the side with the smaller force and decreases the loss rate for the larger side. At a 3+ to 1 ratio, the larger attacking force's loss rate is decreased 30 percent (.7). At a 1 to 7+ ratio, the smaller attacking force's basic daily loss rate is increased 60 percent (1.6). At 1 to 1, there is no effect. Examples: A 3+ to 1 ratio would be a force of 30,000 (or more) versus a force of 10,000. A 1 to 7+ ratio would be a force of 1,000 versus a force of 7,000 or more. But all things are not equal. It is rare for troops of two different armies to have equal combat value. Before force ratios can be calculated, a unit's combat power must be calculated. This is described in Chart 24-3, Factors Modifying Unit Combat Power.

TIME OF DAY has not always been an important consideration. In more civilized times, battles almost always took place during the day. Fighting at night is safer, however, and cuts your daily loss rate in half. The reasons are quite simple—you can't shoot accurately at what you cannot see. If you are getting the worst of it, you can more easily hide.

MAIN EFFORT indicates the intensity of combat. This is usually dictated by the attacker. If the level of activity is increased, the defender must respond. This new

24-1 Basic Daily Loss Rate

Modified by the Following Factors	Max Effect	Min Effect	Attacker 1.0% Cumulative Max Effect	Min Effect	Defender 3.0% Cumulative Max Effect	Min Effect
Size of Force	200%	50%	2.0%	0.50%	6.0%	1.50%
Posture	100%	30%	2.0%	0.15%	6.0%	0.45%
Force Ratio	160%	70%	3.2%	0.11%	9.6%	0.32%
Time of Day	100%	50%	3.2%	0.05%	9.6%	0.16%
Main Effort	150%	70%	4.8%	0.04%	14.4%	0.11%
Supply	200%	100%	9.6%	0.04%	28.8%	0.11%

level of activity is typically defined by more artillery fire and around-the-clock patrol and assault. For this the attacker increases his basic daily loss rate 50 percent. The defender has his basic daily loss rate increased 20 percent. Withdrawal actions usually force the basic daily loss rate up 30 percent to 50 percent.

SUPPLY represents adequate, or degrees of inadequate, material. If one side is lacking supplies of ammunition, fuel, food, etc., it will suffer more casualties as it substitutes people for material.

Examples and Worst Cases

Chart 24-1 demonstrates that there is a wide range of possible daily casualty rates. All of these combinations of attacker and defender rates have some basis in reality, no matter how bizarre some may appear. Take the extreme case of a 4,000-man force. Lacking supplies, making a main-effort attack in daylight against a 100,000-man force, it then proceeds to retreat. The attacker would suffer losses of 9.6 percent a day (384 men), the defender .31 percent (310 men). A plausible rationale for this action would be a smaller force trying to pin down a larger one to prevent it from moving off to a more important battle. It happens all the time. A more common situation has the larger, well-supplied force making a main-effort attack against the smaller one in daylight. The unsupplied defender does the wise thing and withdraws. In this case, the attackers' daily loss rate would be .53 percent (530 men) and the defenders 4.5 percent (180 men). If the defender stood his ground, his daily loss rate would go up to 19 percent (760 men). Normally, a 4,000-man force outnumbered 25 to 1 would not last long. In terms of actual casualties, though, the above figures are historically accurate. It is also historically accurate that the 4,000-man defending force would soon be run right off the battlefield. Naturally, you can run only so far before there is nowhere else to hide. Other possibilities include being surrounded. Being deprived of supply and attacked on all sides further increases your casualties. A week of this and there is little left of the defender. Often, the attacker will simply leave a detachment of 5,000 men to surround the smaller defender and move on with the main force. Other factors can enter into the equation. If the smaller force is defending a mountain pass or other constricted area, the larger force cannot bring all of its combat superiority to bear. A 4,000-man guerrilla force is even more difficult to bring to battle. All this demonstrates that there is more to warfare than simple attrition.

A Multitude of Exceptions

Some armies are more prone to attrition than others. Some wars are likewise more prone to higher casualties. Such an unfortunate matchup occurred during World War I. Some armies consistently produced attrition rates three and four times the above rates. No one during World War I had less than double those rates. It is feared that the next big war will again see the basic rates doubled, even without chemical or nuclear weapons. This assumes that everyone does not run out of these highly destructive, and expensive, munitions.

Armies that put a premium on skill and/or technology in place of masses of troops tend to use the basic attrition rates. Nations without the skill or technology go with rates two or three times the basic one. The Japanese, Chinese, North Vietnamese, Koreans (North and South), and Soviets all experienced doubled rates the last time they fought major wars. The armies of the industrialized nations are more sparing in their use of manpower. During World War II, even though the Germans lost millions of troops, the losses were according to the basic rates. The Soviets lost at twice the rate. Of course, the Soviets won the war. But so did Britain and the United States. The Japanese, who had a somewhat callous attitude toward casualties, also lost. There is no gainsaying that the road to victory, or defeat, is paved with dead bodies.

Unmodified Historical Casualty Rate

Chart 24-2 gives the United States' casualty experience in World War II. It demonstrates the rapidity with which combat units melt away due to normal casualties. The figures are for infantry, tank, or reconnaissance battalions; combat units of 500 to 1,000 men. These units comprise 50 percent of a division's strength but incur 80 percent to 90 percent of the division's casualties. This means that these rates are at least 20 percent higher than those for a regiment (3,200 men) and 50 percent higher than those of a division (15,000 men). From this you can deduce that there is a lot of inactivity in battle for divisions to attain the overall average 2 percent per day loss rate.

TYPE OF ACTION names the types of combat activities that would produce the different rates of loss.

MEETING ENGAGEMENT is a meeting engagement. Both sides are marching, on foot or in vehicles, when they encounter each other. The side that takes the initiative and becomes the attacker suffers proportionately less than in other types of engagements. These actions are rather confused affairs with less artillery and more infantry and tank firepower used.

ATTACK OF POSITION (DAY 1) is the first day of a normal attack, that is, an attack in which the defender is prepared. This first day is generally the day of heaviest fighting. The attacker knows that a quick decision is preferable, and the defenders are fresh. The defender wants to prolong the fight, as this will allow time for defender reinforcements.

ATTACK OF POSITION (DAY 2 +) represents subsequent days of fighting if the first day's push fails to decide the issue. This is attrition fighting, which favors the defense.

ATTACK FORTIFICATIONS (DAY 1) is similar to the position attack, but the defender is better prepared, and the attacker is making a more substantial effort.

ATTACK FORTIFICATIONS (DAY 2 +). Grinding into enemy fortifications is even more expensive, and risky, than going after normal defensive positions. Prepared fortifications are often prepared in great depth. Multiple lines of fortifications over a depth of several kilometers is not unusual.

PURSUIT is combat between a rapidly advancing attacker and a defender attempting to delay this pursuit. Ample opportunities for defenders to prepare ambushes are available. The attacker has such a high degree of initiative that the defender is not able to take full advantage of the attacker's often reckless movements.

INACTIVE is opposing forces in contact, not actively fighting but aggressively maintaining one's positions. There is still a lot of artillery and small-arms activity from time to time. Patrolling also takes a heavy toll as both sides attempt to keep tabs on each other.

ATTACKER and DEFENDER indicate the daily loss rates, as a percentage of current personnel strength, for the attacking and defending force, respectively. The units involved are the combat battalions doing the fighting.

RATIO is the ratio of attacker-to-defender losses. The attacker often loses more men. This ratio shows that the attacker is better off in some types of actions than in others.

Factors Modifying Unit Combat Power

Chart 24-3 shows how various factors can lower the combat power of an army unit. The adjusted combat values show that units of equal size and equipment are not equal. A unit's basic combat power resides in the destructive power of its weapons and the ability of the weapons users to apply that firepower efficiently. Various formulas exist for calculating the raw combat power of a weapon. Adding the human element is a bit more complex and provides more of a moving target. For one overall calculation of combat power, see the charts in this chapter showing casualty rates by branch. For more detail on the relative combat power of weapons, see Chapters 28 and 29 on weapons and armies.

There is nothing fundamentally complex about calculating basic combat power. Most nations have the same standards of organization and levels of equipment.

24-2 Unmodified Historical Casualty Rate

Type of Action	Combat Battalion Daily Losses		
	Attacker	Defender	Ratio
Meeting Engagement	7.5%	4.9%	1.5
Attack of Position (Day 1)	11.5%	6.1%	1.9
Attack of Position (Day 2+)	6.1%	3.5%	1.7
Attack Fortifications (Day 1)	18.7%	9.8%	1.9
Attack Fortifications (Day 2+)	9.8%	5.2%	1.9
Pursuit (Ambushes, etc.)	4.3%	3.2%	1.3
Inactive (Patrols, etc.)	2.6%	2.6%	1.0

24-3 Factors Modifying Unit Combat Power

Factor		Cumulative Effect	
	Minimizing	Worst	Average
Natural Elements	Effect	Case	Case
Terrain	50%	50%	75%
Climate	80%	40%	68%
Command Elements			
Air Superiority	90%	36%	64%
Leadership	60%	22%	51%
Posture	60%	13%	41%
Surprise	60%	8%	33%
Supply	50%	4%	25%
Training	30%	1%	16%
Command, Control & Commo	30%	0.35%	10%
Morale	20%	0.07%	6%

Percentages show portion
of unit's original combat
value remaining after
factors applied

The most powerful individual army weapons today are tanks and artillery. Assigning each tank a value of, say, 40 to 100 and each artillery piece a value of 20 to 50, a rough combat power for a unit can rapidly be calculated. To put these values in perspective, an infantry squad with its assault rifles, machine guns, and other weapons would have a value of 1. If this squad had an armored personnel carrier, the vehicle itself would have a value of 5 to 40+ depending on the weapons carried. An antitank missile system would have a value of 8 to 25. Calculating precise capabilities of weapons is an inexact science. A precise calculation would be irrelevant anyway, as the basic combat value of a unit is a small fraction of its eventual combat value. Many other factors modify the basic values, and the mastery of these modifiers is the key to success in combat. Note that the techniques of calculating combat values of units and the effects of modifiers was derived from experience designing historical simulations (wargames) of military operations. The techniques are valid only because they could constantly be tested using the known outcome of the historical events being simulated.

NATURAL ELEMENTS are the elements over which man has no control. The effects of natural factors on combat performance will generally persist only as long as the natural element is present.

TERRAIN is the effect of geography. Some terrains are more difficult to fight in than others. Terrain becomes difficult by creating three conditions favorable for the defender. Mobility is reduced by rough terrain (mountains, hills, riverbanks) as well as by soft ground (swamp, sand dunes) and numerous obstructions (forests, built-up areas). The range of weapons is cut by obstructions, particularly by forests, underbrush, hills, and buildings. Observation is cut by obstructions that allow the defender to conceal himself more easily and to prepare the classic ambush combat troops fear so much. Terrain can cause these losses of attacker effectiveness: mountains, 25 percent to 50 percent; swamps, 20 to 40 percent; hilly terrain, 0 to 20 percent; flat terrain (soft ground and sand make it worse), 0 percent to 20 percent; built-up areas, 10 percent to 20 percent. Each type may also contain forests, which tend to aid the defender.

WEATHER. Here we are talking about fog, temperature, winds, and the like. Weather affects performance in three ways (in order of performance). Rain, snow, and excessive humidity cut mobility and the efficiency of weapons and troops. Fog, clouds, and mist obstruct observation. Fog aids the attacker by masking his troops from enemy weapons. Many nations have sensors that can overcome this problem, if the troops have them and the gadgets are in working order. However, what you can't see, you can't shoot at, and this allows the attacker to get closer before being fired upon. Extremes in hot and cold temperatures have adverse effects on troops and machines, as will high winds.

COMMAND ELEMENTS are the human factors. These are more important, because human factors persist where natural factors come and go. The first two factors in this category (leadership and training) are more controllable than the remaining "battlefield" factors.

AIR SUPERIORITY is the impact of air control and the ability to go after the enemy with aircraft. For the side without air superiority, mobility is impaired as units move and operate more cautiously to avoid air strikes. For the side with air superiority, operations proceed more smoothly as a result of superior reconnaissance, inferior enemy air recon, and relative freedom from air strikes.

LEADERSHIP is defined here as the quality of the unit commanders. Good leadership, given enough time, can train troops properly. On short notice, good leadership gets the most out of poorly motivated or ill-trained soldiers. Good unit leaders often overcome the debilitating effects of an inefficient high command. Good leadership and good training often go together. Cases of well-trained troops and poor leaders are not unknown, and result in good troops being poorly used.

POSTURE is the nature of the unit's activity when the combat takes place. Other things being equal, it is easier to defend than to attack. The stronger the defensive posture, the more it will decrease the attacker's combat power. The weakest defensive posture is a retreat, either just to escape or to delay the attacker's advance. Then, in ascending order, are hasty, prepared, and fortified defense. The attacker has a similar set of postures. If a force deployed for attack is suddenly forced to defend by the approach of a larger force, it will be at a disadvantage. Troops assume different formations for attack and defense.

SURPRISE is another often underrated factor. Surprise comes in various degrees. It increases the effectiveness of the attacker's weapons and mobility while decreasing the defenders. Basically, the force with the advantage of surprise gets to beat on its opponent for some time without reprisal. Usually, it is the attacker who has the surprise advantage, although on occasion the defender has it.

SUPPLY—the lack of it—stops a successful army from doing anything. Normally, this is not a critical factor, as many commanders do pay attention to logistics. At least they avoid reasonable risks for fear of supply problems. The effects of supply problems are typically sporadic, as they can arise from chaos in the supply system as well as shortages.

TRAINING is the extent to which troops are taught effectively to use their weapons and equipment. Not until this combination of men and machines is put into combat is the training quality conclusively revealed.

COMMAND, CONTROL, COMMUNICATIONS (C^3) is the commander's ability to effectively control his army. If control is lost, the ability to respond to enemy action and coordinate one's own forces is also lost. Blitzkrieg warfare is aimed at destroying the enemy's C^3, rather than undertaking the more formidable task of destroying the army itself.

MORALE is often underrated. This is the state of mind of the troops; their attitude toward their prospects of success and confidence in their side's abilities. Large relative differences in morale have a devastating effect on combat performance. Morale is modified by leadership, training, situation, politics, weather, and numerous other factors, probably including the phases of the moon.

MINIMIZING EFFECT is the maximum minimizing effect or deflation of the unit's base combat power. The basic combat value of a unit is multiplied by these deflators to determine the actual combat value. For example, if a unit had a basic value of 400, and it was operating in the worst possible terrain conditions (a deflator of .5), then the unit's actual combat value would be 200. As the other factors are applied, this value can decline still further.

CUMULATIVE EFFECT is the percentage of the unit's original strength remaining after the factor has effected it. With each factor, the worst case is given to show the extremes to which a unit's theoretical strength can be reduced. The average effect is also given.

Calculating Who Is Winning

The above values allow you to calculate the effective combat power of each side in a conflict. These values are used on the basic daily loss rate chart to determine casualties. We know how many people are likely to be injured. But who will win? Defeat goes to the side that quits first. This means that some wars are bloodier than others. The elusive "resolve" often determines the victor.

For a rough-and-ready rule as to who will win, consider the "force ratio," that of the stronger force to the weaker one. Assume two forces each contain 10,000 men, 200 tanks, 300 APCs, 50 artillery pieces, etc. Assume each one's basic combat value is 30,000. Let us make the following assumptions about the effect of various factors on the attacking force:

- Natural Factors—No loss of effectiveness.
- Command Elements—Losses 20 percent (deflator of .8). Brings actual combat value to 24,000 (.8 × 30,000).

Let us make the following assumptions about the effect of various factors on the defending force:

- Natural Factors—No loss of effectiveness.
- Command Elements—Less well trained and led (with deflators of .7 and .8 creates a deflator of .56) brings the basic value down to 16,800 (.56 × 30,000). Morale is not as high (.8 × 16,800 = 13,440). They do not have air superiority (.9 × 13,440 = 12,096). They are surprised (.6 × 12,096 = 7,258). This gives the attacker a force ratio of over 3 to 1 (24,000 to 7,258 or 3.3 to 1). After a few days of fighting, both sides have lost about 5 percent of their strength. The ratio of forces is now 22,800 to 6,895 or 3.3 to 1. The attacker has disrupted the defender's supplies (.7 × 6,895 = 4,826) and gotten into the defender's rear area and disrupted his command and control (.5 × 4,826 = 2,413). The ratio is now 22,800 to 2,413 or 9.4 to 1. There is little chance of recovery from such an unfavorable ratio. History has shown that as the force ratio approaches 10 to 1, another factor becomes important: the breakpoint. At a certain point in a battle, the side facing a large deficiency in force ratio simply falls apart. The exact point at which a unit collapses depends on

a combination of casualties, leadership, unit disintegration, and troop training. Well-trained and well-led units can continue resistance until it is almost wiped out. Less well endowed units will collapse after less than 10 percent of them have been injured. Eventually, all defending units see the handwriting on the wall. Bloody-minded commanders will infrequently attempt fighting to the last man. The troops have a different agenda. Even if the entire unit does not give up, parts of it will. This makes the force ratio worse for the weaker side. That's how battles normally proceed. This description could very well have been the debacle in Russia during 1941, or the Sinai campaigns of 1967 and 1973. Or it could be somewhere else tomorrow. Before you rush off to calculate World War III, keep in mind that these calculations are most accurate in hindsight. Do the calculations to recreate Desert Storm to see how mismatched the forces were in that battle. There is also a lot of variability in battles not yet fought. This is sometimes called luck, chance, or the "Fortunes of War." Don't underestimate it.

On the Ocean and in the Air

Most of the above factors also apply to naval and air forces. Weather is the same. Terrain has some interesting similarities; water is not all the same. Read Chapters 9 and 10 for more detail on the differing composition of water. Operating near land favors the defender. Small patrol boats armed with cruise missiles can be quite effective. In areas with hot climates, another aspect of naval "terrain" becomes evident. A zone up to 100 feet thick, where the hot air meets the cooler water, creates a space where long-range radar doesn't work too well. In effect, low-flying cruise missiles become difficult to detect. Coastal submarines also benefit from heat effects when under water. Many layers of different-temperature water confounds sonar. Shoals and reefs provide additional hiding places. In addition, we have the familiar sight of storms churning the sea into awesome shapes. Yes, there is terrain at sea.

In the air, we find basically three flavors of terrain: high, medium, and low altitude. The high altitudes, over 10,000 meters, have thin air, which harms engine performance and the maneuverability of aircraft not built for operating under those conditions. The low altitudes, less than 1,000 meters, have a thicker atmosphere. When on the deck (100 meters or less), debris can be sucked into the engine. Birds can hit the canopy and injure the pilot. These are the minor risks of operating close to the ground. The most serious problem is sheer fatigue. More concentration is required when operating at 100 meters' altitude and moving along at 200 or more meters a second. In the middle altitudes, there are still problems. Clouds are more common, and these not only provide concealment and the opportunity for collision, but often confound heat-seeking missiles. All the other factors apply.

Supply effects are immediate for aircraft. If you run out of fuel, you hit the ground. Not a lot of ammunition is carried, perhaps four missiles and 20 seconds' worth of cannon shells. Bomb loads are heavier, although the average is only a few tons. More important for air-force logistics is the amount of supplies getting to the air bases. Most bases are surrounded by dozens of supply dumps containing thousands of tons of fuel, munitions, spares, and other supplies. That's why these complexes are called air bases instead of airfields. Aircraft carriers are more restricted, carrying supplies for less than 1,000 sorties, depending on how many strike sorties are flown. Strike missions use up more fuel than patrols. Naval supply is limited by carrying capacity. Many smaller ships must be refueled once a week. There is rarely sufficient munitions on board for more than a few full-scale battles. Most smaller warships (especially those of Soviet design) carry no reloads for many of their weapons.

Attrition is similar to the land situation. Air losses are calculated in losses per 1,000 sorties. A loss of more than 2 percent (20 per 1,000) is dangerous to unit integrity and morale. Aircraft may fly more than one sortie per day. See the chart on aircraft attrition.

Naval losses tend to be more catastrophic, partially because you have fewer "vehicles." Unlike ships in the last major naval war (1939–45), most modern ships are not armored. Peacetime accidents and limited combat experience indicates that wartime losses are likely to be higher than in the past. Training, especially in damage control, becomes a critical factor. Training, leadership, morale, C³, are all areas in which Western navies have a comfortable, but not invincible, lead over potential opponents.

Noncombat Casualties

AVERAGE (CONSTANT) is the percentage of a unit's strength that will be out of action due to noncombat injuries at any one time. This is an average of operations in all climates and conditions. Disease, including venereal, and accidents are the cause. Eighty-five percent of those affected will return to duty after an average 10-day absence, compared to 100 days for combat casualties. Medical services will devote more than 35 percent of their efforts to treating noncombat injuries. As long as medical services function, there will be daily, cumulative losses of only 15 percent of those afflicted. Because the average time in the hospital is 10 days, only 200 men out of 100,000 need get sick to represent a 2 percent daily loss. Thus, some 15 percent (30 men) will not return to service. This represents a permanent daily loss rate of 30 men per 100,000, or .03 percent.

CLIMATE can modify the loss rate considerably. Temperate climates can reduce the loss rate. Deserts, jungles, severe cold, and other unhealthy environments will

24-4 Noncombat Casualties

	Multi-plier	Daily Sick Rate	Daily Perm Losses	Permanent Losses per Daily	100,000 Men Monthly
Average (Constant)		2.0%	0.30%	300	9,150
Variable Factors Increasing Losses					
Climate	1.5	3.0%	0.45%	450	13,725
Living Conditions	1.5	4.5%	0.68%	675	20,588
Medical Care Level	2	9.0%	1.35%	1,350	41,175

cause more disease and injury. Tropical rain forests are possibly the worst. Any area is a bad climate if disease conditions are harmful to the troops operating in it. For example, troops from tropical areas would suffer somewhat in temperate areas. Any troops going from their own "disease pool" to an area of unaccustomed diseases will suffer. Troops from industrialized nations going to out-of-the-way parts of the world will encounter diseases they are unfamiliar with and more susceptible to.

LIVING CONDITIONS represents the level of sanitation and general living conditions. Living in tents is more injurious to health than living under more substantial cover. Sleeping on the ground is not healthy. Lack of regular, nutritious meals and clean, dry clothing can eventually become critical.

LEVEL OF MEDICAL CARE is the crucial factor. Without medical services, minor afflictions become major ones. Even in temperate zones, lack of medical services, particularly public sanitation, will rapidly increase the rate of losses.

MULTIPLIER is the multiplier effect of climate, living conditions, and level of medical care on the average noncombat casualty rate. At the extreme end, all the troops will be afflicted with disease severe enough to require hospitalization. Under such conditions, few, if any, will receive medical attention. This occurred during the Korean War, especially among Chinese troops, who had a lax attitude toward battlefield medical care. The Germans, during their first winter in Russia, were similarly unprepared and suffered accordingly.

PERMANENT LOSSES (DAILY) is the percentage of disease and injury that results in permanent loss. These losses include death and permanent incapacity for military service. When these losses are high, many troops will simply become ineffective. Without good leadership and training, units will disintegrate or cease to function.

PERMANENT DAILY LOSSES PER 100,000 is the number of noncombat dead, or permanently incapacitated, per day for a force of 100,000 troops.

PERMANENT MONTHLY LOSSES is the number of dead, or permanently incapacitated, for a force of 100,000 over a period of a month. These complications show that without effective measures to control noncombat casualties, an army will disappear without ever seeing the enemy.

Navies and Air Forces

Navies and air forces are more dependent on weapons and equipment readiness than armies. Air forces often suffer up to 1 percent aircraft losses per year in peacetime. These losses are a result of training accidents and just plain accidents. Western air forces have lower rates, while Third World and Soviet-style air forces have higher, often considerably higher, loss rates. Western rates are lower because the aircraft are better maintained and the pilots are more experienced, flying from 200 to 500 hours a year. Western pilots also have access to realistic aircraft simulators. Soviet aircraft are more accident-prone because of design defects. Peacetime personnel losses are lower in air forces because these troops work out of fixed installations and spend little time under field conditions. In wartime, air bases are rapidly created in many godforsaken parts of the world. Despite their fixed nature, air-force personnel suffer noncombat losses just like the combat troops while the base is being built. If the established base can eliminate unhealthy conditions, noncombat losses will decline accordingly.

Navies also suffer from peacetime attrition. Normally, 15 to 25 percent of a fleet's ships are in port for various degrees of repair and maintenance. At sea, they suffer a loss rate approaching one percent a year, depending on skill and intensity of use. Disease is a lesser danger because of the controlled environment on ships. Injuries from accidents are somewhat higher because of cramped conditions and constant working with heavy, complex, and often dangerous equipment.

National Differences

Some armies are more efficient, or callous, than others in dealing with non-combat casualties. During World War II, 89 percent of German hospital admissions were noncombat casualties, while in the U.S. Army the figure was 96 percent. Precise data for the Soviet and Japanese armed forces are lacking, but available information indicates that noncombat admissions were closer to 60 percent. The Soviets and Japanese suffered more frequent and overwhelming casualties and had fewer hospital beds available. Both nations' armed forces also had lower standards of public sanitation and disease control. Post–World War II practices did not change a great deal in the Soviet Army. A Soviet combat division had only 60 hospital beds, clearly insufficient to care for peacetime injuries and disease. Even support from higher units would not enable the Soviets to do more than simply attempt to care for combat casualties. This is another example of how wealth can enable an armed force to literally buy lives with money.

Air Combat Attrition

PERIOD/THEATER is the time frame in which the air combat took place and the area in which the fighting took place. The years 1939–1945 include all air operations in Europe; 1942 was the beginning of the large-scale bombing offensive in Europe; 1943–44 was the height of the bomber offensive; 1945 was the height of fighter-bomber operations; 1950–51 was the Korean War; 1966–68 were three critical years of the air war in Vietnam; 1971 was the India-Pakistan War; 1973 was the Arab-Israeli War; 1982 was the Falklands and Lebanon wars; 1986–87 was the Afghan War after the Afghans got surface-to-air missiles; 1987 was also the Iran-Iraq War; 1991 was the Gulf War.

LOSS RATE PER 100,000 SORTIES is the number of aircraft lost for each 100,000 sorties (one aircraft flying one mission).

NATION (ATTACKER) is the nationality of the air force that was doing the attacking and incurred the losses. "Allied" means Britain and the United States.

24-5 Historical Attrition in Air Operations

Period/Theater	Loss Rate per 100,000 Sorties	Nation (Attacker	A/C Type	Defender Loss Caused by Enemy
1939-45/Germany	900	Allied	All	All
1942/Germany	200	Allied	Bombers	Flak
1943-44/Germany	400	Allied	Bombers	Flak
1945/Germany	650	Allied	FtrBmbrs	Flak
1950-51/China-N K	440	USA	All	Aircraft
1966/N Vietnam	350	USA	All	All
1967/N Vietnam	300	USA	All	All
1968/N Vietnam	150	USA	All	All
1971/Pakistan	1,250	India	All	Aircraft
1971/India	1,700	Pakistan	All	Aircraft
1973/Egypt-Syria	800	Israel	All	80% Flak
1973/Egypt-Syria	1,200	Israel	A-4	Flak
1982/Syria	10	Israel	All	Flak
1985/Afghans	100	Russia	All	Flak
1987/Afghans	200	Russia	All	Flak, Stinger SAM
1986/Iran	100	Iraq	F1	Flak, SAM
1991/Iraq	40	Allies	All	Flak, SAM

AIRCRAFT TYPE is the type of aircraft that took the losses. "All" means all types. Bombers are primarily four-engine bombers (B-17, B-24). FtrBmbrs are fighter bombers (P-47, Typhoon, F-4, etc.) appropriate to the period. A-4 is an American light bomber used by Israel. F1 is the Mirage F1 fighter bomber, as well as other types used by Iraq.

DEFENDER LOSS CAUSED BY ENEMY is the type of enemy weapon that caused the loss. All is aircraft and antiaircraft artillery (flak). "80% Flak" means that 80 percent of aircraft losses were caused by enemy antiaircraft weapons and 20 percent by enemy aircraft.

Changes Through History

The majority of aircraft combat losses in World War II were caused by other aircraft. As the German Air Force became weaker, its flak effectiveness increased. More resources were devoted to flak in the last year of the war, and a higher proportion of Allied aircraft were brought down by flak. This still resulted in relatively lower Allied aircraft losses, as flak could be avoided more easily than enemy fighters. After World War II, the attrition rate continued to decline. In

Korea, there was less flak than in World War II. Political considerations prevented the air war from escalating too far. Communist pilots were greatly overmatched by veteran U.S. pilots. This was not a high-intensity war. In Vietnam, the attrition rate declined still further. The flak defenses, however, were the heaviest ever deployed. American forces responded by mounting massive flak-suppression operations, thereby lowering aircraft losses to flak. This was not a representative situation, as it was a war between unequal opponents. The North Vietnamese were in no position to force the issue. American air operations had none of the time pressure experienced during World War II. This was an unusual war in the air. The war between India and Pakistan was frighteningly intense. The air forces were more evenly matched. The war was fought with Korean War vintage aircraft.

It was also fought with great vigor and skill by evenly matched pilots. The loss rate was disturbing. In the 1973 Arab-Israeli War, the Israelis had a substantial edge. The Egyptians made the best of a bad situation and built up their ground-based air defense. Unlike the Americans in Vietnam, the Israelis discounted this development. Once the war began, Israel did not have time to systematically eliminate the formidable Arab flak defenses, and ran up large losses. The air battles in the Falklands and Lebanon again showed that well-trained pilots and thoughtfully designed aircraft and weapons will swamp less prepared opposition. The success of Afghan irregulars with portable surface-to-air missiles bodes ill for air forces operating over large concentrations of these weapons. The decades of preparation to take on the massive Soviet air defenses in Central Europe paid off for the largely NATO air units in the 1991 Gulf War. Iraq's largely Soviet-supplied air-defense system was handily shut down by coalition air forces, and a new low in attacker air-loss rates was achieved.

In most periods, however, noncombat losses equaled or exceeded combat losses. Landing accidents are most common, and as recently as Vietnam and Afghanistan, accidents and equipment failure have accounted for 2 or 3 percent losses per month. Most observers concentrate on combat losses without doing a little arithmetic to discover that a lot of aircraft were going into the combat zone, avoiding enemy fire, and never coming out again. The Gulf War was an exception, primarily because of the high training levels of the pilots and ground crews as well as the first combat use of the AWACS control aircraft. This led to the unprecedented absence of any air-to-air collisions, a common wartime occurrence in airspace swarming with combat aircraft.

Casualty Rates by Branch

Chart 24-6 shows the levels of casualties of the components of combat divisions: infantry, armor, artillery, and support. Two division types are shown, U.S. infantry and Soviet (now Russian) tank divisions. Two casualty levels are shown (0 and 30 percent), along with the resulting personnel and combat losses of each branch. These combat effects are averages based on historical experience. It is assumed that such elements as leadership, surprise, training, etc., are equal; they usually aren't.

OVERALL CASUALTY RATE OF % is the overall personnel casualty rate for the division in that chart.

COMBAT STRENGTH LOST % is the percentage of the division's combat power lost, given the above level of personnel loss.

BRANCH is the four major job-specialty segments of a division. Each has a different function, loss rate, amount of combat power per man, and size.

INFANTRY is the branch with the most casualties. This category also includes reconnaissance troops. Contemporary divisions consist of less than 50 percent infantry, often closer to one third. As recently as World War II, infantry comprised nearly two thirds of personnel in many divisions.

ARMOR is the branch with the most firepower per man. Armor combat strength declines rapidly because the heavy combat vehicles tend to break down easily.

ARTILLERY is the combat branch that inflicts the most casualties and receives the least. As the armor and infantry waste away in combat, artillery becomes the principal provider of combat power.

ALL OTHER includes the support troops that may come under fire but do not regularly confront the enemy in combat.

MEN is the number of men assigned to each branch. These men have jobs described as infantrymen, tank crews, artillerymen. For the most part, these men are found in battalions composed exclusively of troops of that branch. Where appropriate, the troops of a particular branch are counted as part of their branch no matter where they are. In the many Soviet-type armies, artillery is often assigned to infantry units. Most armies equip their infantry units with mortars. Mortars, because of their short range and limited ammunition supplies, are considered infantry weapons.

% OF DIVISION (MEN) is the percentage of men in a division assigned to each branch category.

COMBAT STRENGTH is the amount of combat strength of each branch based on the average capabilities of that branch's usual weapons and equipment.

% OF DIVISION (COMBAT STRENGTH) is the percentage of combat strength in a division provided by each branch category.

MEN LOST is the number of men lost given the overall casualty rate.

% OF ALL LOSSES is the percentage of total casualties each branch has received. The infantry obviously takes the most losses. The greater the proportion of infantry in a division, the fewer the casualties for the other branches.

CASUALTY RATE is the percentage of each branch lost. The branch casualty rate differs considerably from the overall division rate, as each branch experiences a different degree of exposure and vulnerability to enemy fire.

SURVIVORS is the number of men in each branch still available for service after casualty losses.

% OF DIVISION is the number of survivors of each branch as a percentage of the division total. Compare this with the % OF DIVISION (MEN) to see how quickly some branches disappear in combat.

SURVIVING COMBAT STRENGTH is each branch's surviving combat strength. For armor, combat strength declines faster than personnel strength because the armored vehicles fail more quickly than the crews are wounded or killed.

% OF DIVISION is the amount of surviving combat strength as a percentage of the division total.

Combat Power and Patterns of Combat Losses

The Soviets put most of their efforts into providing many tanks, a trend that proved mistaken. Seventy-two percent of the combat power of a full-strength Soviet tank division came from its tank forces. Although this seems high, the lowest value is 52 percent, for a U.S. infantry division. This is a crucial factor in modern warfare. Heavy combat vehicles, tanks and APCs, break down more quickly than the troops. After a division has taken 30 percent personnel casualties, tank forces suffer more in lost combat power. At that point, divisions have lost 42 percent to 50 percent of their combat strength. Armor branch forces will have lost over 60 percent. The infantry troops suffer even greater damage at the 30 percent divisional casualty level. The division is left with a lot of tanks needing repairs, some infantry, some usable armored vehicles, and a relatively large amount of artillery.

Some strange things happen after combat has converted a division to this new, smaller format. One day of heavy combat or several days of lighter action against a determined opponent can result in losses as high as 10 percent. At this point, the heavier loss rates in infantry and armor branches begin to show. At 30 percent loss levels, divisions show serious signs of disintegration. This is the optimal time to take a division out of battle and rebuild its combat branches. Combat beyond this point will practically wipe out a division's combat power. It is anticipated that in a future war, divisions will routinely be pushed beyond the 30 percent level.

During the Gulf War, the Iraqi divisions were pummeled to the 50 percent level by air power before coalition ground forces attacked. Attacks from the air reduce a division's strength differently. Support, tank, and artillery units get the most attention from aircraft. The idea being that the surviving infantry will notice that they have little support and quickly surrender. At the very least, infantry in that situation will be much less capable of putting up an effective defense. Once the 50 percent level is reached through ground combat, there is little left but support troops. In

24-6 Casualty Rates by Branch

Russian Type Tank Division

Overall Casualty Rate: 30%   Combat Strength Lost: 50%

Branch	Full Strength % of Men	Men	Combat Strength	% of Cmbt Str	Men Lost	% of All Losses	Casualty Rate %	Survivors	% of Division	Surviving Combat Strength	% of All Cmbt	Branch
Infantry	20%	2,451	42	6%	1,794	48%	73%	657	8%	11	3%	Inf
Armor	29%	3,544	528	72%	1,063	29%	30%	2,481	29%	211	57%	Armor
Artillery	20%	2,455	152	21%	206	6%	8%	2,249	26%	139	38%	Arty
Other	32%	3,930	8	1%	650	18%	17%	3,280	38%	6	2%	Other
	100%	12,380	729	100%	3,714	100%	30%	8,666	100%	368	100%	

US Mechanized Infantry Division

Overall Casualty Rate: 30%   Combat Strength Lost: 42%

Branch	Full Strength % of Men	Men	Combat Strength	% of Cmbt Str	Men Lost	% of All Losses	Casualty Rate %	Survivors	% of Division	Surviving Combat Strength	% of All Cmbt	Branch
Infantry	34%	4,211	114	11%	2,779	56%	66%	1,432	12%	39	6%	Inf
Armor	19%	2,345	553	52%	704	14%	30%	1,642	14%	221	36%	Armor
Artillery	31%	3,876	379	36%	326	7%	8%	3,550	31%	347	56%	Arty
Other	50%	6,168	19	2%	1,172	24%	19%	4,996	43%	15	2%	Other
	134%	16,600	1,065	100%	4,980	100%	30%	11,620	100%	623	100%	

most cases, support troops will then be serving, without enthusiasm, as infantry. Most tanks, although not all crews, will be out of action. Only the artillery will be largely intact. Without infantry to protect them, the artillery will soon be overrun and lost. Continuing to fight beyond the 50 percent level quickly results in the complete destruction of the division. Because the support troops are less effective as infantry, they will more quickly be destroyed. Their skills as technicians are generally more difficult to replace than infantry and tank crews. With no one to protect the division's support equipment, the division ceases to exist. Russian-type armies are armies of extremes. Their infantry divisions are built to take enormous losses and still retain remnants of all their combat arms. Their tank divisions, in similar situations, are quickly reduced to some artillery, with tank crews and support troops serving as infantry. The more highly trained support troops do not serve in divisions, but are retained in nondivisional units.

Combat divisions are resilient, if they are not hit with too much combat power in too short a time. Most of their casualties return to duty within a month. Losses average 2 percent a day when facing a combative opponent. The lesson here is that after two weeks of combat, a division should be withdrawn for up to a month so that the lightly wounded can be returned, replacements can be integrated into their units, and vehicles repaired. You then have a unit of the same strength as before but with a lot more practical experience. Warfare rarely allows for such efficient use of a division. Units often are kept under fire for extended periods and are not given sufficient time to recover. Warfare is a debilitating process.

A recent example of the above was in the 1991 Gulf War. The Iraqi divisions were isolated in the desert and blasted with accurate air and artillery fire for six weeks. Without access to replacements or regular supply, most of these divisions lost their combat power, their cohesion, and, in many cases, their will to fight. Coalition ground forces advanced against little organized resistance, and that advance quickly turned into a pursuit. Coalition troops never had to face sustained combat, so effective was the preliminary bombardment by air and artillery firepower.

25

Victory Goes to the Bigger Battalions

The Cost of War

Peace is cheaper than war, but often not by much. People don't complain as much about the cost of war while the shooting is going on. When things settle down, taxpayers become more boisterous. As well they should. Peace is a more common condition than war. The cost of maintaining armed forces for the next war is often more expensive than the war itself. Yet as much as people complain about the expense, victory almost always goes to the bigger battalions. Those battalions are built during peacetime. To put it another way, victory is a property of the wealthy. Battles may be won by a David, but the Goliaths win the wars.

The wealthier nations tend to be conscious of their material advantage and are quick to arm themselves in self-defense. By 1945, the United States was maintaining 12 million troops at an average annual cost of over $35,000 per soldier. More than 40 years later, 4 million were still directly involved in military affairs at nearly double the cost per individual. (Unless otherwise noted, all prices and costs are given in 1993 dollars.) After 1985, annual defense spending in the United States began to decline again, but not by a great deal. Aside from the debatable cost effectiveness of this expensive situation, there is some doubt as to whether the United States could afford another war of the magnitude of World War II. Since 1945, per capita income, adjusted for inflation, has increased more than four times. The wealth is there; what might not be available is the time to hammer all those goodies into weapons.

Can We Afford Peace?

Peace can be more destructive to a nation's economy than a war. The high human costs and economic costs limit the duration of wars. Peace lasts longer, and eventually costs more. During 1993, the nations of the world spent nearly a trillion dollars ($1,000,000,000,000) on armed forces. This is more than was spent during the peak year of World War II (1944). Half is still spent by just two nations, the United States and Russia. Until the end of the Cold War, NATO represented nearly half the remainder, and the Warsaw Pact about a quarter. The Third World managed to account for less than 15 percent of all world arms expenditures. In the post–Cold War world, the United States and the NATO nations (plus Japan) are responsible for two thirds of this spending, with Russia accounting for only 10 percent and the rest of the world the remainder.

Defense spending accounts for 5 percent of global GNP (Gross National Product). The percentage varies from nation to nation. Russia still leads with more than 10 percent. It's 6 percent for the United States as of the early 1990s. Both the United States and Russia will continue to cut their defense spending through the 1990s. The rest of the industrialized nations spend from 1 to 4 percent, while most other nations average a bit less. A major war will generally consume 30 percent to 50 percent of GNP for as long as the war lasts. One year of a major war equals 3 to 30 years of peace. From an economic point of view, World War II has been refought more than five times since 1945. Defense spending since 1945 was different from spending in the previous century. For one thing, there was more to spend. We tend to forget that industrialization, and all the wealth it creates, is relatively recent. Britain went through it first, in the early 1800s. Then came the United States and most of Europe in the late 1800s. Russia didn't really get started until the 1920s. Japan was also a late starter, getting into gear only in the 1950s. But something happened after 1945 that severely limited the economic strength of the two superpowers, the United States and the Soviet Union. Both of these nations began putting enormous portions of their capital funds into military spending.

Without getting too far into economic theory, let us explain this by comparing national economies to an apartment house. Both are similar. A national economy provides all that is needed to sustain the population. The apartment house provides shelter for people. The apartment house lasts a long time, if properly maintained. This maintenance is largely a rebuilding process that eventually results in most major components of the building being replaced as these items wear out or are supplanted by more efficient components. If these repairs and modifications are not made, the building becomes less efficient, or even uninhabitable. The money for these expenses comes from rents. If the apartment-house owners hire a security guard, this will not bankrupt the building. But if they hire a dozen guards and neglect routine maintenance, the building will eventually fall apart. Moreover, tenants will move out, while new ones will be reluctant to move in and rent income will fall.

This is what happened with the United States and Russia. As of 1980, the United States was spending 20 percent of its new capital for defense. Japan was spending 3.5 percent. Germany was spending 16 percent, France 21 percent, and Britain 24 percent. Russia was spending over 40 percent. The nations that can spend more on rebuilding and replacing their factories and other productive assets are more competitive in world markets. To get back to our hypothetical apartment house, people will obviously be attracted to the higher quality and lower rents of the Japanese apartments. If you want security, go live in the well-guarded Soviet apartment bunker. Be careful, though, as the plumbing doesn't work very well and the elevators rarely run.

Japan has other advantages, primarily the tendency of its people to save more of their income. These savings can be invested in still more productive assets. Generally, a nation can spend its production on capital goods (to produce more), maintenance (of people and their tools), and consumption (second homes, larger cars and homes, vacations, generally having a good time). Defense falls into the consumption category because it neither produces anything nor maintains productive assets.

We live in an uneasy and violent world. History shows that you have to defend yourself. But armed forces become counterproductive if their maintenance destroys the economy they are there to protect. This has military implications. Military security requires that you be able to build adequate weapons, or obtain them from a reliable ally who can. The Soviet Union was unable to keep up with Western military technology and compensated with larger quantities of weapons and equipment. As Japan eclipses the United States in more military-related technologies, America will have to go to Japan for key components of its high-tech weapons. This situation should come as no surprise. Through the 1980s, most of Japan's exports to the United States were manufactured goods. Most of America's exports to Japan have been raw materials. In just a century, the United States has gone from a supplier of raw materials, to a supplier of manufactured goods, right back to producing primarily raw materials exports, and now to a major exporter of services (a category that hardly existed a century ago).

Those nations that regularly spend more than 10 percent of their GNP on defense are not noted for economic vigor and stability. Among these 10 percenters are Russia, Iraq, Israel, Jordan, Saudi Arabia, Iran, China, Syria, and North Korea. Low-spending nations, like Japan and most industrialized nations, live in the protection of high spenders like the United

States. Think of this as a form of foreign aid, not to mention a great deal of trust and lack of paranoia.

The high Soviet military spending at the expense of civil-sector capital investment began only in the 1960s. At that time, Russia's economy was still booming from the post–World War II reconstruction programs. The leadership decided to divert capital funds to the military even though this change could not be sustained indefinitely. Eventually, the national economy would decline through lack of new factories and production equipment. At this point, there was less capital available for everyone, including the military. By the 1980s, this process had caused massive damage to the civilian economy, and even the military was feeling the effects. The only benefit from this Soviet economic policy was a military buildup and a larger military establishment that was, in effect, temporary. Such a buildup could not be sustained into the 1990s. By the late 1980s, it became obvious that if the civilian economy was not revived, military spending would go down, and down. On top of the capital-spending problem was the intrinsic inefficiency of the communist-style command economy. Together, these two forces—excessive military spending and a command economy—brought on the collapse of the Soviet Union.

The Soviet armed forces did not disappear in late 1991, but as they were parceled out among the successor states, particularly Russia and the Commonwealth of Independent States, the byzantine Soviet military-budget system collapsed. In the wake of the changeover, former Soviet officials admitted that they had no clear idea how much was spent on the military, much less where it came from. The new states emerging out of the Soviet Union grabbed all the funds they could in a scramble to reform their reeling economies. Most of the former Soviet military immediately found themselves with uncertain funding. Factories that had long produced items for the military discovered that their customers could no longer pay. As a result, the industrial side of the Soviet military-industrial complex began to shift away from weapons work to civilian production that could be sold to customers who could pay. As was the Soviet custom, many of these military-oriented industrial centers were self-contained communities that took care of far more than providing jobs and producing military equipment. These "collectives" also controlled the local civilian economy and government. In the economic chaos following the Soviet Union collapse, these collectives, in effect, were separated from the military. A harsher situation faced the military units themselves, which also operated as "collectives." Most military organizations tried to associate themselves with some government entity that could collect taxes and support the troops and their families. As about a third of the Soviet military were long-term professional troops, these people had nowhere to go if they left the military. Many of the conscript troops went home (with or without permission), and an increasing number of new conscripts chose not to show up for service.

Going into the 1990s, the former Soviet military has lost its morale, many of its conscripts, most of its cohesion, and more than half its funding. In 1992 and 1993, many of the old Soviet units still existed on paper, but all but a few were but a shadow of their former combat capability. Weapons production and research and development on new systems was shrinking rapidly. Many of the most capable professionals were leaving for more lucrative civilian opportunities. The successor states of the Soviet Union were even less capable of supporting this military-industrial complex, causing the Soviet military to go from the world's largest to one barely in the top five within the space of a few years. The result is a vivid example of what excessive military spending can do to a nation.

What do nations get for their defense dollar? Often one never really finds out. Wars are not that frequent, and the results are not always conclusive. The German Army, for example, has lost every war it has fought for over 100 years and is still highly regarded. The Soviet Army has won most of its wars during the same period and is held in lower regard. Quality will prevail only up to a point. In most cases, the economically stronger nation, the "bigger battalions," will prevail. The remainder of this chapter will cover what money can buy when you want to make war.

Why Does Everything Cost So Much?

Weapons have always been expensive; they have also tended to become more complex and less reliable over time. This has become more of a problem as new weapons came into being before the previous generation could be fully mastered. The first weapons were rocks. A rock is quite simple. It can also be quite cheap. No doubt the first weapon cost overrun occurred when the chiseling of special war rocks took longer than anticipated. Military hardware tends to get more complex and expensive as users continually strive for that extra edge in performance. In life-and-death combat situations, every advantage counts. Consider, for example, radar in fighter aircraft. Basic radar with a 30-kilometers range that can track air targets would cost about $210,000. By raising the price to $450,000, we obtain a 40-kilometers range, better accuracy, some resistance to countermeasures, and the ability to guide missiles to a target. For $600,000, you get some more range (70 kilometers), so perhaps the enemy has a hard time shooting back. Raise the price to $1 million, and you add accurate ground tracking, which allows the aircraft to safely fly close to the ground in bad weather. This would also include a data link to ground stations for better coordination and navigation. For nearly $2 million, you get 180-kilometer range, better resistance to countermeasures, and more bells and whistles in general. As things become more expensive and complex, they become less reliable. Reliability is a quality that is often overlooked, particularly as combat conditions involve previously unencountered stresses and less stringent maintenance. Studies have shown the following statistical relationships between electronic component cost and MTBF (Mean Time Between Failure). A radar set might have hundreds or thousands of such components. Most of them are rather inexpensive and reliable. A few are quite expensive, critical, and more prone to failure. A component costing less than $1,000 fails, on average, once every 1,500 hours. Unless another component can pick up the slack, the entire system fails or is degraded in performance. A $5,000 component fails every 250 hours. A $10,000 component fails every 120 hours. More theoretical $100,000 components fail every 12 hours, and an unlikely million-dollar component fails before it gets warmed up. Using duplicates of more failure-prone components increases reliability but at greater cost, weight, and size. Most modern combat aircraft have electronics systems that fail, on the average, every 10 hours or less. It is difficult to predict exactly when the electronics will go, forcing you to be ready for failure at the worst possible moment.

Repairs can take hours to minutes, depending on the design of the system. Extremely expensive items like the space-shuttle flight-control systems use five identical computers as protection against failure or accident. At least one space-shuttle launch was held up because one of these computers failed checkout. High-performance aircraft often have triplicates of key systems. In wartime, these aircraft can go into action with one or two of these systems inoperable. This increases the risk of losing the aircraft or inability to complete the mission. This is considered a normal wartime risk. Examples of past weapons that became more complex and less reliable are numerous. When spears replaced rocks, there were new problems with warped shafts and loose stone spearheads. Then came swords, where impure metals caused brittleness and failure during the stresses of combat. Bows were prone to broken strings and warped arrows. The age of gunpowder brought forth very delicate trigger mechanisms, defective powder, wet powder, and impure metal in barrels. This was a portent of what was to come. Very reliable rifles took more than two centuries to come along. Early machine guns were very vulnerable to mechanical breakdown. Aircraft, electronics, and guided missiles merely compounded these earlier problems.

If complexity is held constant, cost will decline and reliability will increase. In the last 50 years, technological advances and military requirements have replaced weapons before they could obtain these cost and reliability advantages. The average weapons system (tank, aircraft, missile, etc.) becomes obsolete in 10 years or less. In the United States, it takes an average of eight years to bring a new system from idea to troop use. New weapons must be constantly produced to keep up with those of your opponents. American project managers in the early 1980s had an average tenure of 30 months, causing a lack of development continuity. Other Western nations have similar, although less severe, problems here. However, the United States is still leading the technology parade. Where American technology stumbles, all nations that follow tend to do likewise. New

weapons often reach the troops shortly before they become obsolete and
typically never see use in combat. Many systems produced in the last 40
years saw little or no combat. The common pattern is to replace systems
that have not yet worked all their bugs out by even more problem-prone
and equally untried weapons. Another common pattern is to extensively
modify major systems to the extent that they become essentially new systems. Take the U.S. M-60 tank. The initial M-60A1 was a refinement of a
late–World War II heavy tank. The M-60A1 cost $960,000, including
$51,000 for the fire-control system. The M-60A3 came out 10 years later
in 1973. It cost $1,200,000, including $260,000 for the fire-control system.
In the early 1980s, there was the M-1 tank costing $1,700,000 including a
$620,000 fire-control system. These costs do not include development or
operating costs, which normally triples the ultimate cost.

The M-60A3 was a greater improvement over the M-60A1 than the "all
new" M-1 was over the M-60A3. Different versions of the same weapon
often differ more from each other than from the next new model of that
type. Soviet weapons-development policy tended to follow gradual improvements, even though new models are identified as new systems. The
Soviets would have called the M-60A3 the M-65. This Soviet identification
policy often alarmed many in the West for no good reason beyond ignorance
of the other side's slightly different way of naming new vehicles.

Escalating costs are a very intractable problem. While it may be technically possible to calculate accurately the cost of a new weapon system,
political pressures and human nature conspire to prevent it. No one who
is supposed to know the cost of a new system will admit to ignorance. An
initial cost is conjured up and then modified by political considerations.
This is of little consequence, as the price will invariably rise. Indeed, any
American project will cost, on the average, twice the original estimate.
The original estimated cost implies a threshold of intolerance, a price that,
if exceeded, will result in project cancellation. The threshold is a natural
reaction if a handful of new programs obliterates all other projects. The
formula for this threshold, based on past experience, is:

$$10^{10}/(\text{number of units to be produced})^{1.2}$$

In plain English, this means that if there is to be only one item, it can
cost $10 billion. Two items can cost no more than $4.3 billion, 10 items
can each cost $631 million, 100 items $40 million each, 1,000 items $2.5
million each, 10,000 items $158,000 each, 100,000 items $10,000 each, 1
million items $631 each. The averages were made from dozens of weapon
systems and were based on 1993 dollars. This phenomenon has another
insidious aspect. Costs rise toward the limit even if there is no other reason.
A more expensive tank tends to have more expensive components (driver's
seat, heater, paint job, etc.) than a less expensive one. There is no other
reason for these components to be more expensive than that a more ex-

pensive system attracts higher prices for inherently cheap components. As unit prices of weapons increase, there is a tendency to test less. Tests often require weapons to be destroyed. Expensive weapons require expensive testing. Expensive weapons tend to be less reliable and require more testing. As absurd as this might appear, it is common to cut corners on testing of expensive systems in order to reduce the howls of anguish over high cost. If the weapons infrequently see combat, and avoid the ultimate test, this is taken into account. It's a dirty little secret that is no secret. The so-called more effective weapons tend to be less effective. For example, an-tiaircraft cannon have been around for 70 years, but the missile has been used in combat only during the past four decades. Extensive combat experience has shown that cheaper cannon systems account for a higher proportion of aircraft damage than more expensive missile systems. So why continue to build missile systems? Partially because they are possible. They also force aircraft to fly lower, where cannon are more effective. And as history, and the 1991 Gulf War, demonstrated, the new weapons eventually get some age on them and become effective. New weapons also force design changes on existing weapons systems. Some helicopters have been made very resistant to light cannon, but not as much to light missiles. Now most helicopters are equipped with a number of missile warning and an-timissile systems. Also, once a new weapon appears, it acquires a life of its own. New systems are rarely killed until newer and usually more expensive systems appear. Missiles are currently in danger of being replaced by "death ray" systems using lasers or charged particle beams. Another $10 billion, please. The longer a project takes, the more expensive it becomes. The more expensive a project becomes, the more complex it becomes. Greater complexity breeds still more complexity. It is often a violent process to get a weapon system away from the development people and into the hands of the troops.

The Peace Dividend

With the Cold War ending so suddenly, the nearly half-century-long arms race it spawned has led to some rather bizarre consequences. As President Eisenhower warned in the late 1950s, as the arms race was just getting started, the "military-industrial complex" was going to be a growing problem in the future. This became blatantly obvious when, as the Cold War came to an abrupt conclusion, weapons manufacturers pleaded successfully that defense production could not be drastically cut because unemployment would result. The military-industrial people had long stressed this economic angle, and now, as it was the only one they had, they played it off on the politicians to good effect. Weapons production and the maintenance of large armed forces now became a form of public works. President Eisenhower, who had spent most of his adult life as an army officer, was certainly onto something and can be faulted only for not being able to impress on the American public just how unyielding the Cold War defense budget, and its benefactors, would be to an outbreak of peace.

While the Cold War defense budgets may be unyielding to cuts, they are not invulnerable. The Cold War ended as the United States was in the midst of a recession, a presidential election, and several politically embarrassing scandals in Congress. The legislators were reluctant to take the heat for any lost jobs resulting from defense cuts. This was a knee-jerk reaction, as defense cuts benefit the economy in the medium and long term. Defense spending ties up a lot of vital human and economic resources while producing little of economic value. While it does cost something to convert that defense spending to civilian use, the resulting economic activity produces more jobs and greater overall economic benefits. Defense spending tends to use more highly educated workers and produce things in an economically wasteful manner. There is always a shortage of highly educated workers in the civilian economy, and the ones released from defense work are quickly absorbed into nondefense work. The market-driven, highly competitive economy of the civilian sector also makes for much more effective use of capital than for defense production.

WHAT KIND OF POST–COLD WAR MILITARY WILL WE END UP WITH?

The successor states of the Soviet Union have serious economic and political problems. When the Soviet Union broke up, the old Communist party bureaucrats who became the new leaders realized that the economy and government institutions were not going to be untangled easily or quickly. Sorting out the economy was one thing, but the military was another matter because most of the officers were Russians and the units had a mixture of the Soviet Union's 100+ nationalities. Moreover, these units were distributed throughout the former Soviet Union. The first proposal was that the armed forces remain a united force, and this was one of the ideas behind the creation of the Commonwealth of Independent States (CIS). The concept didn't last long, as within a year all the member nations had formed their own armed forces. This still left most of the strategic weapons (nuclear missiles, long range bombers, larger combat ships) under control of the CIS military. But the result was to tear apart the military organization the communists had spent 70 years putting together. Making matters worse was the collapse of the military-controlled portion of the economy that provided everything from weapons to consumer goods and housing for the troops. Some units literally began selling their weapons and equipment to foreign nations (or local gangsters) in order to survive. While the troops and equipment of the Red Army still existed after the summer of 1991, the social and political glue that held this force together quickly dissipated. What was left was a collection of confused and demoralized national armies that would take several years to sort themselves out. The CIS forces were spending most of their energies looking after the economic needs of the troops and destroying most of their nuclear weapons. This last item, the great nuclear disarmament of the 1990s, came about for three reasons:

1. The series of disarmament treaties signed by the United States and the USSR in the late 1980s and right up to the collapse of the Soviet Union in the summer of 1991.
2. The inability to, and unwillingness to, support all those nuclear weapons because of the economic cost. This was acknowledged by most Soviet leaders up until the 1991 collapse, but after the Communists were out of power, it became an article of faith. With the Cold War over, there was no need for all those nukes.
3. The Western nations made it known that they would be far more generous to the successor states of the Soviet Union if a lot of the Soviet nukes were destroyed. It was not hard to sell this idea to the former Soviets, as they didn't want to pay for the upkeep of all those weapons, and they certainly wanted to encourage generosity in the West.

Even the U.S. military publicly recognized that the formidable military force it and its allies had been preparing to fight since the 1950s had suddenly become but a shadow of its former self. Through most of the 1990s, the biggest danger the former Red Army will pose is to the nations it still resides in. The threat of civil war and general unrest has increased the urgency to disarm and disband the remains of the Red Army.

In the West, the military did not collapse. Moreover, a large contingent of the NATO forces that had long confronted the Red Army in Central Europe managed to show off its superior skills by making short work of the Soviet-equipped Iraqi Army. But without a Red Army to fight, the Western military now had to face a much more formidable foe: its own citizens and taxpayers. Throughout the Cold War, most Western taxpayers put up with the large defense budgets needed to support armed opposition to the Red Army. With the Red Menace defanged, the Western generals and admirals are having a difficult time maintaining the force levels they have become accustomed to for several decades. While the former Soviets had little choice but to cut their military strength, the Western nations can still pay their bills. Nevertheless, the cuts were under way within a year of the Soviet Union's collapse. The major holdout was the United States, where the military budget had become a form of political patronage, and it was the politicians who were having a difficult time with cutting the military budget.

By the middle of the decade, the extent of the defense cuts in the West will be clear. The final result will be smaller, but still professional and effective forces. This will be in sharp contrast to the bits and pieces of military power the Soviet successor states were able to cobble together. The officers of the former Soviet military make no secret of their desire to emulate the Western armed forces. This means fewer conscripts, more quality in training and equipment, and discarding their 70-year-old Communist military tradition. The Third World nations that used the Soviet military as their model are equally dismayed with what they ended up with, and many of these nations are also looking to the West for a more effective military model. But the Western nations have a significant advantage in their use of professional troops. A "Western"-type armed forces requires easy access to a highly industrialized economy and a well-educated pool of recruits. Only the Western nations have both of these elements. The images of Western troops quickly devastating the Russian-style Iraqi Army in 1991 will long haunt Third World military leaders. While the image may not be entirely accurate, it will influence military thinking in all nations for the rest of the decade.

Anatomy of an Arms Race

The Cold War was hot in one area: the development and production of weapons. Now that the Cold War is over, and before another one begins, it would be instructive to take a closer look at what happened last time around.

Weapon-development projects are typically begun in response to a perceived rather than actual threat. Because it takes nearly 10 years to develop a new weapon, work must begin before the enemy version appears. Most of the really new weapons came from the West, because this is where most new technology came from. To keep up, the Soviets often applied Western technology to weapons before Western nations did. This meant that the Soviet systems were typically less reliable and capable than Western versions. Although combat experience constantly demonstrated this, Western nations often responded to Soviet developments and touched off still another round of development.

The result was a large number of weapon systems begun and precious few canceled. After its first year of existence, an American system had a 4 percent chance of cancellation each year right up until it went into production. This has been the experience during the past 40 years. Soviet systems experienced even less chance of cancellation. Ineptly implemented or no longer needed Soviet systems went into limited production anyway. These turkeys then either faded away or were converted to other uses. A good example was the U.S. B-70 bomber. This was an early 1960s project, a replacement for the B-52, which would be 10 years old and "obsolete" in the late 1960s. ICBMs seemed a better investment, and the B-70, which showed every sign of being hideously expensive, was canceled. The Soviets, in the meantime, began developing an aircraft to counter the B-70: the MiG-25 Foxbat. The MiG-25 was not canceled and was available in 1970. Without a fast, high-flying bomber to intercept, the MiG-25 didn't have much to do. It could fly fast and high, although not very far. It was a cranky aircraft without carrying capacity, not very maneuverable, and feared by its pilots. It was specialized for one job, going after fast, high-flying bombers, and this job no longer existed. Initially, the MiG-25 was turned into a camera-carrying reconnaissance plane. Operating alone, it could fly high and fast into an area, take photos, and get out with less risk of interception. The MiG-25 eventually evolved into the MiG-31, an interceptor that depended on look-down radar and new air-to-air missiles. In the West, the MiG-25 was viewed with alarm. Here was this huge, fast, ominous-looking plane. Something had to be done. No one mentioned that something had already been done when the B-70 was canceled. It was ignored that the MiG-25 had only one useful mission left, and that was to frighten Western governments into countering the MiG-25's mythical capabilities. The result was a number of very capable, and expensive, Western aircraft and missile systems.

The Soviets, not unmindful of its technological and financial disadvantages versus the West, compensated in several ways:

1. The Soviets copied Western technology extensively. Although Soviet industry was often incapable of duplicating Western technology, it came close enough by producing a large number of less sophisticated weapons that cleverly work around what they couldn't duplicate.
2. The Soviets did not leap from one technological breakthrough to another. They allowed their systems to evolve gradually. Seemingly new systems would eventually be revealed as progressive upgrades of the previous model. Their tanks and aircraft were noted for this approach.
3. The Soviets often mass-produced weapon designs that were not technologically advanced and were simply not made by Western armed forces anymore or in large quantities. This enabled them to achieve some capability in areas where they were technically inferior. Depth-charge throwers and many types of missiles were examples.
4. Soviet commanders accepted a higher discrepancy between actual and theoretical performance than Western nations. This outburst of pragmatism came from their realization that their systems tended to be perfected in use, often carrying uncorrected defects through their entire lifetimes, were produced to lower industrial standards, and had less capable operators.
5. Soviet doctrine called for heavy use of the particularly Soviet quality known as quantity. This became more difficult as the Russians tried to match Western technology and unit cost escalated. Western nations had the same problems with high technology, but the ratio of

Soviet to Western systems did not change appreciably. The effort to keep up in the technology race was killing the Soviets' economy, and eventually forced them to rethink their approach to defense spending.

6. Soviet planning was long term. It dealt in 10-, 20-, and 20+-year planning cycles. As alien as this is to Westerners, it was a necessary practice in the Soviet Union. The entire Soviet economy was centrally planned and required long lead times to accomplish complex tasks. This planning was not detailed. The tank-building plan would assume a new version of the Soviets' main battle tank every five or six years. The required manpower and resources would be set aside for that task. What exactly the tank would be like was left up to the designers. If this does not leave enough engine-building capacity to expand automobile production, then the planners knew that they wouldn't get the additional cars. Military production came first, but within the planned limits. Resources were made available for opportunistic projects. The reactive armor added to Soviet tanks in the mid-1980s was an example.

The United States responded to the arms race by doing what it had always done best: developing new technology and spending a lot of money. As in the past, this approach worked. It was not a cheap victory, the financial cost of the Cold War being greater than all other U.S. wars combined.

THE UNITED STATES: THE HIGH COST OF BEING FIRST

When the United States put a man on the moon in the 1960s, a very expensive myth was born: that with sufficient funds, any technological feat could be accomplished. Weapons development turned out to be different. The budgets are smaller, public support often nonexistent, and the problems less well defined and the tasks often more difficult than staging a lunar press conference. The resulting weapons often do not perform as expected and cost more than anticipated. They cost more than the budget can sustain, so fewer are produced and/or corners are cut in the design. Making fewer systems or reducing performance is compounded by not providing sufficient spare parts for wartime use. This is a flaw that will not be fully appreciated until the shooting starts. The spare-parts shortage was present in the 1991 Gulf War and would have gotten really ugly if the fighting had lasted more than a few weeks.

All of this gives new technology a bad name and makes it difficult for deserving projects to get funds. The escalation of claims causes bigger lies to be told in a vicious circle that makes it difficult for anyone to speak honestly. Being first is very expensive, and not just in terms of money. The system changes considerably when a war breaks out, because you now have a means of determining what works and what doesn't. Much of the indecisiveness and overbuilding of weapons stops. Because new weapons are needed quickly, less time is available to spend money. Because more of each type is built, the unit cost comes down. Typically, if you are building a new tank and planned to produce 10,000 for peacetime use, producing three times as many during a war reduces unit cost 20 percent just for lower development expense. This is because development cost typically represents 30 percent of the total. During wartime, as little as a year is needed for development, thus cutting the development bill by more than half. Costs are reduced further because feedback from the combat troops produces a simpler and more effective design. This produces a weapon that does more of what you need to do and has less gold plating to provide for endless contingencies. Overall, wartime weapons cost less than half as much as peacetime systems. Peril is an excellent motivator. There is no such motivation in peacetime. The most recent example of lower weapons development cost occurred during the brief 1991 Gulf War. Shortly after the air phase of the war began, it was discovered that the Iraqis had bunkers buried so deeply that no current bomb could get to them. A new weapon was needed, and the 19-foot-long, 4,700-pound GBU-28 was developed, tested, and delivered in six weeks at a cost of $335,000 each. Of the 30 delivered, 2 were actually used (2 others were used in testing). During testing, the GBU-28 penetrated over 100 feet into the earth during one test and 22 feet of concrete in another. Two more bombs were used for testing after the war. The other 24 will remain in the air-force inventory. The cost was kept low because discarded barrels from army eight-inch guns were used as the bomb body. A specially hardened front end was attached, and the bomb was filled with 650 pounds of explosive. Normally, producing such a new weapon takes at least two years.

All nations suffer to a certain extent from the inefficiencies of peacetime procurement. But the United States has developed a particularly insidious and expensive host of problems. For starters, the American military has lost control of weapons procurement. The legislature has seized effective control because of the vast funds that can be channeled into their constituencies when defense funds are handed out. The military cannot be too rough with the legislators; otherwise, they may find their budgets cut. The legislative control over defense budgets also prevents long production runs, as the quantity of weapons to be produced is largely at the whim of political requirements. These requirements change every year. During the Korean War, the habit of developing weapons in a hurry was institutionalized. This meant building the production facilities before the design of the system was finished. These crash projects were useful in wartime, but in peacetime there is no incentive to quickly finish them. The expense of changing the production facilities was added to the normal expense of redesigning the weapons. The high costs associated with doing everything at once continues for years, further driving up the costs. This made defense business uncertain and discouraged competition. Lack of competition reduced the need to be efficient. Wartime style "cost plus (profit fee)" does not, in the long run, encourage efficient production. The oldest and least efficient production facilities are to be found in defense plants. Worse yet, the military personnel that supervise the projects are not procurement professionals. Other nations make procurement a career path. In the United States, an officer slips into procurement for a few years and then goes on to something else or retires (and often ends up working for a defense supplier). It gets worse. The U.S. defense procurement bureaucracy has grown to the point where dozens of committees and individual officials must pass on, make suggestions about, and generally impede the progress of new systems. The net result is U.S. weapons costing several times more than they should. Often, needed weapons do not survive the process, and the required systems never get built.

Paying for the Next War

Despite wartime economies of scale, the cost of fighting a war today will be substantially higher than peacetime operations. This is largely due to the high cost of ammunition. Currently, a ton of conventional ammunition costs about $8,500. A ton of missile munitions costs over $600,000. ICM (Improved Conventional Munitions) cost at least 10 times more than old-fashioned bombs and shells. The high cost of ICM and missiles represents two things. One is the greater development cost. Second, their greater complexity requires a more elaborate manufacturing process. Under wartime conditions, economies of scale and expediency could reduce the cost by five or more times. Still, the price of an average ton of munitions would be $40,000 and up. With U.S. divisions consuming at least 1,000 tons a day, the bill would be over $50 million per division per day just for munitions. Intensive combat can up the daily munitions expenditure to 5,000 tons. Fuel, at $1,000 a ton, would be only a million dollars. Fuel would represent as much weight as munitions. Replacing lost and damaged equipment, assuming 2 percent daily losses, plus food, spare parts, wages, and everything else, brings the daily bill to more than $100 million a day. The eight U.S. divisions that found themselves fighting during the 1991 Gulf War, in only three days of combat, used up several billion dollars' worth of resources. The air force, at several hundred thousand dollars per sortie, cost over $40 billion during the seven weeks of active air operation. Transportation and naval expenses are included.

The six months of operations in the Persian Gulf cost over $60 billion. That included seven weeks of air combat, three days of ground combat, and six months of getting ready. The cost was more than 20 percent of the annual defense budget. If there had been more combat, the costs would have escalated sharply. One month of heavy ground combat can easily cost over $100 billion for this same eight-division force.

While the Gulf War was a major operation, it fell far short of the kind of operations the United States has been getting ready for since the 1950s. The United States has considerable economic resources, and was, and still is, ready to mobilize most of it for a major war. Consider the overall situation for a major war. The U.S. economy, if mobilized for war, could increase its GNP by perhaps a third to nearly $8,000 billion. Half of this could be devoted to military needs. A ground force of 30 divisions, each in combat for 120 days, would cost more than $400 billion. Over $300 billion would be required to operate 3,600 aircraft for 120 days. Air operations have always been more expensive than ground operations. A hundred aircraft are generally considered to cost about the same as a division. Looking at it this way, twice the resources are devoted to aircraft, despite the fact that an air-force unit of 100 aircraft requires one third the manpower of an army division. Air power is more expensive, but less costly in human life, at least for the user. Taken in this context, the Gulf War saw air-force resources exceeding ground forces by more than 50 percent. While you'll always need ground forces to go in and finish a war, the Gulf War demonstrated that, if you have the material and financial resources, you can do most of the work with air forces.

A navy of more than 300 combat ships and 1,400 aircraft in combat would consume more than $200 billion in 120 days. Over 60 percent of this would be for aircraft operations (both land- and carrier-based). With the Soviet Navy rapidly losing its former capabilities, there is no major opponent for the U.S. Navy. Thus, the 300 combat-ship operation is less likely to occur. But a naval effort of half that size remains a possibility. Combat would not likely be continuous, or even intense, but we could still see a cost of more than a billion dollars a day to keep the ships out there, ready for anything.

If operations were carried out at the above levels, the direct cost would be more than $800 billion for four months of operations. Only about 10 percent of this is for replacement of destroyed equipment. The majority would be for munitions. Guided missiles and other so-called smart munitions would account for most of the ammunition cost. With no major opponents left on the planet, such enormous expenditures will not be needed. Iraq was one of the few nations that possessed large quantities of armored vehicles, which are the primary target of all those expensive, high-tech munitions. The cost of the Gulf War is still the likely model for wars the United States and its Western allies will face in the next decade.

In addition, there will be no additional expense of building more ships, aircraft, and weapons to replace stuff lost in combat or for new divisions. There will also be less expense for aiding allies, replacing lost satellites, caring for the wounded, and compensating for any damage done to domestic facilities and populations. The tempo of a future war will still be dictated by the ability to produce these expensive and complex munitions as well as the high-technology weapons that use them. But unlike the Cold War era, all you have to do is have a stockpile handy for the next "little war."

Getting Ready for the Next War

The U.S. munitions budget was about $12 billion a year at the end of the Cold War. Stockpiles represented less than $100 billion worth of munitions at current prices. It was understood, but rarely acknowledged too loudly, that this would not last long in a major war. If you ended up blowing off nearly $100 billion worth of munitions a month for three or four months, only a fraction would come off the shelf. The rest has to be manufactured, but only after you build the factories and train the workers. This means increasing manufacturing capacity severalfold. Manufacturing managers and engineers are very resourceful people, but a first-year increase in munitions production would most likely create less than a quarter of the requirements for a major war. Something has to give. What happens is that either one side wins very quickly, or the war settles down to a staring contest while the factories come on line. If peace has not broken out yet, a war of attrition ensues. This is not based on speculation, but observation. World War I followed this pattern, as did our own Civil War, the first of the modern industrial wars. World War II has a different story, as it began in fits and starts. Moreover, the major combatants started mobilizing several years before they came to blows. Throughout both wars, battles often ground to a halt when both sides ran out of munitions or fuel. The same pattern appeared during the 1973 Arab-Israeli War. If the 1991 Gulf War had gone on for another month or so, the United States would have run out of several types of high-tech munitions. This surprises some people. It shouldn't.

Most nations perceive the solution to this problem to be the quick victory. This is another myth regularly worshiped by military planners. While possible, a short war is unlikely against most foes. The Iraqis cooperated by letting themselves be embargoed and then leaving their army out in the desert.

Vietnam was a more likely case, where weapons of mass destruction were avoided, and a war of attrition ensued against an elusive and resilient foe. Vietnams will be avoided by the United States and other nations for another generation or two, at least until that sorry affair becomes a dim memory.

It should also not be forgotten that a major war, while unlikely, is still a possibility. Mobilizing for a major war would take several years. If we entered a major war tomorrow, there would be a severe munitions shortage within a month or two. You need several years to create the tools and train the staff to produce large quantities of munitions, weapons, and military equipment. Training the troops also takes longer than in the past, especially the larger number of technicians. Industrial mobilization for war has been a serious problem for the past century and has been getting worse. The problem tends to solve itself if the combatants cannot. The root cause is the difficulty in maintaining large peacetime stocks of munitions. Not only is ammunition expensive, it doesn't last long in storage. The stuff may look okay in the warehouse, but let's face it, progressive deterioration soon sets in. The rot is not apparent until you use it. It's one of the dirty little secrets of military life. When you use old ammunition, a lot of it lands with a thud, not a bang.

Meanwhile, we have a lot of little wars. Gold-plated little wars are even more expensive than less-than-total total wars. Here, the natural temptation to use weapons that are safer to users, and more expensive ones, will be difficult to resist. Vietnam was such a war, and expensive munitions were just starting to get really expensive. Warfare has never been cheap; Vietnam showed that it can only get more expensive, and the 1991 Gulf War proved it.

The Price of Things to Come

Several cost trends have been inexorably progressing through this century. Aircraft costs, for example, have been increasing four times every 10 years for the past 80 years. During the past 30 years, this disease has spread to land and naval weapons. Currently, aircraft cost an average of $1,200 a pound. Armored vehicles cost $25 a pound and ships $70. These three items also cost two to four times their acquisition cost for operations and maintenance over their 10- to 20-year peacetime life. Missiles cost three to ten times more than aircraft on a per-pound basis. Satellites cost over $10,000 a pound to build and over $3,000 a pound to put into orbit. The chief culprit is electronics. Promising a lot, and sometimes delivering it, electronics tend to become so complex that mere humans cannot easily ensure their reliability. During World War II, combat aircraft had less than 100 pounds of electronic gear. Today, a ton, 2,200 pounds, is the norm in Western aircraft and rising rapidly. In the last 20 years, tank fire-control systems have gone from 6 percent (M-60A1) of total vehicle cost to nearly 40 percent (M-1). As one calculation pointed out, if the trends of the last 80 years persist, by the middle of the next century the entire defense budget of the United States will be spent on one combat aircraft. Something has to give. The end of the Cold War has provided something of an escape hatch. With less money to spend, there will be more incentive to spend it more effectively.

Let us also examine the relationship between cost and effectiveness. Compare a modern carrier task force with one of World War II vintage.

Task Force 58, in 1944, cost $600 million and had 112 ships, over 40,000 men and nearly 1,000 aircraft. These aircraft could deliver 400 tons of ordnance. A modern task force of 9 ships and 90 aircraft and nearly 9,000 men costs $14 billion. Its aircraft carry the same amount of ordnance. The aircraft cost twice as much and require less than 10 percent as many aircrew. The modern aircraft can fly more frequently and have fewer accidents. A hundred fewer ships are needed to support this air capability. Task Force 58 costs much more after adjusting for inflation and other costs. It required nearly five times more manpower. Costs have increased, but potential capability has increased faster. More important, far fewer men are needed to man the weapons. When the cost of training and maintaining manpower is added, the modern task force is actually cheaper. The only drawback to all this is that unit costs are increasing far faster than the ability of national economies. Modern warfare is becoming something other than World War II with faster aircraft and fewer ships.

The future is already here; fewer weapons were being purchased even before the Cold War ended. The Soviet Union, and to a lesser extent the United States, crippled their economies with huge arms expenditures. Japan, spending 1 percent of its GNP on arms, compared with over 6 percent in the United States, used the difference to build up industries producing a wide range of industrial and consumer goods. Japan takes one high-tech market after another from the United States. Soviet industry was so far behind, it was hardly in the race anymore by the end of the Cold War. An arms race is a luxury few can afford, and even then not for long. An arms race contains the seeds of its own destruction, either through a war or the stagnation of the economy supporting it. The lost economic growth that pays for the arms race eventually catches up with you. Arms races exist only when there is a lot of wealth and weapons to spend it on. These conditions have been prevalent more in the past century than at any other time in history. Fear and paranoia produce these spasms of excessive arms spending. It's a hard habit to break. In addition to the diversion of resources from the economy, arms building produces one-third fewer jobs than does nonarms spending.

The result of all this spending is often of dubious value. There is always the tendency to seek technological solutions to problems that are the result of ill-trained personnel and poor leadership.

The primary objective of peacetime arms expenditures often appears to be just spending money. Those nations that can break out of this cycle will not only be better defended but considerably wealthier. The ultimate cost of excessive military spending has been political unrest rather than nuclear war. This happened in the Soviet Union first, where the ill effects of arms spending reached crisis proportions. High military spending also caused political unrest in the United States and Western Europe. One way or the other, the cost of war is felt even in times of peace.

Theory and Practice

The Soviets stockpiled two to three times as many munitions as their Western opponents. Unfortunately for them, a lot of this stuff was so old and ill cared for that it proved as dangerous to its users as to their opponents. This created a major ecological disaster along the former East German border. That was where the Soviets kept a lot of their best stuff. Some of the smaller NATO nations kept dangerously skimpy ammo stockpiles, giving them in some categories only a week's supply if ever there were a war. These two extremes pretty well define the approach of most nations to paying for wars not yet fought.

The end of the Cold War has left the world awash in cheap arms. These weapons may not go to fuel another world war, but they will nourish many small wars.

The Future

The industrialized nations are running out of soldiers and taxes. In a familiar pattern, rising living standards have led to lower birthrates. The pinch is felt most in the armed forces, where large numbers of increasingly scarce young males are needed. The money shortage is caused by increasing competition with more recently industrialized nations. The classic example is Japan capturing markets from the United States and Europe. This competition forces the heavily militarized Americans and Europeans to cut back on defense spending in order to make their industries more competitive. Military power begins with economic power. Lose your productivity, and the armed forces shrink accordingly. The armed forces must get by with fewer people and less money. Those nations that don't adapt to this situation will see their combat power and economic strength suffer. The Cold War ended just in time for the industrialized nations of NATO.

China has demobilized over a million troops in order to pay for more high-tech weapons, and the Soviets announced a similar solution before the 1991 collapse. The future holds a hard decision between guns or butter. Many nations are learning to compromise. Older systems are rebuilt and updated instead of replaced with new weapons. Big-ticket items, particularly strategic nuclear-weapons systems, no longer have the blank-check authority of the past. Disarmament was caused by fiscal exhaustion as well as fear. The Soviets had an additional problem with their centrally planned economy slipping further into terminal stagnation. All the planned (socialist) economies have encountered this stagnation problem. While the end of the Cold War has lifted the economic burden of the arms race from the West, it has left standing a curious change in these enormous "postindustrial" economies. This is a change that has yet to be tested during a major war, but may still be: a postindustrial economy that employs a lot more people providing services and fewer actually producing goods. A major war in the future would reveal some curious insights into postindustrial economies. Going into World War II and through the 1950s, the United States was a manufacturing economy. Primarily of goods, but there was also substantial construction and processing of raw materials. But in the 1980s America has lost nearly a third of this manufacturing capacity. More economic effort goes into services. It is difficult to find a place in a war economy for bankers, insurance agents, and lawyers. Perhaps we can use them to improve the quality of the infantry. Some of the new economic activity is transferable to military uses. The hundreds of thousands of additional computer specialists and medical specialists can have an impact. This will create a military effort unlike any currently envisioned.

As a historical example, consider World War II. In 1940 and 1941, there were plans to build a lot of large warships. But shipbuilding takes time. Building more plants to produce "heavy metal" goods also takes time. What the United States did have was a lot of skilled workers and light-metal fabricating capability. So America built a lot of aircraft, which could be manufactured quickly and put right into action. The massive effort to build the atomic bomb was also an application of abundant scientific resources.

Mobilizing for another world war today would find even more emphasis on building what could be put together quickly and to the best effect. This would again mean more aircraft, light combat vehicles, simplified missiles, and electronic weapons. A future war would test the theory that Western engineers could rapidly retool their appliance production for some kind of effective weapons. Russia already has an enormous heavy-metals industry with which it builds lots of armored vehicles. World War III, or any war of the 1991 Persian Gulf War class, if it happened and lasted long, would be a curious contrast in styles and substance. High tech versus heavy metal. Place your bets.

Cost of War

Chart 25-1 shows the cost of conducting a war for U.S. forces, and Western-armed forces in general. The costs cover a period of one month's fighting. Costs are expressed in dollars and in tonnage of supply that must be transported to the theater of operations. This chart is divided into five sections:

1. Land operations covering all land combat not involving the air force
2. Air operations in support of ground forces
3. Air operations in support of naval forces

4. Naval operations, not including transport of amphibious forces, or their combat on land
5. A summary of all the above operations

LAND OPERATIONS

COMBAT DIVISIONS are the number of divisions involved in combat. There would also be from one tenth to one half again as many divisions not in combat. These would be in the process of formation, rebuilding, or used as garrison forces. These units use less than one tenth the munitions and replacements and less than half the fuel.

COMBAT DAYS, the number of days hostilities persist. Combat does not go on all the time.

DAILY LOSS RATE % is the average percentage of personnel strength lost for each day. A day of combat between equally matched forces causes an average of 2 percent loss per division. To calculate the number of days of combat, divide two into the value shown here and multiply by COMBAT DAYS. Losses of weapons and equipment are tied to it.

COST OF DIVISION (MILLION) is the cost to arm and equip a division with new and repaired equipment. This is used to calculate replacement costs.

SUPPLIES are the various categories of goods and services the division requires in and out of combat.

TONS are the tons of consumable supplies required per division per combat day.

COST PER TON ($1,000) is the average cost of each ton of supplies in thousands of dollars.

TOTAL COST (MILLION) is the total cost of each category of supplies; % is the percentage of total cost each category of supplies represents.

TOTAL TONS (THOUSANDS) is the total tonnage of each category of supplies.

AMMUNITION is all munitions used in combat.

FUEL is all fuel used for vehicles, generators, aircraft, etc.

MAINTENANCE is spare parts and other supplies required to maintain equipment. Also includes food, wages, clothing, and other material.

NONCOMBAT MAINTENANCE is the supplies required to maintain the equipment of noncombat support.

NONCOMBAT SUPPORT is the cost of maintaining noncombat support troops.

25-1 Cost of War

Land Operations

Combat Divisions	10	
Combat Days	30	
Daily Loss Rate	0.5%	
Cost of Division (million)	$4,519	

Supplies	Tons	Cost per Ton ($1,000)	Total Cost (million)	%	Total Tons (thousands)
Ammunition	1,135	$40.00	$13,620	36.1%	341
Fuel	273	$1.00	$82	0.2%	82
Maintenance	147	$15.00	$661	1.8%	44
Replacement			$6,778	18.0%	38
Noncombat maint.			$4,569	12.1%	305
Noncombat support			$12,000	31.8%	800
Total			$38 (billion)		1,609

Cost Per Division Combat Day	$75	Million
All Casualties	35,700	
Losses (Personnel)	8,925	
As % of Division Strength	5%	
Combat Casualties	25,500	
As % of Division Strength	15%	

Air Operations in Support of Ground Forces
(Air Force & Marine Corps)

Combat Aircraft	1,800
Sorties per Aircraft	30
Total Sorties	54,000
Sortie Loss Rate	0.2%
Cost of Aircraft (avg)	$35 (million)

Supplies	Tons	Cost per Ton (x1,000)	Total Cost (million)	%	Total Tons (thousands)	%
Ammunition	2	$259	$27,972	57%	108	7%
Fuel	5	$1.0	$270	1%	270	17%
Maintenance	1	$20	$1,080	2%	54	3%
Replacement	20	$1.0	$3,780	8%	1,080	69%
Noncombat Support	1	$0.30	$16,200	33%	54	3%
Total			$49 (billion)		1,566	

Aircraft Lost	108

Aircrew Casualties	76
Ground Crew Casualties	756

Total Casualties	832

Sorties per Division Combat Day	175

Cost per Sortie ($1,000)	$913
Tons per Sortie	29

Air Operations in Support of Naval Forces

Combat Aircraft	600
Sorties per Aircraft	60
Total Sorties	36,000
Sortie Loss Rate %	0.10%
Cost of Aircraft (avg)	$35 (million)

Supplies	Tons	Cost per Ton ($1,000)	Total Cost (million)		Total Tons (thousands)		
				%			%
Ammunition	2	$250	$18,000	71%	72		4%
Fuel	15	$1.0	$540	2%	540		26%
Maintenance	1	$20	$720	3%	36		2%
Replacement	25	$1.4	$1,260	5%	1,350		66%
Noncombat Support	1	$8	$4,800	19%	54		3%
Total		Billion	$25		2,052		

Aircraft Lost	36

Aircrew Casualties	122
Ground Crew Casualties	894

Total Casualties	1,016

Cost per Sortie ($1,000)	$703
Tons per Sortie	57

Naval Operations

Major Combat Ships	198
Fleet Overhead per Ton per 100 Days	$7,000
Sea Days per Ship	30
Average Ship Size (tons)	10,512
Replacement Cost (per ton)	$120,000
Loss Rate per 100 Ship Days	0.5%
Replacement Costs (million)	$375
Supply per Ship (1,000 tons)	247
Cost per Ton of Supply ($100)	$2.52
Total Ship Supply (1,000 tons)	1,467
Supply Cost (million)	$3,700
Overhead Cost (million)	$14,570
Total Cost (billion)	$19

Summary

	Billions	% of Total				
Total Land-Oriented Costs	$87	66%				
Total Naval-Oriented Costs	$44	34%				
Land Operations Only	$38	29%				
Air Operations Only	$75	57%				
Ship Operations Only	$19	14%				
All Cost	$131	100%			Ships Required to Transport	
Combat Unit Consumption Only	Tons x 1,000	%	Billion	%		
Fuel	2,066	31%	$2	1%	58	Tankers
Ammunition	667	10%	$62	47%	33	Dry Cargo Ships
Parts, replacements & other	3,961	59%	$67	51%	198	Dry Cargo Ships
Total Supply Tonnage (x100)	6,694	100%	$131	100%	290	Total Shiploads

TOTAL gives the total cost in billions of dollars and thousands of tons for all divisions for both combat and noncombat days.

COST PER DIVISION COMBAT DAY is the cost (in millions of dollars) of one day's combat for one division. Combat casualties are the annual casualties for all combat and noncombat units.

AS % OF DIVISION STRENGTH, total combat-unit casualties as a percentage of division strength, indicates the severity of personnel losses (see Chapter 24 for more details).

AIR OPERATIONS IN SUPPORT OF GROUND COMBAT

This is the cost of air operations in support of ground combat. Most of the missions represented here are ground attack, air superiority, or reconnaissance.

COMBAT AIRCRAFT is the number of aircraft involved in operations. In this case, strategic bombers are included, as they are quite effective with conventional munitions.

SORTIES PER AIRCRAFT is the average number of times each aircraft takes off in a year. In wartime, the readiness level—percentage of aircraft not out for repairs or maintenance—will vary from 10 to 50+ percent. Modern aircraft can fly as many as three or more sorties a day. This peak performance is called "surge." On many days, an aircraft will not fly at all. Most sorties will be flown on days the divisions are in combat.

SORTIE LOSS RATE % is the percentage of aircraft lost per 100 sorties. The figure .2 means 2 aircraft lost per 1,000 sorties. Depending on pilot quality, level of aircraft maintenance, and flying conditions, the noncombat loss rate can be less than 1 per 1,000 sorties, or higher, especially in Soviet-style air forces.

COST OF AIRCRAFT is the average cost of the aircraft in millions of dollars. This is used to calculate replacement costs.

SUPPLIES, TONS, COST PER TON, %, TOTAL TONS are the same for land operations above.

AMMUNITION includes missiles, cannon shells, bombs, and any other disposable items, like chaff or flares to avoid enemy missiles. Although the majority of sorties will carry ground-attack munitions, many will be for reconnaissance and air superiority. These missions carry lower weights. Therefore, the average weight carried is less than half the average maximum carrying capacity.

FUEL is the average fuel carried on each sortie.

MAINTENANCE is primarily spare parts, but also includes supplies necessary to support personnel (food, clothing, etc.).

REPLACEMENT is the cost of replacement aircraft. There is no weight given, as these aircraft fly in under their own power.

NONCOMBAT SUPPORT is the cost of all other support operations, particularly those in the homeland where air and ground crew are trained.

AIRCRAFT LOST are the number of aircraft destroyed or damaged beyond repair. Such craft can sometimes serve as a source of cannibalized parts. As you can see, the tempo of operations would quickly destroy many of the air units. Given the present annual U.S. production of under 1,000 aircraft, such losses would quickly reduce the level of air operations.

AIRCREW CASUALTIES are aircraft crew killed, seriously injured, or taken prisoner. Not every lost aircraft results in total aircrew loss. The percentage of aircrew lost varies with pilot quality and the size, construction, and mission of the aircraft. Western aircraft are more resistant to Soviet-type weapons than the reverse. Western aircraft are generally larger and more robust. A mission places aircraft high and over friendly territory (good) or low and over enemy territory (bad). Depending on all these factors, the percentage of aircrew emerging unhurt from a lost aircraft varies from 30 percent to more than 90 percent.

GROUND-CREW CASUALTIES are losses to ground crew and other air-base support personnel. In all past wars, and even more in current ones, air bases are a priority target. Enemy aircraft are easier to destroy on the ground. The increasing complexity of modern aircraft has also increased their vulnerability to loss of ground-support facilities and technicians.

SORTIES PER DIVISION COMBAT DAY are the total number of sorties divided by the number of division combat days. Not all these sorties would be in direct support of the division. Many would be against enemy air bases, airborne aircraft, and communications targets. More than half, however, would support the division. Air operations are substantial on noncombat days, too. Reconnaissance in particular proceeds at all times.

COST PER SORTIE is the average cost of a sortie in thousands of dollars. Also given is the average tonnage of supply needed. Even in peacetime, when minimal amounts of ammunition are used, the cost per sortie is about 30 percent of the wartime cost.

AIR OPERATIONS IN SUPPORT OF NAVAL FORCES

This section follows the same format as the air operations in support of ground forces. Differences exist between naval-support and ground-support air operations. At sea, aircraft spend more of their time on patrol in search of enemy naval forces (surface or submarine) or in defense of friendly shipping. Although most naval aircraft are armed, they use these weapons far less frequently than land-oriented aircraft. Naval aircraft suffer lower attrition because, at sea, they are less likely to encounter other aircraft. Most of the combat is against targets that can't shoot back: cruise missiles, submarines, merchant ships. Against armed ships, U.S. naval aircraft unleash a large array of electronic countermeasures and long-range weapons. Naval aircraft tend to be larger, with larger crews. They are more expensive and fly more sorties. They have a higher noncombat loss rate because of the risk of carrier landings and takeoffs.

NAVAL OPERATIONS

Warfare at sea does not lend itself as easily as air or ground combat to terms like "combat days" and "sorties." Combat is irregular, if it occurs at all. Antisubmarine operations are the closest to attrition warfare. The bulk of naval warfare is little more than keeping ships at sea and ready to fight. This is not an easy task. The supply requirements are enormous. The largest item, by weight, is fuel. More expensive weapons and equipment have made naval items the most expensive.

MAJOR COMBAT SHIPS are the combat ships (over 1,000 tons displacement) that can "maintain station"—stay at sea for long periods. This number does not include amphibious ships and other transports. The amphibious ships tend to be massed at port and then sent off for a landing, from which they return as soon as possible. Other transports spend their time going to and fro delivering supplies.

FLEET OVERHEAD PER COMBAT SHIP is the annual cost (in millions of dollars) to each ship of the fleet overhead, including the establishment of land bases and support (including amphibious) ships.

SEA DAYS PER SHIP is the average number of days per year each ship stays at sea. A ship will spend at least 10 percent to 20 percent of its time in port for mandatory maintenance. The crew needs some time ashore to maintain morale. Without such respite, both ship and crew performance declines.

AVERAGE SHIP SIZE (TONS) is the average tonnage (displacement) of each ship.

SUPPLY PER SHIP (1,000 TONS) is the average tonnage of supply a ship requires per day at sea.

COST PER TON OF SUPPLY ($1,000) is the average cost per ton of supply in thousands of dollars.

TOTAL SHIP SUPPLY (1,000 TONS) is the total daily supply for all ships per day when at sea.

SUPPLY COST ($MILLION) is the total cost of supplying all ships at sea for one day.

OTHER COSTS ($MILLION) are all other costs, including payroll, shore-based support, repair, and replacement.

SUMMARY

This section gives the total costs for land, naval, and air operations in billions of dollars. Also given is a summary of the supply tonnage in thousands of tons, its cost, and the number of ships required to carry it. The cost of replacement troops and the movement of seriously wounded back to the homeland is included in the various overheads and supply movement. Several patterns emerge. The most expensive single item is ammunition, accounting for over two thirds of the cost. By weight, fuel accounts for over half.

25-2 Distribution of Manpower

US Armed Forces Manpower (Cold War High: 1990)

Service	Active	Civilian	Paid Reserve	Total	Major Units	Men per unit
Army	771	400	735	1,906	40	47,650
Navy	571	307	193	1,071	480	2,231
Marines	196	22	43	261	4	65,250
Air Force	605	249	182	1,036	5,800	179
Total	2,143	978	1,153	4,274		
% of Tot.	50%	23%	27%	100%		

Percentage Distribution of Manpower

Service	Active	Civilian	Paid Reserve	Total
Army	18%	9%	17%	45%
Navy	13%	7%	5%	25%
Marines	5%	1%	1%	6%
Air Force	14%	6%	4%	24%
Total	50%	23%	27%	100%

Cost of Manpower

Chart 25-2 shows the extent and distribution of armed-forces manpower and spending in the United States.

SERVICE is the branch of the armed forces.

ARMY represents the land-combat forces.

NAVY represents seagoing forces.

MARINES. The U.S. Navy has built up substantial land forces since World War II. These units, the U.S. Marine Corps, comprise a significant portion of U.S. land combat capability. Although the USMC belongs to the U.S. Navy, it is recognized as a de facto separate service.

AIR FORCE shows air units. This does not mean the air force represents all air units. The U.S. Navy, in particular, has substantial air units, as do the army and marines. The U.S. Air Force provides ground support for the army, as well as having strategic bombers, and a few interceptors. As happened in Vietnam, all U.S. Air Force units, including strategic bombers, can be applied to supporting ground combat. The U.S. armed forces have over 20,000 aircraft, including helicopters. The U.S. Air Force has less than half as many aircraft of all types.

ARMED FORCES MANPOWER

Armed forces manpower (in thousands) tends to fluctuate with the number of military-age men available and the needs of the economy. Military manpower in the United States remained stable during the 1980s as the economy has boomed.

PERCENTAGE DISTRIBUTION OF MANPOWER. U.S. forces are largely organized for offensive operations. With a large navy and air force, manpower can be moved anywhere in the world more quickly than ground forces.

ACTIVE is full-time uniformed troops.

CIVILIAN represents the full-time civilian employees who work for the armed forces. Because so few of the uniformed soldiers are in combat units, many perform jobs that could just as easily be held by civilians. It has long been common for highly technical jobs to be held by civilians. For example, when artillery was introduced 500 years ago, the guns were manned by civilian contractors. This tradition persisted for several centuries. Even today, many of the more complex missile systems and aircraft are maintained, at least partially, by civilians. The reason is simple: People with sufficient technical skills cannot always be persuaded to stay in uniform.

PAID RESERVE represents soldiers who spend most of their time as civilians. See Chapter 5 for more details.

PARAMILITARY. These are combat troops used for border patrol and internal security. See Chapter 5 for more details.

MAJOR UNITS are the major combat units for each branch of the armed forces. These figures are used to calculate the cost of maintaining combat power. For the army and marines, major units include fully equipped combat divisions or groups of smaller units equivalent to divisions. This includes reserve divisions. For the navy, it includes major combat ships (more than 1,000 tons). For the air force, it means combat aircraft and ballistic-missile launchers.

MEN PER UNIT is the average number of personnel for each major unit.

Armed Forces Annual Costs

Annual costs (in millions of 1993 dollars) are the anticipated spending levels for the early 1990s. The data given in Chart 25-3 are a composite based on the past few years' spending and what is likely for the next few years. Military budgets are always subject to severe shifts from year to year. The United States is experiencing severe problems with its economy because of high defense spending and cries for cuts in the wake of the Cold War's ending. It is likely that the figures shown will decline by a third or more over the next few years. During the 1970s, U.S. spending averaged $180 billion a year. American spending increased considerably during the 1980s, contributing to economic and legislative budget crises in 1987. These costs can be broken down in many ways. One alternative to this way is by functional categories, for example:

General-purpose forces (traditional army, navy, air force)—37 percent

Strategic forces (ICBMs)—8 percent

Airlift and sealift forces—2 percent

Reserve forces (added to general-purpose forces in wartime)—5 percent

Intelligence and communications—7 percent

Research and development—9 percent

Central supply and maintenance—10 percent

All other support—22 percent.

PAY is the wages and other allowances paid to the troops.

PROCURE is procurement, the purchase of new weapons and equipment. A typical breakdown would be:
   Aircraft—36 percent

   Missiles (primarily ICBMs or for aircraft)—16 percent

   Ships—14 percent

   Combat vehicles (tanks, etc.)—6 percent

   Electronics and communications—8 percent

   Everything else (including munitions other than missiles and torpedoes)—11 percent.

OPERATE is the cost of operations and maintenance. This covers everything from food and fuel to clothing and spare parts.

SUPPORT includes research, development, testing, administration, pensions, and construction. Research is a high-expense item for Western armed forces. Construction costs also tend to be high. Pensions are a growing expense, where they are currently in excess of $30 billion a year.

25-3 Manpower and Costs

US Armed Forces (Cold War Peak: 1990)
Annual Costs (x $1,000,000)

Service	Pay	Procure	Operate	Support	Total	% of Total	Major Units	Cost per Unit (Million)
Army	$31,300	$16,100	$14,900	$4,100	$66,400	29	40	$1,660
Navy	$16,600	$29,000	$18,100	$8,200	$71,900	31	480	$150
Marines	$3,700	$1,200	$2,800	$2,100	$9,800	4	4	$2,450
Air Force	$20,400	$33,100	$19,100	$11,500	$84,100	36	5,800	$15
Total	$72,000	$79,400	$54,900	$25,900	$232,200	100		
% of Total	31	34	24	11	100			

COST PER UNIT ($\times$ $1,000,000) is the annual cost of maintaining each combat unit. This is more than simply paying, feeding, and maintaining the troops, and buying and maintaining equipment. It includes every cost incurred by the armed forces. This is something like the input/output matrix used by economists to show the entirety of a nation's economic activity. Here we want to show the entire cost of military forces. There is no miscellaneous category to hide things in. The United States is an extreme example of a military system. No other country pays as much per unit for armed forces. The United States cannot buy better weapons from anyone else (with a few minor exceptions). So the United States develops new weapons itself to ensure that it does not lose its qualitative standing with any real or potential rival. Therefore, the high costs of developing and building new weapons become part of maintaining armed forces. An additional unique cost is the development and maintenance of nuclear weapons, strategic missiles, and chemical and biological weapons. Finally, few other nations maintain their forces at such a high level of readiness.

ARMED FORCES COST PER MAN

This section puts the spending into perspective. Cost per man is the average cost per man for pay, procurement, operations, and support. The categories are the same as for the armed forces' annual costs.

Cost of Raising a Division

The basic units of land combat are the divisions. They are expensive creatures. The costs shown here cover only hardware, weapons, and equipment. The cost of recruiting and training personnel equal a third to half the personnel cost. In addition, there is the cost of housing a division in peacetime, which equals at least half the hardware cost. Personnel and housing about double the hardware cost. Support facilities for maintenance and training, plus specialized units for combat

25-4 Cost of a Combat Division

| | | US Mechanized Infantry | | |
| | | Avg Unit | Total | % of |
Item	Quantity	Cost	Cost	Total
APCs	727	$900	$654,300	14.5%
Tanks	290	$3,000	$870,000	19.3%
Munitions, Tons, 30 Days	34,050	$40	$1,362,000	30.1%
Aircraft	143	$5,000	$715,000	15.8%
Misc Equipment & Supplies			$140,000	3.1%
Trucks	3,500	$70	$245,000	5.4%
Communications & EW Equipment			$120,000	2.7%
Air Defense Weapons	108	$800	$86,400	1.9%
Field Artillery	143	$900	$128,700	2.8%
ATGM	660	$150	$99,000	2.2%
Personal Equipment	16,600	$3.0	$49,800	1.1%
Infantry Weapons	24,000	$1.0	$24,000	0.5%
Fuel Stocks (30 Day Supply)	8,184	$1.0	$8,184	0.2%
Food Stocks (30 Day Supply)	2,184	$7.5	$16,380	0.4%
Total (Millions of Dollars)			$4,519	100%

Summaries

Combat Vehicles	$2,239,300	50%
Other Weapons	$338,100	7%
Other Equipment	$554,800	12%
Supplies	$1,386,564	31%

support and noncombat units for medical, supply, and transportation units, also add to the final cost of a division, which can be up to three times the hardware cost shown. Training time to obtain qualified staff varies from a few months for the simplest jobs to years for the more technical ones. Time spent in schools and other training programs can amount to several "division man-years" (the number of people in the division times 2,000 hours). These trainees must be paid and maintained. Their instructors are an additional expense. Even on-the-job training can be costly as you must divert trained people from their normal duties so that they can instruct the new troops. Training adds to equipment cost, as equipment is worn out by the trainees and must be replaced. Equipment without qualified personnel to operate it is useless. To operate a division's equipment requires 12,000 to 16,000 men. Some 20 percent are the cadre—the officers and noncommissioned officers (NCOs). These troops require years of experience and six months to a year of training. Most of them, NCOs and lower-grade officers, can be created in a year or two. Senior officers (majors, colonels, and up) usually need 5 to 10 years as senior officers to be most effective. Competent civilian managers can often fill in with only a year or two of training and experience. The quality of the cadre determines the quality of the remaining troops in the division. About half the division's troops can be trained to an adequate degree of competence in six months.

These troops handle fairly basic tasks that people of average skill and intelligence can handle. These are the combat troops and "common" technicians. Any skill that can be learned in a few months falls into this category. Another 30 percent, the specialist technicians, require a year or more of training and experience. These specialists can often be obtained directly from the civilian economy. Armed forces must constantly cope with an inadequate supply of cadre and specialists. A specialist shortage can be covered with a number of expensive but reliable alternatives. The most common is using more equipment. Without sufficient repair personnel, or enough experienced operators, you go through a lot more equipment. This leads to one of the more insidious peacetime practices, pretending that everything is all right. A fresh coat of paint often stands in for good maintenance. The cadre problem is the most critical because there is no easy way to overcome it. Careful selection of leaders and adequate training programs are a good first step. Unfortunately, few nations are very successful in either selection or training of leaders.

ITEM is the main equipment category.

QUANTITY is the quantity of that item found in the division. Division types shown are U.S. mechanized-infantry division and Soviet motor-rifle division (a common unit organization that will survive the demise of the Soviet Union for a decade or more).

AVG UNIT COST is the average unit cost of each item of equipment in thousands of 1993 dollars. Only new equipment is considered. Where the range of item types within a category is too great to be meaningful, no number appears in this column.

TOTAL COST is the total cost of all items in that category.

% OF TOTAL is each item's percentage of the total cost of the division.

SUMMARIES show general categories of the division's equipment.

COMBAT VEHICLES comprise the largest single expense for most modern armies. Until recently, tanks represented the bulk of this category. With the development of the IFV (Infantry Fighting Vehicle), the armored vehicles for the infantry are looming larger in the equation. IFVs are becoming tanks in their own right. Compared with many tanks of 40 to 50 years ago, modern IFVs have equal or superior firepower. Aircraft assigned directly to the division have become a major factor. More capable drone aircraft accelerate this trend. Currently, armies devote about half their divisional equipment budget to combat vehicles. This ratio is not likely to increase.

OTHER WEAPONS consist primarily of artillery, particularly antitank and antiaircraft artillery. This includes missiles, whose cost is rapidly overwhelming conventional artillery.

OTHER EQUIPMENT is a rapidly growing category, as it includes many electronic items.

SUPPLIES are often overlooked items. Thirty-day stock for the early stage of a war is the accepted standard, although many armies skimp. Such frugality is fatal if a war breaks out. Another potentially serious problem is improper storage and maintenance of these supplies. All these items are perishable and must be rotated. Fuel is the most perishable of all and is generally the best cared for. Ammunition must be fired off regularly and replaced. This is becoming expensive as the cost of missiles and ICM escalates. Often these munitions are rebuilt to incorporate new developments. Storage is another problem, since there is a temptation not to disperse these supplies in protected areas in order to save money. Supply dumps are no secret from the enemy and make ideal targets for aircraft, artillery, and missiles.

PART SEVEN
MOVING
THE GOODS

ONE OF THE more momentous revolutions in warfare during the past century has been the greater capacity to move things. You can't have a world war unless you can quickly move combat forces around the globe.

26

The Navy:
The Tonnage War

IN THE LAST THREE centuries, some nations have found it possible to increase their wealth and military power through the use of extensive naval trade. These nations became known as the oceanic powers. Britain was the first major modern example; Japan and the United States are the latest. Those nations capable of achieving great wealth without naval trade are known as continental powers. First France, then Germany, followed by the Soviet Union, China, and now Russia have assumed this position. When oceanic powers come into conflict with continental powers, the battle comes down to the land-based nation attempting to disrupt the naval trade of the oceanic nation. For over 70 years, the submarine has been the chief means of assaulting naval trade. Guess who still has the world's largest submarine fleet?

The navy is responsible for mobilizing and protecting the civilian merchant fleets in wartime. These merchant ships are needed for moving and maintaining air and ground forces, supplying the navy, and providing the nation's industries with raw materials.

The Tonnage Numbers

Most of the world's merchant shipping, over two thirds, is devoted to moving raw materials in bulk. Over 40 percent of these materials are petroleum. About 30 percent of available shipping can be used to move military supplies and equipment, in addition to tankers taken over to move military fuel. Shipping available for military equipment and supplies equals more than 100 million gross register tons (GRT). To simplify a bit, one gross register ton equals one metric ton of dry military cargo. Want to move a ground-combat division? You'll need 250,000 GRT. Keep it supplied for a month? Another 30,000 to 50,000 GRT, depending on how intense operations are. What about nondivisional troops? Ten GRT per man to get them there. Figure 40,000 nondivisional troops per division, including air force. That's 400,000 GRT. One GRT per man per month for support, another 40,000 GRT. In summary, getting one new division overseas will require 650,000 GRT initially and up to 100,000 GRT a month for support, most of which is tankers. Air-force units require much less shipping, but consume more fuel and munitions during combat. Naval operations are also consumers of enormous resources. Assume one GRT for every two or three displacement tons of combat ships. This will vary, especially with the carriers, according to the intensity of operations and the distance from bases.

To lessen this burden, and save shipping time, the United States has prepositioned the equipment for three divisions in Germany, with smaller stockpiles in Diego Garcia (Indian Ocean) and Guam (Pacific Ocean). Only the troops have to be flown over to make the divisions fully functional. These troops leave 500,000 GRT of divisional equipment behind. This material, and that of up to nine other divisions, can be whipped into shape and shipped within 90 days. Other equipment, and a lot of supply, must be shipped quickly to replace losses and keep the battle going. With the end of the Cold War, the European stockpiles' future is in doubt. Also doubtful are the plans to send massive reinforcements to Europe. By the mid-1990s, the decades-old plans for reinforcements will no longer be possible because of cuts in the defense budgets.

Getting Organized

The navy is responsible for mobilizing, supervising, and safeguarding these movements. Until the end of the Cold War, it was expected that such movements would be made via the stormy North Atlantic and through a gauntlet of Soviet subs. The post–Cold War world poses different problems, the primary ones being the movement of troops and supplies quickly. However, lest we forget, it's important to keep in mind the worst-case situation. Twice in this century, merchant ships have had to fight their way across a submarine-infested Atlantic Ocean. It could happen again.

From the navy's point of view, the biggest problem is lack of control. Although the merchant-shipping fleets are vast, they are not normally under any central control. More than 60 percent of the world's merchant fleet is under the control of companies in eight Western nations. Companies using flags of economic and legal convenience (Liberia, Panama, etc.) control over 25 percent of all shipping. These flags of convenience are largely owned and controlled by U.S. and British companies and often have crews partially composed of U.S. and British citizens. This control does little for the ability to muster these vessels quickly into military service. Let us examine the problems of mobilizing merchant shipping fleets in a military emergency.

1. *Assembling Crews.* Aside from possible problems with unions or noncitizen crews, there is the very basic problem of convincing merchant seamen to serve in a war zone. As losses to enemy action increase, it becomes more difficult to man the ships. It is especially difficult to do so in the winter, when a dunk in the frigid North Atlantic is certain death. Each time a ship goes down, about 25 percent of the crew dies, varying with the severity of the weather and the volatility of the cargoes. The government can offer inducements, such as danger pay and conscription. The best inducement is the ability to protect the ships from enemy attack. All these measures will take a while. Meanwhile, some of the ships, lacking crews, may not move. Modern merchant seaman are primarily technicians; unskilled substitutes will not work.

2. *Mobilizing Merchant Ships.* The bulk of the world's shipping travels a few routes. Two thirds of the total shipping activity moves between North America, Europe, and the Persian Gulf. Add Japan and Australia, and you cover 80 percent of the shipping movements. Less than 3 percent of these ships are needed immediately to support a worst-case situation, a major nonnuclear war in Europe. Certain ships are already under contract to switch over to military service in wartime. However, these ships, as well as most others, are engaged in normal shipping activities and are thus scattered all over the world. The quickest way to get ships is to grab whatever is close by. This disrupts commercial schedules and requires some quick work on the part of governments. Another complication is that few ships are suitable for moving combat vehicles. Most merchant ships are designed to carry liquids, bulk raw materials, or containers. Moreover, many of the tankers are equipped to load and unload at only a few specialized terminals, thus limiting their flexibility. The RoRo (Roll On, Roll Off) ships are needed to most efficiently carry tanks and other military vehicles. Many of these ships are also equipped with loading ramps that can only be used at certain port facilities. How successfully the initial muddle phase is passed will determine how quickly the reinforcing units arrive in the war zone.

3. *Forming Convoys.* This procedure is practiced only during wartime. Forming convoys is like any other technical operation; make mistakes and you pay for it. The basic cost is a lot of ships waiting around for the convoy to proceed. A considerable amount of coordination

has to take place between the military planners, the war material producers, and the convoy-control staff. Based on World War II experience, a convoy schedule would be established. Every few days, so many thousand GRT would go east or west. Coastal-feeder convoys would leave ports up and down the coast for transoceanic-convoy assembly points. So that the scarce and valuable escorts' time would not be wasted, ships that don't make it to the assembly point would have to wait for the next convoy. All this discipline and coordination is not unknown to modern shipping operations. Since World War II, ships have become more conscious that time is money.

4. *Moving Convoys*. The navy cannot afford the expense of much practice with civilian merchant shipping. Some exercises are held to give escorts practice. The biggest problem will be getting civilian shipmasters to conform to the discipline of convoy operations. Steaming in formation and staying calm under combat stress are qualities not usually expected of civilian skippers and crews. Nothing quite prepares one for carrying on while merchant and combat ships explode about you. Mistakes will be made, unnecessary losses will be taken, and eventually hard experience will be won.

Time and Space Variables

In order to organize merchant shipping on a war footing, reallocations will have to be made, quickly. The warship escorts are normally in or near their home ports. Most of the merchant ships are scattered over the worldwide trade routes. It will be an interesting exercise as ships are brought in to the ports from which military units are to embark. It would take a week or two for the military equipment to be moved by rail from their bases to the ports. How efficiently this is handled will not be known until it actually has to happen. There is very little practice for this sort of thing in peacetime. These exercises are expensive and time-consuming. One nation that has practiced this extensively, the United States, was able to move divisions expeditiously to the Persian Gulf in 1990. No other nation has as much experience as the United States in these kinds of moves, and such experience evaporates quickly if the training isn't constantly repeated.

Once convoy operations are under way, the chief variable will be the distances to be traveled and the time urgency of getting the movement done. Steaming at 20 knots (36 kilometers per hour) merchant shipping can move 800 kilometers per day. In wartime, there will be a certain amount of going to and fro to avoid suspected enemy submarines, or land-based air or surface ships. Forming into, and operating as, convoys will lose more travel time. Figure on making some 500 kilometers-per-day headway. Without the threat of enemy action, and using the fastest available commercial shipping, daily headway can be more than doubled.

From the East Coast of the United States to Europe, you must travel 5,500 kilometers. That's 12 days of convoy travel. Depending on the condition of the ports on each end, a few days are needed for loading and unloading. A group of ships and their escorts could make one round trip a month. In the Pacific, it's 8,800 kilometers from the West Coast of the United States to Korea. That's 18 days at sea or two round trips every three months.

Going to the Persian Gulf, and unable to use the Suez Canal, requires a 21,600-kilometer trip from the East Coast of the United States and around South Africa. That's a 44-day journey, or three-and-a-half round trips each year. If the seas are swept free of enemy ships and loading and unloading at each end is optimal, these transit times can be cut by more than half. A common premise is that 90 percent of the tonnage going to a major European war will have to go by sea and the rest by air. This will require 6,000 ships, about 72 million GRT, over a period of six months. At the same time, there will be several times more shipping going each way to support nonmilitary activity, primarily support of the economics on both sides of the ocean.

Theory and Practice

We'll never know how well the Soviet submarine forces could have done in shutting down the North Atlantic shipping lanes. Assuming the Soviets were able to deploy all of their subs against Western shipping, each would have had to sink 20 ships in 90 days to seriously impede NATO operations. This translates to more than six ships sunk per sub per month. It is doubtful that Soviet subs would have been 10 times as effective as the Germans were with their subs in World War II. In their best months during World War II, the Germans barely destroyed one ship for each sub at sea. During their best sustained period, they sank about .7 ships per sub at sea per month. During all of World War II, the Germans managed to sink about two ships for each sub lost. The Soviets, starting World War II with the world's largest submarine fleet, managed to sink less than one ship for each sub lost during 1941–45. Some differences exist between today and the 1940s. Subs have nuclear power and missiles. Antisubmarine forces also have access to nuclear weapons and vastly improved sensors and weapons. Soviet subs also have to get past an array of Western minefields, searching aircraft and waiting subs. It is unlikely that Soviet subs would have sunk anywhere near the required 3,000 ships in 90 days, or 900 days. Even the use of their nuclear torpedoes was unlikely, as this could have caused an escalation that no one would have benefited from.

Further complications arise from the way submarines are deployed during peacetime. The Soviets normally had no more than 20 percent of their subs at sea. To deploy all of them would have been something of an act of war, or a strong indication of same. The Soviets had other options, particularly mines. The Soviets had the world's largest stock of mines and equipped all their subs, ships, and aircraft to deliver them. It doesn't take too many mines to shut down a port. If the ports are too well protected, or equipped with minesweeping equipment, mines can then be dropped in the numerous shallow portions of shipping lanes. All major wars of this century have been decided by the battle against merchant shipping. Whoever wins control of the merchant-shipping lanes wins the war.

So much for a now-defunct future. Since the 1970s, plans had been made for a major shipping effort to the Persian Gulf. During the 1980s, special ships were bought and legal and financial arrangements made to get control of merchant ships to take cargo into a combat zone. Some 20 percent of the cargo arrived in foreign-flag ships. These ships served when called upon, and the legislation already enacted allowing the U.S. government to requisition foreign-flag (but U.S.–owned) ships did not have to be used. These efforts paid off. Without all this behind-the-scenes work, the ground forces would have taken months more to get there; the aircraft would have had fewer bombs to drop and less fuel and fewer spare parts to get them into the air. The war wouldn't have been such a world-class and low-casualty effort without the behind-the-scenes logistical planning and preparations.

To support the war effort, the Allies moved 7 million tons of material to Saudi Arabia. Most came by sea from U.S. ports, while 900,000 tons came from U.S. armed forces stocks in Europe. This was largely stocks of the U.S. 7th Army stationed there since World War II. Throughout the air war, each combat sortie used up more than 10 tons of fuel, munitions, and spare parts (in that order). That's nearly 200,000 tons a day when you include the supplies to support the 130,000 air-force personnel. The ground forces had 30 days of supplies stockpiled for an offensive that, fortunately, was over in a few days.

Fuel turned out to be the major item of supply to be moved. More than 5 million tons of fuel was used, and while much of it was procured locally, a lot had to be shipped in. Before Desert Shield and Desert Storm were over, more than 200 merchant ships were used to move all the ground and air units to the Persian Gulf. Nearly 50 shiploads of material were offloaded in Saudi ports. This included more than 7 million tons of cargo, a third of which was fuel. Although Saudi Arabia is awash in oil, it did not have refineries to produce all the fuels combat units needed. Worse yet, in January half of Saudi Arabia's refining capacity was knocked out by a fire.

By August 15, more than 30,000 marines had been flown into Saudi Arabia and, after a week's steaming from the tiny island of Diego Garcia 2,500 miles to the south, 10 MPS (Maritime Prepositioning Ships) arrived in Saudi ports, and the marines unloaded their equipment, which included trucks, tanks, artillery, and supplies. All this equipment had been stored for years in the air-conditioned holds of the MPS ships. Checked regularly, and thoroughly gone over every 30 months, it was in working order because the marines made the effort to make sure it was always ready.

The first heavy army division to arrive would have to come from North America, more than 15,000 kilometers away. For this purpose, the navy had purchased eight high-speed cargo ships during the 1980s. These civilian ships were capable of steaming at high speed and could carry heavy vehicles (like tanks). The first of these ships arrived at a U.S. port on August 11 and arrived in Saudi Arabia on August 27 with its load of trucks and armored vehicles for the troops of the 24th Infantry Division that had already been flown over. Seven of these fast cargo ships could move one army tank or mechanized division (which are organized almost identically) every 31 days. And this they did, including side trips to Europe to get the U.S. 7th Corps and to replace most of the M-1 tanks previously delivered to Saudi Arabia with the more powerful M-1A1.

The U.S. Navy maintains 24 ships loaded with ground-combat gear (mainly for the marines, but any trained infantry unit can use it). Also held in readiness are two hospital ships and two aviation-support ships, to provide maintenance support for more than 1,000 land-based Marine Corps aircraft and helicopters that can be flown into the combat zone.

The Future

Merchant ships are not likely to get any faster, so increasing reliance will be placed on transport aircraft, amphibious ships, and prepositioning of heavy equipment in order to get combat forces to distant areas quickly. Each of these three options has serious limitations. When push comes to shove, extensive merchant-ship movements are needed to carry the day for any war lasting more than a month. It still takes time to get these movements organized. The United States maintains a special staff that keeps an eye on the world situation and what ships are available for a sudden deployment of forces from North America. Without this organization, the six months available to mass coalition forces in Saudi Arabia during the 1990–91 war would not have been enough.

Prepositioning equipment paid off in the 1991 Gulf War, but you can't preposition equipment everywhere. Amphibious ships carry a limited number of troops (about a division's worth) and are typically scattered all over the globe. Transport aircraft are in limited supply, and require landing facilities at the other end. American transport aircraft can deliver about one infantry division (with most of its heavy equipment) in a few weeks.

Future wars will depend on all of the above to maximize chances of success. But for anything less than a very small military operation, lots of merchant ships will have to be found, loaded with troops and supplies and sent chugging off to the distant battlefield. Any operation that needs more than a division of troops for more than a few weeks will have to fall back on this old standby.

In the wake of the Gulf War, seaborne movement of military forces suddenly got a lot of attention. Specific plans are:

1. The U.S. Navy is building 4–6 more RoRo (Roll On, Roll Off truck and armored-vehicle carriers) ships. This will be added to the eight already available.
2. There already exist 13 Maritime Prepositioning Ships (RoRos with equipment and vehicles stored on board). These can support three U.S. Marine brigades (a total of 50,000 troops) for 30 days.
3. There are also 11 Afloat Prepositioning Ships (nine cargo, two tanker) with supplies for army, navy, and air-force units).
4. The ready reserve of ship transports is being increased from the current 96 ships (83 cargo, 11 tanker, two troop transports) to 142 ships by 1994 (roughly the same ratio). These ships have been held in readiness to be activated in 5, 10, or 20 days. Seventy of these ships were activated for Desert Storm.

World Shipping Capacity and Port Activity

RANK is the ranking of nations by the size of their merchant-marine fleets. Liberia, Panama, and other "flags of convenience" are not included, as the ships flying their flags are not actually controlled by those countries but by shipping companies from Western nations. Britain does include the "flags of convenience" fleets of its colonies.

NATION is the nation of the government or company headquarters controlling the shipping.

MILLION GRT SHIPPING is the amount of shipping controlled, expressed in millions of gross registered tons. Unfortunately, four widely used methods of expressing a ship's size exist. Displacement, how many tons of water the ship displaces, is primarily used for warwhips. Deadweight tonnage is the ship's total carrying capacity in metric tons. A measurement ton is 40 cubic feet of cargo space. Gross register tons are 100 cubic feet of cargo space. One ton (2,200 pounds) of average military cargo takes up 102 cubic feet (approximately one register ton). The deadweight carrying capacity of most ships is closer to 1.6 deadweight tons per register ton. Much military cargo is bulky and not heavy, like trucks, electronic equipment, etc.

% CARGO is the percentage of that nation's shipping that consists of dry cargo vessels, which can carry anything that is prepackaged in bales, boxes, containers. This is a typical cargo, or break bulk, ship. More modern dry cargo ships are designed to carry containers. For example, an eight-by-eight-by-eight-foot container can hold five register tons. Most containers come in variations of this size, being

26-1 Merchant Shipping

Rank	Nation	Million GRT Shipping	% Cargo	% Tanker	% Bulk	Total % of World	Million Tons of Port Activity	% of World
1	Japan	23	19%	37%	43%	5.6%	640	13.20
2	Greece	20	10%	39%	51%	4.7%	30	0.62%
3	Britain	17	20%	44%	36%	4.2%	148	3.05%
4	US	16	42%	54%	4%	3.8%	425	8.76%
5	Norway	16	7%	58%	35%	3.8%	18	0.37%
6	China	13	49%	14%	37%	3.1%	75	1.55%
7	Russia	12	50%	25%	25%	2.9%	450	9.28%
8	Philippines	9	16%	4%	80%	2.1%	25	0.52%
9	Korea (So.)	7	23%	12%	64%	1.8%	130	2.68%
10	Singapore	7	33%	40%	27%	1.7%	72	1.48%
	Flags of Convenience							
	Liberia	47	9%	59%	32%	11.4%	1	0.02%
	Panama	44	32%	26%	41%	10.5%	2	0.04%
	Cyprus	17	20%	27%	53%	4.0%	3	0.06%
	Bahamas	11	15%	59%	26%	2.7%	9	0.19%
	Malta	4	19%	42%	39%	0.9%	1	0.02%
	All Other	152	24%	23%	54%	36.7%	2,821	58.16
	Top 10+	261	23%	39%	38%	63.3%	2,029	41.84
	World Total	413	23%	33%	44%	100%	4,850	
			Cargo	Tanker	Bulk			
	Ships	22,600	12,200	5,100	5,300			
	Per Ship Avg GRT	18,274	7,787	26,863	34,151			

eight-by-eight feet and multiples of eight feet in length. Another increasingly popular type is the RoRo ship (Roll On, Roll Off). These are basically floating parking lots for moving vehicles, both automobiles and cargo trucks. These are ideal for military cargo, and the U.S. Navy bought eight of them during the 1980s. LASH ships carry their own landing craft for loading and unloading at ports that cannot handle large ships. LASH ships are available in break-bulk and container versions and are also well suited for military use. The older "tramp" freighters weigh in at less than 10,000 deadweight tons; many weigh 2,000 tons or less. These smaller ships are found largely in coastal and short-range trade. The more modern RoRo and LASH ships vary from 10,000 to 20,000 tons.

% TANKER is the percentage of that nation's shipping that is capable of carrying only liquids, primarily petroleum, but also sulfur and liquid natural gas. These are very heavy ships; some weigh up to 500,000 deadweight tons. The average is closer to 100,000 tons. Most of these ships move from the Persian Gulf to Europe and Japan.

% BULK is the percentage of that nation's shipping that carries dry bulk cargo only. Typical loads are ores, coal, and grain. These are not as large as tankers but tend to be larger than break-bulk ships.

TOTAL % OF WORLD is the percentage of all the world's shipping controlled by that nation. Liberia, Panama, and so on are flags of convenience; shipping companies establish nominal headquarters in those countries to avoid taxes, high union-wage rates, and other regulations. Most of these ships are owned by companies of the top 10 nations. In wartime, these ships can be brought back under the control of the nations that own them with a little arm-twisting and legislation.

MILLION TONS OF PORT ACTIVITY is the annual activity of that nation's ports in terms of tons of cargo loaded or unloaded. This is a good indication of a nation's dependence on seaborne commerce.

% OF WORLD is the percentage of the world's port activity each nation represents.

ALL OTHER includes the shipping of all other nations not shown in the chart. Note that this group controls only 17 percent of the world's shipping, yet handles more than 50 percent of the world's port activity. These are primarily raw-material-producing nations, the Persian Gulf nations being prime examples.

TOP 10+ are the top 10 countries shown above plus Flags of Convenience. This, in effect, is the merchant fleet of the industrialized Western nations. Three quarters of the world's shipping and nearly half the port activity is found in these nations.

27

The Air Force: Air Freight

SPEED, getting there first with the most, is a valuable military advantage. Air-force transport units exist to deliver this advantage. Technical advances in the last 50 years have made air transportation only about twice as expensive, over long distances, as land movement. This is not a very extravagant expense by military standards. The primary limitation to air transport is the lack of aircraft and the weight and size of military equipment.

Mechanics of Air Transport

The major military nations have large fleets of specialized cargo aircraft. The military and civilian air-transport fleets of the former Soviet Union are still largely intact under the control of Russia. However, the collapse of the Soviet Union's industrial support for the military means that this once-mighty air-transport fleet will gradually waste away before the end of the decade. In any event, in the mid-1990s, Russia and the United States together account for more than 80 percent of all military air-transport capability. Most nations have also made arrangements to militarize their civilian-transport fleets in the event of war. Russian- and U.S.-controlled aircraft account for more than 80 percent of the civilian aircraft that can be taken into military service. How much capacity is available? The U.S. military air transport fleet could lift more than 40,000 tons 5,000 kilometers in one flight. The Russian fleet could lift less than half that. The U.S.-

Allied civilian fleet could lift over 50,000 tons; the former Soviet civilian fleet less than half that. The Soviet civilian fleet is now distributed among the successor states of the Soviet Union, although Russia ended up with more than half the aircraft capacity. A U.S. mechanized-infantry battalion weighs about 2,500 tons, a Russian battalion about 1,500 tons. These weights include the APCs, which can be carried only by large cargo aircraft. The air transports would also carry ammunition, fuel, and other supplies for two or three days' combat. Aircraft-carrying capacity is restricted by size ("cube" or cubic feet) as well as weight. Thus, the movement of commonly used, but large and lightweight, military equipment wastes capacity. Therefore, it will take about 60 C-141 or C-5 aircraft to move a U.S. battalion's vehicles. Civilian aircraft can be used to move most of the remaining men and supplies. Only three wide-bodied passenger aircraft would be required to move the battalion's 900 men, including their personal equipment, weapons, and supplies in the aircraft's cargo containers. Nearly 100 military and civilian aircraft would be required to move this one mechanized-infantry battalion complete with weapons and equipment. You could not move more than five battalions at a time because only about 300 aircraft are available that can carry the armored personnel carriers. Forget about tanks—only the C-5 can carry them, and only one at a time. A tank battalion has 58 tanks, the U.S. Air Force has about that many C-5s ready to fly at any one time. The Russians are somewhat better off. Because of smaller battalions and fewer support vehicles, they require only about 50 aircraft to lift a battalion. They can lift four battalions 5,000 kilometers at any one time. Better yet, Russia's geographical position is closer to any likely areas of conflict. Russia's hot spots are on its frontiers, easily reached from a large network of air bases along its borders. This situation allows the use of shorter-range AN-12 aircraft, thus giving wings to another eight battalions. Because there is no road connection between Moscow and Russia east of the Urals, and only one railroad, air transport assumes critical strategic importance.

If you are content to carry only nonmotorized infantry, the carrying capacity increases quite a bit. War can be waged without tanks, particularly when defending. Antitank missiles (ATGM) weigh, at most, 50 pounds each; mortars can fit into a cargo container. Except in primitive areas, you can commandeer local trucks. Thus, a light-infantry battalion of 900 men armed with 18 120mm mortars, 90 tons of mortar ammo, 60 ATGM launchers and 1,000 missiles, 50 tons of mines plus the usual armament of machine guns, rifles, grenades, sensors, and other supplies, will require only 20 wide-bodied civilian aircraft.

Lift-Capacity Restrictions

These theoretical lift capacities are misleading for several reasons. First, what you can lift is dependent on how far you are going. With an average cruise speed of 500 to 800 kilometers per hour, a 5,000-kilometers "hop" would take seven hours. Landing, unloading, refueling, and reloading take another hour or two. Round-trip flight time: 14 hours. And that's without any but the most routine and perfunctory maintenance. The following typical distances in hours of flying time (at 800 kilometers per hour) do not include refueling stops every 6 to 10 hours for aircraft that cannot refuel in the air.

From Washington D.C. to Berlin—8.5 hours; to Cairo—12; to Istanbul—10.5; to London—7.5; to Madrid—7.5; to Teheran—13; to Persian Gulf—12; to South Africa—16.

From San Francisco to New Delhi—15.5 hours; to Hawaii—5; to Hong Kong—14; to Tokyo—10.5; to Peking—12; to Singapore—17; to Saigon—16.

From Moscow to Berlin—2 hours; to Tokyo—9.5; to Teheran—3; to Nairobi—8; to South Africa—12.5; to Peking—7.5.

It takes seven hours, and 84 tons of fuel, to get a 747 across the North Atlantic. Lift capacity also depends on refueling opportunities. American military aircraft can refuel in the air, most Russian aircraft cannot. No civilian aircraft can refuel in the air. A Boeing-747 wide-body jet burns 12 tons of fuel per hour of flight. There has to be fuel at both ends of the trip, as well as a stock of spares, technicians, and maintenance facilities. There aren't many airfields around capable of handling large transports. These large fields make such good targets for enemy aircraft, missiles, and ground forces. Europe has about 50 that can support long-range aircraft, but most of the refueling and maintenance capacity is concentrated in 30. Losing an airfield is bad enough, when the maintenance and refueling facilities are gone you are worse off because these items are harder to replace. Russia has airfields at no less than 1,000-kilometer intervals along the entire border of the former Soviet Union, except in the arctic north. Russian aircraft can often operate from unpaved fields and with less ground equipment. For example, many Russian aircraft can be refueled without fuel pumps. This takes longer, but eliminates another piece of ground equipment. Russian aircraft often travel with a larger crew containing both flight and maintenance personnel. These aircraft have a lower readiness level for sustained operations, but they can operate under more primitive conditions than Western aircraft. Within Russia, one finds many primitive areas that can be reached only by air and must be serviced by aircraft of this type. For these reasons, Soviet (now Russian) aircraft are favored by many Third World nations, which possess largely primitive support facilities. For this reason, Russia continues to produce and sell some of these Soviet designs.

Helicopters are often used for transport. They can land just about anywhere, but have low carrying capacity (usually under three tons) and short ranges (typically less than 500 kilometers). The entire U.S. helicopter fleet of over 8,000 aircraft could lift about 7,000 tons of weapons and equipment at one time. In function, helicopters have more in common with trucks and APCs than they do with aircraft. Helicopters generally fly within the combat zone, and their bases are also located there. Unlike transport aircraft, they are often armed. Most helicopters perform primarily as combat systems or in direct support of combat units. Not all aircraft are available at all times. As many as 20 percent will be out of service for maintenance. This figure will be higher for most Third World armed forces.

With sufficient flight and ground crews, an aircraft can theoretically be kept going 24 hours a day for a month. After a 12-hour maintenance check, it can go up for another month. Every 3,000 to 4,000 hours the aircraft must be pulled out of service for several hundred hours of overhaul. As a practical matter, such a tempo of operations would soon exhaust available maintenance personnel. Soviet–type aircraft also require maintenance and overhaul more frequently, often three to five times more often, than Western machines. A more practical use pattern is 10 to 12 hours of operations a day, with occasional surges of longer activity and breaks for the 4,000-hour overhauls. This can go on until the 20,000–30,000-hour flight lifetime of an aircraft is reached.

Theory and Practice

During the 1991 Gulf War, the military air transport got a thorough workout. More than 15,000 flights were made by military and civilian aircraft. These delivered nearly 600,000 troops. By March 25, 1991, more than 590,000 tons of cargo had been shipped in by air. Within Saudi Arabia, short-range transports (mainly C-130s) made more than 7,000 flights carrying troops and equipment. Some 65 percent of the personnel and 20 percent of the cargo came in by commercial airliners. Getting the troops out after the war saw commercial airliners moving 85 percent of the personnel and 45 percent of the cargo. At its peak, 110 commercial aircraft were being used for Gulf operations. Because of the tempo of operations, with aircraft in use more than 15 hours a day, four crews were required for each aircraft, and often this was not enough.

Several hundred civilian transport pilots were also air-force reserve pilots. Scheduling gets tricky once these lads are called up. The several months of peak activity during the 1990–91 Gulf operations were handled by shuffling people around a lot and getting permission to have pilots sometimes fly more hours per month than normally allowed.

Military transports are built somewhat differently than civilian transports and thus have dissimilar operating characteristics. Civil transports are built to operate continually from well-equipped commercial airports. They are also built to carry passengers, plus cargo in containers. Some aircraft are freighters; others are convertible from freighter to passenger service. Military transports are built to operate more spasmodically from crude airfields. Their layout is for loading vehicles and a secondary mission of carrying passengers. Keeping commercial airports intact will pay large dividends in a future war as it will allow civil transports to carry a lot of the load and preserve the military transports for those missions only they can perform. A major advantage in the Gulf War was the availability of first-class commercial airports in Saudi Arabia. Without these facilities, the amount of people and cargo landed would have been much less.

Most of the technology for air transports comes from the United States, the leading producer of such aircraft. The Soviet Union followed the United States in this area as best it could, copying and adapting American technology. As a result, Soviet aircraft were less efficient load carriers. Ton for ton of aircraft weight, Western aircraft can carry greater loads longer distances and with more reliability. Soviet aircraft required more ground support to sustain the same level of operations. Most Western aircraft require three or four man-hours of maintenance per flight hour. Soviet aircraft required more than that. Even so, Soviet aircraft were more prone to breakdowns and accidents. Soviet aircraft often had an additional crewmember just to keep an eye on potential maintenance problems.

In the wake of the Soviet Union's collapse, the Soviet aircraft industry is rebuilding itself along Western lines. Some aspects of Soviet transport design were quite good, especially the airframes. It was Soviet engines that caused the most problems. Like many non-U.S. aircraft manufacturers, the Russians (who inherited most of the Soviet aircraft industry) are buying engines from the West and negotiating to build Western engines in their plants under license. The Russians are also making the most of their technological lead in building rugged transports to specialize in this area. Short-range transports, built to land at primitive front-line fields, may become a Russian specialty.

Aircraft maintenance is a massive undertaking, requiring extensive facilities, skilled technicians, and large stocks of spares. More recent aircraft designs are notable for their lower maintenance requirements. In many respects, the Soviet designs had pulled up close to Western standards. They were forced to put more effort into automated maintenance equipment because of their general lack of competent mechanics and maintenance supervisors. These efforts were hobbled by the usual Soviet problems in manufacturing reliable equipment. Yet this was a typically pragmatic Soviet reaction to a problem. It didn't work as well as it could, but it worked.

All transport aircraft have instruments that continually monitor all systems whenever the aircraft is operating. Before takeoff, crew and maintenance personnel run through checklists of items to be monitored. Every 50 or 60 flight hours, the maintenance personnel spend several hours going over the aircraft more thoroughly. Marginal items are fixed before they become critical. Every 300 to 600 flight hours, an overnight check is performed, requiring about 100 man-hours. Expendable items are often replaced, and some major items are partially disassembled. Sometimes more serious conditions are discovered, and more extensive maintenance is performed. This is also one of those times when some upgrades and equipment modifications are performed. On many older Soviet aircraft, this check often requires replacement of entire engines, a tangible aspect of their deficiencies in engine technology.

After 3,000 to 4,000 hours, the aircraft disappears into the hangar for several days. Most major components are disassembled, and many items are replaced. This is when major maintenance and upgrades take place; items such as new interiors, paint jobs, or electronics are installed. It is at this point that many Western aircraft replace engines, which are then rebuilt for installation in another aircraft.

The average Western civilian aircraft flies 3,000 to 4,000 hours a year and has a useful life of 20 or more years. This level of activity requires six different air crews working the aircraft in shifts. Because aircraft are so well taken care of, and practically rebuilt over their lifetime, many are still performing reliably after 40 years of service. A classic example is the 50-year-old DC-3. This twin-engine transport is still the backbone of many small Third World airlines. With good maintenance, this aircraft can continue flying into the next century. Many twenty-year-old four-engine 707s are still flying. Of the 9,000 commercial jets built since 1959, nearly 70 percent are still in use. Fewer than 400 have been lost to accidents. The loss rate per 100,000 flight hours has been less than .3. This is about one-tenth the loss rate of combat aircraft in peacetime. Commercial aircraft are worked hard, and maintained with equal diligence. Military aircraft are equally durable. Thirty-year-old B-52s and 20-year-old F-4s are common. The biggest danger to military aircraft are the rigors of practicing for combat. Military transports are not used as intensively as their civilian counterparts. Military transports often fly less than 1,000 hours a year, most of it just for training. While civil transports require an average of seven mechanics to keep them going, lower military usage allows for half the number of mechanics to keep the aircraft operational.

The Future

The V-22 Osprey, an aircraft that combines the best characteristics of a helicopter and a fixed-wing transport, was due for wide use in the early

1990s for short-range tactical transportation. Even before the Cold War abruptly ended, the V-22 was in trouble because of its cost. After 1991, the V-22 became a political issue, with the Congress wanting it for the patronage its manufacturing jobs created and the Pentagon not wanting it because it felt there were other items that were more needed in the age of rapidly shrinking defense budgets. If the V-22 is forced upon the military, it won't be the first time this sort of thing happened. The impact of the V-22 will not be major, as it's unlikely the politicians can force the military to build a lot of them. Those few helicopter carriers that do get the V-22 will have a more potent aircraft capability. Before the end of the decade, we may even see what the V-22 can do under fire.

America is also planning to introduce the C-17, a replacement for the C-141. This aircraft would halve the time it would take to land a light-infantry division in a Third World country. Budget problems—that is, not enough money to buy everything the armed forces wants—will delay the replacement of the C-141 by the C-17. By the end of the decade, C-17s will still be dribbling off the production lines.

The Western commercial aircraft fleet is still growing and is currently nearly 7,000 aircraft, 15 percent of which are heavy long-distance models. Western air forces continue to push for closer cooperation between military transport services and civil air lines. In general, no major breakthroughs are coming in air transport. More efficient engines, easier maintenance, and lower operating costs are what the future holds for this maturing industry.

Strategic Military Airlift

Chart 27-1 shows the strategic military transport aircraft available to the major military powers. Only the United States has a significant fleet of strategic-transport aircraft. The Russian (formerly Soviet) strategic-transport aircraft fleet is closely integrated with the national airline, Aeroflot. However, Aeroflot was taken apart to a large extent with the breakup of the Soviet Union, and many of its aircraft are now owned and operated by the other (than Russian) successor states of the Soviet Union. The U.S. Air Force fleet could be called the world's largest airline, at least in terms of lift capacity. Not included are the twin-engined tactical transports that equip most other nations' air-transport fleets. Most of these lift five tons or less. Few nations have more than 20 or 30 of them. These are transports designed for combat-zone movement of men, equipment, and supply. This is short-range work, 1,000 kilometers or less.

OF AIRCRAFT simply adds up the total number of aircraft each nation has of the types shown on the chart. Many types are still in production or extensive overhaul and upgrade. The AN-72 was designed for very short landing and takeoff.

TONS CARGO (X 1000). Total cargo-carrying capacity times 1,000 tons.

TOTAL IN USE is all aircraft in service.

U.S. % of TOTAL shows the United States' advantage over Russia. Substantial qualifications exist to this seeming advantage. Nearly half of the U.S. aircraft are tankers (KC-135, KC-10). These can also carry cargo, but the bulk are assigned to provide air refueling for combat aircraft. These tankers are frequently shifted to support of transports. Another factor to consider is that transport-carrying capacity decreases as range increases.

AIRCRAFT CHARACTERISTICS give the operating characteristics of each type of aircraft.

PASSENGERS are the number of seats installed and available for troops. These seats are usually temporary, easily removed, or folded into the wall to make room for cargo.

CARGO (TONS) is the average cargo load that can be carried. Containers are often used, although military transports are primarily designed to accommodate military vehicles. The largest military transport aircraft can even move tanks (C-5, Il-76, AN-2, AN-124), although rarely more than two at a time. It is far more efficient to carry lighter military vehicles like trucks, APCs, guided-missile launchers, and artillery, moving by air, etc. The Soviets employed just such an airlift when they went into Afghanistan in 1979. Pallets of ammunition are another favorite cargo. Most of these aircraft have large doors in the rear that can be opened in flight. Their cargoes can be landed with parachutes.

AVERAGE RANGE (KM) is the average range with a full cargo load. An empty aircraft with a full load of fuel can go 20 percent to 60 percent beyond its full-load range. An important difference between civil and military transports is that civil aircraft operate one-way trips. They refuel at their destination. Military transports normally drop or land their cargo and then return without refueling. Typically, their only refueling opportunity along the way is in flight with a tanker.

EMPTY WEIGHT (TONS) is aircraft weight without fuel or payload. A glance at the potential fuel capacity, possible cargo capacity, and maximum takeoff weight shows the trade-offs that have to be made. Military transports must be able to move very heavy loads for short distances or lighter loads over long hauls. They carry extra weight in their structure to support the heavy loads, and this heavier structure makes them less efficient than comparable, and lighter, civil transports.

MAX TAKEOFF WEIGHT (TONS) is the maximum takeoff weight of the aircraft. This indicates the aircraft's size. The C-5 (347 tons), for example, is 245 feet long, 65 feet high, with a wingspan of 223 feet. The C-141B (155 tons) is 168 feet long, 39 feet high, with a wingspan of 160 feet. The C-17A (265 tons) is 174 feet long, 55 feet high, with a wingspan of 165 feet. The AN-22 (250 tons) is 190 feet long, 41 feet high, and has a span of 211 feet. The C-130 (79 tons) is 98 feet long, 38 feet high, and has a span of 133 feet.

MAX FUEL LOAD (TONS) demonstrates that the primary cargo of military transport aircraft is fuel. Large quantities can be carried without sacrificing space by putting almost all fuel in the wings. A major problem in wartime is getting these large quantities of fuel where they are needed when they are needed.

MINIMUM AIRFIELD LENGTH (M) is the minimum-size airstrip needed for takeoff. Takeoff always requires a longer airfield than landing. Taking off with maximum load requires 30 percent to 40 percent more space than that in the chart. To get off the ground in the shortest possible space, the aircraft will have to go half-loaded.

IN-FLIGHT REFUELING? This indicates whether or not the aircraft can refuel in flight. The tankers transfer more of their own fuel than the additional fuel they carry in their cargo spaces. The KC-135, a militarized 707, normally carries 73 tons of fuel plus another 15 tons as cargo. The aircraft can draw upon all fuel carried for its own engines. Depending on how far the aircraft has to travel, it can transfer up to 90 percent of its total fuel load. The larger KC-10 normally carries 108 tons, plus another 53 tons as cargo. Of this 161 tons, some 90 tons are available for transfer. The most efficient use of tankers is to allow aircraft to take off with maximum weapons or cargo load, but not maximum fuel load. Once airborne, the fuel tanks can be filled to the point that the aircraft can still fly, but would actually be too heavy to take off. Tankers can also meet aircraft returning from a mission and refuel those that are short of fuel. This is often the case with aircraft that have had to use high-speed, high-fuel-consumption maneuvers in combat. Cargo aircraft can be refueled on long flights so they won't have to land and refuel. Sometimes there is no place to land, and in-flight refueling is the only option. The quantity of fuel that large aircraft carry is shown on this chart and on the similar one for civilian transports. By far the worst offender is the B-52, which carries 141 tons of fuel. For this reason, two tankers are typically assigned to each B-52. Smaller combat aircraft are at the other extreme. Fuel load for the F-4 is 6 tons; for the F-16, 3 tons; for the F-15, 5 tons; for the F-18, 5 tons; for the A-6, 7 tons, and for the F-14, 7 tons. To accommodate the larger number of combat aircraft that can be refueled by one tanker, the KC-10 may be equipped to refuel three aircraft at once.

Wartime Use of Civilian Aircraft, Long-Range Heavy-Lift Models

Chart 27-2 shows the heavy-lift aircraft available for military use. The aircraft shown are those that can be easily and quickly militarized. These are primarily the long-range fleets of the major airlines. The United States manufactures over 90 percent of the aircraft in the West. Russia manufactures all those shown as East. American airlines have access to nearly 50 percent of Western aircraft, and could probably make arrangements to charter more of the remainder. Russia has similar access to more than 80 percent of Eastern aircraft. It is assumed that local air service will be maintained with shorter-range aircraft not shown on this chart— Boeing-727, DC-9/MD-80, Boeing-737, etc. Under (major) wartime conditions, all nonessential travel will be curtailed, and aircraft will fly with nearly all seats occupied, instead of 50 percent in peacetime.

27-1 Strategic Military Airlift

Aircraft Lift

Nation	# of Aircraft	Tons Cargo (x,1000)	Pass.
Russia	817	28	83
US	1,579	60	245
Totals	2,396	88	328
US % of Total	66%	68%	75%

"Russia" includes all former USSR as of 1990.

Aircraft Types (Long Range, Heavy Lift Models)

Nation	C5	C141	C130	KC135	C123K	KC10	C17	An74	IL76	An124	An22	An26	An12
Russia								12	420	25	50	210	100
US	112	250	510	650	0	55	2						

Aircraft Characteristics

	C5	C141B	C130	KC135	C123K	KC10	C17	An74	IL76	An124	An22	An26	An12
Passengers	345	168	220	80	260	0	102	32	90	415	330	40	100
Cargo (tons)	120	41	34	22	38	85	59	8	40	150	80	5	20
Average Range (km)	4,800	6,400	4,600	3,700	2,200	7,000	5,200	1,000	6,000	5,000	5,000	2,400	4,000
Empty Weight (tons)	151	66	33	45	14	109	117	16	100	170	110	15	28
Max Takeoff Weight (tons)	349	156	79	135	27	268	258	30	170	405	250	24	61
Max Fuel Load (tons)	130	72	30	73	12	53	62	6	66	230	43	6	15
Minimum Airfield Length (m)	2,600	1,000	1,100	2,800	1,100	3,300	1,000	500	850	3,000	1,300	800	700
In-flight Refueling?	Yes	Yes	No	No	No	No	Yes	No	No	No	No	No	No

Average Tons per man for Division Types: US Light Infantry-1.2, US Mech Infantry- 1.8 Russian Mech Infantry- 1.6, Airborne (all nations)- .4

OF AIRCRAFT simply adds up the total number of aircraft of the types shown on the chart. Of these types, most are still in production.

TONS CARGO is given in thousands of tons. Civilian aircraft are designed to carry passengers plus cargo containers in those spaces not suitable for passengers. About 20 percent are equipped to carry cargo only. Even these aircraft normally carry only freight containers that are preloaded to improve efficiency. Civilian aircraft operate on a fast turnaround. This container system limits the military cargo that a civilian aircraft can carry. Most military equipment is too big to fit in these containers. However, many items of military equipment can fit in the containers, including electronic parts, some missiles, spare parts, some munitions and so on.

PASS is the passengers, given in thousands. The transportation of troops makes civilian aircraft very valuable. The United States has proposed sending light-infantry units, troops and weapons together, overseas using only civilian aircraft. Each passenger represents about 300 pounds of load. You can substitute about 500 pounds of cargo for each passenger in convertible aircraft. The "convertibles" are aircraft designed to fly either passengers or cargo by changing modules inside the aircraft.

TOTALS show the total cargo and passenger capacity.

TOTAL "WEST" includes all those nations that use Western aircraft.

TOTAL "EAST" includes all those nations that use Russian (formerly Soviet) aircraft.

AIRCRAFT CHARACTERISTICS gives the average characteristics of each type of aircraft. More so than military aircraft, civilian aircraft are built in many variations. Averages are perfectly suitable if you are dealing with large numbers of aircraft.

PASSENGERS are the number of seats installed for peacetime operations. Given enough time, more seats could be put in with a less luxurious standard. Yes, fellow air travelers, it can get worse.

CARGO (TONS) is the average cargo load that can be carried in their cargo spaces, in containers. Modern aircraft are weight, not space, limited.

AVERAGE RANGE (KM) is the average range with a full passenger load. An empty aircraft with a full load of fuel can go 20 to 60 percent farther. Commercial aircraft must maintain fuel reserves to allow for landing at another airport in case of foul weather or heavy traffic. These reserves can add up to 1,000 kilometers to an aircraft's range.

EMPTY WEIGHT (TONS) is aircraft weight without fuel or payload. A glance at the potential passenger load (at 300 pounds each), fuel capacity, possible cargo capacity, and maximum takeoff weight reveals that everything won't go into the

27-2 Civilian Transport Aircraft

Aircraft Types

Aircraft Lift

	# of Aircraft	Tons Cargo (x1,000)	Pass.
Total "West"	2,475	110	621
Total "East"	1,770	32	193

Aircraft Characteristics

	Boeing 757	767	Airbus A300	747	L-1011	DC-10	DC-8	707	IL-86	IL-76	IL-62M	TU-154	AN-26	AN-12
Passengers	180	211	220	350	220	260	200	150	240	90	170	160	40	100
Cargo	20	34	34	75	38	46	30	12	42	40	23	18	5	20
Average Range (km)	4,400	5,200	4,600	9,000	6,000	6,000	7,000	7,200	4,200	6,000	8,000	3,200	2,400	4,000
Empty Weight (tons)	59	74	78	177	110	120	65	65	120	100	68	51	15	28
Max Fuel (tons)	33	48	44	150	73	112	71	73	65	66	85	40	6	15
Max Takeoff Weight (tons)	108	136	150	370	210	252	152	153	195	170	162	94	24	61
Max Load Capacity (tons)	80	114	111	278	144	197	131	108	143	120	134	82	17	50
Practical Load (tons)	49	62	72	193	100	132	87	88	75	70	94	43	9	33
With Full Fuel (tons)	16	14	28	43	27	20	16	15	10	4	9	3	4	18

Flight Distances (km)

NY to Paris-5798/Montreal to Ireland-4600/London to Rome-1420/Rome to Cairo-2120/Cairo to Tehran-2000/Moscow to Berlin-1650/Moscow to Baghdad-2600/Montreaal to Iceland-3800/Iceland to London-2000/Moscow to Beijing-5900/California to Hawaii-3900/Hawaii to Tokyo-6200/Tokyo to Beijing-2100/NY to Cairo- 9100 air at once. This is intentional when the plane is designed; tradeoffs must be made during aircraft operations.

MAX FUEL LOAD (TONS) demonstrates that the primary cargo of commercial aircraft is fuel. Most of this fuel is carried within the wings, leaving other space for crew and cargo.

MAX TAKEOFF WEIGHT (TONS) is the maximum takeoff weight of the aircraft. It indicates the aircraft's size. The 747 (370 tons), for example, is 232 feet long, 63 feet high, with a wingspan of 196 feet. The 707 (151 tons) is 153 feet long, 42 feet high, with a span of 146 feet. The Tu-154 (94 tons) is 157 feet long, 37 feet high, with a span of 123 feet. The AN-26 (24 tons) is 78 feet long, 28 feet high, with a span of 96 feet. We are dealing with very large machines.

MAX LOAD CAPACITY (TONS) is the weight of everything you can get onto the aircraft. It includes passengers, cargo, and fuel. Because of takeoff weight limits, you can't take it all. This number gives a good indication of the aircraft's capacity and flexibility.

PRACTICAL LOAD (TONS) is what you can get off the ground as cargo and fuel. This is the maximum takeoff weight less the weight of the empty aircraft. This is an indicator of the aircraft's actual lift capacity.

WITH FULL FUEL (TONS) is the practical load when carrying a full fuel load. It indicates the long-distance carrying capacity of the aircraft.

FLIGHT DISTANCES (KM) give point-to-point flying distances in kilometers. What this points out is that with sufficient airfields along the way, it is possible to cover long distances with short-range aircraft or with long-range aircraft carrying heavier loads. For this reason, Iceland is very important to the United States and Western Europe. Hawaii is important to the United States. Russia's internal network of airfields in remote, unsettled areas is a considerable advantage.

PART EIGHT

TOOLS OF THE TRADE

WITH MORE THAN 100 million active and reserve troops under arms, nearly a trillion dollars a year in military spending, and tens of thousands of tanks, aircraft, ships, and other major items of equipment, we must summarize.

28

The Weapons of the World

THE STATISTICS OF weapons performance, by themselves, will do you little good. At best, analytical and subjective evaluations of weapons will tell you what they can, or simply might, do. This chapter will briefly discuss the general effectiveness of weapons. More important, one must consider why weapons often do not work. Of even greater interest and importance is the frequency with which weapons do not function as the users think they are functioning.

Untried Technology

Weapons are often conceived, designed, manufactured, and used in a triumph of hope over experience. This was less true in the past, when weapon designs persisted for hundreds of years. When weapons were around for centuries, their capabilities became well known. Changes were minor, and generally made small improvements in performance. All this has changed in the past century. Weapons rarely work as intended the first time they are used. History is full of examples. The first machine guns overlooked the fact that the barrel would soon overheat from use. More changes, but not fast enough for the troops using them first. The first bayonets were attached to the musket by plugging them into the barrel. Fine in theory, but troops would forget to take them out before firing their weapons. The results were disastrous, and the design was soon changed.

The use of bayonets revealed a more subtle form of misperception. For all their fearsome reputation, bayonets cause few casualties. When longer-range rifles were introduced in the 1850s, bayonets were used even less. Yet bayonets are issued and troops trained in their use to this day. Slowly, leaders learned that bayonets were less a weapon than a morale-building device and battlefield tool. For most of this century, the bayonet was actually a hazard to its users. In hand-to-hand fighting, troops tend to use their rifles as a club. With a bayonet attached and swung like a club, the bayonet had a tendency to cut the user. This is what the troops reported, at least the survivors.

Often the misperceptions are expensive. The modern battleship, heavily armored, with many large guns and a price tag to match, were built in large quantities. Some 170 were built between 1906 and 1945 at a cost of 200 billion 1993 dollars. These were supposed to be the primary naval weapon, yet most never saw action against another battleship. Battleships were rarely exposed to combat; they were literally too expensive to lose. Although 55 sank, only 5 were sunk by other battleships. Some 17 percent of the losses were accidents, usually by an explosion while in port. Aircraft got 44 percent. Submarines, torpedo boats, and other ships got 10 percent. Torpedoes accounted for 38 percent, generally delivered by an aircraft. Originally designed to secure control of the oceans, they spent most of their time fearfully hiding out in port. Cheaper weapons—aircraft, submarines, and mines—made the high seas too dangerous for the big ships. During World War II, the aircraft carrier decisively demonstrated the ineffectiveness of battleships as the premier warship. Before this lesson was learned, a record was set for expenditure on a weapon for so little return in battlefield effectiveness. The battleship fiasco was bad, but electronics set the stage for truly monumental high costs and low benefits. Electronics have become the major component of aircraft, ships, and, increasingly, land weapons. Electronics, because of their expense and complexity, are tested less thoroughly than cheaper weapons. Rapid developments in electronics make weapons using them obsolete more quickly. Entire classes of weapons are developed, built, and retired without ever seeing combat. Unlike battleships, most electronics-based weapons cannot be replaced with something simpler and cheaper. This creates a ruinously expensive competition that no one can afford to drop out of. While the expense strains budgets, the uncertain effectiveness of these weapons confronts commanders with unprecedented problems. Not knowing with any certainty how their electronic weapons, or those of their opponents, will perform, battlefield leaders have a more difficult time planning for combat. The nature of the uncertainty is complicated by the extent and nature of countermeasures used. This is a problem that will only get worse. The more flexible soldiers will prevail, but only after a lot of headaches and frustration. Testing weapons successfully has become the most important battleground for armed forces. War is a sometime event; peacetime conditions are more the norm. The urgency of effective testing is slowly becoming accepted. America has taken the lead in this area, mandating greater use of simulators and testing of weapons against facsimiles of anticipated opponents' systems. Taking testing to its logical solution and using large quantities of weapons during tests is still horrendously expensive. The lesson of sweating more in peacetime so as to bleed less on the battlefield is a lesson not yet fully accepted.

World War II Versus Today

When we think of a future war between the major powers, we think of World War II. World War II was the last war between major nations and the last war involving large-scale air, land, and naval forces. However, World War II is less and less likely as a benchmark for future conflict because of the increasing accumulation of changes in the nearly half-century that has passed since that last large-scale war. Although massive wars in the Third World still appear remarkably like World War II battles, the major powers have not unleashed their heavily refurbished arsenals on each other during that period. With this in mind, we can still compare today's armed forces to the last "Big War."

INFANTRY WEAPONS

These have changed little since World War II, except for a lot more automatic weapons being used. Nearly every infantryman now has an automatic weapon, a policy the Germans were implementing at the end of World War II. Since most troops have been equipped with automatic weapons, they have become more likely to use their weapons. This has created problems with uncontrolled use of weapons and, at times, ammunition-supply problems. Mortars, grenades, and machine guns are basically the same, with many incremental improvements. The only radically new items have been electronic. These are primarily sensors, especially radars and night scopes, plus navigation and communications gear. The new sensors are used primarily in prepared defenses. The new communications equipment is also not widely used. But for U.S. and other Western armies that do have GPS and jam-resistant radios, the average infantryman on patrol, or otherwise on his own, has seen electronics become a major factor in making battlefield life easier.

Antitank weaponry has seen a major jump in performance, and has moved away from being an infantry weapon. The World War II rocket launchers are still with us, although improved in performance. Tanks have developed thicker skins, and this gave rise to the antitank guided missile. Some of these weapons were not portable at all, but required a vehicle to carry them. Those that were portable were only marginally so. Meanwhile, tanks became better protected. Not just thicker armor, but better armor, like composite (Chobham) and add-on armor (spaced or reactive). More important for the infantry are the changes in tank tactics. To make themselves less vulnerable to nuclear weapons and other wide-area munitions, tanks now operate spread out, with distances up to 100 meters separating them. Moreover, tanks have learned that they must operate in close cooperation with infantry. In other words, the situations where infantry face tanks alone would be the exception. Moreover, the portable antitank weapons the infantry possess are, like their World War II counterparts, best used against the sides or rear of tanks. The rear shot in particular gives the infantry a good chance of evening the odds. Because tank crews can see little from inside their vehicles, a rear shot is not impossibly difficult to arrange in a confused situation. In line with the changes in antitank warfare, there has also been a wholesale mechanization of infantry since World War II. While the troops spend most of their time outside their armored vehicles, their APCs and IFVs are always handy, along with the heavier weapons they carry. These vehicles often have small turrets with automatic cannon. In effect, these vehicles often function like light tanks. Indeed, many are heavier than most tanks used in the early days of World War II. Experience so far has shown that the infantry is still most effective when outside their armored vehicles. The modern battlefield is crowded with a lot more armored vehicles. The only place you find infantry operating alone is in terrain unsuitable for armored vehicles.

TANKS

During World War II, there were frequent instances where one side had a tank model possessing frontal armor that was invulnerable to the other side's antitank weapons, at least for a while. This can still happen, as was the case in the 1991 Gulf War. The invulnerability of U.S. tanks in the Gulf was largely a result of the Iraqis using homemade tank shells against the latest U.S. armor design. Moreover, the fighting in the desert made it more difficult for the defending Iraqi tanks to get shots at the thinner side or rear armor of U.S. tanks. Generally, however, the little ditty "What you can see, you hit, and what you hit, you kill" succinctly sums up the situation in tank warfare. At least for tanks and their large guns. The unarmored antitank weapons used by the infantry are the first to fall short when a new defensive measure is introduced for tanks. Aside from being more vulnerable, tanks have more company. Far more are available today than during World War II, in addition to an even larger number of lighter armored vehicles. In some respects, this is helpful. All these additional armored vehicles "draw fire," as armored vehicles always have. Thus, individual armored vehicles don't stand out as much today as they did during World War II. Alas, all those heavy, tracked vehicles tear up the battlefield to such an extent that everyone has a hard time getting around. Since World War II, tanks have become twice as heavy and not quite twice as fast, agile, or reliable. Modern tanks contain far more electronics and have smaller crews. The latest generation of tanks has shown uncommon ability to flit around the battlefield. American combat-training devices, the ones that use lasers to score hits, have provided realistic training that, in turn, has revealed that these new tanks can operate remarkably more efficiently in combat. These same vehicles have mature and well-tested fire-control devices that are far more effective than anything available in the past. These new training devices combined with the new tanks produced amazing results on the battlefield during the 1991 Gulf War.

ARTILLERY

More artillery is self-propelled. The average caliber is now closer to 155mm than 105mm. Improved transportation allows greater tonnages of munitions to be fired, and fired farther. The munitions themselves have become two, three, or more times as effective thanks to ICM (Improved Conventional Munitions). Because of the cost of the modern stuff, many armies still have essentially World War II–era guns firing World War II–style munitions. Such nations are at a great disadvantage against modern artillery, particularly because of the more efficient artillery-spotting radars and computer-controlled fire. The rich guys have some very deadly stuff. The Iraqis discovered this in 1991.

THE AIR FORCE

Dramatic changes have taken place since World War II. Modern aircraft fly more than three times faster, more than 50 percent higher, and carry more than three times more munitions. Range and reliability have increased, and the most common air-to-air weapon is now the missile. For all this, air combat has changed little. Because of physical restrictions, combat usually takes place at speeds only about 50 percent greater than World War II. Bombing still takes place at slow speeds, primarily because the pilot can't see much if they go any faster. Electronic bombing and air-combat aids have helped, but have not proved a perfect solution to the complications of air warfare. Despite the repeated promises that electronics will make it all better, pragmatic pilots retain their cannon and skills at close-in fighting. Munitions, particularly bombs, have become up to five times as effective as their World War II predecessors. It also takes far fewer people to do the work. A World War II four-engine bomber, the B-17, weighed 25 tons and carried 7 tons of bombs and a crew of 11. A 25-ton F-15E fighter carries over 11 tons of bombs and a crew of 2. The replacement for the B-17, the 35-year-old B-52, can carry over 25 tons of bombs. Far fewer aircraft are available today, and they take five times longer to build (at wartime rates). The F-15, for example, takes 18 months to build in peacetime. In wartime, that might be brought down to three months, but no one has tried it, so no one really knows.

THE NAVY

In World War I, navies put most of their money into battleships, although submarines did most of the fighting. During World War II, aircraft carriers received most of the attention, although it was submarines that shut down the Japanese economy and came close to doing the same to Britain's. If a major war started tomorrow, aircraft carriers would still be the most prominent symbol of naval power, along with their numerous escorts. But today the biggest threat is from nuclear-powered submarines. However, submarines have serious problems. For one thing, they don't communicate too well when submerged. And most of the time, they are under water. Although subs are equipped with missiles that can attack land and naval targets at long ranges, they carry fewer munitions than surface ships. Basically, a nuclear submarine functions best as a lone operator, stalking prey in its own killing zone. A nuclear sub has a difficult time telling if the ship it is going after is enemy or friendly. You don't direct the operations of submarines; you unleash them to sweep an area clear of any ships or subs. Think of a nuclear submarine as a mobile naval mine with a well-trained and intelligent crew. All of this is even more troublesome because nuclear subs have no wartime experience. A British nuclear sub's sinking of an Argentine cruiser in 1982 is all the combat experience these boats have. Under wartime conditions, changes will be made in the face of the unexpected. This is as it has always been, and nuclear submarines and sailors in general feel a bit uneasy over it.

The other dramatic change in navies since World War II has been the enormous growth of electronics in every area of naval operations. The computer operators and technicians are the naval warriors of today. Seamanship had been playing a declining role in naval operations for over a century. This trend continues. Electronics can tell ships how to avoid nasty weather but still does not provide a cure for seasickness when the ocean reminds sailors whose backyard they are playing in.

AMPHIBIOUS OPERATIONS

It's comforting to see that some things don't change. Aside from improved amphibious shipping and landing craft, the only new development has been helicopters. The marines also have whatever new weapons and equipment their land-based brethren have. Amphibious operations are faster and, because of the threat of nuclear and chemical weapons, plan on being smaller than those during World War II.

AIR DEFENSE

Current air-defense composition is an odd mixture of the familiar World War II and a form of science fiction known as SAM (Surface-to-Air Missiles). The World War II cannon type of air defense is still used, in some cases with original weapons. More often, the small-caliber (under 75mm) cannon is controlled by radar and computerized fire-control systems. Manual override keeps these systems honest, and minimally effective. It still requires several tons of cannon shell for each aircraft brought down. SAMs have great potential. At least 1 in 50 will hit its target. Radar screens blink, obscure jargon is muttered, at times sounding like prayers, and, far from the darkened rooms, missiles climb skyward by remote control. So far, the electronic-warfare countermeasures and pilot agility have held the upper hand. This is small comfort to pilots, who must entrust their lives to a lot of black boxes. Aircraft are hit by SAMs. And the SAMs are getting better. Most of the SAM's bad reputation comes from the well-publicized failures of Soviet systems in Vietnam and the Middle East. Less well known is how much more effective Western systems have been. The trend is to let pilotless aircraft penetrate areas well covered by SAMs and cannon. Let the machines kill each other off. This may be a portent of the future.

AT THE MOVIES

We gather our impressions of weapon effectiveness from our daily exposure to the media. The worst offenders are films and TV shows. First, films quite naturally depict World War II more frequently than potential contemporary conflict. Because the appearance of World War II weapons does not differ radically from current ones, we tend to equate their performance with what we can expect in current wars. This is not too far off the mark, as the rest of this chapter demonstrates. But weapons have changed. To further muddle our perceptions, films enhance weapon effects in order to increase their visual impact on the screen. Weapons effects in films are more like fireworks displays than reality. For example, real artillery explosions are smaller and lack flames. When bullets pass close by, they make a pronounced crack as they break the sound barrier, a sound that is no doubt deleted in films so as not to disturb the dialogue. Films show bullets hitting the ground and walls with little explosions. This is because small explosives are used to produce this effect. In reality, most of those bullets hit with dull little thuds. Some of these are people getting hit. Of course, films cannot re-create the most crucial elements of combat, such as fatigue, the smell, and paralyzing fear. All this extra noise is no doubt suppressed so that the dialogue can be heard. Real combat is noisy, although all many soldiers hear is their hearts pounding loudly. Real combat is distracting, making it difficult to follow any plot. Real combat is not very entertaining, even if you are only an observer. Worst of all, soldiers always appear more in control of the situation in films than they are in real battles. This is a dangerous misconception for the young soldier entering his first battle. Watching *Rambo* is misleading; watching the movie *Platoon* is a lot more accurate. *Platoon*'s combat sequences may appear confusing, but that's what combat is all about. Those who rise above the confusion most effectively generally win.

National Differences

Two major weapons-design philosophies exist in the world, represented by the two major sources of weapons production. First, there is the more familiar "Western" school, which emphasizes complex, up-to-date, and sturdy technology. The "Soviet" school is less well understood. Soviet weapons are designed primarily to meet the conditions expected during the defense of Russia itself. For example, Russia is a nation of few roads and horrendous weather conditions. Vehicles can expect to face deep snow, weeks of muddy ground, and dry, dusty weather during the brief summer. Because of these conditions, Soviet equipment tended to be lighter, simpler, and with more engine power than equivalent Western systems. Russia also has a large number of rivers and streams running north to south. Many more Soviet vehicles were amphibious in order to cope with this situation, and the relative lack of bridges within Russia. Soviet soldiers, compared to their Western counterparts, received less training and were not noted for their scrupulous attention to detail. Thus, Soviet equipment was made simple and sturdy.

The Soviet Union's divisions required several million reservists to bring them up to strength. These reservists are men discharged within the past five years, and in that time most of them have had nothing to do with military equipment. For this system to succeed, the equipment must be simple enough for former users to pick up on quickly.

Another characteristic of Soviet life, particularly after the Communists eliminated incentives to do things right, was a lackadaisical attitude toward maintenance and upkeep of weapons and equipment. Soviet material was designed to require a minimum of either. As a consequence of all this, Soviet equipment often appeared similar to Western models. But in reality the Soviet version was less capable and often significantly more durable when abused or ignored. Taking good care of Western equipment will produce splendid results, while the same attention lavished on Soviet equipment won't make as much difference. Unfortunately, ill-maintained Soviet equipment would eventually fail and would often do so in combat. The Soviets attempted to use their equipment as little as possible during peacetime in order to preserve its shorter useful life for combat. They preferred not to retire older equipment but tended to put it in "storage" for use by reserve units should another major war occur. Forty years ago, you could get away with this by packing everything in grease and dropping some canvas over it. Modern equipment is made of much more complex devices that are not as easily preserved. Reports from users of Soviet equipment indicated that the march of technology was constantly being hobbled by lack of maintenance.

Through the 1980s, there was an increasing number of Soviet officers urging that the Soviet Union's military policies be reexamined. After 1991, and the disappearance of the Soviet Union, the former Soviet officers proceeded to attempt salvaging the best of the remains of the Red Army and adapting the superior techniques of Western forces. This would not be the first time Russia has gone through such a military reformation. In the past, the results have always been interesting and effective. This time around should be no different.

Theory and Practice

Everything is not what it seems. Nuclear weapons are considered the ultimate weapons. They are, if they work. Nuclear weapons are highly dependent on complex electronics and precisely engineered components. The chief means of delivering nuclear weapons, missiles, are equally complex. At least the missiles are tested more often, and have achieved an overall effectiveness of more than 80 percent. Perhaps not more than 80 percent, as none of these missiles have been used under combat conditions. Don't put a lot of faith in press releases about weapons with no past. Nearly all modern weapons have experienced problems, just as many weapons introduced during World War II did. The primary flaw in most weapons' development is the reluctance to go as far as one should in testing. It's quite common for testing to be one of the first items reduced when development budgets come under pressure. Realistic testing is not only expensive, but it requires a fair amount of imagination to devise tests that will adequately mimic battlefield realities. There is also the political pressure to get the weapon into service with a minimum of fuss and embarrassment. Because most shortcomings are discovered during a war, the urgency to get things working correctly overwhelms any desire to hold an inquest and punish the guilty. During World War II, there were machine guns that jammed with the least amount of dirt, tank gun-stabilization systems that were more trouble than they were worth, torpedo warheads that didn't explode, and aircraft more dangerous to their pilots than to the ememy. All of these failures could have been avoided with a little more diligent testing. No matter—few remember these disasters. We tend to recall only the good things. This is one aspect of human nature that becomes very expensive if no one maintains a memory of the failures. The opportunity for rapid technological change has produced sprinters and plodders, as well as many nations that simply sit out the race. On the fast track is the United States, being first in most weapons' technologies. The leading edge of technology is often the bleeding edge. Compounding this is the American tendency to ignore the greater military experience of its friends and allies. A "We can do it better" attitude escalates this hubris into an unending stream of marginal weapons. This expensive, and often humbling, experience has produced better systems in the last 10 years. But old habits die hard. A lot of gold-plated lemons still exist, waiting to bedevil the troops these overpriced clunkers are intended to help. Being first in a dark room will always be risky, and easier for those who follow. America's allies, especially the Europeans, take a more circumspect approach. They have the additional advantages of greater experience in military matters and America's technological leadership to show what to avoid.

The Soviet Union took the same approach, although the Soviets were less capable than other Europeans in handling precision technology. This was no problem for them if they were turning out large quantities that didn't require immense complexity. Infantry weapons, artillery, and basic armored vehicles fit this category. As electronics and precision instruments become more the norm, the older Soviet approach staggered along uncertainly. Don't believe everything you read about the effectiveness of Soviet high tech. Experience has demonstrated that Soviet technical prowess fell somewhat short when the shooting started.

An ominous development that arose from the 1991 Gulf War, one that did not generate a lot of attention, was the tradeoff between high defense expenditures and low casualties. The U.S. military had, for most of the 20th century, expended material in return for lower casualties to their own troops. The Gulf War was the pinnacle of that approach, being the first war in nearly a century where a Western army had suffered more deaths from noncombat causes (in this case, accidents rather than disease) than from enemy fire. The trillion dollars the United States spent on defense during the 1980s bought unprecedented amounts of training as well as high-tech weapons. This "bought" the lives of hundreds, if not thousands, of American and coalition troops. In the wake of this striking victory, no one made an issue of this, even though the United States was even then cutting its defense budget in response to the Cold War's ending. Few politicians want to put this hot potato into play. The lives of the troops is a very sensitive issue, and one that has existed as long as there have been organized armed forces. Part of the sensitivity comes from the reluctance of the military and political leaders to take responsibility for screwing up before the war. There is usually a lot of blame to go around, especially when it comes to buying the wrong weapons and not spending enough on training. Watch this issue very carefully in the 1990s, and observe what decisions are made concerning weapons and training expenditures. The results of those decisions won't be known until after the dust settles in the wake of the next war.

Another aspect of the Gulf War was that it was a relatively cheap "reality check" on the effectiveness of the armed forces of the major powers. It has been nearly half a century since the major powers have gone to war with one another, an unprecedented period of peace in this millennium. With the end of the Cold War, it might have been several decades before there would have been a battlefield test of how effective all those decades of military spending had been. The Gulf War allowed the Western powers, particularly the United States, to take their Cold War forces and run what amounted to a live-fire battlefield test against an army using their Cold War opponent's weapons. Of course, it wasn't a perfect test, as the Iraqis were not Soviets. Moreover, the war was fought in a desert, not the rolling woodlands and urban areas of Central Europe. But, despite all that, it was possible to measure the effectiveness of Western military forces. The results revealed that Soviet military doctrine was nearly as remiss as Soviet economic and social policies. Going into what, one hopes, is another half-century of major-power peace, the world's armed forces will look to the Gulf War as a vindication of the NATO style of warfare. Combat is the final arbiter of what military doctrine is correct and worth emulating, and the Gulf War was a convincing demonstration.

The Future

Weapons developments go through cycles of quality and quantity. First there is the development of a new weapon that represents an increase in performance quality. These new weapons are expensive and not as reliable as existing ones, so they are not produced in large quantities. As the bugs are worked out, more are produced, and older models are replaced. This cycle has been quite stable for the last century, the only variation being an understandable speedup during major wars. To demonstrate this, let us consider the changes at 20-year intervals since 1900.

1900 At the beginning of this century, the principal land weapons were masses of infantry, armed with bolt-action rifles, not too many machine guns, and somewhat more light-artillery pieces (primarily 75mm). At sea, the principal weapon was the armored cruiser equipped with 155mm guns.

1920 The ground forces still had a lot of people walking around with bolt-action rifles, but there were a lot more machine guns, plus many mortars and heavier artillery (105mm). There were also primitive armored vehicles and many trucks. Chemical weapons had been developed and used, but few wanted to use them again. Horses still hauled most of the heavy equipment. At sea, the principal ship was the battleship. The new weapon was the submarine, which was basically a small torpedo boat that could travel submerged for a few hours. Surface ships had only a primitive form of sonar and depth charges to deal with subs. In the air, there were totally new weapons: wood-and-fabric biplanes carrying machine guns and a few small bombs. All services made extensive use of radio and telephones.

1940 Ground forces had more and better-armored vehicles, and 5 to 10 percent of the troops were in mechanized units that moved about without horses or walking. At sea, there were now aircraft carriers and a lot more submarines. The battleships were on their way out. In the air, there were metal, prop-driven predecessors of modern fighters, as well as four-engine bombers. The ground forces and navy had thousands of machine guns and cannon for the express purpose of destroying aircraft. There were a lot more radios along with the newly developed radar and improved sonar.

1960 The horse was gone, and nuclear weapons were all over the place. Armored vehicles had gotten bigger and more numerous. Major nations had completely mechanized armies. The average artillery caliber was 155mm, and much of it was self-propelled. The army was using a lot more electronics, especially radar and more capable radios. The navies had recognized the supremacy of the aircraft carrier, but the first nuclear submarines had put to sea, and change was at hand. Antisubmarine warfare had reached new heights of effectiveness with hundreds of four-engine, computer-equipped patrol aircraft plus stationary underwater sensors. The air force was beginning to develop long-range nuclear missiles and already had supersonic fighters armed with missiles as well as heavy jet-propelled bombers.

1980 Ground forces had introduced more capable versions of 1960 weapons and equipment. New items were antitank guided missiles and efficient body armor. The major navies had more nuclear submarines than aircraft carriers. The air forces had more capable, and expensive, aircraft. The missiles were more complex and effective. Long-range bombers had been supplanted by ICBMs and other missiles of various ranges. All services were beginning to introduce robotic weapons that can fight on their own.

2000 The trends of the last 40 years will continue. Computerized weapons are maturing along with the technology that spawned them. There will be more robotic weapons. Combat between machines, without human intervention, will become more common. If there is no major war by 2000, the most crucial element will be the length of time that has passed since the last large-scale conflict. As history has repeatedly shown, these long periods of inactivity create wider gaps between the theory and reality of actual combat. There has never been so large a quantity of automated weapons available before. In the past, when the troops quickly realized that the battlefield was not like they were told it would be, the survivors quickly adapted. Machines have to be modified. This is going to be interesting.

You can see how trends in military equipment work. Large wars force things to happen more quickly. Long periods of peacetime are more evolutionary. We are living in one of the longest evolutionary periods ever experienced. The last evolutionary period extended from 1871 to 1914: 43

years. The current one is over 43 years old and likely to continue for several more decades. Consider the surprises encountered during the opening battles of 1914. World War I is largely remembered for the stalemates resulting from faulty understanding of new technology. Despite the experience of the Gulf War, it's still possible to forget. It's happened before; it will happen again.

29

The Armed Forces
of the World

ARMED FORCES EXIST primarily, or at least initially, for self-defense. Some nations go overboard, and some feel the best way to defend against a real or imagined threat is to attack it. Armed forces also serve as one more bargaining chip in a state's international diplomacy. If war comes, the armed forces have failed in their primary purpose, to appear too strong to be successfully attacked. Therefore, armed forces pay a lot of attention to appearing strong. If substance is sacrificed to enhance apparent strength, why not? An apparently stronger armed force is more valuable in diplomacy than a less capable appearing one. Actual combat capability is difficult to measure. It is too easy to just count the number of tanks, ships, aircraft, and men in uniform. Numbers make the loudest noise when you must rattle the saber. Should bluff fail, and you are forced to wage war, well, that's another set of problems.

Doctrine Versus Reality

Doctrine is the plan, reality is the performance. Most nations' military planning rests on their appraisals of their own military ability. This appraisal reaches a low point just before arms budgets are voted on and rises swiftly during international crises and reelection campaigns.

When actual warfare approaches, the military becomes more realistic. It is always a touchy matter when the generals must confront the national leader, who is either inflamed by patriotic optimism or crestfallen by doubt, to present a sober appraisal of the situation. One of the more poignant examples was in 1914. The German kaiser, after declaring war, began to realize the enormity of his action. He asked his generals to stop the mobilization. They informed him that this would put Germany at a grave disadvantage, as it would totally disorganize the armed forces. The war proceeded, and millions of lives were lost.

The peacetime gap between doctrine and reality is recognized, if only vaguely, by most national leaders. Unfortunately, people sometimes forget or are overtaken by events. Most nations have traditional armed forces, capable of some form of warfare. Countries look at their neighbors' past history and finances and build up their armed forces accordingly. The usual idea is to have forces that can successfully resist one or more potentially unfriendly neighbors. Border disputes and excess wealth are the most common causes of building up armed forces above the levels needed for self-defense. The Middle East is a good example. Israel's existence is a border dispute in the eyes of Arab nations. The size of armed forces in the region has grown accordingly. Excess wealth in the region has also led to excessive armed forces. The more wealth one has, the more concerned one becomes about keeping it. As with good health, no price is too high for security, particularly if you have deep pockets. As doctors are concentrated in wealthy neighborhoods, so arms dealers flock to the oil-rich Middle East. It was just such a case of envy that caused Iraq to invade Kuwait in 1990.

As a nation's apparent military capabilities grow, doctrine tends to follow. One defensive plan is to have armed forces mobilize near the borders to repel invaders. Increasing strength leads one to contemplate taking the war to the aggressor's homeland. An invasion has three attractions:

1. The fighting is shifted to the enemy's territory.
2. Your forces have something to negotiate with (enemy territory).
3. Retribution is made. Never underestimate the power of revenge in world affairs.

Most armed forces are capable of mustering a defense. An attack, especially an invasion into hostile territory, is considerably more difficult. In the defense, you dig trenches and wait. An attack requires moving large numbers of troops and all their equipment. Eventually, defenders start shooting at you. Troops, difficult to control under any circumstances, are more so while moving and being shot at. Keeping large numbers of troops fed and healthy becomes more difficult in unfriendly territory. More supplies must be moved farther. Enemy attacks on these supplies create still more problems. All that movement uses and wastes more supply than if you stay in your own territory. Thus, attacking usually consumes more supply than defending. Commanding, controlling, and communicating with moving forces in enemy territory is enormously more difficult than defending. Gathering information on enemy forces is obviously easier for the defenders in their homeland. It is common for a defender to defeat an invader soundly and then suffer an equally disastrous defeat during a pursuit into the invader's homeland. A recent example of this was Iraq's 1980 invasion of Iran, which was followed by Iran's seven-year attempt to invade Iraq in turn.

Attrition Versus Maneuver

There are two ways to fight a war: plain (attrition) and fancy (maneuver). The stronger military power has the option of which method to use. If the stronger power has little military experience, it simply opts for the meat-grinder approach known as attrition. Any nation with solid military experience and a desire to do it right will choose the maneuver approach. Maneuver kills fewer people on both sides and gets the job done more quickly, if you do it right. Through most of its wars, the United States successfully used the attrition approach. It is easier to be proficient at this type of warfare. You need master only the simplest military skills and possess enormous quantities of arms and munitions. Russia has also opted for attrition through most of its wars, despite continuing efforts to master maneuver warfare on a more than temporary basis. Maneuver warfare means being more agile and efficient than your opponent. Instead of engaging in a mutual slaughter, you destroy your opponent's will to fight. This involves everything from stunning him into surrender with your fancy footwork to the more mundane destruction of enemy headquarters and supplies. Maneuver warfare is waged against leadership, the troops' confidence, and their sense of security. Maneuver warfare also implies a degree of success. Unsuccessful attempts at maneuver warfare are simply failure, and often disastrous failure at that. Maneuver warfare is for able players only. Inept practitioners need not apply. Most nations recognize their limitations in this area and go with attrition. Most nations have no choice.

Maneuver warfare is very risky, a gambler's game. Attrition is slower, plodding, and more predictable. Just the sort of thing your average bureaucrat leans toward. The United States has managed to practice maneuver warfare in several smaller conflicts or portions of larger wars. In the war with Mexico in the 1840s, small U.S. forces invaded and outmaneuvered the opposition. During the American Civil War, several campaigns were notable for their successful application of maneuver warfare. But that entire conflict was permeated by, and won with, attrition. In particular, the Confederate forces managed to keep the war going by successful use of maneuver warfare. They won many battles, but were ground down by attrition. Like any superior technique, maneuver warfare is not a panacea if you are grossly outnumbered. In one of the more interesting ironies of military affairs, the Soviets were a fervent proponent of maneuver warfare. The Soviet Union was one of the first nations to mechanize portions of its armed forces in the 1930s. They used British theory, American engineering, and German advisers. All of this fell apart when the Germans invaded in 1941. But the Soviets were resilient, and industrious, pupils. By 1943, they were demonstrating their growing prowess in mobile warfare. By 1945, Soviet troops were quite good at maneuver warfare. They were mindful of their teachers, and adopted still more German organization, techniques, and weapons after 1945. Soviet commanders were also mindful that they defeated the Germans primarily through a mobile war of attrition. The most crucial lesson the Soviets learned in World War II was that despite their massive preparations for mobile warfare in the 1930s, they still had to relearn all they thought they knew once the war began. The experience in World War II merely confirmed what military leaders have known for thousands of years: military power is mass times velocity. All things being equal, the more mobile force will prevail. Up to a point, a smaller, more mobile force will defeat a larger one. But only up to a point. Unless the smaller, more mobile force wins quickly, the proverbial big battalions will prevail.

The Difference Between Wars and Disorder

There are wars and there are wars. Much of what we currently call war is merely well-armed disorder. It is simply insurrection, guerrilla activity, or general disorder involving the armed forces. This is an important distinction, as a great deal of military skill is not needed to create armed disorder. You don't need trained troops to create a proper insurrection or civil war. All you need are angry people and some weapons.

A war, as is meant in this book, is more than slaughter, mayhem, and senseless destruction. A certain amount of skill is implied, perhaps even a reasonable excuse for the exercise. Not all the armed forces described in this chapter possess skill. Military skill is more than uniforms, display, and awesome-looking equipment. Most of the military violence in the world is nothing more than large-scale disorder, banditry, or worse. Uganda, the Sudan, Lebanon, El Salvador, Somalia, the Balkans, Mozambique, the Caucasus, and Afghanistan are examples of disorder, even if some of the participants are trying to put up an organized fight. In such conflicts, combat takes on a different meaning. For example, during a disorder in which one side is clearly stronger than the other, the weaker side fights when and where it has a chance of success. When faced with overwhelming military power, the weaker force will turn into civilians, or otherwise seek sanctuary. Afghanistan again comes to mind. If the Soviets put a million troops into the country, 10 times the initial number sent in, the Afghans would still have simply waited them out. Sufficient outrages would have occurred to keep the populace in a properly hateful frame of mind.

A war is fought to a conclusion. Disorders may go on for years, decades, or centuries. Wars are fought by powerful, and expensive, armed forces. Disorders are fought with whatever deadly force is handy, plus the legendary hearts and minds. Making disorder is simpler than making war, which is why it is more common.

The Future

For the last 20 years, and into the foreseeable future, each major world region is dominated by one local superpower. The chart shows this rather vividly. The degree of dominance can be expected to change in the future.

Europe. The NATO alliance, having come out on the winning side of the Cold War, now dominates Europe militarily. But that doesn't mean a whole lot. After suffering wars and threats of wars for most of this century, Europeans are making the most of the first true peace in the continent since, well, since before written records were kept. While fighting broke out in the Balkans in the wake of the Cold War ending, this is normal by European standards. There has *always* been some kind of conflict going on in the Balkans. That's been an ugly condition, but an ancient and persistent one just the same. As Europe moves inexorably to economic and political unification in the 1990s, there have also been attempts to form permanent multinational armed forces. It's a new era for Europe, and even the successor states of the Soviet Union want to join in. German reunification raised some fears of a German military hegemony. Germany has shown no interest in this, and without nuclear weapons, Germany would stand little chance against nuclear-armed Britain, France, and Russia.

Middle East. Israel has been increasing its military domination of the Middle East throughout the 1980s. This has been accomplished more by increasing technical skill and technology than by adding weapons. The Iran-Iraq and Lebanese wars plus the decline of oil prices have sapped Arab military and economic resources. The Iraqi invasion of Kuwait in 1990 shattered what anti-Israeli cohesion there was among Arab nations. That war also set back Iraqi military power a decade or more. The end of the Cold War also denied many Arab nations a major patron. The successor states of the Soviet Union have shown no enthusiasm for Middle Eastern politics. On the downside, the end of the Cold War has also led to a lessening of support from Israel's major ally, the United States. But on balance, the Israelis have come out ahead, and will likely continue to be the leading military power in the region.

East Asia. The situation in Asia is a bit more complex. As a result of the 40 years of fighting in Indochina, Vietnam emerged as an uncharacteristically strong regional military power. This has been done at the expense of its economy, leaving Vietnam one of the poorest nations in the world. Meanwhile, China is undergoing an economic renaissance. Vietnam's military power can be expected to decline, while China's will grow, restoring the more normal balance of military capability in the region.

South Asia. India continues to maintain its relatively dominant position and even improve it against its primary antagonist, Pakistan. With Pakistan acquiring nuclear weapons, we also have a situation where two antagonistic nuclear powers glare at each other across contested borders. So far, both sides have shown considerable restraint. Indeed, commentators on both sides of the border have made much of the fact that neither nation can afford the economic disruption that even a war with conventional weapons would entail.

Africa. South Africa's well-trained and well-equipped armed forces dominate the less well turned-out troops of neighboring countries. South Africa's major danger is internal disorder, which will likely increase as that nation approaches full democracy. Multiculturalism is the curse of Africa, and South Africa is no different. The Afrikaner tribe has kept the lid on things for many generations, but this tribal-domination approach has its limitations. Democracy is a much sought after goal, but it is a slippery beast. If you go for it but can't hold it together, you end up with armed disorder.

Americas. The United States will continue to be the dominant power, although Brazil's military power continues to increase along with its economy.

Armed Forces of the World

Chart 29-1 gives evaluations of the quantity and quality of each nation's armed forces. The quantity of each combat unit has been derived from various open sources. Quality has been determined by evaluating historical performance. All armed forces are not equal, and this inequality has been expressed numerically. In calculating the numerical value of total strength, it is important to differentiate between what floats and what doesn't. Aircraft carriers and tank divisions are very different instruments of destruction. Both cost about the same, but a carrier cannot march on Moscow, nor can a tank division hunt submarines in the Atlantic. For this reason, land and naval force capabilities are listed separately. In reality, they are not entirely separate. Naval forces, particularly carriers, can support ground combat. Tank divisions can seize ports needed by naval forces for their sustenance. Destructive effect was the main consideration in assigning values. This was modified by the mobility and flexibility of the system. Tank divisions can move over a wide area to fight, while most air-defense forces are limited in their capabilities and mobility. While the numbers of men and weapons are fairly accurate, estimates of quality factors are subjective. Readers may impose their own evaluations. The assessments given are based on current conditions and historical experience. Don't underestimate the historical trends.

Naval forces are shown in detail on their own chart, while on the Armed Forces

29-1 World Armed Forces: 1995

Country	Rnk	Combat Power		Tot Qual	Tot Pop	GDP	Act Men	Mil Bud	Bud Man	Mbl Army Men	Eqtd Divs	AFV	Aircraft Cmbt
		Land	Naval										
Averages & Totals		15,741	5,271	25%	5,477	$20,972	25,980	$606,897	$23	37,843	1,318	323,653	39,436
Western Bloc		1,592	913	33%	562	$2,140	2,788	$84,549	$30	4,878	157	40,440	4,188
NATO		1,125	1,603	42%	376	$6,048	1,682	$189,005	$112	1,926	63	35,198	6,024
NATO (w/o US)		305	44	28%	126	$348	512	$25,205	$49	990	38	10,238	798
United States		1,051	3,119	48%	260	$6,500	1,500	$210,000	$140	1,200	32	32,000	6,700
Pacific Allies		171	41	32%	248	$532	441	$3,996	$9	442	16	3,535	582
Percentage Analysis													
Western Bloc		10%	17%	31%	10%	10%	11%	14%	30%	13%	12%	12%	11%
NATO		7%	30%	65%	7%	29%	6%	31%	381%	5%	5%	11%	15%
NATO (w/o US)		2%	1%	12%	2%	2%	2%	4%	111%	3%	3%	3%	2%
United States		7%	59%	89%	5%	31%	6%	35%	499%	3%	2%	10%	17%
Pacific Allies		1%	1%	26%	5%	3%	2%	1%	-61%	1%	1%	1%	1%
Africa		534	10	19%	502	$267	905	$7,108	$8	1,385	80	10,866	1,011
Americas		1,265	1,726	32%	729	$7,265	2,700	$181,216	$67	2,546	117	33,923	6,862
Europe		5,786	1,986	21%	803	$8,387	9,201	$261,740	$28	13,881	449	158,959	15,338
Middle East		2,007	356	15%	346	$672	4,099	$67,770	$17	6,152	196	67,900	4,591
South Asia		969	72	30%	1,239	$398	2,122	$10,188	$5	2,276	92	8,491	1,639
East Asia		5,179	1,120	35%	1,858	$3,983	6,952	$78,875	$11	11,603	384	43,514	9,995
Percentage Analysis													
Africa		3.4%	0.2%	-25%	9.2%	1.3%	3.5%	1.2%	-66%	3.7%	6.0%	3.4%	2.6%
Americas		8.0%	32.8%	25%	13.3%	34.6%	10.4%	29.9%	187%	6.7%	8.9%	10.5%	17.4%
Europe		36.8%	37.7%	-18%	14.7%	40.0%	35.4%	43.1%	22%	36.7%	34.0%	49.1%	38.9%
Middle East		12.8%	6.8%	-42%	6.3%	3.2%	15.8%	11.2%	-29%	16.3%	14.9%	21.0%	11.6%
South Asia		6.2%	1.4%	19%	22.6%	1.9%	8.2%	1.7%	-79%	6.0%	7.0%	2.6%	4.2%
East Asia		32.9%	21.2%	37%	33.9%	19.0%	26.8%	13.0%	-51%	30.7%	29.2%	13.4%	25.3%

Country	Rnk	Combat Power Land	Combat Power Naval	Tot Qual	Tot Pop	GDP	Act Men	Mil Bud	Bud Man	Mbl Army Men	Eqtd Divs	AFV	Aircraft Cmbt
European Nations													
Russia	1	1,139	580	28%	150	$1,200.0	2,000	$90,000	$45	3,000	95	45,000	5,500
Germany	2	698	51	75%	80.0	$1,600.0	370	$28,000	$76	700	15	16,000	700
Turkey	3	421	28	44%	59.0	$180.0	654	$2,050	$3	830	24	7,100	480
Sweden	4	339	13	43%	8.6	$140.0	785	$3,500	$4	700	24	2,300	570
France	5	295	161	40%	57.0	$900.0	489	$22,560	$46	586	29	6,600	870
United Kingdom	6	281	271	53%	57	$890.0	311	$26,852	$86	390	16	6,100	780
Italy	7	257	88	52%	58.0	$860.0	388	$8,900	$23	380	11	6,100	500
Switzerland	8	253	0	40%	6.8	$130.0	1,124	$2,800	$2	580	18	2,700	270
Poland	9	248	5	47%	38.0	$145.0	402	$7,800	$19	400	15	8,000	450
Ukraine	10	187	1	18%	53	$245.0	400	7000	$18	800	25	11,000	1,300
Greece	11	141	21	34%	10.1	$77.0	210	$2,300	$11	340	20	4,200	370
Netherlands	12	135	51	51%	15.1	$230.0	105	$5,800	$55	210	5	3,600	180
US Europe	13	126	624	48%			180	$25,200	$140	144	4	3,840	804
Finland	14	119	2	51%	5.0	$80.0	35	$1,100	$31	210	9	1,200	105
Romania	15	117	2	29%	24.0	$60.0	190	$1,322	$7	330	15	4,700	190
Spain	16	103	35	41%	40.0	$440.0	311	$6,300	$20	200	8	2,700	230
Norway	17	99	15	41%	4.3	$76.0	37	$1,800	$49	228	9	600	80
Belgium	18	98	4	39%	10.0	$150.0	91	$2,500	$27	210	7	2,200	175
Bulgaria	19	91	2	31%	9.0	$50.0	148	$1,600	$11	240	13	3,200	220
Serbia	20	87	0	12%	13.2	$25.0	210	$1,100	$5	650	15	2,200	300
Hungary	21	83	0	34%	10.8	$70.0	105	$2,300	$22	200	6	3,135	140
Austria	22	74	0	40%	7.7	$120.0	55	$1,300	$24	172	12	730	42
Denmark	23	67	16	41%	5.2	$80.0	30	$1,700	$57	143	6	1,100	71
Czech Republic	24	64	0	36%	10.4	$250.0	60	$1,200	$20	125	5	2,200	300
Georgia	25	42	0	16%	5.6	$19.0	50	700	$14	250	4	1,600	30
Portugal	26	34	15	33%	10.5	$58.0	68	$950	$14	90	6	410	90
Belarus	27	33	0	10%	10.5	$60.0	90	1200	$13	250	7	4,500	250
Armenia	28	24	0	15%	3.6	$14.0	25	300	$12	150	2	900	30
Lithuania	29	19	0	9%	4.2	$18.0	40	500	$13	200	3	1,500	0
Croatia	30	19	0	8%	4.8	$14.0	25	250	$10	220	2	400	0

29-1 World Armed Forces: 1995

Country	Rnk	Combat Power Land	Combat Power Naval	Tot Qual	Tot Pop	GDP	Act Men	Mil Bud	Bud Man	Mbl Army Men	Eqtd Divs	AFV	Aircraft Cmbt
European Nations													
Albania	31	15	0	20%	3.4	$4.0	42	$256	$6	65	3	280	42
Moldova	32	13	0	7%	4.5	$15.0	10	$200	$20	180	1	250	50
Cyprus (Greek)	33	12	0	21%	0.7	$5.4	13	$65	$5	55	3	265	0
Latvia	34	10	0	9%	2.7	$16.0	40	$500	$13	110	3	250	0
Slovak Republic	35	9	0	9%	5.5	$95.0	40	$900	$23	70	3	1,400	150
Estonia	36	8	0	9%	1.7	$9.0	12	$150	$13	85	1	300	40
Bosnia	37	8	0	4%	.4	$5.0	12	$200	$17	200	1	200	0
Ireland	38	7	0	23%	3.6	$34.0	14	$360	$26	28	2	134	9
Cyprus (Turkish)	39	5	0	24%	0.20	$0.5	5	$5	$1	20	0	20	0
Macedonia	40	3	0	3%	2	$4.0	5	$40	$8	80	1	40	0
Slovenia	41	2	0	4%	2	$5.0	20	$100	$5	55	2		20
Luxembourg	42	1	0	27%	0.4	$7.0	1	$60	$86	2	0	5	0
Malta	43	1	0	21%	0.4	$2.4	1	$15	$15	3	0	0	0
Iceland	44	0	0	18%	0.2	$4.0	0.1	$5	$50	1	0	0	0
Middle East Nations													
Iran	1	435	6	46%	60.0	$85.0	940	$6,000	$6	890	34	2,300	220
Israel	2	422	17	55%	4.6	$48.0	149	$5,500	$37	600	21	11,600	570
Iraq	3	351	1	38%	20.0	$30.0	845	$9,000	$11	800	36	8,700	380
Egypt	4	204	12	41%	55.0	$39.0	445	$5,300	$12	380	15	6,600	550
Syria	5	128	1	25%	13.0	$19.0	390	$3,700	$9	360	11	7,800	660
Uzbekistan	6	66	0	8%	21	$50.0	125	$900	$7	800	8	5,100	120
Algeria	7	50	1	24%	27.0	$55.0	168	$1,200	$7	170	8	2,100	227
Morocco	8	43	1	21%	26.4	$26.0	204	$850	$4	180	5	1,200	130
Jordan	9	36	0	35%	3.7	$5.0	70	$750	$11	70	5	2,200	110
Lebanon	10	34	0	22%	3.4	$4.0	40	$600	$15	150	4	400	15
Libya	11	34	1	20%	4.3	$20.0	70	$1,100	$16	75	6	4,700	500
Saudi Arabia	12	33	2	34%	17.0	$90.0	78	$18,000	$231	50	3	2,200	240
Azerbaijan	13	31	0	10%	7.3	$25.0	70	$900	$13	300	6	1,600	40
Kazakstan	14	29	0	4%	17	$50.0	120	$700	$6	600	9	4,200	50
US Middle East	15	21	312	48%			30	4,200	$140	24	1	640	134
Yemen	16	20	0	25%	10.1	$5.5	37	$600	$16	55	5	1,100	150
Sudan	17	13	0	21%	27.5	$8.0	57	$160	$3	55	4	450	40
Tunisia	18	10	1	20%	8.4	$10.0	40	$600	$15	40	2	300	45
United Arab Emir	19	9	0	15%	2.4	$29.0	43	$2,000	$47	44	2	400	130

Country	Rnk	Combat Power Land	Naval	Tot Qual	Tot Pop	GDP	Act Men	Mil Bud	Bud Man	Mbl Army Men	Eqtd Divs	AFV	Aircraft Cmbt
Middle East Nations													
Kuwait	20	9	1	21%	1.4	$20.0	12	$2,200	$177	24	1	700	94
Tadzhikistan	21	9	0	4%	5.4	$11.0	55	600	$11	180	4	1,200	12
Kyrgizia	22	9	0	4%	4.6	$11.0	45	600	$13	180	4	1,100	20
Oman	23	5	0	22%	1.6	$9.0	22	$1,600	$73	18	1	80	50
Turkmenistan	24	5	0	5%	3.7	$11.0	35	400	$11	100	3	900	60
Qatar	25	1	0	15%	0.5	$7.0	6	$170	$28	5	0	200	20
Bahrain	26	1	0	20%	0.5	$4.0	3	$140	$52	2	0	130	24
East Asian Nations													
China	1	1,742	156	38%	1,200	$460.0	2,800	$12,000	$4	3,800	110	17,400	5,900
Korea, South	2	985	35	46%	43.5	$250.0	601	$5,100	$8	2,020	49	2,400	750
Vietnam	3	841	2	40%	68.0	$16.0	900	$2,100	$2	2,000	65	4,500	350
Taiwan	4	574	45	48%	21.0	$160.0	424	$4,300	$10	1,100	33	2,600	650
Korea, North	5	375	14	31%	22.0	$24.0	840	$4,200	$5	1,100	52	5,100	600
Japan	6	164	188	63%	124	$2,400.0	243	$21,000	$86	197	14	1,900	460
Singapore	7	87	1	40%	2.8	$40.0	56	$1,400	$25	190	5	1,100	150
Indonesia	8	84	10	28%	196	$98.0	281	$2,100	$7	280	9	840	80
US Pacific	9	84	624	48%			120	16,800	$140	96	3	2,560	536
Thailand	10	67	6	22%	57.0	$70.0	256	$1,600	$6	280	15	1,200	140
Australia	11	46	34	61%	17.0	$320.0	71	$4,800	$68	58	2	900	90
Malaysia	12	42	1	28%	18.0	$44.0	110	$1,700	$15	135	4	700	70
Philippines	13	32	2	24%	66.0	$48.0	115	$550	$5	120	6	350	105
Laos	14	22	0	19%	4.2	$0.6	53	$85	$2	110	7	120	30
Mongolia	15	16	0	22%	2.3	$2.3	25	$240	$9	55	4	1,500	20
Cambodia	16	9	0	22%	7.3	$1.0	35	$60	$2	35	5	200	23
New Zealand	17	8	2	47%	3.4	$42.0	13	$480	$38	13	1	100	35
Papua-New Guinea	18	1	0	15%	4.0	$2.8	3	$35	$11	5	0	0	0
Fiji	19	1	0	15%	0.8	$1.4	3	$15	$6	5	0	0	0
Brunei	20	1	0	15%	0.40	$3.2	4	$310	$78	4	0	44	6

29-1 World Armed Forces: 1995

Country	Rnk	Combat Power Land	Combat Power Naval	Tot Qual	Tot Pop	GDP	Act Men	Mil Bud	Bud Man	Mbl Army Men	Eqtd Divs	AFV	Aircraft Cmbt
American Nations													
United States	1	820	1,559	48%	250	$5,700.0	1,170	$163,800	$140	936	25	24,960	5,226
Brazil	2	114	30	35%	150	$400.0	284	$1,100	$4	280	8	1,600	340
Chile	3	50	27	30%	14.0	$30.0	100	$1,300	$13	150	7	850	104
Cuba	4	45	2	16%	11.0	$12.0	121	$1,125	$9	240	22	1,050	300
Colombia	5	34	1	21%	34.0	$44.0	66	$330	$5	155	5	290	55
Mexico	6	30	6	18%	91.0	$250.0	260	$1,200	$5	155	10	250	110
Peru	7	30	22	21%	22.5	$20.0	128	$660	$5	125	6	770	110
Canada	8	27	44	39%	28.0	$600.0	72	$6,240	$87	41	2	1,440	138
Argentina	9	22	24	34%	33.0	$75.0	75	$1,400	$19	40	4	1,100	124
Nicaragua	10	19	0	24%	3.8	$2.0	72	$600	$8	75	4	310	12
Venezuela	11	17	1	23%	20.2	$47.0	71	$980	$14	60	4	420	90
El Salvador	12	9	0	21%	5.6	$6.0	43	$188	$4	40	4	55	47
UK in America	13	9	9		10		10	$868	$86		0		
Paraguay	14	8	0	16%	4.8	$5.0	16	$82	$5	44	3	50	20
Ecuador	15	7	0	14%	11.0	$12.0	42	$230	$5	42	3	250	54
Honduras	16	6	0	15%	5.0	$5.0	19	$95	$5	39	2	95	40
Guatemala	17	5	0	12%	9.4	$11.5	32	$190	$6	40	2	50	30
Uruguay	18	4	0	16%	3.2	$9.3	30	$160	$5	21	2	130	30
Bolivia	19	4	0	16%	7.2	$5.0	28	$220	$8	20	1	110	4
Dominican Rep.	20	2	0	12%	7.5	$7.4	21	$70	$3	13	1	42	12
Costa Rica	21	1	0	16%	3.3	$5.7	9	$22	$2	6	0	3	0
Guyana	22	1	0	11%	0.8	$0.3	5	$48	$9	8	1	8	0
Haiti	23	1	0	10%	6.4	$2.0	7	$33	$5	6	0	17	6
Jamaica	24	1	0	19%	2.6	$4.0	2	$27	$13	3	0	15	0
Panama	25	0	0	14%	2.6	$5.0	12	$120	$10	2	0	28	10
Suriname	26	0	0	10%	0.4	$1.4	3	$44	$18	3	0	30	0
Trinidad	27	0	0	12%	1.3	$5.0	2	$80	$36	2	0	0	0
Belize	28	0	0	12%	0.25	$0.3	1	$4	$7	1	0	0	0

Country	Rnk	Combat Power Land	Naval	Tot Qual	Tot Pop	GDP	Act Men	Mil Bud	Bud Man	Mbl Army Men	Eqtd Divs	AFV	Aircraft Cmbt
African Nations													
South Africa	1	311	7	68%	41.0	$105.0	106	$2,100	$20	390	15	3,900	260
Ethiopia	2	81	1	23%	54.0	$7.0	228	$420	$2	320	23	1,750	66
Nigeria	3	37	2	39%	89	$29.0	94	$1,000	$11	80	4	430	90
Angola	4	20	0	18%	9.0	$8.0	55	$1,100	$20	88	6	900	140
Zimbabwe	5	14	0	20%	11.0	$6.0	41	$290	$7	60	3	166	70
Somalia	6	11	0	15%	7.0	$1.4	43	$140	$3	60	3	770	44
Tanzania	7	8	0	16%	27.0	$6.0	40	$110	$3	49	4	166	30
Zaire	8	6	0	11%	38.0	$7.0	50	$60	$1	47	3	230	18
Mozambique	9	4	0	13%	15.3	$2.0	16	$280	$18	28	2	450	20
Chad	10	4	0	24%	5.3	$1.1	14	$38	$3	18	1	44	5
Kenya	11	4	0	21%	25.5	$8.8	14	$260	$19	12	1	180	50
Ghana	12	4	0	17%	16.0	$6.0	11	$66	$6	20	2	75	10
Uganda	13	3	0	14%	19.0	$5.0	10	$40	$4	20	1	50	2
Madagascar	14	3	0	12%	12.2	$2.6	21	$56	$3	20	1	70	12
Liberia	15	2	0	12%	2.8	$0.8	7	$28	$4	18	1	12	0
Zambia	16	2	0	10%	8.6	$5.0	16	$105	$7	15	1	133	41
Guinea	17	2	0	10%	7.6	$3.0	10	$80	$8	18	1	135	10
Senegal	18	2	0	18%	8.0	$5.0	10	$65	$6	9	1	100	6
Gambia	19	2	0	18%	1.0	$0.2	10	$65	$6	9	1	100	2
Cameroon	20	2	0	16%	11.5	$14.0	7	$140	$19	7	0	100	16
Congo	21	1	0	11%	2.5	$2.2	9	$150	$17	8	0	190	21
Mauretania	22	1	0	10%	2.0	$1.0	9	$6	$1	10	1	106	8
Ivory Coast	23	1	0	14%	13.0	$9.5	13	$92	$7	8	0	28	4
Mali	24	1	0	14%	8.4	$2.0	5	$40	$8	6	1	100	12
Namibia	25	1	0	10%	1.6	$2.0	6	$25	$4	10	1	12	0
Gabon	26	1	0	19%	1.2	$5.5	3	$77	$29	2	0	70	22
Guinea-Bisseau	27	1	0	14%	1.1	$0.2	9	$9	$1	6	0	90	3
Burundi	28	1	0	11%	6.0	$1.3	6	$40	$7	6	0	45	3
Niger	29	1	0	15%	8.3	$2.3	2	$14	$6	4	0	54	0
Rwanda	30	1	0	12%	8.0	$2.2	5	$24	$5	5	0	22	4
Burkina Faso	31	1	0	10%	9.5	$1.8	4	$32	$8	4	0	100	16
Togo	32	1	0	10%	3.9	$1.4	5	$21	$5	4	0	60	15

29-1 World Armed Forces: 1995

Country	Rnk	Combat Power Land	Naval	Tot Qual	Tot Pop	GDP	Act Men	Mil Bud	Bud Man	Mbl Army Men	Eqtd Divs	AFV	Aircraft Cmbt
African Nations													
Malawi	33	1	0	10%	9.5	$1.5	5	$20	$4	5	0	20	2
Botswana	34	0	0	12%	1.4	$3.3	3	$27	$9	3	0	70	5
Sierra Leone	35	0	0	14%	4.3	$1.4	3	$22	$7	3	0	12	0
Djibouti	36	0	0	12%	0.6	$0.4	3	$3	$1	3	0	34	0
Benin	37	0	0	10%	5.0	$1.8	4	$24	$7	3	0	22	0
Equatorial Guinea	38	0	0	12%	0.4	$0.2	2	$3	$2	2	0	20	0
Swaziland	39	0	0	11%	0.9	$0.6	1	$1	$1	2	0	0	2
Central Afr Rep	40	0	0	10%	3.1	$1.4	2	$20	$9	2	0	32	0
Seychelle Is	41	0	0	10%	0.10	$0.2	1	$8	$8	1	0	10	2
Lesotho	42	0	0	12%	1.8	$0.4	1	$2	$2	1	0	0	0
Cape Verde Is	43	0	0	10%	0.4	$0.3	1	$4	$3	1	0	8	0
Sao Tome	44	0	0	10%	0.13	$0.5	0.20	$1	$5		0	0	0
Comoro Is	45	0	0	10%	0.5	$0.3	1	$1	$1	1	0	0	0
South Asian Nations													
India	1	640	50	44%	900	$300.0	1,250	$7,000	$6	1,300	39	4,500	950
Pakistan	2	227	20	37%	118	$44.0	481	$2,100	$4	550	23	2,500	400
Myanmar	3	41	1	21%	43.0	$17.0	186	$250	$1	190	14	110	60
Bangladesh	4	28	1	24%	120	$22.0	91	$170	$2	110	6	56	59
Afghanistan	5	18	0	26%	17.0	$3.0	40	$300	$8	45	5	1,100	130
Nepal	5	8	0	26%	20.0	$3.2	30	$35	$1	30	2	25	0
Sri Lanka	6	6	0	15%	17.5	$6.0	38	$330	$9	30	2	200	40
Bhutan	7	2	0	10%	1.7	$0.3	4	$1	$0	19	1	0	0
Mauritius	8	0	0	10%	1.1	$2.0	1	$1	$1	1	0	0	0
Maldives	9	0	0	11%	0.2	$0.1	1	$1	$1	1	0	0	0

chart they are seen as a component of total nation power. Naval power is difficult to compare to land power, as it is with land power that you ultimately defend yourself or overwhelm an opponent. For nations that are not dependent on seaborne trade, naval power is less important than for those that are. For most industrial nations, and many Third World countries that have periodic food shortages, loss of sea trade is a serious problem. Fortunately for the nations dependent on seaborne trade, they have a substantial naval advantage over less dependent nations. In other words, Western navies are collectively considerably larger than those controlled by continental powers.

The first page of the Armed Forces chart gives regional summaries, world totals, superpower totals, and summaries for the major alliances. The Percentage Analysis shows the proportion each group of nations has of the total or average (as appropriate) resources displayed in each column.

Following pages give breakdowns by nation.

COUNTRY lists every nation with a combat value of 1 or more. Nations with a combat value of less than 1 have little more than national police capability. Many smaller countries, especially those that lack a threatening neighbor, use their forces primarily for internal security. These lesser military powers often repel an invasion most effectively simply by arming the population. Nations are grouped into six regions: Europe; Middle East, Africa; South Asia and East Asia; and the Americas. The United States, Russia, and several other nations have a peculiar problem with their armed forces. These countries have armed forces stationed at widely separated locations. In effect, they have separate forces committed to areas so far from one another that their overall armed forces cannot realistically be considered one large military force. This is often overlooked in evaluating combat strength. Military and political leaders are acutely aware of this problem. Russia possesses three major groups of military forces. The largest is in Western Russia. Russia's Asiatic forces are deployed between the Ural Mountains and Mongolia.

Facing China are the Far Eastern land, air, and naval forces. Each of these military commands have local populations and economies organized to support their wartime activities. Moscow, in the center of all this, is a strategic reserve of land and air units. Showing these groups as separate entities is a more accurate reflection of Russia's strategic military situations. Each of these three groups have their own local political, diplomatic, and military problems. It is impossible to completely strip any one of these areas to assist another. Some forces can be transferred, but only with some risk. Russia has been forced into this situation because of its enormous borders, and the traditional hostility of most of its neighbors. Note that Russia's situation is quite similar to that of the Soviet Union. The major difference is the elimination of forces facing the Balkans (replaced by Ukraine) and the Middle East (replaced by the new Central Asian nations). Russia contains about half of the former Soviet Union's population, but about two thirds of the Soviet Union's military and economic power. Russia remains a formidable military power; it is still the major military power in Europe. In contrast, the United States has voluntarily deployed substantial forces in far-flung parts of the world. Substantial American forces are stationed in Europe and the Pacific. Because these foreign-based forces consist primarily of combat troops, their combat value per man is higher than the national average. The only other nations with significant overseas forces are France and Britain.

RNK is the ranking of each nation within its region.

COMBAT POWER LAND is the total combat capability of the nation's armed forces except for their navies. Certain nations like Israel, Sweden, and Switzerland have a rapid mobilization capability that achieves the combat value shown within three days of mobilization. Their normal, unmobilized combat value is less than one third of the value shown. As explained elsewhere, combat value is modified by geographical, climate, and political factors. The value given here is a combination of the quantity and quality of manpower, equipment, and weapons. This raw combat value is then multiplied by the force multiplier (see below) to combat value shown in this column.

NAVAL capability is separate from land value and is brought over from the Naval Forces chart.

TOT QUAL (total force quality) is a fraction by which raw (theoretical) combat power should be multiplied to account for imperfect leadership, component-of-force quality, support, training, and other "soft" factors. Think of it as an efficiency rating, with "100" being perfect and "55" being a more common 55 percent efficiency.

TOT POP (population in millions) indicates the nation's relative military manpower resources. Population is also a more meaningful indicator of a nation's size than territory.

GDP (Gross Domestic Product) is a rough gauge of the nation's economic power. This does not translate immediately into military power because of the time needed to convert industry from civilian to military production. Mobilization of some types of military equipment takes years. Other types of weapons, especially those using electronics, can be brought to bear in months.

ACT MEN (active military manpower in thousands) is the total uniformed, paid manpower organized into combat and support units. Because of the widely varying systems of organizing military manpower, this figure is at best a good indicator of the personnel devoted to the military. Industrialized nations hire many civilians to perform support duties, while other nations flesh out skeleton units with ill-prepared reserves. The use of reserve troops varies considerably; see Chapter 6 for more details.

MIL BUD (military budget in millions of dollars) is the current annual armed-forces spending of that nation. All nations use somewhat different accounting systems for defense spending. Efforts are made to eliminate some of the more gross attempts at hiding arms expenditures. Some of the figures, particularly for smaller nations, may be off by 10 percent either way.

BUD MAN is the annual cost per man for armed forces in dollars. This is an excellent indicator of the quantity and, to a lesser extent, the quality of weapons and equipment. Some adjustments should be made for different levels of personnel costs, research and development, strategic weapons, and waste. The United States, in particular, is prone to all four afflictions. The precise adjustments for these factors are highly debatable. One possible adjustment would be to cut the U.S. cost per man by at least one third. Other nations with strategic programs and large R&D establishments (Russia, Britain, France, China, etc.) should be adjusted with deductions of no more than 15 percent. Britain could also take another 5 or 10 percent cut because of its all-volunteer forces' higher payroll. At the other extreme, many nations produce a credible defense force using far less wealth. Low-paid conscripts, good leadership, and the sheer need to improvise enables many of these poorer nations to overcome their low budgets. However, most nations end up with what they pay for.

MBL ARMY MEN is the manpower in the land forces, in thousands, once the reserves have been called up for war.

EQTD DIVS (equivalent divisions) represent the number of ground-combat divisions maintained by each nation. The figure includes marines. These are fully equipped, although not always fully manned, units. Most nations rely on reserves to fill out many of these units in wartime. Equivalent divisions are combinations of lesser units that could be used in combination to form a division-size unit. A division normally has 10,000 to 20,000 troops. See Chapter 2 for more details.

AFV (Armored Fighting Vehicles). These include tanks, armored personnel carriers, and most other armored combat and support vehicles. AFV are the primary components of a ground offensive, and greatly enhance chances of success.

AIRCRAFT CMBT are the number of combat aircraft devoted to land operations. This, like AFV, is a good indicator of raw power. The quality of the aircraft, their pilots, ground crew, and leadership are the most important factors in the air power's overall value.

Current Potentials for War

Each region varies in its potential for wars and in the type of war likely to be fought there.

EUROPE This area has more potential for wars since the end of the Cold War, and is one place where a conflict would be extremely destructive. There is more combat power concentrated in Europe than in any other region. The nations controlling these forces are keenly aware of the powder keg they have created. Much diplomatic effort is spent ensuring that the situation remains calm. The potential for war between Greece and Turkey festers as it has for the past 1,000 years. Yugoslavia's internal problems finally boiled over in the early 1990s and continue to provoke the intervention of other European powers. Eastern Europe's liberation from four decades of Soviet hegemony has a dark side. The region is a hodgepodge of multicultural animosity. Ethnic populations are dispersed across national borders, and the borders themselves are not as settled as those in Western Europe. Yugoslavia was simply the worst of the multicultural catastrophes waiting to happen. Romania and Hungary have much potential for outright warfare. Czechoslovakia has split into its Czech and Slovak parts. Bulgaria and Poland both have claims on their neighbors, as do Belarus and the Ukraine. The successor states of the Soviet Union all have substantial Russian minorities. There may be no major war in Europe's future, but there is a lot of potential for a number of little wars.

MIDDLE EAST is the most volatile region. The Arabs' animosity towards Israel runs a close second to their disputes with each other and non-Arab groups like Iran, the Kurds, and Black Africans. While there have been five Arab-Israeli wars, there have been may other wars between Arabs and other groups. The United States has an interest in Middle Eastern unrest because the West gets much of its oil from the region. It is quite likely that more wars will occur in this area. Because none of the nations are major military powers, it is possible for these wars to be restricted. Iraq's and Iran's attempts to acquire nuclear weapons will eventually succeed, but these weapons are most likely to be used locally, if at all.

ASIA is an area where things can get out of hand. The biggest danger is on the border one hears little about: China and Russia's. Russia fears China retaking the Far Eastern territories that Russia seized in the 19th century. Russia has a long history of bad relations with its eastern neighbors. Even the prospect of nuclear war has not entirely diminished this uneasiness between Russians and Orientals. But just as the Russians have an imperialist past in the regions, so does the other major power, China. Korea, Vietnam, Japan, and even India have reason to fear persistent Chinese ambitions. There is also Taiwan, the wayward province now held by the wealthy and powerful losers of the last Chinese civil war. China now hopes to recover Taiwan by negotiation and has played down a military attempt. The border with India, astride the world's tallest mountains, is relatively quiet. Vietnam is another matter, with troops on the border and low-level but persistent fighting. Vietnam is hardly the victim, having fought with Cambodia for centuries over who will control Indochina. China's borders have never been peaceful, and are not likely to be in the future. The central Asian tribes have been waging war with anyone within reach for thousands of years. Only in the last century has Russia finally subdued and conquered them, and now these Central Asian peoples are once more independent. Except for Russia and Japan, most of the armed forces in Asia are low tech. Warfare consists of a lot of infantry and some artillery flailing away at each other. Any war in Asia could easily become nuclear, because the two major powers, Russia and China, have lots of nuclear weapons.

INDIA is a nation similar in size and population to Europe. India also has the same ethnic diversity, but has managed to remain united. This unity is always threatened by ethnic and/or regional disputes. There is also the ancient antagonism with the peoples of the northwest (Pakistan) who, for thousands of years, have periodically invaded India. For all this, India has been significantly more peaceful than any other region of the world. Warfare in this subcontinent is most likely to be in the form of civil disorder.

AFRICA, south of the Sahara, is a political and economic mess. The region is dominated by South Africa. This nation monopolizes military and economic power in the region as well as being the most politically stable country around. South Africa will likely undergo a political transformation in the 1990s, as all elements are allowed to vote. It's still up in the air what this will do to South Africa's political stability and economic viability. Militarily, Africa presents lots of opportunity for low-level wars. Most of these wars are wars in name only. Civil disorders are a more apt description. There is also a lot of random violence by one ethnic group against another. When one ethnic group is in power, which is a common occurrence, the violence against the civilian population tends to be more systematic and relentless.

AMERICAS are insulated from the rest of the world by two oceans and the United States. Most of the warfare has, and will probably continue to be, internal disorder. There is some revolutionary activity. Large-scale military activity is discouraged by the generally small armed forces maintained by all nations except the United States. The United States has actively discouraged large wars and foreign intervention for nearly two centuries. This has had a lasting effect in disposing most nations toward negotiation rather than sustained combat. Not having used their armed forces in a war for many decades has left most nations with suspect combat capability. Argentina's performance against Britain in the 1982 Falklands War is indicative of this.

How to Determine the Losers of Future Wars

In predicting who will win a war, the past is indeed a window to the future. Past performance, however, is not enough. Several problems must be overcome. For example, armed forces are used infrequently. Yet they must train constantly, practicing every task except the most crucial one, combat. This appears to keep military thought and practice essentially conservative. The troops are always more prepared to refight their last war. This makes the task of prediction easier. Uncertainties still exist, but applying proven techniques with some precision, common sense, and systematic persistence will make the results quite accurate. These techniques have been used by military analysts and historical wargame designers successfully. I used it successfully during the 1991 Gulf War (as well as during the 1973 Arab-Israeli War, not to mention the Cold War). The major stipulation is not to become mesmerized by numbers. Counting resources and computing odds will take you only so far. The following procedure will take you a little farther.

1. *Select the nations that will go to war and what they are fighting over.* Determining the causes of a war, and what each side's goals are, is often difficult. It is essential to find out why this war is happening so you can calculate how far each nation will go in supporting the conflict. A minor border squabble is less likely to escalate than an attempt by one nation to completely take over a neighbor. More important issues encourage a nation to keep at it longer and to resist efforts to settle the matter peacefully.
2. *Determine the mode of combat.* That is, will it be land, or naval, or both? Which side will initially be attacking? A large army will be no help to a nation fighting a naval war. The attacker, as we have already learned, must be significantly stronger than the defender in order to succeed.
3. *How much of a nation's forces will be committed to this war, and why?* Nations at war generally do not, and often cannot, commit the whole of their armed

strength against one enemy. There are often other threats, internal as well as external. It is also prudent to retain substantial forces as a reserve to reinforce some unanticipated success, or to recover from an unexpected disaster. Moreover, a nation's armed forces are not normally concentrated together as they would be for combat. In peacetime, combat units are scattered throughout the nation. This is done for political and economic reasons. Going to war means gathering a substantial portion of these forces on another nation's border. This is usually considered an unfriendly act. The other guy will start mobilizing his forces. Therefore, this "mobilization on the frontiers" must be done as quickly as possible lest you end up facing a defender larger than yourself. When waging an offensive war, you cannot expect to be capable of gathering more than 40 to 70 percent of your forces for the initial attack. Defenders will often gather an even larger portion of their forces. After all, they are going to basically stand still and resist your advance. Another problem with marshaling forces for an attack is the need to occupy enemy territory. Unfriendly civilians can be troublesome unless sufficiently cowed by armed force. Occupation forces, such as your own police, or locals acting as collaborators, can often be used instead of troops. In the best of circumstances, 200 troops per million enemy civilians will be needed to keep the conquered population under control. In a worst case, 2,000 troops per million will be needed.

4. *Look at the combat values for each nation as shown on the charts.* The objective of an attacker is to obtain a better than 1-to-1 ratio of his strength to the defender's. A ratio of 6+ to 1 assures an almost instant victory. Anything below 1 to 1 means almost certain failure. But doing this simple calculation requires the armchair strategist to take into account the probable effect of geography, surprise, and human factors. Note that most human factors (training, leadership, etc.) have already been calculated to produce the combat values on the charts.

5. *Calculate the effect of combined operations.* Most nations have separate ground, air, and naval forces. Each of these forces fights a separate war while simultaneously cooperating with each other. If one nation can obtain air superiority, it can more than double the effectiveness of its ground and naval forces. The degree of increased effectiveness depends on the terrain. It's lower if the war is being fought over "busy" terrain (forests, urban areas, jungle) and higher if the terrain is more open (plains, unforested mountains, and especially deserts). Air superiority also guarantees naval superiority. Control of the air goes to the force with more and higher-quality aircraft.

6. *Account for the effect of climate and geography.* Some terrain favors defense; other terrain makes it easier for the attacker. Severe terrain conditions can double the effectiveness of defending troops. Add severe climatic conditions, and the defenders' combat value can be tripled. An attacker would be handicapped by invading Switzerland or Afghanistan in the winter. Other environments that favor the defender are the urban sprawl that covers most of Germany. Jungles or other thick forests also make defense more effective. An attacker coming across open terrain in dry weather has an advantage. Deserts are particularly difficult to defend.

7. *Estimate the effect of surprise, if any.* Surprise can benefit anyone, but the attacker normally has it. A maximum degree of surprise can multiply the attacker's combat capability five times. This is rarely attained. The Japanese came close in 1941. A more likely degree of surprise will multiply the attacker's strength two or three times. At the start of a war, the side that opens hostilities will usually obtain some surprise advantage, at least 10 percent to 50 percent. Basically, surprise means attacking enemy forces before they are prepared to resist. Examples are air attacks that catch enemy aircraft still on the ground. At sea, submarines are the preeminent surprise weapon. Ground combat finds surprise more difficult, but not impossible, to achieve. At the start of a war, the defender first has to determine that there is a war going on. After that, there are the problems of:

- Alerting the combat units
- Getting them on the road
- Getting them to the border
- Establishing defensive positions

If the attacker has concealed his preparations, the invader can be crossing the frontier before the hapless defender knows what is going on. Such a degree of surprise depends on defender deficiencies as well as energetic moves on the attacker's part. Such surprise is not unknown. Iraq achieved it in 1990, the anti-Iraq coalition in 1991, Egypt in 1973, Israel in 1967, North Korea in 1950, and Germany in 1941. Difficult, but not impossible. Surprise does not end when the attacker's intentions are revealed. Carefully planned attacks on defenders' airfields and transportation network can sustain the surprise effect. If the defender does not have a well-thought-out plan to counter these moves, the effects of the surprise will endure.

In the age of technology, there are surprises of a purely technological nature. Underestimating or being ignorant of enemy technical accomplishments can deal out lethal surprises. Israel misread the effectiveness of Egyptian antiaircraft weapons in 1973 and paid a high price in aircraft and lives. The Germans misread the Allied use of radar several times during World War II, both in the air and at sea, and took higher losses because of it. The Germans demonstrated another form of surprise when they unleashed the blitzkrieg tactics on their opponents. This was doctrinal surprise. Future wars will be full of opportunities for doctrinal and technological surprise. Some of the surprise will be self-inflicted, as nations use untried weapons and techniques. Even the Germans tripped over themselves when they first used their blitzkrieg tactics, but they were fortunate in that they had a few smaller actions to get the bugs out before they went up against a major opponent. During the first battles of World War I, everyone was green. Thus, 1914 was full of bloody embarrassments. Future wars will likely open with the same errors of inexperience. Whoever is better prepared to cope with these surprises will have an edge.

8. *What is the quality of the armed forces' leader on each side?* This is typically a factor only in a small armed force—say, under 100,000. A very good, or bad, leader of a smaller force will have a greater impact. Larger armed forces tend to be institutional, where individuals have less effect and then only over a long time. You apply this factor by multiplying the combat value by anything

from .9 (exceptionally good leader) to .1 (very bad). An example of this would be Libya's Qaddafi, a particularly inept military leader who causes Libya's armed forces' strength to be multiplied by only .2 or .3. If a better military leader came to power in Libya, he would improve the situation by replacing many unit commanders with more capable people, introducing new training methods, doctrine, and other practices. This can turn things around in weeks. Within a few months, the multiplier can go up to .6 or .7. Quite a difference. When in doubt, and for larger armed forces not affected by this, multiply by .5.

9. *What impact will time have on the war?* Time is the defender's strongest ally. If the attacker doesn't win quickly, several problems inevitably arise. First, the effects of whatever surprise the attacker had wear off. Next, if the attacker has penetrated into the defender's territory, the attacking force is operating under the adverse conditions one would expect in unfriendly territory. The attacking troops are somewhat demoralized by the fact that they have not quickly won, and the defending troops are likewise encouraged by this lack of success. The attacker's failure to win quickly does not assure a defender victory, but it does guarantee a longer war. In a long war, victory goes to the nation with the more robust economic strength. An extreme example of how this works can be seen in Israel, Sweden, and Switzerland. Each of these nations mobilizes a large segment of its male population in wartime. This mobilization strips key people from most economic activities in the nation. As a result, these nations connot continue fighting at their fully mobilized strength for more than a few months without substantial outside assistance.

Examples

The Arab-Israeli War of 1973 found Israel weaker and Egypt stronger than they are today. Still, Israel had a value of 200, Egypt about 75, and Syria 20. If Israel had launched a surprise attack, as it had in 1967, it would have had an advantage of more than 4 to 1 and virtual assurance of quick victory. However, it was Syria, and especially Egypt, that launched the surprise attack. Moreover, only a small portion of Israel's strength was on the border. Although the Israelis were sitting in bunkers behind the Suez Canal, it was not enough. Egypt had an advantage of more than 6 to 1 on the first day of the attack. Israel recovered quickly, the Arab advantage quickly evaporated, and the advantage shifted to Israel within a week. Part of this rapid shift has to do with the structure of Israel's armed forces. Less than 30 percent of their strength is active in peacetime. Within 24 hours, their peacetime strength doubles, and after 72 hours it triples. Most of the fighting took place on flat, largely hard desert terrain, giving the counterattacking Israelis the advantage. The method the Egyptians used to initially deceive the Israelis was quite simple; several times in the past they had sent their forces to the border and gone through the preparations for an attack. Each time they then withdrew these forces, except on the last occasion, when they actually launched the attack. Israel could not afford to partially mobilize their forces each time Egypt went through this "practice" drill. The last time Egypt did it, the drill turned into the real thing. However, the Arabs were not able to withstand the Israeli counterattack. The final battles of this war saw the Israelis maintaining a combat ratio of better than 3 to 1. The Arabs had no reserves left, except possibly Soviet paratroopers, and the war soon ended.

A more recent example was the Falklands in 1982. Argentina sent a small portion of its ground forces to occupy the Falkland Islands. These troops were supported by air power from the mainland, plus a few aircraft stationed on the islands. Britain sent a large naval task force whose ground troops retook the islands. On paper (the first edition of this book), Britain had a land value of 98, a naval value of 88, and a value per man of 54. Argentina had land value of 7, naval value of 15, and value per man of 15. Argentina put 11,000 men on the island and provided support with mainland-based aircraft representing another 10,000 men. The aircraft were the most effective, sinking and damaging 16 British ships. The Argentine Navy was kept at bay by British nuclear submarines. It came down to the 28,000-man British task force versus the 21,000 Argentine defenders. Although Argentina had another quarter-million men under arms, it could not get them past the British nuclear submarines. British ship-based aircraft prevented significant reinforcement of the islands. All the Argentines could do from the mainland was launch air strikes. The British put 7,000 men ashore and quickly defeated the isolated and demoralized Argentine garrison. If you use the value-per-man figures (54 and 15), multiplied times the men actually involved (28,000 and 21,000), you find the British with a ratio of nearly 5 to 1. The British could have lost, but it would have been very unlikely.

The most recent example was the Persian Gulf in 1990–91. This was actually two wars. The first was Iraq's invasion of Kuwait in the summer of 1990, followed by five months of inaction. In January, the anti-Iraq coalition began its six-week air bombardment of Iraqi forces in Kuwait followed by a three-day ground offensive. Using the data from the second (1988) edition of this book, we have a land-combat value for the Iraqis of 356. This was the value of the Iraqis at the height of the Iran-Iraq War, which ended about the time the 1988 edition of this book was published. The Iraqis demobilized much of this army after the war and then re-mobilized the discharged veterans in 1990. Between 1988 and 1990, the Iraqis lost some of their combat edge, giving them a 1990 value of about 300. The Kuwaitis were only 9, and the United States was 1,412. The Iraqis put about 20 percent of their combat forces into the initial invasion of Kuwait, giving them a superiority of 60 to 9. It was actually higher (more like 100 to 9), as the Iraqis had achieved surprise. A subsequent invasion of Saudi Arabia was a real possibility, as the Saudis and the other Gulf nations couild muster no more than 20–30 in combat value to oppose the Iraqis. After the Iraqis took Kuwait, they immediately began pouring in additional forces to occupy the country. This left the initial attack force free to continue on to Saudi Arabia. Fortunately, the Iraqi troops were not well organized or efficient (as shown by their total quality rating of 38 percent). The U.S. total quality rating was only 26 percent higher (48 percent versus 38 percent). But as the 1988 edition pointed out, the U.S. military was in the midst of reforming itself, and until these reformed forces were put to the test, the new value was uncertain (although a 10–40 percent increase could be expected). It was higher, by about a third, but this was not the principal reason the Iraqis were outclassed. The United States put about 30 percent of its total ground-combat power into the Gulf. That gave the United States a combat value of 420 (plus another 100 from allies) using the 1988 values. Using "1990" values, the United States had a 560 combat value,

29-2 World Naval Forces: 1995

Nation	Combat Value	% of Total	1,000 Tons	Ships	Man-power	Avg Weight	Quality Pers	Quality Wpns	Ship Types CV	SSB	SSN	SS	C	E	P	Mine Ops.	Aircraft
United States	3,119	59.22%	3,283	282	530	11.64	95	100	28	23	74	0	92	0	20	28	2,200
Russia	580	11.01%	1,183	249	440	4.75	70	70	5	10	49	19	2	106	40	150	500
Britain	286	5.43%	318	85	60	3.74	100	90	2	2	12	4	1	12	8	36	70
Japan	188	3.56%	232	98	48	2.36	90	90				20	8	16	11	48	180
France	175	3.33%	258	65	60	3.96	80	85	3	4	7	4	7	20	10	24	150
China	156	2.96%	371	811	170	0.46	70	60		2	5	80		35	665	130	800
Italy	88	1.67%	147	57	50	2.58	80	75	2			8	5	12	12	16	40
Netherlands	51	0.97%	71	24	14	2.96	90	80				4				24	55
Germany	51	0.97%	63	70	35	0.90	90	90				18			40	55	140
India	50	0.96%	122	73	45	1.67	75	55	1			12	1	8	35	24	125
Taiwan	45	0.86%	87	88	36	0.99	80	65				2		6	60	8	44
Canada	44	0.84%	80	26	9	3.08	85	65				3		11		2	33
Korea, South	35	0.67%	78	120	22	0.65	70	65				6		30	80	9	60
Spain	35	0.66%	83	41	54	2.02	70	60	1			8		6	12	12	56
Australia	34	0.64%	57	35	15	1.63	85	70				6			15	6	16
Brazil	30	0.57%	84	66	48	1.27	60	60	1			6		4	40	6	16
Turkey	28	0.53%	78	78	51	1.00	65	55				8		4	48	38	38
Chile	27	0.51%	75	31	28	2.42	60	60				6	5		12		10
Argentina	24	0.46%	73	33	23	2.21	55	60				7		9	10	6	50
Peru	22	0.43%	74	36	24	2.06	55	55				10	2	4	12		21
Greece	21	0.41%	52	56	19	0.93	75	55				8		14	22	16	16
Pakistan	20	0.38%	62	67	15	0.92	65	50				6	1	0	46	2	18

Country																	
Israel	17	0.33%	24	98	6	0.25	90	80					5	3	90		
Denmark	16	0.31%	25	87	5	0.29	85	75					5	9	73	8	8
Norway	15	0.29%	26	69	7	0.38	85	70					16	5	48	7	
Portugal	15	0.28%	36	48	13	0.75	75	55					3	14	28		
Korea, North	14	0.26%	50	319	25	0.16	60	45					16	3	300	20	
Sweden	13	0.26%	24	56	15	0.43	80	70					12		44	22	15
Egypt	12	0.23%	37	60	20	0.62	65	50					12	6	42	12	18
Indonesia	10	0.20%	46	48	36	0.96	45	50					2	20	26	2	36
South Africa	7	0.13%	13	42	7	0.31	80	65					3	7	32	9	
Thailand	6	0.12%	19	126	21	0.15	60	55						6	120	6	36
Mexico	6	0.12%	23	92	20	0.25	60	45						10	80		10
Iran	6	0.11%	19	23	15	0.84	60	50						5	15	3	11
Poland	5	0.10%	13	17	18	0.76	75	55					3	1	12	18	4
Belgium	4	0.08%	9	4	4	2.25	70	70						4		21	
Cuba	2	0.05%	11	70	8	0.16	55	40					3	2	65	12	
Romania	2	0.03%	8	53	6	0.15	55	40					1	2	50	22	
Philippines	2	0.03%	7	19	14	0.37	60	40						4	15		6
Bulgaria	2	0.03%	9	21	7	0.41	45	40					1	2	18	22	12
Totals	5,266	100%	7,329	3,743	2,043	1.96	72	63	43	41	147	327	124	400	2,256	824	4,794

plus the 100 from allies. Against the 660 of combat value, about 600 was used for the liberation of Kuwait. The Iraqis built up their forces in Kuwait and southern Iraq. By the end of 1990, Iraq had sent about half its armed forces to the Kuwait Theater of Operations (KTO). Most of these troops were ordered to the Saudi border, which was desert wasteland. Most of the Allied troops were stationed under far less rigorous conditions. The Iraqis lacked the logistical and technical support for their troops, who suffered much while building fortifications in the desert. Opposite these Iraqi lines were, for the most part, a thin screen of Saudi desert troops, who found the horrid climate quite normal. The Iraqis were not desert people, coming from the mountains up north or the Tigris-Euphrates river valleys. By the time the Allied air offensive began in January of 1991, the Iraqi force had a combat value of about 100. Desertions, illness, and the wear and tear of living in the summer desert had taken its toll. After six weeks of Allied bombing, the Iraqi combat strength had been reduced to about 50. The Allies then unleashed the ground offensive, which, because of the element of surprise, sent a combat value of about 800 against an Iraqi strength of 50. At odds of 16 to 1, it's no surprise that the battle was over in less than a week. What was surprising was the amount of misinformation spread around in the media between August 1990 and February 1991. Myths such as the "million-man, battle-hardened Iraqi desert army" and the "huge U.S. casualties expected" stayed fresh and credible for a long time. This despite published accounts throughout the 1980s that convincingly disproved these myths. Apparently, a lot of people don't read much anymore, not counting you and me, of course.

Armed Forces of the World: Naval Forces

Chart 29-2 shows the world's 40 most powerful fleets, which represent 98 percent of the world's naval power. The fleets are ranked in order of combat value.

NATION is the nation of the ships displayed. The figures include coast-guard ships if they have a wartime combat capability. Amphibious shipping is included (for details, see Chapter 9).

COMBAT VALUE is the numerical combat value of the nation's fleet. This value reflects the overall quantity and quality of ships and crew when used only for naval combat. Included is the effectiveness of support and the fleet's system of bases. Aside from the known quantities of ship numbers, tonnages, and manpower, less firm data on quality have been taken into consideration. To put it more crudely, it comes down to who is more capable of doing what they say they can do. The quality factor was derived from historical experience, a less than perfect guide.

% OF TOTAL is the percentage of the world's total combat value each fleet represents. 1,000 TONS is the weight of the nation's fleet in thousands of tons' full-load displacement.

SHIPS is the total number of ships.

MANPOWER is the number of men in the navy, in thousands. This includes naval air power and support.

AVG WEIGHT is the average weight of the fleet's ships, in thousands of tons. This indicates whether the navy goes in for large or small ships.

QUALITY PERS WPNS

SHIP TYPES are the number of each ship type the nation possesses.

CV are carriers using fixed-wing aircraft.

SSB are ballistic-missile submarines (most are nuclear-powered).

SSN are nuclear-attack subs, including those equipped with cruise missiles.

SS are nonnuclear-powered attack subs.

C are cruisers, here defined as surface warships of over 5000 tons' displacement.

E are escort type ships (1,000 to 3,000 tons).

P are patrol ships less than 1,000 tons armed with missiles or torpedoes.

MINE OPS are mine-warfare operations ships.

AIRCRAFT are naval fixed-wing combat aircraft.

TOTALS gives the totals for each column.

Victory at Sea

The end of the Cold War has made the U.S. Navy (USN) the preeminent maritime power on the planet. No other navy or combination of navies can match the USN. Moreover, the USN is a truly global force. Even with the elimination of many overseas bases, the USN still has sufficient presence and reach to make its power felt in any corner of the globe. Post–Cold War budget cuts may eventually reduce the U.S. fleet to less than half its late-1980s size. Cuts of that magnitude still won't change the USN's position of naval superiority. The Soviet Union was always a long shot as a naval superpower. With the Soviet Union gone, Russia no longer has the Black Sea bases that supported much of its naval power. In the Pacific, the enormous expense of maintaining a major fleet far from the Russian heartland can no longer be supported. Russia's northern fleet in subarctic Murmansk is another economic burden that will have to be sacrificed to economic viability and political stability on the home front.

The only remaining continental power potentially capable of creating a large fleet, China, has shown little interest in doing so.

The 20th century, which had a series of wars (World Wars I and II, the Cold War) that saw Britain as the principal naval power at the beginning, finds the USN holding that position at the end. The planet has gotten a lot smaller during that period. In the future, "Victory at Sea" will lose its meaning as future fleets head for orbital space.

Glossary: Dictionary of Military Terms (Official and Otherwise)

AAM—Air-to-Air Missile
ABM—AntiBallistic Missile
AGM—Air-to-Ground Missile
ALCM—Air-Launched Cruise Missile
AM-39—Exocet Missile
APDS—Armor-Piercing Discarding Sabot
APS—Armor-Piercing Shot
ARM—AntiRadiation Missile
ASW—AntiSubmarine Warfare
ATACMS—Army TACtical Missile System
ATGM—AntiTank Guided Missile
AWACS—Airborne Warning And Control System
BB—Battleship
BMD—Ballistic Missile Defense
CA—Cruiser, Armored
CAS/BAI—Close Air Support/BAttlefield Interdiction
CEP—Circular Error Probable
DD—Destroyer
DIVAD—DIVision Air Defense system
ECM—Electronic CounterMeasures
ELINT—ELectronic INTelligence
EW—Electronic Warfare
FAAD—Forward-Area Air Defense

Flak—Antiaircraft guns (from German word)
FLOT—Forward Line of Own Troops
FROG—Free Rocket Over Ground (NATO name for Soviet-designed system)
GRT—Gross Register Tons
GTO—Geosynchronous Transit Orbit, high stationary orbit
Grunt—U.S. infantryman
HEAT—High Explosive AntiTank Shell (shaped charge)
ICBM—InterContinental Ballistic Missile
ICM—Improved Conventional Munitions
JSTARS—Joint Surveillance and Target-Attack Radar System
MARV—MAneuverable Reentry Vehicle
MBT—Main Battle Tank
MIRV—Multiple Independently targetable Reentry Vehicle
MRBM—Medium-Range Ballistic Missile
MTBF—Mean Time Between Failure
NCO—NonCommissioned Officer (sergeants and corporals)
NRO—National Reconnaissance Office, controls U.S. recon satellites
OTH RADAR—Over The Horizon Radar
Radar—Detects objects by interpreting microwaves as it bounces off them
RV—Reentry Vehicle
SAM—Surface-to-Air Missile
SDI—Strategic Defense Initiative, Star Wars
SIGINT—SIGnal INTelligence
SLBM—Sea-Launched Ballistic Missile
SLCM—Sea-Launched Cruise Missile
SOF—Special Operations Forces (commandos, rangers, etc.)
Sonar—Underwater radar, uses sound instead of microwaves
SOSUS—U.S. sonar system on the continental shelf
SS—Nonnuclear-attack submarine
SSBN—Nuclear ballistic-missile submarine
SSM—Surface-to-Surface Missile
SSN—Nuclear attack submarine
TOT—Time On Target
WWMCCS—World-Wide Military Command-and-Control System

Sources and Suggested Readings

INFORMATION for a work such as this is highly perishable. There are, however, several periodicals that provide a constant stream of up-to-date material.

Air Force Magazine—Semiofficial journal of the U.S. Air Force Association, 1750 Pennsylvania Ave., Washington, DC 20006.

Air Historian—Excellent material on history of air operations. Available from Sky Books, 48 East 50th St., New York, NY 10017.

Armor—Journal of the U.S. Army Armor School, Fort Knox, KY.

Armed Forces—Ian Allen publication. Available from Sky Books, 48 East 50th St., New York, NY 10017.

Aviation Week and Space Technology—U.S. weekly on civil and military aviation. Box 503, Hightstown, NJ 08520.

Defense Monitor is published 10 times a year by the Center for Defense Information (1500 Massachusetts Ave. NW, Washington, DC 20005). This outfit is run by retired military officers and can be loosely described as antiwar and pro–military reform. Good research and often startling insights.

Field Artillery Journal—Journal of the U.S. Army Field Artillery school, Fort Sill, OK.

Flight International—Weekly journal on civil and military aviation. Available from Sky Books, 48 East 50th St., New York, NY 10017.

Infantry—Journal of the U.S. Army Infantry School, Fort Benning, GA.

International Defense Review—A monthly that covers military matters in somewhat more depth and detail than *Jane's Defense Weekly*. Its publisher was bought out by Jane's in 1987. Jane's Information Group, 1340 Braddock Place, Alexandria, VA 22313.

Jane's Annuals—A series of exhaustive annuals on various military topics. Includes *Jane's Fighting Ships, Jane's All the World's Aircraft, Jane's Weapons Systems, Jane's Infantry Weapons,* and others. These are expensive, running over $200 a volume. Jane's Information Group, 1340 Braddock Place, Alexandria, VA 22313.

Jane's Defense Weekly—a weekly magazine covering all aspects of organized mayhem (including the political ones). Jane's Information Group, 1340 Braddock Place, Alexandria, VA 22313.

Jane's Intelligence Review—A monthly publication like *Jane's Weekly,* but covers items in more detail. Jane's Information Group, 1340 Braddock Place, Alexandria, VA 22313.

Marine Corps Gazette—Best journal on amphibious warfare. Box 1775, Quantico, VA 22134.

Military Affairs—Published by the U.S. Army Command and General Staff School at Fort Leavenworth, KS 66027.

Military Balance—An annual review of world military power. Published by the International Institute for Strategic Studies in London, England. Available from Pergamon/Brasseys.

Military Technology—Germany-based journal on military technology. Available from Sky Books, 48 East 50th St., New York, NY 10017.

Naval Forces—United Kingdom–based naval journal. Available from Sky Books, 48 East 50th St., New York, NY 10017.

Soldier of Fortune—Despite its reputation as a refuge for closet Rambos, does contain good firsthand accounts of current military activities. Widely read by military-intelligence professionals for that reason.

Strategy & Tactics—Military history, including a lot of contemporary stuff and a simulation in each issue. Decision Games, Box 4049, Lancaster, CA 93539-4049.

Time-Life Books: The New Face of War. This is a book series that will probably be available throughout the 1990s. Good information and well illustrated. Each 160-page volume costs about $20. Order via (800) 621-7026.

United States Naval Institute Proceedings—Authoritative journal on U.S. Navy. Annapolis, MD 21402.

Weyer's Warships of the World—Published every two years. More compact, and cheaper, than Jane's.

World Armaments and Disarmament Yearbook—Published by the Stockholm International Peace Institute.

World Armies—A book by John Keegan covering all the world's armies. There have been two editions, as the information is perishable.

Keegan also has a number of other books in print, all of which are worthwhile.

There are numerous other publications.

Books

Books on modern warfare are a problem as they are quickly out of date. Most of the truly useful books are periodically updated. When books on modern warfare are published, they usually don't stay in print very long and are thereafter available only in specialized libraries. Your best source of other books on modern warfare is major research libraries. Large cities, as well as many major universities, have these. A stroll through the stacks would present most of what is currently available. Governments are often a source of useful publications. The U.S. Government Publishing Office offers catalogs of books on military matters. The *U.S. Congressional Record* is also a treasure trove of material, but requires a lot of digging. The CIA has prepared numerous Fact Books that can be obtained through the U.S. government.

There are certain authors who continually put out material of use to anyone in this area. A partial list would include John Keegan, Trevor Dupuy, Martin van Creevald, Harriet Scott, A. A. Nofi, Stephen Patrick, and many others.

Official Publications

Government publications are often a good source of detail on modern military affairs. The U.S. Government Printing Office offers regularly updated lists of what they have available. The publications can be ordered by mail. The U.S. military also has numerous unclassified publications that civilians can legally possess. Unfortunately, the official drill is to make a Freedom of Information Act request, which can turn into a tedious process.

People in the Business

It's become something of an open secret that secrets are not always kept very secret. Classified military information is regularly leaked to journalists in order to further one political agenda or another. Vows are regularly taken to tighten up on the flow of sensitive data, but it never seems to work. As a result, people in the business are frequently more talkative than they are supposed to be. As long as you don't ask for secret information, you are fairly safe while it is being dumped into your lap.

Index

615